LOCATION OF VIDEONOTES IN THE TEXT

VideoNote

(continued on next page)

LOCATION OF VIDEONOTES IN THE TEXT (continued)

STARTING OUT WITH

C++

From Control Structures through Objects

6th Edition Brief Version

Tony Gaddis

PEARSON

Addison
Wesley

Boston San Francisco New York
London Toronto Sydney Tokyo Singapore Madrid
Mexico City Munich Paris Cape Town Hong Kong Montreal

Editor-in-Chief:	Michael Hirsch
Editorial Assistant:	Stephanie Sellinger
Managing Editor:	Jeffrey Holcomb
Senior Production Supervisor:	Marilyn Lloyd
Marketing Manager:	Erin Davis
Marketing Coordinator:	Kathryn Ferranti
Senior Media Buyer:	Ginny Michaud
Media Producer:	Katelyn Boller
Senior Manufacturing Buyer:	Carol Melville
Project Coordination:	Sherrill Redd/Aptara, Inc.
Production Services:	Aptara®, Inc.
Art Director, Cover:	Linda Knowles
Cover Designer:	Joyce Cosentino Wells/JWells Design
Cover Image:	Getty Images/Photographer: David Muir

Access the latest information about Addison-Wesley Computer Science titles from our World Wide Web site: http://www.pearsonhighered.com/cs

Many of the designations used by manufacturers and sellers to distinguish their products are claimed as trademarks. Where those designations appear in this book, and Addison-Wesley was aware of a trademark claim, the designations have been printed in initial caps or all caps.

The programs and applications presented in this book have been included for their instructional value. They have been tested with care but are not guaranteed for any particular purpose. The publisher does not offer any warranty or representation, nor does it accept any liabilities with respect to the programs or applications.

The interior of this book was composed in Aptara, Inc. The basal text font is set in Sabon 10/12.5; the chapter titles, headings, running heads, and folios are all set in Stone Sans; the programming code is set in Courier10 Pitch BT 9/11.

Library of Congress Cataloging-in-Publication Data

Gaddis, Tony.
Starting out with C++ : from control structures through objects / Tony Gaddis. — 6th ed., brief version.
   p. cm.
ISBN-13: 978-0-13-602253-4
ISBN-10: 0-13-602253-7
1. C++ (Computer program language) I. Title.

QA76.73.C153G33 2010
005.13'3—dc22
           2009036124

Addison-Wesley
is an imprint of

www.pearsonhighered.com

ISBN 13: 978-0-13-602253-4
ISBN 10:   0-13-602253-7
1 2 3 4 5 6 7 8 9 10—EB—12 11 10 09

Contents at a Glance

Student CD   The following appendices are on the accompanying Student CD.

Contents

Preface

Welcome to the Brief Version of *Starting Out with C++: From Control Structures through Objects, 6th edition*. This book is intended for use in a one or two-semester C++ programming course. Students new to programming, as well as those with prior course work in other languages, will find this text beneficial. The fundamentals of programming are covered for the novice, while the details, pitfalls, and nuances of the C++ language are explored in-depth for both the beginner and more experienced student. The book is written with clear, easy-to-understand language and it covers all the necessary topics for an introductory programming course. This text is rich in example programs that are concise, practical, and real-world oriented, ensuring that the student not only learns how to implement the features and constructs of C++, but why and when to use them.

Changes in the Sixth Edition

This book's pedagogy, organization, and clear writing style remain the same as in the previous edition. Many improvements have been made, which are summarized here:

- **Improved Organization in Chapter 4**
  The section covering the `if/else if` statement has been simplified, and now appears immediately following the section on nested `if` statements. These sections have been rewritten to highlight the similarities between an `if/else if` statement and a nested `if` statement.

- **New Chapter on Sorting and Searching Arrays**
  The bonus chapter on sorting and searching arrays that was previously included on the Student CD is now included in the book as Chapter 8. The chapter covers the Bubble Sort, Selection Sort, Linear Search, and Binary Search algorithms. There is also a section on sorting and searching STL vector objects.

- **New *In the Spotlight* Sections**
  Many of the chapters have new sections titled *In the Spotlight*. Each of these provides a programming problem and a detailed, step-by-step analysis showing the student how to solve it.

- **Online videonotes**
  An extensive series of online videos have been developed to accompany this text. Throughout the book, video note icons alert the student to videos covering

VideoNote

specific topics. Additionally, one Programming Challenge at the end of each chapter now has an accompanying video note explaining how to develop the problem's solution. The videos are available at www.pearsonhighered.com/gaddis.

- **Additional Programming Problems**
  Additional Programming Challenge problems have been added to most chapters. Several of these are simple games that will challenge and motivate students.

Organization of the Text

This text teaches C++ in a step-by-step fashion. Each chapter covers a major set of topics and builds knowledge as the student progresses through the book. Although the chapters can be easily taught in their existing sequence, some flexibility is provided. The diagram shown in Figure P-1 suggests possible sequences of instruction.

Chapter 1 covers fundamental hardware, software, and programming concepts. You may choose to skip this chapter if the class has already mastered those topics. Chapters 2 through 7 cover basic C++ syntax, data types, expressions, selection structures, repetition structures, functions, and arrays. Each of these chapters builds on the previous chapter and should be covered in the order presented.

After Chapter 7 has been covered, you may proceed to Chapter 8, or jump to either Chapter 9 or Chapter 12. (If you jump to Chapter 12 at this point, you will need to postpone sections 12.7, 12.8, and 12.10 until Chapters 9 and 11 have been covered.)

After Chapter 9 has been covered, either of Chapters 10 or 11 may be covered. After Chapter 11, you may cover Chapters 13 through 15 in sequence.

This text's approach starts with a firm foundation in structured, procedural programming before delving fully into object-oriented programming and advanced data structures.

Brief Overview of Each Chapter

Chapter 1: Introduction to Computers and Programming

This chapter provides an introduction to the field of computer science and covers the fundamentals of programming, problem solving, and software design. The components of programs, such as key words, variables, operators, and punctuation are covered. The tools of the trade, such as pseudocode, flow charts, and hierarchy charts are also presented.

Chapter 2: Introduction to C++

This chapter gets the student started in C++ by introducing data types, identifiers, variable declarations, constants, comments, program output, simple arithmetic operations, and C-strings. Programming style conventions are introduced and good programming style is modeled here, as it is throughout the text. An optional section explains the difference between ANSI standard and pre-standard C++ programs.

Figure P-1

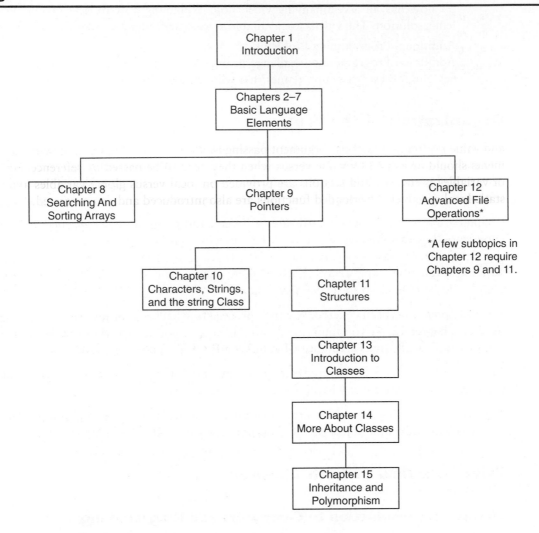

Chapter 3: Expressions and Interactivity

In this chapter the student learns to write programs that input and handle numeric, character, and C-string data. The use of arithmetic operators and the creation of mathematical expressions are covered in greater detail, with emphasis on operator precedence. Debugging is introduced, with a section on hand tracing a program. Sections are also included on using sequential files, on simple output formatting, on data type conversion and type casting, and on using library functions that work with numbers.

Chapter 4: Making Decisions

Here the student learns about relational operators, relational expressions and how to control the flow of a program with the if, if/else, and if/else if statements. The conditional operator and the switch statement are also covered. Crucial applications of these constructs are covered, such as menu-driven programs and the validation of input.

Chapter 5: Looping

This chapter covers repetition control structures. The `while` loop, `do-while` loop, and `for` loop are taught, along with common uses for these devices. Counters, accumulators, running totals, sentinels, and other application-related topics are discussed. A section on file I/O discusses how to use a loop to read from a file until the end of the file is encountered.

Chapter 6: Functions

In this chapter the student learns how and why to modularize programs, using both `void` and value returning functions. Argument passing is covered, with emphasis on when arguments should be passed by value versus when they need to be passed by reference. Scope of variables is covered and sections are provided on local versus global variables and on static local variables. Overloaded functions are also introduced and demonstrated.

Chapter 7: Arrays

In this chapter the student learns to create and work with single and multidimensional arrays. Many examples of array processing are provided including examples illustrating how to find the sum, average, highest and lowest values in an array and how to sum the rows, columns, and all elements of a two-dimensional array. Programming techniques using parallel arrays are also demonstrated and the student is shown how to use a data file as an input source to populate an array. STL vectors are introduced and compared to arrays.

Chapter 8: Sorting and Searching Arrays

Here the student learns the basics of sorting arrays and searching for data stored in them. The chapter covers the Bubble Sort, Selection Sort, Linear Search, and Binary Search algorithms. There is also a section on sorting and searching STL `vector` objects.

Chapter 9: Pointers

This chapter explains how to use pointers. Pointers are compared to and contrasted with reference variables. Other topics include pointer arithmetic, initialization of pointers, relational comparison of pointers, pointers and arrays, pointers and functions, dynamic memory allocation, and more.

Chapter 10: Characters, C-strings, and the Standard `string` Class

This chapter focuses on library functions that manipulate or test characters or strings. A review of the internal storage of C-strings is given. An extensive discussion of the standard `string` class is also presented.

Chapter 11: Structured Data

The student is introduced to abstract data types and taught how to create them using structures, unions, and enumerated data types. Discussions and examples include using pointers to structures, passing structures to functions, and returning structures from functions.

Chapter 12: Advanced File Operations

This chapter covers sequential access, random access, text, and binary files. The various modes for opening files are discussed, as well as the many methods for reading and writing file contents. Advanced output formatting is also covered.

Chapter 13: Introduction to Classes

The student now shifts focus to the object-oriented paradigm. This chapter covers the fundamental concepts of classes. Member variables and functions are discussed. The student learns about private and public access specifications, and reasons to use each. The topics of constructors, overloaded constructors, and destructors are also presented. The chapter presents a section modeling classes with UML, and how to find the classes in a particular problem.

Chapter 14: More About Classes

This chapter continues the study of classes. Static members, friends, memberwise assignment, and copy constructors are discussed. The chapter also includes in-depth sections on operator overloading, object conversion, and object aggregation. There is also a section on class collaborations and the use of CRC cards.

Chapter 15: Inheritance and Polymorphism

The study of classes continues in this chapter with the subjects of inheritance, polymorphism, and virtual member functions. The topics covered include base and derived class constructors and destructors, virtual member functions, base class pointers, static and dynamic binding, multiple inheritance, and class hierarchies.

Appendix A: ASCII Character Set

A list of the ASCII and Extended ASCII characters and their codes.

Appendix B: Operator Precedence and Associativity

A chart showing the C++ operators and their precedence.

The following appendices are on the accompanying Student CD:

Appendix C: Introduction to Flowcharting

A brief introduction to flowcharting. This tutorial discusses sequence, selection, case, repetition, and module structures.

Appendix D: Using UML in Class Design

This appendix shows the student how to use the Unified Modeling Language to design classes. Notation for showing access specification, data types, parameters, return values, overloaded functions, composition, and inheritance are included.

Appendix E: Namespaces

This appendix explains namespaces and their purpose. Examples showing how to define a namespace and access its members are given.

Appendix F: Writing Managed C++ Code for the .NET Framework

This appendix introduces the student to the concepts surrounding managed C++ in Microsoft's .NET environment.

Appendix G: Passing Command Line Arguments

Teaches the student how to write a C++ program that accepts arguments from the command line. This appendix will be useful to students working in a command line environment, such as Unix, Linux, or the Windows MS-DOS prompt console.

Appendix H: Header File and Library Function Reference

This appendix provides a reference for the C++ library functions and header files discussed in the book.

Appendix I: Binary Numbers and Bitwise Operations

A guide to the C++ bitwise operators, as well as a tutorial on the internal storage of integers.

Appendix J: Multi-Source File Programs

Provides a tutorial on creating programs that consist of multiple source files. Function header files, class specification files, and class implementation files are discussed.

Appendix K: Stream Member Functions for Formatting

Covers stream member functions for formatting such as `setf`.

Appendix L: Introduction to Microsoft Visual C++ 2008 Express Edition

A tutorial on how to start a project in Microsoft Visual C++ 2008 Express Edition, compile a program, save source files, and more.

Appendix M: Answers to Checkpoints

Students may test their own progress by comparing their answers to the checkpoint exercises against this appendix. The answers to all Checkpoints are included.

Appendix N: Answers to Odd-Numbered Review Questions

Another tool that students can use to gauge their progress.

Features of the Text

Concept Statements	Each major section of the text starts with a concept statement. This statement summarizes the ideas of the section.
Example Programs	The text has over 300 complete example programs, each designed to highlight the topic currently being studied. In most cases, these are practical, real-world examples. Source code for these programs is provided so that students can run the programs themselves.
Program Output	After each example program there is a sample of its screen output. This immediately shows the student how the program should function.
In the Spotlight	Each of these sections provides a programming problem and a detailed, step by step analysis showing the student how to solve it.
videonotes	A series of online videos, developed specifically for this book, are available for viewing at http://www.pearsonhighered.com/gaddis. Icons appear throughout the text alerting the student to videos about specific topics.
Checkpoints	Checkpoints are questions placed throughout each chapter as a self-test study aid. Answers for all Checkpoint questions are provided on the student CD so students can check how well they have learned a new topic.
Notes	Notes appear at appropriate places throughout the text. They are short explanations of interesting or often misunderstood points relevant to the topic at hand.
Warnings	Warnings are notes that caution the student about certain C++ features, programming techniques, or practices that can lead to malfunctioning programs or lost data.
Case Studies	Case studies that simulate real-world applications appear in many chapters throughout the text, with complete code provided for each one on the student CD. These case studies are designed to highlight the major topics of the chapter in which they appear.
Review Questions and Exercises	Each chapter presents a thorough and diverse set of review questions, such as fill-in-the-blank and short answer, that check the student's mastery of the basic material presented in the chapter. These are followed by exercises requiring problem solving and analysis, such as the *Algorithm Workbench*, *Predict the Output*, and *Find the Errors* sections. Answers to the odd numbered review questions and review exercises are provided on the student CD.

Programming Challenges	Each chapter offers a pool of programming exercises designed to solidify the student's knowledge of the topics currently being studied. In most cases the assignments present real-world problems to be solved. When applicable, these exercises include input validation rules.
Group Projects	There are several group programming projects throughout the text, intended to be constructed by a team of students. One student might build the program's user interface, while another student writes the mathematical code, and another designs and implements a class the program uses. This process is similar to the way many professional programs are written and encourages team work within the classroom.
C++ Quick Reference Guide	For easy access, a quick reference guide to the C++ language is printed on the last page of the book and the inside back cover.

Supplements

Student CD

This CD includes:

- Turbo C++ 2006 Explorer Edition
- Answers to all Checkpoint questions (Appendix M)
- Answers to all odd-numbered Review Questions and Exercises (Appendix N)
- Complete source code for every program included in the book
- Additional case studies, complete with source code
- A full set of appendices that accompany the book

If a CD did not come with your book or you can't locate your CD, you can access most of these items at http://www.aw.com/cssupport/

Other CDs Upon Request

Professors should contact their campus Addison-Wesley representative for the specific ISBN to order this book packaged with Microsoft Visual C++ 2008 Express Edition.

MyCodeMate—Your Own T.A. Just a Click Away

Addison-Wesley's *MyCodeMate* is a book-specific Web resource that provides tutorial help and evaluation of student programs. Example programs throughout the book and selected

Programming Challenges from every chapter have been integrated into *MyCodeMate*. Using this tool, a student is able to write and compile programs from any computer with Internet access, and receive guidance and feedback on how to proceed and on how to address compiler error messages. Instructors can track each student's progress on Programming Challenges from the text or can develop projects of their own. **A complimentary subscription to *MyCodeMate* is offered when the access code is ordered in a package with a new copy of this text.** Subscriptions can also be purchased online. For more information visit `http://www.mycodemate.com`, or contact your campus Addison-Wesley representative.

Instructor Resources

The following supplements are available to qualified instructors only:

- Answers to all Review Questions in the text
- Solutions for all Programming Challenges in the text
- PowerPoint presentation slides for every chapter
- Computerized test bank
- Answers to all Student Lab Manual questions
- Solutions for all Student Lab Manual programs

Visit the Addison-Wesley Instructor Resource Center (`http://www.pearsonhighered.com/irc`) or send an email to `computing@aw.com` for information on how to access them.

Textbook Web site

A Web site for the *Starting Out with* C++ series of books is located at the following URL: `www.pearsonhighered.com/gaddisbooks`

Get this book the way you want it!

This book is part of Pearson Education's custom database for Computer Science textbooks. Use our online PubSelect system to select just the chapters you need from this, and other, Pearson Education CS textbooks. You can edit the sequence to exactly match your course organization and teaching approach. Visit `www.pearsoncustom.com/cs` for details.

Which Gaddis C++ book is right for you?

The Starting Out with C++ Series includes three books, one of which is sure to fit your course:

- *Starting Out with C++: From Control Structures through Objects*
- *Starting Out with C++: Early Objects*
- *Brief Version of Starting Out with C++: From Control Structures through Objects.*

The following chart will help you determine which book is right for your course.

■ FROM CONTROL STRUCTURES THROUGH OBJECTS ■ BRIEF VERSION	■ EARLY OBJECTS
LATE INTRODUCTION OF OBJECTS Classes are introduced in Chapter 13, after control structures, functions, arrays, and pointers. Advanced OOP topics, such as inheritance and polymorphism, are covered in Chapters 14 and 15.	**EARLIER INTRODUCTION OF OBJECTS** Classes are introduced in Chapter 7, after control structures and functions, but before arrays and pointers. Their use is then integrated into the remainder of the text. Advanced OOP topics, such as inheritance and polymorphism, are covered in Chapters 11 and 15.
USE OF C-STRINGS Null-terminated C-strings are used throughout, with the C++ `string` class covered briefly.	**USE OF `string` OBJECTS** Standard library `string` class objects are used throughout, with C-strings covered briefly.
INTRODUCTION OF DATA STRUCTURES AND RECURSION Linked lists, stacks and queues, and binary trees are introduced in the final chapters of the full text. Recursion is covered after stacks and queues, but before binary trees. These topics are not covered in the brief text.	**INTRODUCTION OF DATA STRUCTURES AND RECURSION** Linked lists, stacks and queues, and binary trees are introduced in the final chapters of the text, after the chapter on recursion.

Acknowledgments

There have been many helping hands in the development and publication of this text. We would like to thank the following faculty reviewers for their helpful suggestions and expertise.

Ahmad Abuhejleh
University of Wisconsin, River Falls

David Akins
El Camino College

Steve Allan
Utah State University

Vicki Allan
Utah State University

Karen M. Arlien
Bismark State College

Mary Astone
Troy University

Ijaz A. Awan
Savannah State University

Robert Baird
Salt Lake Community College

Don Biggerstaff
Fayetteville Technical Community College

Michael Bolton
Northeastern Oklahoma State University

Bill Brown
Pikes Peak Community College

Charles Cadenhead
Richland Community College

Randall Campbell
Morningside College

Wayne Caruolo
Red Rocks Community College

Cathi Chambley-Miller
Aiken Technical College

C.C. Chao
Jacksonville State University

Joseph Chao
Bowling Green State University

Royce Curtis
Western Wisconsin Technical College

Joseph DeLibero
Arizona State University

Jeanne Douglas
University of Vermont

Michael Dowell
Augusta State U

Judy Etchison
Southern Methodist University

Dennis Fairclough
Utah Valley State College

Richard Flint
North Central College

Ann Ford
Florida State University

James Gifford
University of Wisconsin, Stevens Point

Leon Gleiberman
Touro College

Ranette Halverson, Ph.D.
Midwestern State University

Carol Hannahs
University of Kentucky

Dennis Heckman
Portland Community College

Ric Heishman
George Mason University

Michael Hennessy
University of Oregon

Ilga Higbee
Black Hawk College

Patricia Hines
Brookdale Community College

Mike Holland
Northern Virginia Community College

Mary Hovik
Lehigh Carbon Community College

Richard Hull
Lenoir-Rhyne College

Chris Kardaras
North Central College

Willard Keeling
Blue Ridge Community College

A.J. Krygeris
Houston Community College

Sheila Lancaster
Gadsden State Community College

Ray Larson
Inver Hills Community College

Jennifer Li
Ohlone College

Norman H. Liebling
San Jacinto College

Zhu-qu Lu
University of Maine, Presque Isle

Heidar Malki
University of Houston

Debbie Mathews
J. Sargeant Reynolds

Rick Matzen
Northeastern State University

Robert McDonald
East Stroudsburg University

James McGuffee
Austin Community College

Dean Mellas
Cerritos College

Lisa Milkowski
Milwaukee School of Engineering

Marguerite Nedreberg
Youngstown State University

Lynne O'Hanlon
Los Angeles Pierce College

Frank Paiano
Southwestern Community College

Theresa Park
Texas State Technical College

Mark Parker
Shoreline Community College

Tino Posillico
SUNY Farmingdale

Frederick Pratter
Eastern Oregon University

Susan L. Quick
Penn State University

Alberto Ramon
Diablo Valley College

Bazlur Rasheed
Sault College of Applied Arts and Technology

Farshad Ravanshad
Bergen Community College

Dolly Samson
Weber State University

Ruth Sapir
SUNY Farmingdale

Jason Schatz
City College of San Francisco

Dr. Sung Shin
South Dakota State University

Bari Siddique
University of Texas at Brownsville

William Slater
Collin County Community College

Shep Smithline
University of Minnesota

Caroline St. Claire
North Central College

Kirk Stephens
Southwestern Community College

Cherie Stevens
South Florida Community College

Dale Suggs
Campbell University

Mark Swanson
Red Wing Technical College

Martha Tillman
College of San Mateo

Ralph Tomlinson
Iowa State University

David Topham
Ohlone College

Robert Tureman
Paul D. Camp Community College

Arisa K. Ude
Richland College

Peter van der Goes
Rose State College

Stewart Venit
California State University, Los Angeles

Judy Walters
North Central College

John H. Whipple
Northampton Community College

Aurelia Williams
Norfolk State University

Vida Winans
Illinois Institute of Technology

I also want to thank everyone at Pearson Addison-Wesley for making the *Starting Out with* series so successful. I have worked so closely with the team at Pearson Adddison-Wesley that I consider them among my closest friends. I am extremely grateful that Michael Hirsch is my editor. Stephanie Sellinger, editorial assistant, managed the revision of this book and made the entire process a pleasure. I am also thankful to have Erin Davis as marketing manager. Her energy and creativity are truly inspiring. The production team worked tirelessly to make this book a reality, and includes Marilyn Lloyd, Jeff Holcomb, Katelyn Boller, Carol Melville, and Linda Knowles. Thanks to you all!

Last, but not least, I want to thank my family for all the patience, love, and support they have shown me throughout this and my many other projects.

About the Author

Tony Gaddis is the principal author of the *Starting Out with* series of textbooks. He has nearly two decades of experience teaching computer science courses, primarily at Haywood Community College. Tony is a highly acclaimed instructor who was previously selected as the North Carolina Community College Teacher of the Year, and has received the Teaching Excellence award from the National Institute for Staff and Organizational Development. The *Starting Out With* series includes introductory textbooks covering Programming Logic and Design, Alice, C++, Java™, Microsoft® Visual Basic®, and Python, all published by Addison-Wesley.

1 Introduction to Computers and Programming

TOPICS

1.1 Why Program?

CONCEPT: Computers can do many different jobs because they are programmable.

Every profession has tools that make its job easier to do. Carpenters use hammers, saws, and measuring tapes. Mechanics use wrenches, screwdrivers, and ratchets. Electronics technicians use probes, scopes, and meters. Some tools are unique and can be categorized as belonging to a single profession. For example, surgeons have certain tools that are designed specifically for surgical operations. Those tools probably aren't used by anyone other than surgeons. There are some tools, however, that are used in several professions. Screwdrivers, for instance, are used by mechanics, carpenters, and many others.

The computer is a tool that is used by so many professions that it cannot be easily categorized. It can perform so many different jobs that it is perhaps the most versatile tool ever made. To the accountant, computers balance books, analyze profits and losses, and prepare tax reports. To the factory worker, computers control manufacturing machines and track production. To the mechanic, computers analyze the various systems in an automobile and pinpoint hard-to-find problems.

What makes the computer so useful? Quite simply, the computer can do such a wide variety of tasks because it can be *programmed*. It is a machine specifically designed to follow instructions.

Because of the computer's programmability, it doesn't belong to any single profession. Computers are designed to do whatever task their programs, or *software*, tell them to do.

Computer programmers do a very important job. They create software that transforms computers into the specialized tools of many trades. Without programmers, the users of computers would have no software, and without software, computers would not be able to do anything.

Computer programming is both an art and a science. It is an art because every aspect of a program should be carefully designed. Listed below are a few of the things that must be designed for any real-world computer program:

- The logical flow of the instructions
- The mathematical procedures
- The appearance of the screens
- The way information is presented to the user
- The program's "user-friendliness"
- Manuals and other forms of written documentation

There is also a scientific, or engineering, side to programming. Because programs rarely work right the first time they are written, a lot of testing, correction, and redesigning is required. This demands patience and persistence from the programmer. Writing software demands discipline as well. Programmers must learn special languages like C++ because computers do not understand English or other human languages. Languages such as C++ have strict rules that must be carefully followed.

Both the artistic and scientific nature of programming make writing computer software like designing a car: Both cars and programs should be functional, efficient, powerful, easy to use, and pleasing to look at.

1.2 Computer Systems: Hardware and Software

CONCEPT: All computer systems consist of similar hardware devices and software components. This section provides an overview of standard computer hardware and software organization.

Hardware

Hardware refers to the physical components that a computer is made of. A computer, as we generally think of it, is not an individual device, but a system of devices. Like the instruments in a symphony orchestra, each device plays its own part. A typical computer system consists of the following major components:

1. The central processing unit (CPU)
2. Main memory
3. Secondary storage devices
4. Input devices
5. Output devices

The organization of a computer system is depicted in Figure 1-1.

Figure 1-1

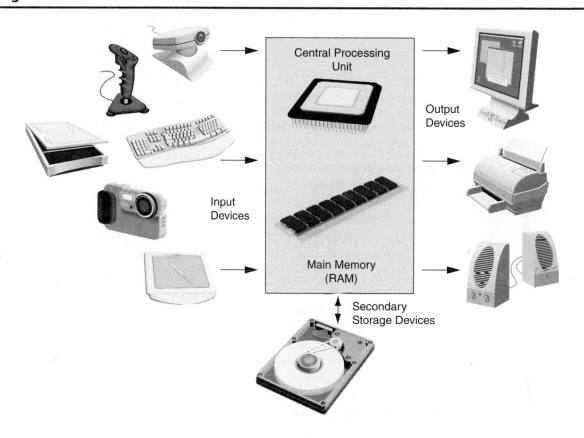

The CPU

At the heart of a computer is its *central processing unit*, or *CPU*. The CPU's job is to fetch instructions, follow the instructions, and produce some result. Internally, the central processing unit consists of two parts: the *control unit* and the *arithmetic and logic unit (ALU)*. The control unit coordinates all of the computer's operations. It is responsible for determining where to get the next instruction and regulating the other major components of the computer with control signals. The arithmetic and logic unit, as its name suggests, is designed to perform mathematical operations. The organization of the CPU is shown in Figure 1-2.

Figure 1-2

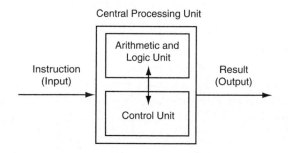

A program is a sequence of instructions stored in the computer's memory. When a computer is running a program, the CPU is engaged in a process known formally as the *fetch/decode/execute cycle*. The steps in the fetch/decode/execute cycle are as follows:

Fetch   The CPU's control unit fetches, from main memory, the next instruction in the sequence of program instructions.

Decode   The instruction is encoded in the form of a number. The control unit decodes the instruction and generates an electronic signal.

Execute   The signal is routed to the appropriate component of the computer (such as the ALU, a disk drive, or some other device). The signal causes the component to perform an operation.

These steps are repeated as long as there are instructions to perform.

Main Memory

Commonly known as *random-access memory*, or *RAM*, the computer's main memory is a device that holds information. Specifically, RAM holds the sequences of instructions in the programs that are running and the data those programs are using.

Memory is divided into sections, or cells, that each hold an equal amount of data. Each cell is made of eight "switches" that may be either on or off. A switch that is in the on position usually represents the number 1, while a switch in the off position usually represents the number 0. The computer stores data by setting the switches in a memory cell to a pattern that represents a character of information. Each of these switches is known as a *bit*, which stands for *binary digit*. Each cell, which is a collection of eight bits, is known as a *byte*. Each byte is assigned a unique number known as an *address*. The addresses are ordered from lowest to highest. A byte is identified by its address in much the same way a post office box is identified by an address. Figure 1-3 shows a group of memory cells with their addresses. In the illustration, sample data is stored in memory. The number 149 is stored in the cell with the address 16, and the number 72 is stored at address 23.

Figure 1-3

RAM is usually a volatile type of memory, used only for temporary storage. When the computer is turned off, the contents of RAM are erased.

Secondary Storage

Secondary storage is a type of memory that can hold data for long periods of time—even when there is no power to the computer. Frequently used programs are stored in secondary memory and loaded into main memory as needed. Important information, such as word processing documents, payroll data, and inventory figures, is saved to secondary storage as well.

The most common type of secondary storage device is the disk drive. A *disk drive* stores data by magnetically encoding it onto a circular disk. Most computers have a disk drive mounted inside their case. External disk drives, which connect to one of the computer's communication ports, are also available. External disk drives can be used to create backup copies of important data or to move data to another computer.

In addition to external disk drives, many types of devices have been created for copying data, and for moving it to other computers. For many years floppy disk drives were popular. A *floppy disk drive* records data onto a small floppy disk, which can be removed from the drive. The use of floppy disk drives has declined dramatically in recent years, in favor of superior devices such as USB drives. *USB drives* are small devices that plug into the computer's USB (universal serial bus) port, and appear to the system as a disk drive. USB drives, which use *flash memory* to store data, are inexpensive, reliable, and small enough to be carried in your pocket.

Optical devices such as the *CD* (compact disc) and the *DVD* (digital versatile disc) are also popular for data storage. Data is not recorded magnetically on an optical disc, but is encoded as a series of pits on the disc surface. CD and DVD drives use a laser to detect the pits and thus read the encoded data. Optical discs hold large amounts of data, and because recordable CD and DVD drives are now commonplace, they are good mediums for creating backup copies of data.

Input Devices

Input is any information the computer collects from the outside world. The device that collects the information and sends it to the computer is called an *input device*. Common input devices are the keyboard, mouse, scanner, digital camera, and microphone. Disk drives, CD/DVD drives, and USB drives can also be considered input devices because programs and information are retrieved from them and loaded into the computer's memory.

Output Devices

Output is any information the computer sends to the outside world. It might be a sales report, a list of names, or a graphic image. The information is sent to an *output device*, which formats and presents it. Common output devices are monitors, printers, and speakers. Output sent to a monitor is sometimes called "softcopy," while output sent to a printer is called "hardcopy." Disk drives, USB drives, and CD/DVD recorders can also be considered output devices because the CPU sends them information to be saved.

Software

As previously mentioned, software refers to the programs that run on a computer. There are two general categories of software: *operating systems* and *application software*. An operating system is a set of programs that manages the computer's hardware devices and controls their processes. Operating systems fall into one of the following categories.

Single tasking   A single tasking operating system is capable of running only one program at a time. The computer devotes all its hardware resources and CPU time to each program as it executes. MS-DOS is an example of a single tasking operating system.

Multitasking   A multitasking operating system is capable of running multiple programs at once. Through a technique called *time sharing*, the system
divides the allocation of hardware resources and the attention of the
CPU among all the executing programs. UNIX, Windows XP, and
Windows Vista are multitasking operating systems.

In addition, operating systems fall into one of the following categories, which describe the
number of users they can accommodate.

Single user   This type of system allows only one user to operate the computer at a
time. MS-DOS and older versions of Windows are single user operating
systems.

Multiuser   Multiuser systems allow several users to run programs and operate the
computer at once. Most variations of the UNIX operating system are
multiuser systems.

Application software refers to programs that make the computer useful to the user. These
programs solve specific problems or perform general operations that satisfy the needs of
the user. Word processing, spreadsheet, and database programs are all examples of application software.

 ## Checkpoint

1.1   Why is the computer used by so many different people, in so many different
       professions?

1.2   List the five major hardware components of a computer system.

1.3   Internally, the CPU consists of what two units?

1.4   Describe the steps in the fetch/decode/execute cycle.

1.5   What is a memory address? What is its purpose?

1.6   Explain why computers have both main memory and secondary storage.

1.7   What are the two general categories of software?

1.8   What is the difference between a single tasking system and a multitasking system?

1.9   What is the difference between a single user system and a multiuser system?

 # 1.3   Programs and Programming Languages

CONCEPT: A program is a set of instructions a computer follows in order to perform
a task. A programming language is a special language used to write
computer programs.

What Is a Program?

Computers are designed to follow instructions. A computer program is a set of instructions that tells the computer how to solve a problem or perform a task. For example, suppose we want the computer to calculate someone's gross pay. Here is a list of things the
computer should do:

1. Display a message on the screen asking "How many hours did you work?"

2. Wait for the user to enter the number of hours worked. Once the user enters a number, store it in memory.

3. Display a message on the screen asking "How much do you get paid per hour?"

4. Wait for the user to enter an hourly pay rate. Once the user enters a number, store it in memory.

5. Multiply the number of hours by the amount paid per hour, and store the result in memory.

6. Display a message on the screen that tells the amount of money earned. The message must include the result of the calculation performed in Step 5.

Collectively, these instructions are called an *algorithm*. An algorithm is a set of well-defined steps for performing a task or solving a problem. Notice these steps are sequentially ordered. Step 1 should be performed before Step 2, and so forth. It is important that these instructions be performed in their proper sequence.

Although you and I might easily understand the instructions in the pay-calculating algorithm, it is not ready to be executed on a computer. A computer's CPU can only process instructions that are written in *machine language*. If you were to look at a machine language program, you would see a stream of *binary numbers* (numbers consisting of only 1s and 0s). The binary numbers form machine language instructions, which the CPU interprets as commands. Here is an example of what a machine language instruction might look like:

    1011010000000101

As you can imagine, the process of encoding an algorithm in machine language is very tedious and difficult. In addition, each different type of CPU has its own machine language. If you wrote a machine language program for computer A and then wanted to run it on computer B, which has a different type of CPU, you would have to rewrite the program in computer B's machine language.

Programming languages, which use words instead of numbers, were invented to ease the task of programming. A program can be written in a programming language, such as C++, which is much easier to understand than machine language. Programmers save their programs in text files, and then use special software to convert their programs to machine language.

Program 1-1 shows how the pay-calculating algorithm might be written in C++.

The "Program Output with Example Input" shows what the program will display on the screen when it is running. In the example, the user enters 10 for the number of hours worked and 15 for the hourly pay rate. The program displays the earnings, which are $150.

NOTE: The line numbers that are shown in Program 1-1 are *not* part of the program. This book shows line numbers in all program listings to help point out specific parts of the program.

Program 1-1

```
1   // This program calculates the user's pay.
2   #include <iostream>
3   using namespace std;
4
5   int main()
6   {
7      double hours, rate, pay;
8
9      // Get the number of hours worked.
10     cout << "How many hours did you work? ";
11     cin >> hours;
12
13     // Get the hourly pay rate.
14     cout << "How much do you get paid per hour? ";
15     cin >> rate;
16
17     // Calculate the pay.
18     pay = hours * rate;
19
20     // Display the pay.
21     cout << "You have earned $" << pay << endl;
22     return 0;
23  }
```

Program Output with Example Input Shown in Bold
```
How many hours did you work? 10 [Enter]
How much do you get paid per hour? 15 [Enter]
You have earned $150
```

Programming Languages

In a broad sense, there are two categories of programming languages: low-level and high-level. A low-level language is close to the level of the computer, which means it resembles the numeric machine language of the computer more than the natural language of humans. The easiest languages for people to learn are *high-level languages*. They are called "high-level" because they are closer to the level of human-readability than computer-readability. Figure 1-4 illustrates the concept of language levels.

Many high-level languages have been created. Table 1-1 lists a few of the well-known ones.

In addition to the high-level features necessary for writing applications such as payroll systems and inventory programs, C++ also has many low-level features. C++ is based on the C language, which was invented for purposes such as writing operating systems and compilers. Since C++ evolved from C, it carries all of C's low-level capabilities with it.

Figure 1-4

High level (Close to human language)

```
cout << "Enter the number ";
cout << "of hours worked: ";
cin >> hours;
cout << "Enter the hourly ";
cout << "pay rate: ";
cin >> payRate;
```

Low level (machine language)

10100010 11101011

Table 1-1

Language	Description
BASIC	Beginners All-purpose Symbolic Instruction Code. A general programming language originally designed to be simple enough for beginners to learn.
FORTRAN	Formula Translator. A language designed for programming complex mathematical algorithms.
COBOL	Common Business-Oriented Language. A language designed for business applications.
Pascal	A structured, general-purpose language designed primarily for teaching programming.
C	A structured, general-purpose language developed at Bell Laboratories. C offers both high-level and low-level features.
C++	Based on the C language, C++ offers object-oriented features not found in C. Also invented at Bell Laboratories.
C#	Pronounced "C sharp." A language invented by Microsoft for developing applications based on the Microsoft .NET platform.
Java	An object-oriented language invented at Sun Microsystems. Java may be used to develop programs that run over the Internet, in a Web browser.
JavaScript	JavaScript can be used to write small programs that run in Web pages. Despite its name, JavaScript is not related to Java.
Python	Python is a general purpose language created in the early 1990s. It has become popular in both business and academic applications.
Ruby	Ruby is a general purpose language that was created in the 1990s. It is increasingly becoming a popular language for programs that run on Web servers.
Visual Basic	A Microsoft programming language and software development environment that allows programmers to quickly create Windows-based applications.

C++ is popular not only because of its mixture of low- and high-level features, but also because of its *portability*. This means that a C++ program can be written on one type of computer and then run on many other types of systems. This usually requires the program to be recompiled on each type of system, but the program itself may need little or no change.

> **NOTE:** Programs written for specific graphical environments often require significant changes when moved to a different type of system. Examples of such graphical environments are Windows, the X-Window System, and the Mac OS X operating system.

Source Code, Object Code, and Executable Code

When a C++ program is written, it must be typed into the computer and saved to a file. A *text editor*, which is similar to a word processing program, is used for this task. The statements written by the programmer are called *source code*, and the file they are saved in is called the *source file*.

After the source code is saved to a file, the process of translating it to machine language can begin. During the first phase of this process, a program called the *preprocessor* reads the source code. The preprocessor searches for special lines that begin with the # symbol. These lines contain commands that cause the preprocessor to modify the source code in some way. During the next phase the *compiler* steps through the preprocessed source code, translating each source code instruction into the appropriate machine language instruction. This process will uncover any *syntax errors* that may be in the program. Syntax errors are illegal uses of key words, operators, punctuation, and other language elements. If the program is free of syntax errors, the compiler stores the translated machine language instructions, which are called *object code*, in an *object file*.

Although an object file contains machine language instructions, it is not a complete program. Here is why: C++ is conveniently equipped with a library of prewritten code for performing common operations or sometimes-difficult tasks. For example, the library contains hardware-specific code for displaying messages on the screen and reading input from the keyboard. It also provides routines for mathematical functions, such as calculating the square root of a number. This collection of code, called the *run-time library*, is extensive. Programs almost always use some part of it. When the compiler generates an object file, however, it does not include machine code for any run-time library routines the programmer might have used. During the last phase of the translation process, another program called the *linker* combines the object file with the necessary library routines. Once the linker has finished with this step, an *executable file* is created. The executable file contains machine language instructions, or *executable code*, and is ready to run on the computer.

Figure 1-5 illustrates the process of translating a C++ source file into an executable file.

The entire process of invoking the preprocessor, compiler, and linker can be initiated with a single action. For example, on a Linux system, the following command causes the C++ program named `hello.cpp` to be preprocessed, compiled, and linked. The executable code is stored in a file named `hello`.

```
g++ -o hello hello.cpp
```

Figure 1-5

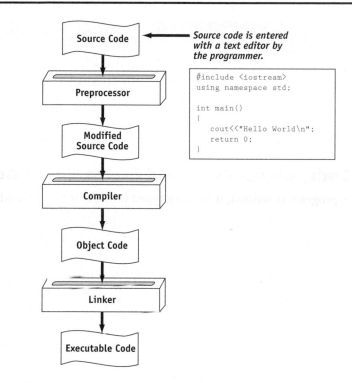

Appendix F on the Student CD explains how compiling works in .Net.

Many development systems, particularly those on personal computers, have *integrated development environments (IDEs)*. These environments consist of a text editor, compiler, debugger, and other utilities integrated into a package with a single set of menus. Preprocessing, compiling, linking, and even executing a program is done with a single click of a button, or by selecting a single item from a menu. Figure 1-6 shows a screen from the Microsoft Visual C++ IDE.

Checkpoint

1.10   What is an algorithm?

1.11   Why were computer programming languages invented?

1.12   What is the difference between a high-level language and a low-level language?

1.13   What does *portability* mean?

1.14   Explain the operations carried out by the preprocessor, compiler, and linker.

1.15   Explain what is stored in a source file, an object file, and an executable file.

1.16   What is an integrated development environment?

Figure 1-6

 1.4

What Is a Program Made of?

CONCEPT: There are certain elements that are common to all programming languages.

Language Elements

All programming languages have a few things in common. Table 1-2 lists the common elements you will find in almost every language.

Let's look at some specific parts of Program 1-1 (the pay-calculating program) to see examples of each element listed in the table above. For your convenience, Program 1-1 is listed again.

Table 1-2

Language Element	Description
Key Words	Words that have a special meaning. Key words may only be used for their intended purpose. Key words are also known as reserved words.
Programmer-Defined Identifiers	Words or names defined by the programmer. They are symbolic names that refer to variables or programming routines.
Operators	Operators perform operations on one or more operands. An operand is usually a piece of data, like a number.
Punctuation	Punctuation characters that mark the beginning or ending of a statement, or separate items in a list.
Syntax	Rules that must be followed when constructing a program. Syntax dictates how key words and operators may be used, and where punctuation symbols must appear.

Program 1-1

```
1   // This program calculates the user's pay.
2   #include <iostream>
3   using namespace std;
4
5   int main()
6   {
7       double hours, rate, pay;
8
9       // Get the number of hours worked.
10      cout << "How many hours did you work? ";
11      cin >> hours;
12
13      // Get the hourly pay rate.
14      cout << "How much do you get paid per hour? ";
15      cin >> rate;
16
17      // Calculate the pay.
18      pay = hours * rate;
19
20      // Display the pay.
21      cout << "You have earned $" << pay << endl;
22      return 0;
23  }
```

Key Words (Reserved Words)

Three of C++'s key words appear on lines 3 and 5: using, namespace, and int. The word double, which appears on line 7, is also a C++ key word. These words, which are always written in lowercase, each have a special meaning in C++ and can only be used for their intended purposes. As you will see, the programmer is allowed to make up his or her own names for certain things in a program. Key words, however, are reserved and cannot be used for anything other than their designated purposes. Part of learning a programming language is learning what the key words are, what they mean, and how to use them.

NOTE: The `#include <iostream>` statement in line 2 is a preprocessor directive.

NOTE: In C++, key words are written in all lowercase.

Programmer-Defined Identifiers

The words `hours`, `rate`, and `pay` that appear in the program on lines 7, 11, 15, 18, and 21 are programmer-defined identifiers. They are not part of the C++ language but rather are names made up by the programmer. In this particular program, these are the names of variables. As you will learn later in this chapter, variables are the names of memory locations that may hold data.

Operators

On line 18 the following code appears:

```
pay = hours * rate;
```

The = and * symbols are both operators. They perform operations on pieces of data known as operands. The * operator multiplies its two operands, which in this example are the variables `hours` and `rate`. The = symbol is called the assignment operator. It takes the value of the expression on the right and stores it in the variable whose name appears on the left. In this example, the = operator stores in the `pay` variable the result of the `hours` variable multiplied by the `rate` variable. In other words, the statement says, "Make the `pay` variable equal to `hours` times `rate`, or "`pay` is assigned the value of `hours` times `rate`."

Punctuation

Notice that lines 3, 7, 10, 11, 14, 15, 18, 21, and 22 all end with a semicolon. A semicolon in C++ is similar to a period in English: It marks the end of a complete sentence (or statement, as it is called in programming jargon). Semicolons do not appear at the end of every line in a C++ program, however. There are rules that govern where semicolons are required and where they are not. Part of learning C++ is learning where to place semicolons and other punctuation symbols.

Lines and Statements

Often, the contents of a program are thought of in terms of lines and statements. A "line" is just that—a single line as it appears in the body of a program. Program 1-1 is shown with each of its lines numbered. Most of the lines contain something meaningful; however, some of the lines are empty. The blank lines are only there to make the program more readable.

A statement is a complete instruction that causes the computer to perform some action. Here is the statement that appears in line 10 of Program 1-1:

```
cout << "How many hours did you work? ";
```

This statement causes the computer to display the message "How many hours did you work?" on the screen. Statements can be a combination of key words, operators, and programmer-defined symbols. Statements often occupy only one line in a program, but sometimes they are spread out over more than one line.

Variables

A variable is a named storage location in the computer's memory for holding a piece of information. The information stored in variables may change while the program is running (hence the name "variable"). Notice that in Program 1-1 the words hours, rate, and pay appear in several places. All three of these are the names of variables. The hours variable is used to store the number of hours the user has worked. The rate variable stores the user's hourly pay rate. The pay variable holds the result of hours multiplied by rate, which is the user's gross pay.

> **NOTE:** Notice the variables in Program 1-1 have names that reflect their purpose. In fact, it would be easy to guess what the variables were used for just by reading their names. This is discussed further in Chapter 2.

Variables are symbolic names that represent locations in the computer's random-access memory (RAM). When information is stored in a variable, it is actually stored in RAM. Assume a program has a variable named length. Figure 1-7 illustrates the way the variable name represents a memory location.

Figure 1-7

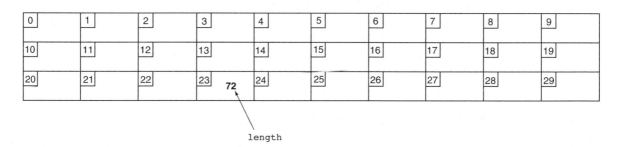

length

In Figure 1-7, the variable length is holding the value 72. The number 72 is actually stored in RAM at address 23, but the name length symbolically represents this storage location. If it helps, you can think of a variable as a box that holds information. In Figure 1-7, the number 72 is stored in the box named length. Only one item may be stored in the box at any given time. If the program stores another value in the box, it will take the place of the number 72.

Variable Definitions

In programming, there are two general types of data: numbers and characters. Numbers are used to perform mathematical operations and characters are used to print data on the screen or on paper.

Numeric data can be categorized even further. For instance, the following are all whole numbers, or integers:

```
5
7
-129
32154
```

The following are real, or floating-point numbers:

```
3.14159
6.7
1.0002
```

When creating a variable in a C++ program, you must know what type of data the program will be storing in it. Look at line 7 of Program 1-1:

```
double hours, rate, pay;
```

The word `double` in this statement indicates that the variables `hours`, `rate`, and `pay` will be used to hold double precision floating-point numbers. This statement is called a *variable definition*. It is used to *define* one or more variables that will be used in the program, and to indicate the type of data they will hold. The variable definition causes the variables to be created in memory, so all variables must be defined before they can be used. If you review the listing of Program 1-1, you will see that the variable definitions come before any other statements using those variables.

NOTE: Programmers often use the term "variable declaration" to mean the same thing as "variable definition." Strictly speaking, there is a difference between the two terms. A definition statement always causes a variable to be created in memory. Some types of declaration statements, however, do not cause a variable to be created in memory. You will learn more about declarations later in this book.

1.5 Input, Processing, and Output

CONCEPT: The three primary activities of a program are input, processing, and output.

Computer programs typically perform a three-step process of gathering input, performing some process on the information gathered, and then producing output. Input is information a program collects from the outside world. It can be sent to the program from the user, who is entering data at the keyboard or using the mouse. It can also be read from disk files or hardware devices connected to the computer. Program 1-1 allows the user to enter two pieces of information: the number of hours worked and the hourly pay rate. Lines 11 and 15 use the `cin` (pronounced "see in") object to perform these input operations:

```
cin >> hours;
cin >> rate;
```

Once information is gathered from the outside world, a program usually processes it in some manner. In Program 1-1, the hours worked and hourly pay rate are multiplied in line 18 and the result is assigned to the `pay` variable:

```
pay = hours * rate;
```

Output is information that a program sends to the outside world. It can be words or graphics displayed on a screen, a report sent to the printer, data stored in a file, or information sent to any device connected to the computer. Lines 10, 14, and 21 in Program 1-1 all perform output:

```
cout << "How many hours did you work? ";
cout << "How much do you get paid per hour? ";
cout << "You have earned $" << pay << endl;
```

These lines use the `cout` (pronounced "see out") object to display messages on the computer's screen. You will learn more details about the `cin` and `cout` objects in Chapter 2.

 Checkpoint

1.17   Describe the difference between a key word and a programmer-defined identifier.

1.18   Describe the difference between operators and punctuation symbols.

1.19   Describe the difference between a program line and a statement.

1.20   Why are variables called "variable"?

1.21   What happens to a variable's current contents when a new value is stored there?

1.22   What must take place in a program before a variable is used?

1.23   What are the three primary activities of a program?

 # 1.6 The Programming Process

CONCEPT: The programming process consists of several steps, which include design, creation, testing, and debugging activities.

Designing and Creating a Program

Now that you have been introduced to what a program is, it's time to consider the process of creating a program. Quite often, when inexperienced students are given programming assignments, they have trouble getting started because they don't know what to do first. If you find yourself in this dilemma, the steps listed in Figure 1-8 may help. These are the steps recommended for the process of writing a program.

Figure 1-8

1. Clearly define what the program is to do.
2. Visualize the program running on the computer.
3. Use design tools such as a hierarchy chart, flowcharts, or pseudocode to create a model of the program.
4. Check the model for logical errors.
5. Type the code, save it, and compile it.
6. Correct any errors found during compilation. Repeat Steps 5 and 6 as many times as necessary.
7. Run the program with test data for input.
8. Correct any errors found while running the program. Repeat Steps 5 through 8 as many times as necessary.
9. Validate the results of the program.

The steps listed in Figure 1-8 emphasize the importance of planning. Just as there are good ways and bad ways to paint a house, there are good ways and bad ways to create a program. A good program always begins with planning.

With the pay-calculating program as our example, let's look at each of the steps in more detail.

1. Clearly define what the program is to do.

This step requires that you identify the purpose of the program, the information that is to be input, the processing that is to take place, and the desired output. Let's examine each of these requirements for the example program:

Purpose	To calculate the user's gross pay.
Input	Number of hours worked, hourly pay rate.
Process	Multiply number of hours worked by hourly pay rate. The result is the user's gross pay.
Output	Display a message indicating the user's gross pay.

2. Visualize the program running on the computer.

Before you create a program on the computer, you should first create it in your mind. Step 2 is the visualization of the program. Try to imagine what the computer screen looks like while the program is running. If it helps, draw pictures of the screen, with sample input and output, at various points in the program. For instance, here is the screen produced by the pay-calculating program:

```
How many hours did you work? 10
How much do you get paid per hour? 15
You have earned $150
```

In this step, you must put yourself in the shoes of the user. What messages should the program display? What questions should it ask? By addressing these concerns, you will have already determined most of the program's output.

3. **Use design tools such as a hierarchy chart, flowcharts, or pseudocode to create a model of the program.**

While planning a program, the programmer uses one or more design tools to create a model of the program. Three common design tools are hierarchy charts, flowcharts, and pseudocode. A *hierarchy chart* is a diagram that graphically depicts the structure of a program. It has boxes that represent each step in the program. The boxes are connected in a way that illustrates their relationship to one another. Figure 1-9 shows a hierarchy chart for the pay-calculating program.

Figure 1-9

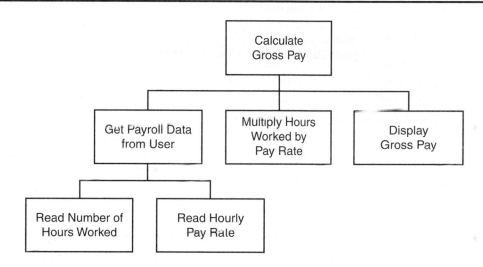

A hierarchy chart begins with the overall task, and then refines it into smaller subtasks. Each of the subtasks is then refined into even smaller sets of subtasks, until each is small enough to be easily performed. For instance, in Figure 1-9, the overall task "Calculate Gross Pay" is listed in the top-level box. That task is broken into three subtasks. The first subtask, "Get Payroll Data from User," is broken further into two subtasks. This process of "divide and conquer" is known as *top-down design*.

VideoNote

Introduction to Flowcharting

A *flowchart* is a diagram that shows the logical flow of a program. It is a useful tool for planning each operation a program performs, and the order in which the operations are to occur. For more information see Appendix C, Introduction to Flowcharting.

Pseudocode is a cross between human language and a programming language. Although the computer can't understand pseudocode, programmers often find it helpful to write an algorithm in a language that's "almost" a programming language, but still very similar to natural language. For example, here is pseudocode that describes the pay-calculating program:

VideoNote

Designing a Program with Pseudocode

Get payroll data.
Calculate gross pay.
Display gross pay.

Although the pseudocode above gives a broad view of the program, it doesn't reveal all the program's details. A more detailed version of the pseudocode follows.

Display "How many hours did you work?".
Input hours.
Display "How much do you get paid per hour?".
Input rate.
Store the value of hours times rate in the pay variable.
Display the value in the pay variable.

Notice the pseudocode contains statements that look more like commands than the English statements that describe the algorithm in Section 1.4 (What Is a Program Made of?). The pseudocode even names variables and describes mathematical operations.

4.   Check the model for logical errors.

Logical errors are mistakes that cause the program to produce erroneous results. Once a hierarchy chart, flowchart, or pseudocode model of the program is assembled, it should be checked for these errors. The programmer should trace through the charts or pseudocode, checking the logic of each step. If an error is found, the model can be corrected before the next step is attempted.

5.   Type the code, save it, and compile it.

Once a model of the program (hierarchy chart, flowchart, or pseudocode) has been created, checked, and corrected, the programmer is ready to write source code on the computer. The programmer saves the source code to a file, and begins the process of translating it to machine language. During this step the compiler will find any syntax errors that may exist in the program.

6.   Correct any errors found during compilation. Repeat Steps 5 and 6 as many times as necessary.

If the compiler reports any errors, they must be corrected. Steps 5 and 6 must be repeated until the program is free of compile-time errors.

7.   Run the program with test data for input.

Once an executable file is generated, the program is ready to be tested for run-time errors. A run-time error is an error that occurs while the program is running. These are usually logical errors, such as mathematical mistakes.

Testing for run-time errors requires that the program be executed with sample data or sample input. The sample data should be such that the correct output can be predicted. If the program does not produce the correct output, a logical error is present in the program.

8.   Correct any run-time errors found while running the program. Repeat Steps 5 through 8 as many times as necessary.

When run-time errors are found in a program, they must be corrected. You must identify the step where the error occurred and determine the cause. Desk-checking is a process that can help locate run-time errors. The term *desk-checking* means the programmer starts reading the program, or a portion of the program, and steps through each statement. A sheet of paper is often used in this process to jot down the current contents of all variables and sketch what the screen looks like after each output operation. When a variable's contents change, or information is displayed on the screen, this is noted. By stepping through each statement, many errors can be located and corrected. If an error is a result of incorrect logic (such as an improperly stated math formula), you must correct the statement or statements involved in the logic. If an error is due to an incomplete understanding of the program requirements, then you must restate the program purpose and modify the hierarchy and/or flowcharts, pseudocode, and source code. The program must then be saved, re-compiled and retested. This means Steps 5 though 8 must be repeated until the program reliably produces satisfactory results.

9. **Validate the results of the program.**

When you believe you have corrected all the run-time errors, enter test data and determine whether the program solves the original problem.

What Is Software Engineering?

The field of software engineering encompasses the whole process of crafting computer software. It includes designing, writing, testing, debugging, documenting, modifying, and maintaining complex software development projects. Like traditional engineers, software engineers use a number of tools in their craft. Here are a few examples:

- Program specifications
- Charts and diagrams of screen output
- Hierarchy charts and flowcharts
- Pseudocode
- Examples of expected input and desired output
- Special software designed for testing programs

Most commercial software applications are very large. In many instances one or more teams of programmers, not a single individual, develop them. It is important that the program requirements be thoroughly analyzed and divided into subtasks that are handled by individual teams, or individuals within a team.

In Step 3 of the programming process, you were introduced to the hierarchy chart as a tool for top-down design. The subtasks that are identified in a top-down design can easily become modules, or separate components of a program. If the program is very large or complex, a team of software engineers can be assigned to work on the individual modules. As the project develops, the modules are coordinated to finally become a single software application.

Procedural and Object-Oriented Programming

CONCEPT: Procedural programming and object-oriented programming are two ways of thinking about software development and program design.

C++ is a language that can be used for two methods of writing computer programs: *procedural programming* and *object-oriented programming*. This book is designed to teach you some of both.

In procedural programming, the programmer constructs procedures (or functions, as they are called in C++). The procedures are collections of programming statements that perform a specific task. The procedures each contain their own variables and commonly share variables with other procedures. This is illustrated by Figure 1-10.

Figure 1-10

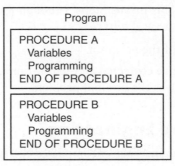

Procedural programming is centered on the procedure, or function. Object-oriented programming (OOP), on the other hand, is centered on the object. An object is a programming element that contains data and the procedures that operate on the data. It is a self-contained unit. This is illustrated in Figure 1-11.

Figure 1-11

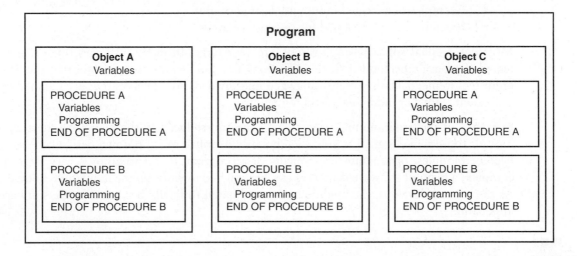

The objects contain, within themselves, both information and the ability to manipulate the information. Operations are carried out on the information in an object by sending the object a *message*. When an object receives a message instructing it to perform some operation, it carries out the instruction. As you study this text, you will encounter many other aspects of object-oriented programming.

 Checkpoint

1.24   What four items should you identify when defining what a program is to do?

1.25   What does it mean to "visualize a program running"? What is the value of such an activity?

1.26   What is a hierarchy chart?

1.27   Describe the process of desk-checking.

1.28   Describe what a compiler does with a program's source code.

1.29   What is a run-time error?

1.30   Is a syntax error (such as misspelling a key word) found by the compiler or when the program is running?

1.31   What is the purpose of testing a program with sample data or input?

1.32   Briefly describe the difference between procedural and object-oriented programming.

Review Questions and Exercises

Short Answer

1. Both main memory and secondary storage are types of memory. Describe the difference between the two.

2. What is the difference between operating system software and application software?

3. Indicate all the categories that the following operating systems belong to.

   System A   This system allows multiple users to run multiple programs simultaneously.

   System B   Only one user may access the system at a time, but multiple programs can be run simultaneously.

   System C   Only one user may access the system at a time, and only one program can be run on the system at a time.

4. Why must programs written in a high-level language be translated into machine language before they can be run?

5. Why is it easier to write a program in a high-level language than in machine language?

6. Explain the difference between an object file and an executable file.

7. What is the difference between a syntax error and a logical error?

Fill-in-the-Blank

8. Computers can do many different jobs because they can be _____.

9. The job of the _____ is to fetch instructions, carry out the operations commanded by the instructions, and produce some outcome or resultant information.

10. Internally, the CPU consists of the _____ and the _____.

11. A(n) _____ is an example of a secondary storage device.

12. The two general categories of software are _____ and _____.

13. A program is a set of _____.

14. Since computers can't be programmed in natural human language, algorithms must be written in a(n) _____ language.

15. _____ is the only language computers really process.

16. _____ languages are close to the level of humans in terms of readability.

17. _____ languages are close to the level of the computer.

18. A program's ability to run on several different types of computer systems is called _____.

19. Words that have special meaning in a programming language are called _____.

20. Words or names defined by the programmer are called _____.

21. _____ are characters or symbols that perform operations on one or more operands.

22. _____ characters or symbols mark the beginning or ending of programming statements, or separate items in a list.

23. The rules that must be followed when constructing a program are called _____.

24. A(n) _____ is a named storage location.

25. A variable must be _____ before it can be used in a program.

26. The three primary activities of a program are _____, _____, and _____.

27. _____ is information a program gathers from the outside world.

28. _____ is information a program sends to the outside world.

29. A(n) _____ is a diagram that graphically illustrates the structure of a program.

Algorithm Workbench

Draw hierarchy charts or flowcharts that depict the programs described below. (See Appendix C for instructions on creating flowcharts.)

30. Available Credit

    The following steps should be followed in a program that calculates a customer's available credit:

    1. Display the message "Enter the customer's maximum credit."

    2. Wait for the user to enter the customer's maximum credit.

    3. Display the message "Enter the amount of credit used by the customer."

    4. Wait for the user to enter the customer's credit used.

    5. Subtract the used credit from the maximum credit to get the customer's available credit.

    6. Display a message that shows the customer's available credit.

31. Sales Tax

    Design a hierarchy chart or flowchart for a program that calculates the total of a retail sale. The program should ask the user for:
    - The retail price of the item being purchased
    - The sales tax rate

    Once these items have been entered, the program should calculate and display:
    - The sales tax for the purchase
    - The total of the sale

VideoNote

Designing the
Account
Balance
Program

32. Account Balance

    Design a hierarchy chart or flowchart for a program that calculates the current balance in a savings account. The program must ask the user for:
    – The starting balance
    – The total dollar amount of deposits made
    – The total dollar amount of withdrawals made
    – The monthly interest rate

    Once the program calculates the current balance, it should be displayed on the screen.

Predict the Result

Questions 33–35 are programs expressed as English statements. What would each display on the screen if they were actual programs?

VideoNote

Predicting the
Result of
Problem 33

33. The variable x starts with the value 0.
    The variable y starts with the value 5.
    Add 1 to x.
    Add 1 to y.
    Add x and y, and store the result in y.
    Display the value in y on the screen.

34. The variable j starts with the value 10.
    The variable k starts with the value 2.
    The variable l starts with the value 4.
    Store the value of j times k in j.
    Store the value of k times l in l.
    Add j and l, and store the result in k.
    Display the value in k on the screen.

35. The variable a starts with the value 1.
    The variable b starts with the value 10.
    The variable c starts with the value 100.
    The variable x starts with the value 0.
    Store the value of c times 3 in x.
    Add the value of b times 6 to the value already in x.
    Add the value of a times 5 to the value already in x.
    Display the value in x on the screen.

Find the Error

36. The following *pseudocode algorithm* has an error. The program is supposed to ask the user for the length and width of a rectangular room, and then display the room's area. The program must multiply the width by the length in order to determine the area. Find the error.

    area = width × length.
    Display "What is the room's width?".
    Input width.
    Display "What is the room's length?".
    Input length.
    Display area.

TOPICS

2.1 The Parts of a C++ Program

CONCEPT: C++ programs have parts and components that serve specific purposes.

Every C++ program has an anatomy. Unlike human anatomy, the parts of C++ programs are not always in the same place. Nevertheless, the parts are there and your first step in learning C++ is to learn what they are. We will begin by looking at Program 2-1.

Let's examine the program line by line. Here's the first line:

```
// A simple C++ program
```

The // marks the beginning of a *comment*. The compiler ignores everything from the double slash to the end of the line. That means you can type anything you want on that line and the compiler will never complain! Although comments are not required, they are very important to programmers. Most programs are much more complicated than the example in Program 2-1, and comments help explain what's going on.

Program 2-1

```
1   // A simple C++ program
2   #include <iostream>
3   using namespace std;
4
5   int main()
6   {
7      cout << "Programming is great fun!";
8      return 0;
9   }
```

The output of the program is shown below. This is what appears on the screen when the program runs.

Program Output
```
Programming is great fun!
```

Line 2 looks like this:

```
#include <iostream>
```

Because this line starts with a #, it is called a *preprocessor directive*. The preprocessor reads your program before it is compiled and only executes those lines beginning with a # symbol. Think of the preprocessor as a program that "sets up" your source code for the compiler.

The #include directive causes the preprocessor to include the contents of another file in the program. The word inside the brackets, iostream, is the name of the file that is to be included. The iostream file contains code that allows a C++ program to display output on the screen and read input from the keyboard. Because this program uses cout to display screen output, the iostream file must be included. The contents of the iostream file are included in the program at the point the #include statement appears. The iostream file is called a *header file,* so it should be included at the head, or top, of the program.

Line 3 reads:

```
using namespace std;
```

Programs usually contain several items with unique names. In this chapter you will learn to create variables. In Chapter 6 you will learn to create functions. In Chapter 13 you will learn to create objects. Variables, functions, and objects are examples of program entities that must have names. C++ uses *namespaces* to organize the names of program entities. The statement using namespace std; declares that the program will be accessing entities whose names are part of the namespace called std. (Yes, even namespaces have names.) The reason the program needs access to the std namespace is because every name created by the iostream file is part of that namespace. In order for a program to use the entities in iostream, it must have access to the std namespace.

Line 5 reads:

```
int main()
```

This marks the beginning of a function. A *function* can be thought of as a group of one or more programming statements that collectively has a name. The name of this function is *main,* and the set of parentheses that follows the name indicate that it is a function. The word `int` stands for "integer." It indicates that the function sends an integer value back to the operating system when it is finished executing.

Although most C++ programs have more than one function, every C++ program must have a function called `main`. It is the starting point of the program. If you are ever reading someone else's C++ program and want to find where it starts, just look for the function named `main`.

> **NOTE:** C++ is a case-sensitive language. That means it regards uppercase letters as being entirely different characters than their lowercase counterparts. In C++, the name of the function `main` must be written in all lowercase letters. C++ doesn't see "Main" the same as "main," or "INT" the same as "int." This is true for all the C++ key words.

Line 6 contains a single, solitary character:

    {

This is called a left-brace, or an opening brace, and it is associated with the beginning of the function `main`. All the statements that make up a function are enclosed in a set of braces. If you look at the third line down from the opening brace you'll see the closing brace. Everything between the two braces is the contents of the function `main`.

> **WARNING!** Make sure you have a closing brace for every opening brace in your program!

After the opening brace you see the following statement in line 7:

    cout << "Programming is great fun!";

To put it simply, this line displays a message on the screen. You will read more about `cout` and the `<<` operator later in this chapter. The message "Programming is great fun!" is printed without the quotation marks. In programming terms, the group of characters inside the quotation marks is called a *string literal* or *string constant.*

> **NOTE:** This is the only line in the program that causes anything to be printed on the screen. The other lines, like `#include <iostream>` and `int main()`, are necessary for the framework of your program, but they do not cause any screen output. Remember, a program is a set of instructions for the computer. If something is to be displayed on the screen, you must use a programming statement for that purpose.

At the end of the line is a semicolon. Just as a period marks the end of a sentence, a semicolon marks the end of a complete statement in C++. Comments are ignored by the compiler, so the semicolon isn't required at the end of a comment. Preprocessor directives, like `#include` statements, simply end at the end of the line and never require semicolons. The beginning of a function, like `int main()`, is not a complete statement, so you don't place a semicolon there either.

It might seem that the rules for where to put a semicolon are not clear at all. Rather than worry about it now, just concentrate on learning the parts of a program. You'll soon get a feel for where you should and should not use semicolons.

Line 8 reads:

```
return 0;
```

This sends the integer value 0 back to the operating system upon the program's completion. The value 0 usually indicates that a program executed successfully.

Line 9 contains the closing brace:

```
}
```

This brace marks the end of the main function. Since main is the only function in this program, it also marks the end of the program.

In the sample program you encountered several sets of special characters. Table 2-1 provides a short summary of how they were used.

Table 2-1   Special Characters

Character	Name	Description
//	Double slash	Marks the beginning of a comment.
#	Pound sign	Marks the beginning of a preprocessor directive.
< >	Opening and closing brackets	Encloses a filename when used with the #include directive.
( )	Opening and closing parentheses	Used in naming a function, as in int main()
{ }	Opening and closing braces	Encloses a group of statements, such as the contents of a function.
" "	Opening and closing quotation marks	Encloses a string of characters, such as a message that is to be printed on the screen.
;	Semicolon	Marks the end of a complete programming statement.

 Checkpoint

2.1   The following C++ program will not compile because the lines have been mixed up.

```
int main()
}
// A crazy mixed up program
return 0;
#include <iostream>
cout << "In 1492 Columbus sailed the ocean blue.";
{
using namespace std;
```

When the lines are properly arranged the program should display the following on the screen:

```
In 1492 Columbus sailed the ocean blue.
```

Rearrange the lines in the correct order. Test the program by entering it on the computer, compiling it, and running it.

2.2 The cout Object

CONCEPT: Use the cout object to display information on the computer's screen.

In this section you will learn to write programs that produce output on the screen. The simplest type of screen output that a program can display is *console output*, which is merely plain text. The word *console* is an old computer term. It comes from the days when a computer operator interacted with the system by typing on a terminal. The terminal, which consisted of a simple screen and keyboard, was known as the *console*.

On modern computers, running graphical operating systems such as Windows or Mac OS X, console output is usually displayed in a window such as the one shown in Figure 2-1. In C++ you use the cout object to produce console output. (You can think of the word cout as meaning console output.)

Figure 2-1　A Console Window

VideoNote
Using cout

cout is classified as a *stream object*, which means it works with streams of data. To print a message on the screen, you send a stream of characters to cout. Let's look at line 7 from Program 2-1:

```
cout << "Programming is great fun!";
```

Notice that the << operator is used to send the string "Programming is great fun!" to cout. When the << symbol is used this way, it is called the *stream insertion operator*. The item immediately to the right of the operator is sent to cout and then displayed on the screen.

The stream insertion operator is always written as two less-than signs with no space between them. Because you are using it to send a stream of data to the cout object, you can think of the stream insertion operator as an arrow that must point toward cout. This is illustrated in Figure 2-2.

Program 2-2 is another way to write the same program.

Figure 2-2

```
cout << "Programming is great fun!";
```

Think of the stream insertion operator as an
arrow that points toward cout.

```
cout ◄── "Programming is great fun!";
```

Program 2-2

```cpp
1   // A simple C++ program
2   #include <iostream>
3   using namespace std;
4
5   int main()
6   {
7      cout << "Programming is " << "great fun!";
8      return 0;
9   }
```

Program Output

```
Programming is great fun!
```

As you can see, the stream-insertion operator can be used to send more than one item to cout. The output of this program is identical to that of Program 2-1. Program 2-3 shows yet another way to accomplish the same thing.

Program 2-3

```cpp
1    // A simple C++ program
2    #include <iostream>
3    using namespace std;
4
5    int main()
6    {
7       cout << "Programming is ";
8       cout << "great fun!";
9       return 0;
10   }
```

Program Output

```
Programming is great fun!
```

An important concept to understand about Program 2-3 is that, although the output is broken up into two programming statements, this program will still display the message on a single line. Unless you specify otherwise, the information you send to cout is displayed in a continuous stream. Sometimes this can produce less-than-desirable results. Program 2-4 is an example.

The layout of the actual output looks nothing like the arrangement of the strings in the source code. First, notice there is no space displayed between the words "sellers" and "during," or between "June:" and "Computer." cout displays messages exactly as they are sent. If spaces are to be displayed, they must appear in the strings.

Program 2-4

```
1   // An unruly printing program
2   #include <iostream>
3   using namespace std;
4
5   int main()
6   {
7       cout << "The following items were top sellers";
8       cout << "during the month of June:";
9       cout << "Computer games";
10      cout << "Coffee";
11      cout << "Aspirin";
12      return 0;
13  }
```

Program Output

```
The following items were top sellersduring the month of June:Computer gamesCoff
eeAspirin
```

Second, even though the output is broken into five lines in the source code, it comes out as one long line of output. Because the output is too long to fit on one line on the screen, it wraps around to a second line when displayed. The reason the output comes out as one long line is because cout does not start a new line unless told to do so. There are two ways to instruct cout to start a new line. The first is to send cout a *stream manipulator* called endl (which is pronounced "end-line" or "end-L"). Program 2-5 is an example.

Program 2-5

```
1   // A well-adjusted printing program
2   #include <iostream>
3   using namespace std;
4
5   int main()
6   {
7       cout << "The following items were top sellers" << endl;
8       cout << "during the month of June:" << endl;
9       cout << "Computer games" << endl;
10      cout << "Coffee" << endl;
11      cout << "Aspirin" << endl;
12      return 0;
13  }
```

(program output continues)

Program 2-5   *(continued)*

Program Output

```
The following items were top sellers
during the month of June:
Computer games
Coffee
Aspirin
```

 NOTE: The last character in endl is the lowercase letter L, *not* the number one.

Every time cout encounters an endl stream manipulator it advances the output to the beginning of the next line for subsequent printing. The manipulator can be inserted anywhere in the stream of characters sent to cout, outside the double quotes. The following statements show an example.

```
cout << "My pets are" << endl << "dog";
cout << endl << "cat" << endl << "bird" << endl;
```

Another way to cause cout to go to a new line is to insert an *escape sequence* in the string itself. An escape sequence starts with the backslash character (\\), and is followed by one or more control characters. It allows you to control the way output is displayed by embedding commands within the string itself. Program 2-6 is an example.

Program 2-6

```
 1   // Yet another well-adjusted printing program
 2   #include <iostream>
 3   using namespace std;
 4
 5   int main()
 6   {
 7      cout << "The following items were top sellers\n";
 8      cout << "during the month of June:\n";
 9      cout << "Computer games\nCoffee";
10      cout << "\nAspirin\n";
11      return 0;
12   }
```

Program Output

```
The following items were top sellers
during the month of June:
Computer games
Coffee
Aspirin
```

The *newline escape sequence* is \\n. When cout encounters \\n in a string, it doesn't print it on the screen, but interprets it as a special command to advance the output cursor to the next line. You have probably noticed inserting the escape sequence requires less typing than inserting endl. That's why many programmers prefer it.

A common mistake made by beginning C++ students is to use a forward slash (/) instead of a backslash (\) when trying to write an escape sequence. This will not work. For example, look at the following code.

```
// Error!
cout << "Four Score/nAnd seven/nYears ago./n";
```

In this code, the programmer accidentally wrote /n when he or she meant to write \n. The cout object will simply display the /n characters on the screen. This code will display the following output:

```
Four Score/nAnd seven/nYears ago./n
```

Another common mistake is to forget to put the \n inside quotation marks. For example, the following code will not compile.

```
// Error! This code will not compile.
cout << "Good" << \n;
cout << "Morning" << \n;
```

This code will result in an error because the \n sequences are not inside quotation marks. We can correct the code by placing the \n sequences inside the string literals, as shown here:

```
// This will work.
cout << "Good\n";
cout << "Morning\n";
```

There are many escape sequences in C++. They give you the ability to exercise greater control over the way information is output by your program. Table 2-2 lists a few of them.

Table 2-2 Common Escape Sequences

Escape Sequence	Name	Description
\n	Newline	Causes the cursor to go to the next line for subsequent printing.
\t	Horizontal tab	Causes the cursor to skip over to the next tab stop.
\a	Alarm	Causes the computer to beep.
\b	Backspace	Causes the cursor to back up, or move left one position.
\r	Return	Causes the cursor to go to the beginning of the current line, not the next line.
\\	Backslash	Causes a backslash to be printed.
\'	Single quote	Causes a single quotation mark to be printed.
\"	Double quote	Causes a double quotation mark to be printed.

 WARNING! When using escape sequences, do not put a space between the backslash and the control character.

2.3   The #include Directive

CONCEPT: The #include directive causes the contents of another file to be inserted into the program.

Now is a good time to expand our discussion of the #include directive. The following line has appeared near the top of every example program.

```
#include <iostream>
```

The header file iostream must be included in any program that uses the cout object. This is because cout is not part of the "core" of the C++ language. Specifically, it is part of the *input–output stream library*. The header file, iostream, contains information describing iostream objects. Without it, the compiler will not know how to properly compile a program that uses cout.

Preprocessor directives are not C++ statements. They are commands to the preprocessor, which runs prior to the compiler (hence the name "preprocessor"). The preprocessor's job is to set programs up in a way that makes life easier for the programmer.

For example, any program that uses the cout object must contain the extensive setup information found in iostream. The programmer could type all this information into the program, but it would be too time consuming. An alternative would be to use an editor to "cut and paste" the information into the program, but that would quickly become tiring as well. The solution is to let the preprocessor insert the contents of iostream automatically.

WARNING! Do not put semicolons at the end of processor directives. Because preprocessor directives are not C++ statements, they do not require semicolons. In many cases an error will result from a preprocessor directive terminated with a semicolon.

An #include directive must always contain the name of a file. The preprocessor inserts the entire contents of the file into the program at the point it encounters the #include directive. The compiler doesn't actually see the #include directive. Instead it sees the code that was inserted by the preprocessor, just as if the programmer had typed it there.

The code contained in header files is C++ code. Typically it describes complex objects like cout. Later you will learn to create your own header files.

 Checkpoint

2.2   The following C++ program will not compile because the lines have been mixed up.

```
cout << "Success\n";
cout << " Success\n\n";
int main()
cout << "Success";
}
using namespace std;
// It's a mad, mad program
```

```
#include <iostream>
cout << "Success\n";
{
return 0;
```

When the lines are properly arranged the program should display the following on the screen:

Program Output
```
Success
Success Success

Success
```

Rearrange the lines in the correct order. Test the program by entering it on the computer, compiling it, and running it.

2.3   Study the following program and show what it will print on the screen.

```
// The Works of Wolfgang
#include <iostream>
using namespace std;

int main()
{
    cout << "The works of Wolfgang\ninclude the following";
    cout << "\nThe Turkish March" << endl;
    cout << "and Symphony No. 40 ";
    cout << "in G minor." << endl;
    return 0;
}
```

2.4   On paper, write a program that will display your name on the first line, your street address on the second line, your city, state, and ZIP code on the third line, and your telephone number on the fourth line. Place a comment with today's date at the top of the program. Test your program by entering, compiling, and running it.

2.4 Variables and Literals

CONCEPT: Variables represent storage locations in the computer's memory. Literals are constant values that are assigned to variables.

As you discovered in Chapter 1, variables allow you to store and work with data in the computer's memory. They provide an "interface" to RAM. Part of the job of programming is to determine how many variables a program will need and what types of information they will hold. Program 2-7 is an example of a C++ program with a variable. Take a look at line 7:

```
int number;
```

VideoNote
Variable
Definitions

This is called a *variable definition*. It tells the compiler the variable's name and the type of data it will hold. This line indicates the variable's name is number. The word int stands for integer, so number will only be used to hold integer numbers. Later in this chapter you will learn all the types of data that C++ allows.

Program 2-7

```
 1  // This program has a variable.
 2  #include <iostream>
 3  using namespace std;
 4
 5  int main()
 6  {
 7     int number;
 8
 9     number = 5;
10     cout << "The value in number is " << number << endl;
11     return 0;
12  }
```

Program Output

```
The value in number is 5
```

 NOTE: You must have a definition for every variable you intend to use in a program. In C++, variable definitions can appear at any point in the program. Later in this chapter, and throughout the book, you will learn the best places to define variables.

Notice that variable definitions end with a semicolon. Now look at line 9:

```
number = 5;
```

This is called an *assignment*. The equal sign is an operator that copies the value on its right (5) into the variable named on its left (number). After this line executes, number will be set to 5.

 NOTE: This line does not print anything on the computer's screen. It runs silently behind the scenes, storing a value in RAM.

Look at line 10.

```
cout << "The value in number is " << number << endl;
```

The second item sent to cout is the variable name number. When you send a variable name to cout it prints the variable's contents. Notice there are no quotation marks around number. Look at what happens in Program 2-8.

Program 2-8

```
 1  // This program has a variable.
 2  #include <iostream>
 3  using namespace std;
 4
 5  int main()
 6  {
 7     int number;
 8
```

(program continues)

Program 2-8   *(continued)*

```
 9     number = 5;
10     cout << "The value in number is " << "number" << endl;
11     return 0;
12  }
```

Program Output
```
The value in number is number
```

When double quotation marks are placed around the word number it becomes a string literal, and is no longer a variable name. When string literals are sent to cout they are printed exactly as they appear inside the quotation marks. You've probably noticed by now that the endl stream manipulator has no quotation marks around it, for the same reason.

Sometimes a Number Isn't a Number

As shown in Program 2-8, just placing quotation marks around a variable name changes the program's results. In fact, placing double quotation marks around anything that is not intended to be a string literal will create an error of some type. For example, in Program 2-8 the number 5 was assigned to the variable number. It would have been incorrect to perform the assignment this way:

```
number = "5";
```

In this line, 5 is no longer an integer, but a string literal. Because number was defined as an integer variable, you can only store integers in it. The integer 5 and the string literal "5" are not the same thing.

The fact that numbers can be represented as strings frequently confuses students who are new to programming. Just remember that strings are intended for humans to read. They are to be printed on computer screens or paper. Numbers, however, are intended primarily for mathematical operations. You cannot perform math on strings. Before numbers can be displayed on the screen, they must first be converted to strings. (Fortunately, cout handles the conversion automatically when you send a number to it.)

Literals

A variable is called a "variable" because its value may be changed. A literal, on the other hand, is a value that does not change during the program's execution. Program 2-9 contains both literals and a variable.

Program 2-9

```
1  // This program has literals and a variable.
2  #include <iostream>
3  using namespace std;
4
5  int main()
6  {
```

(program continues)

Program 2-9   *(continued)*

```
7      int apples;
8
9      apples = 20;
10     cout << "Today we sold " << apples << " bushels of apples.\n";
11     return 0;
12  }
```

Program Output

```
Today we sold 20 bushels of apples.
```

Of course, the variable is `apples`. It is defined as an integer. Table 2-3 lists the literals found in the program.

Table 2-3

Literal	Type of Literal
20	Integer literal
"Today we sold "	String literal
"bushels of apples.\n"	String literal
0	Integer literal

What are literals used for? As you can see from this program, they are commonly used to store known values in variables and display messages on the screen or a printout.

NOTE: Literals are also called constants.

Checkpoint

2.5   Examine the following program.

```
// This program uses variables and literals.
#include <iostream>
using namespace std;

int main()
{
    int little;
    int big;

    little = 2;
    big = 2000;
    cout << "The little number is " << little << endl;
    cout << "The big number is " << big << endl;
    return 0;
}
```

List all the variables and literals that appear in the program.

2.6   What will the following program display on the screen?

```
#include <iostream>
using namespace std;
```

```
int main()
{
    int number;

    number = 712;
    cout << "The value is " << "number" << endl;
    return 0;
}
```

2.5 Identifiers

CONCEPT: Choose variable names that indicate what the variables are used for.

An *identifier* is a programmer-defined name that represents some element of a program. Variable names are examples of identifiers. You may choose your own variable names in C++, as long as you do not use any of the C++ *key words*. The key words make up the "core" of the language and have specific purposes. Table 2-4 shows a complete list of the C++ key words. Note that they are all lowercase.

Table 2-4   The C++ Key Words

and	continue	goto	public	try
and_eq	default	if	register	typedef
asm	delete	inline	reinterpret_cast	typeid
auto	do	int	return	typename
bitand	double	long	short	union
bitor	dynamic_cast	mutable	signed	unsigned
bool	else	namespace	sizeof	using
break	enum	new	static	virtual
case	explicit	not	static_cast	void
catch	export	not_eq	struct	volatile
char	extern	operator	switch	wchar_t
class	false	or	template	while
compl	float	or_eq	this	xor
const	for	private	throw	xor_eq
const_cast	friend	protected	true	

You should always choose names for your variables that give an indication of what the variables are used for. You may be tempted to define variables with names like this:

```
int x;
```

The rather nondescript name, x, gives no clue as to the variable's purpose. Here is a better example.

```
int itemsOrdered;
```

The name `itemsOrdered` gives anyone reading the program an idea of the variable's use. This way of coding helps produce self-documenting programs, which means you get an understanding of what the program is doing just by reading its code. Because real-world programs usually have thousands of lines, it is important that they be as self-documenting as possible.

You probably have noticed the mixture of uppercase and lowercase letters in the name itemsOrdered. Although all of C++'s key words must be written in lowercase, you may use uppercase letters in variable names.

The reason the O in itemsOrdered is capitalized is to improve readability. Normally "items ordered" is two words. Unfortunately you cannot have spaces in a variable name, so the two words must be combined into one. When "items" and "ordered" are stuck together you get a variable definition like this:

```
int itemsordered;
```

Capitalization of the first letter of the second word and succeeding words makes itemsOrdered easier to read. It should be mentioned that this style of coding is not required. You are free to use all lowercase letters, all uppercase letters, or any combination of both. In fact, some programmers use the underscore character to separate words in a variable name, as in the following.

```
int items_ordered;
```

Legal Identifiers

Regardless of which style you adopt, be consistent and make your variable names as sensible as possible. Here are some specific rules that must be followed with all identifiers.

- The first character must be one of the letters a through z, A through Z, or an underscore character (_).
- After the first character you may use the letters a through z or A through Z, the digits 0 through 9, or underscores.
- Uppercase and lowercase characters are distinct. This means ItemsOrdered is not the same as itemsordered.

Table 2-5 lists variable names and tells whether each is legal or illegal in C++.

Table 2-5   Some Variable Names

Variable Name	Legal or Illegal?
dayOfWeek	Legal.
3dGraph	Illegal. Variable names cannot begin with a digit.
_employee_num	Legal.
June1997	Legal.
Mixture#3	Illegal. Variable names may only use letters, digits, or underscores.

2.6   Integer Data Types

CONCEPT: There are many different types of data. Variables are classified according to their data type, which determines the kind of information that may be stored in them. Integer variables can only hold whole numbers.

Computer programs collect pieces of data from the real world and manipulate them in various ways. There are many different types of data. In the realm of numeric information, for example, there are whole numbers and fractional numbers. There are negative numbers and positive numbers. And there are numbers so large, and others so small, that they don't even have a name. Then there is textual information. Names and addresses, for instance, are stored as groups of characters. When you write a program you must determine what types of information it will be likely to encounter.

If you are writing a program to calculate the number of miles to a distant star, you'll need variables that can hold very large numbers. If you are designing software to record microscopic dimensions, you'll need to store very small and precise numbers. Additionally, if you are writing a program that must perform thousands of intensive calculations, you'll want variables that can be processed quickly. The data type of a variable determines all of these factors.

Although C++ offers many data types, in the very broadest sense there are only two: numeric and character. Numeric data types are broken into two additional categories: integer and floating point. Integers are whole numbers like 12, 157, –34, and 2. Floating point numbers have a decimal point, like 23.7, 189.0231, and 0.987. Additionally, the integer and floating point data types are broken into even more classifications. Before we discuss the character data type, let's carefully examine the variations of numeric data.

Your primary considerations for selecting a numeric data type are:

- The largest and smallest numbers that may be stored in the variable
- How much memory the variable uses
- Whether the variable stores signed or unsigned numbers
- The number of decimal places of precision the variable has

The size of a variable is the number of bytes of memory it uses. Typically, the larger a variable is, the greater the range it can hold.

Table 2-6 shows the C++ integer data types with their typical sizes and ranges.

 NOTE. The data type sizes and ranges shown in Table 2-6 are typical on many systems. Depending on your operating system, the sizes and ranges may be different.

Table 2-6 Integer Data Types, Sizes, and Ranges

Data Type	Size	Range
short	2 bytes	–32,768 to +32,767
unsigned short	2 bytes	0 to +65,535
int	4 bytes	–2,147,483,648 to +2,147,483,647
unsigned int	4 bytes	0 to 4,294,967,295
long	4 bytes	–2,147,483,648 to +2,147,483,647
unsigned long	4 bytes	0 to 4,294,967,295

Here are some examples of variable definitions:

```
int days;
unsigned speed;
short month;
unsigned short amount;
long deficit;
unsigned long insects;
```

Unsigned data types can only store nonnegative values. They can be used when you know your program will not encounter negative values. For example, variables that hold ages or weights would rarely hold numbers less than 0.

 NOTE: An unsigned int variable can also be defined using only the word unsigned. For example, the following variable definitions are equivalent.

```
unsigned int days;
unsigned days;
```

Notice in Table 2-6 that the int and long data types have the same sizes and ranges, and that the unsigned int data type has the same size and range as the unsigned long data type. This is not always true because the size of integers is dependent on the type of system you are using. Here are the only guarantees:

- Integers are at least as big as short integers.
- Long integers are at least as big as integers.
- Unsigned short integers are the same size as short integers.
- Unsigned integers are the same size as integers.
- Unsigned long integers are the same size as long integers.

Later in this chapter you will learn to use the sizeof operator to determine how large all the data types are on your computer.

As mentioned before, variables are defined by stating the data type key word followed by the name of the variable. In Program 2-10 an integer, an unsigned integer, and a long integer have been defined.

Program 2-10

```
 1   // This program has variables of several of the integer types.
 2   #include <iostream>
 3   using namespace std;
 4
 5   int main()
 6   {
 7      int checking;
 8      unsigned int miles;
 9      long days;
10
11      checking = -20;
12      miles = 4276;
13      days = 189000;
14      cout << "We have made a long journey of " << miles;
15      cout << " miles.\n";
16      cout << "Our checking account balance is " << checking;
17      cout << "\nAbout " << days << " days ago Columbus ";
18      cout << "stood on this spot.\n";
19      return 0;
20   }
```

Program Output

```
We have made a long journey of 4276 miles.
Our checking account balance is -20
About 189000 days ago Columbus stood on this spot.
```

In most programs you will need more than one variable of any given data type. If a program uses two integers, `length` and `width`, they could be defined separately, like this:

```
int length;
int width;
```

It is easier, however, to combine both variable definitions on one line:

```
int length, width;
```

You can define several variables of the same type like this, simply separating their names with commas. Program 2-11 illustrates this.

Program 2-11

```
 1   // This program shows three variables defined on the same line.
 2   #include <iostream>
 3   using namespace std;
 4
 5   int main()
 6   {
 7      int floors, rooms, suites;
 8
 9      floors = 15;
10      rooms = 300;
11      suites = 30;
12      cout << "The Grande Hotel has " << floors << " floors\n";
13      cout << "with " << rooms << " rooms and " << suites;
14      cout << " suites.\n";
15      return 0;
16   }
```

Program Output

```
The Grande Hotel has 15 floors
with 300 rooms and 30 suites.
```

Integer and Long Integer Literals

Look at lines 9, 10, and 11 in Program 2-11:

```
floors = 15;
rooms = 300;
suites = 30;
```

Each of these lines contains an integer literal. In C++, integer literals are normally stored in memory just as an `int`. On a system that uses 2 byte integers and 4 byte longs, the literal 50000 is too large to be stored as an `int`, so it is stored as a `long`.

One of the pleasing characteristics of the C++ language is that it allows you to control almost every aspect of your program. If you need to change the way something is stored in memory, the tools are provided to do that. For example, what if you are in a situation where you have an integer literal, but you need it to be stored in memory as a long integer? (Rest assured, this is a situation that does arise.) C++ allows you to force an integer literal to be stored as a long integer by placing the letter L at the end of the number. Here is an example:

```
32L
```

On a computer that uses 2-byte integers and 4-byte long integers, this literal will use 4 bytes. This is called a long integer literal.

NOTE: You can use either an uppercase or lowercase L. The lowercase l looks too much like the number 1, so you should always use the uppercase L.

If You Plan to Continue in Computer Science: Hexadecimal and Octal Literals

Programmers commonly express values in numbering systems other than decimal (or base 10). Hexadecimal (base 16) and octal (base 8) are popular because they make certain programming tasks more convenient than decimal numbers do.

By default, C++ assumes that all integer literals are expressed in decimal. You express hexadecimal numbers by placing 0x in front of them. (This is zero-x, not oh-x.) Here is how the hexadecimal number F4 would be expressed in C++:

```
0xF4
```

Octal numbers must be preceded by a 0 (zero, not oh). For example, the octal 31 would be written

```
031
```

NOTE: You will not be writing programs for some time that require this type of manipulation. It is important, however, that you understand this material. Good programmers should develop the skills for reading other people's source code. You may find yourself reading programs that use items like long integer, hexadecimal, or octal literals.

Checkpoint

2.7 Which of the following are illegal variable names, and why?

```
x
99bottles
july97
theSalesFigureForFiscalYear98
r&d
grade_report
```

2.8 Is the variable name `Sales` the same as `sales`? Why or why not?

2.9   Refer to the data types listed in Table 2-6 for these questions.

   A) If a variable needs to hold numbers in the range 32 to 6,000, what data type would be best?

   B) If a variable needs to hold numbers in the range –40,000 to +40,000, what data type would be best?

   C) Which of the following literals uses more memory? 20 or 20L

2.10   On any computer, which data type uses more memory, an integer or an unsigned integer?

2.7 The char Data Type

You might be wondering why there isn't a 1-byte integer data type. Actually there is. It is called the char data type, which gets its name from the word "character." As its name suggests, it is primarily for storing characters, but strictly speaking, it is an integer data type.

> **NOTE:** On some systems the char data type is larger than 1 byte.

The reason an integer data type is used to store characters is because characters are internally represented by numbers. Each printable character, as well as many nonprintable characters, is assigned a unique number. The most commonly used method for encoding characters is ASCII, which stands for the American Standard Code for Information Interchange. (There are other codes, such as EBCDIC, which is used by many IBM mainframes.)

When a character is stored in memory, it is actually the numeric code that is stored. When the computer is instructed to print the value on the screen, it displays the character that corresponds with the numeric code.

You may want to refer to Appendix A, which shows the ASCII character set. Notice that the number 65 is the code for A, 66 is the code for A, and so on. Program 2-12 demonstrates that when you work with characters, you are actually working with numbers.

Program 2-12

```
 1   // This program demonstrates the close relationship between
 2   // characters and integers.
 3   #include <iostream>
 4   using namespace std;
 5
 6   int main()
 7   {
 8      char letter;
 9
10      letter = 65;
11      cout << letter << endl;
12      letter = 66;
13      cout << letter << endl;
14      return 0;
15   }
```

(program output continues)

Program 2-12 *(continued)*

Program Output
```
A
B
```

Figure 2-3 illustrates that when characters, such as A, B, and C, are stored in memory, it is really the numbers 65, 66, and 67 that are stored.

Character Literals

Although Program 2-12 nicely illustrates the way characters are represented by numbers, it isn't necessary to work with the ASCII codes themselves. Program 2-13 is another version that works that same way.

Figure 2-3

Program 2-13 assigns character literals to the variable letter. Any time a program works with a character, it internally works with the code that represents that character, so this program is still assigning the values 65 and 66 to letter.

Program 2-13

```cpp
 1   // This program uses character literals.
 2   #include <iostream>
 3   using namespace std;
 4
 5   int main()
 6   {
 7      char letter;
 8
 9      letter = 'A';
10      cout << letter << endl;
11      letter = 'B';
12      cout << letter << endl;
13      return 0;
14   }
```

Program Output
```
A
B
```

Notice in lines 9 and 11 that the character literals are enclosed in single quotation marks. It is important that you do not confuse character literals with string literals, which are enclosed in double quotation marks. String literals cannot be assigned to standard char variables, because of the way string literals are stored internally.

Strings are a series of characters stored in consecutive memory locations. The problem with strings is that they can be virtually any length. This means that there must be some way for the program to know how long the string is. In C++ an extra byte is appended to the end of most strings. In this last byte, the number 0 is stored. This *null terminator* or *null character* marks the end of the string. Strings that are stored in memory in this fashion, with the null terminator appended to their end, are called *C-strings*. They are called C-strings because this storage technique was initially used in the C programming language.

Don't confuse the null terminator with the character '0'. If you look at Appendix A, you will see that ASCII code 48 corresponds to the character '0', whereas the null terminator is the same as the ASCII code 0. If you want to print the character 0 on the screen, you use ASCII code 48. If you want to mark the end of a string, however, you use ASCII code 0.

Let's look at an example of how a string is stored in memory. Figure 2-4 depicts the way the string "Sebastian" would be stored.

Figure 2-4

| S | e | b | a | s | t | i | a | n | \0 |

First, notice the quotation marks are not stored with the string. They are simply a way of marking the beginning and end of the string in your source code. Second, notice the very last byte of the string. It contains the null terminator, which is represented by the \0 character. The addition of this last byte means that although the string "Sebastian" is 9 characters long, it occupies 10 bytes of memory.

The null terminator is another example of something that sits quietly in the background. It doesn't print on the screen when you display a string, but nevertheless, it is there silently doing its job.

NOTE: C++ automatically places the null terminator at the end of string literals.

Now let's compare the way a string and a char are stored. Suppose you have the literals 'A' and "A" in a program. Figure 2-5 depicts their internal storage.

Figure 2-5

'A' is stored as

| A |

"A" is stored as

| A | \0 |

As you can see, 'A' is a 1-byte element and "A" is a 2-byte element. Since characters are really stored as ASCII codes, Figure 2-6 shows what is actually being stored in memory.

Figure 2-6

'A' is stored as   `65`

"A" is stored as   `65` `0`

Because char variables are only large enough to hold one character, you cannot assign string literals to them. For example, the following code defines a char variable named letter. The character literal 'A' can be assigned to the variable, but the string literal "A" cannot.

```
char letter;
letter = 'A';  // This will work.
letter = "A";  // This will not work!
```

You are probably wondering what kind of variable is used to hold strings in C++. You must define a variable that is made of several 1-byte elements, enough for the entire string and its null terminator. We will discuss this in Chapter 3.

One final topic about characters should be discussed. You have learned that some strings look like a single character but really aren't. It is also possible to have a character that looks like a string. A good example is the newline character, \n. Although it is represented by two characters, a slash and an n, it is internally represented as one character. In fact, all escape sequences, internally, are just 1 byte.

Program 2-14 shows the use of \n as a character literal, enclosed in single quotation marks. If you refer to the ASCII chart in Appendix A, you will see that ASCII code 10 is the linefeed character. This is the code C++ uses for the newline character.

Program 2-14

```
 1   // This program uses character literals.
 2   #include <iostream>
 3   using namespace std;
 4
 5   int main()
 6   {
 7      char letter;
 8
 9      letter = 'A';
10      cout << letter << '\n';
11      letter = 'B';
12      cout << letter << '\n';
13      return 0;
14   }
```

Program Output

A

B

Let's review some important points regarding characters and strings:

- Printable characters are internally represented by numeric codes. Most computers use ASCII codes for this purpose.
- Characters normally occupy a single byte of memory.
- Strings are consecutive sequences of characters that occupy consecutive bytes of memory.
- C-strings always have a null terminator at the end. This marks the end of the string.
- Character literals are enclosed in single quotation marks.
- String literals are enclosed in double quotation marks.
- Escape sequences are stored internally as a single character.

 Checkpoint

2.11   What are the ASCII codes for the following characters? (Refer to Appendix A)

        C
        F
        W

2.12   Which of the following is a character literal?

        'B'
        "B"

2.13   Assuming the char data type uses 1 byte of memory, how many bytes do the following literals use?

        'Q'
        "Q"
        "Sales"
        '\n'

2.14   Write a program that has the following character variables: `first`, `middle`, and `last`. Store your initials in these variables and then display them on the screen.

2.15   What is wrong with the following program?

```
#include <iostream>
using namespace std;

int main()
{
    char letter;

    letter = "Z";
    cout << letter << endl;
    return 0;
}
```

2.8   Floating-Point Data Types

CONCEPT: Floating-point data types are used to define variables that can hold real numbers.

Whole numbers are not adequate for many jobs. If you are writing a program that works with dollar amounts or precise measurements, you need a data type that allows fractional values. In programming terms, these are called *floating-point* numbers.

Internally, floating-point numbers are stored in a manner similar to *scientific notation*. Take the number 47,281.97. In scientific notation this number is 4.728197×10^4. (10^4 is equal to 10,000, and $4.728197 \times 10,000$ is 47,281.97.) The first part of the number, 4.728197, is called the *mantissa*. The mantissa is multiplied by a power of ten.

Computers typically use *E notation* to represent floating-point values. In E notation, the number 47,281.97 would be 4.728197E4. The part of the number before the E is the mantissa, and the part after the E is the power of 10. When a floating point number is stored in memory, it is stored as the mantissa and the power of 10.

Table 2-7 shows other numbers represented in scientific and E notation.

Table 2-7   Floating Point Representations

Decimal Notation	Scientific Notation	E Notation
247.91	2.4791×10^2	`2.4791E2`
0.00072	7.2×10^{-4}	`7.2E-4`
2,900,000	2.9×10^6	`2.9E6`

In C++ there are three data types that can represent floating-point numbers. They are

```
float
double
long double
```

The `float` data type is considered *single precision*. The `double` data type is usually twice as big as `float`, so it is considered *double precision*. As you've probably guessed, the `long double` is intended to be larger than the `double`. Of course, the exact sizes of these data types are dependent on the computer you are using. The only guarantees are:

- A `double` is at least as big as a `float`.
- A `long double` is at least as big as a `double`.

Table 2-8 shows the sizes and ranges of floating-point data types usually found on PCs.

Table 2-8   Floating Point Data Types on PCs

Data Type	Key Word	Description
Single precision	`float`	4 bytes. Numbers between ±3.4E-38 and ±3.4E38
Double precision	`double`	8 bytes. Numbers between ±1.7E-308 and ±1.7E308
Long double precision	`long double*`	8 bytes. Numbers between ±1.7E-308 and ±1.7E308

*Some compilers use 10 bytes for long doubles. This allows a range of ±3.4E-4932 to ±1.1E4832

You will notice there are no unsigned floating point data types. On all machines, variables of the `float`, `double`, and `long double` data types can store positive or negative numbers.

Floating Point Literals

Floating point literals may be expressed in a variety of ways. As shown in Program 2-15, E notation is one method. When you are writing numbers that are extremely large or extremely small, this will probably be the easiest way. E notation numbers may be expressed with an uppercase E or a lowercase e. Notice that in the source code the literals were written as 1.495979E11 and 1.989E30, but the program printed them as 1.49598e+ 011 and 1.989e+30. The two sets of numbers are equivalent. (The plus sign in front of the exponent is also optional.) In Chapter 3 you will learn to control the way `cout` displays E notation numbers.

Program 2-15

```
1   // This program uses floating point data types.
2   #include <iostream>
3   using namespace std;
4
5   int main()
6   {
7      float distance;
8      double mass;
9
10     distance = 1.495979E11;
11     mass = 1.989E30;
12     cout << "The Sun is " << distance << " meters away.\n";
13     cout << "The Sun\'s mass is " << mass << " kilograms.\n";
14     return 0;
15   }
```

Program Output
```
The Sun is 1.49598e+011 meters away.
The Sun's mass is 1.989e+030 kilograms.
```

You can also express floating-point literals in decimal notation. The literal 1.495979E11 could have been written as

```
149597900000.00
```

Obviously the E notation is more convenient for lengthy numbers, but for numbers like 47.39, decimal notation is preferable to 4.739E1.

All of the following floating-point literals are equivalent:

```
1.4959E11
1.4959e11
1.4959E+11
1.4959e+11
149590000000.00
```

Floating-point literals are normally stored in memory as `doubles`. But remember, C++ provides tools for handling just about any situation. Just in case you need to force a literal to be stored as a `float`, you can append the letter F or f to the end of it. For example, the following literals would be stored as `floats`:

```
1.2F
45.907f
```

> **NOTE:** Because floating-point literals are normally stored in memory as `doubles`, many compilers issue a warning message when you assign a floating-point literal to a `float` variable. For example, assuming num is a `float`, the following statement might cause the compiler to generate a warning message:
>
> ```
> num = 14.725;
> ```
>
> You can suppress the warning message by appending the f suffix to the floating-point literal, as shown below:
>
> ```
> num = 14.725f;
> ```

If you want to force a value to be stored as a `long double`, append an L or l to it, as in the following examples:

```
1034.56L
89.21
```

The compiler won't confuse these with long integers because they have decimal points. (Remember, the lowercase L looks so much like the number 1 that you should always use the uppercase L when suffixing literals.)

Assigning Floating-Point Values to Integer Variables

When a floating-point value is assigned to an integer variable, the fractional part of the value (the part after the decimal point) is discarded. For example, look at the following code.

```
int number;
number = 7.5;   // Assigns 7 to number
```

This code attempts to assign the floating-point value 7.5 to the integer variable `number`. As a result, the value 7 will be assigned to `number`, with the fractional part discarded. When part of a value is discarded, it is said to be *truncated*.

Assigning a floating-point variable to an integer variable has the same effect. For example, look at the following code.

```
int i;
float f;
f = 7.5;
i = f;          // Assigns 7 to i.
```

When the `float` variable f is assigned to the `int` variable i, the value being assigned (7.5) is truncated. After this code executes i will hold the value 7 and f will hold the value 7.5.

NOTE: When a floating-point value is truncated, it is not rounded. Assigning the value 7.9 to an `int` variable will result in the value 7 being stored in the variable.

WARNING! Floating-point variables can hold a much larger range of values than integer variables can. If a floating-point value is being stored in an integer variable, and the whole part of the value (the part before the decimal point) is too large for the integer variable, an invalid value will be stored in the integer variable.

2.9 The `bool` Data Type

CONCEPT: Boolean variables are set to either `true` or `false`.

Expressions that have a `true` or `false` value are called *Boolean* expressions, named in honor of English mathematician George Boole (1815–1864).

The `bool` data type allows you to create small integer variables that are suitable for holding `true` or `false` values. Program 2-16 demonstrates the definition and assignment of a `bool` variable.

Program 2-16

```
1   // This program demonstrates boolean variables.
2   #include <iostream>
3   using namespace std;
4
5   int main()
6   {
7      bool boolValue;
8
9      boolValue = true;
10     cout << boolValue << endl;
11     boolValue = false;
12     cout << boolValue << endl;
13     return 0;
14  }
```

Program Output

```
1
0
```

As you can see from the program output, the value `true` is represented in memory by the number 1, and `false` is represented by 0. You will not be using `bool` variables until Chapter 4, however, so just remember they are useful for evaluating conditions that are either true or false.

2.10   Determining the Size of a Data Type

CONCEPT: The `sizeof` operator may be used to determine the size of a data type on any system.

Chapter 1 discussed the portability of the C++ language. As you have seen in this chapter, one of the problems of portability is the lack of common sizes of data types on all machines. If you are not sure what the sizes of data types are on your computer, C++ provides a way to find out.

A special operator called `sizeof` will report the number of bytes of memory used by any data type or variable. Program 2-17 illustrates its use. The first line that uses the operator is line 10:

```
cout << "The size of an integer is " << sizeof(int);
```

The name of the data type or variable is placed inside the parentheses that follow the operator. The operator "returns" the number of bytes used by that item. This operator can be invoked anywhere you can use an unsigned integer, including in mathematical operations.

Program 2-17

```
 1    // This program determines the size of integers, long
 2    // integers, and long doubles.
 3    #include <iostream>
 4    using namespace std;
 5
 6    int main()
 7    {
 8       long double apple;
 9
10       cout << "The size of an integer is " << sizeof(int);
11       cout << " bytes.\n";
12       cout << "The size of a long integer is " << sizeof(long);
13       cout << " bytes.\n";
14       cout << "An apple can be eaten in " << sizeof(apple);
15       cout << " bytes!\n";
16       return 0;
17    }
```

Program Output
```
The size of an integer is 4 bytes.
The size of a long integer is 4 bytes.
An apple can be eaten in 8 bytes!
```

Checkpoint

2.16   Yes or No: Is there an unsigned floating point data type? If so, what is it?

2.17   How would the following number in scientific notation be represented in E notation?

$$6.31 \times 10^{17}$$

2.18   Write a program that defines an integer variable named `age` and a `float` variable named `weight`. Store your age and weight, as literals, in the variables. The program should display these values on the screen in a manner similar to the following:

Program Output
My age is 26 and my weight is 180 pounds.

(Feel free to lie to the computer about your age and your weight—it'll never know!)

2.11 Variable Assignments and Initialization

> **CONCEPT:** An assignment operation assigns, or copies, a value into a variable. When a value is assigned to a variable as part of the variable's definition, it is called an initialization.

As you have already seen in several examples, a value is stored in a variable with an *assignment statement*. For example, the following statement copies the value 12 into the variable unitsSold.

```
unitsSold = 12;
```

The = symbol is called the *assignment operator*. Operators perform operations on data. The data that operators work with are called *operands*. The assignment operator has two operands. In the previous statement, the operands are unitsSold and 12.

In an assignment statement, C++ requires the name of the variable receiving the assignment to appear on the left side of the operator. The following statement is incorrect.

```
12 = unitsSold;     // Incorrect!
```

In C++ terminology, the operand on the left side of the = symbol must be an *lvalue*. It is called an lvalue because it is a value that may appear on the left side of an assignment operator. An lvalue is something that identifies a place in memory whose contents may be changed. Most of the time this will be a variable name. The operand on the right side of the = symbol must be an *rvalue*. An rvalue is any expression that has a value. The assignment statement takes the value of the rvalue and puts it in the memory location of the object identified by the lvalue.

You may also assign values to variables as part of the definition. This is called *initialization*. Program 2-18 shows how it is done.

Program 2-18

```
1    // This program shows variable initialization.
2    #include <iostream>
3    using namespace std;
4
5    int main()
6    {
7       int month = 2, days = 28;
8
9       cout << "Month " << month << " has " << days << " days.\n";
10      return 0;
11   }
```

Program Output
Month 2 has 28 days.

As you can see, this simplifies the program and reduces the number of statements that must be typed by the programmer. Here are examples of other definition statements that perform initialization.

```
double interestRate = 12.9;
char stockode = 'D';
long customerNum = 459L;
```

Of course, there are always variations on a theme. C++ allows you to define several variables and only initialize some of them. Here is an example of such a definition:

```
int flightNum = 89, travelTime, departure = 10, distance;
```

The variable `flightNum` is initialized to 89 and `departure` is initialized to 10. The variables `travelTime` and `distance` remain uninitialized.

2.12 Scope

CONCEPT: A variable's scope is the part of the program that has access to the variable.

Every variable has a *scope*. The scope of a variable is the part of the program where the variable may be used. The rules that define a variable's scope are complex, and you will only be introduced to the concept here. In other sections of the book we will revisit this topic and expand on it.

The first rule of scope you should learn is that a variable cannot be used in any part of the program before the definition. Program 2-19 illustrates this.

Program 2-19

```
 1   // This program can't find its variable.
 2   #include <iostream>
 3   using namespace std;
 4
 5   int main()
 6   {
 7      cout << value; // ERROR! value not defined yet!
 8
 9      int value = 100;
10      return 0;
11   }
```

The program will not work because line 7 attempts to send the contents of the variable value to cout before the variable is defined. The compiler reads your program from top to bottom. If it encounters a statement that uses a variable before the variable is defined, an error will result. To correct the program, the variable definition must be put before any statement that uses it.

2.13 Arithmetic Operators

CONCEPT: There are many operators for manipulating numeric values and performing arithmetic operations.

C++ offers a multitude of operators for manipulating data. Generally, there are three types of operators: *unary*, *binary*, and *ternary*. These terms reflect the number of operands an operator requires.

Unary operators only require a single operand. For example, consider the following expression:

VideoNote

Assignment
Statements and
Simple Math
Expressions

-5

Of course, we understand this represents the value negative five. The literal 5 is preceded by the minus sign. The minus sign, when used this way, is called the *negation operator*. Since it only requires one operand, it is a unary operator.

Binary operators work with two operands. The assignment operator is in this category. Ternary operators, as you may have guessed, require three operands. C++ only has one ternary operator, which will be discussed in Chapter 4.

Arithmetic operations are very common in programming. Table 2-9 shows the common arithmetic operators in C++.

Table 2-9   Fundamental Arithmetic Operators

Operator	Meaning	Type	Example
+	Addition	Binary	`total = cost + tax;`
–	Subtraction	Binary	`cost = total - tax;`
*	Multiplication	Binary	`tax = cost * rate;`
/	Division	Binary	`salePrice = original / 2;`
%	Modulus	Binary	`remainder = value % 3;`

Each of these operators works as you probably expect. The addition operator returns the sum of its two operands. In the following assignment statement, the variable `amount` will be assigned the value 12:

```
amount = 4 + 8;
```

The subtraction operator returns the value of its right operand subtracted from its left operand. This statement will assign the value 98 to `temperature`:

```
temperature = 112 - 14;
```

The multiplication operator returns the product of its two operands. In the following statement, `markUp` is assigned the value 3:

```
markUp = 12 * 0.25;
```

The division operator returns the quotient of its left operand divided by its right operand. In the next statement, `points` is assigned the value 5:

```
points = 100 / 20;
```

 WARNING! When both operands of a division statement are integers, the statement will perform *integer division*. This means the result of the division will be an integer as well. If there is a remainder, it will be discarded. For example, in the following statement, `parts` is assigned the value 5:

```
parts = 17 / 3;
```

This may seem like an annoyance, but it can actually be useful in some programs. Remember, C++ gives you the tools to solve just about any problem! If you want to make sure a statement, like the one shown above, performs regular division, express one of the numbers as a floating point. Here is an example:

```
parts = 17.0 / 3;
```

In the statement above, since 17.0 is interpreted as a floating point number, the division operation will return a floating point number. The result of the division is 5.66667.

The modulus operator, which only works with integer operands, returns the remainder of an integer division. The following statement assigns 2 to `leftOver`:

```
leftOver = 17 % 3;
```

In Chapter 3 you will learn how to use these operators in more complex mathematical formulas. For now we will concentrate on their basic usage. For example, suppose we need to write a program that calculates and displays an employee's total wages for the week. The regular hours for the work week are 40, and any hours worked over 40 are considered overtime. The employee earns $18.25 per hour for regular hours, and $27.78 per hour for overtime hours. The employee has worked 50 hours this week. The following pseudocode algorithm shows the program's logic.

Regular wages = base pay rate × regular hours
Overtime wages = overtime pay rate × overtime hours
Total wages = regular wages + overtime wages
Display the total wages

Program 2-20 shows the C++ code for the program

Program 2-20

```cpp
 1   // This program calculates hourly wages, including overtime.
 2   #include <iostream>
 3   using namespace std;
 4
 5   int main()
 6   {
 7      double regularWages,              // To hold regular wages
 8             basePayRate = 18.25,       // Base pay rate
 9             regularHours = 40.0,       // Hours worked less overtime
10             overtimeWages,             // To hold overtime wages
11             overtimePayRate = 27.78,   // Overtime pay rate
12             overtimeHours = 10,        // Overtime hours worked
13             totalWages;                // To hold total wages
14
15      // Calculate the regular wages.
16      regularWages = basePayRate * regularHours;
17
18      // Calculate the overtime wages.
19      overtimeWages = overtimePayRate * overtimeHours;
20
21      // Calculate the total wages.
22      totalWages = regularWages + overtimeWages;
23
24      // Display the total wages.
25      cout << "Wages for this week are $" << totalWages << endl;
26      return 0;
27   }
```

Program Output

```
Wages for this week are $1007.8
```

Let's take a closer look at the program. As mentioned in the comments, there are variables for regular wages, base pay rate, regular hours worked, overtime wages, overtime pay rate, overtime hours worked, and total wages.

Here is line 16, which multiplies `basePayRate` times `regularHours` and stores the result in `regularWages`:

```
regularWages = basePayRate * regularHours;
```

Here is line 19, which multiplies `overtimePayRate` times `overtimeHours` and stores the result in `overtimeWages`:

```
overtimeWages = overtimePayRate * overtimeHours;
```

Line 22 adds the regular wages and the overtime wages and stores the result in `totalWages`:

```
totalWages = regularWages + overtimeWages;
```

Line 25 displays the message on the screen reporting the week's wages.

In the Spotlight:
Calculating Percentages and Discounts

Determining percentages is a common calculation in computer programming. Although the % symbol is used in general mathematics to indicate a percentage, most programming languages (including C++) do not use the % symbol for this purpose. In a program, you have to convert a percentage to a floating-point number, just as you would if you were using a calculator. For example, 50 percent would be written as 0.5 and 2 percent would be written as 0.02.

Let's look at an example. Suppose you earn $6,000 per month and you are allowed to contribute a portion of your gross monthly pay to a retirement plan. You want to determine the amount of your pay that will go into the plan if you contribute 5 percent, 7 percent, or 10 percent of your gross wages. To make this determination you write the program shown in Program 2-21.

Program 2-21

```
 1    // This program calculates the amount of pay that
 2    // will be contributed to a retirement plan if 5%,
 3    // 7%, or 10% of monthly pay is withheld.
 4    #include <iostream>
 5    using namespace std;
 6
 7    int main()
 8    {
 9       // Variables to hold the monthly pay and the
10       // amount of contribution.
11       double monthlyPay = 6000.0, contribution;
12
13       // Calculate and display a 5% contribution.
```

```
14     contribution = monthlyPay * 0.05;
15     cout << "5 percent is $" << contribution
16          << " per month.\n";
17
18     // Calculate and display a 7% contribution.
19     contribution = monthlyPay * 0.07;
20     cout << "7 percent is $" << contribution
21          << " per month.\n";
22
23     // Calculate and display a 10% contribution.
24     contribution = monthlyPay * 0.1;
25     cout << "10 percent is $" << contribution
26          << " per month.\n";
27
28     return 0;
29 }
```

Program Output
```
5 percent is $300 per month.
7 percent is $420 per month.
10 percent is $600 per month.
```

Line 11 defines two variables: monthlyPay and contribution. The monthlyPay variable, which is initialized with the value 6000.0, holds the amount of your monthly pay. The contribution variable will hold the amount of a contribution to the retirement plan.

The statements in lines 14 through 16 calculate and display 5 percent of the monthly pay. The calculation is done in line 14, where the monthlyPay variable is multiplied by 0.05. The result is assigned to the contribution variable, which is then displayed in line 15.

Similar steps are taken in Lines 18 through 21, which calculate and display 7 percent of the monthly pay, and lines 24 through 26, which calculate and display 10 percent of the monthly pay.

Calculating a Percentage Discount

Another common calculation is determining a percentage discount. For example, suppose a retail business sells an item that is regularly priced at $59.95, and is planning to have a sale where the item's price will be reduced by 20 percent. You have been asked to write a program to calculate the sale price of the item.

To determine the sale price you perform two calculations:

- First, you get the amount of the discount, which is 20 percent of the item's regular price.
- Second, you subtract the discount amount from the item's regular price. This gives you the sale price.

Program 2-22 shows how this is done in C++.

Program 2-22

```cpp
 1  // This program calculates the sale price of an item
 2  // that is regularly priced at $59.95, with a 20 percent
 3  // discount subtracted.
 4  #include <iostream>
 5  using namespace std;
 6
 7  int main()
 8  {
 9      // Variables to hold the regular price, the
10      // amount of a discount, and the sale price.
11      double regularPrice = 59.95, discount, salePrice;
12
13      // Calculate the amount of a 20% discount.
14      discount = regularPrice * 0.2;
15
16      // Calculate the sale price by subtracting the
17      // discount from the regular price.
18      salePrice = regularPrice - discount;
19
20      // Display the results.
21      cout << "Regular price: $" << regularPrice << endl;
22      cout << "Discount amount: $" << discount << endl;
23      cout << "Sale price: $" << salePrice << endl;
24      return 0;
25  }
```

Program Output
```
Regular price: $59.95
Discount amount: $11.99
Sale price: $47.96
```

Line 11 defines three variables. The `regularPrice` variable holds the item's regular price, and is initialized with the value 59.95. The `discount` variable will hold the amount of the discount once it is calculated. The `salePrice` variable will hold the item's sale price.

Line 14 calculates the amount of the 20 percent discount by multiplying `regularPrice` by 0.2. The result is stored in the `discount` variable. Line 18 calculates the sale price by subtracting `discount` from `regularPrice`. The result is stored in the `salePrice` variable. The `cout` statements in lines 21 through 23 display the item's regular price, the amount of the discount, and the sale price.

 Checkpoint

2.19   Is the following assignment statement valid or invalid? If it is invalid, why?

```cpp
72 = amount;
```

2.20 How would you consolidate the following definitions into one statement?

```
int x = 7;
int y = 16;
int z = 28;
```

2.21 What is wrong with the following program? How would you correct it?

```
#include <iostream>
using namespace std;

int main()
{
    number = 62.7;
    double number;
    cout << number << endl;
    return 0;
}
```

2.22 Is the following an example of integer division or floating-point division? What value will be stored in portion?

```
portion = 70 / 3;
```

2.14 Comments

CONCEPT: Comments are notes of explanation that document lines or sections of a program. Comments are part of the program, but the compiler ignores them. They are intended for people who may be reading the source code.

It may surprise you that one of the most important parts of a program has absolutely no impact on the way it runs. In fact, the compiler ignores this part of a program. Of course, I'm speaking of the comments.

As a beginning programmer, you might be resistant to the idea of liberally writing comments in your programs. After all, it can seem more productive to write code that actually does something! It is crucial, however, that you develop the habit of thoroughly annotating your code with descriptive comments. It might take extra time now, but it will almost certainly save time in the future.

Imagine writing a program of medium complexity with about 8,000 to 10,000 lines of C++ code. Once you have written the code and satisfactorily debugged it, you happily put it away and move on to the next project. Ten months later you are asked to make a modification to the program (or worse, track down and fix an elusive bug). You open the file that contains your source code and stare at thousands of statements that now make no sense at all. If only you had left some notes to yourself explaining the program's code. Of course it's too late now. All that's left to do is decide what will take less time: figuring out the old program or completely rewriting it!

This scenario might sound extreme, but it's one you don't want to happen to you. Real world programs are big and complex. Thoroughly documented code will make your life easier, not to mention the other programmers who may have to read your code in the future.

Single-Line Comments

You have already seen one way to place comments in a C++ program. You simply place two forward slashes (//) where you want the comment to begin. The compiler ignores everything from that point to the end of the line. Program 2-23 shows that comments may be placed liberally throughout a program.

Program 2-23

```
1   // PROGRAM: PAYROLL.CPP
2   // Written by Herbert Dorfmann
3   // This program calculates company payroll
4   // Last modification: 8/20/2010
5   #include <iostream>
6   using namespace std;
7
8   int main()
9   {
10     double payRate;    // Holds the hourly pay rate
11     double hours;      // Holds the hours worked
12     int employNumber;  // Holds the employee number
```

(The remainder of this program is left out.)

In addition to telling who wrote the program and describing the purpose of variables, comments can also be used to explain complex procedures in your code.

Multi-Line Comments

The second type of comment in C++ is the multi-line comment. *Multi-line comments* start with /* (a forward slash followed by an asterisk) and end with */ (an asterisk followed by a forward slash). Everything between these markers is ignored. Program 2-24 illustrates how multi-line comments may be used. Notice that a multi-line comment starts in line 1 with the /* symbol, and it ends in line 6 with the */ symbol.

Program 2-24

```
1   /*
2       PROGRAM: PAYROLL.CPP
3       Written by Herbert Dorfmann
4       This program calculates company payroll
5       Last modification: 8/20/2010
6   */
7
8   #include <iostream>
9   using namespace std;
10
```

```
11   int main()
12   {
13      double payRate;    // Holds the hourly pay rate
14      double hours;      // Holds the hours worked
15      int employNumber;  // Holds the employee number
```

(The remainder of this program is left out.)

Unlike a comment started with `//`, a multi-line comment can span several lines. This makes it more convenient to write large blocks of comments because you do not have to mark every line. Consequently, the multi-line comment is inconvenient for writing single-line comments because you must type both a beginning and ending comment symbol.

> **NOTE:** Many programmers use a combination of single-line comments and multi-line comments in their programs. Convenience usually dictates which style to use.

Remember the following advice when using multi-line comments:

- Be careful not to reverse the beginning symbol with the ending symbol.
- Be sure not to forget the ending symbol.

Both of these mistakes can be difficult to track down, and will prevent the program from compiling correctly.

2.15 Focus on Software Engineering: Programming Style

CONCEPT: Programming style refers to the way a programmer uses identifiers, spaces, tabs, blank lines, and punctuation characters to visually arrange a program's source code. These are some, but not all, of the elements of programming style.

In Chapter 1 you learned that syntax rules govern the way a language may be used. The syntax rules of C++ dictate how and where to place key words, semicolons, commas, braces, and other components of the language. The compiler's job is to check for syntax errors and, if there are none, generate object code.

When the compiler reads a program it processes it as one long stream of characters. The compiler doesn't care that each statement is on a separate line, or that spaces separate operators from operands. Humans, on the other hand, find it difficult to read programs that aren't written in a visually pleasing manner. Consider Program 2-25 for example.

Program 2-25

```
1   #include <iostream>
2   using namespace std;int main(){double shares=220.0;
3   double avgPrice=14.67;cout<<"There were "<<shares
4   <<" shares sold at $"<<avgPrice<<" per share.\n";
5   return 0;}
```

Program Output

```
There were 220 shares sold at $14.67 per share.
```

Although the program is syntactically correct (it doesn't violate any rules of C++), it is very difficult to read. The same program is shown in Program 2-26, written in a more reasonable style.

Program 2-26

```
1    // This example is much more readable than Program 2-25.
2    #include <iostream>
3    using namespace std;
4
5    int main()
6    {
7       double shares = 220.0;
8       double avgPrice = 14.67;
9
10      cout << "There were " << shares << " shares sold at $";
11      cout << avgPrice << " per share.\n";
12      return 0;
13   }
```

Program Output

```
There were 220 shares sold at $14.67 per share.
```

Programming style refers to the way source code is visually arranged. Ideally, it is a consistent method of putting spaces and indentions in a program so visual cues are created. These cues quickly tell a programmer important information about a program.

For example, notice in Program 2-26 that inside the function main's braces each line is indented. It is a common C++ style to indent all the lines inside a set of braces. You will also notice the blank line between the variable definitions and the cout statements. This is intended to visually separate the definitions from the executable statements.

 NOTE: Although you are free to develop your own style, you should adhere to common programming practices. By doing so, you will write programs that visually make sense to other programmers.

Another aspect of programming style is how to handle statements that are too long to fit on one line. Because C++ is a free-flowing language, it is usually possible to spread a statement over several lines. For example, here is a cout statement that uses five lines:

```
cout << "The Fahrenheit temperature is "
     << fahrenheit
     << " and the Celsius temperature is "
     << celsius
     << endl;
```

This statement will work just as if it were typed on one line. Here is an example of variable definitions treated similarly:

```
int fahrenheit,
    celsius,
    kelvin;
```

There are many other issues related to programming style. They will be presented throughout the book.

If You Plan to Continue in Computer Science: Standard and Prestandard C++

CONCEPT: C++ programs written before the language became standardized may appear slightly different from programs written today.

C++ is now a standardized programming language, but it hasn't always been. The language has evolved over the years and, as a result, there is a "newer style" and an "older style" of writing C++ code. The newer style is the way programs are written with standard C++, while the older style is the way programs were typically written using prestandard C++. Although the differences between the older and newer styles are subtle, it is important that you recognize them. When you go to work as a computer science professional, it is likely that you will see programs written in the older style. It is also possible that your workplace's programming tools only support the older conventions, and you may need to write programs using the older style.

Older Style Header Files

In older style C++, all header files end with the ".h" extension. For example, in a prestandard C++ program the statement that includes the `iostream.h` header file is written as:

```
#include <iostream.h>
```

Absence of `using namespace std;`

Another difference between the newer and older styles is that older style programs typically do not use the `using namespace std;` statement. In fact, some older compilers do not support namespaces at all, and will produce an error message if a program has that statement.

An Older Style Program

To illustrate these differences, look at the program below. It is a modification of Program 2-1, written in the older style.

```
// A simple C++ program
#include <iostream.h>

int main()
{
    cout << "Programming is great fun!";
    return 0;
}
```

Most standard C++ compilers support programs written in the older style. Prestandard compilers, however, may not support programs written in the newer style.

Review Questions and Exercises

Short Answer

1. How many operands does each of the following types of operators require?

    _____ Unary

    _____ Binary

    _____ Ternary

2. How may the `float` variables `temp`, `weight`, and `age` be defined in one statement?

3. How may the `int` variables `months`, `days`, and `years` be defined in one statement, with `months` initialized to 2 and `years` initialized to 3?

4. Write assignment statements that perform the following operations with the variables a, b, and c.

    A) Adds 2 to a and stores the result in b.

    B) Multiplies b times 4 and stores the result in a.

    C) Divides a by 3.14 and stores the result in b.

    D) Subtracts 8 from b and stores the result in a.

    E) Stores the value 27 in a.

    F) Stores the character 'K' in c.

    G) Stores the ASCII code for 'B' in c.

5. Is the following comment written using single-line or multi-line comment symbols?

    ```
    /* This program was written by M. A. Codewriter*/
    ```

6. Is the following comment written using single-line or multi-line comment symbols?

    ```
    // This program was written by M. A. Codewriter
    ```

7. Modify the following program so it prints two blank lines between each line of text.

    ```
    #include <iostream>
    using namespace std;
    ```

```cpp
int main()
{
    cout << "Two mandolins like creatures in the";
    cout << "dark";
    cout << "Creating the agony of ecstasy.";
    cout << "                    - George Barker";
    return 0;
}
```

8. What will the following programs print on the screen?

   A)
```cpp
#include <iostream>
using namespace std;

int main()
{
    int freeze = 32, boil = 212;
    freeze = 0;
    boil = 100;
    cout << freeze << endl << boil << endl;
    return 0;
}
```

   B)
```cpp
#include <iostream>
using namespace std;

int main()
{
    int x = 0, y = 2;
    x = y * 4;
    cout << x << endl << y << endl;
    return 0;
}
```

   C)
```cpp
#include <iostream>
using namespace std;

int main()
{
    cout << "I am the incredible";
    cout << "computing\nmachine";
    cout << "\nand I will\namaze\n";
    cout << "you.";
    return 0;
}
```

   D)
```cpp
#include <iostream>
using namespace std;

int main()
{
    cout << "Be careful\n";
    cout << "This might/n be a trick ";
    cout << "question\n";
    return 0;
}
```

```
E)  #include <iostream>
    using namespace std;

    int main()
    {
       int a, x = 23;

       a = x % 2;
       cout << x << endl << a << endl;
       return 0;
    }
```

Multiple Choice

9. Every complete statement ends with a

   A) period

   B) # symbol

   C) semicolon

   D) ending brace

10. Which of the following statements is correct?

    A) `#include (iostream)`

    B) `#include {iostream}`

    C) `#include <iostream>`

    D) `#include [iostream]`

    E) All of the above

11. Every C++ program must have a

    A) cout statement.

    B) function main.

    C) #include statement.

    D) All of the above

12. Preprocessor directives begin with a

    A) #

    B) !

    C) <

    D) *

    E) None of the above

13. The following data
    ```
    72
    'A'
    "Hello World"
    2.8712
    ```

are all examples of

A) Variables

B) Literals or constants

C) Strings

D) None of the above

14. A group of statements, such as the contents of a function, is enclosed in

A) Braces `{}`

B) Parentheses `()`

C) Brackets `<>`

D) All of the above will do

15. Which of the following are *not* valid assignment statements? (Circle all that apply.)

A) `total = 9;`

B) `72 = amount;`

C) `profit = 129`

D) `letter = 'W';`

16. Which of the following are *not* valid cout statements? (Circle all that apply.)

A) `cout << "Hello World";`

B) `cout << "Have a nice day"\n;`

C) `cout < value;`

D) `cout << Programming is great fun;`

17. Assume w = 5, x = 4, y = 8, and z = 2. What value will be stored in `result` in each of the following statements?

A) `result = x + y;`

B) `result = z * 2;`

C) `result = y / x;`

D) `result = y - z;`

E) `result = w % 2;`

18. How would each of the following numbers be represented in E notation?

A) 3.287×10^6

B) -978.65×10^{12}

C) 7.65491×10^{-3}

D) -58710.23×10^{-4}

19. The negation operator is

A) Unary

B) Binary

C) Ternary

D) None of the above

20. When do preprocessor directives execute?

    A) Before the compiler compiles your program

    B) After the compiler compiles your program

    C) At the same time as the compiler compiles your program

    D) None of the above

True or False

21. T   F   A variable must be defined before it can be used.

22. T   F   Variable names may begin with a number.

23. T   F   Variable names may be up to 31 characters long.

24. T   F   A left brace in a C++ program should always be followed by a right brace later in the program.

Algorithm Workbench

25. Convert the following pseudocode to C++ code. Be sure to define the appropriate variables.

    > Store 20 in the *speed* variable.
    > Store 10 in the *time* variable.
    > Multiply *speed* by time and store the result in the *distance* variable.
    > Display the contents of the *distance* variable.

26. Convert the following pseudocode to C++ code. Be sure to define the appropriate variables.

    > Store 172.5 in the *force* variable.
    > Store 27.5 in the *area* variable.
    > Divide area by *force* and store the result in the *pressure* variable.
    > Display the contents of the *pressure* variable.

Find the Error

27. There are a number of syntax errors in the following program. Locate as many as you can.

```
*/ What's wrong with this program? /*
#include iostream
using namespace std;

int main();
}
    int a, b, c\\ Three integers
    a = 3
    b = 4
    c = a + b
    Cout < "The value of c is %d" < C;
    return 0;
{
```

Programming Challenges

1. Sum of Two Numbers

Write a program that stores the integers 62 and 99 in variables, and stores the sum of these two in a variable named `total`.

2. Sales Prediction

The East Coast sales division of a company generates 62 percent of total sales. Based on that percentage, write a program that will predict how much the East Coast division will generate if the company has $4.6 million in sales this year.

3. Sales Tax

Write a program that will compute the total sales tax on a $52 purchase. Assume the state sales tax is 4 percent and the county sales tax is 2 percent.

4. Restaurant Bill

Write a program that computes the tax and tip on a restaurant bill for a patron with a $44.50 meal charge. The tax should be 6.75 percent of the meal cost. The tip should be 15 percent of the total after adding the tax. Display the meal cost, tax amount, tip amount, and total bill on the screen.

5. Average of Values

To get the average of a series of values, you add the values up and then divide the sum by the number of values. Write a program that stores the following values in five different variables: 28, 32, 37, 24, and 33. The program should first calculate the sum of these five variables and store the result in a separate variable named `sum`. Then, the program should divide the sum variable by 5 to get the average. Display the average on the screen.

TIP: Use the double data type for all variables in this program.

6. Annual Pay

Suppose an employee gets paid every two weeks and earns $1700.00 each pay period. In a year the employee gets paid 26 times. Write a program that defines the following variables:

`payAmount`   This variable will hold the amount of pay the employee earns each pay period. Initialize the variable with 1700.0.

`payPeriods`   This variable will hold the number of pay periods in a year. Initialize the variable with 26.

`annualPay`   This variable will hold the employee's total annual pay, which will be calculated.

The program should calculate the employee's total annual pay by multiplying the employee's pay amount by the number of pay periods in a year, and store the result in the `annualPay` variable. Display the total annual pay on the screen.

7. Ocean Levels

Assuming the ocean's level is currently rising at about 1.5 millimeters per year, write a program that displays:

- The number of millimeters higher than the current level that the ocean's level will be in 5 years

- The number of millimeters higher than the current level that the ocean's level will be in 7 years
- The number of millimeters higher than the current level that the ocean's level will be in 10 years

8. **Total Purchase**

   A customer in a store is purchasing five items. The prices of the five items are:

   Price of item 1 = $12.95
   Price of item 2 = $24.95
   Price of item 3 = $6.95
   Price of item 4 = $14.95
   Price of item 5 = $3.95

   Write a program that holds the prices of the five items in five variables. Display each item's price, the subtotal of the sale, the amount of sales tax, and the total. Assume the sales tax is 6%.

9. **Cyborg Data Type Sizes**

   You have been given a job as a programmer on a Cyborg supercomputer. In order to accomplish some calculations, you need to know how many bytes the following data types use: `char`, `int`, `float`, and `double`. You do not have any manuals, so you can't look this information up. Write a C++ program that will determine the amount of memory used by these types and display the information on the screen.

10. **Miles per Gallon**

    A car holds 12 gallons of gasoline and can travel 350 miles before refueling. Write a program that calculates the number of miles per gallon the car gets. Display the result on the screen.

    Hint: Use the following formula to calculate miles per gallon (MPG):

    MPG = Miles Driven / Gallons of Gas Used

11. **Distance per Tank of Gas**

    A car with a 20-gallon gas tank averages 21.5 miles per gallon when driven in town and 26.8 miles per gallon when driven on the highway. Write a program that calculates and displays the distance the car can travel on one tank of gas when driven in town and when driven on the highway.

    Hint: The following formula can be used to calculate the distance:

    Distance = Number of Gallons × Average Miles per Gallon

12. **Land Calculation**

    One acre of land is equivalent to 43,560 square feet. Write a program that calculates the number of acres in a tract of land with 389,767 square feet.

13. **Circuit Board Price**

    An electronics company sells circuit boards at a 40 percent profit. Write a program that will calculate the selling price of a circuit board that costs $12.67. Display the result on the screen.

14. **Personal Information**

Write a program that displays the following pieces of information, each on a separate line:

Your name
Your address, with city, state, and ZIP code
Your telephone number
Your college major

Use only a single cout statement to display all of this information.

15. **Triangle Pattern**

Write a program that displays the following pattern on the screen:

```
   *
  ***
 *****
*******
```

16. **Diamond Pattern**

Write a program that displays the following pattern:

```
   *
  ***
 *****
*******
 *****
  ***
   *
```

17. **Stock Commission**

Kathryn bought 600 shares of stock at a price of $21.77 per share. She must pay her stock broker a 2 percent commission for the transaction. Write a program that calculates and displays the following:

- The amount paid for the stock alone (without the commission)
- The amount of the commission
- The total amount paid (for the stock plus the commission)

18. **Energy Drink Consumption**

A soft drink company recently surveyed 12,467 of its customers and found that approximately 14 percent of those surveyed purchase one or more energy drinks per week. Of those customers who purchase energy drinks, approximately 64 percent of them prefer citrus flavored energy drinks. Write a program that displays the following:

- The approximate number of customers in the survey who purchase one or more energy drinks per week
- The approximate number of customers in the survey who prefer citrus flavored energy drinks

3 Expressions and Interactivity

TOPICS

3.1 The cin Object

CONCEPT: The cin object can be used to read data typed at the keyboard.

VideoNote

Reading Input with cin

So far you have written programs with built-in data. Without giving the user an opportunity to enter his or her own data, you have initialized the variables with the necessary starting values. These types of programs are limited to performing their task with only a single set of starting data. If you decide to change the initial value of any variable, the program must be modified and recompiled.

In reality, most programs ask for values that will be assigned to variables. This means the program does not have to be modified if the user wants to run it several times with different sets of data. For example, a program that calculates payroll for a small business might ask the user to enter the name of the employee, the hours worked, and the hourly pay rate. When the paycheck for that employee has been printed, the program could start over again and ask for the name, hours worked, and hourly pay rate of the next employee.

Just as cout is C++'s standard output object, cin is the standard input object. It reads input from the console (or keyboard) as shown in Program 3-1.

Program 3-1

```
 1   // This program asks the user to enter the length and width of
 2   // a rectangle. It calculates the rectangle's area and displays
 3   // the value on the screen.
 4   #include <iostream>
 5   using namespace std;
 6
 7   int main()
 8   {
 9      int length, width, area;
10
11      cout << "This program calculates the area of a ";
12      cout << "rectangle.\n";
13      cout << "What is the length of the rectangle? ";
14      cin >> length;
15      cout << "What is the width of the rectangle? ";
16      cin >> width;
17      area = length * width;
18      cout << "The area of the rectangle is " << area << ".\n";
19      return 0;
20   }
```

Program Output with Example Input Shown in Bold
```
This program calculates the area of a rectangle.
What is the length of the rectangle? 10 [Enter]
What is the width of the rectangle? 20 [Enter]
The area of the rectangle is 200.
```

Instead of calculating the area of one rectangle, this program can be used to get the area of any rectangle. The values that are stored in the length and width variables are entered by the user when the program is running. Look at lines 13 and 14:

```
cout << "What is the length of the rectangle? ";
cin >> length;
```

In line 13, the cout object is used to display the question "What is the length of the rectangle?" This question is known as a *prompt*, and it tells the user what data he or she should enter. Your program should always display a prompt before it uses cin to read input. This way, the user will know that he or she must type a value at the keyboard.

Line 14 uses the cin object to read a value from the keyboard. The >> symbol is the *stream extraction operator*. It gets characters from the stream object on its left and stores them in the variable whose name appears on its right. In this line, characters are taken from the cin object (which gets them from the keyboard) and are stored in the length variable.

Gathering input from the user is normally a two-step process:

1. Use the cout object to display a prompt on the screen.

2. Use the cin object to read a value from the keyboard.

The prompt should ask the user a question, or tell the user to enter a specific value. For example, the code we just examined from Program 3-1 displays the following prompt:

```
What is the length of the rectangle?
```

When the user sees this prompt, he or she knows to enter the rectangle's length. After the prompt is displayed, the program uses the cin object to read a value from the keyboard and store the value in the length variable.

Notice that the << and >> operators appear to point in the direction that data is flowing. In a statement that uses the cout object, the << operator always points toward cout. This indicates that data is flowing from a variable or a literal to the cout object. In a statement that uses the cin object, the >> operator always points toward the variable that is receiving the value. This indicates that data is flowing from cin to a variable. This is illustrated in Figure 3-1.

Figure 3-1

```
cout << "What is the length of the rectangle? ";
cin >> length;
```

Think of the << and >> operators as arrows that point in
the direction that data is flowing.

```
cout ← "What is the length of the rectangle? ";
cin → length;
```

The cin object causes a program to wait until data is typed at the keyboard and the **[Enter]** key is pressed. No other lines in the program will be executed until cin gets its input.

cin automatically converts the data read from the keyboard to the data type of the variable used to store it. If the user types 10, it is read as the characters '1' and '0'. cin is smart enough to know this will have to be converted to an int value before it is stored in the length variable. cin is also smart enough to know a value like 10.7 cannot be stored in an integer variable. If the user enters a floating-point value for an integer variable, cin will not read the part of the number after the decimal point.

NOTE: You must include the iostream file in any program that uses cin.

Entering Multiple Values

The cin object may be used to gather multiple values at once. Look at Program 3-2, which is a modified version of Program 3-1.

Line 15 waits for the user to enter two values. The first is assigned to length and the second to width.

```
cin >> length >> width;
```

Program 3-2

```
 1   // This program asks the user to enter the length and width of
 2   // a rectangle. It calculates the rectangle's area and displays
 3   // the value on the screen.
 4   #include <iostream>
 5   using namespace std;
 6
 7   int main()
 8   {
 9      int length, width, area;
10
11      cout << "This program calculates the area of a ";
12      cout << "rectangle.\n";
13      cout << "Enter the length and width of the rectangle ";
14      cout << "separated by a space.\n";
15      cin >> length >> width;
16      area = length * width;
17      cout << "The area of the rectangle is " << area << endl;
18      return 0;
19   }
```

Program Output with Example Input Shown in Bold
```
This program calculates the area of a rectangle.
Enter the length and width of the rectangle separated by a space.
```
10 20 [Enter]
```
The area of the rectangle is 200
```

In the example output, the user entered 10 and 20, so 10 is stored in length and 20 is stored in width.

Notice the user separates the numbers by spaces as they are entered. This is how cin knows where each number begins and ends. It doesn't matter how many spaces are entered between the individual numbers. For example, the user could have entered

    10   20

 NOTE: The **[Enter]** key is pressed after the last number is entered.

cin will also read multiple values of different data types. This is shown in Program 3-3.

Program 3-3

```
 1   // This program demonstrates how cin can read multiple values
 2   // of different data types.
 3   #include <iostream>
 4   using namespace std;
 5
```

```
 6   int main()
 7   {
 8       int whole;
 9       double fractional;
10       char letter;
11
12       cout << "Enter an integer, a double, and a character: ";
13       cin >> whole >> fractional >> letter;
14       cout << "Whole: " << whole << endl;
15       cout << "Fractional: " << fractional << endl;
16       cout << "Letter: " << letter << endl;
17       return 0;
18   }
```

Program Output with Example Input Shown in Bold
Enter an integer, a double, and a character: **4 5.7 b [Enter]**
Whole: 4
Fractional: 5.7
Letter: b

As you can see in the example output, the values are stored in their respective variables. But what if the user had responded in the following way?

Enter an integer, a double, and a character: **5.7 4 b [Enter]**

When the user types values at the keyboard, those values are first stored in an area of memory known as the *keyboard buffer*. So, when the user enters the values 5.7, 4, and b, they are stored in the keyboard buffer as shown in Figure 3-2.

Figure 3-2

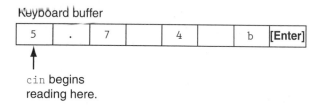

When the user presses the Enter key, cin reads the value 5 into the variable whole. It does not read the decimal point because whole is an integer variable. Next it reads .7 and stores that value in the double variable fractional. The space is skipped and 4 is the next value read. It is stored as a character in the variable letter. Because this cin statement reads only three values, the b is left in the keyboard buffer. So, in this situation the program would have stored 5 in whole, 0.7 in fractional, and the character '4' in letter. It is important that the user enters values in the correct order.

Reading Strings

The cin object can read a string as input and store it in memory as a C-string. C-strings are commonly stored in *character arrays*. In this section we will briefly touch on the topic of character arrays so you can perform some basic operations with C-strings.

An array is like a group of variables with a single name, located together in memory. Here is an example of a character array definition:

```
char company[12];
```

The number inside the brackets indicates the size of the array. The name of the array is company, and it is large enough to hold 12 characters. Remember, however, that C-strings have the null terminator at the end, so this array is large enough to hold a C-string that is 11 characters long.

 NOTE: If a character array is intended to hold strings, it must be at least one character larger than the largest string that will be stored in it. This extra character is for the null terminator.

Program 3-4 shows how cin may be used to read a string into a character array.

Program 3-4

```
 1    // This program demonstrates how cin can read a string into
 2    // a character array.
 3    #include <iostream>
 4    using namespace std;
 5
 6    int main()
 7    {
 8       char name[21];
 9
10       cout << "What is your name? ";
11       cin >> name;
12       cout << "Good morning " << name << endl;
13       return 0;
14    }
```

Program Output with Example Input Shown in Bold
```
What is your name? Charlie [Enter]
Good morning Charlie
```

Let's examine the array definition in line 8:

```
char name[21];
```

The name of the array is name and it is large enough to hold 21 characters. The null terminator at the end of a C-string is a character, so the longest string that may be stored in this array is 20 characters.

WARNING! The user can enter a string larger than the array can hold. If this happens, the string will overflow the array's boundaries and destroy other data in memory.

Notice in lines 11 and 12 for the brackets and the size indicator name are left out.

```
cin >> name;
cout << "Good morning " << name << endl;
```

When reading a string into an array, you use the name of the array only. You would not get the desired result if you wrote these lines as:

```
cin >> name[21];  //Incorrect!
cout << "Good morning " << name[21] << endl;  //Incorrect!
```

Program 3-5 shows another example of using character arrays in a program.

Program 3-5

```
1   // This program reads two strings into two character arrays.
2   #include <iostream>
3   using namespace std;
4
5   int main()
6   {
7       char first[16], last[16];
8
9       cout << "Enter your first and last names and I will\n";
10      cout << "reverse them.\n";
11      cin >> first >> last;
12      cout << last << ", " << first << endl;
13      return 0;
14  }
```

Program Output with Example Input Shown in Bold
```
Enter your first and last names and I will
reverse them.
```
Johnny Jones [Enter]
```
Jones, Johnny
```

The arrays `first` and `last` are large enough to hold strings of 15 characters. Line 11 reads a string into each array:

```
cin >> first >> last;
```

Just as before, spaces separate the two items.

 NOTE: If you wish the user to enter a string that has spaces in it, you cannot use this input method. Later in this chapter you will learn how to accomplish this.

Checkpoint

3.1   What header file must be included in programs using `cin`?

3.2   What type of variable is used to hold a C-string?

3.3   Write a definition statement for a character array named `customer`. It should be large enough to hold a string 52 characters in length.

3.4   TRUE or FALSE: `cin` requires the user to press the **[Enter]** key when finished entering data.

3.5   Assume `value` is an integer variable. If the user enters 3.14 in response to the following programming statement, what will be stored in `value`?

        cin >> value;

        A) 3.14

        B) 3

        C) 0

        D) Nothing. An error message is displayed.

3.6   A program has the following variable definitions.

```
long miles;
int feet;
float inches;
```

Write one `cin` statement that reads a value into each of these variables.

3.7   The following program will run, but the user will have difficulty understanding what to do. How would you improve the program?

```
// This program multiplies two numbers and displays the result.
#include <iostream>
using namespace std;

int main()
{
   double first, second, product;

   cin >> first >> second;
   product = first * second;
   cout << product;
   return 0;
}
```

3.8   Examine the following program.

```
#include <iostream>
using namespace std;

int main()
{
   char name[21];

   cout << "What is your name? ";
   cin >> name;
   cout << "Hello " << name << endl;
   return 0;
}
```

If Jill runs this program and enters her full name, Jill Birkenstock, what will be displayed on the screen? How can the program be improved?

3.9   Complete the following program skeleton so it asks for the user's weight (in pounds) and displays the equivalent weight in kilograms.

```cpp
#include <iostream>
using namespace std;

int main()
{
    double pounds, kilograms;

    // Write code here that prompts the user
    // to enter his or her weight and reads
    // the input into the pounds variable.

    // The following line does the conversion.
    kilograms = pounds / 2.2;

    // Write code here that displays the user's weight
    // in kilograms.
    return 0;
}
```

3.2   Mathematical Expressions

CONCEPT: C++ allows you to construct complex mathematical expressions using multiple operators and grouping symbols.

In Chapter 2 you were introduced to the basic mathematical operators, which are used to build mathematical expressions. An *expression* is a programming statement that has a value. Usually, an expression consists of an operator and its operands. Look at the following statement:

```cpp
sum = 21 + 3;
```

Since 21 + 3 has a value, it is an expression. Its value, 24, is stored in the variable sum. Expressions do not have to be in the form of mathematical operations. In the following statement, 3 is an expression.

```cpp
number = 3;
```

Here are some programming statements where the variable result is being assigned the value of an expression:

```cpp
result = x;
result = 4;
result = 15 / 3;
result = 22 * number;
result = sizeof(int);
result = a + b + c;
```

In each of these statements, a number, variable name, or mathematical expression appears on the right side of the = symbol. A value is obtained from each of these and stored in the variable result. These are all examples of a variable being assigned the value of an expression.

Program 3-6 shows how mathematical expressions can be used with the cout object.

Program 3-6

```
 1   // This program asks the user to enter the numerator
 2   // and denominator of a fraction and it displays the
 3   // decimal value.
 4
 5   #include <iostream>
 6   using namespace std;
 7
 8   int main()
 9   {
10      double numerator, denominator;
11
12      cout << "This program shows the decimal value of ";
13      cout << "a fraction.\n";
14      cout << "Enter the numerator: ";
15      cin >> numerator;
16      cout << "Enter the denominator: ";
17      cin >> denominator;
18      cout << "The decimal value is ";
19      cout << (numerator / denominator) << endl;
20      return 0;
21   }
```

Program Output with Example Input Shown in Bold
```
This program shows the decimal value of a fraction.
Enter the numerator: 3 [Enter]
Enter the denominator: 16 [Enter]
The decimal value is 0.1875
```

The cout object will display the value of any legal expression in C++. In Program 3-6, the value of the expression numerator / denominator is displayed.

NOTE: The example input for Program 3-6 shows the user entering 3 and 16. Since these values are assigned to double variables, they are stored as the double values 3.0 and 16.0.

NOTE: When sending an expression that consists of an operator to cout, it is always a good idea to put parentheses around the expression. Some advanced operators will yield unexpected results otherwise.

Operator Precedence

It is possible to build mathematical expressions with several operators. The following statement assigns the sum of 17, x, 21, and y to the variable `answer`.

```
answer = 17 + x + 21 + y;
```

Some expressions are not that straightforward, however. Consider the following statement:

```
outcome = 12 + 6 / 3;
```

What value will be stored in `outcome`? 6 is used as an operand for both the addition and division operators. `outcome` could be assigned either 6 or 14, depending on whether the addition operation or the division operation takes place first. The answer is 14 because the division operator has higher *precedence* than the addition operator.

Mathematical expressions are evaluated from left to right. When two operators share an operand, the operator with the highest precedence works first. Multiplication and division have higher precedence than addition and subtraction, so the statement above works like this:

A) 6 is divided by 3, yielding a result of 2

B) 12 is added to 2, yielding a result of 14

It could be diagrammed in the following way:

```
outcome = 12 + 6 / 3
                  \ /
outcome = 12 +    2

outcome = 14
```

Table 3-1 shows the precedence of the arithmetic operators. The operators at the top of the table have higher precedence than the ones below them.

Table 3-1   Precedence of Arithmetic Operators (Highest to Lowest)

(unary negation) –
* / %
+   –

The multiplication, division, and modulus operators have the same precedence. This is also true of the addition and subtraction operators. Table 3-2 shows some expressions with their values.

Table 3-2   Some Simple Expressions and Their Values

Expression	Value
5 + 2 * 4	13
10 / 2 – 3	2
8 + 12 * 2 – 4	28
4 + 17 % 2 – 1	4
6 – 3 * 2 + 7 – 1	6

Associativity

An operator's *associativity* is either left to right, or right to left. If two operators sharing an operand have the same precedence, they work according to their associativity. Table 3-3 lists the associativity of the arithmetic operators. As an example, look at the following expression:

```
5 - 3 + 2
```

Both the − and + operators in this expression have the same precedence, and they have left to right associativity. So, the operators will work from left to right. This expression is the same as:

```
((5 - 3) + 2)
```

Here is another example:

```
12 / 6 * 4
```

Because the / and * operators have the same precedence, and they have left to right associativity, they will work from left to right. This expression is the same as:

```
((12 / 6) * 4)
```

Table 3-3   Associativity of Arithmetic Operators

Operator	Associativity
(unary negation) −	Right to left
* / %	Left to right
+ −	Left to right

Grouping with Parentheses

Parts of a mathematical expression may be grouped with parentheses to force some operations to be performed before others. In the following statement, the sum of a + b is divided by 4.

```
result = (a + b) / 4;
```

Without the parentheses, however, b would be divided by 4 and the result added to a. Table 3-4 shows more expressions and their values.

Table 3-4   More Simple Expressions and Their Values

Expression	Value
(5 + 2) * 4	28
10 / (5 - 3)	5
8 + 12 * (6 - 2)	56
(4 + 17) % 2 - 1	0
(6 - 3) * (2 + 7) / 3	9

Converting Algebraic Expressions to Programming Statements

In algebra it is not always necessary to use an operator for multiplication. C++, however, requires an operator for any mathematical operation. Table 3-5 shows some algebraic expressions that perform multiplication and the equivalent C++ expressions.

Table 3-5   Algebraic and C++ Multiplication Expressions

Algebraic Expression	Operation	C++ Equivalent
$6B$	6 times B	`6 * B`
$(3)(12)$	3 times 12	`3 * 12`
$4xy$	4 times x times y	`4 * x * y`

When converting some algebraic expressions to C++, you may have to insert parentheses that do not appear in the algebraic expression. For example, look at the following expression:

$$x = \frac{a + b}{c}$$

To convert this to a C++ statement, $a + b$ will have to be enclosed in parentheses:

```
x = (a + b) / c;
```

Table 3-6 shows more algebraic expressions and their C++ equivalents.

Table 3-6   Algebraic and C++ Expressions

Algebraic Expression	C++ Expression
$y = 3\dfrac{x}{2}$	`y = x / 2 * 3;`
$z = 3bc + 4$	`z = 3 * b * c + 4;`
$a = \dfrac{3x + 2}{4a - 1}$	`a = (3 * x + 2) / (4 * a - 1)`

No Exponents Please!

Unlike many programming languages, C++ does not have an exponent operator. Raising a number to a power requires the use of a *library function*. The C++ library isn't a place where you check out books, but a collection of specialized functions. Think of a library function as a "routine" that performs a specific operation. One of the library functions is called `pow`, and its purpose is to raise a number to a power. Here is an example of how it's used:

```
area = pow(4.0, 2.0);
```

This statement contains a *call* to the `pow` function. The numbers inside the parentheses are *arguments*. Arguments are data being sent to the function. The `pow` function always raises the first argument to the power of the second argument. In this example, 4 is raised to the power of 2. The result is *returned* from the function and used in the statement where the function call appears. In this case, the value 16 is returned from `pow` and assigned to the variable `area`. This is illustrated in Figure 3-3.

Figure 3-3

$$area = \overset{\underset{16.0}{\longleftarrow}}{\underset{\text{return value}}{}} \quad pow(4.0, \; 2.0) \; ;$$

arguments

The statement `area = pow(4.0, 2.0)` is equivalent to the following algebraic statement:

$$area = 4^2$$

Here is another example of a statement using the `pow` function. It assigns 3 times 6^3 to `x`:

```
x = 3 * pow(6.0, 3.0);
```

And the following statement displays the value of 5 raised to the power of 4:

```
cout << pow(5.0, 4.0);
```

It might be helpful to think of `pow` as a "black box" that you plug two numbers into, and that then sends a third number out. The number that comes out has the value of the first number raised to the power of the second number, as illustrated in Figure 3-4:

Figure 3-4

There are some guidelines that should be followed when the `pow` function is used. First, the program must include the `cmath` header file. Second, the arguments that you pass to the `pow` function should be `doubles`. Third, the variable used to store `pow`'s return value should be defined as a `double`. For example, in the following statement the variable `area` should be a `double`:

```
area = pow(4.0, 2.0);
```

Program 3-7 solves a simple algebraic problem. It asks the user to enter the radius of a circle and then calculates the area of the circle. The formula is

$$Area = \pi r^2$$

which is expressed in the program as

```
area = 3.14159 * pow(radius, 2.0);
```

Program 3-7

```
 1  // This program calculates the area of a circle.
 2  // The formula for the area of a circle is Pi times
 3  // the radius squared. Pi is 3.14159.
 4  #include <iostream>
 5  #include <cmath>    // needed for pow function
 6  using namespace std;
 7
 8  int main()
 9  {
10     double area, radius;
11
12     cout << "This program calculates the area of a circle.\n";
13     cout << "What is the radius of the circle? ";
14     cin >> radius;
15     area = 3.14159 * pow(radius, 2.0);
16     cout << "The area is " << area << endl;
17     return 0;
18  }
```

Program Output with Example Input Shown in Bold

```
This program calculates the area of a circle.
What is the radius of the circle? 10 [Enter]
The area is 314.159
```

NOTE: Program 3-7 is presented as a demonstration of the pow function. In reality, there is no reason to use the pow function in such a simple operation. The math statement could just as easily be written as

```
area = 3.14159 * radius * radius;
```

The pow function is useful, however, in operations that involve larger exponents.

In the Spotlight:
Calculating an Average

Determining the average of a group of values is a simple calculation: You add all of the values and then divide the sum by the number of values. Although this is a straightforward calculation, it is easy to make a mistake when writing a program that calculates an average. For example, let's assume that a, b, and c are double variables. Each of the variables holds a value and we want to calculate the average of those values. If we are careless, we might write a statement such as the following to perform the calculation:

```
average = a + b + c / 3.0;
```

Can you see the error in this statement? When it executes, the division will take place first. The value in c will be divided by 3.0, and then the result will be added to the sum of a + b. That is not the correct way to calculate an average. To correct this error we need to put parentheses around a + b + c, as shown here:

```
average = (a + b + c) / 3.0;
```

Let's step through the process of writing a program that calculates an average. Suppose you have taken three tests in your computer science class, and you want to write a program that will display the average of the test scores. Here is the algorithm in pseudocode:

Get the first test score.
Get the second test score.
Get the third test score.
Calculate the average by adding the three test scores and dividing the sum by 3.
Display the average.

In the first three steps we prompt the user to enter three test scores. Let's say we store those test scores in the `double` variables `test1`, `test2`, and `test3`. Then in the fourth step we calculate the average of the three test scores. We will use the following statement to perform the calculation and store the result in the `average` variable, which is a `double`:

```
average = (test1 + test2 + test3) / 3.0;
```

The last step is to display the average. Program 3-8 shows the program.

Program 3-8

```
 1  // This program calculates the average
 2  // of three test scores.
 3  #include <iostream>
 4  #include <cmath>
 5  using namespace std;
 6
 7  int main()
 8  {
 9      double test1, test2, test3;  // To hold the scores
10      double average;              // To hold the average
11
12      // Get the three test scores.
13      cout << "Enter the first test score: ";
14      cin >> test1;
15      cout << "Enter the second test score: ";
16      cin >> test2;
17      cout << "Enter the third test score: ";
18      cin >> test3;
19
20      // Calculate the average of the scores.
21      average = (test1 + test2 + test3) / 3.0;
22
23      // Display the average.
24      cout << "The average score is: " << average << endl;
25      return 0;
26  }
```

Program Output with Example Input Shown in Bold
```
Enter the first test score: 90 [Enter]
Enter the second test score: 80 [Enter]
Enter the third test score: 100 [Enter]
The average score is 90
```

Checkpoint

3.10   Complete the table below by writing the value of each expression in the "Value" column.

Expression	Value
`6 + 3 * 5`	
`12 / 2 - 4`	
`9 + 14 * 2 - 6`	
`5 + 19 % 3 - 1`	
`(6 + 2) * 3`	
`14 / (11 - 4)`	
`9 + 12 * (8 - 3)`	
`(6 + 17) % 2 - 1`	
`(9 - 3) * (6 + 9) / 3`	

3.11   Write C++ expressions for the following algebraic expressions:

$$y = 6x$$

$$a = 2b + 4c$$

$$y = x^2$$

$$g = \frac{x + 2}{z^2}$$

$$y = \frac{x^2}{z^2}$$

3.12   Study the following program and complete the table.

```cpp
#include <iostream>
#include <cmath>
using namespace std;

int main()
{
   double value1, value2, value3;

   cout << "Enter a number: ";
   cin >> value1;
   value2 = 2 * pow(value1, 2.0);
   value3 = 3 + value2 / 2 - 1;
   cout << value3 << endl;
   return 0;
}
```

If the User Enters...	The Program Will Display What Number (Stored in `value3`)?
2	
5	
4.3	
6	

3.13   Complete the following program skeleton so it displays the volume of a cylindrical fuel tank. The formula for the volume of a cylinder is

Volume = $\pi r^2 h$

where

π is 3.14159

r is the radius of the tank

h is the height of the tank

```cpp
#include <iostream>
#include <cmath>
using namespace std;

int main()
{
    double volume, radius, height;

    cout << "This program will tell you the volume of\n";
    cout << "a cylinder-shaped fuel tank.\n";
    cout << "How tall is the tank? ";
    cin >> height;
    cout << "What is the radius of the tank? ";
    cin >> radius;

    // You must complete the program.
}
```

3.3   When You Mix Apples and Oranges: Type Conversion

CONCEPT: When an operator's operands are of different data types, C++ will automatically convert them to the same data type. This can affect the results of mathematical expressions.

If an int is multiplied by a float, what data type will the result be? What if a double is divided by an unsigned int? Is there any way of predicting what will happen in these instances? The answer is yes. C++ follows a set of rules when performing mathematical operations on variables of different data types. It's helpful to understand these rules to prevent subtle errors from creeping into your programs.

Just like officers in the military, data types are ranked. One data type outranks another if it can hold a larger number. For example, a float outranks an int. Table 3-7 lists the data types in order of their rank, from highest to lowest.

Table 3-7   Data Type Ranking

long double
double
float
unsigned long
long
unsigned int
int

One exception to the ranking in Table 3-7 is when an `int` and a `long` are the same size. In that case, an `unsigned int` outranks `long` because it can hold a higher value.

When C++ is working with an operator, it strives to convert the operands to the same type. This automatic conversion is known as *type coercion*. When a value is converted to a higher data type, it is said to be *promoted*. To *demote* a value means to convert it to a lower data type. Let's look at the specific rules that govern the evaluation of mathematical expressions.

Rule 1: `chars`, `shorts`, and `unsigned shorts` are automatically promoted to `int`.

You will notice that `char`, `short`, and `unsigned short` do not appear in Table 3-7. That's because anytime they are used in a mathematical expression, they are automatically promoted to an `int`. The only exception to this rule is when an `unsigned short` holds a value larger than can be held by an `int`. This can happen on systems where `shorts` are the same size as `ints`. In this case, the `unsigned short` is promoted to `unsigned int`.

Rule 2: When an operator works with two values of different data types, the lower-ranking value is promoted to the type of the higher-ranking value.

In the following expression, assume that `years` is an `int` and `interestRate` is a `float`:

```
years * interestRate
```

Before the multiplication takes place, `years` will be promoted to a `float`.

Rule 3: When the final value of an expression is assigned to a variable, it will be converted to the data type of that variable.

In the following statement, assume that `area` is a `long int`, while `length` and `width` are both `ints`:

```
area = length * width;
```

Since `length` and `width` are both `ints`, they will not be converted to any other data type. The result of the multiplication, however, will be converted to `long` so it can be stored in `area`.

Watch out for situations where an expression results in a fractional value being assigned to an integer variable. Here is an example:

```
int x, y = 4;
float z = 2.7;
x = y * z;
```

In the expression y * z, y will be promoted to `float` and 10.8 will result from the multiplication. Since x is an integer, however, 10.8 will be truncated and 10 will be stored in x.

Integer Division

When you divide an integer by another integer in C++, the result is always an integer. If there is a remainder, it will be discarded. For example, in the following code, `parts` is assigned the value 2.0:

```
double parts;
parts = 15 / 6;
```

Even though 15 divided by 6 is really 2.5, the .5 part of the result is discarded because we are dividing an integer by an integer. It doesn't matter that parts is declared as a double because the fractional part of the result is discarded *before* the assignment takes place. In order for a division operation to return a floating-point value, at least one of the operands must be of a floating-point data type. For example, the previous code could be written as:

```
double parts;
parts = 15.0 / 6;
```

In this code the literal value 15.0 is interpreted as a floating-point number, so the division operation will return a floating-point number. The value 2.5 will be assigned to parts.

3.4   Overflow and Underflow

CONCEPT: When a variable is assigned a value that is too large or too small in range for that variable's data type, the variable overflows or underflows.

Trouble can arise when a variable is being assigned a value that is too large for its type. Here is a statement where a, b, and c are all short integers:

```
a = b * c;
```

If b and c are set to values large enough, the multiplication will produce a number too big to be stored in a. To prepare for this, a should have been defined as an int, or a long int.

When a variable is assigned a number that is too large for its data type, it *overflows*. Likewise, assigning a value that is too small for a variable causes it to *underflow*. Program 3-9 shows what happens when an integer overflows or underflows. (The output shown is from a system with two-byte short integers.)

Program 3-9

```
 1   // This program demonstrates integer overflow and underflow.
 2   #include <iostream>
 3   using namespace std;
 4
 5   int main()
 6   {
 7      // testVar is initialized with the maximum value for a short.
 8      short testVar = 32767;
 9
10      // Display testVar.
11      cout << testVar << endl;
12
13      // Add 1 to testVar to make it overflow.
14      testVar = testVar + 1;
15      cout << testVar << endl;
16
```

```
17      // Subtract 1 from testVar to make it underflow.
18      testVar = testVar - 1;
19      cout << testVar << endl;
20      return 0;
21  }
```

Program Output

```
32767
-32768
32767
```

Typically, when an integer overflows, its contents wrap around to that data type's lowest possible value. In Program 3-9, testVar wrapped around from 32,767 to –32,768 when 1 was added to it. When 1 was subtracted from testVar, it underflowed, which caused its contents to wrap back around to 32,767. No warning or error message is given, so be careful when working with numbers close to the maximum or minimum range of an integer. If an overflow or underflow occurs, the program will use the incorrect number, and therefore produce incorrect results.

When floating-point variables overflow or underflow, the results depend upon how the compiler is configured. Your system may produce programs that do any of the following:

- Produces an incorrect result and continues running.
- Prints an error message and immediately stops when either floating point overflow or underflow occurs.
- Prints an error message and immediately stops when floating point overflow occurs, but stores a 0 in the variable when it underflows.
- Gives you a choice of behaviors when overflow or underflow occurs.

You can find out how your system reacts by compiling and running Program 3-10.

Program 3-10

```
1   // This program can be used to see how your system handles
2   // floating point overflow and underflow.
3   #include <iostream>
4   using namespace std;
5
6   int main()
7   {
8      float test;
9
10     test = 2.0e38 * 1000;    // Should overflow test.
11     cout << test << endl;
12     test = 2.0e-38 / 2.0e38; // Should underflow test.
13     cout << test << endl;
14     return 0;
15  }
```

3.5 Type Casting

CONCEPT: Type casting allows you to perform manual data type conversion.

A *type cast expression* lets you manually promote or demote a value. The general format of a type cast expression is

```
static_cast<DataType>(Value)
```

where *Value* is a variable or literal value that you wish to convert and *DataType* is the data type you wish to convert *Value* to. Here is an example of code that uses a type cast expression:

```
double number = 3.7;
int val;
val = static_cast<int>(number);
```

This code defines two variables: number, a double, and val, an int. The type cast expression in the third statement returns a copy of the value in number, converted to an int. When a double is converted to an int, the fractional part is truncated so this statement stores 3 in val. The original value in number is not changed, however.

Type cast expressions are useful in situations where C++ will not perform the desired conversion automatically. Program 3-11 shows an example where a type cast expression is used to prevent integer division from taking place. The statement that uses the type cast expression is

```
perMonth = static_cast<double>(books) / months;
```

Program 3-11

```
 1   // This program uses a type cast to avoid integer division.
 2   #include <iostream>
 3   using namespace std;
 4
 5   int main()
 6   {
 7      int books;        // Number of books to read
 8      int months;       // Number of months spent reading
 9      double perMonth;  // Average number of books per month
10
11      cout << "How many books do you plan to read? ";
12      cin >> books;
13      cout << "How many months will it take you to read them? ";
14      cin >> months;
15      perMonth = static_cast<double>(books) / months;
16      cout << "That is " << perMonth << " books per month.\n";
17      return 0;
18   }
```

Program Output with Example Input Shown in Bold
How many books do you plan to read? **30 [Enter]**
How many months will it take you to read them? **7 [Enter]**
That is 4.28571 books per month.

The variable books is an integer, but its value is converted to a double before the division takes place. Without the type cast expression in line 15, integer division would have been performed resulting in an incorrect answer.

 WARNING! In Program 3-11, the following statement would still have resulted in integer division:

```
perMonth = static_cast<double>(books / months);
```

The result of the expression books / months is 4. When 4 is converted to a double, it is 4.0. To prevent the integer division from taking place, one of the operands should be converted to a double prior to the division operation. This forces C++ to automatically convert the value of the other operand to a double.

Program 3-12 further demonstrates the type cast expression.

Program 3-12

```
 1   // This program uses a type cast expression to print a character
 2   // from a number.
 3   #include <iostream>
 4   using namespace std;
 5
 6   int main()
 7   {
 8       int number = 65;
 9
10       // Display the value of the number variable.
11       cout << number << endl;
12
13       // Display the value of number converted to
14       // the char data type.
15       cout << static_cast<char>(number) << endl;
16       return 0;
17   }
```

Program Output
65
A

Let's take a closer look at this program. In line 8 the int variable number is initialized with the value 65. In line 11, number is sent to cout, causing 65 to be displayed. In line 15, a type cast expression is used to convert the value in number to the char data type.

Recall from Chapter 2 that characters are stored in memory as integer ASCII codes. The number 65 is the ASCII code for the letter 'A', so this statement causes the letter 'A' to be displayed.

> **NOTE:** C++ provides several different type cast expressions. `static_cast` is the most commonly used type cast expression, so we will primarily use it in this book.

If You Plan to Continue in Computer Science: C-Style and Prestandard Type Cast Expressions

C++ also supports two older methods of creating type cast expressions: the C-style form and the prestandard C++ form. The C-style cast is the name of a data type enclosed in parentheses, preceding the value that is to be converted. For example, the following statement converts the value in `number` to an `int`.

```
val = (int)number;
```

The following statement shows another example.

```
perMonth = (double)books / months;
```

In this statement the value in the `books` variable is converted to a `double` before the division takes place.

The prestandard C++ form of the type cast expression appears as a data type name followed by a value inside a set of parentheses. Here is an example:

```
val = int(number);
```

The type cast in this statement returns a copy of the value in `number`, converted to an `int`. Here is another example:

```
perMonth = double(books) / months;
```

Although the `static_cast` expression is preferable to either the C-style or the prestandard C++ form of the type cast expression, you will probably see code in the workplace that uses these older styles.

Checkpoint

3.14   Assume the following variable definitions:

```
int a = 5, b = 12;
double x = 3.4, z = 9.1;
```

What are the values of the following expressions?

A) `b / a`

B) `x * a`

C) `static_cast<double>(b / a)`

D) `static_cast<double>(b) / a`

E) `b / static_cast<double>(a)`

F) `static_cast<double>(b) / static_cast<double>(a)`

G) `b / static_cast<int>(x)`

H) `static_cast<int>(x) * static_cast<int>(z)`

I) `static_cast<int>(x * z)`

J) `static_cast<double>(static_cast<int>(x) *`
   `                        static_cast<int>(z))`

3.15   Complete the following program skeleton so it asks the user to enter a character. Store the character in the variable letter. Use a type cast expression with the variable in a cout statement to display the character's ASCII code on the screen.

```cpp
#include <iostream>
using namespace std;
int main()
{
    char letter;

    //  Finish this program
    //  as specified above.
    return 0;
}
```

3.16   What will the following program display?

```cpp
#include <iostream>
using namespace std;

int main()
{
    int integer1, integer2;
    double result;

    integer1 = 19;
    integer2 = 2;
    result = integer1 / integer2;
    cout << result << endl;
    result = static_cast<double>(integer1) / integer2;
    cout << result << endl;
    result = static_cast<double>(integer1 / integer2);
    cout << result << endl;
    return 0;
}
```

3.6   Named Constants

CONCEPT: Literals may be given names that symbolically represent them in a program.

In Chapter 2 you learned about numbers and strings being expressed as literals. For example, the following statement contains the numeric literal 0.129:

```cpp
newAmount = balance * 0.129;
```

Let's assume this statement appears in a banking program that calculates data pertaining to loans. In such a program, two potential problems arise. First, it is not clear to anyone other than the original programmer what 0.129 is. It appears to be an interest rate, but in some situations there are fees associated with loan payments. How can the purpose of this statement be determined without painstakingly checking the rest of the program?

The second problem occurs if this number is used in other calculations throughout the program and must be changed periodically. Assuming the number is an interest rate, what if the rate changes from 12.9 percent to 13.2 percent? The programmer will have to search through the source code for every occurrence of the number.

Both of these problems can be addressed by using named constants. A *named constant* is like a variable, but its content is read-only, and cannot be changed while the program is running. Here is a definition of a named constant:

```
const double INTEREST_RATE = 0.129;
```

It looks just like a regular variable definition except that the word `const` appears before the data type name, and the name of the variable is written in all uppercase characters. The key word `const` is a qualifier that tells the compiler to make the variable read-only. Its value will remain constant throughout the program's execution. It is not required that the variable name be written in all uppercase characters, but many programmers prefer to write them this way so they are easily distinguishable from regular variable names.

An initialization value must be given when defining a variable with the `const` qualifier, or an error will result when the program is compiled. A compiler error will also result if there are any statements in the program that attempt to change the value of a named constant.

An advantage of using named constants is that they make programs more self-documenting. The following statement

```
newAmount = balance * 0.129;
```

can be changed to read

```
newAmount = balance * INTEREST_RATE;
```

A new programmer can read the second statement and know what is happening. It is evident that `balance` is being multiplied by the interest rate. Another advantage to this approach is that widespread changes can easily be made to the program. Let's say the interest rate appears in a dozen different statements throughout the program. When the rate changes, the initialization value in the definition of the named constant is the only value that needs to be modified. If the rate increases to 13.2% the definition is changed to the following:

```
const double INTEREST_RATE = 0.132;
```

The program is then ready to be recompiled. Every statement that uses `INTEREST_RATE` will then use the new value.

It is also useful to define named constants for common values that are difficult to remember. For example, Program 3-7 calculated the area of a circle. The number 3.14159 is used for `pi` in the formula. This value could easily be defined as a named constant, as shown in Program 3-13.

Program 3-13

```
 1   // This program calculates the area of a circle.
 2   // The formula for the area of a circle is PI times
 3   // the radius squared. PI is 3.14159.
 4   #include <iostream>
 5   #include <cmath>    // needed for pow function
 6   using namespace std;
 7
 8   int main()
 9   {
10      const double PI = 3.14159;
11      double area, radius;
12
13      cout << "This program calculates the area of a circle.\n";
14      cout << "What is the radius of the circle? ";
15      cin >> radius;
16      area = PI * pow(radius, 2.0);
17      cout << "The area is " << area << endl;
18      return 0;
19   }
```

Earlier in this chapter you saw how to create a char array for the purpose of holding a C-string. It is a common practice to use a named constant to indicate the array's size. Here is an example:

```
const int SIZE = 21;
char name[SIZE];
```

This practice can make the program easier to maintain. When we store the size of the array in a named constant, we can use the named constant rather than a literal number in any statement that must refer to the size of the array. Then, if we ever need to change the array's size, we need only to change the initialization value of the named constant.

If You Plan to Continue in Computer Science: The #define Directive

The older C-style method of creating named constants is with the #define preprocessor directive. Although it is preferable to use the const modifier, there are programs with the #define directive still in use. In addition, Chapter 13 teaches other uses of the #define directive, so it is important to understand.

In Chapter 2 you learned that the #include directive causes the preprocessor to include the contents of another file in your program. Program 3-14 shows how the preprocessor can be used to create a named constant.

Program 3-14

```
 1   // This program calculates the area of a circle.
 2   // The formula for the area of a circle is PI times
 3   // the radius squared. PI is 3.1459.
 4   #include <iostream>
 5   #include <cmath>    // needed for pow function
```

(program continues)

Program 3-14 *(continued)*

```
 6  using namespace std;
 7
 8  #define PI 3.14159
 9
10  int main()
11  {
12     double area, radius;
13
14     cout << "This program calculates the area of a circle.\n";
15     cout << "What is the radius of the circle? ";
16     cin >> radius;
17     area = PI * pow(radius, 2.0);
18     cout << "The area is " << area << endl;
19     return 0;
20  }
```

Remember, the preprocessor scans your program before it is compiled. It looks for directives, which are lines that begin with the # symbol. Preprocessor directives cause your source code to be modified prior to being compiled. The #define directive in line 8 reads

```
#define PI 3.14159
```

The word PI is a named constant and 3.14159 is its value. Anytime PI is used in the program, it will be replaced by the value 3.14159. Line 17, which reads

```
area = PI * pow(radius, 2.0);
```

will be modified by the preprocessor to read

```
area = 3.14159 * pow(radius, 2.0);
```

If there had been a line that read

```
cout << PI << endl;
```

it would have been modified to read

```
cout << 3.14159 << endl;
```

It is important to realize the difference between const variables and constants created with the #define directive. const variables are defined like regular variables. They have a data type and a specific storage location in memory. They are like regular variables in every way except that you cannot change their value while the program is running. Constants created with the #define directive, however, are not variables at all, but text substitutions. Each occurrence of the named constant in your source code is removed and the value of the constant is written in its place.

Be careful not to put a semicolon at the end of a #define directive. The semicolon will actually become part of the value of the constant. If the #define directive in line 8 of Program 3-14 had read like this:

```
#define PI 3.14159;
```

The mathematical statement

```
area = PI * pow(radius, 2.0);
```

would have been modified to read

```
area = 3.14159; * pow(radius, 2.0);
```

Because of the semicolon, the preprocessor would have created a syntax error in the statement above and the compiler would have given an error message when trying to process this statement.

> **NOTE:** `#define` directives are intended for the preprocessor and C++ statements are intended for the compiler. The preprocessor does not look for semicolons to terminate directives.

Checkpoint

3.17 Write statements using the `const` qualifier to create named constants for the following literal values:

Literal Value	Description
2.71828	Euler's number (known in mathematics as e)
5.256E5	Number of minutes in a year
32.2	The gravitational acceleration constant (in feet per second^2)
9.8	The gravitational acceleration constant (in meters per second^2)
1609	Number of meters in a mile

3.18 Write `#define` directives for the literal values listed in Question 3.17.

3.19 Assuming the user enters 6 in response to the question, what will the following program display on the screen?

```cpp
#include <iostream>
using namespace std;

#define GREETING1 "This program calculates the number "
#define GREETING2 "of candy pieces sold."
#define QUESTION "How many jars of candy have you sold? "
#define RESULTS "The number of pieces sold: "
#define YOUR_COMMISSION "Candy pieces you get for commission: "
#define COMMISSION_RATE .20
int main()
{
    const int PER_JAR = 1860;
    int jars, pieces;
    double commission;

    cout << GREETING1;
    cout << GREETING2 << endl;
    cout << QUESTION;
    cin >> jars;
    pieces = jars * PER_JAR;
    cout << RESULTS << pieces << endl;
    commission = pieces * COMMISSION_RATE;
    cout << YOUR_COMMISSION << commission << endl;
    return 0;
}
```

3.20   Complete the following program skeleton so it properly converts a speed entered in miles per hour to feet per second. One mile per hour is 1.467 feet per second. (*Hint*: To convert a value in miles per hour to feet per second, multiply it by 1.467.)

```cpp
#include <iostream>
using namespace std;

int main()
{
    // Define a named constant named CONVERSION
    // with the value 1.467.
    double milesPerHour, feetPerSecond;

    cout << "This program converts miles per hour to\n";
    cout << "feet per second.\n";
    cout << "Enter a speed in MPH: ";
    cin >> milesPerHour;

    // Calculate feet per second.
    // One mile per hour equals 1.467 feet per second.

    cout << "That is " << feetPerSecond
         << " feet per second.\n";
    return 0;
}
```

3.7 Multiple Assignment and Combined Assignment

CONCEPT: Multiple assignment means to assign the same value to several variables with one statement.

C++ allows you to assign a value to multiple variables at once. If a program has several variables, such as a, b, c, and d, and each variable needs to be assigned a value, such as 12, the following statement may be constructed:

```cpp
a = b = c = d = 12;
```

The value 12 will be assigned to each variable listed in the statement.*

Combined Assignment Operators

Quite often, programs have assignment statements of the following form:

```cpp
number = number + 1;
```

The expression on the right side of the assignment operator gives the value of number plus 1. The result is then assigned to number, replacing the value that was previously stored there. Effectively, this statement adds 1 to number. In a similar fashion, the following statement subtracts 5 from number.

```cpp
number = number - 5;
```

---

* The assignment operator works from right to left. 12 is first assigned to d, then to c, then to b, then to a.

If you have never seen this type of statement before, it might cause some initial confusion because the same variable name appears on both sides of the assignment operator. Table 3-8 shows other examples of statements written this way.

Table 3-8   (Assume x = 6)

Statement	What It Does	Value of x After the Statement
x = x + 4;	Adds 4 to x	10
x = x - 3;	Subtracts 3 from x	3
x = x * 10;	Multiplies x by 10	60
x = x / 2;	Divides x by 2	3
x = x % 4	Makes x the remainder of x / 4	2

These types of operations are very common in programming. For convenience, C++ offers a special set of operators designed specifically for these jobs. Table 3-9 shows the *combined assignment operators,* also known as *compound operators,* and *arithmetic assignment operators.*

Table 3-9

Operator	Example Usage	Equivalent to
+=	x += 5;	x = x + 5;
-=	y -= 2;	y = y - 2;
*=	z *= 10;	z = z * 10;
/=	a /= b;	a = a / b;
%=	c %= 3;	c = c % 3;

As you can see, the combined assignment operators do not require the programmer to type the variable name twice. Also, they give a clear indication of what is happening in the statement. Program 3-15 uses combined assignment operators.

Program 3-15

```
1   // This program tracks the inventory of three widget stores
2   // that opened at the same time. Each store started with the
3   // same number of widgets in inventory. By subtracting the
4   // number of widgets each store has sold from its inventory,
5   // the current inventory can be calculated.
6   #include <iostream>
7   using namespace std;
8
9   int main()
10  {
11      int begInv,     // Beginning inventory for all stores
12          sold,       // Number of widgets sold
13          store1,     // Store 1's inventory
14          store2,     // Store 2's inventory
15          store3;     // Store 3's inventory
16
17      // Get the beginning inventory for all the stores.
18      cout << "One week ago, 3 new widget stores opened\n";
```

(program continues)

Program 3-15   *(continued)*

```
19        cout << "at the same time with the same beginning\n";
20        cout << "inventory. What was the beginning inventory? ";
21        cin >> begInv;
22
23        // Set each store's inventory.
24        store1 = store2 = store3 = begInv;
25
26        // Get the number of widgets sold at store 1.
27        cout << "How many widgets has store 1 sold? ";
28        cin >> sold;
29        store1 -= sold; // Adjust store 1's inventory.
30
31        // Get the number of widgets sold at store 2.
32        cout << "How many widgets has store 2 sold? ";
33        cin >> sold;
34        store2 -= sold; // Adjust store 2's inventory.
35
36        // Get the number of widgets sold at store 3.
37        cout << "How many widgets has store 3 sold? ";
38        cin >> sold;
39        store3 -= sold; // Adjust store 3's inventory.
40
41        // Display each store's current inventory.
42        cout << "\nThe current inventory of each store:\n";
43        cout << "Store 1: " << store1 << endl;
44        cout << "Store 2: " << store2 << endl;
45        cout << "Store 3: " << store3 << endl;
46        return 0;
47    }
```

Program Output with Example Input Shown in Bold

```
One week ago, 3 new widget stores opened
at the same time with the same beginning
inventory. What was the beginning inventory? 100 [Enter]
How many widgets has store 1 sold? 25 [Enter]
How many widgets has store 2 sold? 15 [Enter]
How many widgets has store 3 sold? 45 [Enter]

The current inventory of each store:
Store 1: 75
Store 2: 85
Store 3: 55
```

More elaborate statements may be expressed with the combined assignment operators. Here is an example:

```
result *= a + 5;
```

In this statement, result is multiplied by the sum of a + 5. When constructing such statements, you must realize the precedence of the combined assignment operators is lower than that of the regular math operators. The statement above is equivalent to

```
result = result * (a + 5);
```

which is different from

```
result = result * a + 5;
```

Table 3-10 shows other examples of such statements and their assignment statement equivalencies.

Table 3-10

Example Usage	Equivalent to
x += b + 5;	x = x + (b + 5);
y -= a * 2;	y = y - (a * 2);
z *= 10 - c;	z = z * (10 - c);
a /= b + c;	a = a / (b + c);
c %= d - 3;	c = c % (d - 3);

 Checkpoint

3.21   Write a multiple assignment statement that assigns 0 to the variables `total`, `subtotal`, `tax`, and `shipping`.

3.22   Write statements using combined assignment operators to perform the following:

A)   Add 6 to `x`.

B)   Subtract 4 from `amount`.

C)   Multiply `y` by 4.

D)   Divide `total` by 27.

E)   Store in `x` the remainder of `x` divided by 7.

F)   Add `y * 5` to `x`.

G)   Subtract `discount` times 4 from `total`.

H)   Multiply `increase` by `salesRep` times 5.

I)   Divide `profit` by `shares` minus 1000.

3.23   What will the following program display?

```cpp
#include <iostream>
using namespace std;

int main()
{
    int unus, duo, tres;

    unus = duo = tres = 5;
    unus += 4;
    duo *= 2;
    tres -= 4;
    unus /= 3;
    duo += tres;
    cout << unus << endl;
    cout << duo << endl;
    cout << tres << endl;
    return 0;
}
```

3.8   Formatting Output

CONCEPT: The `cout` object provides ways to format data as it is being displayed. This affects the way data appears on the screen.

The same data can be printed or displayed in several different ways. For example, all of the following numbers have the same value, although they look different:

```
720
720.0
720.00000000
7.2e+2
+720.0
```

The way a value is printed is called its *formatting*. The `cout` object has a standard way of formatting variables of each data type. Sometimes, however, you need more control over the way data is displayed. Consider Program 3-16, for example, which displays three rows of numbers with spaces between each one.

Program 3-16

```cpp
 1   // This program displays three rows of numbers.
 2   #include <iostream>
 3   using namespace std;
 4
 5   int main()
 6   {
 7      int num1 = 2897, num2 = 5,    num3 = 837,
 8          num4 = 34,   num5 = 7,    num6 = 1623,
 9          num7 = 390,  num8 = 3456, num9 = 12;
10
11      // Display the first row of numbers
12      cout << num1 << "   " << num2 << "   " << num3 << endl;
13
14      // Display the second row of numbers
15      cout << num4 << "   " << num5 << "   " << num6 << endl;
16
17      // Display the third row of numbers
18      cout << num7 << "   " << num8 << "   " << num9 << endl;
19      return 0;
20   }
```

Program Output

```
2897   5   837
34   7   1623
390   3456   12
```

Unfortunately, the numbers do not line up in columns. This is because some of the numbers, such as 5 and 7, occupy one position on the screen, while others occupy two or three positions. `cout` uses just the number of spaces needed to print each number.

To remedy this, `cout` offers a way of specifying the minimum number of spaces to use for each number. A stream manipulator, `setw`, can be used to establish print fields of a specified width. Here is an example of how it is used:

```
value = 23;
cout << setw(5) << value;
```

The number inside the parentheses after the word `setw` specifies the *field width* for the value immediately following it. The field width is the minimum number of character positions, or spaces, on the screen to print the value in. In the example above, the number 23 will be displayed in a field of 5 spaces. Since 23 only occupies 2 positions on the screen, 3 blank spaces will be printed before it. To further clarify how this works, look at the following statements:

```
value = 23;
cout << "(" << setw(5) << value << ")";
```

This will cause the following output:

```
(   23)
```

Notice that the number occupies the last two positions in the field. Since the number did not use the entire field, `cout` filled the extra 3 positions with blank spaces. Because the number appears on the right side of the field with blank spaces "padding" it in front, it is said to be *right-justified*.

Program 3-17 shows how the numbers in Program 3-16 can be printed in columns that line up perfectly by using `setw`.

Program 3-17

```
 1  // This program displays three rows of numbers.
 2  #include <iostream>
 3  #include <iomanip>        // Required for setw
 4  using namespace std;
 5
 6  int main()
 7  {
 8      int num1 = 2897, num2 = 5,    num3 = 837,
 9          num4 = 34,   num5 = 7,    num6 = 1623,
10          num7 = 390,  num8 = 3456, num9 = 12;
11
12      // Display the first row of numbers
13      cout << setw(6) << num1 << setw(6)
14          << num2 << setw(6) << num3 << endl;
15
16      // Display the second row of numbers
17      cout << setw(6) << num4 << setw(6)
18          << num5 << setw(6) << num6 << endl;
19
20      // Display the third row of numbers
21      cout << setw(6) << num7 << setw(6)
22          << num8 << setw(6) << num9 << endl;
23      return 0;
24  }
```

(program output continues)

Program 3-17   *(continued)*

Program Output

```
2897     5   837
  34     7  1623
 390  3456    12
```

By printing each number in a field of 6 positions, they are displayed in perfect columns.

> **NOTE:** A new header file, `iomanip`, is included in Program 3-17. It must be used in any program that uses `setw`.

Notice how a `setw` manipulator is used with each value because `setw` only establishes a field width for the value immediately following it. After that value is printed, `cout` goes back to its default method of printing.

You might wonder what will happen if the number is too large to fit in the field, as in the following statement:

```
value = 18397;
cout << setw(2) << value;
```

In cases like this, `cout` will print the entire number. `setw` only specifies the minimum number of positions in the print field. Any number larger than the minimum will cause `cout` to override the `setw` value.

You may specify the field width of any type of data. Program 3-18 shows `setw` being used with an integer, a floating-point number, and a string.

Program 3-18

```
 1   // This program demonstrates the setw manipulator being
 2   // used with values of various data types.
 3   #include <iostream>
 4   #include <iomanip>
 5   using namespace std;
 6
 7   int main()
 8   {
 9      int intValue = 3928;
10      double doubleValue = 91.5;
11      const int ARRAY_SIZE = 14;
12      char cStringValue[ARRAY_SIZE] = "John J. Smith";
13
14      cout << "(" << setw(5) << intValue << ")" << endl;
15      cout << "(" << setw(8) << doubleValue << ")" << endl;
16      cout << "(" << setw(16) << cStringValue << ")" << endl;
17      return 0;
18   }
```

Program Output
```
( 3928)
(   91.5)
(   John J. Smith)
```

Program 3-18 can be used to illustrate the following points:
- The field width of a floating-point number includes a position for the decimal point.
- The field width of a string includes all characters in the string, including spaces.
- The values printed in the field are right-justified by default. This means they are aligned with the right side of the print field, and any blanks that must be used to pad it are inserted in front of the value.

VideoNote
Formatting Numbers with setprecision

The setprecision Manipulator

Floating-point values may be rounded to a number of *significant digits*, or *precision*, which is the total number of digits that appear before and after the decimal point. You can control the number of significant digits with which floating-point values are displayed by using the setprecision manipulator. Program 3-19 shows the results of a division operation displayed with different numbers of significant digits.

Program 3-19

```
 1   // This program demonstrates how setprecision rounds a
 2   // floating point value.
 3   #include <iostream>
 4   #include <iomanip>
 5   using namespace std;
 6
 7   int main()
 8   {
 9      double quotient, number1 = 132.364, number2 = 26.91;
10
11      quotient = number1 / number2;
12      cout << quotient << endl;
13      cout << setprecision(5) << quotient << endl;
14      cout << setprecision(4) << quotient << endl;
15      cout << setprecision(3) << quotient << endl;
16      cout << setprecision(2) << quotient << endl;
17      cout << setprecision(1) << quotient << endl;
18      return 0;
19   }
```

Program Output
```
4.91877
4.9188
4.919
4.92
4.9
5
```

The first value is displayed in line 12 without the `setprecision` manipulator. (By default, the system in the illustration displays floating-point values with 6 significant digits.) The subsequent `cout` statements print the same value, but rounded to 5, 4, 3, 2, and 1 significant digits.

If the value of a number is expressed in fewer digits of precision than specified by `setprecision`, the manipulator will have no effect. In the following statements, the value of `dollars` only has four digits of precision, so the number printed by both `cout` statements is 24.51.

```
double dollars = 24.51;
cout << dollars << endl;                 // Displays 24.51
cout << setprecision(5) << dollars << endl;    // Displays 24.51
```

Table 3-11 shows how `setprecision` affects the way various values are displayed.

Table 3-11

Number	Manipulator	Value Displayed
28.92786	setprecision(3)	28.9
21	setprecision(5)	21
109.5	setprecision(4)	109.5
34.28596	setprecision(2)	34

Unlike field width, the precision setting remains in effect until it is changed to some other value. As with all formatting manipulators, you must include the header file `iomanip` to use `setprecision`.

Program 3-20 shows how the `setw` and `setprecision` manipulators may be combined to fully control the way floating point numbers are displayed.

Program 3-20

```
 1   // This program asks for sales figures for 3 days. The total
 2   // sales are calculated and displayed in a table.
 3   #include <iostream>
 4   #include <iomanip>
 5   using namespace std;
 6
 7   int main()
 8   {
 9      double day1, day2, day3, total;
10
11      // Get the sales for each day.
12      cout << "Enter the sales for day 1: ";
13      cin >> day1;
14      cout << "Enter the sales for day 2: ";
15      cin >> day2;
16      cout << "Enter the sales for day 3: ";
17      cin >> day3;
18
19      // Calculate the total sales.
20      total = day1 + day2 + day3;
```

```
21
22      // Display the sales figures.
23      cout << "\nSales Figures\n";
24      cout << "-------------\n";
25      cout << setprecision(5);
26      cout << "Day 1: " << setw(8) << day1 << endl;
27      cout << "Day 2: " << setw(8) << day2 << endl;
28      cout << "Day 3: " << setw(8) << day3 << endl;
29      cout << "Total: " << setw(8) << total << endl;
30      return 0;
31  }
```

Program Output with Example Input Shown in Bold
```
Enter the sales for day 1: 321.57 [Enter]
Enter the sales for day 2: 269.62 [Enter]
Enter the sales for day 3: 307.77 [Enter]

Sales Figures
-------------
Day 1:    321.57
Day 2:    269.62
Day 3:    307.77
Total:    898.96
```

The `fixed` Manipulator

The `setprecision` manipulator can sometimes surprise you in an undesirable way. When the precision of a number is set to a lower value, numbers tend to be printed in scientific notation. For example, here is the output of Program 3-20 with larger numbers being input:

Program 3-20

Program Output with Example Input Shown in Bold
```
Enter the sales for day 1: 145678.99 [Enter]
Enter the sales for day 2: 205614.85 [Enter]
Enter the sales for day 3: 198645.22 [Enter]

Sales Figures
-------------
Day 1: 1.4568e+005
Day 2: 2.0561e+005
Day 3: 1.9865e+005
Total: 5.4994e+005
```

Another stream manipulator, `fixed`, forces cout to print the digits in *fixed-point notation,* or decimal. Program 3-21 shows how the `fixed` manipulator is used.

Program 3-21

```
 1   // This program asks for sales figures for 3 days. The total
 2   // sales are calculated and displayed in a table.
 3   #include <iostream>
 4   #include <iomanip>
 5   using namespace std;
 6
 7   int main()
 8   {
 9      double day1, day2, day3, total;
10
11      // Get the sales for each day.
12      cout << "Enter the sales for day 1: ";
13      cin >> day1;
14      cout << "Enter the sales for day 2: ";
15      cin >> day2;
16      cout << "Enter the sales for day 3: ";
17      cin >> day3;
18
19      // Calculate the total sales.
20      total = day1 + day2 + day3;
21
22      // Display the sales figures.
23      cout << "\nSales Figures\n";
24      cout << "-------------\n";
25      cout << setprecision(2) << fixed;
26      cout << "Day 1: " << setw(8) << day1 << endl;
27      cout << "Day 2: " << setw(8) << day2 << endl;
28      cout << "Day 3: " << setw(8) << day3 << endl;
29      cout << "Total: " << setw(8) << total << endl;
30      return 0;
31   }
```

Program Output with Example Input Shown in Bold
```
Enter the sales for day 1:   1321.87 [Enter]
Enter the sales for day 2:   1869.26 [Enter]
Enter the sales for day 3:   1403.77 [Enter]

Sales Figures
-------------
Day 1:   1321.87
Day 2:   1869.26
Day 3:   1403.77
Total:   4594.90
```

The statement in line 25 uses the fixed manipulator:

```
cout << setprecision(2) << fixed;
```

When the fixed manipulator is used, all floating point numbers that are subsequently printed will be displayed in fixed point notation, with the number of digits to the right of the decimal point specified by the setprecision manipulator.

When the `fixed` and `setprecision` manipulators are used together, the value specified by the `setprecision` manipulator will be the number of digits to appear after the decimal point, not the number of significant digits. For example, look at the following code.

```
double x = 123.4567;
cout << setprecision(2) << fixed << x << endl;
```

Because the `fixed` manipulator is used, the `setprecision` manipulator will cause the number to be displayed with two digits after the decimal point. The value will be displayed as 123.46.

The `showpoint` Manipulator

By default, floating-point numbers are not displayed with trailing zeroes, and floating-point numbers that do not have a fractional part are not displayed with a decimal point. For example, look at the following code.

```
double x = 123.4, y = 456.0;
cout << setprecision(6) << x << endl;
cout << y << endl;
```

The cout statements will produce the following output.

```
123.4
456
```

Although six significant digits are specified for both numbers, neither number is displayed with trailing zeroes. If we want the numbers padded with trailing zeroes, we must use the `showpoint` manipulator as shown in the following code.

```
double x = 123.4, y = 456.0;
cout << setprecision(6) << showpoint << x << endl;
cout << y << endl;
```

These cout statements will produce the following output.

```
123.400
456.000
```

> **NOTE:** With most compilers, trailing zeroes are displayed when the `setprecision` and `fixed` manipulators are used together.

The `left` and `right` Manipulators

Normally output is right justified. For example, look at the following code.

```
double x = 146.789, y = 24.2, z = 1.783;
cout << setw(10) << x << endl;
cout << setw(10) << y << endl;
cout << setw(10) << z << endl;
```

Each of the variables, x, y, and z, is displayed in a print field of 10 spaces. The output of the cout statements is

```
146.789
     24.2
    1.783
```

Notice that each value is right-justified, or aligned to the right of its print field. You can cause the values to be left-justified by using the left manipulator, as shown in the following code.

```
double x = 146.789, y = 24.2, z = 1.783;
cout << left << setw(10) << x << endl;
cout << setw(10) << y << endl;
cout << setw(10) << z << endl;
```

The output of these cout statements is

```
146.789
24.2
1.783
```

In this case, the numbers are aligned to the left of their print fields. The left manipulator remains in effect until you use the right manipulator, which causes all subsequent output to be right-justified.

Table 3-12 summarizes the manipulators we have discussed.

Table 3-12

Stream Manipulator	Description
setw(*n*)	Establishes a print field of *n* spaces.
fixed	Displays floating-point numbers in fixed point notation.
showpoint	Causes a decimal point and trailing zeroes to be displayed, even if there is no fractional part.
setprecision(*n*)	Sets the precision of floating-point numbers.
left	Causes subsequent output to be left justified.
right	Causes subsequent output to be right justified.

 Checkpoint

3.24   Write cout statements with stream manipulators that perform the following:

A) Display the number 34.789 in a field of nine spaces with two decimal places of precision.

B) Display the number 7.0 in a field of five spaces with three decimal places of precision.

The decimal point and any trailing zeroes should be displayed.

C) Display the number 5.789e+12 in fixed point notation.

D) Display the number 67 left justified in a field of seven spaces.

3.25   The following program will not compile because the lines have been mixed up.

```
#include <iomanip>
}
cout << person << endl;
char person[15] = "Wolfgang Smith";
int main()
cout << person << endl;
{
#include <iostream>
return 0;
cout << left;
using namespace std;
cout << setw(20);
cout << right;
```

When the lines are properly arranged the program should display the following:

```
        Wolfgang Smith
Wolfgang Smith
```

Rearrange the lines in the correct order. Test the program by entering it on the computer, compiling it, and running it.

3.26   The following program skeleton asks for an angle in degrees and converts it to radians. The formatting of the final output is left to you.

```
#include <iostream>
#include <iomanip>
using namespace std;

int main()
{
    const double PI = 3.14159;
    double degrees, radians;

    cout << "Enter an angle in degrees and I will convert it\n";
    cout << "to radians for you: ";
    cin >> degrees;
    radians = degrees * PI / 180;
    // Display the value in radians left justified, in fixed
    // point notation, with 4 places of precision, in a field
    // 5 spaces wide, making sure the decimal point is always
    // displayed.
    return 0;
}
```

3.9 Formatted Input

CONCEPT: The `cin` object provides ways of controlling string and character input.

The `cin` object has formatting tools similar to those of `cout`. For instance, an input field width may be set with the `setw` manipulator. This is most helpful when `cin` is reading a string and storing it in a character array. You may recall that `cin` has no way of knowing how large the array is. If the user types more characters than the array will hold, `cin` will store the string in the array anyway, overwriting whatever is in memory next to the array. This type of error is known as a *buffer overrun*, and can lead to serious problems if not prevented. An input field width solves this problem by telling `cin` how many characters to read.

Here is a statement defining an array of 10 characters and a `cin` statement reading no more characters than the array will hold:

```cpp
char word[10];
cin >> setw(10) >> word;
```

The field width specified is 10. `cin` will read one character less than this, leaving room for the null character at the end. Program 3-22 illustrates the use of the `setw` manipulator with `cin`.

Program 3-22

```cpp
 1  // This program uses setw with the cin object.
 2  #include <iostream>
 3  #include <iomanip>
 4  using namespace std;
 5
 6  int main()
 7  {
 8     const int SIZE = 5;
 9     char word[SIZE];
10
11     cout << "Enter a word: ";
12     cin >> setw(SIZE) >> word;
13     cout << "You entered " << word << endl;
14     return 0;
15  }
```

Program Output with Example Input Shown in Bold
```
Enter a word: Eureka [Enter]
You entered Eure
```

In this program, `cin` only reads 4 characters into the `word` array. Without the field width, `cin` would have written the entire word "Eureka" into the array, overflowing it. Figure 3-5 illustrates the way memory would have been affected by this. The shaded area is the 5 bytes of memory used by the array. The word "Eureka" with its null terminator would spill over into the adjacent memory. Anything that was stored there would be destroyed.

Figure 3-5

There are two important points to remember about the way `cin` handles field widths:

- The field width only pertains to the very next item entered by the user.
- `cin` stops reading input when it encounters a *whitespace* character. Whitespace characters include the **[Enter]** key, space, and tab.

Reading a "Line" of Input

`cin` provides a member function to read a string containing spaces. The function is called `getline`, and its purpose is to read an entire "line" of text, until the **[Enter]** key is pressed. Here is an example of how it is used:

```
cin.getline(sentence, 20);
```

The `getline` function takes two arguments separated by a comma. The first argument is the name of the array that the string is to be stored in. In the statement above, the name of the array is `sentence`. The second argument is the size of the array. `cin` will read up to one character less than this number, leaving room for the null terminator. This eliminates the need for using the `setw` manipulator. The statement above will read up to 19 characters and the null terminator will automatically be placed in the array, after the last character. Program 3-23 shows the `getline` member function being used to read a sentence of up to 80 characters.

Program 3-23

```
 1   // This program demonstrates cin's getline member function.
 2   #include <iostream>
 3   using namespace std;
 4
 5   int main()
 6   {
 7      const int SIZE = 81;
 8      char sentence[SIZE];
 9
10      cout << "Enter a sentence: ";
11      cin.getline(sentence, SIZE);
12      cout << "You entered " << sentence << endl;
13      return 0;
14   }
```

Program Output with Example Input Shown in Bold
```
Enter a sentence: To be, or not to be, that is the question. [Enter]
You entered To be, or not to be, that is the question.
```

Reading a Character

Sometimes you want to read only a single character of input. For example, some programs display a menu of items for the user to choose from. Often the selections will be denoted by the letters A, B, C, and so forth. The user chooses an item from the menu by typing a character. The simplest way to read a single character is with the >> operator, as shown in the following code.

```
char ch;        // Define a character variable.
cout << "Type a character and press Enter: ";
cin >> ch;    // Read a character.
cout << "You entered " << ch << endl;
```

If the user types the character A and presses Enter, `cin` will store the character 'A' in the variable `ch`. Remember, `cin` is smart enough to know the data type of the variable it is storing data into. Since ch is a `char` variable, it will only store the single character 'A' there. If ch had been a `char` array, `cin` would have stored the string "A" with its null terminator there.

Using `cin.get`

A limiting characteristic of the >> operator with `char` variables is that it requires a character to be entered and it ignores all leading whitespace characters. This means the program will not continue past the `cin` statement until some character other than the spacebar, the tab key, or the **[Enter]** key has been pressed. (The **[Enter]** key must still be pressed after the character has been typed.) Programs that ask the user to "press the enter key to continue" cannot use the >> operator to read only the pressing of the **[Enter]** key.

In those situations another of `cin`'s member functions, `get`, becomes useful. The `get` function reads a single character including any whitespace character. Here is an example:

```
char ch;            // Define a character variable.
cout << "Type a character and press Enter: ";
cin.get(ch);    // Read a character.
cout << "You entered " << ch << endl;
```

If the user types the character A and presses Enter, the `cin.get` function will store the character 'A' in the variable `ch`. If the user simply presses the Enter key, the `cin.get` function will store the newline character ('\n') in the variable `ch`. Program 3-24 shows the function being used to pause a program.

Program 3-24

```
 1   // This program demonstrates cin.get.
 2   #include <iostream>
 3   using namespace std;
 4
 5   int main()
 6   {
 7      char ch;
 8
 9      cout << "This program has paused. Press Enter to continue.";
10      cin.get(ch);
11      cout << "Thank you!" << endl;
12      return 0;
13   }
```

Program Output

```
This program has paused. Press Enter to continue. [Enter]
Thank you!
```

The only difference between the get function and the >> operator is that get reads the first character typed, even if it is a space, tab, or the **[Enter]** key.

Mixing `cin >>` and `cin.get`

Mixing `cin.get` with `cin >>` can cause an annoying and hard-to-find problem. For example, look at the following statements:

```
char ch;            // Define a character variable.
int number;         // Define an integer variable.
cout << "Enter a number: ";
cin >> number;      // Read an integer.
cout << "Enter a character: ";
cin.get(ch);        // Read a character.
cout << "Thank You!\n";
```

These statements may allow the user to enter a number, but not a character. It will appear that the `cin.get` statement is skipped. This happens because both `cin >>` and `cin.get` read the user's keystrokes from the keyboard buffer. After the user enters a number, in response to the first prompt, he or she presses the Enter key. Pressing the Enter key causes a newline character ('\n') to be stored in the keyboard buffer. For example, suppose the user enters 100 and presses Enter. The input will be stored in the keyboard buffer as shown in Figure 3-6.

Figure 3-6

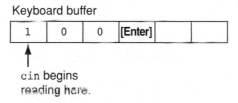

When the `cin >>` statement reads data from the keyboard buffer, it stops reading at the newline character that was generated by the Enter key. This newline character is left in the keyboard buffer. That means the first character read by `cin.get` will be the newline character. So, the `cin.get` statement will read only the newline character left in the keyboard buffer, and it will appear that the `cin.get` statement did not execute. You can remedy this situation by using the `cin.ignore` function, described in the following section.

Using `cin.ignore`

To solve the problem previously described, the `cin.ignore` member function can be used. `cin.ignore` tells the `cin` object to skip characters in the keyboard buffer. Here is its general form:

```
cin.ignore(n, c);
```

The arguments shown in the parentheses are optional. If they are used, *n* is an integer and *c* is a character. They tell `cin` to skip *n* number of characters, or until the character *c* is encountered. For example, the following statement causes `cin` to skip the next 20 characters, or until a newline is encountered, whichever comes first:

```
cin.ignore(20, '\n');
```

If no arguments are used, `cin` will only skip the very next character. Here's an example:

```
cin.ignore();
```

The previous statements that mix `cin >>` and `cin.get` can be repaired by inserting a `cin.ignore` statement after the `cin >>` statement:

```
char ch;              // Define a character variable.
int number;           // Define an integer variable.
cout << "Enter a number: ";
cin >> number;        // Read an integer.
cin.ignore();         // Skip the newline character.
cout << "Enter a character: ";
cin.get(ch);          // Read a character.
cout << "Thank You!" << endl;
```

3.10 Focus on Object-Oriented Programming: More About Member Functions

CONCEPT: A member function is a procedure, written in C++ code, that is part of an object. A member function causes the object it is a member of to perform an action.

The concept of object-oriented programming (OOP) was introduced in Chapter 1, Section 1.7 (*Procedural and Object-Oriented Programming*). Recall from that section that objects are programming elements containing both data and procedures that operate on the data. The packaging together of data and the data's related procedures within an object is known as *encapsulation*.

In C++, the procedures that are part of an object are known as *member functions*. They are called member functions because they are functions that are members of, or belong to, an object. The use of member functions simplifies programming and reduces errors. Anywhere an object is used, it contains not only data, but also the correct algorithms and operations for working with the data. If you are the user of an object (as you are the user of `cout` and `cin`) you do not need to write your own code to manipulate the object's data. All that is necessary is that you learn the object's member functions and how to use them.

In this chapter you have used the following member functions of the `cin` object:

- `getline`
- `get`
- `ignore`

Calling an object's member function causes the object to perform some operation. For example, calling `cin`'s `getline` member function causes `cin` to read a line of input from the keyboard.

In OOP terminology, calling a member function is also described as *passing a message* to the object. For example, you can think of the following statement as sending a message to the cin object, instructing it to read a character from the keyboard and then store the character in the ch variable.

```
cin.get(ch);
```

All of cin's member functions are written in C++ code. In Chapter 13 you will learn to design your own objects, complete with member functions.

3.11 More Mathematical Library Functions

CONCEPT: The C++ runtime library provides several functions for performing complex mathematical operations.

Earlier in this chapter you learned to use the pow function to raise a number to a power. The C++ library has numerous other functions that perform specialized mathematical operations. These functions are useful in scientific and special-purpose programs. Table 3-13 shows several of these, each of which requires the cmath header file.

Table 3-13

Function	Example	Description
abs	y = abs(x);	Returns the absolute value of the argument. The argument and the return value are integers.
cos	y = cos(x);	Returns the cosine of the argument. The argument should be an angle expressed in radians. The return type and the argument are doubles.
exp	y = exp(x);	Computes the exponential function of the argument, which is x. The return type and the argument are doubles.
fmod	y = fmod(x, z);	Returns, as a double, the remainder of the first argument divided by the second argument. Works like the modulus operator, but the arguments are doubles. (The modulus operator only works with integers.) Take care not to pass zero as the second argument. Doing so would cause division by zero.
log	y = log(x);	Returns the natural logarithm of the argument. The return type and the argument are doubles.
log10	y = log10(x);	Returns the base-10 logarithm of the argument. The return type and the argument are doubles.
sin	y = sin(x);	Returns the sine of the argument. The argument should be an angle expressed in radians. The return type and the argument are doubles.
sqrt	y = sqrt(x);	Returns the square root of the argument. The return type and argument are doubles.
tan	y = tan(x);	Returns the tangent of the argument. The argument should be an angle expressed in radians. The return type and the argument are doubles.

Each of these functions is as simple to use as the pow function. The following program segment demonstrates the sqrt function, which returns the square root of a number:

```
cout << "Enter a number: ";
cin >> num;
s = sqrt(num);
cout << "The square root of " << num << " is " << s << endl;
```

Here is the output of the program segment, with 25 as the number entered by the user:

```
Enter a number: 25
The square root of 25 is 5
```

Program 3-25 shows the sqrt function being used to find the hypotenuse of a right triangle. The program uses the following formula, taken from the Pythagorean theorem:

$$c = \sqrt{a^2 + b^2}$$

In the formula, c is the length of the hypotenuse, and a and b are the lengths of the other sides of the triangle.

Program 3-25

```
 1   // This program asks for the lengths of the two sides of a
 2   // right triangle. The length of the hypotenuse is then
 3   // calculated and displayed.
 4   #include <iostream>
 5   #include <iomanip>    // For setprecision
 6   #include <cmath>      // For the sqrt and pow functions
 7   using namespace std;
 8
 9   int main()
10   {
11      double a, b, c;
12
13      cout << "Enter the length of side a: ";
14      cin >> a;
15      cout << "Enter the length of side b: ";
16      cin >> b;
17      c = sqrt(pow(a, 2.0) + pow(b, 2.0));
18      cout << "The length of the hypotenuse is ";
19      cout << setprecision(2) << c << endl;
20      return 0;
21   }
```

Program Output with Example Input Shown in Bold
```
Enter the length of side a: 5.0 [Enter]
Enter the length of side b: 12.0 [Enter]
The length of the hypotenuse is 13
```

The following statement, taken from Program 3-25, calculates the square root of the sum of the squares of the triangle's two sides:

```
c = sqrt(pow(a, 2.0) + pow(b, 2.0));
```

Notice that the following mathematical expression is used as the sqrt function's argument:

```
pow(a, 2.0) + pow(b, 2.0)
```

This expression calls the pow function twice: once to calculate the square of a and again to calculate the square of b. These two squares are then added together, and the sum is sent to the sqrt function.

Random Numbers

Some programming techniques require the use of randomly generated numbers. The C++ library has a function, rand(), for this purpose. (rand() requires the header file cstdlib). The number returned by the function is an int. Here is an example of its usage:

```
y = rand();
```

After this statement executes, the variable y will contain a random number. In actuality, the numbers produced by rand() are pseudorandom. The function uses an algorithm that produces the same sequence of numbers each time the program is repeated on the same system. For example, suppose the following statements are executed.

```
cout << rand() << endl;
cout << rand() << endl;
cout << rand() << endl;
```

The three numbers displayed will appear to be random, but each time the program runs, the same three values will be generated. In order to randomize the results of rand(), the srand() function must be used. srand() accepts an unsigned int argument, which acts as a seed value for the algorithm. By specifying different seed values, rand() will generate different sequences of random numbers.

A common practice for getting unique seed values is to call the time function, which is part of the standard library. The time function returns the number of seconds that have elapsed since midnight, January 1, 1970. The time function requires the ctime header file, and you pass 0 as an argument to the function. Program 3-26 demonstrates. The program should generate three different random numbers each time it is executed.

Program 3-26

```
 1   // This program demonstrates random numbers.
 2   #include <iostream>
 3   #include <cstdlib>    // For rand and srand
 4   #include <ctime>      // For the time function
 5   using namespace std;
 6
 7   int main()
 8   {
 9       // Get the system time.
10       unsigned seed = time(0);
11
12       // Seed the random number generator.
13       srand(seed);
14
```

(program continues)

Program 3-26 *(continued)*

```
15      // Display three random numbers.
16      cout << rand() << endl;
17      cout << rand() << endl;
18      cout << rand() << endl;
19      return 0;
20  }
```

Program Output

```
23861
20884
21941
```

NOTE: If you wish to limit the range of the random number, use the following formula.

```
y = 1 + rand() % maxRange;
```

The `maxRange` value is the upper limit of the range. For example, if you wish to generate a random number in the range of 1 through 100, use the following statement.

```
y = 1 + rand() % 100;
```

This is how the statement works: Look at the following expression.

```
rand() % 100
```

Assuming `rand()` returns 37894, the value of the expression above is 94. That is because 37894 divided by 100 is 378 with a remainder of 94. (The modulus operator returns the remainder.) But, what if `rand()` returns a number that is evenly divisible by 100, such as 500? The expression above will return a 0. If we want a number in the range 1 – 100, we must add 1 to the result. That is why we use the expression `1 + rand() % 100`.

Checkpoint

3.27   Write a short description of each of the following functions:

```
cos     log     sin
exp     log10   sqrt
fmod    pow     tan
```

3.28   Assume the variables `angle1` and `angle2` hold angles stored in radians. Write a statement that adds the sine of `angle1` to the cosine of `angle2`, and stores the result in the variable `x`.

3.29   To find the cube root (the third root) of a number, raise it to the power of $1/3$. To find the fourth root of a number, raise it to the power of $1/4$. Write a statement that will find the fifth root of the variable `x` and store the result in the variable `y`.

3.30   The cosecant of the angle a is

$$\frac{1}{\sin a}$$

Write a statement that calculates the cosecant of the angle stored in the variable a, and stores it in the variable y.

3.12 Focus on Debugging: Hand Tracing a Program

Hand tracing is a debugging process where you pretend that you are the computer executing a program. You step through each of the program's statements one by one. As you look at a statement, you record the contents that each variable will have after the statement executes. This process is often helpful in finding mathematical mistakes and other logic errors.

To hand trace a program you construct a chart with a column for each variable. The rows in the chart correspond to the lines in the program. For example, Program 3-27 is shown with a hand trace chart. The program uses the following four variables: num1, num2, num3, and avg. Notice that the hand trace chart has a column for each variable and a row for each line of code in function main.

Program 3-27

```
1  // This program asks for three numbers, then
2  // displays the average of the numbers.
3  #include <iostream>
4  using namespace std;

5  int main()

6  {

7      double num1, num2, num3, avg;

8      cout << "Enter the first number: ";

9      cin >> num1;

10     cout << "Enter the second number: ";

11     cin >> num2;

12     cout << "Enter the third number: ";

13     cin >> num3;

14     avg = num1 + num2 + num3 / 3;

15     cout << "The average is " << avg << endl;

16     return 0;

17 }
```

num1	num2	num3	avg

This program, which asks the user to enter three numbers and then displays the average of the numbers, has a bug. It does not display the correct average. The output of a sample session with the program follows.

Program Output with Example Input Shown in Bold
```
Enter the first number: 10 [Enter]
Enter the second number: 20 [Enter]
Enter the third number: 30 [Enter]
The average is 40
```

The correct average of 10, 20, and 30 is 20, not 40. To find the error we will hand trace the program. To hand trace this program, you step through each statement, observing the operation that is taking place, and then record the contents of the variables after the statement executes. After the hand trace is complete, the chart will appear as follows. We have written question marks in the chart where we do not know the contents of a variable.

Program 3-27   (with hand trace chart filled)

Line	Code	num1	num2	num3	avg
1	`// This program asks for three numbers, then`				
2	`// displays the average of the numbers.`				
3	`#include <iostream>`				
4	`using namespace std;`				
5	`int main()`				
6	`{`				
7	`    double num1, num2, num3, avg;`	?	?	?	?
8	`    cout << "Enter the first number: ";`	?	?	?	?
9	`    cin >> num1;`	10	?	?	?
10	`    cout << "Enter the second number: ";`	10	?	?	?
11	`    cin >> num2;`	10	20	?	?
12	`    cout << "Enter the third number: ";`	10	20	?	?
13	`    cin >> num3;`	10	20	30	?
14	`    avg = num1 + num2 + num3 / 3;`	10	20	30	40
15	`    cout << "The average is " << avg << endl;`	10	20	30	40
16	`    return 0;`				
17	`}`				

Do you see the error? By examining the statement that performs the math operation in line 14, we find a mistake. The division operation takes place before the addition operations, so we must rewrite that statement as

```
avg = (num1 + num2 + num3) / 3;
```

Hand tracing is a simple process that focuses your attention on each statement in a program. Often this helps you locate errors that are not obvious.

3.13 Focus on Problem Solving: A Case Study

General Crates, Inc. builds custom-designed wooden crates. With materials and labor, it costs GCI $0.23 per cubic foot to build a crate. In turn, they charge their customers $0.50 per cubic foot for the crate. You have been asked to write a program that calculates the volume (in cubic feet), cost, customer price, and profit of any crate GCI builds.

Variables

Table 3-14 shows the variables needed.

Table 3-14

Variable	Description
length	A double variable to hold the length of the crate, which is input by the user.
width	A double variable to hold the width of the crate, which is input by the user.
height	A double variable to hold the height of the crate, which is input by the user.
volume	A double variable to hold the volume of the crate. The value stored in this variable is calculated.
cost	A double variable to hold the cost of building the crate. The value stored in this variable is calculated.
charge	A double variable to hold the amount charged to the customer for the crate. The value stored in this variable is calculated.
profit	A double variable to hold the profit GCI makes from the crate. The value stored in this variable is calculated.

Program Design

The program must perform the following general steps:

1. Ask the user to enter the dimensions of the crate (the crate's length, width, and height).

2. Calculate the crate's volume, the cost of building the crate, the customer's charge, and the profit made.

3. Display the data calculated in Step 2.

A general hierarchy chart for this program is shown in Figure 3-7.

Figure 3-7

The "Get Crate Dimensions" step is shown in greater detail in Figure 3-8.

Figure 3-8

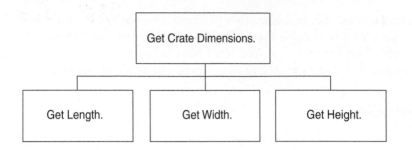

The "Calculate Volume, Cost, Customer Charge, and Profit" step is shown in greater detail in Figure 3-9.

Figure 3-9

The "Display Calculated Data" step is shown in greater detail in Figure 3-10.

Figure 3-10

Pseudocode for the program is as follows:

```
Ask the user to input the crate's length.
Ask the user to input the crate's width.
Ask the user to input the crate's height.
Calculate the crate's volume.
Calculate the cost of building the crate.
Calculate the customer's charge for the crate.
Calculate the profit made from the crate.
Display the crate's volume.
```

Display the cost of building the crate.
Display the customer's charge for the crate.
Display the profit made from the crate.

Calculations

The following formulas will be used to calculate the crate's volume, cost, charge, and profit:

volume = length * width * height
cost = volume * 0.23
charge = volume * 0.5
profit = charge − cost

The Program

The last step is to expand the pseudocode into the final program, which is shown in Program 3-28.

Program 3-28

```cpp
1   // This program is used by General Crates, Inc. to calculate
2   // the volume, cost, customer charge, and profit of a crate
3   // of any size. It calculates this data from user input, which
4   // consists of the dimensions of the crate.
5   #include <iostream>
6   #include <iomanip>
7   using namespace std;
8
9   int main()
10  {
11      double length,    // The crate's length
12             width,     // The crate's width
13             height,    // The crate's height
14             volume,    // The volume of the crate
15             cost,      // The cost to build the crate
16             charge,    // The customer charge for the crate
17             profit;    // The profit made on the crate
18
19      // Set the desired output formatting for numbers.
20      cout << setprecision(2) << fixed << showpoint;
21
22      // Prompt the user for the crate's length, width, and height
23      cout << "Enter the dimensions of the crate (in feet):\n";
24      cout << "Length: ";
25      cin >> length;
26      cout << "Width: ";
27      cin >> width;
28      cout << "Height: ";
29      cin >> height;
30
```

(program continues)

Program 3-28 *(continued)*

```
31      // Calculate the crate's volume, the cost to produce it,
32      // the charge to the customer, and the profit.
33      volume = length * width * height;
34      cost = volume * 0.23;
35      charge = volume * 0.5;
36      profit = charge - cost;
37
38      // Display the calculated data.
39      cout << "The volume of the crate is ";
40      cout << volume << " cubic feet.\n";
41      cout << "Cost to build: $" << cost << endl;
42      cout << "Charge to customer: $" << charge << endl;
43      cout << "Profit: $" << profit << endl;
44      return 0;
45  }
```

Program Output with Example Input Shown in Bold
```
Enter the dimensions of the crate (in feet):
Length: 10 [Enter]
Width: 8 [Enter]
Height: 4 [Enter]
The volume of the crate is 320.00 cubic feet.
Cost to build: $73.60
Charge to customer: $160.00
Profit: $86.40
```

Program Output with Different Example Input Shown in Bold
```
Enter the dimensions of the crate (in feet):
Length: 12.5 [Enter]
Width: 10.5 [Enter]
Height: 8 [Enter]
The volume of the crate is 1050.00 cubic feet.
Cost to build: $241.50
Charge to customer: $525.00
Profit: $283.50
```

3.14 Introduction to File Input and Output

CONCEPT: This section discusses simple techniques to write input and output operations with files.

The programs you have written so far require you to re-enter data each time the program runs. This is because the data stored in RAM disappears once the program stops running or the computer is shut down. If a program is to retain data between the times it runs, it must have a way of saving it. Data is saved in a file, which is usually stored on a computer's disk. Once the data is saved in a file, it will remain there after the program stops running. The data can then be retrieved and used at a later time.

There are always three steps that must be taken when a file is used by a program:

1. The file must be *opened*. If the file does not yet exist, opening it means creating it.

2. Data is then saved to the file, read from the file, or both.

3. When the program is finished using the file, the file must be *closed*.

When a program is actively working with data, the data is located in random-access memory, usually in variables. When data is written into a file, it is copied from the variables. This is illustrated in Figure 3-11.

Figure 3-11

Writing data to a file

Data is copied from variables
into the file.

When data is read from a file, it is copied from the file into variables. Figure 3-12 illustrates this.

Figure 3-12

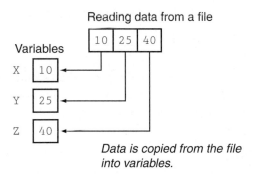

Reading data from a file

Data is copied from the file
into variables.

Setting Up a Program for File Input/Output

Just as cin and cout require the iostream file to be included in the program, C++ file access requires another header file. The file fstream contains all the declarations necessary for file operations. It is included with the following statement:

```
#include <fstream>
```

The next step in setting up a program to perform file I/O is to define one or more *file stream objects*. They are called "stream" objects because a file can be thought of as a stream of data. File stream objects work very much like the cin and cout objects. A stream of data may be sent to cout, which causes values to be displayed on the screen.

A stream of data may be read from the keyboard by cin, and stored in variables. Likewise, streams of data may be sent to a file stream object, which writes the data to a file. Data that is read from a file flows from a file stream object into other variables.

The fstream header file defines the data types ofstream, ifstream, and fstream. Before a C++ program can work with a file, it must define an object of one of these data types. The object will be "linked" with an actual file on the computer's disk, and the operations that may be performed on the file depend on which of these three data types you pick for the file stream object. Table 3-15 lists and describes the file stream data types.

Table 3-15

File Stream Data Type	Description
ofstream	Output file stream. This data type can be used to create files and write data to them. With the ofstream data type, data may only be copied from variables to the file, but not vice versa.
ifstream	Input file stream. This data type can be used to open existing files and read data from them into memory. With the ifstream data type, data may only be copied from the file into variables, not but vice versa.
fstream	File stream. This data type can be used to create files, write data to them, and read data from them. With the fstream data type, data may be copied from variables into a file, or from a file into variables.

NOTE: In this section we only discuss the ofstream and ifstream types. The fstream type is covered in Chapter 12.

Here are example statements that define ofstream and ifstream objects:

```
ofstream outputFile;
ifstream inputFile
```

The statements above define the objects outputFile and inputFile. outputFile is of the ofstream type, so data can be written to any file associated with it. inputFile is of the ifstream type, so data can be read from any file it is associated with.

Opening a File

Before data can be written to or read from a file, the file must be opened. Outside of the C++ program, a file is identified by its name. Inside a C++ program, however, a file stream object identifies a file. The object and the file name are linked when the file is opened.

Files are opened through the open member function of a file stream object. Assume inputFile is an ifstream object, defined as:

```
ifstream inputFile;
```

For example, the following statement uses inputFile to open a file named customer.dat:

```
inputFile.open("customer.dat");
```

The argument to the `open` function in this statement is the name of the file. This links the file `customer.dat` with the stream object `inputFile`. Until `inputFile` is associated with another file, any operations performed with it will be carried out on the file `customer.dat`. (Remember, `ifstream` objects can only perform input operations with files. This means data may only be read from the `customer.dat` file using the `inputFile` stream object.)

Often, when opening a file, you will need to specify its location as well as its name. For example, on a Windows system the following statement opens the file `C:\data\inventory.dat`:

```
outputFile.open("C:\\data\\inventory.dat")
```

In this statement, the file `C:\data\inventory.dat` is opened and linked with `outputFile`.

> **NOTE:** Notice the use of two backslashes in the file's path. As mentioned before in this text, two backslashes are needed to represent one backslash in a string literal.

You may also use a character array as an argument to the open function. For example, the following program segment defines an `ifstream` object and a 20-element character array. The user is asked to enter the name of the file, which is passed to the `open` function.

```
ifstream inputFile;
char fileName[20];
cout << "Enter the name of the file: ";
cin >> filename;
inputFile.open(fileName);
```

The previous examples have shown you how to define a file stream object and then use the open member function to open a file. It is possible to define a file stream object and open a file in one statement. Here is an example:

```
ifstream inputFile("customer.dat");
```

This statement defines an `ifstream` object named `inputFile` and opens the `customer.dat` file.

Closing a File

The opposite of opening a file is closing it. Although a program's files are automatically closed when the program shuts down, it is a good programming practice to write statements that close them. Here are two reasons a program should close files when it is finished using them:

- Most operating systems temporarily store data in a *file buffer* before it is written to a file. A file buffer is a small "holding section" of memory that file-bound data is first written to. When the buffer is filled, all the data stored there is written to the file. This technique improves the system's performance. Closing a file causes any unsaved data that may still be held in a buffer to be saved to its file. This means the data will be in the file if you need to read it later in the same program.

- Some operating systems limit the number of files that may be open at one time. When a program closes files that are no longer being used, it will not deplete more of the operating system's resources than necessary.

Calling the file stream object's `close` member function closes a file. Here is an example:

```
outputFile.close();
```

Writing Data to a File

You already know how to use the stream insertion operator (`<<`) with the `cout` object to write data to the screen. It can also be used with file stream objects to write data to a file. Assuming `outputFile` is a file stream object, the following statement demonstrates using the `<<` operator to write a string to a file:

```
outputFile << "I love C++ programming";
```

VideoNote

Writing Data
to a File

This statement writes the string "I love C++ programming" to the file associated with `outputFile`. As you can see, the statement looks like a `cout` statement, except the file stream object name replaces `cout`. Here is a statement that writes both a string and the contents of a variable to a file:

```
outputFile << "Price: " << price;
```

The statement above writes the stream of data to `outputFile` exactly as `cout` would write it to the screen.

Program 3-29 demonstrates opening a file, writing data to the file, and closing the file.

Program 3-29

```
 1   // This program writes data to a file.
 2   #include <iostream>
 3   #include <fstream>
 4   using namespace std;
 5
 6   int main()
 7   {
 8      ofstream outputFile;
 9      outputFile.open("demofile.txt");
10
11      cout << "Now writing data to the file.\n";
12
13      // Write 4 great names to the file
14      outputFile << "Bach\n";
15      outputFile << "Beethoven\n";
16      outputFile << "Mozart\n";
17      outputFile << "Schubert\n";
18
19      // Close the file
20      outputFile.close();
21      cout << "Done.\n";
22      return 0;
23   }
```

Program Screen Output
```
Now writing data to the file.
Done.
```

Output to File demofile.txt
```
Bach
Beethoven
Mozart
Schubert
```

Reading Data from a File

The >> operator not only reads user input from the cin object, but it can also read data from a file. Assuming inFile is a file stream object, the following statement shows the >> operator reading data from the file into the variable name:

```
inFile >> name;
```

VideoNote

Reading Data from a File

In Program 3-29, the file demofile.txt was created and the following list of names was stored there.

```
Bach
Beethoven
Mozart
Schubert
```

Program 3-30 demonstrates the use of the >> operator to read the names from the file and store them in a variable.

Program 3-30

```
 1   // This program reads data from a file.
 2   #include <iostream>
 3   #include <fstream>
 4   using namespace std;
 5
 6   int main()
 7   {
 8       ifstream inFile;
 9       const int SIZE = 81;
10       char name[SIZE];
11
12       inFile.open("demofile.txt");
13       cout << "Reading data from the file.\n\n";
14
15       inFile >> name;         // Read name 1 from the file
16       cout << name << endl;   // Display name 1
17
```

(program continues)

Program 3-30 *(continued)*

```
18      inFile >> name;          // Read name 2 from the file
19      cout << name << endl;    // Display name 2
20
21      inFile >> name;          // Read name 3 from the file
22      cout << name << endl;    // Display name 3
23
24      inFile >> name;          // Read name 4 from the file
25      cout << name << endl;    // Display name 4
26
27      inFile.close();          // Close the file
28      cout << "\nDone.\n";
29      return 0;
30  }
```

Program Screen Output

```
Reading data from the file.

Bach
Beethoven
Mozart
Schubert

Done.
```

Data is read from files in a sequential manner. When a file is first opened, the file stream object's *read position* is at the first byte of the file. The first read operation extracts data starting at the first byte. As data is read, the file stream object's read position advances through the file.

When the >> operator extracts data from a file, it expects to read pieces of data that are separated by whitespace characters (spaces, tabs, or newlines). In Program 3-30, the following statement reads a string from the file:

```
inFile >> name;
```

In the statement above, the >> operator extracts a string because name is a character array. Figure 3-13 shows the first 5 bytes in the file:

Figure 3-13

| B | a | c | h | \n | ... |

The >> operator will extract all of the characters up to the newline, so "Bach" is the first string read from the file. After "Bach" is extracted, the file stream object will be positioned so the following read operation would extract the string "Beethoven." This procedure is followed until all four strings have been read from the file.

Sometimes, when a program has a substantial amount of input, it is preferable to read the input from a file instead of the keyboard. For example, consider Program 3-31. It reads the length and width of five rectangles from a file and displays the area of each rectangle on the screen.

Program 3-31

```cpp
1   // This program reads rectangle dimensions from a file.
2   #include <iostream>
3   #include <fstream>
4   using namespace std;
5
6   int main()
7   {
8       ifstream inFile;
9       int length, width, area;
10
11      inFile.open("dimensions.txt");
12      cout << "Reading dimensions of 5 rectangles from the file.\n\n";
13
14      // Process rectangle 1
15      inFile >> length;
16      inFile >> width;
17      area = length * width;
18      cout << "Area of rectangle 1: " << area << endl;
19
20      // Process rectangle 2
21      inFile >> length;
22      inFile >> width;
23      area = length * width;
24      cout << "Area of rectangle 2: " << area << endl;
25
26      // Process rectangle 3
27      inFile >> length;
28      inFile >> width;
29      area = length * width;
30      cout << "Area of rectangle 3: " << area << endl;
31
32      // Process rectangle 4
33      inFile >> length;
34      inFile >> width;
35      area = length * width;
36      cout << "Area of rectangle 4: " << area << endl;
37
38      // Process rectangle 5
39      inFile >> length;
40      inFile >> width;
41      area = length * width;
42      cout << "Area of rectangle 5: " << area << endl;
43
44      // Close the file
45      inFile.close();
46      cout << "\nDone.\n";
47      return 0;
48  }
```

Before this program is executed, the file `dimensions.txt` must be created with a text editor (such as Windows Notepad). Here is an example of the file's contents:

```
10 2
5 7
18 9
6 20
8 3
```

Notice that the program first reads a value into `length`, and then reads a value into `width`. It then multiplies `length` by `width` to get the rectangle's area. So, these file contents specify the following dimensions:

```
Rectangle 1: length = 10, width = 2
Rectangle 2: length = 5, width = 7
Rectangle 3: length = 18, width = 9
Rectangle 4: length = 6, width = 20
Rectangle 5: length = 8, width = 3
```

The program's output follows.

Program 3-31

Program Output
```
Reading dimensions of 5 rectangles from the file.

Area of rectangle 1: 20
Area of rectangle 2: 35
Area of rectangle 3: 162
Area of rectangle 4: 120
Area of rectangle 5: 24

Done.
```

Review Questions and Exercises

Short Answer

1. Assuming the array `description` is defined as follows:

   `char description[40];`

   A) How many characters *total* can the array hold?

   B) What is the length of the largest string that may be stored in the array?

   C) Will the following `cin` statement automatically stop reading input when the array is filled?

   `cin >> description;`

2. Write a definition statement for a character array large enough to hold any of the following strings:

   ```
   "Billy Bob's Pizza"
   "Downtown Auto Supplies"
   "Betty Smith School of Architecture"
   "ABC Cabinet Company"
   ```

3. Assume the array `name` is defined as follows:

    ```
    char name[25];
    ```

    A) Using a stream manipulator, write a `cin` statement that will read a string into `name`, but will read no more characters than `name` can hold.

    B) Using the `getline` member function, write a `cin` statement that will read a string into `name`, but will read no more characters than `name` can hold.

4. Assume that the following variables are defined:

    ```
    int age;
    double pay;
    char section;
    ```

    Write a single `cin` statement that will read input into each of these variables.

5. What header files must be included in the following program?

    ```
    int main()
    {
        double amount = 89.7;
        cout << showpoint << fixed;
        cout << setw(8) << amount << endl;
        return 0;
    }
    ```

6. Write a definition statement for a character array named `city`. It should be large enough to hold a string 30 characters in length.

7. Assume the following preprocessor directive appears in a program:

    ```
    #define SIZE 12
    ```

    How will the preprocessor rewrite the following lines?

    A) `price = SIZE * unitCost;`

    B) `cout << setw(SIZE) << 98.7;`

    C) `cout << SIZE;`

8. Complete the following table by writing the value of each expression in the Value column.

Expression	Value
`28 / 4 - 2`	
`6 + 12 * 2 - 8`	
`4 + 8 * 2`	
`6 + 17 % 3 - 2`	
`2 + 22 * (9 - 7)`	
`(8 + 7) * 2`	
`(16 + 7) % 2 - 1`	
`12 / (10 - 6)`	
`(19 - 3) * (2 + 2) / 4`	

9. Write C++ expressions for the following algebraic expressions:

$$a = 12x$$

$$z = 5x + 14y + 6k$$

$$y = x^4$$

$$g = \frac{b + 12}{4k}$$

$$c = \frac{a^3}{b^2 k^4}$$

10. Assume a program has the following variable definitions:

```
int units;
float mass;
double weight;
```

and the following statement:

```
weight = mass * units;
```

Which automatic data type conversion will take place?

A) `mass` is demoted to an `int`, `units` remains an `int`, and the result of `mass * units` is an `int`.

B) `units` is promoted to a `float`, `mass` remains a `float`, and the result of `mass * units` is a `float`.

C) `units` is promoted to a `float`, `mass` remains a `float`, and the result of `mass * units` is a `double`.

11. Assume a program has the following variable definitions:

```
int a, b = 2;
float c = 4.2;
```

and the following statement:

```
a = b * c;
```

What value will be stored in a?

A) 8.4

B) 8

C) 0

D) None of the above

12. Assume that `qty` and `salesReps` are both integers. Use a type cast expression to rewrite the following statement so it will no longer perform integer division.

```
unitsEach = qty / salesReps;
```

13. Rewrite the following variable definition so the variable is a named constant.

    ```
    int rate;
    ```

14. Complete the following table by writing statements with combined assignment operators in the right-hand column. The statements should be equivalent to the statements in the left-hand column.

Statements with Assignment Operator	Statements with Combined Assignment Operator
`x = x + 5;`	
`total = total + subtotal;`	
`dist = dist / rep;`	
`ppl = ppl * period;`	
`inv = inv - shrinkage;`	
`num = num % 2;`	

15. Write a multiple assignment statement that can be used instead of the following group of assignment statements:

    ```
    east = 1;
    west = 1;
    north = 1;
    south = 1;
    ```

16. Write a cout statement so the variable `divSales` is displayed in a field of 8 spaces, in fixed point notation, with a precision of 2 decimal places. The decimal point should always be displayed.

17. Write a cout statement so the variable `totalAge` is displayed in a field of 12 spaces, in fixed point notation, with a precision of 4 decimal places.

18. Write a cout statement so the variable `population` is displayed in a field of 12 spaces, left-justified, with a precision of 8 decimal places. The decimal point should always be displayed.

Fill-in-the-Blank

19. The _____ library function returns the cosine of an angle.

20. The _____ library function returns the sine of an angle.

21. The _____ library function returns the tangent of an angle.

22. The _____ library function returns the exponential function of a number.

23. The _____ library function returns the remainder of a floating point division.

24. The _____ library function returns the natural logarithm of a number.

25. The _____ library function returns the base-10 logarithm of a number.

26. The _____ library function returns the value of a number raised to a power.

27. The _____ library function returns the square root of a number.

28. The _____ file must be included in a program that uses the mathematical functions.

Algorithm Workbench

29. A retail store grants its customers a maximum amount of credit. Each customer's available credit is his or her maximum amount of credit minus the amount of credit used. Write a pseudocode algorithm for a program that asks for a customer's maximum amount of credit and amount of credit used. The program should then display the customer's available credit.

    After you write the pseudocode algorithm, convert it to a complete C++ program.

30. Write a pseudocode algorithm for a program that calculates the total of a retail sale. The program should ask for the amount of the sale and the sales tax rate. The sales tax rate should be entered as a floating-point number. For example, if the sales tax rate is 6 percent, the user should enter 0.06. The program should display the amount of sales tax and the total of the sale.

    After you write the pseudocode algorithm, convert it to a complete C++ program.

Find the Errors

Each of the following programs has some errors. Locate as many as you can.

31.
```cpp
using namespace std;
int main ()
{
    double number1, number2, sum;

    Cout << "Enter a number: ";
    Cin << number1;
    Cout << "Enter another number: ";
    Cin << number2;
    number1 + number2 = sum;
    Cout "The sum of the two numbers is " << sum
    return 0;
}
```

32.
```cpp
#include <iostream>
using namespace std;

int main()
{
    int number1, number2;
    float quotient;
    cout << "Enter two numbers and I will divide\n";
    cout << "the first by the second for you.\n";
    cin >> number1, number2;
    quotient = float<static_cast>(number1) / number2;
    cout << quotient
    return 0;
}
```

33.
```cpp
#include <iostream>;
using namespace std;

int main()
{
    const int number1, number2, product;
```

```
        cout << "Enter two numbers and I will multiply\n";
        cout << "them for you.\n";
        cin >> number1 >> number2;
        product = number1 * number2;
        cout << product
        return 0;
    }
```

34.
```
    #include <iostream>;
    using namespace std;

    main
    {
        int number1, number2;

        cout << "Enter two numbers and I will multiply\n"
        cout << "them by 50 for you.\n"
        cin >> number1 >> number2;
        number1 =* 50;
        number2 =* 50;
        cout << number1 << " " << number2;
        return 0;
    }
```

35.
```
    #include <iostream>;
    using namespace std;

    main
    {
        double number, half;

        cout << "Enter a number and I will divide it\n"
        cout << "in half for you.\n"
        cin >> number1;
        half =/ 2;
        cout << fixedpoint << showpoint << half << endl;
        return 0;
    }
```

36.
```
    #include <iostream>;
    using namespace std;

    int main()
    {
        char name, go;

        cout << "Enter your name: ";
        cin >> setw(20);
        cin.getline >> name;
        cout << "Hi " << name << endl;
        cout "Press the ENTER key to end this program.";
        cin >> go;
        return 0;
    }
```

Predict the Output

What will each of the following programs display? (Some should be hand traced, and require a calculator.)

37. *(Assume the user enters 38700. Use a calculator.)*
```cpp
#include <iostream>
using namespace std;

int main()
{
   double salary, monthly;
   cout << "What is your annual salary? ";
   cin >> salary;
   monthly = static_cast<int>(salary) / 12;
   cout << "Your monthly wages are " << monthly << endl;
   return 0;
}
```

38.
```cpp
#include <iostream>
using namespace std;
int main()
{
   long x, y, z;

   x = y = z = 4;
   x += 2;
   y -= 1;
   z *= 3;
   cout << x << " " << y << " " << z << endl;
   return 0;
}
```

39.
```cpp
#include <iostream>
using namespace std;

#define WHO "Columbus"
#define DID "sailed"
#define WHAT "the ocean blue."
int main()
{
   const int WHEN = 1492;
   cout << "In " << WHEN << " " << WHO << " "
        << DID << " " << WHAT << endl;
   return 0;
}
```

40. *(Assume the user enters George Washington.)*
```cpp
#include <iostream>
#include <iomanip>
using namespace std;

int main()
{
```

```
      const in SIZE = 20;
      char userInput[SIZE];
      cout << "What is your name? ";
      cin >> setw(SIZE) >> userInput;
      cout << "Hello " << userInput << endl;
      return 0;
   }
```

41. (*Assume the user enters George Washington.*)

```
   #include <iostream>
   #include <iomanip>
   using namespace std;

   int main()
   {
      const in SIZE = 20;
      char userInput[SIZE];

      cout << "What is your name? ";
      cin.getline(userInput, SIZE);
      cout << "Hello " << userInput << endl;
      return 0;
   }
```

42. (*Assume the user enters 36720152. Use a calculator.*)

```
   #include <iostream>
   #include <iomanip>
   using namespace std;

   int main()
   {
      long seconds;
      double minutes, hours, days, months, years;

      cout << "Enter the number of seconds that have\n";
      cout << "elapsed since some time in the past and\n";
      cout << "I will tell you how many minutes, hours,\n";
      cout << "days, months, and years have passed: ";
      cin >> seconds;
      minutes = seconds / 60;
      hours = minutes / 60;
      days = hours / 24;
      years = days / 365;
      months = years * 12;
      cout << setprecision(4) << fixed << showpoint << right;
      cout << "Minutes: " << setw(6) << minutes << endl;
      cout << "Hours: " << setw(6) << hours << endl;
      cout << "Days: " << setw(6) << days << endl;
      cout << "Months: " << setw(6) << months << endl;
      cout << "Years: " << setw(6) << years << endl;
      return 0;
   }
```

Programming Challenges

1. Miles per Gallon

Write a program that calculates a car's gas mileage. The program should ask the user to enter the number of gallons of gas the car can hold, and the number of miles it can be driven on a full tank. It should then display the number of miles that may be driven per gallon of gas.

2. Stadium Seating

VideoNote

Solving the Stadium Seating Problem

There are three seating categories at a stadium. For a softball game, Class A seats cost $15, Class B seats cost $12, and Class C seats cost $9. Write a program that asks how many tickets for each class of seats were sold, then displays the amount of income generated from ticket sales. Format your dollar amount in fixed-point notation, with two decimal places of precision, and be sure the decimal point is always displayed.

3. Test Average

Write a program that asks for five test scores. The program should calculate the average test score and display it. The number displayed should be formatted in fixed-point notation, with one decimal point of precision.

4. Average Rainfall

Write a program that calculates the average rainfall for three months. The program should ask the user to enter the name of each month, such as June or July, and the amount of rain (in inches) that fell each month. The program should display a message similar to the following:

The average rainfall for June, July, and August is 6.72 inches.

5. Box Office

A movie theater only keeps a percentage of the revenue earned from ticket sales. The remainder goes to the movie distributor. Write a program that calculates a theater's gross and net box office profit for a night. The program should ask for the name of the movie, and how many adult and child tickets were sold. (The price of an adult ticket is $6.00 and a child's ticket is $3.00.) It should display a report similar to

Movie Name:	"Wheels of Fury"
Adult Tickets Sold:	382
Child Tickets Sold:	127
Gross Box Office Profit:	$ 2673.00
Net Box Office Profit:	$ 534.60
Amount Paid to Distributor:	$ 2138.40

 NOTE: Assume the theater keeps 20 percent of the gross box office profit.

6. How Many Widgets?

The Yukon Widget Company manufactures widgets that weigh 9.2 pounds each. Write a program that calculates how many widgets are stacked on a pallet, based on the total weight of the pallet. The program should ask the user how much the pallet weighs by itself and with the widgets stacked on it. It should then calculate and display the number of widgets stacked on the pallet.

7. **How Many Calories?**

A bag of cookies holds 40 cookies. The calorie information on the bag claims that there are 10 "servings" in the bag and that a serving equals 300 calories. Write a program that asks the user to input how many cookies he or she actually ate and then reports how many total calories were consumed.

8. **How Much Insurance?**

Many financial experts advise that property owners should insure their homes or buildings for at least 80 percent of the amount it would cost to replace the structure. Write a program that asks the user to enter the replacement cost of a building and then displays the minimum amount of insurance he or she should buy for the property.

9. **Automobile Costs**

Write a program that asks the user to enter the monthly costs for the following expenses incurred from operating his or her automobile: loan payment, insurance, gas, oil, tires, and maintenance. The program should then display the total monthly cost of these expenses, and the total annual cost of these expenses.

10. **Celsius to Fahrenheit**

Write a program that converts Celsius temperatures to Fahrenheit temperatures. The formula is

$$F = \frac{9}{5}C + 32$$

F is the Fahrenheit temperature and C is the Celsius temperature.

11. **Currency**

Write a program that will convert U.S. dollar amounts to Japanese Yen and to Euros. To get the most up-to-date exchange rates, search the Internet using the term "currency exchange rate". If you cannot find the most recent exchange rates, use the following:

    1 Dollar = 113.22 Yen
    1 Dollar = 0.6936 Euros

Format your currency amounts in fixed-point notation, with two decimal places of precision, and be sure the decimal point is always displayed.

12. **Monthly Sales Tax**

A retail company must file a monthly sales tax report listing the sales for the month and the amount of sales tax collected. Write a program that asks for the month, the year, and the total amount collected at the cash register (that is, sales plus sales tax). Assume the state sales tax is 4 percent and the county sales tax is 2 percent.

If the total amount collected is known and the total sales tax is 6 percent, the amount of product sales may be calculated as:

$$S = \frac{T}{1.06}$$

S is the product sales and *T* is the total income (product sales plus sales tax).

The program should display a report similar to

```
Month: October
--------------------
Total Collected:     $ 26572.89
Sales:               $ 25068.76
County Sales Tax:    $   501.38
State Sales Tax:     $  1002.75
Total Sales Tax:     $  1504.13
```

13. Property Tax

A county collects property taxes on the assessment value of property, which is 60 percent of the property's actual value. If an acre of land is valued at $10,000, its assessment value is $6,000. The property tax is then 64¢ for each $100 of the assessment value. The tax for the acre assessed at $6,000 will be $38.40. Write a program that asks for the actual value of a piece of property and displays the assessment value and property tax.

14. Senior Citizen Property Tax

Madison County provides a $5,000 homeowner exemption for its senior citizens. For example, if a senior's house is valued at $158,000 its assessed value would be $94,800, as explained above. However, he would only pay tax on $89,800. At last year's tax rate of $2.64 for each $100 of assessed value, the property tax would be $2,370.72. In addition to the tax break, senior citizens are allowed to pay their property tax in four equal payments. The quarterly payment due on this property would be $592.68. Write a program that asks the user to input the actual value of a piece of property and the current tax rate for each $100 of assessed value. The program should then calculate and report how much annual property tax a senior homeowner will be charged for this property and what the quarterly tax bill will be.

15. Math Tutor

Write a program that can be used as a math tutor for a young student. The program should display two random numbers to be added, such as

```
   247
 + 129
```

The program should then pause while the student works on the problem. When the student is ready to check the answer, he or she can press a key and the program will display the correct solution:

```
   247
 + 129
   376
```

16. Interest Earned

Assuming there are no deposits other than the original investment, the balance in a savings account after one year may be calculated as

$$\text{Amount} = \text{Principal} * \left(1 + \frac{\text{Rate}}{\text{T}}\right)^{\text{T}}$$

`Principal` is the balance in the savings account, `Rate` is the interest rate, and `T` is the number of times the interest is compounded during a year (`T` is 4 if the interest is compounded quarterly).

Write a program that asks for the principal, the interest rate, and the number of times the interest is compounded. It should display a report similar to

```
Interest Rate:             4.25%
Times Compounded:             12
Principal:          $ 1000.00
Interest:           $   43.34
Amount in Savings:  $ 1043.34
```

17. Monthly Payments

The monthly payment on a loan may be calculated by the following formula:

$$\text{Payment} = \frac{\text{Rate} * (1 + \text{Rate})^N}{((1 + \text{Rate})^N - 1)} * L$$

`Rate` is the monthly interest rate, which is the annual interest rate divided by 12. (12% annual interest would be 1 percent monthly interest.) `N` is the number of payments and `L` is the amount of the loan. Write a program that asks for these values and displays a report similar to

```
Loan Amount:            $ 10000.00
Monthly Interest Rate:        1%
Number of Payments:           36
Monthly Payment:        $   332.14
Amount Paid Back:       $ 11957.15
Interest Paid:          $  1957.15
```

18. Pizza Pi

Joe's Pizza Palace needs a program to calculate the number of slices a pizza of any size can be divided into. The program should perform the following steps:

A) Ask the user for the diameter of the pizza in inches.

B) Calculate the number of slices that may be taken from a pizza of that size.

C) Display a message telling the number of slices.

To calculate the number of slices that may be taken from the pizza, you must know the following facts:

- Each slice should have an area of 14.125 inches.
- To calculate the number of slices, simply divide the area of the pizza by 14.125.
- The area of the pizza is calculated with this formula:

Area = πr^2

> **NOTE:** π is the Greek letter pi. 3.14159 can be used as its value. The variable r is the radius of the pizza. Divide the diameter by 2 to get the radius.

Make sure the output of the program displays the number of slices in fixed point notation, rounded to one decimal place of precision. Use a named constant for pi.

19. **How Many Pizzas?**

Modify the program you wrote in Programming Challenge 18 (Pizza Pi) so that it reports the number of pizzas you need to buy for a party if each person attending is expected to eat an average of four slices. The program should ask the user for the number of people who will be at the party and for the diameter of the pizzas to be ordered. It should then calculate and display the number of pizzas to purchase.

20. **Angle Calculator**

Write a program that asks the user for an angle, entered in radians. The program should then display the sine, cosine, and tangent of the angle. (Use the sin, cos, and tan library functions to determine these values.) The output should be displayed in fixed-point notation, rounded to four decimal places of precision.

21. **Saving Numbers to a File**

For this assignment you will write two programs:

Program 1   Write a program that asks the user to enter five numbers. Use a float-ing-point data type to hold the numbers. The program should create a file and save all five numbers to the file.

Program 2   Write a program that opens the file created by Program 1, reads the five numbers, and displays them. The program should also calculate and display the sum of the five numbers.

22. **Monthly Sales Tax Modification**

Modify the program you wrote for Programming Challenge 12 (Monthly Sales Tax) so it writes its output to a file instead of the screen.

23. **Average Rainfall Modification**

Modify the program you wrote for Programming Challenge 4 (Average Rainfall) so it reads its input from a file instead of the keyboard.

24. **Stock Transaction Program**

Last month Joe purchased some stock in Acme Software, Inc. Here are the details of the purchase:

- The number of shares that Joe purchased was 1,000.
- When Joe purchased the stock, he paid $32.87 per share.
- Joe paid his stock broker a commission that amounted to 2% of the amount he paid for the stock.

Two weeks later Joe sold the stock. Here are the details of the sale:

- The number of shares that Joe sold was 1,000.
- He sold the stock for $33.92 per share.
- He paid his stock broker another commission that amounted to 2% of the amount he received for the stock.

Write a program that displays the following information:

- The amount of money Joe paid for the stock.
- The amount of commission Joe paid his broker when he bought the stock.
- The amount that Joe sold the stock for.
- The amount of commission Joe paid his broker when he sold the stock.
- Display the amount of profit that Joe made after selling his stock and paying the two commissions to his broker. (If the amount of profit that your program displays is a negative number, then Joe lost money on the transaction.)

25. **Word Game**

Write a program that plays a word game with the user. The program should ask the user to enter the following:

- His or her name
- His or her age
- The name of a city
- The name of a college
- A profession
- A type of animal
- A pet's name

After the user has entered these items, the program should display the following story, inserting the user's input into the appropriate locations:

```
There once was a person named NAME who lived in CITY. At the age of
AGE, NAME went to college at COLLEGE. NAME graduated and went to work
as a PROFESSION. Then, NAME adopted a(n) ANIMAL named PETNAME. They
both lived happily ever after!
```

CHAPTER

4 Making Decisions

TOPICS

4.1 Relational Operators

CONCEPT: Relational operators allow you to compare numeric and char values and determine whether one is greater than, less than, equal to, or not equal to another.

So far, the programs you have written follow this simple scheme:

- Gather input from the user.
- Perform one or more calculations.
- Display the results on the screen.

Computers are good at performing calculations, but they are also quite adept at comparing values to determine if one is greater than, less than, or equal to the other. These types

159

of operations are valuable for tasks such as examining sales figures, determining profit and loss, checking a number to ensure it is within an acceptable range, and validating the input given by a user.

Numeric data is compared in C++ by using relational operators. Each relational operator determines whether a specific relationship exists between two values. For example, the greater-than operator (>) determines if a value is greater than another. The equality operator (==) determines if two values are equal. Table 4-1 lists all of C++'s relational operators.

Table 4-1

Relational Operators	Meaning
>	Greater than
<	Less than
>=	Greater than or equal to
<=	Less than or equal to
==	Equal to
!=	Not equal to

All of the relational operators are binary, which means they use two operands. Here is an example of an expression using the greater-than operator:

    x > y

This expression is called a *relational expression*. It is used to determine whether x is greater than y. The following expression determines whether x is less than y:

    x < y

Table 4-2 shows examples of several relational expressions that compare the variables x and y.

Table 4-2

Expression	What the Expression Means
x > y	Is x greater than y?
x < y	Is x less than y?
x >= y	Is x greater than or equal to y?
x <= y	Is x less than or equal to y?
x == y	Is x equal to y?
x != y	Is x not equal to y?

 NOTE: All the relational operators have left-to-right associativity. Recall that associativity is the order in which an operator works with its operands.

The Value of a Relationship

So, how are relational expressions used in a program? Remember, all expressions have a value. Relational expressions are also known as *Boolean expressions*, which means their value can only be *true* or *false*. If x is greater than y, the expression x > y will be true, while the expression y == x will be false.

The == operator determines whether the operand on its left is equal to the operand on its right. If both operands have the same value, the expression is true. Assuming that a is 4, the following expression is true:

```
a == 4
```

But the following is false:

```
a == 2
```

> **WARNING!** Notice the equality operator is two = symbols together. Don't confuse this operator with the assignment operator, which is one = symbol. The == operator determines whether a variable is equal to another value, but the = operator assigns the value on the operator's right to the variable on its left. There will be more about this later in the chapter.

A couple of the relational operators actually test for two relationships. The >= operator determines whether the operand on its left is greater than *or* equal to the operand on the right. Assuming that a is 4, b is 6, and c is 4, both of the following expressions are true:

```
b >= a
a >= c
```

But the following is false:

```
a >= 5
```

The <= operator determines whether the operand on its left is less than *or* equal to the operand on its right. Once again, assuming that a is 4, b is 6, and c is 4, both of the following expressions are true:

```
a <= c
b <= 10
```

But the following is false:

```
b <= a
```

The last relational operator is !=, which is the not-equal operator. It determines whether the operand on its left is not equal to the operand on its right, which is the opposite of the == operator. As before, assuming a is 4, b is 6, and c is 4, both of the following expressions are true:

```
a != b
b != c
```

These expressions are true because a is *not* equal to b and b is *not* equal to c. But the following expression is false because a *is* equal to c:

```
a != c
```

Table 4-3 shows other relational expressions and their true or false values.

Table 4-3   (Assume x is 10 and y is 7.)

Expression	Value
x < y	False, because x is not less than y.
x > y	True, because x is greater than y.
x >= y	True, because x is greater than or equal to y.
x <= y	False, because x is not less than or equal to y.
y != x	True, because y is not equal to x.

What Is Truth?

The question "what is truth?" is one you would expect to find in a philosophy book, not a C++ programming text. It's a good question for us to consider, though. If a relational expression can be either true or false, how are those values represented internally in a program? How does a computer store *true* in memory? How does it store *false*?

As you saw in Program 2-16, those two abstract states are converted to numbers. In C++, relational expressions represent true states with the number 1 and false states with the number 0.

NOTE: As you will see later in this chapter, 1 is not the only value regarded as true.

To illustrate this more fully, look at Program 4-1.

Program 4-1

```
 1   // This program displays the values of true and false states.
 2   #include <iostream>
 3   using namespace std;
 4
 5   int main()
 6   {
 7      bool trueValue, falseValue;
 8      int x = 5, y = 10;
 9
10      trueValue = x < y;
11      falseValue = y == x;
12
13      cout << "True is  " << trueValue << endl;
14      cout << "False is  " << falseValue << endl;
15      return 0;
16   }
```

Program Output
```
True is 1
False is 0
```

Let's examine the statements containing the relational expressions, in lines 10 and 11, a little closer:

```
trueValue = x < y;
falseValue = y == x;
```

These statements may seem odd because they are assigning the value of a comparison to a variable. In line 10 the variable `trueValue` is being assigned the result of x < y. Since x is less than y, the expression is true, and the variable `trueValue` is assigned the value 1. In line 11 the expression y == x is false, so the variable `falseValue` is set to 0. Table 4-4 shows examples of other statements using relational expressions and their outcomes.

> **NOTE:** Relational expressions have a higher precedence than the assignment operator. In the statement
>
> `z = x < y;`
>
> the expression x < y is evaluated first, and then its value is assigned to z.

Table 4-4 (Assume x is 10, y is 7, and z, a, and b are `ints` or `bools`)

Statement	Outcome
`z = x < y`	z is assigned 0 because x is not less than y.
`cout << (x > y);`	Displays 1 because x is greater than y.
`a = x >= y;`	a is assigned 1 because x is greater than or equal to y.
`cout << (x <= y);`	Displays 0 because x is not less than or equal to y.
`b = y != x;`	b is assigned 1 because y is not equal to x.

When writing statements such as these, it sometimes helps to enclose the relational expression in parentheses, such as:

```
trueValue = (x < y);
falseValue = (y == x);
```

As interesting as relational expressions are, we've only scratched the surface of how to use them. In this chapter's remaining sections you will see how to get the most from relational expressions by using them in statements that take action based on the results of the comparison.

 Checkpoint

4.1   Assuming x is 5, y is 6, and z is 8, indicate by circling the T or F whether each of the following relational expressions is true or false:

    A) `x == 5`   T   F

    B) `7 <= (x + 2)`   T   F

    C) `z < 4`   T   F

    D) `(2 + x) != y`   T   F

    E) `z != 4`   T   F

    F) `x >= 9`   T   F

    G) `x <= (y * 2)`   T   F

4.2   Indicate whether the following statements about relational expressions are correct or incorrect.

A)   `x <= y` is the same as `y > x`.

B)   `x != y` is the same as `y >= x`.

C)   `x >= y` is the same as `y <= x`.

4.3   Answer the following questions with a yes or no.

A)   If it is true that `x > y` and it is also true that `x < z`, does that mean `y < z` is true?

B)   If it is true that `x >= y` and it is also true that `z == x`, does that mean that `z == y` is true?

C)   If it is true that `x != y` and it is also true that `x != z`, does that mean that `z != y` is true?

4.4   What will the following program display?

```cpp
#include <iostream>
using namespace std;

int main ()
{
    int a = 0, b = 2, x = 4, y = 0;

    cout << (a == b) << endl;
    cout << (a != y) << endl;
    cout << (b <= x) << endl;
    cout << (y > a) << endl;
    return 0;
}
```

4.2   The `if` Statement

CONCEPT: The `if` statement can cause other statements to execute only under certain conditions.

VideoNote

The `if` Statement

You might think of the statements in a procedural program as individual steps taken as you are walking down a road. To reach the destination, you must start at the beginning and take each step, one after the other, until you reach the destination. The programs you have written so far are like a "path" of execution for the program to follow.

The type of code in Figure 4-1 is called a *sequence structure*, because the statements are executed in sequence, without branching off in another direction. Programs often need more than one path of execution, however. Many algorithms require a program to execute some statements only under certain circumstances. This can be accomplished with a *decision structure*.

In a decision structure's simplest form, a specific action is taken only when a specific condition exists. If the condition does not exist, the action is not performed. The flowchart in Figure 4-2 shows the logic of a decision structure. The diamond symbol represents a yes/no

Figure 4-1

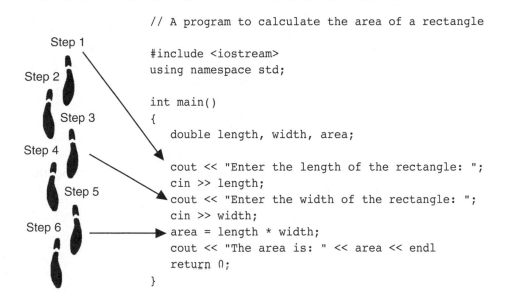

```cpp
// A program to calculate the area of a rectangle

#include <iostream>
using namespace std;

int main()
{
    double length, width, area;

    cout << "Enter the length of the rectangle: ";
    cin >> length;
    cout << "Enter the width of the rectangle: ";
    cin >> width;
    area = length * width;
    cout << "The area is: " << area << endl
    return 0;
}
```

Step 1
Step 2
Step 3
Step 4
Step 5
Step 6

question or a true/false condition. If the answer to the question is yes (or if the condition is true), the program flow follows one path, which leads to an action being performed. If the answer to the question is no (or the condition is false), the program flow follows another path, which skips the action.

Figure 4-2

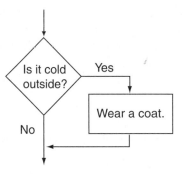

In the flowchart, the action "Wear a coat" is performed only when it is cold outside. If it is not cold outside, the action is skipped. The action is *conditionally executed* because it is performed only when a certain condition (cold outside) exists. Figure 4-3 shows a more elaborate flowchart, where three actions are taken only when it is cold outside.

We perform mental tests like these every day. Here are some other examples:

If the car is low on gas, stop at a service station and get gas.
If it's raining outside, go inside.
If you're hungry, get something to eat.

Figure 4-3

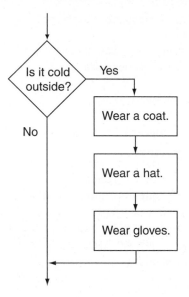

One way to code a decision structure in C++ is with the `if` statement. Here is the general format of the `if` statement:

```
if (expression)
      statement;
```

The `if` statement is simple in the way it works: If the value of the expression inside the parentheses is true, the very next *statement* is executed. Otherwise, it is skipped. The *statement* is *conditionally executed* because it only executes under the condition that the expression in the parentheses is true. Program 4-2 shows an example of an `if` statement. The user enters three test scores and the program calculates their average. If the average is greater than 95, the program congratulates the user on obtaining a high score.

Program 4-2

```
 1   // This program averages three test scores
 2   #include <iostream>
 3   #include <iomanip>
 4   using namespace std;
 5
 6   int main()
 7   {
 8      int score1, score2, score3;   // To hold three test scores
 9      double average;               // To hold the average score
10
```

```
11      // Get the three test scores.
12      cout << "Enter 3 test scores and I will average them: ";
13      cin >> score1 >> score2 >> score3;
14
15      // Calculate and display the average score.
16      average = (score1 + score2 + score3) / 3.0;
17      cout << fixed << showpoint << setprecision(1);
18      cout << "Your average is " << average << endl;
19
20      // If the average is greater than 95, congratulate the user.
21      if (average > 95)
22         cout << "Congratulations! That's a high score!\n";
23      return 0;
24   }
```

Program Output with Example Input Shown in Bold
Enter 3 test scores and I will average them: **80 90 70 [Enter]**
Your average is 80.0

Program Output with Different Example Input Shown in Bold
Enter 3 test scores and I will average them: **100 100 100 [Enter]**
Your average is 100.0
Congratulations! That's a high score!

Lines 21 and 22 cause the congratulatory message to be printed:

```
if (average > 95)
    cout << "Congratulations! That's a high score!\n";
```

The cout statement in line 22 is executed only if the average is greater than 95. If the average is not greater than 95, the cout statement is skipped. Figure 4-4 shows the logic of this if statement.

Figure 4-4

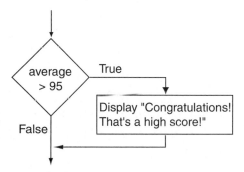

Table 4-5 shows other examples of if statements and their outcomes.

Table 4-5

Statement	Outcome
`if (hours > 40)` `    overTime = true;`	Assigns `true` to the `bool` variable `overTime` only when `hours` is greater than 40
`if (value > 32)` `     cout << "Invalid number\n";`	Displays the message "Invalid number" only when `value` is greater than 32
`if (overTime == true)` `    payRate *= 2;`	Multiplies `payRate` by 2 only when `overTime` is equal to `true`

Be Careful with Semicolons

Semicolons do not mark the end of a line, but the end of a complete C++ statement. The `if` statement isn't complete without the conditionally executed statement that comes after it. So, you must not put a semicolon after the `if (expression)` portion of an `if` statement.

No semicolon goes here.

`if (expression)`
`    statement;`

Semicolon goes here.

If you inadvertently put a semicolon after the `if` part, the compiler will assume you are placing a null statement there. The *null statement* is an empty statement that does nothing. This will prematurely terminate the `if` statement, which disconnects it from the statement that follows it. The statement following the `if` will always execute, as shown in Program 4-3.

Program 4-3

```
 1   // This program demonstrates how a misplaced semicolon
 2   // prematurely terminates an if statement.
 3   #include <iostream>
 4   using namespace std;
 5
 6   int main()
 7   {
 8      int x = 0, y = 10;
 9
10      cout << "x is " << x << " and y is " << y << endl;
11      if (x > y);    // Error! Misplaced semicolon
12         cout << "x is greater than y\n"; //This is always executed.
13      return 0;
14   }
```

Program Output
```
x is 0 and y is 10
x is greater than y
```

Programming Style and the if Statement

Even though if statements usually span more than one line, they are technically one long statement. For instance, the following if statements are identical except in style:

```
if (a >= 100)
    cout << "The number is out of range.\n";
if (a >= 100) cout << "The number is out of range.\n";
```

In both the examples above, the compiler considers the if part and the cout statement as one unit, with a semicolon properly placed at the end. Indention and spacing are for the human readers of a program, not the compiler. Here are two important style rules you should adopt for writing if statements:

- The conditionally executed statement should appear on the line after the if statement.
- The conditionally executed statement should be indented one "level" from the if statement.

NOTE: In most editors, each time you press the tab key, you are indenting one level.

By indenting the conditionally executed statement you are causing it to stand out visually. This is so you can tell at a glance what part of the program the if statement executes. This is a standard way of writing if statements and is the method you should use.

NOTE: Indentation and spacing are for the human readers of a program, not the compiler. Even though the cout statement following the if statement in Program 4-3 is indented, the semicolon still terminates the if statement.

Comparing Floating-Point Numbers

Because of the way that floating-point numbers are stored in memory, rounding errors sometimes occur. This is because some fractional numbers cannot be exactly represented using binary. So, you should be careful when using the equality operator (==) to compare floating point numbers. For example, Program 4-4 uses two double variables, a and b. Both variables are initialized to the value 1.5. Then, the value 0.0000000000000001 is added to a. This should make a's contents different than b's contents. Because of a round-off error, however, the two variables are still the same.

Program 4-4

```
1  // This program demonstrates how floating-point
2  // round-off errors can make equality operations unreliable.
3  #include <iostream>
4  using namespace std;
5
```

(program continues)

```
 6   int main()
 7   {
 8      double a = 1.5;          // a is 1.5.
 9      double b = 1.5;          // b is 1.5.
10
11      a += 0.0000000000000001;   // Add a little to a.
12      if (a == b)
13         cout << "Both a and b are the same.\n";
14      else
15         cout << "a and b are not the same.\n";
16
17      return 0;
18   }
```

Program Output

```
Both a and b are the same.
```

To prevent round-off errors from causing this type of problem, you should stick with greater-than and less-than comparisons with floating-point numbers.

And Now Back to Truth

Now that you've gotten your feet wet with relational expressions and `if` statements, let's look at the subject of truth again. You have seen that a relational expression has the value 1 when it is true and 0 when false. In the world of the `if` statement, however, the concept of truth is expanded. 0 is still false, but all values other than 0 are considered true. This means that any value, even a negative number, represents true as long as it is not 0.

Just as in real life, truth is a complicated thing. Here is a summary of the rules you have seen so far:

- When a relational expression is true it has the value 1.
- When a relational expression is false it has the value 0.
- Any expression that has the value 0 is considered false by the `if` statement. This includes the `bool` value `false`, which is equivalent to 0.
- Any expression that has any value other than 0 is considered true by the `if` statement. This includes the `bool` value `true`, which is equivalent to 1.

The fact that the `if` statement considers any nonzero value as true opens many possibilities. Relational expressions are not the only conditions that may be tested. For example, the following is a legal `if` statement in C++:

```
if (value)
    cout << "It is True!";
```

The `if` statement above does not test a relational expression, but rather the contents of a variable. If the variable, `value`, contains any number other than 0, the message "It is True!" will be displayed. If `value` is set to 0, however, the `cout` statement will be skipped. Here is another example:

```
if (x + y)
    cout << "It is True!";
```

In this statement the sum of x and y is tested like any other value in an if statement: 0 is false and all other values are true. You may also use the return value of function calls as conditional expressions. Here is an example that uses the pow function:

```
if (pow(a, b))
    cout << "It is True!";
```

This if statement uses the pow function to raise a to the power of b. If the result is anything other than 0, the cout statement is executed. This is a powerful programming technique that you will learn more about in Chapter 6.

Don't Confuse == With =

Earlier you saw a warning not to confuse the equality operator (==) with the assignment operator (=), as in the following statement:

```
if (x = 2)  //Caution here!
    cout << "It is True!";
```

The statement above does not determine whether x is equal to 2, it assigns x the value 2! Furthermore, the cout statement will *always* be executed because the expression x = 2 is always true.

This occurs because the value of an assignment expression is the value being assigned to the variable on the left side of the = operator. That means the value of the expression x = 2 is 2. Since 2 is a nonzero value, it represents a true condition. Program 4-5 is a version of Program 4-2 that attempts to test for a perfect average of 100. The = operator, however, was mistakenly used in the if statement.

Program 4-5

```
 1  // This program averages 3 test scores. The if statement
 2  // uses the = operator, but the == operator was intended.
 3  #include <iostream>
 4  #include <iomanip>
 5  using namespace std;
 6
 7  int main()
 8  {
 9     int score1, score2, score3;  // To hold three test scores
10     double average;              // TO hold the average score
11
12     // Get the three test scores.
13     cout << "Enter 3 test scores and I will average them: ";
14     cin >> score1 >> score2 >> score3;
15
16     // Calculate and display the average score.
17     average = (score1 + score2 + score3) / 3.0;
18     cout << fixed << showpoint << setprecision(1);
19     cout << "Your average is " << average << endl;
20
```

(program continues)

Program 4-5   *(continued)*

```
21      // Our intention is to congratulate the user
22      // for having a perfect score. But, this doesn't work.
23      if (average = 100)  // WRONG! This is an assignment!
24         cout << "Congratulations! That's a perfect score!\n";
25      return 0;
26   }
```

Program Output with Example Input Shown in Bold
```
Enter three test scores and I will average them: 80 90 70 [Enter]
Your average is 80.0
Congratulations! That's a perfect score!
```

Regardless of the average score, this program will print the message congratulating the user on a perfect score.

4.3   Flags

> **CONCEPT:** A flag is a Boolean or integer variable that signals when a condition exists.

A *flag* is typically a `bool` variable that signals when some condition exists in the program. When the flag variable is set to `false`, it indicates that the condition does not yet exist. When the flag variable is set to `true`, it means the condition does exist.

For example, suppose a program similar to the previous test averaging program has a `bool` variable named `highScore`, defined and initialized as shown here:

```
bool highScore = false;
```

When we define the variable, we initialize it with `false` because we do not yet know if a high score has been achieved. After the average score is calculated, we can use the following code to determine whether it is greater than 95. If it is, the `highScore` variable is set to `true`.

```
if (average > 95)
   highScore = true;
```

Later, the same program might use code similar to the following to test the `highScore` variable, in order to determine whether a high score has been achieved.

```
if (highScore)
   cout << "Congratulations! That's a high score!";
```

Integer Flags

Integer variables may also be used as flags. This is because in C++ the value 0 is considered false, and any nonzero value is considered true. In a test averaging program we could define the `highScore` variable with the following statement:

```
int highScore = 0;   // 0 means false.
```

As before, we initialize the variable with 0 because we do not yet know whether a high score has been achieved. After the average score is calculated, we can use the following code to determine whether it is greater than 95. If it is, the `highScore` variable is set to a nonzero value.

```
if (average > 95)
    highScore = 1;  // A nonzero value means true.
```

Later in the program we might use code similar to the following to test the `highScore` variable, in order to determine whether a high score has been achieved.

```
if (highScore)
    cout << "Congratulations! That's a high score!";
```

You will find flag variables useful in many circumstances, and we will come back to them in future chapters.

> **NOTE:** Variables that are created inside a function, like `main`, are not automatically initialized. If you need a variable to start with a particular value, you should initialize it to that value.

4.4 Expanding the `if` Statement

CONCEPT: The `if` statement can conditionally execute a block of statements enclosed in braces.

What if you want an `if` statement to conditionally execute a group of statements, not just one line? For instance, what if the test averaging program needed to use several `cout` statements when a high score was reached? The answer is to enclose all of the conditionally executed statements inside a set of braces. Here is the format:

```
if (expression)
{
    statement;
    statement;
    // Place as many statements here as necessary.
}
```

Program 4-6, another modification of the test-averaging program, demonstrates this type of `if` statement.

Program 4-6

```
1   // This program averages 3 test scores.
2   // It demonstrates an if statement executing
3   // a block of statements.
4   #include <iostream>
5   #include <iomanip>
6   using namespace std;
7
```

(program continues)

Program 4-6   *(continued)*

```cpp
 8   int main()
 9   {
10      int score1, score2, score3;   // To hold three test scores
11      double average;               // To hold the average score
12
13      // Get the three test scores.
14      cout << "Enter 3 test scores and I will average them: ";
15      cin >> score1 >> score2 >> score3;
16
17      // Calculate and display the average score.
18      average = (score1 + score2 + score3) / 3.0;
19      cout << fixed << showpoint << setprecision(1);
20      cout << "Your average is " << average << endl;
21
22      // If the average is greater than 95, congratulate the user.
23      if (average > 95)
24      {
25         cout << "Congratulations!\n";
26         cout << "That's a high score.\n";
27         cout << "You deserve a pat on the back!\n";
28      }
29      return 0;
30   }
```

Program Output with Example Input Shown in Bold
Enter 3 test scores and I will average them: **100 100 100 [Enter]**
Your average is 100.0
Congratulations!
That's a high score.
You deserve a pat on the back!

Program Output with Different Example Input Shown in Bold
Enter 3 test scores and I will average them: **80 90 70 [Enter]**
Your average is 80.0

Program 4-6 prints a more elaborate message when the average score is greater than 95. The if statement was expanded to execute three cout statements when highScore is set to true. Enclosing a group of statements inside a set of braces creates a *block* of code. The if statement will execute all the statements in the block, in the order they appear, only when average is greater than 95. Otherwise, the block will be skipped.

Notice all the statements inside the braces are indented. As before, this visually separates the statements from lines that are not indented, making it more obvious they are part of the if statement.

 NOTE: Anytime your program has a block of code, all the statements inside the braces should be indented.

Don't Forget the Braces!

If you intend to conditionally execute a block of statements with an if statement, don't forget the braces. Remember, without a set of braces, the if statement only executes the very next statement. Program 4-7 shows the test-averaging program with the braces inadvertently left out of the if statement's block.

Program 4-7

```
 1   // This program averages 3 test scores. The braces
 2   // were inadvertently left out of the if statement.
 3   #include <iostream>
 4   #include <iomanip>
 5   using namespace std;
 6
 7   int main()
 8   {
 9      int score1, score2, score3;   // To hold three test scores
10      double average;               // To hold the average score
11
12      // Get the three test scores.
13      cout << "Enter 3 test scores and I will average them: ";
14      cin >> score1 >> score2 >> score3;
15
16      // Calculate and display the average score.
17      average = (score1 + score2 + score3) / 3.0;
18      cout << fixed << showpoint << setprecision(1);
19      cout << "Your average is " << average << endl;
20
21      // ERROR! This if statement is missing its braces!
22      if (average > 95)
23         cout << "Congratulations!\n";
24         cout << "That's a high score.\n";
25         cout << "You deserve a pat on the back!\n";
26      return 0;
27   }
```

Program Output with Example Input Shown in Bold

```
Enter 3 test scores and I will average them: 80 90 70 [Enter]
Your average is 80
That's a high score.
You deserve a pat on the back!
```

The cout statements in lines 24 and 25 are always executed, even when average is not greater than 95. Because the braces have been removed, the if statement only controls execution of line 23. This is illustrated in Figure 4-5.

Figure 4-5

Checkpoint

4.5   TRUE or FALSE: Both of the following `if` statements perform the same operation.

```
if (sales > 10000)
   commissionRate = 0.15;

if (sales > 10000) commissionRate = 0.15;
```

4.6   TRUE or FALSE: Both of the following `if` statements perform the same operation.

```
if (calls == 20)
   rate *= 0.5;

if (calls = 20)
   rate *= 0.5;
```

4.7   Although the following code segments are syntactically correct, each contains an error. Locate the error.

A)
```
if (hours > 40);
    cout << hours << " hours qualifies for overtime.\n";
```

B)
```
balance = 1000;
if (interestRate = .07)
   cout << "This account is earning the maximum rate.\n";
```

C)
```
if (interestRate > .07)
   cout << "This account earns a $10 bonus.\n";
   balance += 10.0;
```

4.8   Write an `if` statement that assigns 0 to x if y is equal to 20.

4.9   Write an `if` statement that multiplies `payRate` by 1.5 if hours is greater than 40.

4.10   Write an `if` statement that assigns .20 to `commission` if `sales` is greater than or equal to 10000.00.

4.11   Write an `if` statement that sets the variable `fees` to 50 if the flag variable `max` is set to `true`.

4.5 The `if/else` Statement

> **CONCEPT:** The `if/else` statement will execute one group of statements if the expression is true, or another group of statements if the expression is false.

VideoNote

The `if/else` Statement

The `if/else` statement is an expansion of the `if` statement. Here is its format:

```
if (expression)
    statement or block
else
    statement or block
```

As with the `if` statement, an expression is evaluated. If the expression is true, a statement or block of statements is executed. If the expression is false, however, a separate group of statements is executed. Program 4-8 uses the `if/else` statement along with the modulus operator to determine if a number is odd or even.

Program 4-8

```cpp
 1   // This program uses the modulus operator to determine
 2   // if a number is odd or even. If the number is evenly divisible
 3   // by 2, it is an even number. A remainder indicates it is odd.
 4   #include <iostream>
 5   using namespace std;
 6
 7   int main()
 8   {
 9      int number;
10
11      cout << "Enter an integer and I will tell you if it\n";
12      cout << "is odd or even. ";
13      cin >> number;
14      if (number % 2 == 0)
15         cout << number << " is even.\n";
16      else
17         cout << number << " is odd.\n";
18      return 0;
19   }
```

Program Output with Example Input Shown in Bold
```
Enter an integer and I will tell you if it
is odd or even. 17 [Enter]
17 is odd.
```

The `else` part at the end of the `if` statement specifies a statement that is to be executed when the expression is false. When `number % 2` does not equal 0, a message is printed indicating the number is odd. Note that the program will only take one of the two paths in the `if/else` statement. If you think of the statements in a computer program as steps taken down a road, consider the `if/else` statement as a fork in the road. Instead of being a momentary detour, like an `if` statement, the `if/else` statement causes program execution to follow one of two exclusive paths. The flowchart in Figure 4-6 shows the logic of this `if/else` statement.

Figure 4-6

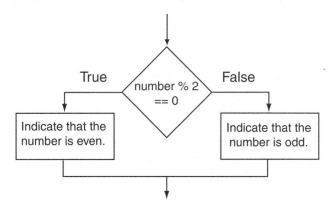

Notice the programming style used to construct the `if/else` statement. The word `else` is at the same level of indention as `if`. The statement whose execution is controlled by `else` is indented one level. This visually depicts the two paths of execution that may be followed.

Like the `if` part, the `else` part controls a single statement. If you wish to control more than one statement with the `else` part, create a block by writing the lines inside a set of braces. Program 4-9 shows this as a way of handling a classic programming problem: *division by zero*.

Division by zero is mathematically impossible to perform and it normally causes a program to crash. This means the program will prematurely stop running, sometimes with an error message. Program 4-9 shows a way to test the value of a divisor before the division takes place.

Program 4-9

```
 1   // This program asks the user for two numbers, num1 and num2.
 2   // num1 is divided by num2 and the result is displayed.
 3   // Before the division operation, however, num2 is tested
 4   // for the value 0. If it contains 0, the division does not
 5   // take place.
 6   #include <iostream>
 7   using namespace std;
 8
 9   int main()
10   {
11       double num1, num2, quotient;
12
```

```
13      // Get the first number.
14      cout << "Enter a number: ";
15      cin >> num1;
16
17      // Get the second number.
18      cout << "Enter another number: ";
19      cin >> num2;
20
21      // If num2 is not zero, perform the division.
22      if (num2 == 0)
23      {
24         cout << "Division by zero is not possible.\n";
25         cout << "Please run the program again and enter\n";
26         cout << "a number other than zero.\n";
27      }
28      else
29      {
30         quotient = num1 / num2;
31         cout << "The quotient of " << num1 << " divided by ",
32         cout<< num2 << " is " << quotient << ".\n";
33      }
34      return 0;
35  }
```

Program Output with Example Input Shown in Bold
(When the user enters 0 for num2)
Enter a number: **10 [Enter]**
Enter another number: **0 [Enter]**
Division by zero is not possible.
Please run the program again and enter
a number other than zero.

The value of num2 is tested in line 22 before the division is performed. If the user enters 0, the lines controlled by the if part execute, displaying a message which indicates that the program cannot perform a division by zero. Otherwise, the else part takes control, which divides num1 by num2 and displays the result.

 Checkpoint

4.12   TRUE or FALSE: The following if/else statements cause the same output to display.

A) if (x > y)
        cout << "x is the greater.\n";
    else
        cout << "x is not the greater.\n";

B) if (y <= x)
        cout << "x is not the greater.\n";
    else
        cout << "x is the greater.\n";

4.13   Write an `if/else` statement that assigns 1 to x if y is equal to 100. Otherwise it should assign 0 to x.

4.14   Write an `if/else` statement that assigns 0.10 to `commission` unless `sales` is greater than or equal to 50000.00, in which case it assigns 0.20 to `commission`.

4.15   Complete the following program skeleton so it computes the correct sales tax. If the customer is an in-state resident, `taxRate` should be set to .05. If the customer is an out-of-state resident, `taxRate` should be set to 0.

```cpp
#include <iostream>
using namespace std;

int main()
{
    double taxRate, saleAmount;
    char residence;

    cout << "Enter the amount of the sale: ";
    cin >> saleAmount;
    cout << "Enter I for in-state residence or O for out-of-\n";
    cout << "state: ";
    cin.get(residence);

    // Write code here that assigns 0 to taxRate if residence
    // is set to 'O' or .05 to taxRate if residence is set
    // to 'I'

    saleAmount += saleAmount * taxRate;
    cout << "The total is " << saleAmount;
    return 0;
}
```

4.6   Nested `if` Statements

CONCEPT: To test more than one condition, an `if` statement can be nested inside another `if` statement.

Sometimes an `if` statement must be nested inside another `if` statement. For example, consider a banking program that determines whether a bank customer qualifies for a special, low interest rate on a loan. To qualify, two conditions must exist: (1) the customer must be currently employed, and (2) the customer must have recently graduated from college (in the past two years). Figure 4-7 shows a flowchart for an algorithm that could be used in such a program.

If we follow the flow of execution in the flowchart, we see that the expression `employed == 'Y'` is tested. If this expression is false, there is no need to perform further tests; we know that the customer does not qualify for the special interest rate. If the expression is true, however, we need to test the second condition. This is done with a nested decision structure that tests the expression `recentGrad == 'Y'`. If this expression is true, then the customer qualifies for the special interest rate. If this expression is false, then the customer does not qualify. Program 4-10 shows the code for the complete program.

Figure 4-7

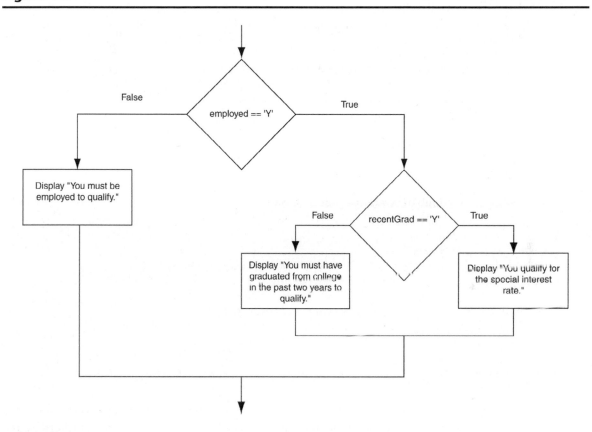

Program 4-10

```
 1   // This program demonstrates the nested if statement.
 2   #include <iostream>
 3   using namespace std;
 4
 5   int main()
 6   {
 7      char employed,   // Currently employed, Y or N
 8           recentGrad; // Recent graduate, Y or N
 9
10      // Is the user employed and a recent graduate?
11      cout << "Answer the following questions\n";
12      cout << "with either Y for Yes or ";
13      cout << "N for No.\n";
14      cout << "Are you employed? ";
15      cin >> employed;
16      cout << "Have you graduated from college ";
17      cout << "in the past two years? ";
18      cin >> recentGrad;
19
```

(program continues)

Program 4-10   *(continued)*

```
20      // Determine the user's loan qualifications.
21      if (employed == 'Y')
22      {
23         if (recentGrad == 'Y') //Nested if
24         {
25            cout << "You qualify for the special ";
26            cout << "interest rate.\n";
27         }
28      }
29      return 0;
30  }
```

Program Output with Example Input Shown in Bold
```
Answer the following questions
with either Y for Yes or N for No.
Are you employed? Y [Enter]
Have you graduated from college in the past two years? Y [Enter]
You qualify for the special interest rate.
```

Program Output with Different Example Input Shown in Bold
```
Answer the following questions
with either Y for Yes or N for No.
Are you employed? Y [Enter]
Have you graduated from college in the past two years? N [Enter]
```

Look at the if statement that begins in line 21. It tests the expression employed == 'Y'. If this expression is true, the if statement that begins in line 23 is executed. Otherwise the program jumps to the return statement in line 29 and the program ends.

Notice in the second sample execution of Program 4-10 that the program output does not inform the user whether he or she qualifies for the special interest rate. If the user enters an 'N' (or any character other than 'Y') for employed or recentGrad, the program does not print a message letting the user know that he or she does not qualify. An else statement should be able to remedy this, as illustrated by Program 4-11.

Program 4-11

```
1   // This program demonstrates the nested if statement.
2   #include <iostream>
3   using namespace std;
4
5   int main()
6   {
7      char employed,   // Currently employed, Y or N
8           recentGrad; // Recent graduate, Y or N
9
10     // Is the user employed and a recent graduate?
11     cout << "Answer the following questions\n";
12     cout << "with either Y for Yes or ";
13     cout << "N for No.\n";
14     cout << "Are you employed? ";
15     cin >> employed;
16     cout << "Have you graduated from college ";
```

```
17       cout << "in the past two years? ";
18       cin >> recentGrad;
19
20       // Determine the user's loan qualifications.
21       if (employed == 'Y')
22       {
23          if (recentGrad == 'Y') // Nested if
24          {
25             cout << "You qualify for the special ";
26             cout << "interest rate.\n";
27          }
28          else // Not a recent grad, but employed
29          {
30             cout << "You must have graduated from ";
31             cout << "college in the past two\n";
32             cout << "years to qualify.\n";
33          }
34       }
35       else // Not employed
36       {
37          cout << "You must be employed to qualify.\n";
38       }
39       return 0;
40    }
```

Program Output with Example Input Shown in Bold

```
Answer the following questions
with either Y for Yes or N for No.
Are you employed? N [Enter]
Have you graduated from college in the past two years? Y [Enter]
You must be employed to qualify.
```

Program Output with Different Example Input Shown in Bold

```
Answer the following questions
with either Y for Yes or N for No.
Are you employed? Y [Enter]
Have you graduated from college in the past two years? N [Enter]
You must have graduated from college in the past two years to qualify.
```

Program Output with Different Example Input Shown in Bold

```
Answer the following questions
with either Y for Yes or N for No.
Are you employed? Y [Enter]
Have you graduated from college in the past two years? Y [Enter]
You qualify for the special interest rate.
```

In this version of the program, both if statements have else clauses that inform the user why he or she does not qualify for the special interest rate.

Programming Style and Nested Decision Structures

For readability and easier debugging, it's important to use proper alignment and indentation in a set of nested `if` statements. This makes it easier to see which actions are performed by each part of the decision structure. For example, the following code is functionally equivalent to lines 21 through 38 in Program 4-11. Although this code is logically correct, it is very difficult to read, and would be very difficult to debug because it is not properly indented.

```cpp
if (employed == 'Y')
{
if (recentGrad == 'Y') // Nested if
{
cout << "You qualify for the special ";
cout << "interest rate.\n";
}
else // Not a recent grad, but employed
{
cout << "You must have graduated from ";
cout << "college in the past two\n";
cout << "years to qualify.\n";
}
}
else // Not employed
{
cout << "You must be employed to qualify.\n";
}
```

Don't write code like this!

Proper indentation and alignment also makes it easier to see which `if` and `else` clauses belong together, as shown in Figure 4-8.

Figure 4-8

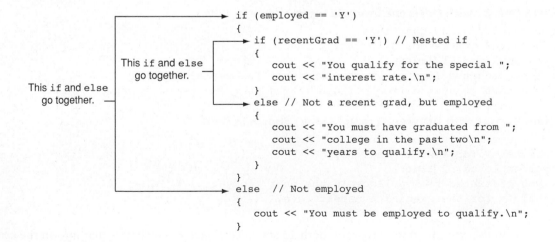

Testing a Series of Conditions

In the previous example you saw how a program can use nested decision structures to test more than one condition. It is not uncommon for a program to have a series of conditions to test, and then perform an action depending on which condition is true. One way to accomplish this is to have a decision structure with numerous other decision structures nested inside it. For example, consider the program presented in the following *In the Spotlight* section.

In the Spotlight:

Multiple Nested Decision Structures

Dr. Suarez teaches a literature class and uses the following 10 point grading scale for all of his exams:

Test Score	Grade
90 and above	A
80–89	B
70–79	C
60–69	D
Below 60	F

He has asked you to write a program that will allow a student to enter a test score and then display the grade for that score. Here is the algorithm that you will use:

Ask the user to enter a test score.
Determine the grade in the following manner:
If the score is less than 60, then the grade is F.
    Otherwise, if the score is less than 70, then the grade is D.
        Otherwise, if the score is less than 80, then the grade is C.
            Otherwise, if the score is less than 90, then the grade is B.
            Otherwise, the grade is A.

You decide that the process of determining the grade will require several nested decisions structures, as shown in Figure 4-9. Program 4-12 shows the code for the complete program. The code for the nested decision structures is in lines 17 through 45.

Figure 4-9   Nested decision structure to determine a grade

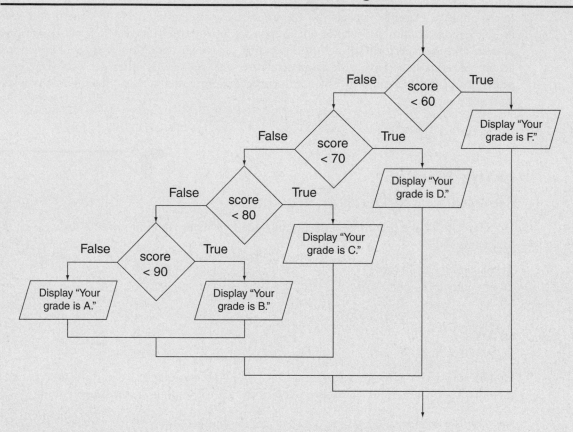

Program 4-12

```
1  // This program uses nested if/else statements to assign a
2  // letter grade (A, B, C, D, or F) to a numeric test score.
3  #include <iostream>
4  using namespace std;
5
6  int main()
7  {
8     int testScore;  // To hold a numeric test score
9
10    // Get the numeric test score.
11    cout << "Enter your numeric test score and I will\n";
12    cout << "tell you the letter grade you earned: ";
13    cin >> testScore;
14
15    // Determine the letter grade.
16    if (testScore < 60)
17    {
18       cout << "Your grade is F.\n";
19    }
20    else
```

```
21   {
22       if (testScore < 70)
23       {
24           cout << "Your grade is D.\n";
25       }
26       else
27       {
28           if (testScore < 80)
29           {
30               cout << "Your grade is C.\n";
31           }
32           else
33           {
34               if (testScore < 90)
35               {
36                   cout << "Your grade is B.\n";
37               }
38               else
39               {
40                   cout << "Your grade is A.\n";
41               }
42           }
43       }
44   }
45
46       return 0;
47 }
```

Program Output with Example Input Shown in Bold

```
Enter your numeric test score and I will
tell you the letter grade you earned: 78 [Enter]
Your grade is C.
```

Program Output with Different Example Input Shown in Bold

```
Enter your numeric test score and I will
tell you the letter grade you earned: 84 [Enter]
Your grade is B.
```

4.7 The if/else if Statement

CONCEPT: The if/else if statement tests a series of conditions. It is often simpler to test a series of conditions with the if/else if statement than with a set of nested if/else statements.

VideoNote

The if/else if Statement

Even though Program 4-12 is a simple example, the logic of the nested decision structure is fairly complex. In C++, and many other languages, you can alternatively test a series of conditions using the if/else if statement. The if/else if statement makes certain types of nested decision logic simpler to write. Here is the general format of the if/else if statement:

```
if (expression_1)
{
    statement
    statement                    }    If expression_1 is true these state-
    etc.                              ments are executed, and the rest of the
                                      structure is ignored.
}
else if (expression_2)
{
    statement
    statement                    }    Otherwise, if expression_2 is true these
    etc.                              statements are executed, and the rest of
                                      the structure is ignored.
}

Insert as many else if clauses as necessary

else
{
    statement
    statement                    }    These statements are executed if
    etc.                              none of the expressions above
                                      are true.
}
```

When the statement executes, *expression_1* is tested. If *expression_1* is true, the block of statements that immediately follows is executed, and the rest of the structure is ignored. If *expression_1* is false, however, the program jumps to the very next `else if` clause and tests *expression_2*. If it is true, the block of statements that immediately follows is executed, and then the rest of the structure is ignored. This process continues, from the top of the structure to the bottom, until one of the expressions is found to be true. If none of the expressions are true, the last `else` clause takes over and the block of statements immediately following it is executed.

The last `else` clause, which does not have an `if` statement following it, is referred to as the *trailing else*. The trailing `else` is optional, but in most cases you will use it.

NOTE: The general format shows braces surrounding each block of conditionally executed statements. As with other forms of the `if` statement, the braces are required only when more than one statement is conditionally executed.

Program 4-13 shows an example of the `if/else if` statement. This program is a modification of Program 4-12, which appears in the previous *In the Spotlight* section.

Program 4-13

```
1 // This program uses an if/else if statement to assign a
2 // letter grade (A, B, C, D, or F) to a numeric test score.
3 #include <iostream>
4 using namespace std;
5
6 int main()
7 {
8     int testScore;  // To hold a numeric test score
```

```
 9
10     // Get the numeric test score.
11     cout << "Enter your numeric test score and I will\n";
12     cout << "tell you the letter grade you earned: ";
13     cin >> testScore;
14
15     // Determine the letter grade.
16     if (testScore < 60)
17        cout << "Your grade is F.\n";
18     else if (testScore < 70)
19        cout << "Your grade is D.\n";
20     else if (testScore < 80)
21        cout << "Your grade is C.\n";
22     else if (testScore < 90)
23        cout << "Your grade is B.\n";
24     else
25        cout << "Your grade is A.\n";
26
27     return 0;
28 }
```

Program Output with Example Input Shown in Bold
Enter your numeric test score and I will
tell you the letter grade you earned: **78 [Enter]**
Your grade is C.

Program Output with Different Example Input Shown in Bold
Enter your numeric test score and I will
tell you the letter grade you earned: **84 [Enter]**
Your grade is B.

Let's analyze how the if/else if statement in lines 16 through 25 works. First, the expression testScore < 60 is tested in line 16:

```
→   if (testScore < 60)
        cout << "Your grade is F.\n";
    else if (testScore < 70)
        cout << "Your grade is D.\n";
    else if (testScore < 80)
        cout << "Your grade is C.\n";
    else if (testScore < 90)
        cout << "Your grade is B.\n";
    else
        cout << "Your grade is A.\n";
```

If testScore is less than 60, the message "Your grade is F.\n" is displayed and the rest of the if/else if statement is skipped. If testScore is not less than 60, the else clause in line 18 takes over and causes the next if statement to be executed:

```
    if (testScore < 60)
        cout << "Your grade is F.\n";;
```

```
    →   else if (testScore < 70)
            cout << "Your grade is D.\n";
        else if (testScore < 80)
            cout << "Your grade is C.\n";
        else if (testScore < 90)
            cout << "Your grade is B.\n";
        else
            cout << "Your grade is A.\n";
```

The first `if` statement handles all of the grades less than 60, so when this `if` statement executes, `testScore` will have a value of 60 or greater. If `testScore` is less than 70, the message `"Your grade is D.\n"` is displayed and the rest of the `if/else if` statement is skipped. This chain of events continues until one of the expressions is found to be true, or the last `else` clause at the end of the statement is encountered.

Notice the alignment and indentation that is used with the `if/else if` statement: The starting `if` clause, the `else if` clauses, and the trailing `else` clause are all aligned, and the conditionally executed statements are indented.

Using the Trailing `else` To Catch Errors

The trailing `else` clause, which appears at the end of the `if/else if` statement, is optional, but in many situations you will use it to catch errors. For example, Program 4-13 will assign the grade 'A' to any test score that is 90 or greater. What if the highest possible test score is 100? We can modify the code as shown in Program 4-14 so the trailing `else` clause catches any value greater than 100 and displays an error message.

Program 4-14

```
 1  // This program uses an if/else if statement to assign a
 2  // letter grade (A, B, C, D, or F) to a numeric test score.
 3  #include <iostream>
 4  using namespace std;
 5
 6  int main()
 7  {
 8     int testScore;  // To hold a numeric test score
 9
10     // Get the numeric test score.
11     cout << "Enter your numeric test score and I will\n";
12     cout << "tell you the letter grade you earned: ";
13     cin >> testScore;
14
15     // Determine the letter grade.
16     if (testScore < 60)
17        cout << "Your grade is F.\n";
18     else if (testScore < 70)
19        cout << "Your grade is D.\n";
20     else if (testScore < 80)
21        cout << "Your grade is C.\n";
22     else if (testScore < 90)
23        cout << "Your grade is B.\n";
```

```
24      else if (testScore <= 100)
25         cout << "Your grade is A.\n";
26      else
27          cout << "We do not give scores higher than 100.\n";
28
29      return 0;
30 }
```

Program Output with Example Input Shown in Bold
Enter your numeric test score and I will
tell you the letter grade you earned: **105 [Enter]**
We do not give scores higher than 100.

The if/else if Statement Compared to a Nested Decision Structure

You never have to use the if/else if statement because its logic can be coded with nested if/else statements. However, a long series of nested if/else statements has two particular disadvantages when you are debugging code:

- The code can grow complex and become difficult to understand.
- Because indenting is important in nested statements, a long series of nested if/else statements can become too long to be displayed on the computer screen without horizontal scrolling. Also, long statements tend to "wrap around" when printed on paper, making the code even more difficult to read.

The logic of an if/else if statement is usually easier to follow than that of a long series of nested if/else statements. And, because all of the clauses are aligned in an if/else if statement, the lengths of the lines in the statement tend to be shorter.

4.8   Menus

CONCEPT: You can use nested if/else statements or the if/else if statement to create menu-driven programs. A *menu-driven* program allows the user to determine the course of action by selecting it from a list of actions.

A menu is a screen displaying a set of choices the user selects from. For example, a program that manages a mailing list might give you the following menu:

1. Add a name to the list.

2. Remove a name from the list.

3. Change a name in the list.

4. Print the list.

5. Quit the program.

The user selects one of the operations by entering its number. Entering 4, for example, causes the mailing list to be printed, and entering 5 causes the program to end. Nested `if/else` statements or an `if/else if` structure can be used to set up such a menu. After the user enters a number, the program compares the number with the available selections and executes the statements that perform that operation.

Program 4-15 calculates the charges for membership in a health club. The club has three membership packages to choose from: standard adult membership, child membership, and senior citizen membership. The program presents a menu that allows the user to choose the desired package and then calculates the cost of the membership.

Program 4-15

```
 1  // This program displays a menu and asks the user to make a
 2  // selection. An if/else if statement determines which item
 3  // the user has chosen.
 4  #include <iostream>
 5  #include <iomanip>
 6  using namespace std;
 7
 8  int main()
 9  {
10      int choice;       // Menu choice
11      int months;       // Number of months
12      double charges;   // Monthly charges
13
14      // Constants for membership rates
15      const double ADULT = 40.0;
16      const double SENIOR = 30.0;
17      const double CHILD = 20.0;
18
19      // Display the menu and get a choice.
20      cout << "\t\tHealth Club Membership Menu\n\n";
21      cout << "1. Standard Adult Membership\n";
22      cout << "2. Child Membership\n";
23      cout << "3. Senior Citizen Membership\n";
24      cout << "4. Quit the Program\n\n";
25      cout << "Enter your choice: ";
26      cin >> choice;
27
28      // Set the numeric output formatting.
29      cout << fixed << showpoint << setprecision(2);
30
31      // Respond to the user's menu selection.
32      if (choice == 1)
33      {
34          cout << "For how many months? ";
35          cin >> months;
36          charges = months * ADULT;
37          cout << "The total charges are $" << charges << endl;
38      }
39      else if (choice == 2)
40      {
```

```
41        cout << "For how many months? ";
42        cin >> months;
43        charges = months * CHILD;
44        cout << "The total charges are $" << charges << endl;
45      }
46      else if (choice == 3)
47      {
48        cout << "For how many months? ";
49        cin >> months;
50        charges = months * SENIOR;
51        cout << "The total charges are $" << charges << endl;
52      }
53      else if (choice == 4)
54      {
55          cout << "Program ending.\n";
56      }
57      else
58      {
59        cout << "The valid choices are 1 through 4. Run the\n";
60        cout << "program again and select one of those.\n";
61      }
62      return 0;
63 }
```

Program Output with Example Input Shown in Bold
```
        Health Club Membership Menu

1. Standard Adult Membership
2. Child Membership
3. Senior Citizen Membership
4. Quit the Program

Enter your choice: 3 [Enter]
For how many months? 6 [Enter]
The total charges are $180.00
```

Notice that three `double` constants `ADULT`, `CHILD`, and `SENIOR` are defined in lines 15 through 17. These constants hold the monthly membership rates for adult, child, and senior citizen memberships.

Also notice that the program lets the user know when an invalid choice is made. If a number other than 1, 2, 3, or 4 is entered, an error message is printed. This is known as *input validation*.

 Checkpoint

4.16   Program 4-14 asks the user for a numeric test score and displays the letter grade for that score. Modify it so an error message is displayed if the user enters a test score less than 0.

4.17   What will the following program display?

```cpp
#include <iostream>
using namespace std;

int main()
{
    int funny = 7, serious = 15;

    funny = serious % 2;
    if (funny != 1)
    {
        funny = 0;
        serious = 0;
    }
    else if (funny == 2)
    {
        funny = 10;
        serious = 10;
    }

    else
    {
        funny = 1;
        serious = 1;
    }
    cout << funny << "" << serious << endl;
    return 0;
}
```

4.18   The following program is used in a bookstore to determine how many discount
coupons a customer gets. Complete the table that appears after the program.

```cpp
#include <iostream>
using namespace std;

int main()
{
    int numBooks, numCoupons;

    cout << "How many books are being purchased? ";
    cin >> numBooks;
    if (numBooks < 1)
        numCoupons = 0;
    else if (numBooks < 3)
        numCoupons = 1;
    else if (numBooks < 5)
        numCoupons = 2;
    else
        numCoupons = 3;
    cout << "The number of coupons to give is " << numCoupons
        << endl;
    return 0;
}
```

If the customer purchases this many books	This many coupons are given.
1	
2	
3	
4	
5	
10	

4.19   Write nested `if` statements that perform the following test: If `amount1` is greater than 10 and `amount2` is less than 100, display the greater of the two.

4.9   Logical Operators

CONCEPT: Logical operators connect two or more relational expressions into one or reverse the logic of an expression.

In the previous section you saw how a program tests two conditions with two `if` statements. In this section you will see how to use logical operators to combine two or more relational expressions into one. Table 4-6 lists C++'s logical operators.

Table 4-6

Operator	Meaning	Effect
&&	AND	Connects two expressions into one. Both expressions must be true for the overall expression to be true.
||	OR	Connects two expressions into one. One or both expressions must be true for the overall expression to be true. It is only necessary for one to be true, and it does not matter which.
!	NOT	The ! operator reverses the "truth" of an expression. It makes a true expression false, and a false expression true.

The && Operator

The `&&` operator is known as the logical AND operator. It takes two expressions as operands and creates an expression that is true only when both sub-expressions are true. Here is an example of an `if` statement that uses the `&&` operator:

```
if (temperature < 20 && minutes > 12)
    cout << "The temperature is in the danger zone.";
```

In the statement above the two relational expressions are combined into a single expression. The `cout` statement will only be executed if `temperature` is less than 20 AND `minutes` is greater than 12. If either relational test is false, the entire expression is false and the `cout` statement is not executed.

TIP: You must provide complete expressions on both sides of the `&&` operator. For example, the following is not correct because the condition on the right side of the `&&` operator is not a complete expression.

```
temperature > 0 && < 100
```

The expression must be rewritten as

```
temperature > 0 && temperature < 100
```

Table 4-7 shows a truth table for the `&&` operator. The truth table lists all the possible combinations of values that two expressions may have, and the resulting value returned by the `&&` operator connecting the two expressions.

Table 4-7

Expression	Value of Expression
`true && false`	false (0)
`false && true`	false (0)
`false && false`	false (0)
`true && true`	true (1)

As the table shows, both sub-expressions must be true for the `&&` operator to return a true value.

NOTE: If the sub-expression on the left side of an `&&` operator is false, the expression on the right side will not be checked. Since the entire expression is false if only one of the sub-expressions is false, it would waste CPU time to check the remaining expression. This is called *short circuit evaluation*.

The `&&` operator can be used to simplify programs that otherwise would use nested `if` statements. Program 4-16 performs a similar operation as Program 4-11, which qualifies a bank customer for a special interest rate. This program uses a logical operator.

Program 4-16

```
1   // This program demonstrates the && logical operator.
2   #include <iostream>
3   using namespace std;
4
5   int main()
6   {
7      char employed,    // Currently employed, Y or N
8           recentGrad;  // Recent graduate, Y or N
9
10     // Is the user employed and a recent graduate?
11     cout << "Answer the following questions\n";
12     cout << "with either Y for Yes or ";
13     cout << "N for No.\n";
```

```
14        cout << "Are you employed? ";
15        cin >> employed;
16        cout << "Have you graduated from college ";
17        cout << "in the past two years? ";
18        cin >> recentGrad;
19
20        // Determine the user's loan qualifications.
21        if (employed == 'Y' && recentGrad == 'Y')
22        {
23           cout << "You qualify for the special ";
24           cout << "interest rate.\n";
25        }
26        else
27        {
28           cout << "You must be employed and have\n";
29           cout << "graduated from college in the\n";
30           cout << "past two years to qualify.\n";
31        }
32        return 0;
33   }
```

Program Output with Example Input Shown in Bold

```
Answer the following questions
with either Y for Yes or N for No.
Are you employed? Y [Enter]
Have you graduated from college in the past two years? N [Enter]
You must be employed and have
graduated from college in the
past two years to qualify.
```

Program Output with Example Input Shown in Bold

```
Answer the following questions
with either Y for Yes or N for No.
Are you employed? N [Enter]
Have you graduated from college in the past two years? Y [Enter]
You must be employed and have
graduated from college in the
past two years to qualify.
```

Program Output with Example Input Shown in Bold

```
Answer the following questions
with either Y for Yes or N for No.
Are you employed? Y [Enter]
Have you graduated from college in the past two years? Y [Enter]
You qualify for the special interest rate.
```

The message "You qualify for the special interest rate" is only displayed when both the expressions employed == 'Y' and recentGrad == 'Y' are true. If either of these is false, the message "You must be employed and have graduated from college in the past two years to qualify." is printed.

NOTE: Although it is similar, Program 4-16 is not the logical equivalent of Program 4-11. For example, Program 4-16 doesn't display the message "You must be employed to qualify."

The || Operator

The || operator is known as the logical OR operator. It takes two expressions as operands and creates an expression that is true when either of the sub-expressions are true. Here is an example of an if statement that uses the || operator:

```
if (temperature < 20 || temperature > 100)
    cout << "The temperature is in the danger zone.";
```

The cout statement will be executed if temperature is less than 20 OR temperature is greater than 100. If either relational test is true, the entire expression is true and the cout statement is executed.

TIP: You must provide complete expressions on both sides of the || operator. For example, the following is not correct because the condition on the right side of the || operator is not a complete expression.

```
temperature < 0 || > 100
```

The expression must be rewritten as

```
temperature < 0 || temperature > 100
```

Table 4-8 shows a truth table for the || operator.

Table 4-8

Expression	Value of the Expression
true || false	true (1)
false || true	true (1)
false || false	false (0)
true || true	true (1)

All it takes for an OR expression to be true is for one of the sub-expressions to be true. It doesn't matter if the other sub-expression is false or true.

NOTE: The || operator also performs short circuit evaluation. If the sub-expression on the left side of an || operator is true, the expression on the right side will not be checked. Since it's only necessary for one of the sub-expressions to be true, it would waste CPU time to check the remaining expression.

Program 4-17 performs different tests to qualify a person for a loan. This one determines if the customer earns at least $35,000 per year, or has been employed for more than five years.

Program 4-17

```
 1   // This program asks the user for annual income and
 2   // the number of years of employment at the current
 3   // job. The || operator is used in an if statement that
 4   // determines if the income is at least $35,000 or the time
 5   // on the job is more than 5 years.
 6   #include <iostream>
 7   using namespace std;
 8
 9   int main()
10   {
11      double income;  // Annual income
12      int years;      // Years at the current job
13
14      // Get the annual income
15      cout << "What is your annual income? ";
16      cin >> income;
17
18      // Get the number of years at the current job.
19      cout << "How many years have you worked at "
20           << "your current job? ";
21      cin >> years;
22
23      // Determine the user's loan qualifications.
24      if (income >= 35000 || years > 5)
25         cout << "You qualify.\n";
26      else
27      {
28         cout << "You must earn at least $35,000 or have\n";
29         cout << "been employed for more than 5 years.\n";
30      }
31      return 0;
32   }
```

Program Output with Example Input Shown in Bold
What is your annual income? **40000 [Enter]**
How many years have you worked at your current job? **2 [Enter]**
You qualify.

Program Output with Example Input Shown in Bold
What is your annual income? **20000 [Enter]**
How many years have you worked at your current job? **7 [Enter]**
You qualify.

Program Output with Example Input Shown in Bold
What is your annual income? **30000 [Enter]**
How many years have you worked at your current job? **3 [Enter]**
You must earn at least $35,000 or have
been employed for more than 5 years.

The message "You qualify\n." is displayed when either or both the expressions income >= 35000 or years > 5 are true. If both of these are false, the disqualifying message is printed.

The ! Operator

The ! operator performs a logical NOT operation. It takes an operand and reverses its truth or falsehood. In other words, if the expression is true, the ! operator returns false, and if the expression is false, it returns true. Here is an if statement using the ! operator:

```
if (!(temperature > 100))
    cout << "You are below the maximum temperature.\n";
```

First, the expression (temperature > 100) is tested to be true or false. Then the ! operator is applied to that value. If the expression (temperature > 100) is true, the ! operator returns false. If it is false, the ! operator returns true. In the example, it is equivalent to asking "is the temperature not greater than 100?"

Table 4-9 shows a truth table for the ! operator.

Table 4-9

Expression	Value of the Expression
!true	false (0)
!false	true (1)

Program 4-18 performs the same task as Program 4-17. The if statement, however, uses the ! operator to determine if the user does *not* make at least $35,000 or has *not* been on the job more than five years.

Program 4-18

```
 1   // This program asks the user for his or her annual income and
 2   // the number years the user been employed at the current
 3   // job. The ! operator reverses the logic of the expression
 4   // in the if/else statement.
 5   #include <iostream>
 6   using namespace std;
 7
 8   int main()
 9   {
10      double income;  // Annual income
11      int years;      // Years at the current job
12
13      // Get the annual income
14      cout << "What is your annual income? ";
15      cin >> income;
16
17      // Get the number of years at the current job.
18      cout << "How many years have you worked at "
19           << "your current job? ";
20      cin >> years;
21
22      // Determine the user's loan qualifications.
```

```
23      if (!(income >= 35000 || years > 5))
24      {
25         cout << "You must earn at least $35,000 or have\n";
26         cout << "been employed for more than 5 years.\n";
27      }
28      else
29         cout << "You qualify.\n";
30      return 0;
31   }
```

The output of Program 4-18 is the same as Program 4-17.

Precedence and Associativity of Logical Operators

Table 4-10 shows the precedence of C++'s logical operators, from highest to lowest.

Table 4-10

Logical Operators in Order of Precedence
!
&&
||

The ! operator has a higher precedence than many of the C++ operators. To avoid an error, you should always enclose its operand in parentheses unless you intend to apply it to a variable or a simple expression with no other operators. For example, consider the following expressions:

```
!(x > 2)
!x > 2
```

The first expression applies the ! operator to the expression x > 2. It is asking "is x not greater than 2?" The second expression, however, applies the ! operator to x only. It is asking "is the logical negation of x greater than 2?" Suppose x is set to 5. Since 5 is non-zero, it would be considered true, so the ! operator would reverse it to false, which is 0. The > operator would then determine if 0 is greater than 2. To avoid a catastrophe like this, always use parentheses!

The && and || operators rank lower in precedence than the relational operators, so precedence problems are less likely to occur. If you feel unsure, however, it doesn't hurt to use parentheses anyway.

```
(a > b) && (x < y)     is the same as     a > b && x < y
(x == y) || (b > a)    is the same as     x == y || b > a
```

The logical operators have left-to-right associativity. In the following expression, a < b is evaluated before y == z.

```
a < b || y == z
```

In the following expression, y == z is evaluated first, however, because the && operator has higher precedence than ||.

```
a < b || y == z && m > j
```

The expression is equivalent to

```
(a < b) || ((y == z) && (m > j))
```

4.10 Checking Numeric Ranges with Logical Operators

CONCEPT: Logical operators are effective for determining whether a number is in or out of a range.

When determining whether a number is inside a numeric range, it's best to use the && operator. For example, the following if statement checks the value in x to determine whether it is in the range of 20 through 40:

```
if (x >= 20 && x <= 40)
    cout << x << " is in the acceptable range.\n";
```

The expression in the if statement will be true only when x is both greater than or equal to 20 AND less than or equal to 40. x must be within the range of 20 through 40 for this expression to be true.

When determining whether a number is outside a range, the || operator is best to use. The following statement determines whether x is outside the range of 20 to 40:

```
if (x < 20 || x > 40)
    cout << x << " is outside the acceptable range.\n";
```

It's important not to get the logic of these logical operators confused. For example, the following if statement would never test true:

```
if (x < 20 && x > 40)
    cout << x << " is outside the acceptable range.\n";
```

Obviously, x cannot be less than 20 and at the same time greater than 40.

NOTE: C++ does not allow you to check numeric ranges with expressions such as 5 < x < 20. Instead, you must use a logical operator to connect two relational expressions, as previously discussed.

Checkpoint

4.20   What is the disadvantage of using the && logical operator in Program 4-16 instead of the nested if statement in Program 4-11?

4.21   The following truth table shows various combinations of the values true and false connected by a logical operator. Complete the table by indicating if the result of such a combination is TRUE or FALSE.

Logical Expression	Result (true or false)
true && false	
true && true	
false && true	
false && false	
true || false	
true || true	
false || true	
false || false	
!true	
!false	

4.22 Assume the variables a = 2, b = 4, and c = 6. Indicate by circling the T or F if each of the following conditions is true or false:

```
a == 4 || b > 2        T    F
6 <= c && a > 3        T    F
1 != b && c != 3       T    F
a >= -1 || a <= b      T    F
!(a > 2)               T    F
```

4.23 Write an `if` statement that prints the message "The number is valid" if the variable `speed` is within the range 0 through 200.

4.24 Write an `if` statement that prints the message "The number is not valid" if the variable `speed` is outside the range 0 through 200.

Focus on Software Engineering: Validating User Input

CONCEPT: As long as the user of a program enters bad input, the program will produce bad output. Programs should be written to filter out bad input.

Perhaps the most famous saying of the computer world is "garbage in, garbage out." The integrity of a program's output is only as good as its input, so you should try to make sure garbage does not go into your programs. *Input validation* is the process of inspecting data given to a program by the user and determining if it is valid. A good program should give clear instructions about the kind of input that is acceptable, and not assume the user has followed those instructions. Here are just a few examples of input validations performed by programs:

- Numbers are checked to ensure they are within a range of possible values. For example, there are 168 hours in a week. It is not possible for a person to be at work longer than 168 hours in one week.
- Values are checked for their "reasonableness." Although it might be possible for a person to be at work for 168 hours per week, it is not probable.
- Items selected from a menu or other sets of choices are checked to ensure they are available options.
- Variables are checked for values that might cause problems, such as division by zero.

Program 4-19 is a modification of Program 4-13, the test scoring program. It rejects any test score less than 0 or greater than 100.

Program 4-19

```cpp
 1  // This program uses an if/else if statement to assign a
 2  // letter grade (A, B, C, D, or F) to a numeric test score.
 3  #include <iostream>
 4  using namespace std;
 5
 6  int main()
 7  {
 8      int testScore;  // To hold a numeric test score
 9
10      // Get the numeric test score.
11      cout << "Enter your numeric test score and I will\n";
12      cout << "tell you the letter grade you earned: ";
13      cin >> testScore;
14
15      if (testScore < 0 || testScore > 100) //Input validation
16      {
17          // An invalid score was entered.
18          cout << testScore << " is an invalid score.\n";
19          cout << "Run the program again and enter a value\n";
20          cout << "in the range of 0 to 100.\n";
21      }
22      else
23      {
24          // Determine the letter grade.
25          if (testScore < 60)
26              cout << "Your grade is F.\n";
27          else if (testScore < 70)
28              cout << "Your grade is D.\n";
29          else if (testScore < 80)
30              cout << "Your grade is C.\n";
31          else if (testScore < 90)
32              cout << "Your grade is B.\n";
33          else if (testScore <= 100)
34              cout << "Your grade is A.\n";
35      }
36
37      return 0;
38  }
```

Program Output with Example Input Shown in Bold
```
Enter your test score and I will tell you
the letter grade you earned: -12 [Enter]
-12 is an invalid score.
Run the program again and enter a value
in the range of 0 to 100.
```

Program Output with Example Input Shown in Bold
```
Enter your test score and I will tell you
the letter grade you earned: 81 [Enter]
Your grade is B
```

4.12 More About Variable Definitions and Scope

CONCEPT: The scope of a variable is limited to the block in which it is defined.

C++ allows you to create variables almost anywhere in a program. Program 4-20 is a modification of Program 4-17, which determines if the user qualifies for a loan. The definitions of the variables income and years have been moved to later points in the program.

Program 4-20

```
 1   // This program demonstrates late variable definition
 2   #include <iostream>
 3   using namespace std;
 4
 5   int main()
 6   {
 7      // Get the annual income.
 8      cout << "What is your annual income? ";
 9      double income;    // Variable definition
10      cin >> income;
11
12      // Get the number of years at the current job.
13      cout << "How many years have you worked at "
14           << "your current job? ";
15      int years;         // Variable definition
16      cin >> years;
17
18      // Determine the user's loan qualifications.
19      if (income >= 35000 || years > 5)
20         cout << "You qualify.\n";
21      else
22      {
23         cout << "You must earn at least $35,000 or have\n";
24         cout << "been employed for more than 5 years.\n";
25      }
26      return 0;
27   }
```

It is a common practice to define all of a function's variables at the top of the function. Sometimes, especially in longer programs, it's a good idea to define variables near the part of the program where they are used. This makes the purpose of the variable more evident.

Recall from Chapter 2 that the scope of a variable is defined as the part of the program where the variable may be used.

In Program 4-20, the scope of the income variable is the part of the program in lines 9 through 26. The scope of the years variable is the part of the program in lines 15 through 26.

The variables income and years are defined inside function main's braces. Variables defined inside a set of braces have *local scope* or *block scope*. They may only be used in the part of the program between their definition and the block's closing brace.

You may define variables inside any block. For example, look at Program 4-21. This version of the loan program has the variable years defined inside the block of the if statement. The scope of years is the part of the program in lines 17 through 26.

Program 4-21

```
1    // This program demonstrates a variable defined in an inner block.
2    #include <iostream>
3    using namespace std;
4
5    int main()
6    {
7       // Get the annual income.
8       cout << "What is your annual income? ";
9       double income;    //variable definition
10      cin >> income;
11
12      if (income >= 35000)
13      {
14         // Get the number of years at the current job.
15         cout << "How many years have you worked at "
16              << "your current job? ";
17         int years;      //variable definition
18         cin >> years;
19
20         if (years > 5)
21            cout << "You qualify.\n";
22         else
23         {
24            cout << "You must have been employed for\n";
25            cout << "more than 5 years to qualify.\n";
26         }
27      }
28      else
29      {
30         cout << "You must earn at least $35,000 to\n";
31         cout << "qualify.\n";
32      }
33      return 0;
34   }
```

Notice the scope of years is only within the block where it is defined. The variable is not visible before its definition or after the closing brace of the block. This is true of any variable defined inside a set of braces.

 NOTE: When a program is running and it enters the section of code that constitutes a variable's scope, it is said that the variable *comes into scope*. This simply means the variable is now visible and the program may reference it. Likewise, when a variable *leaves scope*, it may no longer be used.

Variables with the Same Name

When a block is nested inside another block, a variable defined in the inner block may have the same name as a variable defined in the outer block. As long as the variable in the inner block is visible, however, the variable in the outer block will be hidden. This is illustrated by Program 4-22.

Program 4-22

```
 1   // This program uses two variables with the name number.
 2   #include <iostream>
 3   using namespace std;
 4
 5   int main()
 6   {
 7       // Define a variable named number.
 8       int number;
 9
10       cout << "Enter a number greater than 0: ";
11       cin >> number;
12       if (number > 0)
13       {
14           int number;  // Another variable named number.
15           cout << "Now enter another number: ";
16           cin >> number;
17           cout << "The second number you entered was ";
18           cout << number << endl;
19       }
20       cout << "Your first number was " << number << endl;
21       return 0;
22   }
```

Program Output with Example Input Shown in Bold
```
Enter a number greater than 0: 2 [Enter]
Now enter another number: 7 [Enter]
The second number you entered was 7
Your first number was 2
```

Program 4-22 has two separate variables named number. The cin and cout statements in the inner block (belonging to the if statement) can only work with the number variable defined in that block. As soon as the program leaves that block, the inner number goes out of scope, revealing the outer number variable.

WARNING! Although it's perfectly acceptable to define variables inside nested blocks, you should avoid giving them the same names as variables in the outer blocks. It's too easy to confuse one variable with another.

Checkpoint

4.25   The following program skeleton asks the user for two numbers and then multiplies them. The first should be negative and the second should be positive. Write the input validation code for both numbers.

```cpp
#include <iostream>
using namespace std;

int main()
{
    int first, second, result;

    cout << "Enter a negative integer: ";
    cin >> first;
    cout << "Now enter a positive integer: ";
    cin >> second;
    //
    // Write input validation code
    //
    result = first * second;
    cout << first << " times " << second << " is "
        << result << endl;
    return 0;
}
```

4.26   Find and fix the errors in the following program:

```cpp
#include <iostream>
using namespace std;

int main()
{
    cout << "This program calculates the area of a "
        << "rectangle. Enter the length: ";
    cin >> length;
    cout << "Enter the width: ";
    cin >> width;
    int length, width, area;
    area = length * width;
    cout << "The area is " << area << endl;
    return 0;
}
```

4.27   What will the following program display if the user enters 40 for `test1` and 30 for `test2`?

```cpp
#include <iostream>
using namespace std;

int main()
{
    cout << "Enter your first test score: ";
    int test1;
    cin >> test1;
```

```
        cout << "Enter your second test score: ";
        int test2;
        cin >> test2;
        int sum = test1 + test2;
        if (sum > 50)
        {
            test1 += 10;
            test2 += 10;
            int sum = test1 + test2;
        }
        cout << "test 1: " << test1 << endl;
        cout << "test 2: " << test2 << endl;
        cout << "sum    : " << sum << endl;
        return 0;
    }
```

4.13 Comparing Strings

CONCEPT: You must use the strcmp library function to compare C-strings.

The relational operators can be used to compare numbers, but not C-strings. Program 4-23 asks the user to enter two strings, stores them in arrays as C-strings, and incorrectly tries to compare them using the equality operator.

Program 4-23

```
1   // This program illustrates that you cannot compare C-strings
2   // with relational operators. Although it appears to test the
3   // strings for equality, that is NOT what happens.
4   #include <iostream>
5   using namespace std;
6
7   int main()
8   {
9       const int SIZE = 40;
10      char firstString[SIZE], secondString[SIZE];
11
12      // Get two strings.
13      cout << "Enter a string: ";
14      cin.getline(firstString, SIZE);
15      cout << "Enter another string: ";
16      cin.getline(secondString, SIZE);
17
18      // Can you use the == operator to compare them?
19      if (firstString == secondString)
20          cout << "You entered the same string twice.\n";
21      else
22          cout << "The strings are not the same.\n";
23      return 0;
24  }
```

(program output continues)

Program 4-23   *(continued)*

Program Output with Example Input Shown in Bold
```
Enter a string: Alfonso [Enter]
Enter another string: Alfonso [Enter]
The strings are not the same.
```

Although two identical strings may be entered, the program will always report they are not the same. This is because of the way C++ handles C-strings. When you use the name of an array or a string literal, you are actually working with the *memory address* of the array or literal. In line 19, the following statement is comparing the memory addresses of firstString and secondString:

```
if (firstString == secondString)
```

Because the addresses of firstString and secondString are not the same (the two arrays are not located in the same place in memory), the comparison will always be false.

The strcmp Function

In C++, C-string comparisons are done with the library function strcmp. To use the strcmp function, you must include the cstring header file. Here is the function's general format:

```
strcmp(string1, string2);
```

The function compares the contents of string1 with the contents of string2 and returns one of the following values:

- If the two strings are identical, strcmp returns 0.
- If string1 < string2, strcmp returns a negative number.
- If string1 > string2, strcmp returns a positive number.

In general, strcmp compares the ASCII codes of each character in the two strings. If it goes all the way through both strings finding no characters different, it returns 0. As soon as it finds two corresponding characters that have different codes, however, it stops the comparison. If the ASCII code for the character in string2 is higher than the code in string1, it returns a negative number. But, if the code in string2 is lower than the code in string1, a positive number is returned. Here is the format of an if/else statement using strcmp to determine if two strings are equal:

```
if (strcmp(string1, string2) == 0)
    statement; // The strings are the same
else
    statement; // The strings are NOT the same
```

 TIP: It might help you to think of strcmp as using inverted logic: If the two strings are equal, strcmp returns false (zero). If the two strings are not equal, strcmp returns true (a nonzero value).

Program 4-23, which incorrectly tested two C-strings with a relational operator, can be correctly rewritten with the strcmp function, as shown in Program 4-24.

Program 4-24

```
 1   // This program correctly tests two C-strings for equality
 2   // with the strcmp function.
 3   #include <iostream>
 4   #include <cstring>
 5   using namespace std;
 6
 7   int main()
 8   {
 9      const int SIZE = 40;
10      char firstString[SIZE], secondString[SIZE];
11
12      // Get two strings
13      cout << "Enter a string: ";
14      cin.getline(firstString, SIZE);
15      cout << "Enter another string: ";
16      cin.getline(secondString, SIZE);
17
18      // Compare them with strcmp
19      if (strcmp(firstString, secondString) == 0)
20         cout << "You entered the same string twice.\n";
21      else
22         cout << "The strings are not the same.\n";
23      return 0;
24   }
```

Program Output with Example Input Shown in Bold
```
Enter a string: Alfonso [Enter]
Enter another string: Alfonso [Enter]
You entered the same string twice.
```

The function strcmp is case-sensitive when it compares the two strings. If the user enters "Dog" and "dog" in Program 4-24, it will report they are not the same. Most compilers provide nonstandard versions of strcmp that perform case-insensitive comparisons. For instance, Borland C++ has the stricmp function. It works identically to strcmp except the case of the characters is ignored.

Program 4-25 is a more practical example of how strcmp can be used. It asks the user to enter the part number of the stereo they wish to purchase. The part number contains numbers, letters, and a hyphen, so it must be stored as a string. Once the user enters the part number, the program displays the price of the stereo.

Program 4-25

```
 1   // This program uses strcmp to compare the string entered
 2   // by the user with the valid stereo part numbers.
 3   #include <iostream>
 4   #include <iomanip>
 5   #include <cstring>
 6   using namespace std;
 7
```

(program continues)

Program 4-25   *(continued)*

```
8  int main()
9  {
10     const double APRICE = 249.0, // Price A
11                  BPRICE = 299.0; // Price B
12     const int SIZE = 9;          // Array size
13     char partNum[SIZE];          // To hold the part number
14
15     // Get a part number from the user.
16     cout << "The stereo part numbers are:\n";
17     cout << "\tBoom Box, part number S147-29A\n";
18     cout << "\tShelf Model, part number S147-29B\n";
19     cout << "Enter the part number of the stereo you\n";
20     cout << "wish to purchase: ";
21     cin.width(SIZE);  // Restrict input for code safety.
22     cin >> partNum;
23
24     // Set the numeric output formatting.
25     cout << fixed << showpoint << setprecision(2);
26
27     // Determine and display the correct price.
28     if (strcmp(partNum, "S147-29A") == 0)
29        cout << "The price is $" << APRICE << endl;
30     else if (strcmp(partNum, "S147-29B") == 0)
31        cout << "The price is $" << BPRICE << endl;
32     else
33        cout << partNum << " is not a valid part number.\n";
34     return 0;
35  }
```

Program Output with Example Input Shown in Bold
```
The stereo part numbers are:
   Boom Box, part number S147-29A
   Shelf Model, part number S147-29B
Enter the part number of the stereo you
wish to purchase: S147-29B [Enter]
The price is $299.00
```

Using ! with strcmp

Some programmers prefer to use the logical NOT operator with strcmp when testing strings for equality. Because 0 is considered logically false, the ! operator converts that value to true. The expression !strcmp(string1, string2) will return true when both strings are the same, and false when they are different. The two following statements perform the same operation:

```
if (strcmp(firstString, secondString) == 0)
if (!strcmp(firstString, secondString))
```

Sorting Strings

Programs are frequently written to print alphabetically sorted lists of items. For example, consider a department store computer system that keeps customers' names and addresses in a file. The names do not appear in the file alphabetically, but in the order the operator entered them. If a list were to be printed in this order, it would be very difficult to locate any specific name. The list would have to be sorted before it was printed.

Because strcmp's return value indicates which of the two strings is higher on the ASCII chart, it can be used in programs that sort strings. Program 4-26 asks the user to enter two names. Then it prints the names alphabetically.

Program 4-26

```cpp
 1   // This program uses the return value of strcmp to alphabetically
 2   // sort two strings entered by the user.
 3   #include <iostream>
 4   #include <cstring>
 5   using namespace std;
 6
 7   int main()
 8   {
 9      const int SIZE = 30;
10      char name1[SIZE], name2[SIZE];
11
12      // Get the first name.
13      cout << "Enter a name (last name first): ";
14      cin.getline(name1, SIZE);
15
16      // Get the second name.
17      cout << "Enter another name: ";
18      cin.getline(name2, SIZE);
19
20      // Display them sorted in alphabetical order.
21      cout << "Here are the names sorted alphabetically:\n";
22      if (strcmp(name1, name2) < 0)
23         cout << name1 << endl << name2 << endl;
24      else if (strcmp(name1, name2) > 0)
25         cout << name2 << endl << name1 << endl;
26      else
27         cout << "You entered the same name twice!\n";
28      return 0;
29   }
```

Program Output with Example Input Shown in Bold
```
Enter a name (last name first): Smith, Richard [Enter]
Enter another name: Jones, John [Enter]
Here are the names sorted alphabetically:
Jones, John
Smith, Richard
```

Checkpoint

4.28   Indicate whether the following `strcmp` function calls will return 0, a negative number, or a positive number. Refer to the ASCII table in Appendix A if necessary.

A)   `strcmp("ABC", "abc");`

B)   `strcmp("Jill", "Jim");`

C)   `strcmp("123", "ABC");`

D)   `strcmp("Sammy", "Sally");`

4.29   Complete the `if` statements in the following program skeleton.

```cpp
#include <iostream>
#include <cstring>
using namespace std;

int main()
{
    const int SIZE = 20;
    char iceCream[SIZE];

    cout << "What flavor of ice cream do you like best? ";
    cout << "Chocolate, Vanilla, or Pralines and Pecan? ";
    cin.getline(iceCream, SIZE);
    cout << "Here is the number of fat grams for a half ";
    cout << "cup serving:\n";
    //
    // Finish the following if/else if statement
    // so the program will select the ice cream entered
    // by the user.
    //
    if (/* insert your code here */)
        cout << "Chocolate: 9 fat grams.\n";
    else if (/* insert your code here */)
        cout << "Vanilla: 10 fat grams.\n";
    else if (/* insert your code here */)
        cout << "Pralines & Pecan: 14 fat grams.\n";
    else
        cout << "That's not one of our flavors!\n";
    return 0;
}
```

4.14   The Conditional Operator

CONCEPT: You can use the conditional operator to create short expressions that work like `if/else` statements.

The conditional operator is powerful and unique. It provides a shorthand method of expressing a simple `if/else` statement. The operator consists of the question-mark (?) and the colon(:). Its format is:

```
expression ? expression : expression;
```

Here is an example of a statement using the conditional operator:

```
x < 0 ? y = 10 : z = 20;
```

The statement above is called a *conditional expression* and consists of three sub-expressions separated by the ? and : symbols. The expressions are x < 0, y = 10, and z = 20, as illustrated here:

x < 0	?	y = 10	:	z = 20;

NOTE: Since it takes three operands, the conditional operator is considered a *ternary* operator.

The conditional expression above performs the same operation as the following if/else statement:

```
if (x < 0)
    y = 10;
else
    z = 20;
```

The part of the conditional expression that comes before the question mark is the expression to be tested. It's like the expression in the parentheses of an if statement. If the expression is true, the part of the statement between the ? and the : is executed. Otherwise, the part after the : is executed. Figure 4-10 illustrates the roles played by the three sub-expressions.

Figure 4-10

If it helps, you can put parentheses around the sub-expressions, as in the following:

```
(x < 0) ? (y = 10) : (z = 20);
```

Using the Value of a Conditional Expression

Remember, in C++ all expressions have a value, and this includes the conditional expression. If the first sub-expression is true, the value of the conditional expression is the value of the second sub-expression. Otherwise it is the value of the third sub-expression. Here is an example of an assignment statement using the value of a conditional expression:

```
a = x > 100 ? 0 : 1;
```

The value assigned to a will be either 0 or 1, depending upon whether x is greater than 100. This statement could be expressed as the following if/else statement:

```
if (x > 100)
    a = 0;
else
    a = 1;
```

Program 4-27 can be used to help a consultant calculate her charges. Her rate is $50.00 per hour, but her minimum charge is for five hours. The conditional operator is used in a statement that ensures the number of hours does not go below five.

Program 4-27

```
 1   // This program calculates a consultant's charges at $50
 2   // per hour, for a minimum of 5 hours. The ?: operator
 3   // adjusts hours to 5 if less than 5 hours were worked.
 4   #include <iostream>
 5   #include <iomanip>
 6   using namespace std;
 7
 8   int main()
 9   {
10       const double PAY_RATE = 50.0;
11       double hours, charges;
12
13       cout << "How many hours were worked? ";
14       cin >> hours;
15       hours = hours < 5 ? 5 : hours; //conditional operator
16       charges = PAY_RATE * hours;
17       cout << fixed << showpoint << setprecision(2);
18       cout << "The charges are $" << charges << endl;
19       return 0;
20   }
```

Program Output with Example Input Shown in Bold
```
How many hours were worked? 10 [Enter]
The charges are $500.00
```

Program Output with Example Input Shown in Bold
```
How many hours were worked? 2 [Enter]
The charges are $250.00
```

Here is the statement in line 15, with the conditional expression:

```
hours = hours < 5 ? 5 : hours;
```

If the value in hours is less than 5, then 5 is stored in hours. Otherwise hours is assigned the value it already has. hours will not have a value less than 5 when it is used in the next statement, which calculates the consultant's charges.

As you can see, the conditional operator gives you the ability to pack decision-making power into a concise line of code. With a little imagination it can be applied to many other programming problems. For instance, consider the following statement:

```
cout << "Your grade is: " << (score < 60 ? "Fail." : "Pass.");
```

If you were to use an `if/else` statement, the statement above would be written as follows:

```
if (score < 60)
   cout << "Your grade is: Fail.";
else
   cout << "Your grade is: Pass.";
```

> **NOTE:** The parentheses are placed around the conditional expression because the `<<` operator has higher precedence than the `?:` operator. Without the parentheses, just the value of the expression `score < 60` would be sent to `cout`.

Checkpoint

4.30 Rewrite the following `if/else` statements as conditional expressions:

A)
```
if (x > y)
    z = 1;
else
    z = 20;
```

B)
```
if (temp > 45)
    population = base * 10;
else
    population = base * 2;
```

C)
```
if (hours > 40)
    wages *= 1.5;
else
    wages *= 1;
```

D)
```
if (result >= 0)
    cout << "The result is positive\n";
else
    cout << "The result is negative.\n";
```

4.31 The following statements use conditional expressions. Rewrite each with an `if/else` statement.

A) `j = k > 90 ? 57 : 12;`

B) `factor = x >= 10 ? y * 22 : y * 35;`

C) `total += count == 1 ? sales : count * sales;`

D) `cout << (((num % 2) == 0) ? "Even\n" : "Odd\n");`

4.32 What will the following program display?

```
#include <iostream>
using namespace std;

int main()
{
   const int UPPER = 8, LOWER = 2;
   int num1, num2, num3 = 12, num4 = 3;

   num1 = num3 < num4 ? UPPER : LOWER;
   num2 = num4 > UPPER ? num3 : LOWER;
   cout << num1 << " " << num2 << endl;
   return 0;
}
```

4.15   The switch Statement

CONCEPT: The switch statement lets the value of a variable or expression determine where the program will branch.

A branch occurs when one part of a program causes another part to execute. The if/else if statement allows your program to branch into one of several possible paths. It performs a series of tests (usually relational) and branches when one of these tests is true. The switch statement is a similar mechanism. It, however, tests the value of an integer expression and then uses that value to determine which set of statements to branch to. Here is the format of the switch statement:

```
switch (IntegerExpression)
{
   case ConstantExpression:
        // place one or more
        // statements here

   case ConstantExpression:
        // place one or more
        // statements here

   // case statements may be repeated as many
   // times as necessary

   default:
        // place one or more
        // statements here
}
```

The first line of the statement starts with the word switch, followed by an integer expression inside parentheses. This can be either of the following:

- a variable of any of the integer data types (including char)
- an expression whose value is of any of the integer data types

On the next line is the beginning of a block containing several case statements. Each case statement is formatted in the following manner:

```
case ConstantExpression:
     // place one or more
     // statements here
```

After the word case is a constant expression (which must be of an integer type), followed by a colon. The constant expression may be an integer literal or an integer named constant. The case statement marks the beginning of a section of statements. The program branches to these statements if the value of the switch expression matches that of the case expression.

 WARNING! The expression of each case statement in the block must be unique.

NOTE: The expression following the word case must be an integer literal or constant. It cannot be a variable, and it cannot be an expression such as x < 22 or n == 50.

An optional default section comes after all the case statements. The program branches to this section if none of the case expressions match the switch expression. So, it functions like a trailing else in an if/else if statement.

Program 4-28 shows how a simple switch statement works.

Program 4-28

```
 1   // The switch statement in this program tells the user something
 2   // he or she already knows: the data just entered!
 3   #include <iostream>
 4   using namespace std;
 5
 6   int main()
 7   {
 8      char choice;
 9
10      cout << "Enter A, B, or C: ";
11      cin >> choice;
12      switch (choice)
13      {
14         case 'A': cout << "You entered A.\n";
15                   break;
16         case 'B': cout << "You entered B.\n";
17                   break;
18         case 'C': cout << "You entered C.\n";
19                   break;
20         default:  cout << "You did not enter A, B, or C!\n";
21      }
22      return 0;
23   }
```

Program Output with Example Input Shown in Bold
```
Enter A, B, or C: B [Enter]
You entered B.
```

Program Output with Example Input Shown in Bold
```
Enter A, B, or C: F [Enter]
You did not enter A, B, or C!
```

The first case statement is case 'A':, the second is case 'B':, and the third is case 'C':. These statements mark where the program is to branch to if the variable choice contains the values 'A', 'B', or 'C'. (Remember, character variables and literals are considered integers.) The default section is branched to if the user enters anything other than A, B, or C.

Notice the break statements that are in the case 'A', case 'B', and case 'C' sections.

```cpp
switch (choice)
{
    case 'A':cout << "You entered A.\n";
            break;   ←————
    case 'B':cout << "You entered B.\n";
            break;   ←————
    case 'C':cout << "You entered C.\n";
            break;   ←————
    default: cout << "You did not enter A, B, or C!\n";
}
```

The case statements show the program where to start executing in the block and the break statements show the program where to stop. Without the break statements, the program would execute all of the lines from the matching case statement to the end of the block.

 NOTE: The default section (or the last case section, if there is no default) does not need a break statement. Some programmers prefer to put one there anyway, for consistency.

Program 4-29 is a modification of Program 4-28, without the break statements.

Program 4-29

```cpp
 1   // The switch statement in this program tells the user something
 2   // he or she already knows: the data just entered!
 3   #include <iostream>
 4   using namespace std;
 5
 6   int main()
 7   {
 8      char choice;
 9
10      cout << "Enter A, B, or C: ";
11      cin >> choice;
12      // The following switch is
13      // missing its break statements!
14      switch (choice)
15      {
16         case 'A': cout << "You entered A.\n";
17         case 'B': cout << "You entered B.\n";
18         case 'C': cout << "You entered C.\n";
19         default:  cout << "You did not enter A, B, or C!\n";
20      }
21      return 0;
22   }
```

Program Output with Example Input Shown in Bold
```
Enter A, B, or C: A [Enter]
You entered A.
You entered B.
You entered C.
You did not enter A, B, or C!
```

Without the break statement, the program "falls through" all of the statements below the one with the matching case expression. Sometimes this is what you want. Program 4-30 lists the features of three TV models a customer may choose from. The Model 100 has remote control. The Model 200 has remote control and stereo sound. The Model 300 has remote control, stereo sound, and picture-in-a-picture capability. The program uses a switch statement with carefully omitted breaks to print the features of the selected model.

Program 4-30

```
1  // This program is carefully constructed to use the "fallthrough"
2  // feature of the switch statement.
3  #include <iostream>
4  using namespace std;
5
6  int main()
7  {
8      int modelNum;  // Model number
9
10     // Get a model number from the user.
11     cout << "Our TVs come in three models:\n";
12     cout << "The 100, 200, and 300. Which do you want? ";
13     cin >> modelNum;
14
15     // Display the model's features.
16     cout << "That model has the following features:\n";
17     switch (modelNum)
18     {
19        case 300: cout << "\tPicture-in-a-picture.\n";
20        case 200: cout << "\tStereo sound.\n";
21        case 100: cout << "\tRemote control.\n";
22                  break;
23        default:  cout << "You can only choose the 100,";
24                  cout << "200, or 300.\n";
25     }
26     return 0;
27 }
```

Program Output with Example Input Shown in Bold
Our TVs come in three models:
The 100, 200, and 300. Which do you want? **100 [Enter]**
That model has the following features:
   Remote control.

(program output continues)

Program 4-30   *(continued)*

Program Output with Example Input Shown in Bold
```
Our TVs come in three models:
The 100, 200, and 300. Which do you want? 200 [Enter]
That model has the following features:
   Stereo sound.
   Remote control.
```

Program Output with Example Input Shown in Bold
```
Our TVs come in three models:
The 100, 200, and 300. Which do you want? 300 [Enter]
That model has the following features:
   Picture-in-a-picture.
   Stereo sound.
   Remote control.
```

Program Output with Example Input Shown in Bold
```
Our TVs come in three models:
The 100, 200, and 300. Which do you want? 500 [Enter]
That model has the following features:
You can only choose the 100, 200, or 300.
```

Another example of how useful this "fall through" capability can be is when you want the program to branch to the same set of statements for multiple case expressions. For instance, Program 4-31 asks the user to select a grade of pet food. The available choices are A, B, and C. The switch statement will recognize either upper or lowercase letters.

Program 4-31

```
 1   // The switch statement in this program uses the "fall through"
 2   // feature to catch both uppercase and lowercase letters entered
 3   // by the user.
 4   #include <iostream>
 5   using namespace std;
 6
 7   int main()
 8   {
 9      char feedGrade;
10
11      // Get the desired grade of feed.
12      cout << "Our pet food is available in three grades:\n";
13      cout << "A, B, and C. Which do you want pricing for? ";
14      cin >> feedGrade;
15
16      // Display the price.
17      switch(feedGrade)
18      {
19         case 'a':
20         case 'A': cout << "30 cents per pound.\n";
21                   break;
```

```
22          case 'b':
23          case 'B': cout << "20 cents per pound.\n";
24                    break;
25          case 'c':
26          case 'C': cout << "15 cents per pound.\n";
27                    break;
28          default:  cout << "That is an invalid choice.\n";
29      }
30      return 0;
31  }
```

Program Output with Example Input Shown in Bold

```
Our pet food is available in three grades:
A, B, and C. Which do you want pricing for? b [Enter]
20 cents per pound.
```

Program Output with Example Input Shown in Bold

```
Our pet food is available in three grades:
A, B, and C. Which do you want pricing for? B [Enter]
20 cents per pound.
```

When the user enters 'a' the corresponding case has no statements associated with it, so the program falls through to the next case, which corresponds with 'A'.

```
case 'a':
case 'A':  cout << "30 cents per pound.\n";
           break;
```

The same technique is used for 'b' and 'c'.

Using switch in Menu Systems

The switch statement is a natural mechanism for building menu systems. Recall that Program 4-15 gives a menu to select which health club package the user wishes to purchase. The program uses if/else if statements to determine which package the user has selected and displays the calculated charges. Program 4-32 is a modification of that program, using a switch statement instead of if/else if.

Program 4-32

```
1  // This program displays a menu and asks the user to make a
2  // selection. A switch statement determines which item
3  // the user has chosen.
4  #include <iostream>
5  #include <iomanip>
6  using namespace std;
7
8  int main()
9  {
```

(program continues)

Program 4-32   *(continued)*

```
10      int choice;         // Menu choice
11      int months;         // Number of months
12      double charges;     // Monthly charges
13
14      // Constants for membership rates
15      const double ADULT = 40.0;
16      const double SENIOR = 30.0;
17      const double CHILD = 20.0;
18
19      // Display the menu and get a choice.
20      cout << "\t\tHealth Club Membership Menu\n\n";
21      cout << "1. Standard Adult Membership\n";
22      cout << "2. Child Membership\n";
23      cout << "3. Senior Citizen Membership\n";
24      cout << "4. Quit the Program\n\n";
25      cout << "Enter your choice: ";
26      cin >> choice;
27
28      // Set the numeric output formatting.
29      cout << fixed << showpoint << setprecision(2);
30
31      // Respond to the user's menu selection.
32      switch (choice)
33      {
34         case 1:
35            cout << "For how many months? ";
36            cin >> months;
37            charges = months * ADULT;
38            cout << "The total charges are $" << charges << endl;
39            break;
40
41         case 2:
42            cout << "For how many months? ";
43            cin >> months;
44            charges = months * CHILD;
45            cout << "The total charges are $" << charges << endl;
46            break;
47
48         case 3:
49            cout << "For how many months? ";
50            cin >> months;
51            charges = months * SENIOR;
52            cout << "The total charges are $" << charges << endl;
53            break;
54
55         case 4:
56            cout << "Program ending.\n";
57            break;
58
```

```
59          default:
60              cout << "The valid choices are 1 through 4. Run the\n";
61              cout << "program again and select one of those.\n";
62      }
63
64      return 0;
65  }
```

Program Output with Example Input Shown in Bold
```
        Health Club Membership Menu

1. Standard Adult Membership
2. Child Membership
3. Senior Citizen Membership
4. Quit the Program

Enter your choice: 2 [Enter]
For how many months? 6 [Enter]
The total charges are $120.00
```

 Checkpoint

4.33   Explain why you cannot convert the following if/else if statement into a
        switch statement.

```
if (temp == 100)
    x = 0;
else if (population > 1000)
    x = 1;
else if  (rate < .1)
    x = -1;
```

4.34   What is wrong with the following switch statement?

```
switch (temp)
{
    case temp < 0 : cout << "Temp is negative.\n";
                    break;
    case temp == 0: cout << "Temp is zero.\n";
                    break;
    case temp > 0 : cout << "Temp is positive.\n";
                    break;
}
```

4.35   What will the following program display?

```
#include <iostream>
using namespace std;

int main()
{
    int funny = 7, serious = 15;

    funny = serious * 2;
    switch (funny)
```

```
      {   case 0 : cout << "That is funny.\n";
                    break;
          case 30: cout << "That is serious.\n";
                    break;
          case 32: cout << "That is seriously funny.\n";
                    break;
          default: cout << funny << endl;
      }
      return 0;
}
```

4.36   Complete the following program skeleton by writing a `switch` statement that displays "one" if the user has entered 1, "two" if the user has entered 2, and "three" if the user has entered 3. If a number other than 1, 2, or 3 is entered, the program should display an error message.

```
#include <iostream>
using namespace std;

int main()
{
    int userNum;

    cout << "Enter one of the numbers 1, 2, or 3: ";
    cin >> userNum;
    //
    // Write the switch statement here.
    //
    return 0;
}
```

4.37   Rewrite the following program. Use a `switch` statement instead of the `if/else if` statement.

```
#include <iostream>
using namespace std;

int main()
{
    int selection;

    cout << "Which formula do you want to see?\n\n";
    cout << "1. Area of a circle\n";
    cout << "2. Area of a rectangle\n";
    cout << "3. Area of a cylinder\n"
    cout << "4. None of them!\n";
    cin >> selection;
    if (selection == 1)
       cout << "Pi times radius squared\n";
    else if (selection == 2)
       cout << "Length times width\n";
    else if (selection == 3)
       cout << "Pi times radius squared times height\n";
    else if (selection == 4)
       cout << "Well okay then, good bye!\n";
    else
       cout << "Not good with numbers, eh?\n";
    return 0;
}
```

4.16   Testing for File Open Errors

CONCEPT: When opening a file you can test the file stream object to determine if an error occurred.

In Chapter 3 you were introduced to file operations and saw that the file stream member function open is used to open a file. Sometimes the open member function will not work. For example, the following code will fail if the file info.txt does not exist:

```
ifstream inputFile;
inputFile.open("info.txt");
```

You can determine when a file has failed to open by testing the value of the file stream object with the ! operator. The following program segment attempts to open the file customers.txt. If the file cannot be opened, an error message is displayed:

```
ifstream inputFile;
inputFile.open("customers.txt");
if (!inputFile)
{
    cout << "Error opening file.\n";
}
```

Another way to detect a failed attempt to open a file is with the fail member function, as shown in the following code:

```
ifstream inputFile;
inputFile.open("customers.txt");
if (inputFile.fail())
{
    cout << "Error opening file.\n";
}
```

The fail member function returns true when an attempted file operation is unsuccessful. When using file I/O, you should always test the file stream object to make sure the file was opened successfully. If the file could not be opened, the user should be informed and appropriate action taken by the program. For instance, the following program segment attempts to open the file customer.txt for output. In the event the file cannot be opened, the user is informed and given some clue as to why.

```
ofstream outputFile;
outputFile.open("customer.txt");
if (outputFile.fail())
{
    cout << "The customer.txt file could not be opened.\n";
    cout << "Perhaps the disk is full or you do not have\n";
    cout << "sufficient privileges. Contact your system\n";
    cout << "manager for assistance.\n";
}
```

 Case Study on CD: See the Sales Commission Case Study on the Student CD.

Review Questions and Exercises

Short Answer

1. Describe the difference between the `if/else if` statement and a series of `if` statements.

2. In an `if/else if` statement, what is the purpose of a trailing `else`?

3. What is a flag and how does it work?

4. Can an `if` statement test expressions other than relational expressions? Explain.

5. Briefly describe how the `&&` operator works.

6. Briefly describe how the `||` operator works.

7. Why are the relational operators called relational?

8. Why do most programmers indent the conditionally executed statements in a decision structure?

Fill-in-the-Blank

9. An expression using the greater-than, less-than, greater-than-or-equal to, less-than-or-equal-to, equal, or not-equal to operator is called a(n) _____ expression.

10. A relational expression is either _____ or _____.

11. The value of a relational expression is 0 if the expression is _____ or 1 if the expression is _____.

12. The `if` statement regards an expression with the value 0 as _____.

13. The `if` statement regards an expression with a nonzero value as _____.

14. For an `if` statement to conditionally execute a group of statements, the statements must be enclosed in a set of _____.

15. In an `if/else` statement, the `if` part executes its statement or block if the expression is _____, and the `else` part executes its statement or block if the expression is _____.

16. The trailing `else` in an `if/else if` statement has a similar purpose as the _____ section of a `switch` statement.

17. The `if/else if` statement is actually a form of the _____ if statement.

18. If the sub-expression on the left of the _____ logical operator is false, the right sub-expression is not checked.

19. If the sub-expression on the left of the _____ logical operator is true, the right sub-expression is not checked.

20. The _____ logical operator has higher precedence than the other logical operators.

21. The logical operators have _____ associativity.

22. The _____ logical operator works best when testing a number to determine if it is within a range.

23. The _____ logical operator works best when testing a number to determine if it is outside a range.

24. A variable with _____ scope is only visible when the program is executing in the block containing the variable's definition.

25. The `strcmp` function is used to compare _____.

26. An expression using the conditional operator is called a(n) _____ expression.

27. The expression that follows the `switch` statement must have a(n) _____ value.

28. The expression following a `case` statement must be a(n) _____ _____.

29. A program will "fall through" a `case` section if it is missing the _____ statement.

30. What value will be stored in the variable `t` after each of the following statements executes?

    A) `t = (12 > 1);`_____

    B) `t = (2 < 0);`_____

    C) `t = (5 == (3 * 2));`_____

    D) `t = (5 == 5);`_____

Algorithm Workbench

31. Write an `if` statement that assigns 100 to `x` when `y` is equal to 0.

32. Write an `if/else` statement that assigns 0 to `x` when `y` is equal to 10. Otherwise it should assign 1 to `x`.

33. Using the following chart, write an `if/else if` statement that assigns .10, .15, or .20 to `commission`, depending on the value in `sales`.

Sales	Commission Rate
Up to $10,000	10%
$10,000 to $15,000	15%
Over $15,000	20%

34. Write an `if` statement that sets the variable `hours` to 10 when the flag variable `minimum` is set.

35. Write nested `if` statements that perform the following tests: If `amount1` is greater than 10 and `amount2` is less than 100, display the greater of the two.

36. Write an `if` statement that prints the message "The number is valid" if the variable `grade` is within the range 0 through 100.

37. Write an `if` statement that prints the message "The number is valid" if the variable `temperature` is within the range –50 through 150.

38. Write an `if` statement that prints the message "The number is not valid" if the variable `hours` is outside the range 0 through 80.

39. Write an `if/else` statement that displays the strings in the arrays `title1` and `title2` in alphabetical order.

40. Convert the following `if/else if` statement into a `switch` statement:

```
if (choice == 1)
{
    cout << fixed << showpoint << setprecision(2);
```

```
    }
    else if (choice == 2 || choice == 3)
    {
        cout << fixed << showpoint << setprecision(4);
    }
    else if (choice == 4)
    {
        cout << fixed << showpoint << setprecision(6);
    }
    else
    {
        cout << fixed << showpoint << setprecision(8);
    }
```

41. Match the conditional expression with the `if/else` statement that performs the same operation.

    A) `q = x < y ? a + b : x * 2;`

    B) `q = x < y ? x * 2 : a + b;`

    C) `x < y ? q = 0 : q = 1;`

    ```
    ____  if (x < y)
              q = 0;
          else
              q = 1;

    ____  if (x < y)
              q = a + b;
          else
              q = x * 2;

    ____  if (x < y)
              q = x * 2;
          else
              q = a + b;
    ```

True or False

42. T   F   The = operator and the == operator perform the same operation.

43. T   F   A variable defined in an inner block may not have the same name as a variable defined in the outer block.

44. T   F   A conditionally executed statement should be indented one level from the `if` statement.

45. T   F   All lines in a block should be indented one level.

46. T   F   It's safe to assume that all uninitialized variables automatically start with 0 as their value.

47. T   F   When an `if` statement is nested in the `if` part of another statement, the only time the inner `if` is executed is when the expression of the outer `if` is true.

48. T   F   When an `if` statement is nested in the `else` part of another statement, as in an `if/else if`, the only time the inner `if` is executed is when the expression of the outer `if` is true.

49. T F The scope of a variable is limited to the block in which it is defined.
50. T F Strings may be directly compared by using the == operator.
51. T F `x != y` is the same as `(x > y || x < y)`
52. T F `y < x` is the same as `x >= y`
53. T F `x >= y` is the same as `(x > y && x = y)`

Assume the variables x = 5, y = 6, and z = 8. Indicate by circling the T or F whether each of the following conditions is true or false:

54. T F `x == 5 || y > 3`
55. T F `7 <= x && z > 4`
56. T F `2 != y && z != 4`
57. T F `x >= 0 || x <= y`

Find the Errors

Each of the following programs has errors. Find as many as you can.

58.
```cpp
// This program averages 3 test scores.
// It uses the variable perfectScore as a flag.
include <iostream>
using namespace std;

int main()
{
    cout << "Enter your 3 test scores and I will ";
        << "average them:";
    int score1, score2, score3,
    cin >> score1 >> score2 >> score3;
    double average;
    average = (score1 + score2 + score3) / 3.0;
    if (average = 100);
        perfectScore = true;  // Set the flag variable
    cout << "Your average is " << average << endl;
    bool perfectScore;
    if (perfectScore);
    {
        cout << "Congratulations!\n";
        cout << "That's a perfect score.\n";
        cout << "You deserve a pat on the back!\n";
        return 0;
    }
}
```

59.
```cpp
// This program divides a user-supplied number by another
// user-supplied number. It checks for division by zero.
#include <iostream>
using namespace std;

int main()
{
    double num1, num2, quotient;

    cout << "Enter a number: ";
    cin >> num1;
    cout << "Enter another number: ";
```

```cpp
            cin >> num2;
            if (num2 == 0)
                cout << "Division by zero is not possible.\n";
                cout << "Please run the program again ";
                cout << "and enter a number besides zero.\n";
            else
                quotient = num1 / num2;
                cout << "The quotient of " << num1 <<
                cout << " divided by " << num2 << " is ";
                cout << quotient << endl;
            return 0;
        }
```

60.
```cpp
    // This program uses an if/else if statement to assign a
    // letter grade (A, B, C, D, or F) to a numeric test score.
    #include <iostream>
    using namespace std;

    int main()
    {
        int testScore;

        cout << "Enter your test score and I will tell you\n";
        cout << "the letter grade you earned: ";
        cin >> testScore;
        if (testScore < 60)
            cout << "Your grade is F.\n";
        else if (testScore < 70)
            cout << "Your grade is D.\n";
        else if (testScore < 80)
            cout << "Your grade is C.\n";
        else if (testScore < 90)
            cout << "Your grade is B.\n";
        else
            cout << "That is not a valid score.\n";
        else if (testScore <= 100)
            cout << "Your grade is A.\n";
        return 0;
    }
```

61.
```cpp
    // This program tests two strings for equality.
    #include <iostream>
    using namespace std;

    int main()
    {
        const int SIZE = 40;
        char string1[SIZE], string2[SIZE];

        cout << "Enter a string: ";
        cin.getline(string1, 80);
        cout << "Enter another string: ";
        cin.getline(string2, 80);
        if (string1 == string2)
            cout << "The strings are the same.\n";
        else
```

```
            cout << "The strings are not the same.\n";
        return 0;
    }
```

62. ```
    // This program uses a switch-case statement to assign a
    // letter grade (A, B, C, D, or F) to a numeric test score.
    #include <iostream>
    using namespace std;

    int main()
    {
        double testScore;
        cout << "Enter your test score and I will tell you\n";
        cout << "the letter grade you earned: ";
        cin >> testScore;
        switch (testScore)
        {
            case (testScore < 60.0):
                    cout << "Your grade is F.\n";
                    break;
            case (testScore < 70.0):
                    cout << "Your grade is D.\n";
                    break;
            case (testScore < 80.0):
                    cout << "Your grade is C.\n";
                    break;
            case (testScore < 90.0):
                    cout << "Your grade is B.\n";
                    break;
            case (testScore <= 100.0):
                    cout << "Your grade is A.\n";
                    break;
            default:
                    cout << "That score isn't valid\n";
        return 0;
    }
    ```

63. The following statement should determine if x is not greater than 20. What is wrong with it?

    ```
    if (!x > 20)
    ```

64. The following statement should determine if count is within the range of 0 through 100. What is wrong with it?

    ```
    if (count >= 0 || count <= 100)
    ```

65. The following statement should determine if count is outside the range of 0 through 100. What is wrong with it?

    ```
    if (count < 0 && count > 100)
    ```

66. The following statement should assign 0 to z if a is less than 10, otherwise it should assign 7 to z. What is wrong with it?

    ```
    z = (a < 10) : 0 ? 7;
    ```
    ```

Programming Challenges

1. Minimum/Maximum

Write a program that asks the user to enter two numbers. The program should use the conditional operator to determine which number is the smaller and which is the larger.

2. Roman Numeral Converter

Write a program that asks the user to enter a number within the range of 1 through 10. Use a `switch` statement to display the Roman numeral version of that number.

Input Validation: Do not accept a number less than 1 or greater than 10.

3. Magic Dates

The date June 10, 1960 is special because when we write it in the following format, the month times the day equals the year.

6/10/60

Write a program that asks the user to enter a month (in numeric form), a day, and a two-digit year. The program should then determine whether the month times the day is equal to the year. If so, it should display a message saying the date is magic. Otherwise it should display a message saying the date is not magic.

4. Areas of Rectangles

The area of a rectangle is the rectangle's length times its width. Write a program that asks for the length and width of two rectangles. The program should tell the user which rectangle has the greater area, or if the areas are the same.

5. Body Mass Index

Write a program that calculates and displays a person's body mass index (BMI). The BMI is often used to determine whether a person with a sedentary lifestyle is overweight or underweight for his or her height. A person's BMI is calculated with the following formula:

$$BMI = weight \times 703 / height^2$$

where *weight* is measured in pounds and *height* is measured in inches. The program should display a message indicating whether the person has optimal weight, is underweight, or is overweight. A sedentary person's weight is considered to be optimal if his or her BMI is between 18.5 and 25. If the BMI is less than 18.5, the person is considered to be underweight. If the BMI value is greater than 25, the person is considered to be overweight.

6. Mass and Weight

Scientists measure an object's mass in kilograms and its weight in newtons. If you know the amount of mass that an object has, you can calculate its weight, in newtons, with the following formula:

$$Weight = mass \times 9.8$$

Write a program that asks the user to enter an object's mass, and then calculates and displays its weight. If the object weighs more than 1,000 newtons, display a message indicating that it is too heavy. If the object weighs less than 10 newtons, display a message indicating that the object is too light.

7. **Time Calculator**

VideoNote

Solving the Time Calculator problem

Write a program that asks the user to enter a number of seconds.

- There are 60 seconds in a minute. If the number of seconds entered by the user is greater than or equal to 60, the program should display the number of minutes in that many seconds.
- There are 3,600 seconds in an hour. If the number of seconds entered by the user is greater than or equal to 3,600, the program should display the number of hours in that many seconds.
- There are 86,400 seconds in a day. If the number of seconds entered by the user is greater than or equal to 86,400, the program should display the number of days in that many seconds.

8. **Sorted Names**

Write a program that asks the user to enter three names, and then displays the names sorted in alphabetical order. Assume that none of the names are the same. For example, if the user entered "Charlie," "Leslie," and "Andy," the program would display:

Andy
Charlie
Leslie

9. **Math Tutor**

This is a modification of Programming Challenge 15 from Chapter 3. Write a program that can be used as a math tutor for a young student. The program should display two random numbers that are to be added, such as:

247
+ 129

The program should wait for the student to enter the answer. If the answer is correct, a message of congratulations should be printed. If the answer is incorrect, a message should be printed showing the correct answer.

10. **Software Sales**

A software company sells a package that retails for $99. Quantity discounts are given according to the following table.

Quantity	Discount
10–19	20%
20–49	30%
50–99	40%
100 or more	50%

Write a program that asks for the number of units sold and computes the total cost of the purchase.

Input Validation: Make sure the number of units is greater than 0.

11. **Book Club Points**

Serendipity Booksellers has a book club that awards points to its customers based on the number of books purchased each month. The points are awarded as follows:

- If a customer purchases 0 books, he or she earns 0 points.
- If a customer purchases 1 book, he or she earns 5 points.
- If a customer purchases 2 books, he or she earns 15 points.
- If a customer purchases 3 books, he or she earns 30 points.
- If a customer purchases 4 or more books, he or she earns 60 points.

Write a program that asks the user to enter the number of books that he or she has purchased this month and then displays the number of points awarded.

12. **Bank Charges**

A bank charges $10 per month plus the following check fees for a commercial checking account:

$.10 each for fewer than 20 checks
$.08 each for 20–39 checks
$.06 each for 40–59 checks
$.04 each for 60 or more checks

The bank also charges an extra $15 if the balance of the account falls below $400 (before any check fees are applied). Write a program that asks for the beginning balance and the number of checks written. Compute and display the bank's service fees for the month.

Input Validation: Do not accept a negative value for the number of checks written. If a negative value is given for the beginning balance, display an urgent message indicating the account is overdrawn.

13. **Shipping Charges**

The Fast Freight Shipping Company charges the following rates:

Weight of Package (in Kilograms)	Rate per 500 Miles Shipped
2 Kg or less	$1.10
Over 2 Kg but not more than 6 kg	$2.20
Over 6 Kg but not more than 10 kg	$3.70
Over 10 Kg but not more than 20 kg	$4.80

Write a program that asks for the weight of the package and the distance it is to be shipped, and then displays the charges.

Input Validation: Do not accept values of 0 or less for the weight of the package. Do not accept weights of more than 20 Kg (this is the maximum weight the company will ship). Do not accept distances of less than 10 miles or more than 3,000 miles. These are the company's minimum and maximum shipping distances.

14. Running the Race

Write a program that asks for the names of three runners and the time it took each of them to finish a race. The program should display who came in first, second, and third place.

Input Validation: Be sure the names do not overflow the arrays. Only accept positive numbers for the times.

15. Personal Best

Write a program that asks for the name of a pole vaulter and the dates and vault heights (in meters) of the athlete's three best vaults. It should then report, in order of height (best first), the date on which each vault was made and its height.

Input Validation: Only accept values between 2.0 and 5.0 for the heights.

16. Fat Gram Calculator

Write a program that asks for the number of calories and fat grams in a food. The program should display the percentage of calories that come from fat. If the calories from fat are less than 30% of the total calories of the food, it should also display a message indicating that the food is low in fat.

One gram of fat has 9 calories, so

Calories from fat = fat grams * 9

The percentage of calories from fat can be calculated as

Calories from fat ÷ total calories

Input Validation: Make sure the number of calories and fat grams are not less than 0. Also, the number of calories from fat cannot be greater than the total number of calories. If that happens, display an error message indicating that either the calories or fat grams were incorrectly entered.

17. Spectral Analysis

If a scientist knows the wavelength of an electromagnetic wave, he or she can determine what type of radiation it is. Write a program that asks for the wavelength of an electromagnetic wave in meters and then displays what that wave is according to the chart below. (For example, a wave with a wavelength of 1E-10 meters would be an X-ray.)

18. The Speed of Sound

The following table shows the approximate speed of sound in air, water, and steel.

Medium	Speed
Air	1,100 feet per second
Water	4,900 feet per second
Steel	16,400 feet per second

Write a program that displays a menu allowing the user to select air, water, or steel. After the user has made a selection, he or she should be asked to enter the distance a sound wave will travel in the selected medium. The program will then display the amount of time it will take. (Round the answer to four decimal places.)

Input Validation: Check that the user has selected one of the available choices from the menu. Do not accept distances less than 0.

19. **The Speed of Sound in Gases**

When sound travels through a gas, its speed depends primarily on the density of the medium. The less dense the medium, the faster the speed will be. The following table shows the approximate speed of sound at 0 degrees centigrade, measured in meters per second, when traveling through carbon dioxide, air, helium, and hydrogen.

Medium	Speed (Meters per Second)
Carbon Dioxide	258.0
Air	331.5
Helium	972.0
Hydrogen	1,270.0

Write a program that displays a menu allowing the user to select one of these four gases. After a selection has been made, the user should enter the number of seconds it took for the sound to travel in this medium from its source to the location at which it was detected. The program should then report how far away (in meters) the source of the sound was from the detection location.

Input Validation: Check that the user has selected one of the available menu choices. Do not accept times less than 0 seconds or more than 30 seconds.

20. **Freezing and Boiling Points**

The following table lists the freezing and boiling points of several substances. Write a program that asks the user to enter a temperature, and then shows all the substances that will freeze at that temperature and all that will boil at that temperature. For example, if the user enters –20 the program should report that water will freeze and oxygen will boil at that temperature.

Substance	Freezing Point (°F)	Boiling Point (°F)
Ethyl alcohol	–173	172
Mercury	–38	676
Oxygen	–362	–306
Water	32	212

21. **Geometry Calculator**

Write a program that displays the following menu:

```
Geometry Calculator

    1. Calculate the Area of a Circle
    2. Calculate the Area of a Rectangle
    3. Calculate the Area of a Triangle
    4. Quit

    Enter your choice (1-4):
```

If the user enters 1, the program should ask for the radius of the circle and then display its area. Use the following formula:

$$area = \pi r^2$$

Use 3.14159 for π and the radius of the circle for r. If the user enters 2, the program should ask for the length and width of the rectangle and then display the rectangle's area. Use the following formula:

```
area = length * width
```

If the user enters 3 the program should ask for the length of the triangle's base and its height, and then display its area. Use the following formula:

```
area = base * height * .5
```

If the user enters 4, the program should end.

Input Validation: Display an error message if the user enters a number outside the range of 1 through 4 when selecting an item from the menu. Do not accept negative values for the circle's radius, the rectangle's length or width, or the triangle's base or height.

22. **Long-Distance Calls**

A long-distance carrier charges the following rates for telephone calls:

Starting Time of Call	Rate per Minute
00:00–06:59	0.12
07:00–19:00	0.55
19:01–23:59	0.35

Write a program that asks for the starting time and the number of minutes of the call, and displays the charges. The program should ask for the time to be entered as a floating-point number in the form HH.MM. For example, 07:00 hours will be entered as 07.00, and 16:28 hours will be entered as 16.28.

Input Validation: The program should not accept times that are greater than 23:59. Also, no number whose last two digits are greater than 59 should be accepted. Hint: Assuming num is a floating-point variable, the following expression will give you its fractional part:

```
num - static_cast<int>(num)
```

23. **Internet Service Provider**

    An Internet service provider has three different subscription packages for its customers:

    Package A: For $9.95 per month 10 hours of access are provided. Additional hours are $2.00 per hour.

    Package B: For $14.95 per month 20 hours of access are provided. Additional hours are $1.00 per hour.

    Package C: For $19.95 per month unlimited access is provided.

    Write a program that calculates a customer's monthly bill. It should ask which package the customer has purchased and how many hours were used. It should then display the total amount due.

    Input Validation: Be sure the user only selects package A, B, or C. Also, the number of hours used in a month cannot exceed 744.

24. **Internet Service Provider, Part 2**

    Modify the Program in Programming Challenge 23 so that it also displays how much money Package A customers would save if they purchased packages B or C, and how much money Package B customers would save if they purchased Package C. If there would be no savings, no message should be printed.

25. **Internet Service Provider, Part 3**

    Months with 30 days have 720 hours, and months with 31 days have 744 hours. February, with 28 days, has 672 hours. Enhance the input validation of the Internet Service Provider program by asking the user for the month (by name), and validating that the number of hours entered is not more than the maximum for the entire month. Here is a table of the months, their days, and number of hours in each.

Month	Days	Hours
January	31	744
February	28	672
March	31	744
April	30	720
May	31	744
June	30	720
July	31	744
August	31	744
September	30	720
October	31	744
November	30	720
December	31	744

26. **File Input (Freezing and Boiling Points Modification)**

    Modify the program that you wrote for Programming Challenge 20 (Freezing and Boiling Points) so it reads its input from a file instead of the keyboard. Perform the necessary test to determine if an error occurs when the file is opened. If an error occurs, display a message informing the user.

TOPICS

5.1 The Increment and Decrement Operators

CONCEPT: ++ and -- are operators that add and subtract 1 from their operands.

To *increment* a value means to increase it by one, and to *decrement* a value means to decrease it by one. Both of the following statements increment the variable num:

```
num = num + 1;
num += 1;
```

And num is decremented in both of the following statements:

```
num = num - 1;
num -= 1;
```

241

C++ provides a set of simple unary operators designed just for incrementing and decrementing variables. The increment operator is ++ and the decrement operator is --. The following statement uses the ++ operator to increment num:

        num++;

And the following statement decrements num:

        num--;

> **NOTE:** The expression num++ is pronounced "num plus plus," and num-- is pronounced "num minus minus."

Our examples so far show the increment and decrement operators used in *postfix mode*, which means the operator is placed after the variable. The operators also work in *prefix mode*, where the operator is placed before the variable name:

        ++num;
        --num;

In both postfix and prefix mode, these operators add 1 to or subtract 1 from their operand. Program 5-1 shows how they work.

Program 5-1

```
 1   // This program demonstrates the ++ and -- operators.
 2   #include <iostream>
 3   using namespace std;
 4
 5   int main()
 6   {
 7      int num = 4;    // num starts out with 4.
 8
 9      // Display the value in num.
10      cout << "The variable num is " << num << endl;
11      cout << "I will now increment num.\n\n";
12
13      // Use postfix ++ to increment num.
14      num++;
15      cout << "Now the variable num is " << num << endl;
16      cout << "I will increment num again.\n\n";
17
18      // Use prefix ++ to increment num.
19      ++num;
20      cout << "Now the variable num is " << num << endl;
21      cout << "I will now decrement num.\n\n";
22
23      // Use postfix -- to decrement num.
24      num--;
25      cout << "Now the variable num is " << num << endl;
26      cout << "I will decrement num again.\n\n";
27
```

```
28      // Use prefix -- to increment num.
29      --num;
30      cout << "Now the variable num is " << num << endl;
31      return 0;
32  }
```

Program Output

```
The variable num is 4
I will now increment num.

Now the variable num is 5
I will increment num again.

Now the variable num is 6
I will now decrement num.

Now the variable num is 5
I will decrement num again.

Now the variable num is 4
```

The Difference Between Postfix and Prefix Modes

In the simple statements used in Program 5-1, it doesn't matter if the increment or decrement operator is used in postfix or prefix mode. The difference is important, however, when these operators are used in statements that do more than just incrementing or decrementing. For example, look at the following lines:

```
num = 4;
cout << num++;
```

This cout statement is doing two things: (1) displaying the value of num, and (2) incrementing num. But which happens first? cout will display a different value if num is incremented first than if num is incremented last. The answer depends on the mode of the increment operator.

Postfix mode causes the increment to happen after the value of the variable is used in the expression. In the example, cout will display 4, then num will be incremented to 5. Prefix mode, however, causes the increment to happen first. In the following statements, num will be incremented to 5, then cout will display 5:

```
num = 4;
cout << ++num;
```

Program 5-2 illustrates these dynamics further:

Program 5-2

```
1   // This program demonstrates the prefix and postfix
2   // modes of the increment and decrement operators.
3   #include <iostream>
4   using namespace std;
```

(program continues)

Program 5-2   *(continued)*

```
 5
 6   int main()
 7   {
 8      int num = 4;
 9
10      cout << num << endl;    // Displays 4
11      cout << num++ << endl;  // Displays 4, then adds 1 to num
12      cout << num << endl;    // Displays 5
13      cout << ++num << endl;  // Adds 1 to num, then displays 6
14      cout << endl;           // Displays a blank line
15
16      cout << num << endl;    // Displays 6
17      cout << num-- << endl;  // Displays 6, then subtracts 1 from num
18      cout << num << endl;    // Displays 5
19      cout << --num << endl;  // Subtracts 1 from num, then displays 4
20
21      return 0;
22   }
```

Program Output

```
4
4
5
6

6
6
5
4
```

Let's analyze the statements in this program. In line 8, num is initialized with the value 4, so the cout statement in line 10 displays 4. Then, line 11 sends the expression num++ to cout. Because the ++ operator is used in postfix mode, the value 4 is first sent to cout, and then 1 is added to num, making its value 5.

When line 12 executes, num will hold the value 5, so 5 is displayed. Then, line 13 sends the expression ++num to cout. Because the ++ operator is used in prefix mode, 1 is first added to num (making it 6), and then the value 6 is sent to cout. This same sequence of events happens in lines 16 through 19, except the -- operator is used.

For another example, look at the following code:

```
int x = 1;
int y
y = x++;      // Postfix increment
```

The first statement defines the variable x (initialized with the value 1) and the second statement defines the variable y. The third statement does two things:

- It assigns the value of x to the variable y.
- The variable x is incremented.

The value that will be stored in y depends on when the increment takes place. Because the ++ operator is used in postfix mode, it acts *after* the assignment takes place. So, this code will store 1 in y. After the code has executed, x will contain 2. Let's look at the same code, but with the ++ operator used in prefix mode:

```
int x = 1;
int y;
y = ++x;        // Prefix increment
```

In the third statement, the ++ operator is used in prefix mode, so it acts on the variable x before the assignment takes place. So, this code will store 2 in y. After the code has executed, x will also contain 2.

Using ++ and -- in Mathematical Expressions

The increment and decrement operators can also be used on variables in mathematical expressions. Consider the following program segment:

```
a = 2;
b = 5;
c = a * b++;
cout << a << " " << b << " " << c;
```

In the statement c = a * b++, c is assigned the value of a times b, which is 10. The variable b is then incremented. The cout statement will display

```
2 6 10
```

If the statement were changed to read

```
c = a * ++b;
```

The variable b would be incremented before it was multiplied by a. In this case c would be assigned the value of 2 times 6, so the cout statement would display

```
2 6 12
```

You can pack a lot of action into a single statement using the increment and decrement operators, but don't get too tricky with them. You might be tempted to try something like the following, thinking that c will be assigned 11:

```
a = 2;
b = 5;
c = ++(a * b);    // Error!
```

But this assignment statement simply will not work because the operand of the increment and decrement operators must be an lvalue. Recall from Chapter 2 that an lvalue identifies a place in memory whose contents may be changed. The increment and decrement operators usually have variables for their operands, but generally speaking, anything that can go on the left side of an = operator is legal.

Using ++ and -- in Relational Expressions

Sometimes you will see code where the ++ and -- operators are used in relational expressions. Just as in mathematical expressions, the difference between postfix and prefix mode is critical. Consider the following program segment:

```
x = 10;
if (x++ > 10)
    cout << "x is greater than 10.\n";
```

Two operations are happening in this `if` statement: (1) The value in `x` is tested to determine if it is greater than 10, and (2) `x` is incremented. Because the increment operator is used in postfix mode, the comparison happens first. Since 10 is not greater than 10, the `cout` statement won't execute. If the mode of the increment operator is changed, however, the `if` statement will compare 11 to 10 and the `cout` statement will execute:

```cpp
x = 10;
if (++x > 10)
    cout << "x is greater than 10.\n";
```

Checkpoint

5.1   What will the following program segments display?

A)
```cpp
x = 2;
y = x++;
cout << x << y;
```

B)
```cpp
x = 2;
y = ++x;
cout << x << y;
```

C)
```cpp
x = 2;
y = 4;
cout << x++ << --y;
```

D)
```cpp
x = 2;
y = 2 * x++;
cout << x << y;
```

E)
```cpp
x = 99;
if (x++ < 100)
    cout "It is true!\n";
else
    cout << "It is false!\n";
```

F)
```cpp
x = 0;
if (++x)
    cout << "It is true!\n";
else
    cout << "It is false!\n";
```

5.2   Introduction to Loops: The `while` Loop

CONCEPT: A loop is part of a program that repeats.

VideoNote

The `while` Loop

Chapter 4 introduced the concept of control structures, which direct the flow of a program. A *loop* is a control structure that causes a statement or group of statements to repeat. C++ has three looping control structures: the `while` loop, the `do-while` loop, and the `for` loop. The difference between these structures is how they control the repetition.

The while Loop

The while loop has two important parts: (1) an expression that is tested for a true or false value, and (2) a statement or block that is repeated as long as the expression is true. Figure 5-1 shows the logic of a while loop.

Figure 5-1

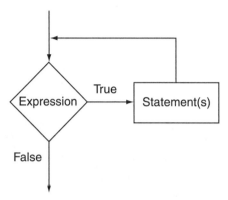

Here is the general format of the while loop:

```
while (expression)
   statement;
```

In the general format, *expression* is any expression that can be evaluated as true or false, and *statement* is any valid C++ statement. The first line shown in the format is sometimes called the *loop header*. It consists of the key word while followed by an *expression* enclosed in parentheses.

Here's how the loop works: the *expression* is tested, and if it is true, the *statement* is executed. Then, the *expression* is tested again. If it is true, the *statement* is executed. This cycle repeats until the *expression* is false.

The statement that is repeated is known as the *body* of the loop. It is also considered a conditionally executed statement, because it is executed only under the condition that the *expression* is true.

Notice there is no semicolon after the expression in parentheses. Like the if statement, the while loop is not complete without the statement that follows it.

If you wish the while loop to repeat a block of statements, its format is:

```
while (expression)
{
   statement;
   statement;
   // Place as many statements here
   // as necessary.
}
```

The while loop works like an if statement that executes over and over. As long as the expression inside the parentheses is true, the conditionally executed statement or block will repeat. Program 5-3 uses the while loop to print "Hello" five times.

Program 5-3

```
 1   // This program demonstrates a simple while loop.
 2   #include <iostream>
 3   using namespace std;
 4
 5   int main()
 6   {
 7      int number = 1;
 8
 9      while (number <= 5)
10      {
11         cout << "Hello\n";
12         number++;
13      }
14      cout << "That's all!\n";
15      return 0;
16   }
```

Program Output
```
Hello
Hello
Hello
Hello
Hello
That's all!
```

Let's take a closer look at this program. In line 7 an integer variable, number, is defined and initialized with the value 1. In line 9 the while loop begins with this statement:

```
while (number <= 5)
```

This statement tests the variable number to determine whether it is less than or equal to 5. If it is, then the statements in the body of the loop (lines 11 and 12) are executed:

```
cout << "Hello\n";
number++;
```

The statement in line 11 prints the word "Hello." The statement in line 12 uses the increment operator to add one to number. This is the last statement in the body of the loop, so after it executes, the loop starts over. It tests the expression number <= 5 again, and if it is true, the statements in the body of the loop are executed again. This cycle repeats until the expression number <= 5 is false. This is illustrated in Figure 5-2.

Each repetition of a loop is known as an *iteration*. This loop will perform five iterations because the variable number is initialized with the value 1, and it is incremented each time the body of the loop is executed. When the expression number <= 5 is tested and found to be false, the loop will terminate and the program will resume execution at the statement that immediately follows the loop. Figure 5-3 shows the logic of this loop.

Figure 5-2

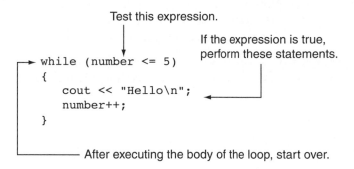

Test this expression.

If the expression is true, perform these statements.

```
while (number <= 5)
{
    cout << "Hello\n";
    number++;
}
```

After executing the body of the loop, start over.

Figure 5-3

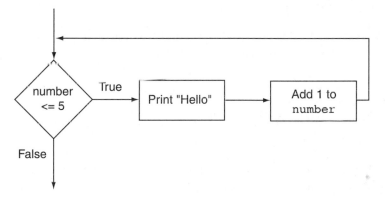

In this example, the number variable is referred to as the *loop control variable* because it controls the number of times that the loop iterates.

The while Loop Is a Pretest Loop

The while loop is known as a *pretest* loop, which means it tests its expression before each iteration. Notice the variable definition in line 7 of Program 5-3:

```
int number = 1;
```

The number variable is initialized with the value 1. If number had been initialized with a value that is greater than 5, as shown in the following program segment, the loop would never execute:

```
int number = 6;
while (number <= 5)
{
    cout << "Hello\n";
    number++;
}
```

An important characteristic of the while loop is that the loop will never iterate if the test expression is false to start with. If you want to be sure that a while loop executes the first time, you must initialize the relevant data in such a way that the test expression starts out as true.

Infinite Loops

In all but rare cases, loops must contain within themselves a way to terminate. This means that something inside the loop must eventually make the test expression false. The loop in Program 5-3 stops when the expression number <= 5 is false.

If a loop does not have a way of stopping, it is called an infinite loop. An *infinite loop* continues to repeat until the program is interrupted. Here is an example of an infinite loop:

```
int number = 1;
while (number <= 5)
{
    cout << "Hello\n";
}
```

This is an infinite loop because it does not contain a statement that changes the value of the number variable. Each time the expression number <= 5 is tested, number will contain the value 1.

It's also possible to create an infinite loop by accidentally placing a semicolon after the first line of the while loop. Here is an example:

```
int number = 1;
while (number <= 5);  // This semicolon is an ERROR!
{
    cout << "Hello\n";
    number++;
}
```

The semicolon at the end of the first line is assumed to be a null statement and disconnects the while statement from the block that comes after it. To the compiler, this loop looks like:

```
while (number <= 5);
```

This while loop will forever execute the null statement, which does nothing. The program will appear to have "gone into space" because there is nothing to display screen output or show activity.

Don't Forget the Braces with a Block of Statements

If you write a loop that conditionally executes a block of statements, don't forget to enclose all of the statements in a set of braces. If the braces are accidentally left out, the while statement conditionally executes only the very next statement. For example, look at the following code.

```
int number = 1;
// This loop is missing its braces!
while (number <= 5)
    cout << "Hello\n";
    number++;
```

In this code the number++ statement is not in the body of the loop. Because the braces are missing, the while statement only executes the statement that immediately follows it. This loop will execute infinitely because there is no code in its body that changes the number variable.

Another common pitfall with loops is accidentally using the = operator when you intend to use the == operator. The following is an infinite loop because the test expression assigns 1 to remainder each time it is evaluated instead of testing whether remainder is equal to 1.

```
while (remainder = 1) // Error: Notice the assignment
{
   cout << "Enter a number: ";
   cin >> num;
   remainder = num % 2;
}
```

Remember, any nonzero value is evaluated as true.

Programming Style and the while Loop

It's possible to create loops that look like this:

```
while (number <= 5) { cout << "Hello\n"; number++; }
```

Avoid this style of programming. The programming style you should use with the while loop is similar to that of the if statement:

- If there is only one statement repeated by the loop, it should appear on the line after the while statement and be indented one additional level.
- If the loop repeats a block, each line inside the braces should be indented.

This programming style should visually set the body of the loop apart from the surrounding code. In general, you'll find a similar style being used with the other types of loops presented in this chapter.

In the Spotlight:
Designing a Program with a while Loop

A project currently underway at Chemical Labs, Inc. requires that a substance be continually heated in a vat. A technician must check the substance's temperature every 15 minutes. If the substance's temperature does not exceed 102.5 degrees Celsius, then the technician does nothing. However, if the temperature is greater than 102.5 degrees Celsius, the technician must turn down the vat's thermostat, wait 5 minutes, and check the temperature again. The technician repeats these steps until the temperature does not exceed 102.5 degrees Celsius. The director of engineering has asked you to write a program that guides the technician through this process.

Here is the algorithm:

1. *Prompt the user to enter the substance's temperature.*

2. *Repeat the following steps as long as the temperature is greater than 102.5 degrees Celsius:*
    a. *Tell the technician to turn down the thermostat, wait 5 minutes, and check the temperature again.*
    b. *Prompt the user to enter the substance's temperature.*

> 3. *After the loop finishes, tell the technician that the temperature is acceptable and to check it again in 15 minutes.*

After reviewing this algorithm, you realize that steps 2a and 2b should not be performed if the test condition (temperature is greater than102.5) is false to begin with. The while loop will work well in this situation, because it will not execute even once if its condition is false. Program 5-4 shows the code for the program.

Program 5-4

```cpp
 1  // This program assists a technician in the process
 2  // of checking a substance's temperature.
 3  #include <iostream>
 4  using namespace std;
 5
 6  int main()
 7  {
 8     const double MAX_TEMP = 102.5;  // Maximum temperature
 9     double temperature;             // To hold the temperature
10
11     // Get the current temperature.
12     cout << "Enter the substance's Celsius temperature: ";
13     cin >> temperature;
14
15     // As long as necessary, instruct the technician
16     // to adjust the thermostat.
17     while (temperature > MAX_TEMP)
18     {
19        cout << "The temperature is too high. Turn the\n";
20        cout << "thermostat down and wait 5 minutes.\n";
21        cout << "Then take the Celsius temperature again\n";
22        cout << "and enter it here: ";
23        cin >> temperature;
24     }
25
26     // Remind the technician to check the temperature
27     // again in 15 minutes.
28     cout << "The temperature is acceptable.\n";
29     cout << "Check it again in 15 minutes.\n";
30
31     return 0;
32  }
```

Program Output with Example Input Shown in Bold
```
Enter the substance's Celsius temperature: 104.7 [Enter]
The temperature is too high. Turn the
thermostat down and wait 5 minutes.
Then take the Celsius temperature again
and enter it here: 103.2 [Enter]
The temperature is too high. Turn the
thermostat down and wait 5 minutes.
Then take the Celsius temperature again
and enter it here: 102.1 [Enter]
The temperature is acceptable.
Check it again in 15 minutes.
```

5.3 Using the while Loop for Input Validation

CONCEPT: The while loop can be used to create input routines that repeat until acceptable data is entered.

Perhaps the most famous saying of the computer industry is "garbage in, garbage out." The integrity of a program's output is only as good as its input, so you should try to make sure garbage does not go into your programs. *Input validation* is the process of inspecting data given to a program by the user and determining if it is valid. A good program should give clear instructions about the kind of input that is acceptable, and not assume the user has followed those instructions.

The while loop is especially useful for validating input. If an invalid value is entered, a loop can require that the user re-enter it as many times as necessary. For example, the following loop asks for a number in the range of 1 through 100:

```
cout << "Enter a number in the range 1-100: ";
cin >> number;
while (number < 1 || number > 100)
{
    cout << "ERROR: Enter a value in the range 1-100: ";
    cin >> number;
}
```

This code first allows the user to enter a number. This takes place just before the loop. If the input is valid, the loop will not execute. If the input is invalid, however, the loop will display an error message and require the user to enter another number. The loop will continue to execute until the user enters a valid number. The general logic of performing input validation is shown in Figure 5-4.

Figure 5-4

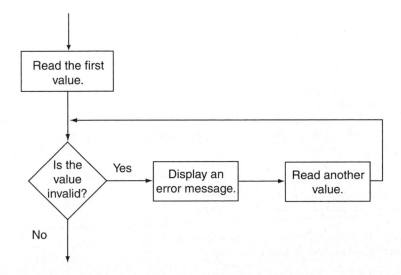

The read operation that takes place just before the loop is called a *priming read*. It provides the first value for the loop to test. Subsequent values are obtained by the loop.

Program 5-5 calculates the number of soccer teams a youth league may create, based on a given number of players and a maximum number of players per team. The program uses while loops (in lines 21 through 27 and lines 34 through 38) to validate the user's input.

Program 5-5

```cpp
1   // This program calculates the number of soccer teams
2   // that a youth league may create from the number of
3   // available players. Input validation is demonstrated
4   // with while loops.
5   #include <iostream>
6   using namespace std;
7
8   int main()
9   {
10     int players,      // Number of available players
11         teamPlayers,  // Number of desired players per team
12         numTeams,     // Number of teams
13         leftOver;     // Number of players left over
14
15     // Get the number of players per team.
16     cout << "How many players do you wish per team?\n";
17     cout << "(Enter a value in the range 9-15): ";
18     cin >> teamPlayers;
19
20     // Validate the input.
21     while (teamPlayers < 9 || teamPlayers > 15)
22     {
23        cout << "You should have at least 9 but no\n";
24        cout << "more than 15 per team.\n";
25        cout << "How many players do you wish per team? ";
26        cin >> teamPlayers;
27     }
28
29     // Get the number of players available.
30     cout << "How many players are available? ";
31     cin >> players;
32
33     // Validate the input.
34     while (players <= 0)
35     {
36        cout << "Please enter a positive number: ";
37        cin >> players;
38     }
39
40     // Calculate the number of teams.
41     numTeams = players / teamPlayers;
42
43     // Calculate the number of leftover players.
44     leftOver = players % teamPlayers;
45
```

```
46      // Display the results.
47      cout << "There will be " << numTeams << " teams with ";
48      cout << leftOver << " players left over.\n";
49      return 0;
50  }
```

Program Output with Example Input Shown in Bold
How many players do you wish per team?
(Enter a value in the range 9-15): **4 [Enter]**
You should have at least 9 but no
more than 15 per team.
How many players do you wish per team? **12 [Enter]**
How many players are available? **–142 [Enter]**
Please enter a positive number: **142 [Enter]**
There will be 11 teams with 10 players left over.

 ## Checkpoint

5.2   Write an input validation loop that asks the user to enter a number in the range of 10 through 25.

5.3   Write an input validation loop that asks the user to enter 'Y', 'y', 'N', or 'n'.

5.4   Write an input validation loop that asks the user to enter "Yes" or "No".

 # 5.4   Counters

CONCEPT: A counter is a variable that is regularly incremented or decremented each time a loop iterates.

Sometimes it's important for a program to control or keep track of the number of iterations a loop performs. For example, Program 5-6 displays a table consisting of the numbers 1 through 10 and their squares, so its loop must iterate 10 times.

Program 5-6

```
1   // This program displays the numbers 1 through 10 and
2   // their squares.
3   #include <iostream>
4   using namespace std;
5
6   int main()
7   {
8       int num = 1; //Initialize the counter.
9
10      cout << "Number Number Squared\n";
```

(program continues)

Program 5-6   *(continued)*

```
11      cout << "-----------------------\n";
12      while (num <= 10)
13      {
14         cout << num << "\t\t" << (num * num) << endl;
15         num++; //Increment the counter.
16      }
17      return 0;
18  }
```

Program Output

```
Number          Number Squared
-----------------------------
1               1
2               4
3               9
4               16
5               25
6               36
7               49
8               64
9               81
10              100
```

In Program 5-6, the variable num, which starts at 1, is incremented each time through the loop. When num reaches 11 the loop stops. num is used as a *counter* variable, which means it is regularly incremented in each iteration of the loop. In essence, num keeps count of the number of iterations the loop has performed.

NOTE: It's important that num be properly initialized. Remember, variables defined inside a function have no guaranteed starting value.

In Program 5-6, num is incremented in the last statement of the loop. Another approach is to combine the increment operation with the relational test, as shown here:

```
int num = 0;
while (num++ < 10)
    cout << num << "\t\t" << (num * num) << endl;
```

This code will produce the same output as Program 5-6.

Notice that num is now initialized to 0, rather than 1, and the relational expression uses the < operator instead of <=. This is because of the way the increment operator works when combined with the relational expression.

The increment operator is used in postfix mode, which means it adds one to num after the relational test. When the loop first executes, num is set to 0, so 0 is compared to 10. The ++ operator then increments num immediately after the comparison. When the cout statement executes, num has the value 1. This is shown in Figure 5-5.

Figure 5-5

num is compared to 10, then it is
incremented. When the **cout** statement
executes, num is 1 greater than it was
in the relational test.

```
while (num++ <10)
   cout << num << "\t\t" << (num * num) << endl;
```

Inside the loop, num always has a value of 1 greater than the value previously compared to 10. That's why the relational operator is < instead of <=. When num is 9 in the relational test, it will be 10 in the cout statement.

5.5 The do-while Loop

CONCEPT: The do-while loop is a posttest loop, which means its expression is tested after each iteration.

The do-while loop looks something like an inverted while loop. Here is the do-while loop's format when the body of the loop contains only a single statement:

```
do
   statement;
while (expression);
```

Here is the format of the do-while loop when the body of the loop contains multiple statements:

```
do
{
   statement;
   statement;
   // Place as many statements here
   // as necessary.
} while (expression);
```

NOTE: The do-while loop must be terminated with a semicolon.

The do-while loop is a *posttest* loop. This means it does not test its expression until it has completed an iteration. As a result, the do-while loop always performs at least one iteration, even if the expression is false to begin with. This differs from the behavior of a while loop, which you will recall is a pretest loop. For example, in the following while loop the cout statement will not execute at all:

```
int x = 1;
while (x < 0)
   cout << x << endl;
```

But the `cout` statement in the following `do-while` loop will execute once because the `do-while` loop does not evaluate the expression `x < 0` until the end of the iteration.

```
int x = 1;
do
    cout << x << endl;
while (x < 0);
```

Figure 5-6 illustrates the logic of the `do-while` loop.

Figure 5-6

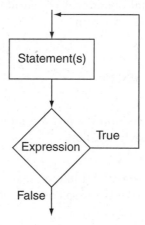

You should use the `do-while` loop when you want to make sure the loop executes at least once. For example, Program 5-7 averages a series of three test scores for a student. After the average is displayed, it asks the user if he or she wants to average another set of test scores. The program repeats as long as the user enters Y for yes.

Program 5-7

```
1    // This program averages 3 test scores. It repeats as
2    // many times as the user wishes.
3    #include <iostream>
4    using namespace std;
5
6    int main()
7    {
8        int score1, score2, score3; // Three scores
9        double average;             // Average score
10       char again;                 // To hold Y or N input
11
12       do
13       {
14           // Get three scores.
15           cout << "Enter 3 scores and I will average them: ";
16           cin >> score1 >> score2 >> score3;
17
18           // Calculate and display the average.
```

```
19        average = (score1 + score2 + score3) / 3.0;
20        cout << "The average is " << average << ".\n";
21
22        // Does the user want to average another set?
23        cout << "Do you want to average another set? (Y/N) ";
24        cin >> again;
25     } while (again == 'Y' || again == 'y');
26     return 0;
27 }
```

Program Output with Example Input Shown in Bold
Enter 3 scores and I will average them: **80 90 70 [Enter]**
The average is 80.
Do you want to average another set? (Y/N) **y [Enter]**
Enter 3 scores and I will average them: **60 75 88 [Enter]**
The average is 74.3333.
Do you want to average another set? (Y/N) **n [Enter]**

When this program was written, the programmer had no way of knowing the number of times the loop would iterate. This is because the loop asks the user if he or she wants to repeat the process. This type of loop is known as a *user-controlled loop*, because it allows the user to decide the number of iterations.

Using do-while with Menus

The do-while loop is a good choice for repeating a menu. Recall Program 4-32, which displayed a menu of health club packages. Program 5-8 is a modification of that program which uses a do-while loop to repeat the program until the user selects item 4 from the menu.

Program 5-8

```
1  // This program displays a menu and asks the user to make a
2  // selection. An if/else if statement determines which item
3  // the user has chosen.
4  #include <iostream>
5  #include <iomanip>
6  using namespace std;
7
8  int main()
9  {
10     int choice;       // Menu choice
11     int months;       // Number of months
12     double charges;   // Monthly charges
13
14     // Constants for membership rates
15     const double ADULT = 40.0;
16     const double SENIOR = 30.0;
17     const double CHILD = 20.0;
18
```

(program continues)

Program 5-8   *(continued)*

```cpp
19    // Set the numeric output formatting.
20    cout << fixed << showpoint << setprecision(2);
21
22    do
23    {
24       // Display the menu and get a choice.
25       cout << "\n\t\tHealth Club Membership Menu\n\n";
26       cout << "1. Standard Adult Membership\n";
27       cout << "2. Child Membership\n";
28       cout << "3. Senior Citizen Membership\n";
29       cout << "4. Quit the Program\n\n";
30       cout << "Enter your choice: ";
31       cin >> choice;
32
33       // Validate the menu selection.
34       while (choice < 1 || choice > 4)
35       {
36          cout << "Please enter 1, 2, 3, or 4: ";
37          cin >> choice;
38       }
39
40       // Respond to the user's menu selection.
41       switch (choice)
42       {
43         case 1:
44            cout << "For how many months? ";
45            cin >> months;
46            charges = months * ADULT;
47            cout << "The total charges are $"
48                 << charges << endl;
49            break;
50
51         case 2:
52             cout << "For how many months? ";
53             cin >> months;
54             charges = months * CHILD;
55             cout << "The total charges are $"
56                  << charges << endl;
57            break;
58
59         case 3:
60            cout << "For how many months? ";
61            cin >> months;
62            charges = months * SENIOR;
63            cout << "The total charges are $"
64                 << charges << endl;
65           break;
66
67         case 4:
68             cout << "Program ending.\n";
```

```
69            break;
70        }
71
72    } while (choice != 4);
73
74    return 0;
75 }
```

Program Output with Example Input Shown in Bold

```
            Health Club Membership Menu

1. Standard Adult Membership
2. Child Membership
3. Senior Citizen Membership
4. Quit the Program

Enter your choice: 1 [Enter]
For how many months? 12 [Enter]
The total charges are $480.00

            Health Club Membership Menu

1. Standard Adult Membership
2. Child Membership
3. Senior Citizen Membership
4. Quit the Program

Enter your choice: 4 [Enter]
Program ending.
```

 Checkpoint

5.5   What will the following program segments display?

A)
```
int count = 10;
do
    cout << "Hello World\n";
while (count++ < 1);
```

B)
```
int v = 0;
do
    cout << v++;
while (v < 5);
```

C)
```
int count = 0, funny = 1, serious = 0, limit = 4;
do
{
    funny++;
    serious += 2;
} while (count++ < limit);
cout << funny << " " << serious << " ";
cout << count << endl;
```

5.6   The for Loop

> **CONCEPT:** The for loop is ideal for performing a known number of iterations.

In general, there are two categories of loops: conditional loops and count-controlled loops. A *conditional loop* executes as long as a particular condition exists. For example, an input validation loop executes as long as the input value is invalid. When you write a conditional loop, you have no way of knowing the number of times it will iterate.

VideoNote

The for Loop

Sometimes you know the exact number of iterations that a loop must perform. A loop that repeats a specific number of times is known as a *count-controlled loop*. For example, if a loop asks the user to enter the sales amounts for each month in the year, it will iterate twelve times. In essence, the loop counts to twelve and asks the user to enter a sales amount each time it makes a count. A count-controlled loop must possess three elements:

1. It must initialize a counter variable to a starting value.

2. It must test the counter variable by comparing it to a maximum value. When the counter variable reaches its maximum value, the loop terminates.

3. It must update the counter variable during each iteration. This is usually done by incrementing the variable.

Count-controlled loops are so common that C++ provides a type of loop specifically for them. It is known as the for loop. The for loop is specifically designed to initialize, test, and update a counter variable. Here is the format of the for loop when it is used to repeat a single statement:

```
for (initialization; test; update)
    statement;
```

The format of the for loop when it is used to repeat a block is

```
for (initialization; test; update)
{
    statement;
    statement;
    // Place as many statements here
    // as necessary.
}
```

The first line of the for loop is the *loop header*. After the key word for, there are three expressions inside the parentheses, separated by semicolons. (Notice there is not a semicolon after the third expression.) The first expression is the *initialization expression*. It is normally used to initialize a counter variable to its starting value. This is the first action performed by the loop, and it is only done once. The second expression is the *test expression*. This is an expression that controls the execution of the loop. As long as this expression is true, the body of the for loop will repeat. The for loop is a pretest loop, so it evaluates the test expression before each iteration. The third expression is the *update expression.* It executes at the end of each iteration. Typically, this is a statement that increments the loop's counter variable.

Here is an example of a simple `for` loop that prints "Hello" five times:

```
for (count = 1; count <= 5; count++)
    cout << "Hello" << endl;
```

In this loop, the initialization expression is `count = 1`, the test expression is `count <= 5`, and the update expression is `count++`. The body of the loop has one statement, which is the `cout` statement. Figure 5-7 illustrates the sequence of events that takes place during the loop's execution. Notice that Steps 2 through 4 are repeated as long as the test expression is `true`.

Figure 5-7

Step 1: Perform the initialization expression.

Step 2: Evaluate the test expression. If it is true, go to Step 3. Otherwise, terminate the loop.

```
for (count = 1; count <= 5; count++)
    cout << "Hello" << endl;
```

Step 3: Execute the body of the loop.

Step 4: Perform the update expression, then go back to Step 2.

Figure 5-8 shows the loop's logic in the form of a flowchart.

Figure 5-8

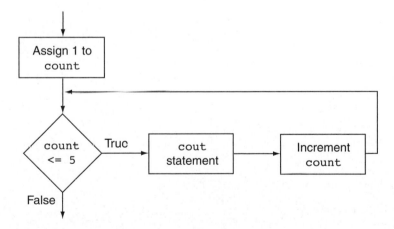

Notice how the counter variable, `count`, is used to control the number of times that the loop iterates. During the execution of the loop, this variable takes on the values 1 through 5, and when the test expression `count <= 5` is `false`, the loop terminates. Also notice that in this example the `count` variable is used only in the loop header, to control the number of loop iterations. It is not used for any other purpose. It is also possible to use the counter variable within the body of the loop. For example, look at the following code:

```
for (number = 1; number <= 10; number++)
   cout << number << " " << endl;
```

The counter variable in this loop is number. In addition to controlling the number of iterations, it is also used in the body of the loop. This loop will produce the following output:

```
1 2 3 4 5 6 7 8 9 10
```

As you can see, the loop displays the contents of the number variable during each iteration. Program 5-9 shows another example of a for loop that uses its counter variable within the body of the loop. This is yet another program that displays a table showing the numbers 1 through 10 and their squares.

Program 5-9

```
 1  // This program displays the numbers 1 through 10 and
 2  // their squares.
 3  #include <iostream>
 4  using namespace std;
 5
 6  int main()
 7  {
 8     int num;
 9
10     cout << "Number      Number Squared\n";
11     cout << "------------------------\n";
12
13     for (num = 1; num <= 10; num++)
14        cout << num << "\t\t" << (num * num) << endl;
15     return 0;
16  }
```

Program Output

```
Number      Number Squared
------------------------
1            1
2            4
3            9
4            16
5            25
6            36
7            49
8            64
9            81
10           100
```

Figure 5-9 illustrates the sequence of events performed by this for loop, and Figure 5-10 shows the logic of the loop as a flowchart.

Figure 5-9

Step 1: Perform the initialization expression.

> **Step 2:** Evaluate the test expression. If it is true, go to Step 3.
>   Otherwise, terminate the loop.

```
for (num = 1; num <= 10; num++)
    cout << num << "\t\t" << (num * num) << endl; ←—— Step 3: Execute the body of the loop.
```

Step 4: Perform the update expression,
            then go back to Step 2.

Figure 5-10

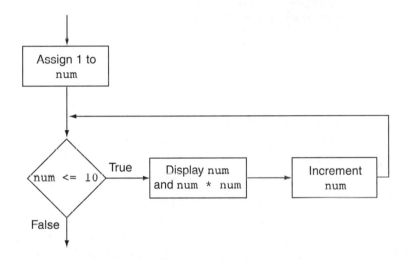

Using the for Loop Instead of while or do-while

You should use the for loop instead of the while or do-while loop in any situation that clearly requires an initialization, uses a false condition to stop the loop, and requires an update to occur at the end of each loop iteration. Program 5-9 is a perfect example. It requires that the num variable be initialized to 1, it stops the loop when the expression num <= 10 is false, and it increments num at the end of each loop iteration.

Recall that when we first introduced the idea of a counter variable we examined Program 5-6, which uses a while loop to display the table of numbers and their squares. Because the loop in that program requires an initialization, uses a false test expression to stop, and performs an increment at the end of each iteration, it can easily be converted to a for loop. Figure 5-11 shows how the while loop in Program 5-6 and the for loop in Program 5-9 each have initialization, test, and update expressions.

Figure 5-11

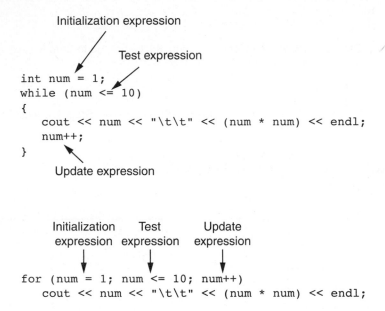

The `for` Loop Is a Pretest Loop

Because the `for` loop tests its test expression before it performs an iteration, it is a pretest loop. It is possible to write a `for` loop in such a way that it will never iterate. Here is an example:

```
for (count = 11; count <= 10; count++)
    cout << "Hello" << endl;
```

Because the variable `count` is initialized to a value that makes the test expression false from the beginning, this loop terminates as soon as it begins.

Avoid Modifying the Counter Variable in the Body of the `for` Loop

Be careful not to place a statement that modifies the counter variable in the body of the `for` loop. All modifications of the counter variable should take place in the update expression, which is automatically executed at the end of each iteration. If a statement in the body of the loop also modifies the counter variable, the loop will probably not terminate when you expect it to. The following loop, for example, increments x twice for each iteration:

```
for (x = 1; x <= 10; x++)
{
    cout << x << endl;
    x++;    // Wrong!
}
```

Other Forms of the Update Expression

You are not limited to using increment statements in the update expression. Here is a loop that displays all the even numbers from 2 through 100 by adding 2 to its counter:

```
for (num = 2; num <= 100; num += 2)
    cout << num << endl;
```

And here is a loop that counts backward from 10 down to 0:

```
for (num = 10; num >= 0; num--)
    cout << num << endl;
```

Defining a Variable in the for Loop's Initialization Expression

Not only may the counter variable be initialized in the initialization expression, it may be defined there as well. The following code shows an example. This is a modified version of the loop in Program 5-9.

```
for (int num = 1; num <= 10; num++)
    cout << num << "\t\t" << (num * num) << endl;
```

In this loop, the num variable is both defined and initialized in the initialization expression. If the counter variable is used only in the loop, it makes sense to define it in the loop header. This makes the variable's purpose more clear.

When a variable is defined in the initialization expression of a for loop, the scope of the variable is limited to the loop. This means you cannot access the variable in statements outside the loop. For example, the following program segment will not compile because the last cout statement cannot access the variable count.

```
for (int count = 1; count <= 10; count++)
    cout << count << endl;
cout << "count is now " << count << endl;    // ERROR!
```

Creating a User Controlled for Loop

Sometimes you want the user to determine the maximum value of the counter variable in a for loop, and therefore determine the number of times the loop iterates. For example, look at Program 5-10. It is a modification of Program 5-9. Instead of displaying the numbers 1 through 10 and their squares, this program allows the user to enter the maximum value to display.

Program 5-10

```
 1  // This program demonstrates a user controlled for loop.
 2  #include <iostream>
 3  using namespace std;
 4
 5  int main()
 6  {
 7      int num;        // Loop counter variable
```

(program continues)

Program 5-10   *(continued)*

```
 8      int maxValue;  // Maximum value to display
 9
10      // Get the maximum value to display.
11      cout << "I will display a table of numbers and\n";
12      cout << "their squares. How high should I go? ";
13      cin >> maxValue;
14
15      cout << "\nNumber     Number Squared\n";
16      cout << "-------------------------\n";
17
18      for (num = 1; num <= maxValue; num++)
19         cout << num << "\t\t" << (num * num) << endl;
20      return 0;
21   }
```

Program Output with Example Input Shown in Bold
```
I will display a table of numbers and
their squares. How high should I go? 5 [Enter]

Number     Number Squared
-------------------------
1              1
2              4
3              9
4              16
5              25
```

Before the loop, this program asks the user to enter the highest value to display. This value is stored in the maxValue variable:

```
cout << "I will display a table of numbers and\n";
cout << "their squares. How high should I go? ";
cin >> maxValue;
```

The for loop's test expression then uses this value as the upper limit for the control variable:

```
for (num = 1; num <= maxValue; num++)
```

In this loop, the num variable takes on the values 1 through maxValue, and then the loop terminates.

Using Multiple Statements in the Initialization and Update Expressions

It is possible to execute more than one statement in the initialization expression and the update expression. When using multiple statements in either of these expressions, simply separate the statements with commas. For example, look at the loop in the following code, which has two statements in the initialization expression.

```
int x, y;
for (x = 1, y = 1; x <= 5; x++)
{
```

```
        cout << x << " plus " << y
             << " equals " << (x + y)
             << endl;
    }
```

This loop's initialization expression is

```
    x = 1, y = 1
```

This initializes two variables, x and y. The output produced by this loop is

```
    1 plus 1 equals 2
    2 plus 1 equals 3
    3 plus 1 equals 4
    4 plus 1 equals 5
    5 plus 1 equals 6
```

We can further modify the loop to execute two statements in the update expression. Here is an example:

```
    int x, y;
    for (x = 1, y = 1; x <= 5; x++, y++)
    {
        cout << x << " plus " << y
             << " equals " << (x + y)
             << endl;
    }
```

The loop's update expression is

```
    x++, y++
```

This update expression increments both the x and y variables. The output produced by this loop is

```
    1 plus 1 equals 2
    2 plus 2 equals 4
    3 plus 3 equals 6
    4 plus 4 equals 8
    5 plus 5 equals 10
```

Connecting multiple statements with commas works well in the initialization and update expressions, but do *not* try to connect multiple expressions this way in the test expression. If you wish to combine multiple expressions in the test expression, you must use the && or || operators.

Omitting the for Loop's Expressions

The initialization expression may be omitted from inside the for loop's parentheses if it has already been performed or no initialization is needed. Here is an example of the loop in Program 5-10 with the initialization being performed prior to the loop:

```
    int num = 1;
    for ( ; num <= maxValue; num++)
       cout << num << "\t\t" << (num * num) << endl;
```

You may also omit the update expression if it is being performed elsewhere in the loop or if none is needed. Although this type of code is not recommended, the following `for` loop works just like a `while` loop:

```
int num = 1;
for ( ; num <= maxValue; )
{
    cout << num << "\t\t" << (num * num) << endl;
    num++;
}
```

You can even go so far as to omit all three expressions from the `for` loop's parentheses. Be warned, however, that if you leave out the test expression, the loop has no built-in way of terminating. Here is an example:

```
for ( ; ; )
    cout << "Hello World\n";
```

Because this loop has no way of stopping, it will display `"Hello World\n"` forever (or until something interrupts the program).

In the Spotlight:

Designing a Count-Controlled Loop with the `for` Statement

Your friend Amanda just inherited a European sports car from her uncle. Amanda lives in the United States, and she is afraid she will get a speeding ticket because the car's speedometer indicates kilometers per hour. She has asked you to write a program that displays a table of speeds in kilometers per hour with their values converted to miles per hour. The formula for converting kilometers per hour to miles per hour is:

$MPH = KPH * 0.6214$

In the formula, *MPH* is the speed in miles per hour and *KPH* is the speed in kilometers per hour.

The table that your program displays should show speeds from 60 kilometers per hour through 130 kilometers per hour, in increments of 10, along with their values converted to miles per hour. The table should look something like this:

KPH	MPH
60	37.3
70	43.5
80	49.7
etc. . . .	
130	80.8

After thinking about this table of values, you decide that you will write a `for` loop that uses a counter variable to hold the kilometer-per-hour speeds. The counter's starting value will be 60, its ending value will be 130, and you will add 10 to the counter variable after each iteration. Inside the loop you will use the counter variable to calculate a speed in miles-per-hour. Program 5-11 shows the code.

Program 5-11

```
1  // This program converts the speeds 60 kph through
2  // 130 kph (in 10 kph increments) to mph.
3  #include <iostream>
4  #include <iomanip>
5  using namespace std;
6
7  int main()
8  {
9     int kph;       // To hold speeds in kph
10    double mph;    // To hold speeds in mph
11
12    // Set the numeric output formatting.
13    cout << fixed << showpoint << setprecision(1);
14
15    // Display the table headings.
16    cout << "KPH\tMPH\n";
17    cout << "--------------\n";
18
19    // Display the speeds.
20    for (kph = 60; kph <= 130; kph += 10)
21    {
22       // Calculate mph
23       mph = kph * 0.6214;
24
25       // Display the speeds in kph and mph.
26       cout << kph << "\t" << mph << endl;
27
28    }
29    return 0;
30 }
```

Program Output

```
KPH        MPH
--------------
60         37.3
70         43.5
80         49.7
90         55.9
100        62.1
110        68.4
120        74.6
130        80.8
```

Checkpoint

5.6   Name the three expressions that appear inside the parentheses in the `for` loop's header.

5.7   You want to write a `for` loop that displays "I love to program" 50 times. Assume that you will use a counter variable named `count`.

A) What initialization expression will you use?

B) What test expression will you use?

C) What update expression will you use?

D) Write the loop.

5.8   What will the following program segments display?

A) ```
for (int count = 0; count < 6; count++)
    cout << (count + count);
```

B)  ```
for (int value = -5; value < 5; value++)
    cout << value;
```

C) ```
int x;
for (x = 5; x <= 14; x += 3)
    cout << x << endl;
cout << x << endl;
```

5.9    Write a `for` loop that displays your name 10 times.

5.10   Write a `for` loop that displays all of the odd numbers, 1 through 49.

5.11   Write a `for` loop that displays every fifth number, zero through 100.

 ## 5.7   Keeping a Running Total

**CONCEPT:** A *running total* is a sum of numbers that accumulates with each iteration of a loop. The variable used to keep the running total is called an *accumulator*.

Many programming tasks require you to calculate the total of a series of numbers. For example, suppose you are writing a program that calculates a business's total sales for a week. The program would read the sales for each day as input and calculate the total of those numbers.

Programs that calculate the total of a series of numbers typically use two elements:

* A loop that reads each number in the series.
* A variable that accumulates the total of the numbers as they are read.

The variable that is used to accumulate the total of the numbers is called an *accumulator*. It is often said that the loop keeps a *running total* because it accumulates the total as it reads each number in the series. Figure 5-12 shows the general logic of a loop that calculates a running total.
```

Figure 5-12   Logic for calculating a running total

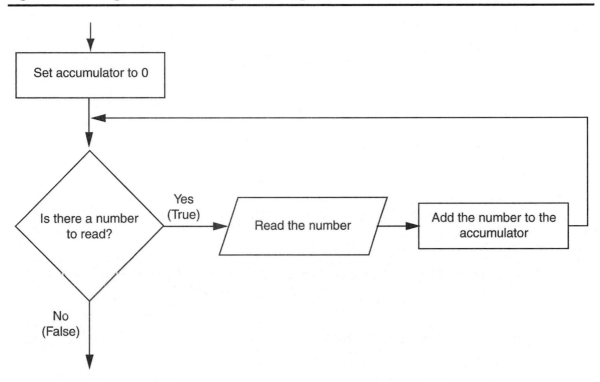

When the loop finishes, the accumulator will contain the total of the numbers that were read by the loop. Notice that the first step in the flowchart is to set the accumulator variable to 0. This is a critical step. Each time the loop reads a number, it adds it to the accumulator. If the accumulator starts with any value other than 0, it will not contain the correct total when the loop finishes.

Let's look at a program that calculates a running total. Program 5-12 calculates a company's total sales over a period of time by taking daily sales figures as input and calculating a running total of them as they are gathered

Program 5-12

```
 1   // This program takes daily sales figures over a period of time
 2   // and calculates their total.
 3   #include <iostream>
 4   #include <iomanip>
 5   using namespace std;
 6
 7   int main()
 8   {
 9      int days;            // Number of days
10      double total = 0.0;  // Accumulator, initialized with 0
11
12      // Get the number of days.
13      cout << "For how many days do you have sales figures? ";
```

(program continues)

Program 5-12   *(continued)*

```
14      cin >> days;
15
16      // Get the sales for each day and accumulate a total.
17      for (int count = 1; count <= days; count++)
18      {
19         double sales;
20         cout << "Enter the sales for day " << count << ": ";
21         cin >> sales;
22         total += sales;   // Accumulate the running total.
23      }
24
25      // Display the total sales.
26      cout << fixed << showpoint << setprecision(2);
27      cout << "The total sales are $" << total << endl;
28      return 0;
29   }
```

Program Output with Example Input Shown in Bold

For how many days do you have sales figures? **5 [Enter]**
Enter the sales for day 1: **489.32 [Enter]**
Enter the sales for day 2: **421.65 [Enter]**
Enter the sales for day 3: **497.89 [Enter]**
Enter the sales for day 4: **532.37 [Enter]**
Enter the sales for day 5: **506.92 [Enter]**
The total sales are $2448.15

Let's take a closer look at this program. Line 9 defines the days variable, which will hold the number of days that we have sales figures for. Line 10 defines the total variable, which will hold the total sales. Because total is an accumulator, it is initialized with 0.0.

In line 14 the user enters the number of days that he or she has sales figures for. The number is assigned to the days variable. Next, the for loop in lines 17 through 23 executes. In the loop's initialization expression, in line 17, the variable count is defined and initialized with 1. The test expression specifies the loop will repeat as long as count is less than or equal to days. The update expression increments count by one at the end of each loop iteration.

Line 19 defines a variable named sales. Because the variable is defined in the body of the loop, its scope is limited to the loop. During each loop iteration, the user enters the amount of sales for a specific day, which is assigned to the sales variable. This is done in line 21. Then, in line 22 the value of sales is added to the existing value in the total variable. (Note that line 22 does *not* assign sales to total, but *adds* sales to total. Put another way, this line increases total by the amount in sales.)

Because total was initially assigned 0.0, after the first iteration of the loop, total will be set to the same value as sales. After each subsequent iteration, total will be increased by the amount in sales. After the loop has finished, total will contain the total of all the daily sales figures entered. Now it should be clear why we assigned 0.0 to total before the loop executed. If total started at any other value, the total would be incorrect.

5.8 Sentinels

> **CONCEPT:** A *sentinel* is a special value that marks the end of a list of values.

Program 5-12, in the previous section, requires the user to know in advance the number of days he or she wishes to enter sales figures for. Sometimes the user has a list that is very long and doesn't know how many items there are. In other cases, the user might be entering several lists and it is impractical to require that every item in every list be counted.

A technique that can be used in these situations is to ask the user to enter a sentinel at the end of the list. A *sentinel* is a special value that cannot be mistaken as a member of the list and signals that there are no more values to be entered. When the user enters the sentinel, the loop terminates.

Program 5-13 calculates the total points earned by a soccer team over a series of games. It allows the user to enter the series of game points, then -1 to signal the end of the list.

Program 5-13

```cpp
 1  // This program calculates the total number of points a
 2  // soccer team has earned over a series of games. The user
 3  // enters a series of point values, then -1 when finished.
 4  #include <iostream>
 5  using namespace std;
 6
 7  int main()
 8  {
 9     int game = 1,    // Game counter
10         points,      // To hold a number of points
11         total = 0;   // Accumulator
12
13     cout << "Enter the number of points your team has earned\n";
14     cout << "so far in the season, then enter -1 when finished.\n\n";
15     cout << "Enter the points for game " << game << ": ";
16     cin >> points;
17
18     while (points != -1)
19     {
20        total += points;
21        game++;
22        cout << "Enter the points for game " << game << ": ";
23        cin >> points;
24     }
25     cout << "\nThe total points are " << total << endl;
26     return 0;
27  }
```

(program output continues)

Program 5-13 *(continued)*

Program Output with Example Input Shown in Bold
```
Enter the number of points your team has earned
so far in the season, then enter -1 when finished.

Enter the points for game 1: 7 [Enter]
Enter the points for game 2: 9 [Enter]
Enter the points for game 3: 4 [Enter]
Enter the points for game 4: 6 [Enter]
Enter the points for game 5: 8 [Enter]
Enter the points for game 6: -1 [Enter]

The total points are 34
```

The value -1 was chosen for the sentinel in this program because it is not possible for a team to score negative points. Notice that this program performs a priming read in line 18 to get the first value. This makes it possible for the loop to immediately terminate if the user enters -1 as the first value. Also note that the sentinel value is not included in the running total.

5.9 Using a Loop to Read Data from a File

CONCEPT: When reading a value from a file with the stream extraction operator, the operator returns a true or false value indicating whether the value was successfully read. This return value can be used to detect when the end of a file has been reached.

A loop can be used to read the items stored in a file. For example, suppose the file numbers.txt exists with the following contents.

```
8
7
3
9
12
```

As you can see, there are five numbers stored in the file. Program 5-14 uses a loop to read the five numbers and display them on the screen.

Program 5-14

```cpp
1   // This program displays five numbers in a file.
2   #include <iostream>
3   #include <fstream>
4   using namespace std;
5
6   int main()
7   {
8       ifstream inputFile;  // File stream object
```

```
 9      int number;           // To hold a value from the file
10      int count = 1;        // Loop counter, initialized with 1
11
12      inputFile.open("numbers.txt");   // Open the file.
13      if (!inputFile)                  // Test for errors.
14         cout << "Error opening file.\n";
15      else
16      {
17         while (count <= 5)
18         {
19            inputFile >> number;      // Read a number.
20            cout << number << endl;   // Display the number.
21            count++;                  // Increment the counter.
22         }
23         inputFile.close();           // Close the file.
24      }
25      return 0;
26   }
```

This program is limited, however, because it depends on the file having five numbers stored in it. If the file contains fewer than five numbers, an error will occur because the program will attempt to read beyond the end of the file. If the file has more than five numbers stored in it, the program will only display the first five. In many cases the exact number of items stored in a file is unknown and the program must have a way of detecting the end of the file. Fortunately, you can use the >> operator to do this.

The stream extraction operator (>>) not only reads data from a file, but it also returns a value indicating whether the data was successfully read or not. If the operator returns true, then a value was successfully read. If the operator returns false, it means that no value was read from the file. For example, look at the following code

```
if (inputFile >> number)
{
   // Data was successfully read from the file.
   cout << "The data read from the file is " << number << endl;
}
else
{
   // No data was read from the file.
   cout << "Could not read an item from the file.\n";
}
```

Notice that the statement that reads an item from the file is also used as the conditional expression in the if statement:

```
if (inputFile >> number)
```

This statement does two things:

1. It uses the expression inputFile >> number to read an item from the file and stores the item in the number variable. The >> operator returns true if the item was successfully read, or false otherwise.

2. It tests the value returned by the stream extraction operator.

You can use the stream extraction operator's return value in a loop to determine when the end of the file has been reached. Here is an example:

```
while (inputFile >> number)
{
    cout << number << endl;
}
```

Because the value returned from the >> operator controls the loop, it will read items from the file until the end of the file has been reached.

Program 5-15 is a modification of Program 5-14. Instead of reading the first five items in the file, however, this program reads all of the items in the file regardless of how many there are.

Program 5-15

```
 1  // This program displays all of the numbers in a file.
 2  #include <iostream>
 3  #include <fstream>
 4  using namespace std;
 5
 6  int main()
 7  {
 8     ifstream inputFile;  // File stream object
 9     int number;          // To hold a value from the file
10
11     inputFile.open("numbers.txt");     // Open the file.
12     if (!inputFile)                    // Test for errors.
13        cout << "Error opening file.\n";
14     else
15     {
16        while (inputFile >> number)     // Read a number
17        {
18           cout << number << endl;      // Display the number.
19        }
20        inputFile.close();              // Close the file.
21     }
22     return 0;
23  }
```

Checkpoint

5.12   Write a for loop that repeats seven times, asking the user to enter a number. The loop should also calculate the sum of the numbers entered.

5.13   In the following program segment, which variable is the counter variable and which is the accumulator?

```
int a, x, y = 0;
for (x = 0; x < 10; x++)
{
    cout << "Enter a number: ";
    cin >> a;
    y += a;
}
cout << "The sum of those numbers is " << y << endl;
```

5.14   Why should you be careful when choosing a sentinel value?

5.15   How would you modify program 5-13 so any negative value is a sentinel?

5.16   Assume that a file named `values.txt` exists and that it contains a series of numbers, one per line in the file. Also assume that a program can successfully execute the following statements to open the file:

```
ifstream inputFile;
inputFile.open("values.txt");
```

Write a loop that reads each number from the file and displays each number on the screen.

Focus on Software Engineering: Deciding Which Loop to Use

CONCEPT: Although most repetitive algorithms can be written with any of the three types of loops, each works best in different situations.

Each of the three C++ loops is ideal to use in different situations. Here's a short summary of when each loop should be used.

- **The `while` loop.** The `while` loop is a conditional loop, which means it repeats as long as a particular condition exists. It is also a pretest loop, so it is ideal in situations where you do not want the loop to iterate if the condition is false from the beginning. For example, validating input that has been read and reading lists of data terminated by a sentinel value are good applications of the `while` loop.
- **The `do-while` loop.** The `do-while` loop is also a conditional loop. Unlike the `while` loop, however, `do-while` is a posttest loop. It is ideal in situations where you always want the loop to iterate at least once. The `do-while` loop is a good choice for repeating a menu.
- **The `for` loop.** The `for` loop is a pretest loop that has built-in expressions for initializing, testing, and updating. These expressions make it very convenient to use a counter variable to control the number of iterations that the loop performs. The initialization expression can initialize the counter variable to a starting value, the test expression can test the counter variable to determine whether it holds the maximum value, and the update expression can increment the counter variable. The `for` loop is ideal in situations where the exact number of iterations is known.

Nested Loops

CONCEPT: A loop that is inside another loop is called a *nested loop*.

A nested loop is a loop that appears inside another loop. A clock is a good example of something that works like a nested loop. The second hand, minute hand, and hour hand all spin around the face of the clock. The hour hand, however, only makes one revolution for every 12 of the minute hand's revolutions. And it takes 60 revolutions of the second hand for the minute hand to make one revolution. This means that for every complete revolution of the hour hand, the second hand has revolved 720 times.

Here is a program segment with a `for` loop that partially simulates a digital clock. It displays the seconds from 0 to 59:

```
cout << fixed << right;
cout.fill('0');
for (int seconds = 0; seconds < 60; seconds++)
   cout << setw(2) << seconds << endl;
```

 NOTE: The `fill` member function of `cout` changes the fill character, which is a space by default. In the program segment above, the `fill` function causes a zero to be printed in front of all single digit numbers.

We can add a `minutes` variable and nest the loop above inside another loop that cycles through 60 minutes:

```
cout << fixed << right;
cout.fill('0');
for (int minutes = 0; minutes < 60; minutes++)
{
    for (int seconds = 0; seconds < 60; seconds++)
    {
        cout << setw(2) << minutes << ":";
        cout << setw(2) << seconds << endl;
    }
}
```

To make the simulated clock complete, another variable and loop can be added to count the hours:

```
cout << fixed << right;
cout.fill('0');
for (int hours = 0; hours < 24; hours++)
{
    for (int minutes = 0; minutes < 60; minutes++)
    {
        for (int seconds = 0; seconds < 60; seconds++)
        {
            cout << setw(2) << hours << ":";
            cout << setw(2) << minutes << ":";
            cout << setw(2) << seconds << endl;
        }
    }
}
```

The output of the previous program segment follows:

```
00:00:00
00:00:01
00:00:02
        .   (The program will count through each second of 24 hours.)
        .
        .
23:59:59
```

The innermost loop will iterate 60 times for each iteration of the middle loop. The middle loop will iterate 60 times for each iteration of the outermost loop. When the outermost loop has iterated 24 times, the middle loop will have iterated 1,440 times and the innermost loop will have iterated 86,400 times!

The simulated clock example brings up a few points about nested loops:

- An inner loop goes through all of its iterations for each iteration of an outer loop.
- Inner loops complete their iterations faster than outer loops.
- To get the total number of iterations of a nested loop, multiply the number of iterations of all the loops.

Program 5-16 is another test-averaging program. It asks the user for the number of students and the number of test scores per student. A nested inner loop, in lines 26 through 33, asks for all the test scores for one student, iterating once for each test score. The outer loop in lines 23 through 37 iterates once for each student.

Program 5-16

```cpp
 1  // This program averages test scores. It asks the user for the
 2  // number of students and the number of test scores per student.
 3  #include <iostream>
 4  #include <iomanip>
 5  using namespace std;
 6
 7  int main()
 8  {
 9     int numStudents,  // Number of students
10         numTests;     // Number of tests per student
11     double total,     // Accumulator for total scores
12            average;   // Average test score
13
14     // Set up numeric output formatting.
15     cout << fixed << showpoint << setprecision(1);
16
17     // Get the number of students.
18     cout << "This program averages test scores.\n";
19     cout << "For how many students do you have scores? ";
20     cin >> numStudents;
21
22     // Get the number of test scores per student.
23     cout << "How many test scores does each student have? ";
24     cin >> numTests;
25
26     // Determine each student's average score.
27     for (int student = 1; student <= numStudents; student++)
28     {
29        total = 0;       // Initialize the accumulator.
30        for (int test = 1; test <= numTests; test++)
31        {
32           double score;
33           cout << "Enter score " << test << " for ";
34           cout << "student " << student << ": ";
```

(program continues)

Program 5-16   *(continued)*

```
35              cin >> score;
36              total += score;
37          }
38          average = total / numTests;
39          cout << "The average score for student " << student;
40          cout << " is " << average << ".\n\n";
41      }
42      return 0;
43  }
```

Program Output with Example Input Shown in Bold
```
This program averages test scores.
For how many students do you have scores? 2 [Enter]
How many test scores does each student have? 3 [Enter]
Enter score 1 for student 1: 84 [Enter]
Enter score 2 for student 1: 79 [Enter]
Enter score 3 for student 1: 97 [Enter]
The average score for student 1 is 86.7.

Enter score 1 for student 2: 92 [Enter]
Enter score 2 for student 2: 88 [Enter]
Enter score 3 for student 2: 94 [Enter]
The average score for student 2 is 91.3.
```

5.12 Breaking Out of a Loop

CONCEPT: The `break` statement causes a loop to terminate early.

WARNING! Use the `break` statement with great caution. Because it bypasses the loop condition to terminate the loop, it makes code difficult to understand and debug. For this reason, you should avoid using `break` when possible. Because it is part of the C++ language, we discuss it briefly in this section.

Sometimes it's necessary to stop a loop before it goes through all its iterations. The `break` statement, which was used with `switch` in Chapter 4, can also be placed inside a loop. When it is encountered, the loop stops and the program jumps to the statement immediately following the loop.

The `while` loop in the following program segment appears to execute 10 times, but the `break` statement causes it to stop after the fifth iteration.

```
int count = 0;
while (count++ < 10)
{
    cout << count << endl;
    if (count == 5)
        break;
}
```

Program 5-17 uses the break statement to interrupt a for loop. The program asks the user for a number and then displays the value of that number raised to the powers of 0 through 10. The user can stop the loop at any time by entering Q.

Program 5-17

```
 1   // This program raises the user's number to the powers
 2   // of 0 through 10.
 3   #include <iostream>
 4   #include <cmath>
 5   using namespace std;
 6
 7   int main()
 8   {
 9      double value;
10      char choice;
11
12      cout << "Enter a number: ";
13      cin >> value;
14      cout << "This program will raise " << value;
15      cout << " to the powers of 0 through 10.\n";
16      for (int count = 0; count <= 10; count++)
17      {
18         cout << value << " raised to the power of ";
19         cout << count << " is " << pow(value, count);
20         cout << "\nEnter Q to quit or any other key ";
21         cout << "to continue. ";
22         cin >> choice;
23         if (choice == 'Q' || choice == 'q')
24            break;
25      }
26      return 0;
27   }
```

Program Output with Example Input Shown in Bold
```
Enter a number: 2 [Enter]
This program will raise 2 to the powers of 0 through 10.
2 raised to the power of 0 is 1
Enter Q to quit or any other key to continue. C [Enter]
2 raised to the power of 1 is 2
Enter Q to quit or any other key to continue. C [Enter]
2 raised to the power of 2 is 4
Enter Q to quit or any other key to continue. Q [Enter]
```

Using break in a Nested Loop

In a nested loop, the break statement only interrupts the loop it is placed in. The following program segment displays five rows of asterisks on the screen. The outer loop controls the number of rows and the inner loop controls the number of asterisks in each row. The inner loop is designed to display 20 asterisks, but the break statement stops it during the eleventh iteration.

```
for (int row = 0; row < 5; row++)
{
   for (int star = 0; star < 20; star++)
   {
```

```
        cout << '*';
        if (star == 10)
            break;
    }
    cout << endl;
}
```

The output of the program segment above is:

```
**********
**********
**********
**********
**********
```

5.13   The continue Statement

CONCEPT: The continue statement causes a loop to stop its current iteration and begin the next one.

> **WARNING!** As with the break statement, use continue with great caution. It makes code difficult to understand and debug. Because it is part of the C++ language, we discuss it briefly in this section.

The continue statement causes the current iteration of a loop to end immediately. When continue is encountered, all the statements in the body of the loop that appear after it are ignored, and the loop prepares for the next iteration.

In a while loop, this means the program jumps to the test expression at the top of the loop. As usual, if the expression is still true, the next iteration begins. In a do-while loop, the program jumps to the test expression at the bottom of the loop, which determines whether the next iteration will begin. In a for loop, continue causes the update expression to be executed, and then the test expression to be evaluated.

The following program segment demonstrates the use of continue in a while loop:

```
int testVal = 0;
while (testVal++ < 10)
{
    if (testVal == 4)
        continue;
    cout << testVal << " ";
}
```

This loop looks like it displays the integers 1 through 10. When testVal is equal to 4, however, the continue statement causes the loop to skip the cout statement and begin the next iteration. The output of the loop is

```
1 2 3 5 6 7 8 9 10
```

Program 5-18 shows a practical application of the continue statement. The program calculates the charges for DVD rentals, where current releases cost $3.50 and all others cost

$2.50. If a customer rents several DVDs, every third one is free. The continue statement is used to skip the part of the loop that calculates the charges for every third DVD.

Program 5-18

```cpp
 1  // This program calculates the charges for DVD rentals.
 2  // Every third DVD is free.
 3  #include <iostream>
 4  #include <iomanip>
 5  using namespace std;
 6
 7  int main()
 8  {
 9     int dvdCount = 1;     // DVD counter
10     int numDVDs;          // Number of DVDs rented
11     double total = 0.0;   // Accumulator
12     char current;         // Current release, Y or N
13
14     // Get the number of DVDs.
15     cout << "How many DVDs are being rented? ";
16     cin >> numDVDs;
17
18     // Determine the charges.
19     do
20     {
21        if ((dvdCount % 3) == 0)
22        {
23           cout << "DVD #" << dvdCount << " is free!\n";
24           continue;  // Immediately start the next iteration
25        }
26        cout << "Is DVD #" << dvdCount;
27        cout << " a current release? (Y/N) ";
28        cin >> current;
29        if (current == 'Y' || current == 'y')
30           total += 3.50;
31        else
32           total += 2.50;
33     } while (dvdCount++ < numDVDs);
34
35     // Display the total.
36     cout << fixed << showpoint << setprecision(2);
37     cout << "The total is $" << total << endl;
38     return 0;
39  }
```

Program Output with Example Input Shown in Bold
```
How many DVDs are being rented? 6 [Enter]
Is DVD #1 a current release? (Y/N) y [Enter]
Is DVD #2 a current release? (Y/N) n [Enter]
DVD #3 is free!
Is DVD #4 a current release? (Y/N) n [Enter]
Is DVD #5 a current release? (Y/N) y [Enter]
DVD #6 is free!
The total is $12.00
```

 Case Study on CD: See the Loan Amortization Case Study on the Student CD.

Review Questions and Exercises

Short Answer

1. Why should you indent the statements in the body of a loop?

2. Describe the difference between pretest loops and posttest loops.

3. Why are the statements in the body of a loop called conditionally executed statements?

4. What is the difference between the `while` loop and the `do-while` loop?

5. Which loop should you use in situations where you wish the loop to repeat until the test expression is false, and the loop should not execute if the test expression is false to begin with?

6. Which loop should you use in situations where you wish the loop to repeat until the test expression is false, but the loop should execute at least one time?

7. Which loop should you use when you know the number of required iterations?

8. Why is it critical that counter variables be properly initialized?

9. Why is it critical that accumulator variables be properly initialized?

10. Why should you be careful not to place a statement in the body of a `for` loop that changes the value of the loop's counter variable?

Fill-in-the-Blank

11. To _____ a value means to increase it by one, and to _____ a value means to decrease it by one.

12. When the increment or decrement operator is placed before the operand (or to the operand's left), the operator is being used in _____ mode.

13. When the increment or decrement operator is placed after the operand (or to the operand's right), the operator is being used in _____ mode.

14. The statement or block that is repeated is known as the _____ of the loop.

15. Each repetition of a loop is known as a(n) _____.

16. A loop that evaluates its test expression before each repetition is a(n) _____ loop.

17. A loop that evaluates its test expression after each repetition is a(n) _____ loop.

18. A loop that does not have a way of stopping is a(n) _____ loop.

19. A(n) _____ is a variable that "counts" the number of times a loop repeats.

20. A(n) _____ is a sum of numbers that accumulates with each iteration of a loop.

21. A(n) _____ is a variable that is initialized to some starting value, usually zero, and then has numbers added to it in each iteration of a loop.

22. A(n) _____ is a special value that marks the end of a series of values.

23. The _____ loop always iterates at least once.

24. The _____ and _____ loops will not iterate at all if their test expressions are false to start with.

25. The _____ loop is ideal for situations that require a counter.

26. Inside the for loop's parentheses, the first expression is the _____ , the second expression is the _____ , and the third expression is the _____.

27. A loop that is inside another is called a(n) _____ loop.

28. The _____ statement causes a loop to terminate immediately.

29. The _____ statement causes a loop to skip the remaining statements in the current iteration.

Algorithm Workbench

30. Write a while loop that lets the user enter a number. The number should be multiplied by 10, and the result stored in the variable product. The loop should iterate as long as product contains a value less than 100.

31. Write a do-while loop that asks the user to enter two numbers. The numbers should be added and the sum displayed. The user should be asked if he or she wishes to perform the operation again. If so, the loop should repeat; otherwise it should terminate.

32. Write a for loop that displays the following set of numbers:

    0, 10, 20, 30, 40, 50 . . . 1000

33. Write a loop that asks the user to enter a number. The loop should iterate 10 times and keep a running total of the numbers entered.

34. Write a nested loop that displays 10 rows of '#' characters. There should be 15 '#' characters in each row.

35. Convert the following while loop to a do-while loop:

```
int x = 1;
while (x > 0)
{
   cout << "enter a number: ";
   cin >> x;
}
```

36. Convert the following do-while loop to a while loop:

```
char sure;
do
{
   cout << "Are you sure you want to quit? ";
   cin >> sure;
} while (sure != 'Y' && sure != 'N');
```

37. Convert the following while loop to a for loop:

```
int count = 0;
while (count < 50)
{
   cout << "count is " << count << endl;
   count++;
}
```

38. Convert the following `for` loop to a `while` loop:

```
for (int x = 50; x > 0; x--)
{
    cout << x << " seconds to go.\n";
}
```

True or False

39. T F The operand of the increment and decrement operators can be any valid mathematical expression.

40. T F The `cout` statement in the following program segment will display 5:

```
int x = 5;
cout << x++;
```

41. T F The `cout` statement in the following program segment will display 5:

```
int x = 5;
cout << ++x;
```

42. T F The `while` loop is a pretest loop.

43. T F The `do-while` loop is a pretest loop.

44. T F The `for` loop is a posttest loop.

45. T F It is not necessary to initialize counter variables.

46. T F All three of the `for` loop's expressions may be omitted.

47. T F One limitation of the `for` loop is that only one variable may be initialized in the initialization expression.

48. T F Variables may be defined inside the body of a loop.

49. T F A variable may be defined in the initialization expression of the `for` loop.

50. T F In a nested loop, the outer loop executes faster than the inner loop.

51. T F In a nested loop, the inner loop goes through all of its iterations for every single iteration of the outer loop.

52. T F To calculate the total number of iterations of a nested loop, add the number of iterations of all the loops.

53. T F The `break` statement causes a loop to stop the current iteration and begin the next one.

54. T F The `continue` statement causes a terminated loop to resume.

55. T F In a nested loop, the `break` statement only interrupts the loop it is placed in.

Find the Errors

Each of the following programs has errors. Find as many as you can.

56.
```
// Find the error in this program.
#include <iostream>
using namespace std;

int main()
{
    int num1 = 0, num2 = 10, result;
```

```cpp
            num1++;
            result = ++(num1 + num2);
            cout << num1 << " " << num2 << " " << result;
            return 0;
        }
```

57.
```cpp
    // This program adds two numbers entered by the user.
    #include <iostream>
    using namespace std;

    int main()
    {
        int num1, num2;
        char again;

        while (again == 'y' || again == 'Y')
            cout << "Enter a number: ";
            cin >> num1;
            cout << "Enter another number: ";
            cin >> num2;
            cout << "Their sum is << (num1 + num2) << endl;
            cout << "Do you want to do this again? ";
            cin >> again;
            return 0;
    }
```

58.
```cpp
    // This program uses a loop to raise a number to a power.
    #include <iostream>
    using namespace std;

    int main()
    {
        int num, bigNum, power, count;

        cout << "Enter an integer: ";
        cin >> num;
        cout << "What power do you want it raised to? ";
        cin >> power;
        bigNum = num;
        while (count++ < power);
            bigNum *= num;
        cout << "The result is << bigNum << endl;
        return 0;
    }
```

59.
```cpp
    // This program averages a set of numbers.
    #include <iostream>
    using namespace std;

    int main()
    {
        int numCount, total;
        double average;

        cout << "How many numbers do you want to average? ";
        cin >> numCount;
```

```cpp
    for (int count = 0; count < numCount; count++)
    {
        int num;
        cout << "Enter a number: ";
        cin >> num;
        total += num;
        count++;
    }
    average = total / numCount;
    cout << "The average is << average << endl;
    return 0;
}
```

60.
```cpp
// This program displays the sum of two numbers.
#include <iostream>
using namespace std;

int main()
{
    int choice, num1, num2;

    do
    {
        cout << "Enter a number: ";
        cin >> num1;
        cout << "Enter another number: ";
        cin >> num2;
        cout << "Their sum is " << (num1 + num2) << endl;
        cout << "Do you want to do this again?\n";
        cout << "1 = yes, 0 = no\n";
        cin >> choice;
    } while (choice = 1)
    return 0;
}
```

61.
```cpp
// This program displays the sum of the numbers 1-100.
#include <iostream>
using namespace std;

int main()
{
    int count = 1, total;

    while (count <= 100)
        total += count;
    cout << "The sum of the numbers 1-100 is ";
    cout << total << endl;
    return 0;
}
```

Programming Challenges

1. Sum of Numbers

Write a program that asks the user for a positive integer value. The program should use a loop to get the sum of all the integers from 1 up to the number entered. For example, if the user enters 50, the loop will find the sum of 1, 2, 3, 4, ... 50.

Input Validation: Do not accept a negative starting number.

2. Characters for the ASCII Codes

Write a program that uses a loop to display the characters for the ASCII codes 0 through 127. Display 16 characters on each line.

3. Ocean Levels

Assuming the ocean's level is currently rising at about 1.5 millimeters per year, write a program that displays a table showing the number of millimeters that the ocean will have risen each year for the next 25 years.

VideoNote

Solving the
Calories
Burned
Problem

4. Calories Burned

Running on a particular treadmill you burn 3.9 calories per minute. Write a program that uses a loop to display the number of calories burned after 10, 15, 20, 25, and 30 minutes.

5. Membership Fees Increase

A country club, which currently charges $2,500 per year for membership, has announced it will increase its membership fee by 4% each year for the next six years. Write a program that uses a loop to display the projected rates for the next six years.

6. Distance Traveled

The distance a vehicle travels can be calculated as follows:

```
distance = speed * time
```

For example, if a train travels 40 miles per hour for 3 hours, the distance traveled is 120 miles.

Write a program that asks the user for the speed of a vehicle (in miles per hour) and how many hours it has traveled. The program should then use a loop to display the distance the vehicle has traveled for each hour of that time period. Here is an example of the output:

```
What is the speed of the vehicle in mph? 40
How many hours has it traveled? 3
Hour    Distance Traveled
--------------------------------
 1              40
 2              80
 3             120
```

Input Validation: Do not accept a negative number for speed and do not accept any value less than 1 for time traveled.

7. **Pennies for Pay**

Write a program that calculates how much a person would earn over a period of time if his or her salary is one penny the first day and two pennies the second day, and continues to double each day. The program should ask the user for the number of days. Display a table showing how much the salary was for each day, and then show the total pay at the end of the period. The output should be displayed in a dollar amount, not the number of pennies.

Input Validation: Do not accept a number less than 1 for the number of days worked.

8. **Math Tutor**

This program started in Programming Challenge 15 of Chapter 3, and was modified in Programming Challenge 9 of Chapter 4. Modify the program again so it displays a menu allowing the user to select an addition, subtraction, multiplication, or division problem. The final selection on the menu should let the user quit the program. After the user has finished the math problem, the program should display the menu again. This process is repeated until the user chooses to quit the program.

Input Validation: If the user selects an item not on the menu, display an error message and display the menu again.

9. **Hotel Occupancy**

Write a program that calculates the occupancy rate for a hotel. The program should start by asking the user how many floors the hotel has. A loop should then iterate once for each floor. In each iteration, the loop should ask the user for the number of rooms on the floor and how many of them are occupied. After all the iterations, the program should display how many rooms the hotel has, how many of them are occupied, how many are unoccupied, and the percentage of rooms that are occupied. The percentage may be calculated by dividing the number of rooms occupied by the number of rooms.

 NOTE: It is traditional that most hotels do not have a thirteenth floor. The loop in this program should skip the entire thirteenth iteration.

Input Validation: Do not accept a value less than 1 for the number of floors. Do not accept a number less than 10 for the number of rooms on a floor.

10. **Average Rainfall**

Write a program that uses nested loops to collect data and calculate the average rainfall over a period of years. The program should first ask for the number of years. The outer loop will iterate once for each year. The inner loop will iterate twelve times, once for each month. Each iteration of the inner loop will ask the user for the inches of rainfall for that month.

After all iterations, the program should display the number of months, the total inches of rainfall, and the average rainfall per month for the entire period.

Input Validation: Do not accept a number less than 1 for the number of years. Do not accept negative numbers for the monthly rainfall.

11. Population

Write a program that will predict the size of a population of organisms. The program should ask the user for the starting number of organisms, their average daily population increase (as a percentage), and the number of days they will multiply. A loop should display the size of the population for each day.

Input Validation: Do not accept a number less than 2 for the starting size of the population. Do not accept a negative number for average daily population increase. Do not accept a number less than 1 for the number of days they will multiply.

12. Celsius to Fahrenheit Table

In Programming Challenge 10 of Chapter 3 you were asked to write a program that converts a Celsius temperature to Fahrenheit. Modify that program so it uses a loop to display a table of the Celsius temperatures 0–20, and their Fahrenheit equivalents.

13. The Greatest and Least of These

Write a program with a loop that lets the user enter a series of integers. The user should enter -99 to signal the end of the series. After all the numbers have been entered, the program should display the largest and smallest numbers entered.

14. Student Line Up

A teacher has asked all her students to line up single file according to their first name. For example, in one class Amy will be at the front of the line and Yolanda will be at the end. Write a program that prompts the user to enter the number of students in the class, then loops to read in that many names. Once all the names have been read in it reports which student would be at the front of the line and which one would be at the end of the line. You may assume that no two students have the same name.

Input Validation: Do not accept a number less than 1 or greater than 25 for the number of students.

15. Payroll Report

Write a program that displays a weekly payroll report. A loop in the program should ask the user for the employee number, gross pay, state tax, federal tax, and FICA withholdings. The loop will terminate when 0 is entered for the employee number. After the data is entered, the program should display totals for gross pay, state tax, federal tax, FICA withholdings, and net pay.

Input Validation: Do not accept negative numbers for any of the items entered. Do not accept values for state, federal, or FICA withholdings that are greater than the gross pay. If the sum state tax + federal tax + FICA withholdings for any employee is greater than gross pay, print an error message and ask the user to re-enter the data for that employee.

16. Savings Account Balance

Write a program that calculates the balance of a savings account at the end of a period of time. It should ask the user for the annual interest rate, the starting balance, and the number of months that have passed since the account was established. A loop should then iterate once for every month, performing the following:

A) Ask the user for the amount deposited into the account during the month. (Do not accept negative numbers.) This amount should be added to the balance.

B) Ask the user for the amount withdrawn from the account during the month. (Do not accept negative numbers.) This amount should be subtracted from the balance.

C) Calculate the monthly interest. The monthly interest rate is the annual interest rate divided by twelve. Multiply the monthly interest rate by the balance, and add the result to the balance.

After the last iteration, the program should display the ending balance, the total amount of deposits, the total amount of withdrawals, and the total interest earned.

NOTE: If a negative balance is calculated at any point, a message should be displayed indicating the account has been closed and the loop should terminate.

17. Sales Bar Chart

Write a program that asks the user to enter today's sales for five stores. The program should then display a bar graph comparing each store's sales. Create each bar in the bar graph by displaying a row of asterisks. Each asterisk should represent $100 of sales.

Here is an example of the program's output.

```
Enter today's sales for store 1: 1000 [Enter]
Enter today's sales for store 2: 1200 [Enter]
Enter today's sales for store 3: 1800 [Enter]
Enter today's sales for store 4: 800 [Enter]
Enter today's sales for store 5: 1900 [Enter]

SALES BAR CHART
(Each * = $100)
Store 1: **********
Store 2: ************
Store 3: ******************
Store 4: ********
Store 5: *******************
```

18. Population Bar Chart

Write a program that produces a bar chart showing the population growth of Prairieville, a small town in the Midwest, at 20-year intervals during the past 100 years. The program should read in the population figures (rounded to the nearest 1,000 people) for 1900, 1920, 1940, 1960, 1980, and 2000 from a file. For each year it should display the date and a bar consisting of one asterisk for each 1,000 people. The data can be found in the `people.dat` file.

Here is an example of how the chart might begin:

```
PRAIRIEVILLE POPULATION GROWTH
(each * represents 1,000 people)
1900 **
1920 ****
1940 *****
```

19. **Budget Analysis**

    Write a program that asks the user to enter the amount that he or she has budgeted for a month. A loop should then prompt the user to enter each of his or her expenses for the month, and keep a running total. When the loop finishes, the program should display the amount that the user is over or under budget.

20. **Random Number Guessing Game**

    Write a program that generates a random number and asks the user to guess what the number is. If the user's guess is higher than the random number, the program should display "Too high, try again." If the user's guess is lower than the random number, the program should display "Too low, try again." The program should use a loop that repeats until the user correctly guesses the random number.

21. **Random Number Guessing Game Enhancement**

    Enhance the program that you wrote for Programming Challenge 20 so it keeps a count of the number of guesses that the user makes. When the user correctly guesses the random number, the program should display the number of guesses.

22. **Square Display**

    Write a program that asks the user for a positive integer no greater than 15. The program should then display a square on the screen using the character 'X'. The number entered by the user will be the length of each side of the square. For example, if the user enters 5, the program should display the following:

    ```
    XXXXX
    XXXXX
    XXXXX
    XXXXX
    XXXXX
    ```

    If the user enters 8, the program should display the following:

    ```
    XXXXXXXX
    XXXXXXXX
    XXXXXXXX
    XXXXXXXX
    XXXXXXXX
    XXXXXXXX
    XXXXXXXX
    XXXXXXXX
    ```

23. **Pattern Displays**

    Write a program that uses a loop to display Pattern A below, followed by another loop that displays Pattern B.

Pattern A	Pattern B
+	++++++++++
++	+++++++++
+++	++++++++
++++	+++++++
+++++	++++++
++++++	+++++
+++++++	++++
++++++++	+++
+++++++++	++
++++++++++	+

24. **Using Files—Numeric Processing**

The Student CD contains a file named random.txt. This file contains a long list of random numbers. Copy the file to your hard drive and then write a program that opens the file, reads all the numbers from the file, and calculates the following:

A) The number of numbers in the file

B) The sum of all the numbers in the file (a running total)

C) The average of all the numbers in the file

The program should display the number of numbers found in the file, the sum of the numbers, and the average of the numbers.

25. **Using Files—Student Line Up**

Modify the Student Line Up program described in Programming Challenge 14 so that it gets the names from a data file. Names should be read in until there is no more data to read. Data to test your program can be found in the LineUp.dat file.

26. **Using Files—Savings Account Balance Modification**

Modify the Savings Account Balance program described in Programming Challenge 16 so that it writes the final report to a file. After the program runs, print the file to hand in to your instructor.

TOPICS

6.1   Focus on Software Engineering: Modular Programming

CONCEPT: A program may be broken up into manageable functions.

A function is a collection of statements that performs a specific task. So far you have experienced functions in two ways: (1) you have created a function named main in every program you've written, and (2) you have used library functions such as pow and strcmp. In this chapter you will learn how to create your own functions that can be used like library functions.

Functions are commonly used to break a problem down into small manageable pieces. Instead of writing one long function that contains all of the statements necessary to solve a problem, several small functions that each solve a specific part of the problem can be written. These small functions can then be executed in the desired order to solve the problem. This approach is sometimes called *divide and conquer* because a large problem is

297

divided into several smaller problems that are easily solved. Figure 6-1 illustrates this idea by comparing two programs: one that uses a long complex function containing all of the statements necessary to solve a problem, and another that divides a problem into smaller problems, each of which are handled by a separate function.

Figure 6-1

This program has one long, complex function containing all of the statements necessary to solve a problem.

In this program the problem has been divided into smaller problems, each of which is handled by a separate function.

```
int main()
{
    statement;
    statement;
    statement;
    statement;
    statement;
    statement;
    statement;
    statement;
    statement;
    statement;
    statement;
    statement;
    statement;
    statement;
    statement;
    statement;
    statement;
    statement;
    statement;
    statement;
    statement;
    statement;
    statement;
}
```

```
int main()
{
    statement;
    statement;            main function
    statement;
}
```

```
void function2()
{
    statement;
    statement;            function 2
    statement;
}
```

```
void function3()
{
    statement;
    statement;            function 3
    statement;
}
```

```
void function4()
{
    statement;
    statement;            function 4
    statement;
}
```

Another reason to write functions is that they simplify programs. If a specific task is performed in several places in a program, a function can be written once to perform that task, and then be executed anytime it is needed. This benefit of using functions is known as *code reuse* because you are writing the code to perform a task once and then reusing it each time you need to perform the task.

6.2 Defining and Calling Functions

CONCEPT: A function call is a statement that causes a function to execute. A function definition contains the statements that make up the function.

When creating a function, you must write its *definition*. All function definitions have the following parts:

Return type: A function can send a value to the part of the program that executed it. The return type is the data type of the value that is sent from the function.

Name: You should give each function a descriptive name. In general, the same rules that apply to variable names also apply to function names.

Parameter list: The program can send data into a function. The parameter list is a list of variables that hold the values being passed to the function.

Body: The body of a function is the set of statements that perform the function's operation. They are enclosed in a set of braces.

Figure 6-2 shows the definition of a simple function with the various parts labeled.

Figure 6-2

```
Return type       Parameter list (This one is empty)
   |  Function name  /
   |       |        /     Function body
   v       v       v
int  main  ()
{
     cout << "Hello World\n";
     return 0;
}
```

The line in the definition that reads `int main()` is called the *function header*.

void Functions

You already know that a function can return a value. The main function in all of the programs you have seen in this book is declared to return an `int` value to the operating system. The `return 0;` statement causes the value 0 to be returned when the main function finishes executing.

It isn't necessary for all functions to return a value, however. Some functions simply perform one or more statements which follows terminate. These are called *void functions*. The `displayMessage` function, which follows is an example.

```
void displayMessage()
{
    cout << "Hello from the function displayMessage.\n";
}
```

The function's name is `displayMessage`. This name gives an indication of what the function does: It displays a message. You should always give functions names that reflect their purpose. Notice that the function's return type is `void`. This means the function does not return a value to the part of the program that executed it. Also notice the function has no `return` statement. It simply displays a message on the screen and exits.

Calling a Function

A function is executed when it is *called*. Function `main` is called automatically when a program starts, but all other functions must be executed by *function call* statements. When a function is called, the program branches to that function and executes the statements in its body. Let's look at Program 6-1, which contains two functions: `main` and `displayMessage`.

Program 6-1

```
 1   // This program has two functions: main and displayMessage
 2   #include <iostream>
 3   using namespace std;
 4
 5   //****************************************
 6   // Definition of function displayMessage  *
 7   // This function displays a greeting.      *
 8   //****************************************
 9
10   void displayMessage()
11   {
12      cout << "Hello from the function displayMessage.\n";
13   }
14
15   //****************************************
16   // Function main                          *
17   //****************************************
18
19   int main()
20   {
21      cout << "Hello from main.\n";
22      displayMessage();
23      cout << "Back in function main again.\n";
24      return 0;
25   }
```

Program Output
```
Hello from main.
Hello from the function displayMessage.
Back in function main again.
```

The function `displayMessage` is called by the following statement in line 22:

```
displayMessage();
```

This statement is the function call. It is simply the name of the function followed by a set of parentheses and a semicolon. Let's compare this with the function header:

Function Header ⟶ `void displayMessage()`
Function Call ⟶ `displayMessage();`

The function header is part of the function definition. It declares the function's return type, name, and parameter list. It is not terminated with a semicolon because the definition of the function's body follows it.

The function call is a statement that executes the function, so it is terminated with a semicolon like all other C++ statements. The return type is not listed in the function call, and, if the program is not passing data into the function, the parentheses are left empty.

 NOTE: Later in this chapter you will see how data can be passed into a function by being listed inside the parentheses.

Even though the program starts executing at `main`, the function `displayMessage` is defined first. This is because the compiler must know the function's return type, the number of parameters, and the type of each parameter before the function is called. One way to ensure the compiler will know this information is to place the function definition before all calls to that function. (Later you will see an alternative, preferred method of accomplishing this.)

 NOTE: You should always document your functions by writing comments that describe what they do. These comments should appear just before the function definition.

Notice how Program 6-1 flows. It starts, of course, in function `main`. When the call to `displayMessage` is encountered, the program branches to that function and performs its statements. Once `displayMessage` has finished executing, the program branches back to function `main` and resumes with the line that follows the function call. This is illustrated in Figure 6-3.

Figure 6-3

Function call statements may be used in control structures like loops, `if` statements, and `switch` statements. Program 6-2 places the `displayMessage` function call inside a loop.

Program 6-2

```
 1   // The function displayMessage is repeatedly called from a loop.
 2   #include <iostream>
 3   using namespace std;
 4
 5   //*****************************************
 6   // Definition of function displayMessage  *
 7   // This function displays a greeting.     *
 8   //*****************************************
 9
10   void displayMessage()
11   {
12      cout << "Hello from the function displayMessage.\n";
13   }
14
15   //*****************************************
16   // Function main                          *
17   //*****************************************
18
19   int main()
20   {
21      cout << "Hello from main.\n";
22      for (int count = 0; count < 5; count++)
23         displayMessage(); // Call displayMessage
24      cout << "Back in function main again.\n";
25      return 0;
26   }
```

Program Output

```
Hello from main.
Hello from the function displayMessage.
Hello from the function displayMessage.
Hello from the function displayMessage.
Hello from the function displayMessage.
Hello from the function displayMessage.
Back in function main again.
```

It is possible to have many functions and function calls in a program. Program 6-3 has three functions: main, first, and second.

Program 6-3

```
 1   // This program has three functions: main, first, and second.
 2   #include <iostream>
 3   using namespace std;
 4
```

```
 5    //****************************************
 6    // Definition of function first          *
 7    // This function displays a message.      *
 8    //****************************************
 9
10    void first()
11    {
12       cout << "I am now inside the function first.\n";
13    }
14
15    //****************************************
16    // Definition of function second         *
17    // This function displays a message.      *
18    //****************************************
19
20    void second()
21    {
22       cout << "I am now inside the function second.\n";
23    }
24
25    //****************************************
26    // Function main                         *
27    //****************************************
28
29    int main()
30    {
31       cout << "I am starting in function main.\n";
32       first();    // Call function first
33       second();   // Call function second
34       cout << "Back in function main again.\n";
35       return 0;
36    }
```

Program Output
```
I am starting in function main.
I am now inside the function first.
I am now inside the function second.
Back in function main again.
```

In lines 32 and 33 of Program 6-3, function main contains a call to first and a call to second:

```
first();
second();
```

Each call statement causes the program to branch to a function and then back to main when the function is finished. Figure 6-4 illustrates the paths taken by the program.

Figure 6-4

Functions may also be called in a hierarchical, or layered fashion. This is demonstrated by Program 6-4, which has three functions: main, deep, and deeper.

Program 6-4

```
 1   // This program has three functions: main, deep, and deeper
 2   #include <iostream>
 3   using namespace std;
 4
 5   //****************************************
 6   // Definition of function deeper          *
 7   // This function displays a message.      *
 8   //****************************************
 9
10   void deeper()
11   {
12      cout << "I am now inside the function deeper.\n";
13   }
14
15   //****************************************
16   // Definition of function deep            *
17   // This function displays a message.      *
18   //****************************************
19
```

```
20  void deep()
21  {
22     cout << "I am now inside the function deep.\n";
23     deeper();   // Call function deeper
24     cout << "Now I am back in deep.\n";
25  }
26
27  //*****************************************
28  // Function main                          *
29  //*****************************************
30
31  int main()
32  {
33     cout << "I am starting in function main.\n";
34     deep();      // Call function deep
35     cout << "Back in function main again.\n";
36     return 0;
37  }
```

Program Output
```
I am starting in function main.
I am now inside the function deep.
I am now inside the function deeper.
Now I am back in deep.
Back in function main again.
```

In Program 6-4, function main only calls the function deep. In turn, deep calls deeper. The paths taken by the program are shown in Figure 6-5.

Figure 6-5

Checkpoint

6.1   Is the following a function header or a function call?

```
calcTotal();
```

6.2   Is the following a function header or a function call?

```
void showResults()
```

6.3   What will the output of the following program be if the user enters 10?

```cpp
#include <iostream>
using namespace std;

void func1()
{
    cout << "Able was I\n";
}

void func2()
{
    cout << "I saw Elba\n";
}

int main()
{
    int input;
    cout << "Enter a number: ";
    cin >> input;
    if (input < 10)
    {
        func1();
        func2();
    }
    else
    {
        func2();
        func1();
    }
    return 0;
}
```

6.4   The following program skeleton determines whether a person qualifies for a
        credit card. To qualify, the person must have worked on his or her current job for
        at least two years and make at least $17,000 per year. Finish the program by writ-
        ing the definitions of the functions qualify and noQualify. The function
        qualify should explain that the applicant qualifies for the card and that the
        annual interest rate is 12%. The function noQualify should explain that the
        applicant does not qualify for the card and give a general explanation why.

```cpp
#include <iostream>
using namespace std;

// You must write definitions for the two functions qualify
// and noQualify.
```

```
int main()
{
   double salary;
   int years;

   cout << "This program will determine if you qualify\n";
   cout << "for our credit card.\n";
   cout << "What is your annual salary? ";
   cin >> salary;
   cout << "How many years have you worked at your ";
   cout << "current job? ";
   cin >> years;
   if (salary >= 17000.0 && years >= 2)
      qualify();
   else
      noQualify();
   return 0;
}
```

6.3 Function Prototypes

CONCEPT: A function prototype eliminates the need to place a function definition before all calls to the function.

Before the compiler encounters a call to a particular function, it must already know the function's return type, the number of parameters it uses, and the type of each parameter. (You will learn how to use parameters in the next section.)

One way of ensuring that the compiler has this information is to place the function definition before all calls to that function. This was the approach taken in Programs 6-1, 6-2, 6-3, and 6-4. Another method is to declare the function with a *function prototype*. Here is a prototype for the `displayMessage` function in Program 6-1:

```
void displayMessage();
```

The prototype looks similar to the function header, except there is a semicolon at the end. The statement above tells the compiler that the function `displayMessage` has a `void` return type (it doesn't return a value) and uses no parameters.

NOTE: Function prototypes are also known as *function declarations*.

WARNING! You must place either the function definition or the function prototype ahead of all calls to the function. Otherwise the program will not compile.

Function prototypes are usually placed near the top of a program so the compiler will encounter them before any function calls. Program 6-5 is a modification of Program 6-3. The definitions of the functions `first` and `second` have been placed after `main`, and a function prototype has been placed after the `using namespace std` statement.

Program 6-5

```cpp
1   // This program has three functions: main, first, and second.
2   #include <iostream>
3   using namespace std;
4
5   // Function Prototypes
6   void first();
7   void second();
8
9   int main()
10  {
11     cout << "I am starting in function main.\n";
12     first();    // Call function first
13     second();   // Call function second
14     cout << "Back in function main again.\n";
15     return 0;
16  }
17
18  //***********************************
19  // Definition of function first.    *
20  // This function displays a message. *
21  //***********************************
22
23  void first()
24  {
25     cout << "I am now inside the function first.\n";
26  }
27
28  //***********************************
29  // Definition of function second.   *
30  // This function displays a message. *
31  //***********************************
32
33  void second()
34  {
35     cout << "I am now inside the function second.\n";
36  }
```

Program Output

(The program's output is the same as the output of Program 6-3.)

When the compiler is reading Program 6-5, it encounters the calls to the functions first and second in lines 12 and 13 before it has read the definition of those functions. Because of the function prototypes, however, the compiler already knows the return type and parameter information of first and second.

 NOTE: Although some programmers make main the last function in the program, many prefer it to be first because it is the program's starting point.

6.4   Sending Data into a Function

CONCEPT: When a function is called, the program may send values into the function.

VideoNote

Functions and
Arguments

Values that are sent into a function are called *arguments*. You're already familiar with how to use arguments in a function call. In the following statement the function pow is being called and two arguments, 2.0 and 4.0, are passed to it:

```cpp
result = pow(2.0, 4.0);
```

By using *parameters*, you can design your own functions that accept data this way. A parameter is a special variable that holds a value being passed into a function. Here is the definition of a function that uses a parameter:

```cpp
void displayValue(int num)
{
    cout << "The value is " << num << endl;
}
```

Notice the integer variable definition inside the parentheses (int num). The variable num is a parameter. This enables the function displayValue to accept an integer value as an argument. Program 6-6 is a complete program using this function.

NOTE: In this text, the values that are passed into a function are called arguments, and the variables that receive those values are called parameters. There are several variations of these terms in use. Some call the arguments *actual parameters* and call the parameters *formal parameters*. Others use the terms *actual argument* and *formal argument*. Regardless of which set of terms you use, it is important to be consistent.

Program 6-6

```cpp
 1  // This program demonstrates a function with a parameter.
 2  #include <iostream>
 3  using namespace std;
 4
 5  // Function Prototype
 6  void displayValue(int);
 7
 8  int main()
 9  {
10     cout << "I am passing 5 to displayValue.\n";
11     displayValue(5);  // Call displayValue with argument 5
12     cout << "Now I am back in main.\n";
13     return 0;
14  }
15
```

(program continues)

Program 6-6   *(continued)*

```
16   //*******************************************************
17   // Definition of function displayValue.                 *
18   // It uses an integer parameter whose value is displayed. *
19   //*******************************************************
20
21   void displayValue(int num)
22   {
23       cout << "The value is " << num << endl;
24   }
```

Program Output
```
I am passing 5 to displayValue.
The value is 5
Now I am back in main.
```

First, notice the function prototype for `displayValue` in line 6:

```
void displayValue(int);
```

It is not necessary to list the name of the parameter variable inside the parentheses. Only its data type is required. The function prototype shown above could optionally have been written as:

```
void displayValue(int num);
```

However, the compiler ignores the name of the parameter variable in the function prototype.

In `main`, the `displayValue` function is called with the argument 5 inside the parentheses. The number 5 is passed into `num`, which is `displayValue`'s parameter. This is illustrated in Figure 6-6.

Figure 6-6

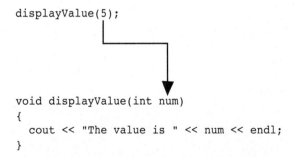

Any argument listed inside the parentheses of a function call is copied into the function's parameter variable. In essence, parameter variables are initialized to the value of their corresponding arguments. Program 6-7 shows the function `displayValue` being called several times with a different argument being passed each time.

Program 6-7

```
 1   // This program demonstrates a function with a parameter.
 2   #include <iostream>
 3   using namespace std;
 4
 5   // Function Prototype
 6   void displayValue(int);
 7
 8   int main()
 9   {
10      cout << "I am passing several values to displayValue.\n";
11      displayValue(5);  // Call displayValue with argument 5
12      displayValue(10); // Call displayValue with argument 10
13      displayValue(2);  // Call displayValue with argument 2
14      displayValue(16); // Call displayValue with argument 16
15      cout << "Now I am back in main.\n";
16      return 0;
17   }
18
19   //**********************************************************
20   // Definition of function displayValue.                   *
21   // It uses an integer parameter whose value is displayed. *
22   //**********************************************************
23
24   void displayValue(int num)
25   {
26      cout << "The value is " << num << endl;
27   }
```

Program Output
```
I am passing several values to displayValue.
The value is 5
The value is 10
The value is 2
The value is 16
Now I am back in main.
```

 WARNING! When passing a variable as an argument, simply write the variable name inside the parentheses of the function call. Do not write the data type of the argument variable in the function call. For example, the following funtion call will cause an error:

```
displayValue(int x); // Error!
```

The function call should appear as

```
displayValue(x);     // Correct
```

Each time the function is called in Program 6-7, num takes on a different value. Any expression whose value could normally be assigned to num may be used as an argument. For example, the following function call would pass the value 8 into num:

```
displayValue(3 + 5);
```

If you pass an argument whose type is not the same as the parameter's type, the argument will be promoted or demoted automatically. For instance, the argument in the following function call would be truncated, causing the value 4 to be passed to num:

```
displayValue(4.7);
```

Often, it's useful to pass several arguments into a function. Program 6-8 shows the definition of a function with three parameters.

Program 6-8

```
 1   // This program demonstrates a function with three parameters.
 2   #include <iostream>
 3   using namespace std;
 4
 5   // Function Prototype
 6   void showSum(int, int, int);
 7
 8   int main()
 9   {
10      int value1, value2, value3;
11
12      // Get three integers.
13      cout << "Enter three integers and I will display ";
14      cout << "their sum: ";
15      cin >> value1 >> value2 >> value3;
16
17      // Call showSum passing three arguments.
18      showSum(value1, value2, value3);
19      return 0;
20   }
21
22   //*********************************************************
23   // Definition of function showSum.                        *
24   // It uses three integer parameters. Their sum is displayed. *
25   //*********************************************************
26
27   void showSum(int num1, int num2, int num3)
28   {
29      cout << (num1 + num2 + num3) << endl;
30   }
```

Program Output with Example Input Shown in Bold
Enter three integers and I will display their sum: **4 8 7 [Enter]**
19

In the function header for showSum, the parameter list contains three variable definitions separated by commas:

```
void showSum(int num1, int num2, int num3)
```

WARNING! Each parameter variable in a parameter list must have a data type listed before its name. For example, a compiler error would occur if the parameter list for the showSum function were defined as shown in the following header:

```
void showSum(int num1, num2, num3) // Error!
```

A data type for all three of the parameter variables must be listed, as shown here:

```
void showSum(int num1, int num2, int num3) // Correct
```

In the function call in line 18, the variables value1, value2, and value3 are passed as arguments:

```
showSum(value1, value2, value3);
```

When a function with multiple parameters is called, the arguments are passed to the parameters in order. This is illustrated in Figure 6-7.

Figure 6-7

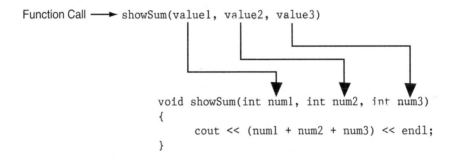

The following function call will cause 5 to be passed into the num1 parameter, 10 to be passed into num2, and 15 to be passed into num3:

```
showSum(5, 10, 15);
```

However, the following function call will cause 15 to be passed into the num1 parameter, 5 to be passed into num2, and 10 to be passed into num3:

```
showSum(15, 5, 10);
```

NOTE: The function prototype must list the data type of each parameter.

NOTE: Like all variables, parameters have a scope. The scope of a parameter is limited to the body of the function that uses it.

6.5 Passing Data by Value

CONCEPT: When an argument is passed into a parameter, only a copy of the argument's value is passed. Changes to the parameter do not affect the original argument.

As you've seen in this chapter, parameters are special-purpose variables that are defined inside the parentheses of a function definition. They are separate and distinct from the arguments that are listed inside the parentheses of a function call. The values that are stored in the parameter variables are copies of the arguments. Normally, when a parameter's value is changed inside a function it has no effect on the original argument. Program 6-9 demonstrates this concept.

Program 6-9

```
 1  // This program demonstrates that changes to a function parameter
 2  // have no effect on the original argument.
 3  #include <iostream>
 4  using namespace std;
 5
 6  // Function Prototype
 7  void changeMe(int);
 8
 9  int main()
10  {
11     int number = 12;
12
13     // Display the value in number.
14     cout << "number is " << number << endl;
15
16     // Call changeMe, passing the value in number
17     // as an argument.
18     changeMe(number);
19
20     // Display the value in number again.
21     cout << "Now back in main again, the value of ";
22     cout << "number is " << number << endl;
23     return 0;
24  }
25
26  //*************************************************************
27  // Definition of function changeMe.                          *
28  // This function changes the value of the parameter myValue. *
29  //*************************************************************
30
```

```
31   void changeMe(int myValue)
32   {
33       // Change the value of myValue to 0.
34       myValue = 0;
35
36       // Display the value in myValue.
37       cout << "Now the value is " << myValue << endl;
38   }
```

Program Output
```
number is 12
Now the value is 0
Now back in main again, the value of number is 12
```

Even though the parameter variable myValue is changed in the changeMe function, the argument number is not modified. The myValue variable contains only a copy of the number variable.

The changeMe function does not have access to the original argument. When only a copy of an argument is passed to a function, it is said to be *passed by value*. This is because the function receives a copy of the argument's value, and does not have access to the original argument.

Figure 6-8 illustrates that a parameter variable's storage location in memory is separate from that of the original argument.

Figure 6-8

 NOTE: Later in this chapter you will learn ways to give a function access to its original arguments.

6.6   Focus on Software Engineering: Using Functions in a Menu-Driven Program

CONCEPT: Functions are ideal for use in menu-driven programs. When the user selects an item from a menu, the program can call the appropriate function.

In Chapters 4 and 5 you saw a menu-driven program that calculates the charges for a health club membership. Program 6-10 shows the program redesigned as a modular program. A *modular* program is broken up into functions that perform specific tasks.

Program 6-10

```cpp
 1  // This is a menu-driven program that makes a function call
 2  // for each selection the user makes.
 3  #include <iostream>
 4  #include <iomanip>
 5  using namespace std;
 6
 7  // Function prototypes
 8  void showMenu();
 9  void showFees(double, int);
10
11  int main()
12  {
13     int choice;        // To hold a menu choice
14     int months;        // To hold a number of months
15
16     // Constants for membership rates
17     const double ADULT = 40.0;
18     const double SENIOR = 30.0;
19     const double CHILD = 20.0;
20
21     // Set up numeric output formatting.
22     cout << fixed << showpoint << setprecision(2);
23
24     do
25     {
26        // Display the menu and get the user's choice.
27        showMenu();
28        cin >> choice;
29
```

```
30          // Validate the menu selection.
31          while (choice < 1 || choice > 4)
32          {
33             cout << "Please enter 1, 2, 3, or 4: ";
34             cin >> choice;
35          }
36
37          if (choice != 4)
38          {
39             // Get the number of months.
40             cout << "For how many months? ";
41             cin >> months;
42
43             // Display the membership fees.
44             switch (choice)
45             {
46                case 1:  showFees(ADULT, months);
47                         break;
48                case 2:  showFees(CHILD, months);
49                         break;
50                case 3:  showFees(SENIOR, months);
51             }
52          }
53       } while (choice != 4);
54       return 0;
55    }
56
57    //*********************************************************************
58    // Definition of function showMenu which displays the menu.          *
59    //*********************************************************************
60
61    void showMenu()
62    {
63       cout << "\n\t\tHealth Club Membership Menu\n\n";
64       cout << "1. Standard Adult Membership\n";
65       cout << "2. Child Membership\n";
66       cout << "3. Senior Citizen Membership\n";
67       cout << "4. Quit the Program\n\n";
68       cout << "Enter your choice: ";
69    }
70
71    //*********************************************************************
72    // Definition of function showFees. The memberRate parameter holds*
73    // the monthly membership rate and the months parameter holds the *
74    // number of months. The function displays the total charges.     *
75    //*********************************************************************
76
77    void showFees(double memberRate, int months)
78    {
79        cout << "The total charges are $"
80             << (memberRate * months) << endl;
81    }
```

(program output continues)

Program 6-10 *(continued)*

Program Output with Example Input Shown in Bold

```
          Health Club Membership Menu

1. Standard Adult Membership
2. Child Membership
3. Senior Citizen Membership
4. Quit the Program

Enter your choice: 1 [Enter]
For how many months? 12 [Enter]
The total charges are $480.00

          Health Club Membership Menu

1. Standard Adult Membership
2. Child Membership
3. Senior Citizen Membership
4. Quit the Program

Enter your choice: 4 [Enter]
```

Let's take a closer look at this program. First notice that the `double` constants `ADULT`, `CHILD`, and `SENIOR` are defined in lines 17 through 19. Recall that these constants hold the monthly membership rates for adult, child, and senior citizen memberships.

Next, notice the `showMenu` function in lines 61 through 69. This function displays the menu, and is called from the `main` function in line 27.

The `showFees` function appears in lines 77 through 81. Its purpose is to display the total fees for a membership lasting a specified number of months. The function accepts two arguments: the monthly membership fee (a `double`) and the number of months of membership (an `int`). The function uses these values to calculate and display the total charges. For example, if we wanted the function to display the fees for an adult membership lasting six months, we would pass the `ADULT` constant as the first argument and 6 as the second argument.

The `showFees` function is called from three different locations in the `switch` statement which is in the `main` function. The first location is line 46. This statement is executed when the user has selected item 1, standard adult membership, from the menu. The `showFees` function is called with the `ADULT` constant and the `months` variable passed as arguments. The second location is line 48. This statement is executed when the user has selected item 2, child membership, from the menu. The `showFees` function is called in this line with the `CHILD` constant and the `months` variable passed as arguments. The third location is line 50. This statement is executed when the user has selected item 3, senior citizen membership, from the menu. The `showFees` function is called with the `SENIOR` constant and the `months` variable passed as arguments. Each time the `showFees` function is called, it displays the total membership fees for the specified type of membership, for the specified number of months.

Checkpoint

6.5   Indicate which of the following is the function prototype, the function header, and the function call:

```
void showNum(double num)

void showNum(double);

showNum(45.67);
```

6.6   Write a function named `timesTen` The function should have an integer parameter named `number`. When `timesTen` is called, it should display the product of `number` times ten. (*Note*: just write the function. Do not write a complete program.)

6.7   Write a function prototype for the `timesTen` function you wrote in Question 6.6.

6.8   What is the output of the following program?

```cpp
#include <iostream>
using namespace std;

void showDouble(int); // Function prototype

int main()
{
    int num;

    for (num = 0; num < 10; num++)
        showDouble(num);
    return 0;
}

// Definition of function showDouble.
void showDouble(int value)
{
    cout << value << "\t" << (value * 2) << endl;
}
```

6.9   What is the output of the following program?

```cpp
#include <iostream>
using namespace std;

void func1(double, int); // Function prototype

int main()
{
    int x = 0;
    double y = 1.5;

    cout << x << " " << y << endl;
    func1(y, x);
    cout << x << " " << y << endl;
    return 0;
}
```

```cpp
void func1(double a, int b)
{
   cout << a << " " << b << endl;
   a = 0.0;
   b = 10;
   cout << a << " " << b << endl;
}
```

6.10   The following program skeleton asks for the number of hours you've worked and your hourly pay rate. It then calculates and displays your wages. The function showDollars, which you are to write, formats the output of the wages.

```cpp
#include <iostream>
using namespace std;

void showDollars(double); // Function prototype

int main()
{
   double payRate, hoursWorked, wages;

   cout << "How many hours have you worked? "
   cin >> hoursWorked;
   cout << "What is your hourly pay rate? ";
   cin >> payRate;
   wages = hoursWorked * payRate;
   showDollars(wages);
   return 0;
}

// You must write the definition of the function showDollars
// here. It should take one parameter of the type double.
// The function should display the message "Your wages are $"
// followed by the value of the parameter. It should be displayed
// with 2 places of precision after the decimal point, in fixed
// notation, and the decimal point should always display.
```

6.7   The return Statement

CONCEPT: The return statement causes a function to end immediately.

When the last statement in a void function has finished executing, the function terminates and the program returns to the statement following the function call. It's possible, however, to force a function to return before the last statement has been executed. When the return statement is encountered, the function immediately terminates and control of the program returns to the statement that called the function. This is demonstrated in Program 6-11. The function divide shows the quotient of arg1 divided by arg2. If arg2 is set to zero, the function returns.

Program 6-11

```
 1    // This program uses a function to perform division. If division
 2    // by zero is detected, the function returns.
 3    #include <iostream>
 4    using namespace std;
 5
 6    // Function prototype.
 7    void divide(double, double);
 8
 9    int main()
10    {
11       double num1, num2;
12
13       cout << "Enter two numbers and I will divide the first\n";
14       cout << "number by the second number: ";
15       cin >> num1 >> num2;
16       divide(num1, num2);
17       return 0;
18    }
19
20    //*************************************************************
21    // Definition of function divide.                           *
22    // Uses two parameters: arg1 and arg2. The function divides arg1*
23    // by arg2 and shows the result. If arg2 is zero, however, the  *
24    // function returns.                                         *
25    //*************************************************************
26
27    void divide(double arg1, double arg2)
28    {
29       if (arg2 == 0.0)
30       {
31          cout << "Sorry, I cannot divide by zero.\n";
32          return;
33       }
34       cout << "The quotient is " << (arg1 / arg2) << endl;
35    }
```

Program Output with Example Input Shown in Bold
```
Enter two numbers and I will divide the first
number by the second number: 12 0 [Enter]
Sorry, I cannot divide by zero.
```

In the example running of the program, the user entered 12 and 0 as input. In line 16 the divide function was called, passing 12 into the arg1 parameter and 0 into the arg2 parameter. Inside the divide function, the if statement in line 29 executes. Because arg2 is equal to 0.0, the code in lines 31 and 32 execute. When the return statement in line 32 executes, the divide function immediately ends. This means the cout statement in line 34 does not execute. The program resumes at line 17 in the main function.

6.8   Returning a Value from a Function

CONCEPT: A function may send a value back to the part of the program that called the function.

You've seen that data may be passed into a function by way of parameter variables. Data may also be returned from a function, back to the statement that called it. Functions that return a value are appropriately known as *value-returning functions*.

VideoNote

Value-Return-
ing Functions

The pow function, which you have already seen, is an example of a value-returning function. Here is an example:

```
double x;
x = pow(4.0, 2.0);
```

The second line in this code calls the pow function, passing 4.0 and 2.0 as arguments. The function calculates the value of 4.0 raised to the power of 2.0 and returns that value. The value, which is 16.0, is assigned to the x variable by the = operator.

Although several arguments may be passed into a function, only one value may be returned from it. Think of a function as having multiple communication channels for receiving data (parameters), but only one channel for sending data (the return value). This is illustrated in Figure 6-9.

Figure 6-9

NOTE: It is possible to return multiple values from a function, but they must be "packaged" in such a way that they are treated as a single value. This is a topic of Chapter 11.

Defining a Value-Returning Function

When you are writing a value-returning function, you must decide what type of value the function will return. This is because you must specify the data type of the return value in the function header, and in the function prototype. Recall that a void function, which does not return a value, uses the key word void as its return type in the function header. A value-returning function will use `int`, `double`, `bool`, or any other valid data type in its header. Here is an example of a function that returns an `int` value:

```
int sum(int num1, int num2)
{
   int result;

   result = num1 + num2;
   return result;
}
```

The name of this function is `sum`. Notice in the function header that the return type is `int`, as illustrated in Figure 6-10.

Figure 6-10

Return Type
↓

```
int sum(int num1, int num2)
```

This code defines a function named `sum` that accepts two `int` arguments. The arguments are passed into the parameter variables `num1` and `num2`. Inside the function, a variable, `result`, is defined. Variables that are defined inside a function are called *local variables*. After the variable definition, the parameter variables `num1` and `num2` are added, and their sum is assigned to the `result` variable. The last statement in the function is

```
return result;
```

This statement causes the function to end, and it sends the value of the `result` variable back to the statement that called the function. A value-returning function must have a return statement written in the following general format:

```
return expression;
```

In the general format, *expression* is the value to be returned. It can be any expression that has a value, such as a variable, literal, or mathematical expression. The value of the expression is converted to the data type that the function returns, and is sent back to the statement that called the function. In this case, the `sum` function returns the value in the `result` variable.

However, we could have eliminated the `result` variable and returned the expression `num1 + num2`, as shown in the following code:

```
int sum(int num1, int num2)
{
   return num1 + num2;
}
```

When writing the prototype for a value-returning function, follow the same conventions that we have covered earlier. Here is the prototype for the sum function:

```
int sum(int, int);
```

Calling a Value-Returning Function

Program 6-12 shows an example of how to call the sum function.

Program 6-12

```
 1   // This program uses a function that returns a value.
 2   #include <iostream>
 3   using namespace std;
 4
 5   // Function prototype
 6   int sum(int, int);
 7
 8   int main()
 9   {
10      int value1 = 20,    // The first value
11          value2 = 40,    // The second value
12          total;          // To hold the total
13
14      // Call the sum function, passing the contents of
15      // value1 and value2 as arguments. Assign the return
16      // value to the total variable.
17      total = sum(value1, value2);
18
19      // Display the sum of the values.
20      cout << "The sum of " << value1 << " and "
21           << value2 << " is " << total << endl;
22      return 0;
23   }
24
25   //*****************************************************
26   // Definition of function sum. This function returns  *
27   // the sum of its two parameters.                     *
28   //*****************************************************
29
30   int sum(int num1, int num2)
31   {
32      return num1 + num2;
33   }
```

Program Output
```
The sum of 20 and 40 is 60
```

Here is the statement in line 17 that calls the sum function, passing value1 and value2 as arguments.

```
total = sum(value1, value2);
```

This statement assigns the value returned by the sum function to the total variable. In this case, the function will return 60. Figure 6-11 shows how the arguments are passed into the function and how a value is passed back from the function.

Figure 6-11

When you call a value-returning function, you usually want to do something meaningful with the value it returns. Program 6-12 shows a function's return value being assigned to a variable. This is commonly how return values are used, but you can do many other things with them. For example, the following code shows a mathematical expression that uses a call to the sum function:

```
int x = 10, y = 15;
double average;
average = sum(x, y) / 2.0;
```

In the last statement, the sum function is called with x and y as its arguments. The function's return value, which is 25, is divided by 2.0. The result, 12.5, is assigned to average. Here is another example:

```
int x = 10, y = 15;
cout << "The sum is " << sum(x, y) << endl;
```

This code sends the sum function's return value to cout so it can be displayed on the screen. The message "The sum is 25" will be displayed.

Remember, a value-returning function returns a value of a specific data type. You can use the function's return value anywhere that you can use a regular value of the same data type. This means that anywhere an int value can be used, a call to an int value-returning function can be used. Likewise, anywhere a double value can be used, a call to a double value-returning function can be used. The same is true for all other data types.

Let's look at another example. Program 6-13, which calculates the area of a circle, has two functions in addition to main. One of the functions is named square, and it returns the square of any number passed to it as an argument. The square function is called in a mathematical statement. The program also has a function named getRadius, which prompts the user to enter the circle's radius. The value entered by the user is returned from the function.

Program 6-13

```
1   // This program demonstrates two value-returning functions.
2   // The square function is called in a mathematical statement.
3   #include <iostream>
4   #include <iomanip>
5   using namespace std;
6
```

(program continues)

Program 6-13   *(continued)*

```cpp
 7   //Function prototypes
 8   double getRadius();
 9   double square(double);
10
11   int main()
12   {
13      const double PI = 3.14159; // Constant for pi
14      double radius;             // To hold the circle's radius
15      double area;               // To hold the circle's area
16
17      // Set the numeric output formatting.
18      cout << fixed << showpoint << setprecision(2);
19
20      // Get the radius of the circle.
21      cout << "This program calculates the area of ";
22      cout << "a circle.\n";
23      radius = getRadius();
24
25      // Caculate the area of the circle.
26      area = PI * square(radius);
27
28      // Display the area.
29      cout << "The area is " << area << endl;
30      return 0;
31   }
32
33   //*********************************************************
34   // Definition of function getRadius.                      *
35   // This function asks the user to enter the radius of     *
36   // the circle and then returns that number as a double.   *
37   //*********************************************************
38
39   double getRadius()
40   {
41      double rad;
42
43      cout << "Enter the radius of the circle: ";
44      cin >> rad;
45      return rad;
46   }
47
48   //*********************************************************
49   // Definition of function square.                         *
50   // This function accepts a double argument and returns    *
51   // the square of the argument as a double.                *
52   //*********************************************************
53
54   double square(double number)
55   {
56      return number * number;
57   }
```

Program Output with Example Input Shown in Bold
```
This program calculates the area of a circle.
Enter the radius of the circle: 10 [Enter]
The area is 314.16
```

First, look at the getRadius function defined in lines 39 through 46. The purpose of the function is to prompt the user to enter the radius of a circle. In line 41 the function defines a local variable, rad. Lines 43 and 44 prompt the user to enter the circle's radius, which is stored in the rad variable. In line 45 the value of the rad value is returned. The getRadius function is called in the main function, in line 23. The value that is returned from the function is assigned to the radius variable.

Next look at the square function, which is defined in lines 54 through 57. When the function is called, a double argument is passed to it. The function stores the argument in the number parameter. The return statement in line 56 returns the value of the expression number * number, which is the square of the number parameter. The square function is called in the main function, in line 26, with the value of radius passed as an argument. The function will return the square of the radius variable, and that value will be used in the mathematical expression.

Assuming the user has entered 10 as the radius, and this value is passed as an argument to the square function, the square function will return the value 100. Figure 6-12 illustrates how the value 100 is passed back to the mathematical expression in line 26. The value 100 will then be used in the mathematical expression.

Figure 6-12

Functions can return values of any type. Both the getRadius and square functions in Program 6-13 return a double. The sum function you saw in Program 6-12 returned an int. When a statement calls a value-returning function, it should properly handle the return value. For example, if you assign the return value of the square function to a variable, the variable should be a double. If the return value of the function has a fractional portion and you assign it to an int variable, the value will be truncated.

In the Spotlight:

Using Functions

Your friend Michael runs a catering company. Some of the ingredients that his recipes require are measured in cups. When he goes to the grocery store to buy those ingredients, however, they are sold only by the fluid ounce. He has asked you to write a simple program that converts cups to fluid ounces.

You design the following algorithm:

1. *Display an introductory screen that explains what the program does.*

2. *Get the number of cups.*

3. *Convert the number of cups to fluid ounces and display the result.*

This algorithm lists the top level of tasks that the program needs to perform, and becomes the basis of the program's main function. The hierarchy chart shown in Figure 6-13 shows how the program will broken down into functions.

Figure 6-13   Hierarchy chart for the program

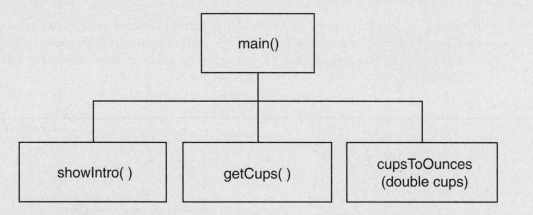

As shown in the hierarchy chart, the main function will call three other functions. Here are summaries of those functions:

- showIntro—This function will display a message on the screen that explains what the program does.
- getCups—This function will prompt the user to enter the number of cups and then will return that value as a double.
- cupsToOunces—This function will accept the number of cups as an argument and then return an equivalent number of fluid ounces as a double.

Program 6-14 shows the code for the program.

Program 6-14

```cpp
1  // This program converts cups to fluid ounces.
2  #include <iostream>
3  #include <iomanip>
4  using namespace std;
5
6  // Function prototypes
7  void showIntro();
8  double getCups();
9  double cupsToOunces(double);
10
11 int main()
12 {
13    // Variables for the cups and ounces.
14    double cups, ounces;
15
16    // Set up numeric output formatting.
17    cout << fixed << showpoint << setprecision(1);
18
19    // Display an intro screen.
20    showIntro();
21
22    // Get the number of cups.
23    cups = getCups();
24
25    // Convert cups to fluid ounces.
26    ounces = cupsToOunces(cups);
27
28    // Display the number of ounces.
29    cout << cups << " cups equals "
30         << ounces << " ounces.\n";
31
32    return 0;
33 }
34
35 //*****************************************
36 // The showIntro function displays an     *
37 // introductory screen.                   *
38 //*****************************************
39
40 void showIntro()
41 {
42    cout << "This program converts measurements\n"
43         << "in cups to fluid ounces. For your\n"
44         << "reference the formula is:\n"
45         << "     1 cup = 8 fluid ounces\n\n";
46 }
47
48 //*****************************************
49 // The getCups function prompts the user  *
50 // to enter the number of cups and then   *
51 // returns that value as a double.        *
52 //*****************************************
53
```

(program continues)

Program 6-14   *(continued)*

```
54 double getCups()
55 {
56    double numCups;
57
58    cout << "Enter the number of cups: ";
59    cin >> numCups;
60    return numCups;
61 }
62
63 //*****************************************
64 // The cupsToOunces function accepts a     *
65 // number of cups as an argument and       *
66 // returns the equivalent number of fluid  *
67 // ounces as a double.                      *
68 //*****************************************
69
70 double cupsToOunces(double numCups)
71 {
72    return numCups * 8.0;
73 }
```

Program Output with Example Input Shown in Bold

```
This program converts measurements
in cups to fluid ounces. For your
reference the formula is:
    1 cup = 8 fluid ounces

Enter the number of cups: 2 [Enter]
2.0 cups equals 16.0 ounces.
```

6.9   Returning a Boolean Value

CONCEPT: Functions may return **true** or **false** values.

Frequently there is a need for a function that tests an argument and returns a **true** or **false** value indicating whether or not a condition exists. Such a function would return a **bool** value. For example, the following function accepts an **int** argument and returns true if the argument is within the range of 1 through 100, or **false** otherwise.

```
bool isValid(int number)
{
   bool status;

   if (number >= 1 && number <= 100)
      status = true;
   else
      status = false;
   return status;
}
```

The following code shows an if/else statement that uses a call to the function:

```cpp
int value = 20;
if (isValid(value))
    cout << "The value is within range.\n";
else
    cout << "The value is out of range.\n";
```

When this code executes, the message "The value is within range." will be displayed.

Program 6-15 shows another example. This program has a function named isEven which returns true if its argument is an even number. Otherwise, the function returns false.

Program 6-15

```cpp
 1  // This program uses a function that returns true or false.
 2  #include <iostream>
 3  using namespace std;
 4
 5  // Function prototype
 6  bool isEven(int);
 7
 8  int main()
 9  {
10      int val;
11
12      // Get a number from the user.
13      cout << "Enter an integer and I will tell you ";
14      cout << "if it is even or odd: ";
15      cin >> val;
16
17      // Indicate whether it is even or odd.
18      if (isEven(val))
19          cout << val << " is even.\n";
20      else
21          cout << val << " is odd.\n";
22      return 0;
23  }
24
25  //*****************************************************************
26  // Definition of function isEven. This function accepts an       *
27  // integer argument and tests it to be even or odd. The function *
28  // returns true if the argument is even or false if the argument *
29  // is odd. The return value is a bool.                           *
30  //*****************************************************************
31
32  bool isEven(int number)
33  {
34      bool status;
35
36      if (number % 2 == 0)
37          status = true;  // The number is even if there is no remainder.
38      else
39          status = false; // Otherwise, the number is odd.
40      return status;
41  }
```

(program output continues)

Program 6-15   *(continued)*

Program Output with Example Input Shown in Bold
Enter an integer and I will tell you if it is even or odd: **5 [Enter]**
5 is odd.

The isEven function is called in line 18, in the following statement:

    if (isEven(val))

When the if statement executes, isEven is called with val as its argument. If val is even, isEven returns true , otherwise it returns false.

 ## Checkpoint

6.11   How many return values may a function have?

6.12   Write a header for a function named distance. The function should return a double and have two double parameters: rate and time.

6.13   Write a header for a function named days. The function should return an int and have three int parameters: years, months, and weeks.

6.14   Write a header for a function named getKey. The function should return a char and use no parameters.

6.15   Write a header for a function named lightYears. The function should return a long and have one long parameter: miles.

 # 6.10   Local and Global Variables

CONCEPT: A local variable is defined inside a function and is not accessible outside the function. A global variable is defined outside all functions and is accessible to all functions in its scope.

Local Variables

Variables defined inside a function are *local* to that function. They are hidden from the statements in other functions, which normally cannot access them. Program 6-16 shows that because the variables defined in a function are hidden, other functions may have separate, distinct variables with the same name.

Program 6-16

```
1   // This program shows that variables defined in a function
2   // are hidden from other functions.
3   #include <iostream>
4   using namespace std;
5
6   void anotherFunction(); // Function prototype
```

```
 7
 8   int main()
 9   {
10      int num = 1;   // Local variable
11
12      cout << "In main, num is " << num << endl;
13      anotherFunction();
14      cout << "Back in main, num is " << num << endl;
15      return 0;
16   }
17
18   //*****************************************************
19   // Definition of anotherFunction                     *
20   // It has a local variable, num, whose initial value  *
21   // is displayed.                                      *
22   //*****************************************************
23
24   void anotherFunction()
25   {
26      int num = 20;  // Local variable
27
28      cout << "In anotherFunction, num is " << num << endl;
29   }
```

Program Output
```
In main, num is 1
In anotherFunction, num is 20
Back in main, num is 1
```

Even though there are two variables named num, the program can only "see" one of them at a time because they are in different functions. When the program is executing in main, the num variable defined in main is visible. When anotherFunction is called, however, only variables defined inside it are visible, so the num variable in main is hidden. Figure 6-14 illustrates the closed nature of the two functions. The boxes represent the scope of the variables.

Figure 6-14

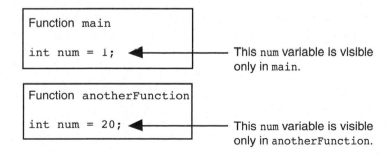

| Function main | |
| int num = 1; ◄ | This num variable is visible only in main. |

| Function anotherFunction | |
| int num = 20; ◄ | This num variable is visible only in anotherFunction. |

Local Variable Lifetime

A function's local variables exist only while the function is executing. This is known as the *lifetime* of a local variable. When the function begins, its local variables and its parameter variables are created in memory, and when the function ends, the local variables and parameter variables are destroyed. This means that any value stored in a local variable is lost between calls to the function in which the variable is declared.

Initializing Local Variables with Parameter Values

It is possible to use a parameter variable to initialize a local variable. Sometimes this simplifies the code in a function. For example, recall the first version of the sum function we discussed earlier:

```
int sum(int num1, int num2)
{
    int result;

    result = num1 + num2;
    return result;
}
```

In the body of the function, the result variable is defined and then a separate assignment statement assigns num1 + num2 to result. We can combine these statements into one, as shown in the following modified version of the function.

```
int sum(int num1, int num2)
{
    int result = num1 + num2;
    return result;
}
```

Because the scope of a parameter variable is the entire function in which it is declared, we can use parameter variables to initialize local variables.

Global Variables and Global Constants

A global variable is any variable defined outside all the functions in a program. The scope of a global variable is the portion of the program from the variable definition to the end. This means that a global variable can be accessed by all functions that are defined after the global variable is defined. Program 6-17 shows two functions, main and anotherFunction, that access the same global variable, num.

Program 6-17

```
1   // This program shows that a global variable is visible
2   // to all the functions that appear in a program after
3   // the variable's declaration.
4   #include <iostream>
5   using namespace std;
6
7   void anotherFunction(); // Function prototype
8   int num = 2;            // Global variable
```

```
 9
10   int main()
11   {
12      cout << "In main, num is " << num << endl;
13      anotherFunction();
14      cout << "Back in main, num is " << num << endl;
15      return 0;
16   }
17
18   //****************************************************
19   // Definition of anotherFunction                   *
20   // This function changes the value of the          *
21   // global variable num.                            *
22   //****************************************************
23
24   void anotherFunction()
25   {
26      cout << "In anotherFunction, num is " << num << endl;
27      num = 50;
28      cout << "But, it is now changed to " << num << endl;
29   }
```

Program Output

```
In main, num is 2
In anotherFunction, num is 2
But, it is now changed to 50
Back in main, num is 50
```

In Program 6-17, num is defined outside of all the functions. Because its definition appears before the definitions of main and anotherFunction, both functions have access to it.

Unless you explicitly initialize numeric global variables, they are automatically initialized to zero. Global character variables are initialized to NULL.* The variable globalNum in Program 6-18 is never set to any value by a statement, but because it is global, it is automatically set to zero.

Program 6-18

```
 1   // This program has an uninitialized global variable.
 2   #include <iostream>
 3   using namespace std;
 4
 5   int globalNum; // Global variable, automatically set to zero
 6
 7   int main()
 8   {
 9      cout << "globalNum is " << globalNum << endl;
10      return 0;
11   }
```

(program output continues)

---

* The NULL character is stored as ASCII code 0.

Program 6-18 *(continued)*

Program Output
```
globalNum is 0
```

Now that you've had a basic introduction to global variables, I must warn you to restrict your use of them. When beginning students first learn to write programs with multiple functions, they are sometimes tempted to make all their variables global. This is usually because global variables can be accessed by any function in the program without being passed as arguments. Although this approach might make a program easier to create, it usually causes problems later. The reasons are as follows:

- Global variables make debugging difficult. Any statement in a program can change the value of a global variable. If you find that the wrong value is being stored in a global variable, you have to track down every statement that accesses it to determine where the bad value is coming from. In a program with thousands of lines of code, this can be difficult.
- Functions that use global variables are usually dependent on those variables. If you want to use such a function in a different program, most likely you will have to redesign it so it does not rely on the global variable.
- Global variables make a program hard to understand. A global variable can be modified by any statement in the program. If you are to understand any part of the program that uses a global variable, you have to be aware of all the other parts of the program that access the global variable.

In most cases, you should declare variables locally and pass them as arguments to the functions that need to access them.

Because of this, you should not use global variables for the conventional purposes of storing, manipulating, and retrieving data. Instead, you should only use them as *global constants*, defining them with the `const` modifier. Because a constant cannot be changed during program execution, you do not have to worry about a global constant's value getting corrupted.

Program 6-19 shows an example of how global constants might be used. The program calculates an employee's gross pay, including overtime. In addition to `main`, this program has two functions: `getBasePay` and `getOvertimePay`. The `getBasePay` function accepts the number of hours worked and returns the amount of pay for the non-overtime hours. The `getOvertimePay` function accepts the number of hours worked and returns the amount of pay for the overtime hours, if any.

Program 6-19

```
1   // This program calculates gross pay.
2   #include <iostream>
3   #include <iomanip>
4   using namespace std;
5
6   // Global constants
7   const double PAY_RATE = 22.55;    // Hourly pay rate
8   const double BASE_HOURS = 40.0;   // Max non-overtime hours
```

```
 9    const double OT_MULTIPLIER = 1.5; // Overtime multiplier
10
11    // Function prototypes
12    double getBasePay(double);
13    double getOvertimePay(double);
14
15    int main()
16    {
17       double hours,            // Hours worked
18              basePay,          // Base pay
19              overtime = 0.0,   // Overtime pay
20              totalPay;         // Total pay
21
22       // Get the number of hours worked.
23       cout << "How many hours did you work? ";
24       cin >> hours;
25
26       // Get the amount of base pay.
27       basePay = getBasePay(hours);
28
29       // Get overtime pay, if any.
30       if (hours > BASE_HOURS)
31          overtime = getOvertimePay(hours);
32
33       // Calculate the total pay.
34       totalPay = basePay + overtime;
35
36       // Set up numeric output formatting.
37       cout << setprecision(2) << fixed << showpoint;
38
39       // Display the pay.
40       cout << "Base pay: $" << basePay << endl;
41       cout << "Overtime pay: $" << overtime << endl;
42       cout << "Total pay: $" << totalPay << endl;
43       return 0;
44    }
45
46    //************************************************
47    // The getBasePay function accepts the number of *
48    // hours worked as an argument and returns the   *
49    // employee's pay for non-overtime hours.        *
50    //************************************************
51
52    double getBasePay(double hoursWorked)
53    {
54       double basePay; // To hold base pay
55
56       // Determine base pay.
57       if (hoursWorked > BASE_HOURS)
58          basePay = BASE_HOURS * PAY_RATE;
59       else
60          basePay = hoursWorked * PAY_RATE;
```

(program continues)

Program 6-19   *(continued)*

```
61
62      return basePay;
63   }
64
65   //*************************************************
66   // The getOvertimePay function accepts the number *
67   // of hours worked as an argument and returns the *
68   // employee's overtime pay.                       *
69   //*************************************************
70
71   double getOvertimePay(double hoursWorked)
72   {
73      double overtimePay; // To hold overtime pay
74
75      // Determine overtime pay.
76      if (hoursWorked > BASE_HOURS)
77      {
78         overtimePay = (hoursWorked - BASE_HOURS) *
79                 PAY_RATE * OT_MULTIPLIER;
80      }
81      else
82         overtimePay = 0.0;
83
84      return overtimePay;
85   }
```

Program Output with Example Input Shown in Bold
```
How many hours did you work? 48 [Enter]
Base pay: $902.00
Overtime pay: $270.60
Total pay: $1172.60
```

Let's take a closer look at the program. Three global constants are defined in lines 7, 8, and 9. The PAY_RATE constant is set to the employee's hourly pay rate, which is 22.55. The BASE_HOURS constant is set to 40, which is the number of hours an employee can work in a week without getting paid overtime. The OT_MULTIPLIER constant is set to 1.5, which is the pay rate multiplier for overtime hours. This means that the employee's hourly pay rate is multiplied by 1.5 for all overtime hours.

Because these constants are global, and are defined before all of the functions in the program, all the functions may access them. For example, the getBasePay function accesses the BASE_HOURS constant in lines 57 and 58, and accesses the PAY_RATE constant in lines 58 and 60. The getOvertimePay function accesses the BASE_HOURS constant in lines 76 and 78, the PAY_RATE constant in line 79, and the OT_MULTIPLIER constant in line 79.

Local and Global Variables with the Same Name

You cannot have two local variables with the same name in the same function. This applies to parameter variables as well. A parameter variable is, in essence, a local variable. So, you cannot give a parameter variable and a local variable in the same function the same name.

However, you can have a local variable or a parameter variable with the same name as a global variable, or a global constant. When you do, the name of the local or parameter variable *shadows* the name of the global variable or global constant. This means that the global variable or constant's name is hidden by the name of the local or parameter variable. For example, look at Program 6-20. This program has a global constant named BIRDS, set to 500. The california function has a local constant named BIRDS, set to 10000.

Program 6-20

```
 1   // This program demonstrates how a local variable
 2   // can shadow the name of a global constant.
 3   #include <iostream>
 4   using namespace std;
 5
 6   // Global constant.
 7   const int BIRDS = 500;
 8
 9   // Function prototype
10   void california();
11
12   int main()
13   {
14      cout << "In main there are " << BIRDS
15          << " birds.\n";
16      california();
17      return 0;
18   }
19
20   //*******************************************
21   // california function                      *
22   //*******************************************
23
24   void california()
25   {
26      const int BIRDS = 10000;
27      cout << "In california there are " << BIRDS
28          << " birds.\n";
29   }
```

Program Output
```
In main there are 500 birds.
In california there are 10000 birds.
```

When the program is executing in the main function, the global constant BIRDS, which is set to 500, is visible. The cout statement in lines 14 and 15 displays "In main there are 500 birds." (My apologies to folks living in Maine for the difference in spelling.) When the program is executing in the california function, however, the local constant BIRDS shadows the global constant BIRDS. When the california function accesses BIRDS, it accesses the local constant. That is why the cout statement in lines 27 and 28 displays "In california there are 10000 birds."

6.11   Static Local Variables

If a function is called more than once in a program, the values stored in the function's local variables do not persist between function calls. This is because the local variables are destroyed when the function terminates and are then re-created when the function starts again. This is shown in Program 6-21.

Program 6-21

```
 1   // This program shows that local variables do not retain
 2   // their values between function calls.
 3   #include <iostream>
 4   using namespace std;
 5
 6   // Function prototype
 7   void showLocal();
 8
 9   int main()
10   {
11      showLocal();
12      showLocal();
13      return 0;
14   }
15
16   //*********************************************************
17   // Definition of function showLocal.                     *
18   // The initial value of localNum, which is 5, is displayed. *
19   // The value of localNum is then changed to 99 before the  *
20   // function returns.                                      *
21   //*********************************************************
22
23   void showLocal()
24   {
25      int localNum = 5; // Local variable
26
27      cout << "localNum is " << localNum << endl;
28      localNum = 99;
29   }
```

Program Output
```
localNum is 5
localNum is 5
```

Even though in line 28 the last statement in the showLocal function stores 99 in localNum, the variable is destroyed when the function returns. The next time the function is called, localNum is re-created and initialized to 5 again.

Sometimes it's desirable for a program to "remember" what value is stored in a local variable between function calls. This can be accomplished by making the variable static.

Static local variables are not destroyed when a function returns. They exist for the lifetime of the program, even though their scope is only the function in which they are defined. Program 6-22 demonstrates some characteristics of `static` local variables:

Program 6-22

```
1   // This program uses a static local variable.
2   #include <iostream>
3   using namespace std;
4
5   void showStatic(); // Function prototype
6
7   int main()
8   {
9      // Call the showStatic function five times.
10     for (int count = 0; count < 5; count++)
11        showStatic();
12     return 0;
13  }
14
15  //**************************************************************
16  // Definition of function showStatic.                         *
17  // statNum is a static local variable. Its value is displayed *
18  // and then incremented just before the function returns.     *
19  //**************************************************************
20
21  void showStatic()
22  {
23     static int statNum;
24
25     cout << "statNum is " << statNum << endl;
26     statNum++;
27  }
```

Program Output
```
statNum is 0
statNum is 1
statNum is 2
statNum is 3
statNum is 4
```

In line 26 of Program 6-22, `statNum` is incremented in the `showStatic` function, and it retains its value between each function call. Notice that even though `statNum` is not explicitly initialized, it starts at zero. Like global variables, all `static` local variables are initialized to zero by default. (Of course, you can provide your own initialization value, if necessary.)

If you do provide an initialization value for a `static` local variable, the initialization only occurs once. This is because initialization normally happens when the variable is created, and `static` local variables are only created once during the running of a program. Program 6-23, which is a slight modification of Program 6-22, illustrates this point.

Program 6-23

```cpp
1   // This program shows that a static local variable is only
2   // initialized once.
3   #include <iostream>
4   using namespace std;
5
6   void showStatic(); // Function prototype
7
8   int main()
9   {
10     // Call the showStatic function five times.
11     for (int count = 0; count < 5; count++)
12        showStatic();
13     return 0;
14  }
15
16  //************************************************************
17  // Definition of function showStatic.                       *
18  // statNum is a static local variable. Its value is displayed *
19  // and then incremented just before the function returns.   *
20  //************************************************************
21
22  void showStatic()
23  {
24     static int statNum = 5;
25
26     cout << "statNum is " << statNum << endl;
27     statNum++;
28  }
```

Program Output
```
statNum is 5
statNum is 6
statNum is 7
statNum is 8
statNum is 9
```

Even though the statement that defines statNum in line 24 initializes it to 5, the initialization does not happen each time the function is called. If it did, the variable would not be able to retain its value between function calls.

 Checkpoint

6.16   What is the difference between a static local variable and a global variable?

6.17   What is the output of the following program?

```cpp
#include <iostream>
using namespace std;

void myFunc();  // Function prototype

int main()
{
```

```
    int var = 100;

    cout << var << endl;
    myFunc();
    cout << var << endl;
    return 0;
}

// Definition of function myFunc
void myFunc()
{
    int var = 50;

    cout << var << endl;
}
```

6.18   What is the output of the following program?

```
#include <iostream>
using namespace std;

void showVar(); // Function prototype

int main()
{
    for (int count = 0; count < 10; count++)
        showVar();
    return 0;
}

// Definition of function showVar
void showVar()
{
    static int var = 10;

    cout << var << endl;
    var++;
}
```

6.12   Default Arguments

CONCEPT: Default arguments are passed to parameters automatically if no argument is provided in the function call.

It's possible to assign *default arguments* to function parameters. A default argument is passed to the parameter when the actual argument is left out of the function call. The default arguments are usually listed in the function prototype. Here is an example:

```
void showArea(double = 20.0, double = 10.0);
```

Default arguments are literal values or constants with an = operator in front of them, appearing after the data types listed in a function prototype. Since parameter names are optional in function prototypes, the example prototype could also be declared as

```
void showArea(double length = 20.0, double width = 10.0);
```

In both example prototypes, the function `showArea` has two `double` parameters. The first is assigned the default argument 20.0 and the second is assigned the default argument 10.0. Here is the definition of the function:

```
void showArea(double length, double width)
{
    double area = length * width;
    cout << "The area is " << area << endl;
}
```

The default argument for `length` is 20.0 and the default argument for `width` is 10.0. Because both parameters have default arguments, they may optionally be omitted in the function call, as shown here:

```
showArea();
```

In this function call, both default arguments will be passed to the parameters. The parameter `length` will take the value 20.0 and `width` will take the value 10.0. The output of the function will be

```
The area is 200
```

The default arguments are only used when the actual arguments are omitted from the function call. In the call below, the first argument is specified, but the second is omitted:

```
showArea(12.0);
```

The value 12.0 will be passed to `length`, while the default value 10.0 will be passed to `width`. The output of the function will be

```
The area is 120
```

Of course, all the default arguments may be overridden. In the function call below, arguments are supplied for both parameters:

```
showArea(12.0, 5.5);
```

The output of the function call above will be

```
The area is 66
```

NOTE: If a function does not have a prototype, default arguments may be specified in the function header. The `showArea` function could be defined as follows:

```
void showArea(double length = 20.0, double width = 10.0)
{
    double area = length * width;
    cout << "The area is " << area << endl;
}
```

WARNING! A function's default arguments should be assigned in the earliest occurrence of the function name. This will usually be the function prototype.

Program 6-24 uses a function that displays asterisks on the screen. Arguments are passed to the function specifying how many columns and rows of asterisks to display. Default arguments are provided to display one row of 10 asterisks.

Program 6-24

```cpp
 1   // This program demonstrates default function arguments.
 2   #include <iostream>
 3   using namespace std;
 4
 5   // Function prototype with default arguments
 6   void displayStars(int = 10, int = 1);
 7
 8   int main()
 9   {
10      displayStars();        // Use default values for cols and rows.
11      cout << endl;
12      displayStars(5);       // Use default value for rows.
13      cout << endl;
14      displayStars(7, 3);  // Use 7 for cols and 3 for rows.
15      return 0;
16   }
17
18   //*****************************************************
19   // Definition of function displayStars.             *
20   // The default argument for cols is 10 and for rows is 1.*
21   // This function displays a square made of asterisks.    *
22   //*****************************************************
23
24   void displayStars(int cols, int rows)
25   {
26      // Nested loop. The outer loop controls the rows
27      // and the inner loop controls the columns.
28      for (int down = 0; down < rows; down++)
29      {
30         for (int across = 0; across < cols; across++)
31            cout << "*";
32         cout << endl;
33      }
34   }
```

Program Output

```
**********

*****

*******
*******
*******
```

Although C++'s default arguments are very convenient, they are not totally flexible in their use. When an argument is left out of a function call, all arguments that come after it must be left out as well. In the `displayStars` function in Program 6-24, it is not possible to omit the argument for `cols` without also omitting the argument for `rows`. For example, the following function call would be illegal:

```cpp
displayStars(, 3); // Illegal function call.
```

It's possible for a function to have some parameters with default arguments and some without. For example, in the following function (which displays an employee's gross pay), only the last parameter has a default argument:

```
// Function prototype
void calcPay(int empNum, double payRate, double hours = 40.0);

// Definition of function calcPay
void calcPay(int empNum, double payRate, double hours)
{
    double wages;

    wages = payRate * hours;
    cout << fixed << showpoint << setprecision(2);
    cout << "Gross pay for employee number ";
    cout << empNum << " is " << wages << endl;
}
```

When calling this function, arguments must always be specified for the first two parameters (empNum and payRate) since they have no default arguments. Here are examples of valid calls:

```
calcPay(769, 15.75);      // Use default arg for 40 hours
calcPay(142, 12.00, 20);  // Specify number of hours
```

When a function uses a mixture of parameters with and without default arguments, the parameters with default arguments must be defined last. In the calcPay function, hours could not have been defined before either of the other parameters. The following prototypes are illegal:

```
// Illegal prototype
void calcPay(int empNum, double hours = 40.0, double payRate);

// Illegal prototype
void calcPay(double hours = 40.0, int empNum, double payRate);
```

Here is a summary of the important points about default arguments:

- The value of a default argument must be a literal value or a named constant.
- When an argument is left out of a function call (because it has a default value), all the arguments that come after it must be left out too.
- When a function has a mixture of parameters both with and without default arguments, the parameters with default arguments must be declared last.

6.13 Using Reference Variables as Parameters

CONCEPT: When used as parameters, reference variables allow a function to access the parameter's original argument. Changes to the parameter are also made to the argument.

Earlier you saw that arguments are normally passed to a function by value, and that the function cannot change the source of the argument. C++ provides a special type of variable called a *reference variable* that, when used as a function parameter, allows access to the original argument.

A reference variable is an alias for another variable. Any changes made to the reference variable are actually performed on the variable for which it is an alias. By using a reference variable as a parameter, a function may change a variable that is defined in another function.

Reference variables are defined like regular variables, except you place an ampersand (&) in front of the name. For example, the following function definition makes the parameter refVar a reference variable:

```
void doubleNum(int &refVar)
{
    refVar *= 2;
}
```

NOTE: The variable refVar is called "a reference to an int."

This function doubles refVar by multiplying it by 2. Since refVar is a reference variable, this action is actually performed on the variable that was passed to the function as an argument. When prototyping a function with a reference variable, be sure to include the ampersand after the data type. Here is the prototype for the doubleNum function:

```
void doubleNum(int &);
```

NOTE: Some programmers prefer not to put a space between the data type and the ampersand. The following prototype is equivalent to the one above:

```
void doubleNum(int&);
```

NOTE: The ampersand must appear in both the prototype and the header of any function that uses a reference variable as a parameter. It does not appear in the function call.

Program 6-25 demonstrates how the doubleNum function works.

Program 6-25

```
 1  // This program uses a reference variable as a function
 2  // parameter.
 3  #include <iostream>
 4  using namespace std;
 5
 6  // Function prototype. The parameter is a reference variable.
 7  void doubleNum(int &);
 8
 9  int main()
```

(program continues)

Program 6-25   *(continued)*

```
10  {
11      int value = 4;
12
13      cout << "In main, value is " << value << endl;
14      cout << "Now calling doubleNum..." << endl;
15      doubleNum(value);
16      cout << "Now back in main. value is " << value << endl;
17      return 0;
18  }
19
20  //*********************************************************
21  // Definition of doubleNum.                               *
22  // The parameter refVar is a reference variable. The value *
23  // in refVar is doubled.                                  *
24  //*********************************************************
25
26  void doubleNum (int &refVar)
27  {
28      refVar *= 2;
29  }
```

Program Output

```
In main, value is 4
Now calling doubleNum...
Now back in main. value is 8
```

The parameter refVar in Program 6-25 "points" to the value variable in function main. When a program works with a reference variable, it is actually working with the variable it references, or points to. This is illustrated in Figure 6-15.

Figure 6-15

Recall that function arguments are normally passed by value, which means a copy of the argument's value is passed into the parameter variable. When a reference parameter is used, it is said that the argument is *passed by reference*.

Program 6-26 is a modification of Program 6-25. The function getNum has been added. The function asks the user to enter a number, which is stored in userNum. userNum is a reference to main's variable value.

Program 6-26

```cpp
 1   // This program uses reference variables as function parameters.
 2   #include <iostream>
 3   using namespace std;
 4
 5   // Function prototypes. Both functions use reference variables
 6   // as parameters.
 7   void doubleNum(int &);
 8   void getNum(int &);
 9
10   int main()
11   {
12      int value;
13
14      // Get a number and store it in value.
15      getNum(value);
16
17      // Double the number stored in value.
18      doubleNum(value);
19
20      // Display the resulting number.
21      cout << "That value doubled is " << value << endl;
22      return 0;
23   }
24
25   //*************************************************************
26   // Definition of getNum.                                      *
27   // The parameter userNum is a reference variable. The user is *
28   // asked to enter a number, which is stored in userNum.       *
29   //*************************************************************
30
31   void getNum(int &userNum)
32   {
33      cout << "Enter a number: ";
34      cin >> userNum;
35   }
36
37   //*************************************************************
38   // Definition of doubleNum.                                   *
39   // The parameter refVar is a reference variable. The value    *
40   // in refVar is doubled.                                      *
41   //*************************************************************
42
43   void doubleNum (int &refVar)
44   {
45      refVar *= 2;
46   }
```

Program Output with Example Input Shown in Bold

```
Enter a number: 12 [Enter]
That value doubled is 24
```

NOTE: Only variables may be passed by reference. If you attempt to pass a nonvariable argument, such as a literal, a constant, or an expression, into a reference parameter, an error will result. Using the doubleNum function as an example, the following statements will generate an error.

```
doubleNum(5);              // Error
doubleNum(userNum + 10);   // Error
```

If a function uses more than one reference variable as a parameter, be sure to place the ampersand before each reference variable name. Here is the prototype and definition for a function that uses four reference variable parameters:

```
// Function prototype with four reference variables
// as parameters.
void addThree(int &, int &, int &, int &);

// Definition of addThree.
// All four parameters are reference variables.
void addThree(int &sum, int &num1, int &num2, int &num3)
{
    cout << "Enter three integer values: ";
    cin >> num1 >> num2 >> num3;
    sum = num1 + num2 + num3;
}
```

WARNING! Don't get carried away with using reference variables as function parameters. Any time you allow a function to alter a variable that's outside the function, you are creating potential debugging problems. Reference variables should only be used as parameters when the situation requires them.

 Checkpoint

6.19   What kinds of values may be specified as default arguments?

6.20   Write the prototype and header for a function called compute. The function should have three parameters: an int, a double, and a long (not necessarily in that order). The int parameter should have a default argument of 5, and the long parameter should have a default argument of 65536. The double parameter should not have a default argument.

6.21   Write the prototype and header for a function called calculate. The function should have three parameters: an int, a reference to a double, and a long (not necessarily in that order.) Only the int parameter should have a default argument, which is 47.

6.22   What is the output of the following program?

```
#include <iostream>
using namespace std;

void test(int = 2, int = 4, int = 6);
```

```cpp
int main()
{
   test();
   test(6);
   test(3, 9);
   test(1, 5, 7);
   return 0;
}

void test (int first, int second, int third)
{
   first += 3;
   second += 6;
   third += 9;
   cout << first << " " << second << " " << third << endl;
}
```

6.23   The following program asks the user to enter two numbers. What is the output of
the program if the user enters 12 and 14?

```cpp
#include <iostream>
using namespace std;

void func1(int &, int &);
void func2(int &, int &, int &);
void func3(int, int, int);

int main()
{
   int x = 0, y = 0, z = 0;

   cout << x << " " << y << " " << z << endl;
   func1(x, y);
   cout << x << " " << y << " " << z << endl;
   func2(x, y, z);
   cout << x << " " << y << " " << z << endl;
   func3(x, y, z);
   cout << x << " " << y << " " << z << endl;
   return 0;
}

void func1(int &a, int &b)
{
   cout << "Enter two numbers: ";
   cin >> a >> b;
}
void func2(int &a, int &b, int &c)
{
   b++;
   c--;
   a = b + c;
}

void func3(int a, int b, int c)
{
   a = b - c;
}
```

6.14 Overloading Functions

CONCEPT: Two or more functions may have the same name, as long as their parameter lists are different.

Sometimes you will create two or more functions that perform the same operation, but use a different set of parameters or parameters of different data types. For instance, in Program 6-13 there is a `square` function that uses a `double` parameter. But, suppose you also wanted a `square` function that works exclusively with integers, accepting an `int` as its argument. Both functions would do the same thing: return the square of their argument. The only difference is the data type involved in the operation. If you were to use both these functions in the same program, you could assign a unique name to each function. For example, the function that squares an `int` might be named `squareInt`, and the one that squares a `double` might be named `squareDouble`. C++, however, allows you to *overload* function names. That means you may assign the same name to multiple functions, as long as their parameter lists are different. Program 6-27 uses two overloaded square functions.

Program 6-27

```
 1   // This program uses overloaded functions.
 2   #include <iostream>
 3   #include <iomanip>
 4   using namespace std;
 5
 6   // Function prototypes
 7   int square(int);
 8   double square(double);
 9
10   int main()
11   {
12      int userInt;
13      double userFloat;
14
15      // Get an int and a double.
16      cout << fixed << showpoint << setprecision(2);
17      cout << "Enter an integer and a floating-point value: ";
18      cin >> userInt >> userFloat;
19
20      // Display their squares.
21      cout << "Here are their squares: ";
22      cout << square(userInt) << " and " << square(userFloat);
23      return 0;
24   }
25
26   //************************************************************
27   // Definition of overloaded function square.               *
28   // This function uses an int parameter, number. It returns the *
29   // square of number as an int.                             *
30   //************************************************************
```

```
31
32  int square(int number)
33  {
34      return number * number;
35  }
36
37  //*****************************************************************
38  // Definition of overloaded function square.                     *
39  // This function uses a double parameter, number. It returns     *
40  // the square of number as a double.                             *
41  //*****************************************************************
42
43  double square(double number)
44  {
45      return number * number;
46  }
```

Program Output with Example Input Shown in Bold

```
Enter an integer and a floating point value: 12 4.2 [Enter]
Here are their squares: 144 and 17.64
```

Here are the headers for the `square` functions used in Program 6-27:

```
int square(int number)
```

```
double square(double number)
```

In C++, each function has a signature. The *function signature* is the name of the function and the data types of the function's parameters in the proper order. The `square` functions in Program 6-27 would have the following signatures:

```
square(int)
```

```
square(double)
```

When an overloaded function is called, C++ uses the function signature to distinguish it from other functions with the same name. In Program 6-27, when an `int` argument is passed to `square`, the version of the function that has an `int` parameter is called. Likewise, when a `double` argument is passed to `square`, the version with a `double` parameter is called.

Note that the function's return value is not part of the signature. The following functions could not be used in the same program because their parameter lists aren't different.

```
int square(int number)
{
    return number * number
}

double square(int number)  // Wrong! Parameter lists must differ
{
    return number * number
}
```

Overloading is also convenient when there are similar functions that use a different number of parameters. For example, consider a program with functions that return the sum of integers. One returns the sum of two integers, another returns the sum of three integers, and yet another returns the sum of four integers. Here are their function headers:

```
int sum(int num1, int num2)

int sum(int num1, int num2, int num3)

int sum(int num1, int num2, int num3, int num4)
```

Because the number of parameters is different in each, they all may be used in the same program. Program 6-28 is an example that uses two functions, each named `calcWeeklyPay`, to determine an employee's gross weekly pay. One version of the function uses an `int` and a `double` parameter, while the other version only uses a `double` parameter.

Program 6-28

```cpp
 1   // This program demonstrates overloaded functions to calculate
 2   // the gross weekly pay of hourly paid or salaried employees.
 3   #include <iostream>
 4   #include <iomanip>
 5   using namespace std;
 6
 7   // Function prototypes
 8   void getChoice(char &);
 9   double calcWeeklyPay(int, double);
10   double calcWeeklyPay(double);
11
12   int main()
13   {
14      char selection;     // Menu selection
15      int worked;         // Hours worked
16      double rate;        // Hourly pay rate
17      double yearly;      // Yearly salary
18
19      // Set numeric output formatting.
20      cout << fixed << showpoint << setprecision(2);
21
22      // Display the menu and get a selection.
23      cout << "Do you want to calculate the weekly pay of\n";
24      cout << "(H) an hourly paid employee, or \n";
25      cout << "(S) a salaried employee?\n";
26      getChoice(selection);
27
28      // Process the menu selection.
29      switch (selection)
30      {
31         // Hourly paid employee
32         case 'H' :
33         case 'h' :  cout << "How many hours were worked? ";
```

```
34                      cin >> worked;
35                      cout << "What is the hourly pay rate? ";
36                      cin >> rate;
37                      cout << "The gross weekly pay is $";
38                      cout << calcWeeklyPay(worked, rate) << endl;
39                      break;
40
41          // Salaried employee
42          case 'S' :
43          case 's' :  cout << "What is the annual salary? ";
44                      cin >> yearly;
45                      cout << "The gross weekly pay is $";
46                      cout << calcWeeklyPay(yearly) << endl;
47                      break;
48      }
49      return 0;
50  }
51
52  //************************************************************
53  // Definition of function getChoice.                        *
54  // The parameter letter is a reference to a char.           *
55  // This function asks the user for an H or an S and returns *
56  // the validated input.                                     *
57  //************************************************************
58
59  void getChoice(char &letter)
60  {
61      // Get the user's selection.
62      cout << "Enter your choice (H or S): ";
63      cin >> letter;
64
65      // Validate the selection.
66      while (letter != 'H' && letter != 'h' &&
67             letter != 'S' && letter != 's')
68      {
69         cout << "Please enter H or S: ";
70         cin >> letter;
71      }
72  }
73
74  //************************************************************
75  // Definition of overloaded function calcWeeklyPay.         *
76  // This function calculates the gross weekly pay of         *
77  // an hourly paid employee. The parameter hours holds the   *
78  // number of hours worked. The parameter payRate holds the  *
79  // hourly pay rate. The function returns the weekly salary. *
80  //************************************************************
```

(program continues)

Program 6-28   *(continued)*

```
81
82   double calcWeeklyPay(int hours, double payRate)
83   {
84      return hours * payRate;
85   }
86
87   //**********************************************************
88   // Definition of overloaded function calcWeeklyPay.        *
89   // This function calculates the gross weekly pay of        *
90   // a salaried employee. The parameter holds the employee's *
91   // annual salary. The function returns the weekly salary.  *
92   //**********************************************************
93
94   double calcWeeklyPay(double annSalary)
95   {
96      return annSalary / 52;
97   }
```

Program Output with Example Input Shown in Bold

```
Do you want to calculate the weekly pay of
(H) an hourly paid employee, or
(S) a salaried employee?
Enter your choice (H or S): H [Enter]
How many hours were worked? 40 [Enter]
What is the hourly pay rate? 18.50 [Enter]
The gross weekly pay is $740.00
```

Program Output with Example Input Shown in Bold

```
Do you want to calculate the weekly pay of
(H) an hourly paid employee, or
(S) a salaried employee?
Enter your choice (H or S): S [Enter]
What is the annual salary? 68000.00 [Enter]
The gross weekly pay is $1307.69
```

6.15   The exit() Function

CONCEPT: The exit() function causes a program to terminate, regardless of which function or control mechanism is executing.

A C++ program stops executing when the return statement in function main is encountered. When other functions end, however, the program does not stop. Control of the program goes back to the place immediately following the function call. Sometimes it's convenient or even necessary to terminate a program in a function other than main. To accomplish this, the exit function is used.

When the exit function is called, it causes the program to stop, regardless of which function contains the call. Program 6-29 demonstrates its use.

Program 6-29

```cpp
1   // This program shows how the exit function causes a program
2   // to stop executing.
3   #include <iostream>
4   #include <cstdlib>    // For exit
5   using namespace std;
6
7   void function();      // Function prototype
8
9   int main()
10  {
11     function();
12     return 0;
13  }
14
15  //**********************************************************
16  // This function simply demonstrates that exit can be used  *
17  // to terminate a program from a function other than main.  *
18  //**********************************************************
19
20  void function()
21  {
22     cout << "This program terminates with the exit function.\n";
23     cout << "Bye!\n";
24     exit(0);
25     cout << "This message will never be displayed\n";
26     cout << "because the program has already terminated.\n";
27  }
```

Program Output

```
This program terminates with the exit function.
Bye!
```

To use the exit function, be sure to include the cstdlib header file. Notice the function takes an integer argument. This argument is the exit code you wish the program to pass back to the computer's operating system. This code is sometimes used outside of the program to indicate whether the program ended successfully or as the result of a failure. In Program 6-29, the exit code zero is passed, which commonly indicates a successful exit. If you are unsure which code to use with the exit function, there are two named constants, EXIT_FAILURE and EXIT_SUCCESS, defined in cstdlib for you to use. The constant EXIT_FAILURE is defined as the termination code that commonly represents an unsuccessful exit under the current operating system. Here is an example of its use:

```cpp
exit(EXIT_FAILURE);
```

The constant EXIT_SUCCESS is defined as the termination code that commonly represents a successful exit under the current operating system. Here is an example:

```cpp
exit(EXIT_SUCCESS);
```

 NOTE: Generally, the exit code is important only if you know it will be tested outside the program. If it is not used, just pass zero, or EXIT_SUCCESS.

Checkpoint

6.24   What is the output of the following program?

```cpp
#include <iostream>
#include <cstdlib>
using namespace std;

void showVals(double, double);

int main()
{

    double x = 1.2, y = 4.5;

    showVals(x, y);
    return 0;
}

void showVals(double p1, double p2)
{
    cout << p1 << endl;
    exit(0);
    cout << p2 << endl;
}
```

6.25   What is the output of the following program?

```cpp
#include <iostream>
using namespace std;

int manip(int);
int manip(int, int);
int manip(int, double);

int main()
{
    int x = 2, y= 4, z;
    double a = 3.1;

    z = manip(x) + manip(x, y) + manip(y, a);
    cout << z << endl;
    return 0;
}
int manip(int val)
{
    return val + val * 2;
}

int manip(int val1, int val2)
{
    return (val1 + val2) * 2;
}

int manip(int val1, double val2)
{
    return val1 * static_cast<int>(val2);
}
```

6.16 Stubs and Drivers

Stubs and *drivers* are very helpful tools for testing and debugging programs that use functions. They allow you to test the individual functions in a program, in isolation from the parts of the program that call the functions.

A *stub* is a dummy function that is called instead of the actual function it represents. It usually displays a test message acknowledging that it was called, and nothing more. For example, if a stub were used for the showFees function in Program 6-10 (the modular health club membership program), it might look like this:

```
void showFees(double memberRate, int months)
{
    cout << "The showFees function was called with "
         << "the following arguments:\n"
         << "memberRate: " << memberRate << endl
         << "months: " << months << endl;
}
```

The following is an example output of the program if it were run with the stub instead of the actual showFees function. (A version of the health club program using this stub function is on the Student CD. The program is named HealthClubWithStub.cpp.)

```
            Health Club Membership Menu

1. Standard Adult Membership
2. Child Membership
3. Senior Citizen Membership
4. Quit the Program

Enter your choice: 1 [Enter]
For how many months? 4 [Enter]
The showFees function was called with the following arguments:
memberRate: 40.00
months: 4


            Health Club Membership Menu

1. Standard Adult Membership
2. Child Membership
3. Senior Citizen Membership
4. Quit the Program

Enter your choice: 4 [Enter]
```

As you can see, by replacing an actual function with a stub, you can concentrate your testing efforts on the parts of the program that call the function. Primarily, the stub allows you to determine whether your program is calling a function when you expect it to, and to confirm that valid values are being passed to the function. If the stub represents a function that returns a value, then the stub should return a test value. This helps you confirm that the return value is being handled properly. When the parts of the program that call a function are debugged to your satisfaction, you can move on to testing and debugging the actual functions themselves. This is where *drivers* become useful.

A driver is a program that tests a function by simply calling it. If the function accepts arguments, the driver passes test data. If the function returns a value, the driver displays the return value on the screen. This allows you to see how the function performs in isolation from the rest of the program it will eventually be part of. Program 6-30 shows a driver for testing the showFees function in the health club membership program.

Program 6-30

```cpp
 1  // This program is a driver for testing the showFees function.
 2  #include <iostream>
 3  using namespace std;
 4
 5  // Prototype
 6  void showFees(double, int);
 7
 8  int main()
 9  {
10      // Constants for membership rates
11      const double ADULT = 40.0;
12      const double SENIOR = 30.0;
13      const double CHILD = 20.0;
14
15      // Perform a test for adult membership.
16      cout << "Testing an adult membership...\n"
17          << "Calling the showFees function with arguments "
18          << ADULT << " and 10.\n";
19      showFees(ADULT, 10);
20
21      // Perform a test for senior citizen membership.
22      cout << "\nTesting a senior citizen membership...\n"
23          << "Calling the showFees function with arguments "
24          << SENIOR << " and 10.\n";
25      showFees(SENIOR, 10);
26
27      // Perform a test for child membership.
28      cout << "\nTesting a child membership...\n"
29          << "\nCalling the showFees function with arguments "
30          << CHILD << " and 10.\n";
31      showFees(CHILD, 10);
32      return 0;
33  }
34
35  //*****************************************************************
36  // Definition of function showFees. The memberRate parameter holds*
37  // the monthly membership rate and the months parameter holds the *
38  // number of months. The function displays the total charges.     *
39  //*****************************************************************
40
41  void showFees(double memberRate, int months)
42  {
43      cout << "The total charges are $"
44          << (memberRate * months) << endl;
45  }
```

Program Output

```
Testing an adult membership...
Calling the showFees function with arguments 40 and 10.
The total charges are $400

Testing a senior citizen membership...
Calling the showFees function with arguments 30 and 10.
The total charges are $300

Testing a child membership...

Calling the showFees function with arguments 20 and 10.
The total charges are $200
```

As shown in Program 6-30, a driver can be used to thoroughly test a function. It can repeatedly call the function with different test values as arguments. When the function performs as desired, it can be placed into the actual program it will be part of.

 Case Study on CD: See High Adventure Travel Agency Part 1 Case Study on the Student CD.

Review Questions and Exercises

Short Answer

1. Why do local variables lose their values between calls to the function in which they are defined?

2. What is the difference between an argument and a parameter variable?

3. Where do you define parameter variables?

4. If you are writing a function that accepts an argument and you want to make sure the function cannot change the value of the argument, what do you do?

5. When a function accepts multiple arguments, does it matter in what order the arguments are passed in?

6. How do you return a value from a function?

7. What is the advantage of breaking your application's code into several small procedures?

8. How would a static local variable be useful?

9. Give an example where passing an argument by reference would be useful.

Fill-in-the-Blank

10. The _____ is the part of a function definition that shows the function name, return type, and parameter list.

11. If a function doesn't return a value, the word _____ will appear as its return type.

12. Either a function's _____ or its _____ must precede all calls to the function.

13. Values that are sent into a function are called _____.

14. Special variables that hold copies of function arguments are called _____.

15. When only a copy of an argument is passed to a function, it is said to be passed by _____.

16. A(n) _____ eliminates the need to place a function definition before all calls to the function.

17. A(n) _____ variable is defined inside a function and is not accessible outside the function.

18. _____ variables are defined outside all functions and are accessible to any function within their scope.

19. _____ variables provide an easy way to share large amounts of data among all the functions in a program.

20. Unless you explicitly initialize global variables, they are automatically initialized to _____.

21. If a function has a local variable with the same name as a global variable, only the _____ variable can be seen by the function.

22. _____ local variables retain their value between function calls.

23. The _____ statement causes a function to end immediately.

24. _____ arguments are passed to parameters automatically if no argument is provided in the function call.

25. When a function uses a mixture of parameters with and without default arguments, the parameters with default arguments must be defined _____.

26. The value of a default argument must be a(n) _____.

27. When used as parameters, _____ variables allow a function to access the parameter's original argument.

28. Reference variables are defined like regular variables, except there is a(n) _____ in front of the name.

29. Reference variables allow arguments to be passed by _____.

30. The _____ function causes a program to terminate.

31. Two or more functions may have the same name, as long as their _____ are different.

Algorithm Workbench

32. Examine the following function header, then write an example call to the function.

```
void showValue(int quantity)
```

33. The following statement calls a function named `half`. The `half` function returns a value that is half that of the argument. Write the function.

```
result = half(number);
```

34. A program contains the following function.

```
int cube(int num)
{
    return num * num * num;
}
```

Write a statement that passes the value 4 to this function and assigns its return value to the variable `result`.

35. Write a function named `timesTen` that accepts an argument. When the function is called, it should display the product of its argument multiplied times 10.

36. A program contains the following function.

```
void display(int arg1, double arg2, char arg3)
{
    cout << "Here are the values: "
         << arg1 << " " << arg2 << " "
         << arg3 << endl;
}
```

Write a statement that calls the procedure and passes the following variables to it:

```
int age;
double income;
char initial;
```

37. Write a function named `getNumber` that uses a reference parameter variable to accept an integer argument. The function should prompt the user to enter a number in the range of 1 through 100. The input should be validated and stored in the parameter variable.

True or False

38. T F Functions should be given names that reflect their purpose.
39. T F Function headers are terminated with a semicolon.
40. T F Function prototypes are terminated with a semicolon.
41. T F If other functions are defined before main, the program still starts executing at function main.
42. T F When a function terminates, it always branches back to main, regardless of where it was called from.
43. T F Arguments are passed to the function parameters in the order they appear in the function call.
44. T F The scope of a parameter is limited to the function which uses it.
45. T F Changes to a function parameter always affect the original argument as well.
46. T F In a function prototype, the names of the parameter variables may be left out.
47. T F Many functions may have local variables with the same name.
48. T F Overuse of global variables can lead to problems.
49. T F Static local variables are not destroyed when a function returns.
50. T F All static local variables are initialized to –1 by default.

51. T F Initialization of static local variables only happens once, regardless of how many times the function in which they are defined is called.

52. T F When a function with default arguments is called and an argument is left out, all arguments that come after it must be left out as well.

53. T F It is not possible for a function to have some parameters with default arguments and some without.

54. T F The `exit` function can only be called from `main`.

55. T F A stub is a dummy function that is called instead of the actual function it represents.

Find the Errors

Each of the following functions has errors. Locate as many errors as you can.

56.
```cpp
void total(int value1, value2, value3)
{
    return value1 + value2 + value3;
}
```

57.
```cpp
double average(int value1, int value2, int value3)
{
    double average;

    average = value1 + value2 + value3 / 3;
}
```

58.
```cpp
void area(int length = 30, int width)
{
    return length * width;
}
```

59.
```cpp
void getValue(int value&)
{
    cout << "Enter a value: ";
    cin >> value&;
}
```

60. *(Overloaded functions)*
```cpp
int getValue()
{
    int inputValue;
    cout << "Enter an integer: ";
    cin >> inputValue;
    return inputValue;
}
double getValue()
{
    double inputValue;
    cout << "Enter a floating-point number: ";
    cin >> inputValue;
    return inputValue;
}
```

Programming Challenges

1. Markup

Write a program that asks the user to enter an item's wholesale cost and its markup percentage. It should then display the item's retail price. For example:

VideoNote

Solving the Markup Problem

- If an item's wholesale cost is 5.00 and its markup percentage is 100%, then the item's retail price is 10.00.
- If an item's wholesale cost is 5.00 and its markup percentage is 50%, then the item's retail price is 7.50.

The program should have a function named `calculateRetail` that receives the wholesale cost and the markup percentage as arguments, and returns the retail price of the item.

Input Validation: Do not accept negative values for either the wholesale cost of the item or the markup percentage.

2. Rectangle Area—Complete the Program

The Student CD contains a partially written program named `AreaRectangle.cpp`. Your job is to complete the program. When it is complete, the program will ask the user to enter the width and length of a rectangle, and then display the rectangle's area. The program calls the following functions, which have not been written:

- `getLength` – This function should ask the user to enter the rectangle's length, and then return that value as a `double`.
- `getWidth` - This function should ask the user to enter the rectangle's width, and then return that value as a `double`.
- `getArea` – This function should accept the rectangle's length and width as arguments, and return the rectangle's area. The area is calculated by multiplying the length by the width.
- `displayData` – This function should accept the rectangle's length, width, and area as arguments, and display them in an appropriate message on the screen.

3. Winning Division

Write a program that determines which of a company's four divisions (Northeast, Southeast, Northwest, and Southwest) had the greatest sales for a quarter. It should include the following two functions, which are called by `main`.

- `double getSales()` is passed the name of a division. It asks the user for a division's quarterly sales figure, validates the input, then returns it. It should be called once for each division.
- `void findHighest()` is passed the four sales totals. It determines which is the largest and prints the name of the high grossing division, along with its sales figure.

Input Validation: Do not accept dollar amounts less than $0.00.

4. **Safest Driving Area**

Write a program that determines which of five geographic regions within a major city (north, south, east, west, and central) had the fewest reported automobile accidents last year. It should have the following two functions, which are called by main.

- `int getNumAccidents()` is passed the name of a region. It asks the user for the number of automobile accidents reported in that region during the last year, validates the input, then returns it. It should be called once for each city region.
- `void findLowest()` is passed the five accident totals. It determines which is the smallest and prints the name of the region, along with its accident figure.

Input Validation: Do not accept an accident number that is less than 0.

5. **Falling Distance**

When an object is falling because of gravity, the following formula can be used to determine the distance the object falls in a specific time period:

$$d = \frac{1}{2} gt^2$$

The variables in the formula are as follows: d is the distance in meters, g is 9.8, and t is the amount of time, in seconds, that the object has been falling.

Write a function named `fallingDistance` that accepts an object's falling time (in seconds) as an argument. The function should return the distance, in meters, that the object has fallen during that time interval. Write a program that demonstrates the function by calling it in a loop that passes the values 1 through 10 as arguments, and displays the return value.

6. **Kinetic Energy**

In physics, an object that is in motion is said to have kinetic energy. The following formula can be used to determine a moving object's kinetic energy:

$$KE = \frac{1}{2} mv^2$$

The variables in the formula are as follows: KE is the kinetic energy, m is the object's mass in kilograms, and v is the object's velocity, in meters per second.

Write a function named `kineticEnergy` that accepts an object's mass (in kilograms) and velocity (in meters per second) as arguments. The function should return the amount of kinetic energy that the object has. Demonstrate the function by calling it in a program that asks the user to enter values for mass and velocity.

7. **Celsius Temperature Table**

The formula for converting a temperature from Fahrenheit to Celsius is

$$C = \frac{5}{9}(F - 32)$$

where F is the Fahrenheit temperature and C is the Celsius temperature. Write a function named `celsius` that accepts a Fahrenheit temperature as an argument. The function should return the temperature, converted to Celsius. Demonstrate the function by calling it in a loop that displays a table of the Fahrenheit temperatures 0 through 20 and their Celsius equivalents.

8. **Coin Toss**

   Write a function named `coinToss` that simulates the tossing of a coin. When you call the function, it should generate a random number in the range of 1 through 2. If the random number is 1, the function should display "heads." If the random number is 2, the function should display "tails." Demonstrate the function in a program that asks the user how many times the coin should be tossed, and then simulates the tossing of the coin that number of times.

9. **Present Value**

   Suppose you want to deposit a certain amount of money into a savings account, and then leave it alone to draw interest for the next 10 years. At the end of 10 years you would like to have $10,000 in the account. How much do you need to deposit today to make that happen? You can use the following formula, which is known as the present value formula, to find out:

   $$P = \frac{F}{(1 + r)^n}$$

   The terms in the formula are as follows:

   - P is the **present value**, or the amount that you need to deposit today.
   - F is the **future value** that you want in the account. (In this case, F is $10,000.)
   - r is the **annual interest rate**.
   - n is the **number of years** that you plan to let the money sit in the account.

   Write a program that has a function named `presentValue` that performs this calculation. The function should accept the future value, annual interest rate, and number of years as arguments. It should return the present value, which is the amount that you need to deposit today. Demonstrate the function in a program that lets the user experiment with different values for the formula's terms.

10. **Lowest Score Drop**

    Write a program that calculates the average of a group of test scores, where the lowest score in the group is dropped. It should use the following functions:

    - `void getScore()` should ask the user for a test score, store it in a reference parameter variable, and validate it. This function should be called by `main` once for each of the five scores to be entered.
    - `void calcAverage()` should calculate and display the average of the four highest scores. This function should be called just once by `main`, and should be passed the five scores.
    - `int findLowest()` should find and return the lowest of the five scores passed to it. It should be called by `calcAverage`, which uses the function to determine which of the five scores to drop.

    Input Validation: Do not accept test scores lower than 0 or higher than 100.

11. **Star Search**

A particular talent competition has five judges, each of whom awards a score between 0 and 10 to each performer. Fractional scores, such as 8.3, are allowed. A performer's final score is determined by dropping the highest and lowest score received, then averaging the three remaining scores. Write a program that uses this method to calculate a contestant's score. It should include the following functions:

- `void getJudgeData()` should ask the user for a judge's score, store it in a reference parameter variable, and validate it. This function should be called by `main` once for each of the five judges.
- `void calcScore()` should calculate and display the average of the three scores that remain after dropping the highest and lowest scores the performer received. This function should be called just once by `main`, and should be passed the five scores.

The last two functions, described below, should be called by `calcScore`, which uses the returned information to determine which of the scores to drop.

- `int findLowest()` should find and return the lowest of the five scores passed to it.
- `int findHighest()` should find and return the highest of the five scores passed to it.

Input Validation: Do not accept judge scores lower than 0 or higher than 10.

12. **Days Out**

Write a program that calculates the average number of days a company's employees are absent. The program should have the following functions:

- A function called by `main` that asks the user for the number of employees in the company. This value should be returned as an `int`. (The function accepts no arguments.)
- A function called by `main` that accepts one argument: the number of employees in the company. The function should ask the user to enter the number of days each employee missed during the past year. The total of these days should be returned as an `int`.
- A function called by `main` that takes two arguments: the number of employees in the company and the total number of days absent for all employees during the year. The function should return, as a `double`, the average number of days absent. (This function does not perform screen output and does not ask the user for input.)

Input Validation: Do not accept a number less than 1 for the number of employees. Do not accept a negative number for the days any employee missed.

13. **Order Status**

The Middletown Wholesale Copper Wire Company sells spools of copper wiring for $100 each. Write a program that displays the status of an order. The program should have a function that asks for the following data:

- The number of spools ordered.
- The number of spools in stock.
- Whether there are special shipping and handling charges.

(Shipping and handling is normally $10 per spool.) If there are special charges, the program should ask for the special charges per spool.

The gathered data should be passed as arguments to another function that displays

- The number of spools ready to ship from current stock.
- The number of spools on backorder (if the number ordered is greater than what is in stock).
- Subtotal of the portion ready to ship (the number of spools ready to ship times $100).
- Total shipping and handling charges on the portion ready to ship.
- Total of the order ready to ship.

The shipping and handling parameter in the second function should have the default argument 10.00.

Input Validation: Do not accept numbers less than 1 for spools ordered. Do not accept a number less than 0 for spools in stock or shipping and handling charges.

14. **Overloaded Hospital**

Write a program that computes and displays the charges for a patient's hospital stay. First, the program should ask if the patient was admitted as an in-patient or an out-patient. If the patient was an in-patient, the following data should be entered:

- The number of days spent in the hospital
- The daily rate
- Hospital medication charges
- Charges for hospital services (lab tests, etc.)

The program should ask for the following data if the patient was an out-patient:

- Charges for hospital services (lab tests, etc.)
- Hospital medication charges

The program should use two overloaded functions to calculate the total charges. One of the functions should accept arguments for the in-patient data, while the other function accepts arguments for out-patient information. Both functions should return the total charges.

Input Validation: Do not accept negative numbers for any data.

 15. **Population**

In a population, the birth rate is the percentage increase of the population due to births and the death rate is the percentage decrease of the population due to deaths. Write a program that displays the size of a population for any number of years. The program should ask for the following data:

- The starting size of a population
- The annual birth rate
- The annual death rate
- The number of years to display

Write a function that calculates the size of the population for a year. The formula is

```
N = P + BP - DP
```

where N is the new population size, P is the previous population size, B is the birth rate, and D is the death rate.

Input Validation: Do not accept numbers less than 2 for the starting size. Do not accept negative numbers for birth rate or death rate. Do not accept numbers less than 1 for the number of years.

16. **Transient Population**

    Modify Programming Challenge 13 to also consider the effect on population caused by people moving into or out of a geographic area. Given as input a starting population size, the annual birth rate, the annual death rate, the number of individuals who typically move into the area each year, and the number of individuals who typically leave the area each year, the program should project what the population will be num-Years from now. You can either prompt the user to input a value for numYears, or you can set it within the program.

    Input Validation: Do not accept numbers less than 2 for the starting size. Do not accept negative numbers for birth rate, death rate, arrivals, or departures.

17. **Paint Job Estimator**

    A painting company has determined that for every 115 square feet of wall space, one gallon of paint and eight hours of labor will be required. The company charges $18.00 per hour for labor. Write a modular program that allows the user to enter the number of rooms that are to be painted and the price of the paint per gallon. It should also ask for the square feet of wall space in each room. It should then display the following data:

    - The number of gallons of paint required
    - The hours of labor required
    - The cost of the paint
    - The labor charges
    - The total cost of the paint job

    Input validation: Do not accept a value less than 1 for the number of rooms. Do not accept a value less than $10.00 for the price of paint. Do not accept a negative value for square footage of wall space.

18. **Using Files—Hospital Report**

    Modify Programming Challenge 14, Overloaded Hospital, to write the report it creates to a file. Print the contents of the file to hand in to your instructor.

19. **Stock Profit**

    The profit from the sale of a stock can be calculated as follows:

    $$\text{Profit} = ((NS \times SP) - SC) - ((NS \times PP) + PC)$$

    where NS is the number of shares, SP is the sale price per share, SC is the sale commission paid, PP is the purchase price per share, and PC is the purchase commission paid. If the calculation yields a positive value, then the sale of the stock resulted in a profit. If the calculation yields a negative number, then the sale resulted in a loss.

    Write a function that accepts as arguments the number of shares, the purchase price per share, the purchase commission paid, the sale price per share, and the sale commission paid. The function should return the profit (or loss) from the sale of stock.

Demonstrate the function in a program that asks the user to enter the necessary data and displays the amount of the profit or loss.

20. **Multiple Stock Sales**

Use the function that you wrote for Programming Challenge 19 (Stock Profit) in a program that calculates the total profit or loss from the sale of multiple stocks. The program should ask the user for the number of stock sales, and the necessary data for each stock sale. It should accumulate the profit or loss for each stock sale and then display the total.

21. **`isPrime` Function**

A prime number is a number that is only evenly divisible by itself and 1. For example, the number 5 is prime because it can only be evenly divided by 1 and 5. The number 6, however, is not prime because it can be divided evenly by 1, 2, 3, and 6.

Write a function name `isPrime`, which takes an integer as an argument and returns true if the argument is a prime number, or false otherwise. Demonstrate the function in a complete program.

TIP: Recall that the % operator divides one number by another, and returns the remainder of the division. In an expression such as num1 % num2, the % operator will return 0 if num1 is evenly divisible by num2.

22. **Prime Number List**

Use the `isPrime` function that you wrote in Programming Challenge 21 in a program that stores a list of all the prime numbers from 1 through 100 in a file.

23. **Rock, Paper, Scissors Game**

Write a program that lets the user play the game of Rock, Paper, Scissors against the computer. The program should work as follows.

1. When the program begins, a random number in the range of 1 through 3 is generated. If the number is 1, then the computer has chosen rock. If the number is 2, then the computer has chosen paper. If the number is 3, then the computer has chosen scissors. (Don't display the computer's choice yet.)

2. The user enters his or her choice of "rock", "paper", or "scissors" at the keyboard. (You can use a menu if you prefer.)

3. The computer's choice is displayed.

4. A winner is selected according to the following rules:

   • If one player chooses rock and the other player chooses scissors, then rock wins. (The rock smashes the scissors.)
   • If one player chooses scissors and the other player chooses paper, then scissors wins. (Scissors cuts paper.)
   • If one player chooses paper and the other player chooses rock, then paper wins. (Paper wraps rock.)
   • If both players make the same choice, the game must be played again to determine the winner.

Be sure to divide the program into functions that perform each major task.

Group Project

24. **Travel Expenses**

This program should be designed and written by a team of students. Here are some suggestions:

- One student should design function main, which will call the other functions in the program. The remainder of the functions will be designed by other members of the team.
- The requirements of the program should be analyzed so each student is given about the same work load.
- The parameters and return types of each function should be decided in advance.
- Stubs and drivers should be used to test and debug the program.
- The program can be implemented as a multifile program, or all the functions can be cut and pasted into the main file.

Here is the assignment: Write a program that calculates and displays the total travel expenses of a businessperson on a trip. The program should have functions that ask for and return the following:

- The total number of days spent on the trip
- The time of departure on the first day of the trip, and the time of arrival back home on the last day of the trip
- The amount of any round-trip airfare
- The amount of any car rentals
- Miles driven, if a private vehicle was used. Calculate the vehicle expense as $0.27 per mile driven
- Parking fees (The company allows up to $6 per day. Anything in excess of this must be paid by the employee.)
- Taxi fees, if a taxi was used anytime during the trip (The company allows up to $10 per day, for each day a taxi was used. Anything in excess of this must be paid by the employee.)
- Conference or seminar registration fees
- Hotel expenses (The company allows up to $90 per night for lodging. Anything in excess of this must be paid by the employee.)
- The amount of *each* meal eaten. On the first day of the trip, breakfast is allowed as an expense if the time of departure is before 7 a.m. Lunch is allowed if the time of departure is before 12 noon. Dinner is allowed on the first day if the time of departure is before 6 p.m. On the last day of the trip, breakfast is allowed if the time of arrival is after 8 a.m. Lunch is allowed if the time of arrival is after 1 p.m. Dinner is allowed on the last day if the time of arrival is after 7 p.m. The program should only ask for the amounts of allowable meals. (The company allows up to $9 for breakfast, $12 for lunch, and $16 for dinner. Anything in excess of this must be paid by the employee.)

The program should calculate and display the total expenses incurred by the businessperson, the total allowable expenses for the trip, the excess that must be reimbursed by the businessperson, if any, and the amount saved by the businessperson if the expenses were under the total allowed.

Input Validation: Do not accept negative numbers for any dollar amount or for miles driven in a private vehicle. Do not accept numbers less than 1 for the number of days. Only accept valid times for the time of departure and the time of arrival.

7 Arrays

TOPICS

7.1 Arrays Hold Multiple Values

CONCEPT: An array allows you to store and work with multiple values of the same data type.

The variables you have worked with so far are designed to hold only one value at a time. Each of the variable definitions in Figure 7-1 causes only enough memory to be reserved to hold one value of the specified data type.

An array works like a variable that can store a group of values, all of the same type. The values are stored together in consecutive memory locations. Here is a definition of an array of integers:

```
int days[6];
```

Figure 7-1

```
int count;    Enough memory for 1 int
                   ┌─────────┐
                   │  12314  │
                   └─────────┘

float price;  Enough memory for 1 float
                   ┌─────────┐
                   │  56.981 │
                   └─────────┘

char letter;  Enough memory for 1 char
                       ┌───┐
                       │ A │
                       └───┘
```

The name of this array is days. The number inside the brackets is the array's *size declarator*. It indicates the number of *elements,* or values, the array can hold. The days array can store six elements, each one an integer. This is depicted in Figure 7-2.

Figure 7-2

days array: enough memory for six int values

   Element 0   Element 1   Element 2   Element 3   Element 4   Element 5

An array's size declarator must be a constant integer expression with a value greater than zero. It can be either a literal, as in the previous example, or a named constant, as shown in the following:

```
const int NUM_DAYS = 6;
int days[NUM_DAYS];
```

Arrays of any data type can be defined. The following are all valid array definitions:

```
float temperatures[100];   // Array of 100 floats
char name[41];             // Array of 41 characters
long units[50];            // Array of 50 long integers
double sizes[1200];        // Array of 1200 doubles
```

Memory Requirements of Arrays

The amount of memory used by an array depends on the array's data type and the number of elements. The hours array, defined here, is an array of six shorts.

```
short hours[6];
```

On a typical PC, a short uses two bytes of memory, so the hours array would occupy 12 bytes. This is shown in Figure 7-3.

Figure 7-3

hours array: Each element uses two bytes

Element 0   Element 1   Element 2   Element 3   Element 4   Element 5

The size of an array can be calculated by multiplying the size of an individual element by the number of elements in the array. Table 7-1 shows the typical sizes of various arrays.

Table 7-1

Array Definition	Number of Elements	Size of Each Element	Size of the Array
char letters[25];	25	1 byte	25 bytes
short rings[100];	100	2 bytes	200 bytes
int miles[84];	84	4 bytes	336 bytes
float temp[12];	12	4 bytes	48 bytes
double distance[1000];	1000	8 bytes	8000 bytes

7.2 Accessing Array Elements

CONCEPT: The individual elements of an array are assigned unique subscripts. These subscripts are used to access the elements.

Even though an entire array has only one name, the elements may be accessed and used as individual variables. This is possible because each element is assigned a number known as a *subscript*. A subscript is used as an index to pinpoint a specific element within an array. The first element is assigned the subscript 0, the second element is assigned 1, and so forth. The six elements in the array hours would have the subscripts 0 through 5. This is shown in Figure 7-4.

Figure 7-4

Subscripts

0   1   2   3   4   5

NOTE: Subscript numbering in C++ always starts at zero. The subscript of the last element in an array is one less than the total number of elements in the array. This means that in the array shown in Figure 7-4, the element hours[6] does not exist. hours[5] is the last element in the array.

Each element in the hours array, when accessed by its subscript, can be used as a short variable. Here is an example of a statement that stores the number 20 in the first element of the array:

```
hours[0] = 20;
```

NOTE: The expression hours[0] is pronounced "hours sub zero." You would read this assignment statement as "hours sub zero is assigned twenty."

Figure 7-5 shows the contents of the array hours after the statement assigns 20 to hours[0].

Figure 7-5

NOTE: Because values have not been assigned to the other elements of the array, question marks will be used to indicate that the contents of those elements are unknown. If an array is defined globally, all of its elements are initialized to zero by default. Local arrays, however, have no default initialization value.

The following statement stores the integer 30 in hours[3].

```
hours[3] = 30;
```

Figure 7-6 shows the contents of the array after the previous statement executes:

Figure 7-6

NOTE: Understand the difference between the array size declarator and a subscript. The number inside the brackets of an array definition is the size declarator. The number inside the brackets of an assignment statement or any statement that works with the contents of an array is a subscript.

Inputting and Outputting Array Contents

Array elements may be used with the cin and cout objects like any other variable. Program 7-1 shows the array hours being used to store and display values entered by the user.

Program 7-1

```
 1  // This program asks for the number of hours worked
 2  // by six employees. It stores the values in an array.
 3  #include <iostream>
 4  using namespace std;
 5
 6  int main()
 7  {
 8      const int NUM_EMPLOYEES = 6;
 9      int hours[NUM_EMPLOYEES];
10
11      // Get the hours worked by each employee.
12      cout << "Enter the hours worked by "
13           << NUM_EMPLOYEES << " employees: ";
14      cin >> hours[0];
15      cin >> hours[1];
16      cin >> hours[2];
17      cin >> hours[3];
18      cin >> hours[4];
19      cin >> hours[5];
20
21      // Display the values in the array.
22      cout << "The hours you entered are:";
23      cout << " " << hours[0];
24      cout << " " << hours[1];
25      cout << " " << hours[2];
26      cout << " " << hours[3];
27      cout << " " << hours[4];
28      cout << " " << hours[5] << endl;
29      return 0;
30  }
```

Program Output with Example Input Shown in Bold
```
Enter the hours worked by 6 employees: 20 12 40 30 30 15 [Enter]
The hours you entered are: 20 12 40 30 30 15
```

Figure 7-7 shows the contents of the array hours with the values entered by the user in the example output above.

Figure 7-7

Even though the size declarator of an array definition must be a constant or a literal, subscript numbers can be stored in variables. This makes it possible to use a loop to "cycle through" an entire array, performing the same operation on each element. For example, look at the following code:

```
const int ARRAY_SIZE = 5;
int numbers[ARRAY_SIZE];

for (int count = 0; count < ARRAY_SIZE; count++)
    numbers[count] = 99;
```

VideoNote

Accessing
Array
Elements
with a Loop

This code first defines a constant `int` named `ARRAY_SIZE` and initializes it with the value 5. Then it defines an `int` array named `numbers`, using `ARRAY_SIZE` as the size declarator. As a result, the `numbers` array will have five elements. The `for` loop uses a counter variable named `count`. This loop will iterate five times, and during the loop iterations the `count` variable will take on the values 0 through 4.

Notice that the statement inside the loop uses the `count` variable as a subscript. It assigns 99 to `numbers[count]`. During the first iteration, 99 is assigned to `numbers[0]`. During the next iteration, 99 is assigned to `numbers[1]`. This continues until 99 has been assigned to all of the array's elements. Figure 7-8 illustrates that the loop's initialization, test, and update expressions have been written so the loop starts and ends the counter variable with valid subscript values (0 through 4). This ensures that only valid subscripts are used in the body of the loop.

Figure 7-8

The variable `count` starts at 0, which is the first valid subscript value.

The loop ends when the variable `count` reaches 5, which is the first invalid subscript value.

```
for (count = 0; count < ARRAY_SIZE; count++)
    numbers[count] = 99;
```

The variable `count` is incremented after each iteration.

Program 7-1 could be simplified by using two `for` loops: one for inputting the values into the array and another for displaying the contents of the array. This is shown in Program 7-2.

Program 7-2

```
1   // This program asks for the number of hours worked
2   // by six employees. It stores the values in an array.
3   #include <iostream>
4   using namespace std;
5
```

```
 6   int main()
 7   {
 8      const int NUM_EMPLOYEES = 6;  // Number of employees
 9      int hours[NUM_EMPLOYEES];     // Each employee's hours
10      int count;                    // Loop counter
11
12      // Input the hours worked.
13      for (count = 0; count < NUM_EMPLOYEES; count++)
14      {
15         cout << "Enter the hours worked by employee "
16              << (count + 1) << ": ";
17         cin >> hours[count];
18      }
19
20      // Display the contents of the array.
21      cout << "The hours you entered are:";
22      for (count = 0; count < NUM_EMPLOYEES; count++)
23         cout << " " << hours[count];
24      cout << endl;
25      return 0;
26   }
```

Program Output with Example Input Shown in Bold
```
Enter the hours worked by employee 1: 20 [Enter]
Enter the hours worked by employee 2: 12 [Enter]
Enter the hours worked by employee 3: 40 [Enter]
Enter the hours worked by employee 4: 30 [Enter]
Enter the hours worked by employee 5: 30 [Enter]
Enter the hours worked by employee 6: 15 [Enter]
The hours you entered are: 20 12 40 30 30 15
```

The first for loop, in lines 13 through 18, prompts the user for each employee's hours. Take a closer look at lines 15 through 17:

```
cout << "Enter the hours worked by employee "
     << (count + 1) << ": ";
cin >> hours[count];
```

Notice that the cout statement uses the expression count + 1 to display the employee number, but the cin statement uses count as the array subscript. This is because the hours for employee number 1 are stored in hours[0], the hours for employee number 2 are stored in hours[1], and so forth.

The loop in lines 22 through 23 also uses the count variable to step through the array, displaying each element.

NOTE: You can use any integer expression as an array subscript. For example, the first loop in Program 7-2 could have been written like this:

```cpp
for (count = 1; count <= NUM_EMPLOYEES; count++)
{
    cout << "Enter the hours worked by employee "
        << count << ": ";
    cin >> hours[count - 1];
}
```

In this code the `cin` statement uses the expression `count - 1` as a subscript.

Inputting data into an array must normally be done one element at a time. For example, the following `cin` statement will not input data into the `hours` array:

```cpp
cin >> hours;  // Wrong! This will NOT work.
```

Instead, you must use multiple `cin` statements to read data into each array element, or use a loop to step through the array, reading data into its elements. Also, outputting an array's contents must normally be done one element at a time. For example, the following `cout` statement will not display the contents of the `hours` array:

```cpp
cout << hours;  // Wrong! This will NOT work.
```

Instead, you must output each element of the array separately.

Reading Data from a File into an Array

In many circumstances you will need to read data from a file and store it in an array. The process is straightforward, and in most cases is best done with a loop. Each iteration of the loop reads an item from the file and stores it in an array element. Program 7-3 demonstrates by opening a file that has 10 numbers stored in it and then reading the file's contents into an array.

Program 7-3

```cpp
 1  // This program reads data from a file into an array.
 2  #include <iostream>
 3  #include <fstream>
 4  using namespace std;
 5
 6  int main()
 7  {
 8     const int ARRAY_SIZE = 10;  // Array size
 9     int numbers[ARRAY_SIZE];    // Array with 10 elements
10     int count;                  // Loop counter variable
11     ifstream inputFile;         // Input file stream object
12
13     inputFile.open("TenNumbers.txt"); // Open the file.
14
```

```
15      // Read the 10 numbers from the file into the array.
16      for (count = 0; count < ARRAY_SIZE; count++)
17         inputFile >> numbers[count];
18
19      // Close the file.
20      inputFile.close();
21
22      // Display the numbers read:
23      cout << "The numbers are: ";
24      for (count = 0; count < ARRAY_SIZE; count++)
25         cout << numbers[count] << " ";
26      cout << endl;
27      return 0;
28   }
```

Program Output

```
The numbers are: 101 102 103 104 105 106 107 108 109 110
```

Writing the Contents of an Array to a File

Writing the contents of an array to a file is also a straightforward matter. Use a loop to step through each element of the array, writing its contents to a file. Program 7-4 demonstrates.

Program 7-4

```
1   // This program writes the contents of an array to a file.
2   #include <iostream>
3   #include <fstream>
4   using namespace std;
5
6   int main()
7   {
8      const int ARRAY_SIZE = 10;   // Array size
9      int numbers[ARRAY_SIZE];     // Array with 10 elements
10     int count;                   // Loop counter variable
11     ofstream outputFile;         // Output file stream object
12
13     // Store values in the array.
14     for (count = 0; count < ARRAY_SIZE; count++)
15        numbers[count] = count;
16
17     // Open a file for output.
18     outputFile.open("SavedNumbers.txt");
19
20     // Write the array contents to the file.
21     for (count = 0; count < ARRAY_SIZE; count++)
22        outputFile << numbers[count] << endl;
23
```

(program continues)

Program 7-4   *(continued)*

```
24      // Close the file.
25      outputFile.close();
26
27      // That's it!
28      cout << "The numbers were saved to the file.\n ";
29      return 0;
30  }
```

Program Output

The numbers were saved to the file.

Contents of the File SavedNumbers.txt

```
0
1
2
3
4
5
6
7
8
9
```

7.3   No Bounds Checking in C++

CONCEPT: C++ gives you the freedom to store data past an array's boundaries.

Historically, one of the reasons for C++'s popularity has been the freedom it gives programmers to work with the computer's memory. Many of the safeguards provided by other languages to prevent programs from unsafely accessing memory are absent in C++. For example, C++ does not perform array bounds checking. This means you can write programs with subscripts that go beyond the boundaries of a particular array. Program 7-5 demonstrates this capability.

    WARNING! Think twice before you compile and run Program 7-5. The program will attempt to write to an area of memory outside the array. This is an invalid operation, and will most likely cause the program to crash.

Program 7-5

```
1   // This program unsafely accesses an area of memory by writing
2   // values beyond an array's boundary.
3   // WARNING: If you compile and run this program, it could crash.
```

```
4   #include <iostream>
5   using namespace std;
6
7   int main()
8   {
9      const int SIZE = 3;   // Constant for the array size
10     int values[SIZE];     // An array of 3 integers
11     int count;            // Loop counter variable
12
13     // Attempt to store five numbers in the three-element array.
14     cout << "I will store 5 numbers in a 3-element array!\n";
15     for (count = 0; count < 5; count++)
16        values[count] = 100;
17
18     // If the program is still running, display the numbers.
19     cout << "If you see this message, it means the program\n";
20     cout << "has not crashed! Here are the numbers:\n";
21     for (count = 0; count < 5; count++)
22        cout << values[count] << endl;
23     return 0;
24  }
```

The values array has three integer elements, with the subscripts 0, 1, and 2. The loop, however, stores the number 100 in elements 0, 1, 2, 3, and 4. The elements with subscripts 3 and 4 do not exist, but C++ allows the program to write beyond the boundary of the array, as if those elements were there. Figure 7-9 depicts the way the array is set up in memory when the program first starts to execute, and what happens when the loop writes data beyond the boundary of the array.

Figure 7-9

The way the `values` array is set up in memory.
The outlined area represents the array.

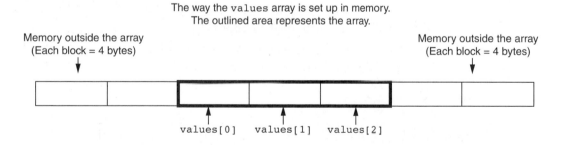

How the numbers assigned to the array overflow the array's boundaries.
The shaded area is the section of memory illegally written to.

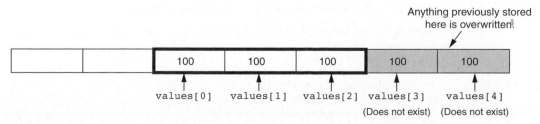

Although C++ provides the programmer a great deal of power and freedom, the absence of safeguards such as array bounds checking usually proves to be a bad thing. It's easy for C++ programmers to make careless mistakes that allow programs to access areas of memory that are supposed to be off-limits. You must always make sure that any time you assign values to array elements, the values are written within the array's boundaries.

Watch for Off-by-One Errors

In working with arrays, a common type of mistake is the *off-by-one error*. This is an easy mistake to make because array subscripts start at 0 rather than 1. For example, look at the following code:

```
// This code has an off-by-one error.
const int SIZE = 100;
int numbers[SIZE];
for (int count = 1; count <= SIZE; count++)
    numbers[count] = 0;
```

The intent of this code is to create an array of integers with 100 elements, and store the value 0 in each element. However, this code has an off-by-one error. The loop uses its counter variable, count, as a subscript with the numbers array. During the loop's execution, the variable count takes on the values 1 through 100, when it should take on the values 0 through 99. As a result, the first element, which is at subscript 0, is skipped. In addition, the loop attempts to use 100 as a subscript during the last iteration. Because 100 is an invalid subscript, the program will write data beyond the array's boundaries.

 Checkpoint

7.1   Define the following arrays:

   A)   empNums, a 100-element array of ints

   B)   payRates, a 25-element array of floats

   C)   miles, a 14-element array of longs

   D)   cityName, a 26-element array of chars

   E)   lightYears, a 1,000-element array of doubles

7.2   What's wrong with the following array definitions?

```
int readings[-1];
float measurements[4.5];
int size;
char name[size];
```

7.3   What would the valid subscript values be in a four-element array of doubles?

7.4   What is the difference between an array's size declarator and a subscript?

7.5   What is "array bounds checking"? Does C++ perform it?

7.6   What is the output of the following code?

```
int values[5], count;
for (count = 0; count < 5; count++)
    values[count] = count + 1;
for (count = 0; count < 5; count++)
    cout << values[count] << endl;
```

7.7 The following program skeleton contains a 20-element array of ints called fish. When completed, the program should ask how many fish were caught by fishermen 1 through 20, and store this data in the array. Complete the program.

```cpp
#include <iostream>
using namespace std;

int main()
{
    const int NUM_FISH = 20;
    int fish[NUM_FISH];
    // You must finish this program. It should ask how
    // many fish were caught by fishermen 1-20, and
    // store this data in the array fish.
    return 0;
}
```

7.4 Array Initialization

CONCEPT: Arrays may be initialized when they are defined.

Like regular variables, C++ allows you to initialize an array's elements when you create the array. Here is an example:

```cpp
const int MONTHS = 12;
int days[MONTHS] = {31, 28, 31, 30, 31, 30, 31, 31, 30, 31, 30, 31};
```

The series of values inside the braces and separated with commas is called an *initialization list*. These values are stored in the array elements in the order they appear in the list. (The first value, 31, is stored in days[0], the second value, 28, is stored in days[1], and so forth.) Figure 7-10 shows the contents of the array after the initialization.

Figure 7-10

Subscripts

0	1	2	3	4	5	6	7	8	9	10	11
31	28	31	30	31	30	31	31	30	31	30	31

Program 7-6 demonstrates how an array may be initialized.

Program 7-6

```cpp
1  // This program displays the number of days in each month.
2  #include <iostream>
3  using namespace std;
4
```

(program continues)

Program 7-6   *(continued)*

```
5   int main()
6   {
7      const int MONTHS = 12;
8      int days[MONTHS] = { 31, 28, 31, 30,
9                           31, 30, 31, 31,
10                          30, 31, 30, 31};
11
12     for (int count = 0; count < MONTHS; count++)
13     {
14        cout << "Month " << (count + 1) << " has ";
15        cout << days[count] << " days.\n";
16     }
17     return 0;
18  }
```

Program Output

```
Month 1 has 31 days.
Month 2 has 28 days.
Month 3 has 31 days.
Month 4 has 30 days.
Month 5 has 31 days.
Month 6 has 30 days.
Month 7 has 31 days.
Month 8 has 31 days.
Month 9 has 30 days.
Month 10 has 31 days.
Month 11 has 30 days.
Month 12 has 31 days.
```

NOTE: Notice that C++ allows you to spread the initialization list across multiple lines. Both of the following array definitions are equivalent:

```
double coins[5] = {0.05, 0.1, 0.25, 0.5, 1.0};
double coins[5] = {0.05,
                   0.1,
                   0.25,
                   0.5,
                   1.0};
```

Program 7-7 shows a character array being initialized with the first ten letters of the alphabet. The array is then used to display those characters' ASCII codes.

Program 7-7

```
1   // This program uses an array of ten characters to store the
2   // first ten letters of the alphabet. The ASCII codes of the
3   // characters are displayed.
4   #include <iostream>
5   using namespace std;
6
```

```
 7   int main()
 8   {
 9      const int NUM_LETTERS = 10;
10      char letters[NUM_LETTERS] = {'A', 'B', 'C', 'D', 'E',
11                                   'F', 'G', 'H', 'I', 'J'};
12
13      cout << "Character" << "\t" << "ASCII Code\n";
14      cout << "---------" << "\t" << "----------\n";
15      for (int count = 0; count < NUM_LETTERS; count++)
16      {
17         cout << letters[count] << "\t\t";
18         cout << static_cast<int>(letters[count]) << endl;
19      }
20      return 0;
21   }
```

Program Output
```
Character        ASCII Code
---------        ----------
A                65
B                66
C                67
D                68
E                69
F                70
G                71
H                72
I                73
J                74
```

NOTE: An array's initialization list cannot have more values than the array has elements.

Partial Array Initialization

When an array is being initialized, C++ does not require a value for every element. It's possible to only initialize part of an array, such as:

```
int numbers[7] = {1, 2, 4, 8};
```

This definition initializes only the first four elements of a seven-element array, as illustrated in Figure 7-11.

Figure 7-11

It's important to note that if an array is partially initialized, the uninitialized elements will be set to zero. This is true even if the array is defined locally. (If a local array is completely uninitialized, its elements will contain "garbage," like all other local variables.) Program 7-8 shows the contents of the array `numbers` after it is partially initialized.

Program 7-8

```
 1   // This program has a partially initialized array.
 2   #include <iostream>
 3   using namespace std;
 4
 5   int main()
 6   {
 7      const int SIZE = 7;
 8      int numbers[SIZE] = {1, 2, 4, 8}; // Initialize first 4 elements
 9
10      cout << "Here are the contents of the array:\n";
11      for (int index = 0; index < SIZE; index++)
12        cout << numbers[index] << " ";
13
14      cout << endl;
15      return 0;
16   }
```

Program Output
```
Here are the contents of the array:
1 2 4 8 0 0 0
```

If you leave an element uninitialized, you must leave all the elements that follow it uninitialized as well. C++ does not provide a way to skip elements in the initialization list. For example, the following is *not* legal:

```
int array[6] = {2, 4, , 8, , 12}; // NOT Legal!
```

Implicit Array Sizing

It's possible to define an array without specifying its size, as long as you provide an initialization list. C++ automatically makes the array large enough to hold all the initialization values. For example, the following definition creates an array with five elements:

```
double ratings[] = {1.0, 1.5, 2.0, 2.5, 3.0};
```

Because the size declarator is omitted, C++ counts the number of items in the initialization list and gives the array that many elements.

> **NOTE:** You *must* specify an initialization list if you leave out the size declarator. Otherwise, C++ doesn't know how large to make the array.

Initializing with Strings

When initializing a character array with a string, simply enclose the string in quotation marks, as shown here:

```
char name[7] = "Warren";
```

Although there are six characters in the string "Warren," the array must have enough elements to also accommodate the null terminator at the end of the string. It's important to note that anytime a string literal is used in C++, the null terminator is automatically included. That's why name is defined above with seven elements. Figure 7-12 shows the contents of name after the initialization:

Figure 7-12

NOTE: Recall from Chapter 2 that '\0' represents the null terminator. '\0' is an escape sequence that is stored in memory as a single character. Its ASCII code is 0.

The null terminator is not automatically included when an array is initialized with individual characters. It must be included in the initialization list, as shown below:

```
char name[7] = {'W', 'a', 'r', 'r', 'e', 'n', '\0'};
```

Program 7-9 shows two character arrays initialized with strings. The first is initialized with a string literal and the second is initialized with individual characters.

Program 7-9

```
 1   // This program displays the contents of two char arrays.
 2   #include <iostream>
 3   using namespace std;
 4
 5   int main()
 6   {
 7      char name1[] = "Holly";
 8      char name2[] = {'W', 'a', 'r', 'r', 'e', 'n', '\0'};
 9
10      cout << name1 << endl;
11      cout << name2 << endl;
12      return 0;
13   }
```

Program Output
```
Holly
Warren
```

In Program 7-9, notice that the size declarators for each array are left out. The compiler will size the arrays just large enough to hold the values they are initialized with. name1 will have six elements because the string "Holly" has five characters, plus the null terminator. name2 will have seven elements because there are seven characters in the initialization list.

In Chapter 2 you were shown that to display a string stored in a character array, you simply use the stream insertion operator to send the name of the array (without the brackets) to the cout object. It's important to point out that character arrays containing null-terminated strings are the only type of array this technique works with. You cannot display the contents of numeric arrays in this fashion. Displaying the contents of a numeric array must be done element-by-element.

7.5   Processing Array Contents

CONCEPT: Individual array elements are processed like any other type of variable.

Processing array elements is no different than processing other variables. For example, the following statement multiplies hours[3] by the variable rate:

```
pay = hours[3] * rate;
```

And the following are examples of pre-increment and post-increment operations on array elements:

```
int score[5] = {7, 8, 9, 10, 11};
++score[2];    // Pre-increment operation on the value in score[2]
score[4]++;    // Post-increment operation on the value in score[4]
```

NOTE: When using increment and decrement operators, be careful not to confuse the subscript with the array element. For example, the following statement decrements the variable count, but does nothing to the value in amount[count]:

```
amount[count--];
```

To decrement the value stored in amount[count], use the following statement:

```
amount[count]--;
```

Program 7-10 demonstrates the use of array elements in a simple mathematical statement. A loop steps through each element of the array, using the elements to calculate the gross pay of five employees.

Program 7-10

```cpp
1    // This program stores, in an array, the hours worked by
2    // employees who all make the same hourly wage.
3    #include <iostream>
4    #include <iomanip>
5    using namespace std;
6
7    int main()
8    {
9       const int NUM_EMPLOYEES = 5;
10      int hours[NUM_EMPLOYEES];
11      double payrate;
12
13      // Input the hours worked.
14      cout << "Enter the hours worked by ";
15      cout << NUM_EMPLOYEES << " employees who all\n";
16      cout << "earn the same hourly rate.\n";
17      for (int index = 0; index < NUM_EMPLOYEES; index++)
18      {
19         cout << "Employee #" << (index + 1) << ": ";
20         cin >> hours[index];
21      }
22
23      // Input the hourly rate for all employees.
24      cout << "Enter the hourly pay rate for all the employees: ";
25      cin >> payrate;
26
27      // Display each employee's gross pay.
28      cout << "Here is the gross pay for each employee:\n";
29      cout << fixed << showpoint << setprecision(2);
30      for (int index = 0; index < NUM_EMPLOYEES; index++)
31      {
32         double grossPay = hours[index] * payrate;
33         cout << "Employee #" << (index + 1);
34         cout << ": $" << grossPay << endl;
35      }
36      return 0;
37   }
```

Program Output with Example Input Shown in Bold

```
Enter the hours worked by 5 employees who all
earn the same hourly rate.
Employee #1: 5 [Enter]
Employee #2: 10 [Enter]
Employee #3: 15 [Enter]
Employee #4: 20 [Enter]
Employee #5: 40 [Enter]
Enter the hourly pay rate for all the employees: 12.75 [Enter]
Here is the gross pay for each employee:
Employee #1: $63.75
Employee #2: $127.50
Employee #3: $191.25
Employee #4: $255.00
Employee #5: $510.00
```

The following statement in line 32 defines the variable grossPay and initializes it with the value of hours[index] times payRate:

```
double grossPay = hours[index] * payRate;
```

Array elements may also be used in relational expressions. For example, the following if statement tests cost[20] to determine whether it is less than cost[0]:

```
if (cost[20] < cost[0])
```

And the following statement sets up a while loop to iterate as long as value[place] does not equal 0:

```
while (value[place] != 0)
```

Thou Shall Not Assign

The following code defines two integer arrays: newValues and oldValues. newValues is uninitialized and oldValues is initialized with 10, 100, 200, and 300:

```
const int SIZE = 4;
int oldValues[SIZE] = {10, 100, 200, 300};
int newValues[SIZE];
```

At first glance, it might appear that the following statement assigns the contents of the array oldValues to newValues:

```
newValues = oldValues;              // Wrong!
```

Unfortunately, this statement will not work. The only way to assign one array to another is to assign the individual elements in the arrays. Usually, this is best done with a loop, such as:

```
for (int count = 0; count < SIZE; count++)
   newValues[count] = oldValues[count];
```

The reason the assignment operator will not work with an entire array at once is complex, but important to understand. Anytime the name of an array is used without brackets and a subscript, *it is seen as the array's beginning memory address*. To illustrate this, consider the definition of the arrays newValues and oldValues above. Figure 7-13 depicts the two arrays in memory.

Figure 7-13

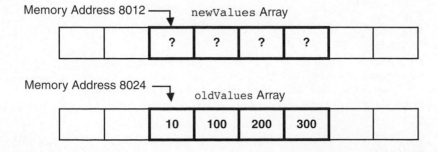

In the figure, `newValues` is shown starting at memory address 8012 and `oldValues` is shown starting at 8024. (Of course, these are just arbitrary addresses, picked for illustration purposes. In reality the addresses would probably be different.) Table 7-2 shows various expressions that use the names of these arrays, and their values.

Table 7-2

Expression	Value
`oldValues[0]`	10 (Contents of Element 0 of `oldValues`)
`oldValues[1]`	100 (Contents of Element 1 of `oldValues`)
`oldValues[2]`	200 (Contents of Element 2 of `oldValues`)
`oldValues[3]`	300 (Contents of Element 3 of `oldValues`)
`newValues`	8012 (Memory Address of `newValues`)
`oldValues`	8024 (Memory Address of `oldValues`)

Because the name of an array without the brackets and subscript stands for the array's starting memory address, the following statement

```
newValues = oldValues;
```

is interpreted by C++ as

```
8012 = 8024;
```

The statement will not work because you cannot change the starting memory address of an array.

Printing the Contents of an Array

Suppose we have the following array definition:

```
const int SIZE = 5;
int array[SIZE] = {10, 20, 30, 40, 50};
```

You now know that an array's name is seen as the array's beginning memory address. This explains why the following statement cannot be used to display the contents of `array`:

```
cout << array << endl;    //Wrong!
```

When this statement executes, `cout` will display the array's memory address, not the array's contents. You must use a loop to display the contents of each of the array's elements, as follows.

```
for (int count = 0; count < SIZE; count++)
   cout << array[count] << endl;
```

The only exception to this rule is when you are displaying the contents of a `char` array that contains a C-string. For example, assume a program has the following code segment:

```
char name[] = "Ruth";
cout << name << endl;
```

This `cout` statement displays the string "Ruth" instead of the array's address. This is because the stream insertion operator is designed to behave differently when it receives the address of a char array. When the stream insertion operator receives the address of a char array, it assumes a C-string is stored at that address, and sends the C-string to cout.

> **WARNING!** Do not pass the name of a char array to cout if the char array does not contain a null-terminated C-string. If you do, cout will display all the characters in memory, starting at the array's address, until it encounters a null terminator.

Summing the Values in a Numeric Array

To sum the values in an array, you must use a loop with an accumulator variable. The loop adds the value in each array element to the accumulator. For example, assume that the following statements appear in a program and that values have been stored in the units array.

```
const int NUM_UNITS = 24;
int units[NUM_UNITS];
```

The following loop adds the values of each element in the array to the total variable. When the code is finished, total will contain the sum of the units array's elements.

```
int total = 0;   // Initialize accumulator
for (int count = 0; count < NUM_UNITS; count++)
   total += units[count];
```

> **NOTE:** The first statement in the code segment sets total to 0. Recall from Chapter 5 that an accumulator variable must be set to 0 before it is used to keep a running total or the sum will not be correct.

Getting the Average of the Values in a Numeric Array

The first step in calculating the average of all the values in an array is to sum the values. The second step is to divide the sum by the number of elements in the array. Assume that the following statements appear in a program and that values have been stored in the scores array.

```
const int NUM_SCORES = 10;
double scores[NUM_SCORES];
```

The following code calculates the average of the values in the scores array. When the code completes, the average will be stored in the average variable.

```
double total = 0;   // Initialize accumulator
double average;      // Will hold the average
for (int count = 0; count < NUM_SCORES; count++)
   total += scores[count];
average = total / NUM_SCORES;
```

Notice that the last statement, which divides total by numScores, is not inside the loop. This statement should only execute once, after the loop has finished its iterations.

Finding the Highest and Lowest Values in a Numeric Array

The algorithms for finding the highest and lowest values in an array are very similar. First, let's look at code for finding the highest value in an array. Assume that the following code exists in a program, and that values have been stored in the array.

```cpp
const int SIZE = 50;
int numbers[SIZE];
```

The code to find the highest value in the array is as follows.

```cpp
int count;
int highest;

highest = numbers[0];
for (count = 1; count < SIZE; count++)
{
   if (numbers[count] > highest)
      highest = numbers[count];
}
```

First we copy the value in the first array element to the variable `highest`. Then the loop compares all of the remaining array elements, beginning at subscript 1, to the value in `highest`. Each time it finds a value in the array that is greater than `highest`, it copies that value to `highest`. When the loop has finished, `highest` will contain the highest value in the array.

The following code finds the lowest value in the array. As you can see, it is nearly identical to the code for finding the highest value.

```cpp
int count;
int lowest;

lowest = numbers[0];
for (count = 1; count < SIZE; count++)
{
   if (numbers[count] < lowest)
      lowest = numbers[count];
}
```

When the loop has finished, `lowest` will contain the lowest value in the array.

Partially Filled Arrays

Sometimes you need to store a series of items in an array, but you do not know the number of items that there are. As a result, you do not know the exact number of elements needed for the array. One solution is to make the array large enough to hold the largest possible number of items. This can lead to another problem, however. If the actual number of items stored in the array is less than the number of elements, the array will be only partially filled. When you process a partially filled array, you must only process the elements that contain valid data items.

A partially filled array is normally used with an accompanying integer variable that holds the number of items stored in the array. For example, suppose a program uses the following code to create an array with 100 elements, and an `int` variable named `count` that will hold the number of items stored in the array:

```
const int SIZE = 100;
int array[SIZE];
int count = 0;
```

Each time we add an item to the array, we must increment `count`. The following code demonstrates.

```
int number;
cout << "Enter a number or -1 to quit: ";
cin >> number;
while (number != -1 && count < SIZE)
{
    count++;
    array[count - 1] = number;
    cout << "Enter a number or -1 to quit: ";
    cin >> number;
}
```

Each iteration of this sentinel-controlled loop allows the user to enter a number to be stored in the array, or -1 to quit. The `count` variable is incremented, and then used to calculate the subscript of the next available element in the array. When the user enters -1, or `count` exceeds 99, the loop stops. The following code displays all of the valid items in the array.

```
for (int index = 0; index < count; index++)
{
    cout << array[index] << endl;
}
```

Notice that this code uses `count` to determine the maximum array subscript to use.

Program 7-11 shows how this technique can be used to read an unknown number of items from a file into an array. The program reads values from the file `numbers.txt`, which is located on the Student CD.

Program 7-11

```
 1   // This program reads data from a file into an array.
 2   #include <iostream>
 3   #include <fstream>
 4   using namespace std;
 5
 6   int main()
 7   {
 8       const int ARRAY_SIZE = 100; // Array size
 9       int numbers[ARRAY_SIZE];    // Array with 100 elements
10       int count = 0;              // Loop counter variable
11       ifstream inputFile;         // Input file stream object
12
```

```
13       inputFile.open("numbers.txt"); // Open the file.
14
15       // Read the numbers from the file into the array.
16       // After this loop executes, the count variable will hold
17       // the number of values that were stored in the array.
18       while (count < ARRAY_SIZE && inputFile >> numbers[count])
19          count++;
20
21       // Close the file.
22       inputFile.close();
23
24       // Display the numbers read.
25       cout << "The numbers are: ";
26       for (int index = 0; index < count; index++)
27          cout << numbers[index] << " ";
28       cout << endl;
29       return 0;
30   }
```

Program Output
The numbers are: 47 89 65 36 12 25 17 8 62 10 87 62

Look closer at the while loop that begins in line 18. It repeats as long as count is less than ARRAY_SIZE and the end of the file has not been encountered. The first part of the while loop's test expression, count < ARRAY_SIZE, prevents the loop from writing outside the array boundaries. Recall from Chapter 4 that the && operator performs short-circuit evaluation, so the second part of the while loop's test expression, inputFile >> values[count], will be executed only if count is less than ARRAY_SIZE.

Comparing Arrays

We have already noted that you cannot simply assign one array to another array. You must assign each element of the first array to an element of the second array. In addition, you cannot use the == operator with the names of two arrays to determine whether the arrays are equal. For example, the following code appears to compare two arrays, but in reality does not.

```
int firstArray[] = { 5, 10, 15, 20, 25 };
int secondArray[] = { 5, 10, 15, 20, 25 };
if (firstArray == secondArray)      // This is a mistake.
   cout << "The arrays are the same.\n";
else
   cout << "The arrays are not the same.\n";
```

When you use the == operator with array names, the operator compares the beginning memory addresses of the arrays, not the contents of the arrays. The two array names in this code will obviously have different memory addresses. Therefore, the result of the expression firstArray == secondArray is false and the code reports that the arrays are not the same.

To compare the contents of two arrays, you must compare the elements of the two arrays. For example, look at the following code.

```cpp
const int SIZE = 5;
int firstArray[SIZE] = { 5, 10, 15, 20, 25  };
int secondArray[SIZE] = { 5, 10, 15, 20, 25  };
bool arraysEqual = true;   // Flag variable
int count = 0;             // Loop counter variable

// Determine whether the elements contain the same data.
while (arraysEqual && count < SIZE)
{
   if (firstArray[count] != secondArray[count])
      arraysEqual = false;
   count++;
}

if (arraysEqual)
   cout << "The arrays are equal.\n";
else
   cout << "The arrays are not equal.\n";
```

This code determines whether `firstArray` and `secondArray` contain the same values. A `bool` variable, `arraysEqual`, which is initialized to `true`, is used to signal whether the arrays are equal. Another variable, `count`, which is initialized to 0, is used as a loop counter variable.

Then a `while` loop begins. The loop executes as long as `arraysEqual` is `true` and the counter variable `count` is less than `SIZE`. During each iteration, it compares a different set of corresponding elements in the arrays. When it finds two corresponding elements that have different values, the `arraysEqual` variable is set to `false`. After the loop finishes, an `if` statement examines the `arraysEqual` variable. If the variable is `true`, then the arrays are equal and a message indicating so is displayed. Otherwise, they are not equal, so a different message is displayed. This code can be found in the program `ArrayCompare.cpp` on the Student CD.

7.6 Focus on Software Engineering: Using Parallel Arrays

CONCEPT: By using the same subscript, you can build relationships between data stored in two or more arrays.

Sometimes it's useful to store related data in two or more arrays. It's especially useful when the related data is of unlike types. For example, Program 7-12 is another variation of the payroll program. It uses two arrays: one to store the hours worked by each employee (as `ints`), and another to store each employee's hourly pay rate (as `doubles`).

Program 7-12

```cpp
1  // This program uses two parallel arrays: one for hours
2  // worked and one for pay rate.
3  #include <iostream>
4  #include <iomanip>
5  using namespace std;
6
7  int main()
8  {
9     const int NUM_EMPLOYEES = 5;    // Number of employees
10    int hours[NUM_EMPLOYEES];       // Holds hours worked
11    double payRate[NUM_EMPLOYEES]; // Holds pay rates
12
13    // Input the hours worked and the hourly pay rate.
14    cout << "Enter the hours worked by " << NUM_EMPLOYEES
15         << " employees and their\n"
16         << "hourly pay rates.\n";
17    for (int index = 0; index < NUM_EMPLOYEES; index++)
18    {
19       cout << "Hours worked by employee #" << (index+1) << ": ";
20       cin >> hours[index];
21       cout << "Hourly pay rate for employee #" << (index+1) << ": ";
22       cin >> payRate[index];
23    }
24
25    // Display each employee's gross pay.
26    cout << "Here is the gross pay for each employee:\n";
27    cout << fixed << showpoint << setprecision(2);
28    for (int index = 0; index < NUM_EMPLOYEES; index++)
29    {
30       double grossPay = hours[index] * payRate[index];
31       cout << "Employee #" << (index + 1);
32       cout << ": $" << grossPay << endl;
33    }
34    return 0;
35 }
```

Program Output with Example Input Shown in Bold
```
Enter the hours worked by 5 employees and their
hourly pay rates.
Hours worked by employee #1: 10 [Enter]
Hourly pay rate for employee #1: 9.75 [Enter]
Hours worked by employee #2: 15 [Enter]
Hourly pay rate for employee #2: 8.62 [Enter]
Hours worked by employee #3: 20 [Enter]
Hourly pay rate for employee #3: 10.50 [Enter]
Hours worked by employee #4: 40 [Enter]
Hourly pay rate for employee #4: 18.75 [Enter]
Hours worked by employee #5: 40 [Enter]
Hourly pay rate for employee #5: 15.65 [Enter]
```

(program output continues)

Program 7-12   *(continued)*

```
Here is the gross pay for each employee:
Employee #1: $97.50
Employee #2: $129.30
Employee #3: $210.00
Employee #4: $750.00
Employee #5: $626.00
```

Notice in the loops that the same subscript is used to access both arrays. That's because the data for one employee is stored in the same relative position in each array. For example, the hours worked by employee #1 are stored in hours[0], and the same employee's pay rate is stored in payRate[0]. The subscript relates the data in both arrays.

This concept is illustrated in Figure 7-14.

Figure 7-14

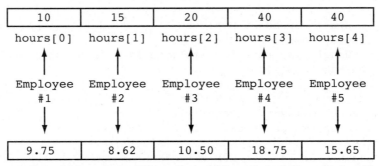

Checkpoint

7.8   Define the following arrays:

A)   ages, a 10-element array of ints initialized with the values 5, 7, 9, 14, 15, 17, 18, 19, 21, and 23.

B)   temps, a 7-element array of floats initialized with the values 14.7, 16.3, 18.43, 21.09, 17.9, 18.76, and 26.7.

C)   alpha, an 8-element array of chars initialized with the values 'J', 'B', 'L', 'A', '*', '$', 'H', and 'M'.

7.9   Is each of the following a valid or invalid array definition? (If a definition is invalid, explain why.)

```
int numbers[10] = {0, 0, 1, 0, 0, 1, 0, 0, 1, 1};
int matrix[5] = {1, 2, 3, 4, 5, 6, 7};
double radii[10] = {3.2, 4.7};
int table[7] = {2, , , 27, , 45, 39};
char codes[] = {'A', 'X', '1', '2', 's'};
int blanks[];
char name[6] = "Joanne";
```

7.10   Given the following array definition:

```
int values[] = {2, 6, 10, 14};
```

What does each of the following display?
A) `cout << values[2];`
B) `cout << ++values[0];`
C) `cout << values[1]++;`
D) `x = 2;`
    `cout << values[++x];`

7.11   Given the following array definition:

```
int nums[5] = {1, 2, 3};
```

What will the following statement display?

```
cout << nums[3];
```

7.12   What is the output of the following code? (You may need to use a calculator.)

```
double balance[5] = {100.0, 250.0, 325.0, 500.0, 1100.0};
const double INTRATE = 0.1;

cout << fixed << showpoint << setprecision(2);
for (int count = 0; count < 5; count++)
    cout << (balance[count] * INTRATE) << endl;
```

7.13   What is the output of the following code? (You may need to use a calculator.)

```
const int SIZE = 5;
int time[SIZE] = {1, 2, 3, 4, 5},
    speed[SIZE] = {18, 4, 27, 52, 100},
    dist[SIZE];

for (int count = 0; count < SIZE; count++)
    dist[count] = time[count] * speed[count];
for (int count = 0; count < SIZE; count++)
{
    cout << time[count] << " ";
    cout << speed[count] << " ";
    cout << dist[count] << endl;
}
```

7.7   Arrays as Function Arguments

CONCEPT: To pass an array as an argument to a function, pass the name of the array.

VideoNote

Passing an Array to a Function

Quite often you'll want to write functions that process the data in arrays. For example, functions could be written to put values in an array, display an array's contents on the screen, total all of an array's elements, or calculate their average. Usually, such functions accept an array as an argument.

When a single element of an array is passed to a function, it is handled like any other variable. For example, Program 7-13 shows a loop that passes one element of the array `numbers` to the function `showValue` each time the loop iterates.

Program 7-13

```
 1    // This program demonstrates that an array element is passed
 2    // to a function like any other variable.
 3    #include <iostream>
 4    using namespace std;
 5
 6    void showValue(int); // Function prototype
 7
 8    int main()
 9    {
10       const int SIZE = 8;
11       int numbers[SIZE] = {5, 10, 15, 20, 25, 30, 35, 40};
12
13       for (int index = 0; index < SIZE; index++)
14          showValue(numbers[index]);
15       return 0;
16    }
17
18    //*********************************************
19    // Definition of function showValue.          *
20    // This function accepts an integer argument.  *
21    // The value of the argument is displayed.     *
22    //*********************************************
23
24    void showValue(int num)
25    {
26       cout << num << " ";
27    }
```

Program Output
```
5 10 15 20 25 30 35 40
```

Each time `showValue` is called in line 14, a copy of an array element is passed into the parameter variable `num`. The `showValue` function simply displays the contents of `num`, and doesn't work directly with the array element itself. (In other words, the array element is passed by value.)

If the function were written to accept the entire array as an argument, however, the parameter would be set up differently. In the following function definition, the parameter `nums` is followed by an empty set of brackets. This indicates that the argument will be an array, not a single value.

```
void showValues(int nums[], int size)
{
   for (int index = 0; index < size; index++)
      cout << nums[index] << " ";
   cout << endl;
}
```

The reason there is no size declarator inside the brackets of nums is because nums is not actually an array. It's a special variable that can accept the address of an array. When an entire array is passed to a function, it is not passed by value, but passed by reference. Imagine the CPU time and memory that would be necessary if a copy of a 10,000-element array were created each time it was passed to a function! Instead, only the starting memory address of the array is passed. Program 7-14 shows the function showValues in use.

NOTE: Notice that in the function prototype, empty brackets appear after the data type of the array parameter. This indicates that showValues accepts the address of an array of integers.

Program 7-14

```
 1   // This program demonstrates an array being passed to a function.
 2   #include <iostream>
 3   using namespace std;
 4
 5   void showValues(int [], int); // Function prototype
 6
 7   int main()
 8   {
 9      const int ARRAY_SIZE = 8;
10      int numbers[ARRAY_SIZE] = {5, 10, 15, 20, 25, 30, 35, 40};
11
12      showValues(numbers, ARRAY_SIZE);
13      return 0;
14   }
15
16   //**************************************************
17   // Definition of function showValue.               *
18   // This function accepts an array of integers and  *
19   // the array's size as its arguments. The contents *
20   // of the array are displayed.                     *
21   //**************************************************
22
23   void showValues(int nums[], int size)
24   {
25      for (int index = 0; index < size; index++)
26         cout << nums[index] << " ";
27      cout << endl;
28   }
```

Program Output
```
5 10 15 20 25 30 35 40
```

In Program 7-14, the function showValues is called in the following statement which appears in line 12:

```
    showValues(numbers, ARRAY_SIZE);
```

The first argument is the name of the array. Remember, in C++ the name of an array without brackets and a subscript is actually the beginning address of the array. In this function call, the address of the `numbers` array is being passed as the first argument to the function. The second argument is the size of the array.

In the `showValues` function, the beginning address of the `numbers` array is copied into the `nums` parameter variable. The `nums` variable is then used to reference the `numbers` array. Figure 7-15 illustrates the relationship between the `numbers` array and the `nums` parameter variable. When the contents of `nums[0]` is displayed, it is actually the contents of `numbers[0]` that appears on the screen.

Figure 7-15

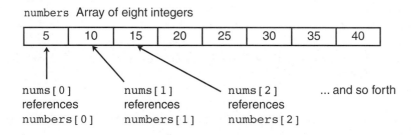

```
numbers  Array of eight integers

┌─────┬─────┬─────┬─────┬─────┬─────┬─────┬─────┐
│  5  │ 10  │ 15  │ 20  │ 25  │ 30  │ 35  │ 40  │
└─────┴─────┴─────┴─────┴─────┴─────┴─────┴─────┘

nums[0]        nums[1]        nums[2]      ... and so forth
references     references     references
numbers[0]     numbers[1]     numbers[2]
```

 NOTE: Although `nums` is not a reference variable, it works like one.

The `nums` parameter variable in the `showValues` function can accept the address of any integer array and can be used to reference that array. So, we can use the `showValues` function to display the contents of any integer array by passing the name of the array and its size as arguments. Program 7-15 uses the function to display the contents of two different arrays.

Program 7-15

```cpp
 1  // This program demonstrates the showValues function being
 2  // used to display the contents of two arrays.
 3  #include <iostream>
 4  using namespace std;
 5
 6  void showValues(int [], int); // Function prototype
 7
 8  int main()
 9  {
10      const int SIZE1 = 8; // Size of set1 array
11      const int SIZE2 = 5; // Size of set2 array
12      int set1[SIZE1] = {5, 10, 15, 20, 25, 30, 35, 40};
13      int set2[SIZE2] = {2, 4, 6, 8, 10};
14
15      // Pass set1 to showValues.
16      showValues(set1, SIZE1);
17
```

```
18        // Pass set2 to showValues.
19        showValues(set2, SIZE2);
20        return 0;
21    }
22
23    //****************************************************
24    // Definition of function showValues.               *
25    // This function accepts an array of integers and   *
26    // the array's size as its arguments. The contents  *
27    // of the array are displayed.                      *
28    //****************************************************
29
30    void showValues(int nums[], int size)
31    {
32        for (int index = 0; index < size; index++)
33            cout << nums[index] << " ";
34        cout << endl;
35    }
```

Program Output

```
5 10 15 20 25 30 35 40
2 4 6 8 10
```

Recall from Chapter 6 that when a reference variable is used as a parameter, it gives the function access to the original argument. Any changes made to the reference variable are actually performed on the argument referenced by the variable. Array parameters work very much like reference variables. They give the function direct access to the original array. Any changes made with the array parameter are actually made on the original array used as the argument. The function doubleArray in Program 7-16 uses this capability to double the contents of each element in the array.

Program 7-16

```
1    // This program uses a function to double the value of
2    // each element of an array.
3    #include <iostream>
4    using namespace std;
5
6    // Function prototypes
7    void doubleArray(int [], int);
8    void showValues(int [], int);
9
10   int main()
11   {
12       const int ARRAY_SIZE = 7;
13       int set[ARRAY_SIZE] = {1, 2, 3, 4, 5, 6, 7};
14
```

(program continues)

Program 7-16   (continued)

```
15      // Display the initial values.
16      cout << "The array's values are:\n";
17      showValues(set, ARRAY_SIZE);
18
19      // Double the values in the array.
20      doubleArray(set, ARRAY_SIZE);
21
22      // Display the resulting values.
23      cout << "After calling doubleArray the values are:\n";
24      showValues(set, ARRAY_SIZE);
25
26      return 0;
27  }
28
29  //*******************************************************
30  // Definition of function doubleArray                  *
31  // This function doubles the value of each element     *
32  // in the array passed into nums. The value passed     *
33  // into size is the number of elements in the array.   *
34  //*******************************************************
35
36  void doubleArray(int nums[], int size)
37  {
38      for (int index = 0; index < size; index++)
39          nums[index] *= 2;
40  }
41
42  //*******************************************************
43  // Definition of function showValues.                  *
44  // This function accepts an array of integers and      *
45  // the array's size as its arguments. The contents     *
46  // of the array are displayed.                         *
47  //*******************************************************
48
49  void showValues(int nums[], int size)
50  {
51      for (int index = 0; index < size; index++)
52          cout << nums[index] << " ";
53      cout << endl;
54  }
```

Program Output

```
The array's values are:
1 2 3 4 5 6 7
After calling doubleArray the values are:
2 4 6 8 10 12 14
```

 WARNING! Like reference variables, array parameters require responsibility. It's important to realize that when an array is passed as an argument, the function has the capability of modifying the original data in the array.

Some Useful Array Functions

Section 7.5 introduced you to algorithms such as summing an array and finding the highest and lowest values in an array. Now that you know how to pass an array as an argument to a function, you can write general purpose functions that perform those operations. The following In the Spotlight section shows an example.

In the Spotlight:
Processing an Array

Dr. LaClaire gives four exams during the semester in her chemistry class. At the end of the semester she drops each student's lowest test score before averaging the scores. She has asked you to write a program that will read a student's four test scores as input, and calculate the average with the lowest score dropped. Here is the pseudocode algorithm that you developed:

Read the student's four test scores.
Calculate the total of the scores.
Find the lowest score.
Subtract the lowest score from the total. This gives the adjusted total.
Divide the adjusted total by 3. This is the average.
Display the average.

Program 7-17 shows the program, which is modularized. Rather than presenting the entire program at once, let's first examine the main function, and then each additional function separately. Here is the first part of the program, including the main function:

Program 7-17 (main function)

```
 1  // This program gets a series of test scores and
 2  // calculates the average of the scores with the
 3  // lowest score dropped.
 4  #include <iostream>
 5  #include <iomanip>
 6  using namespace std;
 7
 8  // Function prototypes
 9  void getTestScores(double[], int);
10  double getTotal(double[], int);
11  double getLowest(double[], int);
12
13  int main()
14  {
15     const int SIZE = 4;        // Array size
16     double testScores[SIZE],   // Array of test scores
17            total,              // Total of the scores
18            lowestScore,        // Lowest test score
19            average;            // Average test score
20
```

(program continues)

Program 7-17   *(continued)*

```
21      // Set up numeric output formatting.
22      cout << fixed << showpoint << setprecision(1);
23
24      // Get the test scores from the user.
25      getTestScores(testScores, SIZE);
26
27      // Get the total of the test scores.
28      total = getTotal(testScores, SIZE);
29
30      // Get the lowest test score.
31      lowestScore = getLowest(testScores, SIZE);
32
33      // Subtract the lowest score from the total.
34      total -= lowestScore;
35
36      // Calculate the average. Divide by 3 because
37      // the lowest test score was dropped.
38      average = total / (SIZE - 1);
39
40      // Display the average.
41      cout << "The average with the lowest score "
42           << "dropped is " << average << ".\n";
43
44      return 0;
45 }
46
```

Lines 15 through 19 define the following items:

- SIZE, an int constant that is used as an array size declarator
- testScores, a double array to hold the test scores
- total, a double variable that will hold the test score totals
- lowestScore, a double variable that will hold the lowest test score
- average, a double variable that will hold the average of the test scores

Line 25 calls the getTestScores function, passing the testScores array and the value of the SIZE constant as arguments. The function gets the test scores from the user and stores them in the array.

Line 28 calls the getTotal function, passing the testScores array and the value of the SIZE constant as arguments. The function returns the total of the values in the array. This value is assigned to the total variable.

Line 31 calls the getLowest function, passing the testScores array and the value of the SIZE constant as arguments. The function returns the lowest value in the array. This value is assigned to the lowestScore variable.

Line 34 subtracts the lowest test score from the total variable. Then, line 38 calculates the average by dividing total by SIZE − 1. (The program divides by SIZE − 1 because the lowest test score was dropped.) Lines 41 and 42 display the average.

The getTestScores function appears next, as shown here:

Program 7-17   **(getTestScores function)**

```
47  //**********************************************************
48  // The getTestScores function accepts an array and its size *
49  // as arguments. It prompts the user to enter test scores,  *
50  // which are stored in the array.                           *
51  //**********************************************************
52
53  void getTestScores(double scores[], int size)
54  {
55     // Loop counter
56     int index;
57
58     // Get each test score.
59     for(index = 0; index <= size - 1; index++)
60     {
61        cout << "Enter test score number "
62             << (index + 1) << ": ";
63        cin >> scores[index];
64     }
65  }
66
```

The getTestScores function has two parameters:

- scores[]—A double array
- size—An int specifying the size of the array that is passed into the scores[] parameter

The purpose of this function is to get a student's test scores from the user and store them in the array that is passed as an argument into the scores[] parameter.

The getTotal function appears next, as shown here:

Program 7-17   **(getTotal function)**

```
67  //*************************************************
68  // The getTotal function accepts a double array    *
69  // and its size as arguments. The sum of the array's *
70  // elements is returned as a double.               *
71  //*************************************************
72
73  double getTotal(double array[], int size)
74  {
75     double total = 0; // Accumulator
76
77     // Add each element to total.
78     for (int count = 0; count < size; count++)
79        total += array[count];
80
81     // Return the total.
82     return total;
83  }
84
```

The getTotal function has two parameters:

- array[]—A double array
- size—An int specifying the size of the array that is passed into the array[] parameter

This function returns the total of the values in the array that is passed as an argument into the array[] parameter.

The getLowest function appears next, as shown here:

Program 7-17   (getLowest **function**)

```
 85  //****************************************************
 86  // The getLowest function accepts a double array and *
 87  // its size as arguments. The lowest value in the    *
 88  // array is returned as a double.                    *
 89  //****************************************************
 90
 91  double getLowest(double array[], int size)
 92  {
 93     double lowest;  // To hold the lowest value
 94
 95     // Get the first array's first element.
 96     lowest = array[0];
 97
 98     // Step through the rest of the array. When a
 99     // value less than lowest is found, assign it
100     // to lowest.
101     for (int count = 1; count < size; count++)
102     {
103        if (array[count] < lowest)
104           lowest = array[count];
105     }
106
107     // Return the lowest value.
108     return lowest;
109  }
```

The getLowest function has two parameters:

- array[]—A double array
- size—An int specifying the size of the array that is passed into the array[] parameter

This function returns the lowest value in the array that is passed as an argument into the array[] parameter. Here is an example of the program's output:

Program 7-17

Program Output with Example Input Shown in Bold
```
Enter test score number 1: 92 [Enter]
Enter test score number 2: 67 [Enter]
Enter test score number 3: 75 [Enter]
Enter test score number 4: 88 [Enter]
The average with the lowest score dropped is 85.0.
```

Checkpoint

7.14   Given the following array definitions

```
double array1[4] = {1.2, 3.2, 4.2, 5.2};
double array2[4];
```

will the following statement work? If not, why?

```
array2 = array1;
```

7.15   When an array name is passed to a function, what is actually being passed?

7.16   When used as function arguments, are arrays passed by value?

7.17   What is the output of the following program? (You may need to consult the ASCII table in Appendix A.)

```cpp
#include <iostream>
using namespace std;

// Function prototypes
void fillArray(char [], int);
void showArray(char [], int);

int main ()
{
    const int SIZE = 8;
    char prodCode[SIZE] = {'0', '0', '0', '0', '0', '0', '0', '0'};

    fillArray(prodCode, SIZE);
    showArray(prodCode, SIZE);
    return 0;
}

// Definition of function fillArray.
// (Hint: 65 is the ASCII code for 'A')

void fillArray(char arr[], int size)
{
    char code = 65;

    for (int k = 0; k < size; code++, k++)
        arr[k] = code;
}

// Definition of function showArray.

void showArray(char codes[], int size)
{
    for (int k = 0; k < size; k++)
        cout << codes[k];
    cout << endl;
}
```

7.18   The following program skeleton, when completed, will ask the user to enter 10 integers, which are stored in an array. The function avgArray, which you must write, is to calculate and return the average of the numbers entered.

```cpp
#include <iostream>
using namespace std;
```

```
// Write your function prototype here

int main()
{
   const int SIZE = 10;
   int userNums[SIZE];

   cout << "Enter 10 numbers: ";
   for (int count = 0; count < SIZE; count++)
   {
      cout << "#" << (count + 1) << " ";
      cin >> userNums[count];
   }
   cout << "The average of those numbers is ";
   cout << avgArray(userNums, SIZE) << endl;
   return 0;
}

//
// Write the function avgArray here.
//
```

7.8   Two-Dimensional Arrays

CONCEPT: A two-dimensional array is like several identical arrays put together. It is useful for storing multiple sets of data.

An array is useful for storing and working with a set of data. Sometimes, though, it's necessary to work with multiple sets of data. For example, in a grade-averaging program a teacher might record all of one student's test scores in an array of doubles. If the teacher has 30 students, that means she'll need 30 arrays of doubles to record the scores for the entire class. Instead of defining 30 individual arrays, however, it would be better to define a two-dimensional array.

The arrays that you have studied so far are one-dimensional arrays. They are called *one-dimensional* because they can only hold one set of data. Two-dimensional arrays, which are sometimes called *2D arrays*, can hold multiple sets of data. It's best to think of a two-dimensional array as having rows and columns of elements, as shown in Figure 7-16. This figure shows an array of test scores, having three rows and four columns.

Figure 7-16

	Column 0	Column 1	Column 2	Column 3
Row 0	scores[0] [0]	scores[0] [1]	scores[0] [2]	scores[0] [3]
Row 1	scores[1] [0]	scores[1] [1]	scores[1] [2]	scores[1] [3]
Row 2	scores[2] [0]	scores[2] [1]	scores[2] [2]	scores[2] [3]

The array depicted in Figure 7-16 has three rows (numbered 0 through 2), and four columns (numbered 0 through 3). There are a total of 12 elements in the array.

To define a two-dimensional array, two size declarators are required. The first one is for the number of rows and the second one is for the number of columns. Here is an example definition of a two-dimensional array with three rows and four columns:

```
double scores[3][4];
```

Rows Columns

The first size declarator specifies the number of rows, and the second size declarator specifies the number of columns. Notice that each number is enclosed in its own set of brackets.

When processing the data in a two-dimensional array, each element has two subscripts: one for its row and another for its column. In the scores array defined above, the elements in row 0 are referenced as

```
scores[0][0]
scores[0][1]
scores[0][2]
scores[0][3]
```

The elements in row 1 are

```
scores[1][0]
scores[1][1]
scores[1][2]
scores[1][3]
```

And the elements in row 2 are

```
scores[2][0]
scores[2][1]
scores[2][2]
scores[2][3]
```

The subscripted references are used in a program just like the references to elements in a single-dimensional array, except now you use two subscripts. The first subscript represents the row position, and the second subscript represents the column position. For example, the following statement assigns the value 92.25 to the element at row 2, column 1 of the scores array:

```
scores[2][1] = 92.25;
```

And the following statement displays the element at row 0, column 2:

```
cout << scores[0][2];
```

Programs that cycle through each element of a two-dimensional array usually do so with nested loops. Program 7-18 is an example.

Program 7-18

```
1   // This program demonstrates a two-dimensional array.
2   #include <iostream>
3   #include <iomanip>
4   using namespace std;
5
```

(program continues)

Program 7-18   *(continued)*

```cpp
 6   int main()
 7   {
 8      const int NUM_DIVS = 3;            // Number of divisions
 9      const int NUM_QTRS = 4;            // Number of quarters
10      double sales[NUM_DIVS][NUM_QTRS]; // Array with 3 rows and 4 columns.
11      double totalSales = 0;             // To hold the total sales.
12      int div, qtr;                      // Loop counters.
13
14      cout << "This program will calculate the total sales of\n";
15      cout << "all the company's divisions.\n";
16      cout << "Enter the following sales information:\n\n";
17
18      // Nested loops to fill the array with quarterly
19      // sales figures for each division.
20      for (div = 0; div < NUM_DIVS; div++)
21      {
22         for (qtr = 0; qtr < NUM_QTRS; qtr++)
23         {
24            cout << "Division " << (div + 1);
25            cout << ", Quarter " << (qtr + 1) << ": $";
26            cin >> sales[div][qtr];
27         }
28         cout << endl; // Print blank line.
29      }
30
31      // Nested loops used to add all the elements.
32      for (div = 0; div < NUM_DIVS; div++)
33      {
34         for (qtr = 0; qtr < NUM_QTRS; qtr++)
35            totalSales += sales[div][qtr];
36      }
37
38      cout << fixed << showpoint << setprecision(2);
39      cout << "The total sales for the company are: $";
40      cout << totalSales << endl;
41      return 0;
42   }
```

Program Output with Example Input Shown in Bold

```
This program will calculate the total sales of
all the company's divisions.
Enter the following sales data:

Division 1, Quarter 1: $31569.45 [Enter]
Division 1, Quarter 2: $29654.23 [Enter]
Division 1, Quarter 3: $32982.54 [Enter]
Division 1, Quarter 4: $39651.21 [Enter]

Division 2, Quarter 1: $56321.02 [Enter]
Division 2, Quarter 2: $54128.63 [Enter]
Division 2, Quarter 3: $41235.85 [Enter]
Division 2, Quarter 4: $54652.33 [Enter]
```

```
Division 3, Quarter 1: $29654.35 [Enter]
Division 3, Quarter 2: $28963.32 [Enter]
Division 3, Quarter 3: $25353.55 [Enter]
Division 3, Quarter 4: $32615.88 [Enter]

The total sales for the company are: $456782.34
```

When initializing a two-dimensional array, it helps to enclose each row's initialization list in a set of braces. Here is an example:

```
int hours[3][2] = {{8, 5}, {7, 9}, {6, 3}};
```

The same definition could also be written as:

```
int hours[3][2] = {{8, 5},
                   {7, 9},
                   {6, 3}};
```

In either case, the values are assigned to hours in the following manner:

```
hours[0][0] is set to 8
hours[0][1] is set to 5
hours[1][0] is set to 7
hours[1][1] is set to 9
hours[2][0] is set to 6
hours[2][1] is set to 3
```

Figure 7-17 illustrates the initialization.

Figure 7-17

	Column 0	Column 1
Row 0	8	5
Row 1	7	9
Row 2	6	3

The extra braces that enclose each row's initialization list are optional. Both of the following statements perform the same initialization:

```
int hours[3][2] = {{8, 5}, {7, 9}, {6, 3}};
int hours[3][2] = {8, 5, 7, 9, 6, 3};
```

Because the extra braces visually separate each row, however, it's a good idea to use them. In addition, the braces give you the ability to leave out initializers within a row without omitting the initializers for the rows that follow it. For instance, look at the following array definition:

```
int table[3][2] = {{1}, {3, 4}, {5}};
```

table[0][0] is initialized to 1, table[1][0] is initialized to 3, table[1][1] is initialized to 4, and table[2][0] is initialized to 5. table[0][1] and table[2][1] are not initialized. Because some of the array elements are initialized, these two initialized elements are automatically set to zero.

Passing Two-Dimensional Arrays to Functions

Program 7-19 demonstrates passing a two-dimensional array to a function. When a two-dimensional array is passed to a function, the parameter type must contain a size declarator for the number of columns. Here is the header for the function showArray, from Program 7-19:

```
void showArray(int array[][COLS], int rows)
```

COLS is a global named constant which is set to 4. The function can accept any two-dimensional integer array, as long as it consists of four columns. In the program, the contents of two separate arrays are displayed by the function.

Program 7-19

```cpp
 1   // This program demonstrates accepting a 2D array argument.
 2   #include <iostream>
 3   #include <iomanip>
 4   using namespace std;
 5
 6   // Global constants
 7   const int COLS = 4;      // Number of columns in each array
 8   const int TBL1_ROWS = 3; // Number of rows in table1
 9   const int TBL2_ROWS = 4; // Number of rows in table2
10
11   void showArray(int [][COLS], int); // Function prototype
12
13   int main()
14   {
15      int table1[TBL1_ROWS][COLS] = {{1, 2, 3, 4},
16                                     {5, 6, 7, 8},
17                                     {9, 10, 11, 12}};
18      int table2[TBL2_ROWS][COLS] = {{10, 20, 30, 40},
19                                     {50, 60, 70, 80},
20                                     {90, 100, 110, 120},
21                                     {130, 140, 150, 160}};
22
23      cout << "The contents of table1 are:\n";
24      showArray(table1, TBL1_ROWS);
25      cout << "The contents of table2 are:\n";
26      showArray(table2, TBL2_ROWS);
27      return 0;
28   }
29
30   //****************************************************************
31   // Function Definition for showArray                            *
32   // The first argument is a two-dimensional int array with COLS  *
33   // columns. The second argument, rows, specifies the number of  *
34   // rows in the array. The function displays the array's contents.*
35   //****************************************************************
36
37   void showArray(int array[][COLS], int rows)
38   {
39      for (int x = 0; x < rows; x++)
40      {
```

```
41          for (int y = 0; y < COLS; y++)
42          {
43             cout << setw(4) << array[x][y] << " ";
44          }
45          cout << endl;
46       }
47    }
```

Program Output

```
The contents of table1 are:
   1    2    3    4
   5    6    7    8
   9   10   11   12
The contents of table2 are:
  10   20   30   40
  50   60   70   80
  90  100  110  120
 130  140  150  160
```

C++ requires the columns to be specified in the function prototype and header because of the way two-dimensional arrays are stored in memory. One row follows another, as shown in Figure 7-18.

Figure 7-18

When the compiler generates code for accessing the elements of a two-dimensional array, it needs to know how many bytes separate the rows in memory. The number of columns is a critical factor in this calculation.

Summing All the Elements of a Two-Dimensional Array

To sum all the elements of a two-dimensional array, you can use a pair of nested loops to add the contents of each element to an accumulator. The following code is an example.

```
const int NUM_ROWS = 5;    // Number of rows
const int NUM_COLS = 5;    // Number of columns
int total = 0;             // Accumulator
int numbers[NUM_ROWS][NUM_COLS] = {{2, 7, 9, 6, 4},
                                   {6, 1, 8, 9, 4},
                                   {4, 3, 7, 2, 9},
                                   {9, 9, 0, 3, 1},
                                   {6, 2, 7, 4, 1}};

// Sum the array elements.
for (int row = 0; row < NUM_ROWS; row++)
{
```

```
      for (int col = 0; col < NUM_COLS; col++)
         total += numbers[row][col];
   }

   // Display the sum.
   cout << "The total is " << total << endl;
```

Summing the Rows of a Two-Dimensional Array

Sometimes you may need to calculate the sum of each row in a two-dimensional array. For example, suppose a two-dimensional array is used to hold a set of test scores for a set of students. Each row in the array is a set of test scores for one student. To get the sum of a student's test scores (perhaps so an average may be calculated), you use a loop to add all the elements in one row. The following code shows an example.

```
const int NUM_STUDENTS = 3;        // Number of students
const int NUM_SCORES = 5;          // Number of test scores
double total;                      // Accumulator is set in the loops
double average;                    // To hold each student's average
double scores[NUM_STUDENTS][NUM_SCORES] = {{88, 97, 79, 86, 94},
                                           {86, 91, 78, 79, 84},
                                           {82, 73, 77, 82, 89}};

// Get each student's average score.
for (int row = 0; row < NUM_STUDENTS; row++)
{
   // Set the accumulator.
   total = 0;

   // Sum a row.
   for (int col = 0; col < NUM_SCORES; col++)
      total += scores[row][col];

   // Get the average.
   average = total / NUM_SCORES;

   // Display the average.
   cout << "Score average for student "
        << (row + 1) << " is " << average <<endl;
}
```

Notice that the total variable, which is used as an accumulator, is set to zero just before the inner loop executes. This is because the inner loop sums the elements of a row and stores the sum in total. Therefore, the total variable must be set to zero before each iteration of the inner loop.

Summing the Columns of a Two-Dimensional Array

Sometimes you may need to calculate the sum of each column in a two-dimensional array. In the previous example a two-dimensional array is used to hold a set of test scores for a set of students. Suppose you wish to calculate the class average for each of the test scores. To do this, you calculate the average of each column in the array. This is accomplished with a set of nested loops. The outer loop controls the column subscript and the inner loop controls the row subscript. The inner loop calculates the sum of a column, which is stored in an accumulator. The following code demonstrates.

```cpp
const int NUM_STUDENTS = 3;      // Number of students
const int NUM_SCORES = 5;        // Number of test scores
double total;                    // Accumulator is set in the loops
double average;                  // To hold each score's class average
double scores[NUM_STUDENTS][NUM_SCORES] = {{88, 97, 79, 86, 94},
                                           {86, 91, 78, 79, 84},
                                           {82, 73, 77, 82, 89}};

// Get the class average for each score.
for (int col = 0; col < NUM_SCORES; col++)
{
    // Reset the accumulator.
    total = 0;

    // Sum a column.
    for (int row = 0; row < NUM_STUDENTS; row++)
        total += scores[row][col];

    // Get the average.
    average = total / NUM_STUDENTS;

    // Display the class average.
    cout << "Class average for test " << (col + 1)
         << " is " << average << endl;
}
```

7.9 Arrays of Strings

CONCEPT: A two-dimensional array of characters can be used as an array of strings.

Because strings are stored in single-dimensional character arrays, an array of strings would be a two-dimensional character array. Figure 7-19 depicts such an array.

Figure 7-19

```cpp
char scientists[4][9] = {"Galileo",
                         "Kepler",
                         "Newton",
                         "Einstein" };
```

G	a	l	i	l	e	o	\0	
K	e	p	l	e	r	\0		
N	e	w	t	o	n	\0		
E	i	n	s	t	e	i	n	\0

The longest string in the array shown above is nine characters (including the null terminator), so the array must have nine columns. The rows with strings of less than nine characters will have unused elements.

Just as the name of an array represents the array's address, a two-dimensional array with only the row subscript represents the address of that row. For instance, in the array defined above, `scientists[0]` represents the address of row 0, `scientists[1]` represents the address of row 1, and so forth. The following `cout` statement will display the string "Einstein" on the screen:

```
cout << scientists[3];
```

Likewise, the following loop will display all the names in the array:

```
for (int count = 0; count < 4; count++)
    cout << scientists[count] << endl;
```

Program 7-20 uses a two-dimensional character array to hold the names of the months and a one-dimensional integer array to hold the number of days in each month.

Program 7-20

```
 1   // This program displays the number of days in each month.
 2   #include <iostream>
 3   using namespace std;
 4
 5   int main()
 6   {
 7      const int NUM_MONTHS = 12;  // The number of months
 8      const int STRING_SIZE = 10; // Maximum size of each string
 9
10      // Array with the names of the months
11      char months[NUM_MONTHS][STRING_SIZE] =
12                   { "January", "February", "March",
13                     "April", "May", "June",
14                     "July", "August", "September",
15                     "October", "November", "December" };
16
17      // Array with the number of days in each month
18      int days[NUM_MONTHS] = {31, 28, 31, 30,
19                              31, 30, 31, 31,
20                              30, 31, 30, 31};
21
22      // Display the months and their numbers of days.
23      for (int count = 0; count < NUM_MONTHS; count++)
24      {
25         cout << months[count] << " has ";
26         cout << days[count] << " days.\n";
27      }
28      return 0;
29   }
```

Program Output
```
January has 31 days.
February has 28 days.
March has 31 days.
April has 30 days.
May has 31 days.
June has 30 days.
July has 31 days.
August has 31 days.
September has 30 days.
October has 31 days.
November has 30 days.
December has 31 days.
```

7.10 Arrays with Three or More Dimensions

CONCEPT: C++ does not limit the number of dimensions that an array may have. It is possible to create arrays with multiple dimensions, to model data that occur in multiple sets.

C++ allows you to create arrays with virtually any number of dimensions. Here is an example of a three-dimensional array definition:

```
double seats[3][5][8];
```

This array can be thought of as three sets of five rows, with each row containing eight elements. The array might be used to store the prices of seats in an auditorium, where there are eight seats in a row, five rows in a section, and a total of three sections.

Figure 7-20 illustrates the concept of a three-dimensional array as "pages" of two-dimensional arrays.

Figure 7-20

Arrays with more than three dimensions are difficult to visualize, but can be useful in some programming problems. For example, in a factory warehouse where cases of widgets are stacked on pallets, an array with four dimensions could be used to store a part number for each widget. The four subscripts of each element could represent the pallet number, case number, row number, and column number of each widget. Similarly, an array with five dimensions could be used if there were multiple warehouses.

> **NOTE:** When writing functions that accept multi-dimensional arrays as arguments, all but the first dimension must be explicitly stated in the parameter list.

Checkpoint

7.19 Define a two-dimensional array of `ints` named `grades`. It should have 30 rows and 10 columns.

7.20 How many elements are in the following array?

```
double sales[6][4];
```

7.21 Write a statement that assigns the value 56893.12 to the first column of the first row of the array defined in Question 7.20.

7.22 Write a statement that displays the contents of the last column of the last row of the array defined in Question 7.20.

7.23 Define a two-dimensional array named `settings` large enough to hold the table of data below. Initialize the array with the values in the table.

12	24	32	21	42
14	67	87	65	90
19	1	24	12	8

7.24 Fill in the table below so it shows the contents of the following array:

```
int table[3][4] = {{2, 3}, {7, 9, 2}, {1}};
```


7.25 Write a function called `displayArray7`. The function should accept a two-dimensional array as an argument and display its contents on the screen. The function should work with any of the following arrays:

```
int hours[5][7];
int stamps[8][7];
int autos[12][7];
int cats[50][7];
```

7.26   A video rental store keeps DVDs on 50 racks with 10 shelves each. Each shelf holds 25 DVDs. Define a three-dimensional array large enough to represent the store's storage system.

7.11   Focus on Problem Solving and Program Design: A Case Study

The National Commerce Bank has hired you as a contract programmer. Your first assignment is to write a function that will be used by the bank's automated teller machines (ATMs) to validate a customer's personal identification number (PIN).

Your function will be incorporated into a larger program that asks the customer to input his or her PIN on the ATM's numeric keypad. (PINs are seven-digit numbers. The program stores each digit in an element of an integer array.) The program also retrieves a copy of the customer's actual PIN from a database. (The PINs are also stored in the database as seven-element arrays.) If these two numbers match, then the customer's identity is validated. Your function is to compare the two arrays and determine whether they contain the same numbers.

Here are the specifications your function must meet:

Parameters   The function is to accept as arguments two integer arrays of seven elements each. The first argument will contain the number entered by the customer. The second argument will contain the number retrieved from the bank's database.

Return value   The function should return a Boolean true value if the two arrays are identical. Otherwise, it should return false.

Here is the pseudocode for the function:

```
For each element in the first array
    Compare the element with the element in the second array
    that is in the corresponding position.
    If the two elements contain different values
        Return false.
    End If.
End For.
Return true.
```

The C++ code is shown below.

```cpp
bool testPIN(int custPIN[], int databasePIN[], int size)
{
    for (int index = 0; index < size; index++)
    {
        if (custPIN[index] != databasePIN[index])
            return false;   // We've found two different values.
    }
    return true;   // If we make it this far, the values are the same.
}
```

Because you have only been asked to write a function that performs the comparison between the customer's input and the PIN that was retrieved from the database, you will also need to design a driver. Program 7-21 shows the complete program.

Program 7-21

```
 1  // This program is a driver that tests a function comparing the
 2  // contents of two int arrays.
 3  #include <iostream>
 4  using namespace std;
 5
 6  // Function Prototype
 7  bool testPIN(int [], int [], int);
 8
 9  int main ()
10  {
11     const int NUM_DIGITS = 7; // Number of digits in a PIN
12     int pin1[NUM_DIGITS] = {2, 4, 1, 8, 7, 9, 0}; // Base set of values.
13     int pin2[NUM_DIGITS] = {2, 4, 6, 8, 7, 9, 0}; // Only 1 element is
14                                                   // different from pin1.
15     int pin3[NUM_DIGITS] = {1, 2, 3, 4, 5, 6, 7}; // All elements are
16                                                   // different from pin1.
17     if (testPIN(pin1, pin2, NUM_DIGITS))
18        cout << "ERROR: pin1 and pin2 report to be the same.\n";
19     else
20        cout << "SUCCESS: pin1 and pin2 are different.\n";
21
22     if (testPIN(pin1, pin3, NUM_DIGITS))
23        cout << "ERROR: pin1 and pin3 report to be the same.\n";
24     else
25        cout << "SUCCESS: pin1 and pin3 are different.\n";
26
27     if (testPIN(pin1, pin1, NUM_DIGITS))
28        cout << "SUCCESS: pin1 and pin1 report to be the same.\n";
29     else
30        cout << "ERROR: pin1 and pin1 report to be different.\n";
31     return 0;
32  }
33
34  //********************************************************************
35  // The following function accepts two int arrays. The arrays are    *
36  // compared. If they contain the same values, true is returned.     *
37  // If they contain different values, false is returned.             *
38  //********************************************************************
39
40  bool testPIN(int custPIN[], int databasePIN[], int size)
41  {
42     for (int index = 0; index < size; index++)
43     {
44        if (custPIN[index] != databasePIN[index])
45           return false; // We've found two different values.
46     }
47     return true; // If we make it this far, the values are the same.
48  }
```

Program Output

```
SUCCESS: pin1 and pin2 are different.
SUCCESS: pin1 and pin3 are different.
SUCCESS: pin1 and pin1 report to be the same.
```

 Case Study on CD: See the Intersection of Sets Case Study on the Student CD.

7.12 If You Plan to Continue in Computer Science: Introduction to the STL vector

CONCEPT: The Standard Template Library offers a vector data type, which in many ways, is superior to standard arrays.

The *Standard Template Library* (STL) is a collection of data types and algorithms that you may use in your programs. These data types and algorithms are *programmer-defined*. They are not part of the C++ language, but were created in addition to the built-in data types. If you plan to continue your studies in the field of computer science, you should become familiar with the STL. This section introduces one of the STL data types.

 NOTE: Many older compilers do not support the STL.

The data types that are defined in the STL are commonly called *containers*. They are called containers because they store and organize data. There are two types of containers in the STL: sequence containers and associative containers. A *sequence container* organizes data in a sequential fashion, similar to an array. *Associative containers* organize data with keys, which allow rapid, random access to elements stored in the container.

In this section you will learn to use the vector data type, which is a sequence container. A vector is like an array in the following ways:

- A vector holds a sequence of values, or elements.
- A vector stores its elements in contiguous memory locations.
- You can use the array subscript operator [ ] to read the individual elements in the vector.

However, a vector offers several advantages over arrays. Here are just a few:

- You do not have to declare the number of elements that the vector will have.
- If you add a value to a vector that is already full, the vector will automatically increase its size to accommodate the new value.
- vectors can report the number of elements they contain.

Defining a `vector`

To use `vectors` in your program, you must include the `vector` header file with the following statement:

```
#include <vector>
```

NOTE: To use the `vector` data type, you must have the `using namespace std;` statement in your program.

Now you are ready to define an actual `vector` object. The syntax for defining a `vector` is somewhat different from the syntax used in defining a regular variable or array. Here is an example:

```
vector<int> numbers;
```

This statement defines `numbers` as a `vector` of `ints`. Notice that the data type is enclosed in angled brackets, immediately after the word `vector`. Because the `vector` expands in size as you add values to it, there is no need to declare a size. You can define a starting size, if you prefer. Here is an example:

```
vector<int> numbers(10);
```

This statement defines `numbers` as a `vector` of 10 `ints`. This is only a starting size, however. Although the `vector` has 10 elements, its size will expand if you add more than 10 values to it.

NOTE: If you specify a starting size for a `vector`, the size declarator is enclosed in parentheses, not square brackets.

When you specify a starting size for a `vector`, you may also specify an initialization value. The initialization value is copied to each element. Here is an example:

```
vector<int> numbers(10, 2);
```

In this statement, `numbers` is defined as a `vector` of 10 `ints`. Each element in `numbers` is initialized to the value 2.

You may also initialize a `vector` with the values in another `vector`. For example, look at the following statement. Assume that `set1` is a `vector` of `ints` that already has values stored in it.

```
vector<int> set2(set1);
```

After this statement executes, `set2` will be a copy of `set1`.

Table 7-3 summarizes the `vector` definition procedures we have discussed.

Table 7-3

Definition Format	Description
`vector<float> amounts;`	Defines amounts as an empty vector of floats.
`vector<int> scores(15);`	Defines scores as a vector of 15 ints.
`vector<char> letters(25, 'A');`	Defines letters as a vector of 25 characters. Each element is initialized with 'A'.
`vector<double> values2(values1);`	Defines values2 as a vector of doubles. All the elements of values1, which is also a vector of doubles, are copied to value2.

Storing and Retrieving Values in a vector

To store a value in an element that already exists in a vector, you may use the array subscript operator [ ]. For example, look at Program 7-22.

Program 7-22

```cpp
 1  // This program stores, in two vectors, the hours worked by 5
 2  // employees, and their hourly pay rates.
 3  #include <iostream>
 4  #include <iomanip>
 5  #include <vector>          // Needed to define vectors
 6  using namespace std;
 7
 8  int main()
 9  {
10     const int NUM_EMPLOYEES = 5;          // Number of employees
11     vector<int> hours(NUM_EMPLOYEES);     // A vector of integers
12     vector<double> payRate(NUM_EMPLOYEES); // A vector of doubles
13     int index;                             // Loop counter
14
15     // Input the data.
16     cout << "Enter the hours worked by " << NUM_EMPLOYEES;
17     cout << " employees and their hourly rates.\n";
18     for (index = 0; index < NUM_EMPLOYEES; index++)
19     {
20        cout << "Hours worked by employee #" << (index + 1);
21        cout << ": ";
22        cin >> hours[index];
23        cout << "Hourly pay rate for employee #";
24        cout << (index + 1) << ": ";
25        cin >> payRate[index];
26     }
27
28     // Display each employee's gross pay.
29     cout << "\nHere is the gross pay for each employee:\n";
30     cout << fixed << showpoint << setprecision(2);
```

(program continues)

Program 7-22   *(continued)*

```
31      for (index = 0; index < NUM_EMPLOYEES; index++)
32      {
33         double grossPay = hours[index] * payRate[index];
34         cout << "Employee #" << (index + 1);
35         cout << ": $" << grossPay << endl;
36      }
37      return 0;
38 }
```

Program Output with Example Input Shown in Bold
```
Enter the hours worked by 5 employees and their hourly rates.
Hours worked by employee #1: 10 [Enter]
Hourly pay rate for employee #1: 9.75 [Enter]
Hours worked by employee #2: 15 [Enter]
Hourly pay rate for employee #2: 8.62 [Enter]
Hours worked by employee #3: 20 [Enter]
Hourly pay rate for employee #3: 10.50 [Enter]
Hours worked by employee #4: 40 [Enter]
Hourly pay rate for employee #4: 18.75 [Enter]
Hours worked by employee #5: 40 [Enter]
Hourly pay rate for employee #5: 15.65 [Enter]

Here is the gross pay for each employee:
Employee #1: $97.50
Employee #2: $129.30
Employee #3: $210.00
Employee #4: $750.00
Employee #5: $626.00
```

Notice that Program 7-22 uses the following statements in lines 11 and 12 to define two vectors.

```
vector<int> hours(NUM_EMPLOYEES);       // A vector of integers
vector<double> payRate(NUM_EMPLOYEES); // A vector of doubles
```

Both of the vectors are defined with the starting size 5, which is the value of the named constant NUM_EMPLOYEES. The program uses the following loop in lines 18 through 26 to store a value in each element of both vectors:

```
for (index = 0; index < NUM_EMPLOYEES; index++)
{
   cout << "Hours worked by employee #" << (index + 1);
   cout << ": ";
   cin >> hours[index];
   cout << "Hourly pay rate for employee #";
   cout << (index + 1) << ": ";
   cin >> payRate[index];
}
```

Because the values entered by the user are being stored in vector elements that already exist, the program uses the array subscript operator [ ], as shown in the following statements, which appear in lines 22 and 25:

```
cin >> hours[index];

cin >> payRate[index];
```

Using the push_back Member Function

You cannot use the [ ] operator to access a vector element that does not exist. To store a value in a vector that does not have a starting size, or that is already full, use the push_back member function. The push_back member function accepts a value as an argument, and stores that value after the last element in the vector. (It pushes the value onto the back of the vector.) Here is an example:

```
numbers.push_back(25);
```

Assuming numbers is a vector of ints, this statement stores 25 as the last element. If numbers is full, the statement creates a new last element, and stores 25 in it. If there are no elements in numbers, this statement creates an element and stores 25 in it.

Program 7-23 is a modification of Program 7-22. This version, however, allows the user to specify the number of employees. The two vectors, hours and payRate, are defined without starting sizes. Because these vectors have no starting elements, the push_back member function is used to store values in the vectors.

Program 7-23

```
 1  // This program stores, in two arrays, the hours worked by 5
 2  // employees, and their hourly pay rates.
 3  #include <iostream>
 4  #include <iomanip>
 5  #include <vector>     // Needed to define vectors
 6  using namespace std;
 7
 8  int main()
 9  {
10      vector<int> hours;       // hours is an empty vector
11      vector<double> payRate;  // payRate is an empty vector
12      int numEmployees;        // The number of employees
13      int index;               // Loop counter
14
15      // Get the number of employees.
16      cout << "How many employees do you have? ";
17      cin >> numEmployees;
18
19      // Input the payroll data.
20      cout << "Enter the hours worked by " << numEmployees;
21      cout << " employees and their hourly rates.\n";
```

(program continues)

Program 7-23 *(continued)*

```
22    for (index = 0; index < numEmployees; index++)
23    {
24        int tempHours;    // To hold the number of hours entered
25        double tempRate;  // To hold the payrate entered
26
27        cout << "Hours worked by employee #" << (index + 1);
28        cout << ": ";
29        cin >> tempHours;
30        hours.push_back(tempHours);      // Add an element to hours
31        cout << "Hourly pay rate for employee #";
32        cout << (index + 1) << ": ";
33        cin >> tempRate;
34        payRate.push_back(tempRate);  // Add an element to payRate
35    }
36
37    // Display each employee's gross pay.
38    cout << "Here is the gross pay for each employee:\n";
39    cout << fixed << showpoint << setprecision(2);
40    for (index = 0; index < numEmployees; index++)
41    {
42        double grossPay = hours[index] * payRate[index];
43        cout << "Employee #" << (index + 1);
44        cout << ": $" << grossPay << endl;
45    }
46    return 0;
47 }
```

Program Output with Example Input Shown in Bold
```
How many employees do you have? 3 [Enter]
Enter the hours worked by 3 employees and their hourly rates.
Hours worked by employee #1: 40 [Enter]
Hourly pay rate for employee #1: 12.63 [Enter]
Hours worked by employee #2: 25 [Enter]
Hourly pay rate for employee #2: 10.35 [Enter]
Hours worked by employee #3: 45 [Enter]
Hourly pay rate for employee #3: 22.65 [Enter]

Here is the gross pay for each employee:
Employee #1: $505.20
Employee #2: $258.75
Employee #3: $1019.2
```

Notice that in lines 40 through 45 the second loop, which calculates and displays each employee's gross pay, uses the [] operator to access the elements of the hours and payRate vectors:

```
for (index = 0; index < numEmployees; index++)
{
    double grossPay = hours[index] * payRate[index];
    cout << "Employee #" << (index + 1);
    cout << ": $" << grossPay << endl;
}
```

This is possible because the first loop in lines 22 through 35 uses the push_back member function to create the elements in the two vectors.

Determining the Size of a vector

Unlike arrays, vectors can report the number of elements they contain. This is accomplished with the size member function. Here is an example of a statement that uses the size member function:

```
numValues = set.size();
```

In this statement, assume that numValues is an int and set is a vector. After the statement executes, numValues will contain the number of elements in set.

The size member function is especially useful when you are writing functions that accept vectors as arguments. For example, look at the following code for the showValues function:

```
void showValues(vector<int> vect)
{
    for (int count = 0; count < vect.size(); count++)
        cout << vect[count] << endl;
}
```

Because the vector can report its size, this function does not need to accept a second argument indicating the number of elements in the vector. Program 7-24 demonstrates this function.

Program 7-24

```
 1  // This program demonstrates the vector size
 2  // member function.
 3  #include <iostream>
 4  #include <vector>
 5  using namespace std;
 6
 7  // Function prototype
 8  void showValues(vector<int>);
 9
10  int main()
11  {
12      vector<int> values;
13
14      // Put a series of numbers in the vector.
15      for (int count = 0; count < 7; count++)
16          values.push_back(count * 2);
17
18      // Display the numbers.
19      showValues(values);
20      return 0;
21  }
22
```

(program continues)

Program 7-24   *(continued)*

```
23 //**************************************************
24 // Definition of function showValues.           *
25 // This function accepts an int vector as its    *
26 // argument. The value of each of the vector's   *
27 // elements is displayed.                        *
28 //**************************************************
29
30 void showValues(vector<int> vect)
31 {
32    for (int count = 0; count < vect.size(); count++)
33       cout << vect[count] << endl;
34 }
```

Program Output
```
0
2
4
6
8
10
12
```

Removing Elements from a vector

Use the pop_back member function to remove the last element from a vector. In the following statement, assume that collection is the name of a vector.

```
collection.pop_back();
```

This statement removes the last element from the collection vector. Program 7-25 demonstrates the function.

Program 7-25

```
1 // This program demonstrates the vector pop_back member function.
2 #include <iostream>
3 #include <vector>
4 using namespace std;
5
6 int main()
7 {
8    vector<int> values;
9
10    // Store values in the vector.
11    values.push_back(1);
12    values.push_back(2);
13    values.push_back(3);
14    cout << "The size of values is " << values.size() << endl;
15
```

```
16    // Remove a value from the vector.
17    cout << "Popping a value from the vector...\n";
18    values.pop_back();
19    cout << "The size of values is now " << values.size() << endl;
20
21    // Now remove another value from the vector.
22    cout << "Popping a value from the vector...\n";
23    values.pop_back();
24    cout << "The size of values is now " << values.size() << endl;
25
26    // Remove the last value from the vector.
27    cout << "Popping a value from the vector...\n";
28    values.pop_back();
29    cout << "The size of values is now " << values.size() << endl;
30    return 0;
31 }
```

Program Output

```
The size of values is 3
Popping a value from the vector...
The size of values is now 2
Popping a value from the vector...
The size of values is now 1
Popping a value from the vector...
The size of values is now 0
```

Clearing a vector

To completely clear the contents of a vector, use the clear member function, as shown in the following statement:

```
numbers.clear();
```

After this statement executes, numbers will be cleared of all its elements. Program 7-26 demonstrates the function.

Program 7-26

```
1 // This program demonstrates the vector clear member function.
2 #include <iostream>
3 #include <vector>
4 using namespace std;
5
6 int main()
7 {
8    vector<int> values(100);
9
10   cout << "The values vector has "
11        << values.size() << " elements.\n";
12   cout << "I will call the clear member function...\n";
13   values.clear();
```

(program continues)

Program 7-26 *(continued)*

```
14     cout << "Now, the values vector has "
15         << values.size() << " elements.\n";
16     return 0;
17 }
```

Program Output

```
The values vector has 100 elements.
I will call the clear member function...
Now, the values vector has 0 elements.
```

Detecting an Empty vector

To determine if a vector is empty, use the empty member function. The function returns true if the vector is empty, and false if the vector has elements stored in it. Assuming set is a vector, here is an example of its use:

```
if (set.empty())
    cout << "No values in set.\n";
```

Program 7-27 uses a function named avgVector, which demonstrates the empty member function.

Program 7-27

```
 1 // This program demonstrates the vector's empty member function.
 2 #include <iostream>
 3 #include <vector>
 4 using namespace std;
 5
 6 // Function prototype
 7 double avgVector(vector<int>);
 8
 9 int main()
10 {
11     vector<int> values;    // A vector to hold values
12     int numValues;         // The number of values
13     double average;        // To hold the average
14
15     // Get the number of values to average.
16     cout << "How many values do you wish to average? ";
17     cin >> numValues;
18
19     // Get the values and store them in the vector.
20     for (int count = 0; count < numValues; count++)
21     {
22         int tempValue;
23         cout << "Enter a value: ";
24         cin >> tempValue;
25         values.push_back(tempValue);
26     }
27
```

```
28      // Get the average of the values and display it.
29      average = avgVector(values);
30      cout << "Average: " << average << endl;
31      return 0;
32  }
33
34  //*************************************************************
35  // Definition of function avgVector.                        *
36  // This function accepts an int vector as its argument. If   *
37  // the vector contains values, the function returns the      *
38  // average of those values. Otherwise, an error message is   *
39  // displayed and the function returns 0.0.                   *
40  //*************************************************************
41
42  double avgVector(vector<int> vect)
43  {
44      int total = 0;     // accumulator
45      double avg;        // average
46
47      if (vect.empty()) // Determine if the vector is empty
48      {
49          cout << "No values to average.\n";
50          avg = 0.0;
51      }
52      else
53      {
54          for (int count = 0; count < vect.size(); count++)
55              total += vect[count];
56          avg = total / vect.size();
57      }
58      return avg;
59  }
```

Program Output with Example Input Shown in Bold
```
How many values do you wish to average? 5 [Enter]
Enter a value: 12
Enter a value: 18
Enter a value: 3
Enter a value: 7
Enter a value: 9
Average: 9
```

Program Output with Different Example Input Shown in Bold
```
How many values do you wish to average? 0 [Enter]
No values to average.
Average: 0
```

Summary of vector Member Functions

Table 7-4 provides a summary of the vector member function we have discussed, as well as some additional ones.

Table 7-4

Member Function	Description
at(*element*)	Returns the value of the element located at *element* in the vector. *Example:* `x = vect.at(5);` This statement assigns the value of the fifth element of vect to x.
capacity()	Returns the maximum number of elements that may be stored in the vector without additional memory being allocated. (This is not the same value as returned by the size member function). *Example:* `x = vect.capacity();` This statement assigns the capacity of vect to x.
clear()	Clears a vector of all its elements. Example: `vect.clear();` This statement removes all the elements from vect.

empty()	Returns true if the vector is empty. Otherwise, it returns false. *Example:*
	
	`if (vect.empty())`
	`    cout << "The vector is empty.";`
	
	This statement displays the message if vect is empty.

pop_back()	Removes the last element from the vector. *Example:* `vect.pop_back();` This statement removes the last element of vect, thus reducing its size by 1.
push_back(*value*)	Stores a value in the last element of the vector. If the vector is full or empty, a new element is created. *Example:* `vect.push_back(7);` This statement stores 7 in the last element of vect.

(table continues)

Table 7-4 *(continued)*

Member Function	Description
reverse()	Reverses the order of the elements in the vector. (The last element becomes the first element, and the first element becomes the last element.) *Example:* vect.reverse(); This statement reverses the order of the element in vect.
resize(*elements, value*)	Resizes a vector by *elements* elements. Each of the new elements is initialized with the value in *value*. *Example:* vect.resize(5, 1); This statement increases the size of vect by five elements. The five new elements are initialized to the value 1.
swap(*vector2*)	Swaps the contents of the vector with the contents of *vector2*. *Example:* vect1.swap(vect2); This statement swaps the contents of vect1 and vect2

 Checkpoint

7.27   What header file must you #include in order to define vector objects?

7.28   Write a definition statement for a vector named frogs. frogs should be an empty vector of ints.

7.29   Write a definition statement for a vector named lizards. lizards should be a vector of 20 floats.

7.30   Write a definition statement for a vector named toads. toads should be a vector of 100 chars, with each element initialized to 'z'.

7.31   gators is an empty vector of ints. Write a statement that stores the value 27 in gators.

7.32   snakes is a vector of doubles, with 10 elements. Write a statement that stores the value 12.897 in element 4 of the snakes vector.

Review Questions and Exercises

Short Answer

1. What is the difference between a size declarator and a subscript?

2. Look at the following array definition.

   ```
   int values[10];
   ```

   How many elements does the array have?
   What is the subscript of the first element in the array?
   What is the subscript of the last element in the array?
   Assuming that an int uses four bytes of memory, how much memory does the array use?

3. Why should a function that accepts an array as an argument, and processes that array, also accept an argument specifying the array's size?

4. Consider the following array definition:

   ```
   int values[5] = { 4, 7, 6, 8, 2 };
   ```

   What does each of the following statements display?

   ```
   cout << values[4] << endl;  _____
   ```

   ```
   cout << (values[2] + values[3]) << endl;  _____
   ```

   ```
   cout << ++values[1] << endl;  _____
   ```

5. How do you define an array without providing a size declarator?

6. Look at the following array definition.

   ```
   int numbers[5] = { 1, 2, 3 };
   ```

   What value is stored in numbers[2]?
   What value is stored in numbers[4]?

7. Assuming that array1 and array2 are both arrays, why is it not possible to assign the contents of array2 to array1 with the following statement?

   ```
   array1 = array2;
   ```

8. Assuming that numbers is an array of doubles, will the following statement display the contents of the array?

   ```
   cout << numbers << endl;
   ```

9. Is an array passed to a function by value or by reference?

10. When you pass an array name as an argument to a function, what is actually being passed?

11. How do you establish a parallel relationship between two or more arrays?

12. Look at the following array definition.

    ```
    char day[] = "Tuesday";
    ```

    How many elements are in the day array?
    Is the string stored in the day array terminated by a null character?

13. Look at the following array definition.

    ```
    double sales[8][10];
    ```

    How many rows does the array have?

    How many columns does the array have?

    How many elements does the array have?

    Write a statement that stores a number in the last column of the last row in the array.

14. When writing a function that accepts a two-dimensional array as an argument, which size declarator must you provide in the parameter for the array?

15. What advantages does a vector offer over an array?

Fill-in-the-Blank

16. The _____ indicates the number of elements, or values, an array can hold.

17. The size declarator must be a(n) _____ with a value greater than _____.

18. Each element of an array is accessed and indexed by a number known as a(n) _____.

19. Subscript numbering in C++ always starts at _____.

20. The number inside the brackets of an array definition is the _____, but the number inside an array's brackets in an assignment statement, or any other statement that works with the contents of the array, is the _____.

21. C++ has no array _____ checking, which means you can inadvertently store data past the end of an array.

22. Starting values for an array may be specified with a(n) _____ list.

23. If an array is partially initialized, the uninitialized elements will be set to _____.

24. If the size declarator of an array definition is omitted, C++ counts the number of items in the _____ to determine how large the array should be.

25. When a character array is initialized with a string literal, the _____ is automatically included at the end.

26. By using the same _____ for multiple arrays, you can build relationships between the data stored in the arrays.

27. You cannot use the _____ operator to copy data from one array to another in a single statement.

28. Any time the name of an array is used without brackets and a subscript, it is seen as _____.

29. To pass an array to a function, pass the _____ of the array.

30. A(n) _____ array is like several arrays of the same type put together.

31. It's best to think of a two-dimensional array as having _____ and _____.

32. To define a two-dimensional array, _____ size declarators are required.

33. When initializing a two-dimensional array, it helps to enclose each row's initialization list in _____.

34. When a two-dimensional array is passed to a function the _____ size must be specified.

35. The _____ is a collection of programmer-defined data types and algorithms that you may use in your programs

36. The two types of containers defined by the STL are _____ and _____.

37. The `vector` data type is a(n) _____ container.

38. To define a `vector` in your program, you must `#include` the _____ header file.

39. To store a value in a `vector` that does not have a starting size, or that is already full, use the _____ member function.

40. To determine the number of elements in a `vector`, use the _____ member function.

41. Use the _____ member function to remove the last element from a `vector`.

42. To completely clear the contents of a `vector`, use the _____ member function.

Algorithm Workbench

43. `names` is an integer array with 20 elements. Write a `for` loop that prints each element of the array.

44. The arrays `numberArray1` and `numberArray2` have 100 elements. Write code that copies the values in `numberArray1` to `numberArray2`.

45. In a program you need to store the identification numbers of 10 employees (as `int`s) and their weekly gross pay (as `double`s).

    A) Define two arrays that may be used in parallel to store the 10 employee identification numbers and gross pay amounts.

    B) Write a loop that uses these arrays to print each employee's identification number and weekly gross pay.

46. Define a two-dimensional array of integers named `grades`. It should have 30 rows and 10 columns.

47. In a program you need to store the populations of 12 countries.

    A) Define two arrays that may be used in parallel to store the names of the countries and their populations.

    B) Write a loop that uses these arrays to print each country's name and its population.

48. The following code totals the values in two arrays: `numberArray1` and `numberArray2`. Both arrays have 25 elements. Will the code print the correct sum of values for both arrays? Why or why not?

```
int total = 0;          // Accumulator
int count;              // Loop counter
// Calculate and display the total of the first array.
for (count = 0; count < 24; count++)
   total += numberArray1[count];
cout << "The total for numberArray1 is " << total << endl;
// Calculate and display the total of the second array.
for (count = 0; count < 24; count++)
```

```
        total += numberArray2[count];
    cout << "The total for numberArray2 is " << total << endl;
```

49. Write a statement that defines a two-dimensional array to hold three strings. Initialize the array with your first, middle, and last names.

50. Look at the following array definition.

    ```
    int numberArray[9][11];
    ```

    Write a statement that assigns 145 to the first column of the first row of this array.

    Write a statement that assigns 18 to the last column of the last row of this array.

51. `values` is a two-dimensional array of `float`s with 10 rows and 20 columns. Write code that sums all the elements in the array and stores the sum in the variable `total`.

52. An application uses a two-dimensional array defined as follows.

    ```
    int days[29][5];
    ```

    Write code that sums each row in the array and displays the results.

    Write code that sums each column in the array and displays the results.

True or False

53. T   F   An array's size declarator can be either a literal, a named constant, or a variable.

54. T   F   To calculate the amount of memory used by an array, multiply the number of elements by the number of bytes each element uses.

55. T   F   The individual elements of an array are accessed and indexed by unique numbers.

56. T   F   The first element in an array is accessed by the subscript 1.

57. T   F   The subscript of the last element in a single-dimensional array is one less than the total number of elements in the array.

58. T   F   The contents of an array element cannot be displayed with cout.

59. T   F   Subscript numbers may be stored in variables.

60. T   F   You can write programs that use invalid subscripts for an array.

61. T   F   Arrays cannot be initialized when they are defined. A loop or other means must be used.

62. T   F   The values in an initialization list are stored in the array in the order they appear in the list.

63. T   F   C++ allows you to partially initialize an array.

64. T   F   If an array is partially initialized, the uninitialized elements will contain "garbage."

65. T   F   If you leave an element uninitialized, you do not have to leave all the ones that follow it uninitialized.

66. T   F   If you leave out the size declarator of an array definition, you do not have to include an initialization list.

67. T   F   In initializing an array with a string, the null terminator is automatically included.

68. T   F   In initializing an array with individual characters, the null terminator is automatically included.

69. T   F   You cannot use the assignment operator to copy one array's contents to another in a single statement.

70. T   F   When an array name is used without brackets and a subscript, it is seen as the value of the first element in the array.

71. T   F   To pass an array to a function, pass the name of the array.

72. T   F   When defining a parameter variable to hold a single-dimensional array argument, you do not have to include the size declarator.

73. T   F   When an array is passed to a function, the function has access to the original array.

74. T   F   A two-dimensional array is like several identical arrays put together.

75. T   F   It's best to think of two-dimensional arrays as having rows and columns.

76. T   F   The first size declarator (in the declaration of a two-dimensional array) represents the number of columns. The second size defintion represents the number of rows.

77. T   F   Two-dimensional arrays may be passed to functions, but the row size must be specified in the definition of the parameter variable.

78. T   F   C++ allows you to create arrays with three or more dimensions.

79. T   F   A vector is an associative container.

80. T   F   To use a vector, you must include the vector header file.

81. T   F   vectors can report the number of elements they contain.

82. T   F   You can use the [ ] operator to insert a value into a vector that has no elements.

83. T   F   If you add a value to a vector that is already full, the vector will automatically increase its size to accommodate the new value.

Find the Error

Each of the following definitions and program segments has errors. Locate as many as you can.

84.
```cpp
int size;
double values[size];
```

85.
```cpp
int collection[-20];
```

86.
```cpp
int table[10];
for (int x = 0; x < 20; x++)
{
   cout << "Enter the next value: ";
   cin >> table[x];
}
```

87.
```cpp
int hours[3] = 8, 12, 16;
```

88.
```cpp
char name[17] = "George Washington";
```

89.
```cpp
int numbers[8] = {1, 2, , 4, , 5};
```

90.
```cpp
float ratings[];
```

91.
```cpp
char greeting[] = {'H', 'e', 'l', 'l', 'o'};
cout << greeting;
```

92. ```
    int array1[4], array2[4] = {3, 6, 9, 12};
    array1 = array2;
    ```

93. ```
    void showValues(int nums)
    {
        for (int count = 0; count < 8; count++)
            cout << nums[count];
    }
    ```

94. ```
    void showValues(int nums[4][])
    {
        for (rows = 0; rows < 4; rows++)
            for (cols = 0; cols < 5; cols++)
                cout << nums[rows][cols];
    }
    ```

Programming Challenges

1. Largest/Smallest Array Values

Write a program that lets the user enter 10 values into an array. The program should then display the largest and smallest values stored in the array.

2. Rainfall Statistics

Write a program that lets the user enter the total rainfall for each of 12 months into an array of `doubles`. The program should calculate and display the total rainfall for the year, the average monthly rainfall, and the months with the highest and lowest amounts.

Input Validation: Do not accept negative numbers for monthly rainfall figures.

3. Chips and Salsa

Write a program that lets a maker of chips and salsa keep track of sales for five different types of salsa: mild, medium, sweet, hot, and zesty. The program should use two parallel 5-element arrays: an array of strings that holds the five salsa names and an array of integers that holds the number of jars sold during the past month for each salsa type. The salsa names should be stored using an initialization list at the time the name array is created. The program should prompt the user to enter the number of jars sold for each type. Once this sales data has been entered, the program should produce a report that displays sales for each salsa type, total sales, and the names of the highest selling and lowest selling products.

VideoNote

Solving the
Chips and
Salsa Problem

Input Validation: Do not accept negative values for number of jars sold.

4. Monkey Business

A local zoo wants to keep track of how many pounds of food each of its three monkeys eats each day during a typical week. Write a program that stores this information in a two-dimensional 3 × 7 array, where each row represents a different monkey and each column represents a different day of the week. The program should first have the user input the data for each monkey. Then it should create a report that includes the following information:

- Average amount of food eaten per day by the whole family of monkeys.
- The least amount of food eaten during the week by any one monkey.
- The greatest amount of food eaten during the week by any one monkey.

Input Validation: Do not accept negative numbers for pounds of food eaten.
    ```

5. **Rain or Shine**

An amateur meteorologist wants to keep track of weather conditions during the past year's three-month summer season and has designated each day as either rainy ('R'), cloudy ('C'), or sunny ('S'). Write a program that stores this information in a 3 × 30 array of characters, where the row indicates the month (0 = June, 1 = July, 2 = August) and the column indicates the day of the month. Note that data are not being collected for the 31st of any month. The program should begin by reading the weather data in from a file. Then it should create a report that displays, for each month and for the whole three-month period, how many days were rainy, how many were cloudy, and how many were sunny. It should also report which of the three months had the largest number of rainy days. Data for the program can be found in the `RainOrShine.dat` file.

6. **Number Analysis Program**

Write a program that asks the user for a file name. Assume the file contains a series of numbers, each written on a separate line. The program should read the contents of the file into an array and then display the following data:

- The lowest number in the array
- The highest number in the array
- The total of the numbers in the array
- The average of the numbers in the array

The Student CD contains a text file named `numbers.txt.` that you can use to test the program.

7. **Lowercase to Uppercase Converter**

Write a program that lets the user enter a string into a character array. The program should then convert all the lowercase letters to uppercase. (If a character is already uppercase, or is not a letter, it should be left alone.) *Hint*: Consult the ASCII chart in Appendix A. Notice that the lowercase letters are represented by the ASCII codes 97 through 122. If you subtract 32 from any lowercase character's ASCII code, it will yield the ASCII code of the uppercase equivalent.

8. **Proper Words**

Write a function that uses an array parameter to accept a string as its argument. It should convert the first letter of each word in the string to uppercase. If any of the letters are already uppercase, they should be left alone. (See the hint in Problem 7 for help on converting lowercase characters to uppercase.) Demonstrate the function in a simple program that asks the user to input a string, passes it to the function, and then displays the string after it has been modified.

9. **Quarterly Sales Statistics**

Write a program that lets the user enter four quarterly sales figures for six divisions of a company. The figures should be stored in a two-dimensional array. Once the figures are entered, the program should display the following data for each quarter:

- A list of the sales figures by division
- Each division's increase or decrease from the previous quarter (This will not be displayed for the first quarter.)
- The total sales for the quarter

- The company's increase or decrease from the previous quarter (This will not be displayed for the first quarter.)
- The average sales for all divisions that quarter
- The division with the highest sales for that quarter

The program should be modular, with functions that calculate the statistics above.

Input Validation: Do not accept negative numbers for sales figures.

10. **Payroll**

    Write a program that uses the following arrays:

    - `empId`: an array of seven long integers to hold employee identification numbers. The array should be initialized with the following numbers:

      ```
      5658845    4520125    7895122    8777541
      8451277    1302850    7580489
      ```

    - `hours`: an array of seven integers to hold the number of hours worked by each employee
    - `payRate`: an array of seven doubles to hold each employee's hourly pay rate
    - `wages`: an array of seven doubles to hold each employee's gross wages

    The program should relate the data in each array through the subscripts. For example, the number in element 0 of the `hours` array should be the number of hours worked by the employee whose identification number is stored in element 0 of the `empId` array. That same employee's pay rate should be stored in element 0 of the `payRate` array.

    The program should display each employee number and ask the user to enter that employee's hours and pay rate. It should then calculate the gross wages for that employee (hours times pay rate) and store them in the `wages` array. After the data has been entered for all the employees, the program should display each employee's identification number and gross wages.

    Input Validation: Do not accept negative values for hours or numbers less than 6.00 for pay rate.

11. **Driver's License Exam**

    The local Driver's License Office has asked you to write a program that grades the written portion of the driver's license exam. The exam has 20 multiple choice questions. Here are the correct answers:

1. B	6. A	11. B	16. C
2. D	7. B	12. C	17. C
3. A	8. A	13. D	18. B
4. A	9. C	14. A	19. D
5. C	10. D	15. D	20. A

    Your program should store the correct answers shown above in an array. It should ask the user to enter the student's answers for each of the 20 questions, and the answers should be stored in another array. After the student's answers have been entered, the program should display a message indicating whether the student passed or failed the exam. (A student must correctly answer 15 of the 20 questions to pass the exam.)

It should then display the total number of correctly answered questions, the total number of incorrectly answered questions, and a list showing the question numbers of the incorrectly answered questions.

Input Validation: Only accept the letters A, B, C, or D as answers.

12. **Exam Grader**

One of your professors has asked you to write a program to grade her final exams, which consist of only 20 multiple-choice questions. Each question has one of four possible answers: A, B, C, or D. The file `CorrectAnswers.txt`, which is on the Student CD, contains the correct answers for all of the questions, each answer written on a separate line. The first line contains the answer to the first question, the second line contains the answer to the second question, and so forth.

Write a program that reads the contents of the `CorrectAnswers.txt` file into a one-dimensional char array, and then reads the contents of another file, containing a student's answers, into a second char array. The Student CD has a file named `StudentAnswers.txt` that you can use for testing purposes. The program should determine the number of questions that the student missed, and then display the following:

- A list of the questions missed by the student, showing the correct answer and the incorrect answer provided by the student for each missed question
- The total number of questions missed
- The percentage of questions answered correctly. This can be calculated as

  Correctly Answered Questions ÷ Total Number of Questions

- If the percentage of correctly answered questions is 70% or greater, the program should indicate that the student passed the exam. Otherwise, it should indicate that the student failed the exam.

13. **Grade Book**

A teacher has five students who have taken four tests. The teacher uses the following grading scale to assign a letter grade to a student, based on the average of his or her four test scores.

Test Score	Letter Grade
90–100	A
80–89	B
70–79	C
60–69	D
0–59	F

Write a program that uses a two-dimensional array of characters to hold the five student names, a single-dimensional array of five characters to hold the five students' letter grades, and five single-dimensional arrays of four `doubles` to hold each student's set of test scores.

The program should allow the user to enter each student's name and his or her four test scores. It should then calculate and display each student's average test score and a letter grade based on the average.

Input Validation: Do not accept test scores less than 0 or greater than 100.

14. **Grade Book Modification**

Modify the grade book application in Programming Challenge 13 so it drops each student's lowest score when determining the test score averages and letter grades.

15. **Lottery Application**

Write a program that simulates a lottery. The program should have an array of five integers named `lottery`, and should generate a random number in the range of 0 through 9 for each element in the array. The user should enter five digits which should be stored in an integer array named `user`. The program is to compare the corresponding elements in the two arrays and keep a count of the digits that match. For example, the following shows the `lottery` array and the `user` array with sample numbers stored in each. There are two matching digits (elements 2 and 4).

lottery array:

7	4	9	1	3

user array:

4	2	9	7	3

The program should display the random numbers stored in the `lottery` array and the number of matching digits. If all of the digits match, display a message proclaiming the user as a grand prize winner.

16. **vector Modification**

Modify the National Commerce Bank case study presented in Program 7-21 so `pin1`, `pin2`, and `pin3` are `vectors` instead of arrays. You must also modify the `testPIN` function to accept a `vector` instead of an array.

17. **Tic-Tac-Toe Game**

Write a program that allows two players to play a game of tic-tac-toe. Use a two-dimensional `char` array with three rows and three columns as the game board. Each element of the array should be initialized with an asterisk (*). The program should run a loop that

- Displays the contents of the board array
- Allows player 1 to select a location on the board for an X. The program should ask the user to enter the row and column number.
- Allows player 2 to select a location on the board for an O. The program should ask the user to enter the row and column number.
- Determines whether a player has won, or a tie has occurred. If a player has won, the program should declare that player the winner and end. If a tie has occurred, the program should say so and end.

Player 1 wins when there are three Xs in a row on the game board. The Xs can appear in a row, in a column, or diagonally across the board. A tie occurs when all of the locations on the board are full, but there is no winner.

18. **2D Array Operations**

Write a program that creates a two-dimensional array initialized with test data. Use any data type you wish. The program should have the following functions:

- **getTotal**. This function should accept a two-dimensional array as its argument and return the total of all the values in the array.
- **getAverage**. This function should accept a two-dimensional array as its argument and return the average of all the values in the array.
- **getRowTotal**. This function should accept a two-dimensional array as its first argument and an integer as its second argument. The second argument should be the subscript of a row in the array. The function should return the total of the values in the specified row.
- **getColumnTotal**. This function should accept a two-dimensional array as its first argument and an integer as its second argument. The second argument should be the subscript of a column in the array. The function should return the total of the values in the specified column.
- **getHighestInRow**. This function should accept a two-dimensional array as its first argument and an integer as its second argument. The second argument should be the subscript of a row in the array. The function should return the highest value in the specified row of the array.
- **getLowestInRow**. This function should accept a two-dimensional array as its first argument and an integer as its second argument. The second argument should be the subscript of a row in the array. The function should return the lowest value in the specified row of the array.

Demonstrate each of the functions in this program.

Group Project

19. **Theater Seating**

This program should be designed and written by a team of students. Here are some suggestions:

- One student should design function `main`, which will call the other functions in the program. The remainder of the functions will be designed by other members of the team.
- The requirements of the program should be analyzed so each student is given about the same work load.
- The parameters and return types of each function should be decided in advance.
- The program can be implemented as a multi-file program, or all the functions can be cut and pasted into the main file.

Here is the assignment: Write a program that can be used by a small theater to sell tickets for performances. The theater's auditorium has 15 rows of seats, with 30 seats in each row. The program should display a screen that shows which seats are available and which are taken. For example, the following screen shows a chart depicting each seat in the theater. Seats that are taken are represented by an * symbol, and seats that are available are represented by a # symbol:

```
                Seats
         12345678901234567890123456789 0
Row 1    ***##***###*##########****####
Row 2    ####***********##########****##
Row 3    **###**********##########****###
Row 4    **########************#*#*****
Row 5    ********#####********#######
Row 6    ##############********######*####
Row 7    #######***********##########
Row 8    ***********##*****###########
Row 9    ##########****##############****
Row 10   #####**********##############
Row 11   #*********##################**
Row 12   ###############*******########*
Row 13   ###********###########**######
Row 14   ##############################
Row 15   ##############################
```

Here is a list of tasks this program must perform:

- When the program begins, it should ask the user to enter the seat prices for each row. The prices can be stored in a separate array. (Alternatively, the prices may be read from a file.)
- Once the prices are entered, the program should display a seating chart similar to the one shown above. The user may enter the row and seat numbers for tickets being sold. Every time a ticket or group of tickets is purchased, the program should display the total ticket prices and update the seating chart.
- The program should keep a total of all ticket sales. The user should be given an option of viewing this amount.
- The program should also give the user an option to see a list of how many seats have been sold, how many seats are available in each row, and how many seats are available in the entire auditorium.

Input Validation: When tickets are being sold, do not accept row or seat numbers that do not exist. When someone requests a particular seat, the program should make sure that seat is available before it is sold.

8 Searching and Sorting Arrays

TOPICS

8.1 Focus on Software Engineering: Introduction to Search Algorithms

CONCEPT: A search algorithm is a method of locating a specific item in a larger collection of data. This section discusses two algorithms for searching the contents of an array.

It's very common for programs not only to store and process data stored in arrays, but to search arrays for specific items. This section will show you two methods of searching an array: the linear search and the binary search. Each has its advantages and disadvantages.

The Linear Search

The *linear search* is a very simple algorithm. Sometimes called a *sequential search*, it uses a loop to sequentially step through an array, starting with the first element. It compares each element with the value being searched for, and stops when either the value is found or the end of the array is encountered. If the value being searched for is not in the array, the algorithm will unsuccessfully search to the end of the array.

Here is the pseudocode for a function that performs the linear search:

```
Set found to false.
Set position to -1.
Set index to 0.
While found is false and index < number of elements
    If list[index] is equal to search value
        found = true.
        position = index.
    End If
    Add 1 to index.
End While.
Return position.
```

The function searchList shown below is an example of C++ code used to perform a linear search on an integer array. The array list, which has a maximum of numElems elements, is searched for an occurrence of the number stored in value. If the number is found, its array subscript is returned. Otherwise, –1 is returned indicating the value did not appear in the array.

```cpp
int searchList(int list[], int numElems, int value)
{
    int index = 0;          // Used as a subscript to search array
    int position = -1;      // To record position of search value
    bool found = false;     // Flag to indicate if the value was found

    while (index < numElems && !found)
    {
        if (list[index] == value)   // If the value is found
        {
            found = true;           // Set the flag
            position = index;       // Record the value's subscript
        }
        index++;                    // Go to the next element
    }
    return position;                // Return the position, or -1
}
```

 NOTE: The reason –1 is returned when the search value is not found in the array is because –1 is not a valid subscript.

Program 8-1 is a complete program that uses the searchList function. It searches the five-element array tests to find a score of 100.

Program 8-1

```cpp
1 // This program demonstrates the searchList function, which
2 // performs a linear search on an integer array.
3 #include <iostream>
4 using namespace std;
5
```

```cpp
 6  // Function prototype
 7  int searchList(int [], int, int);
 8  const int SIZE = 5;
 9
10  int main()
11  {
12     int tests[SIZE] = {87, 75, 98, 100, 82};
13     int results;
14
15     // Search the array for 100.
16     results = searchList(tests, SIZE, 100);
17
18     // If searchList returned -1, then 100 was not found.
19     if (results == -1)
20        cout << "You did not earn 100 points on any test\n";
21     else
22     {
23        // Otherwise results contains the subscript of
24        // the first 100 found in the array.
25        cout << "You earned 100 points on test ";
26        cout << (results + 1) << endl;
27     }
28     return 0;
29  }
30
31  //****************************************************************
32  // The searchList function performs a linear search on an        *
33  // integer array. The array list, which has a maximum of numElems *
34  // elements, is searched for the number stored in value. If the   *
35  // number is found, its array subscript is returned. Otherwise,   *
36  // -1 is returned indicating the value was not in the array.      *
37  //****************************************************************
38
39  int searchList(int list[], int numElems, int value)
40  {
41     int index = 0;        // Used as a subscript to search array
42     int position = -1;    // To record position of search value
43     bool found = false;   // Flag to indicate if the value was found
44
45     while (index < numElems && !found)
46     {
47        if (list[index] == value)  // If the value is found
48        {
49           found = true;           // Set the flag
50           position = index;       // Record the value's subscript
51        }
52        index++;                   // Go to the next element
53     }
54     return position;              // Return the position, or -1
55  }
```

Program Output
```
You earned 100 points on test 4
```

Inefficiency of the Linear Search

The advantage of the linear search is its simplicity. It is very easy to understand and implement. Furthermore, it doesn't require the data in the array to be stored in any particular order. Its disadvantage, however, is its inefficiency. If the array being searched contains 20,000 elements, the algorithm will have to look at all 20,000 elements in order to find a value stored in the last element (so the algorithm actually reads an element of the array 20,000 times).

In an average case, an item is just as likely to be found near the beginning of the array as near the end. Typically, for an array of N items, the linear search will locate an item in N/2 attempts. If an array has 50,000 elements, the linear search will make a comparison with 25,000 of them in a typical case. This is assuming, of course, that the search item is consistently found in the array. (N/2 is the average number of comparisons. The maximum number of comparisons is always N.)

When the linear search fails to locate an item, it must make a comparison with every element in the array. As the number of failed search attempts increases, so does the average number of comparisons. Obviously, the linear search should not be used on large arrays if the speed is important.

VideoNote

The Binary
Search

The Binary Search

The *binary search* is a clever algorithm that is much more efficient than the linear search. Its only requirement is that the values in the array be sorted in order. Instead of testing the array's first element, this algorithm starts with the element in the middle. If that element happens to contain the desired value, then the search is over. Otherwise, the value in the middle element is either greater than or less than the value being searched for. If it is greater, then the desired value (if it is in the list) will be found somewhere in the first half of the array. If it is less, then the desired value (again, if it is in the list) will be found somewhere in the last half of the array. In either case, half of the array's elements have been eliminated from further searching.

If the desired value wasn't found in the middle element, the procedure is repeated for the half of the array that potentially contains the value. For instance, if the last half of the array is to be searched, the algorithm immediately tests *its* middle element. If the desired value isn't found there, the search is narrowed to the quarter of the array that resides before or after that element. This process continues until either the value being searched for is found or there are no more elements to test.

Here is the pseudocode for a function that performs a binary search on an array:

```
Set first index to 0.
Set last index to the last subscript in the array.
Set found to false.
Set position to -1.
While found is not true and first is less than or equal to last
    Set middle to the subscript halfway between array[first]
    and array[last].
    If array[middle] equals the desired value
```

```
        Set found to true.
        Set position to middle.
    Else If array[middle] is greater than the desired value
        Set last to middle - 1.
    Else
        Set first to middle + 1.
    End If.
End While.
Return position.
```

This algorithm uses three index variables: `first`, `last`, and `middle`. The `first` and `last` variables mark the boundaries of the portion of the array currently being searched. They are initialized with the subscripts of the array's first and last elements. The subscript of the element halfway between `first` and `last` is calculated and stored in the `middle` variable. If the element in the middle of the array does not contain the search value, the `first` or `last` variables are adjusted so that only the top or bottom half of the array is searched during the next iteration. This cuts the portion of the array being searched in half each time the loop fails to locate the search value.

The function `binarySearch` shown in the following example is used to perform a binary search on an integer array. The first parameter, `array`, which has a maximum of `numElems` elements, is searched for an occurrence of the number stored in `value`. If the number is found, its array subscript is returned. Otherwise, –1 is returned indicating the value did not appear in the array.

```cpp
int binarySearch(int array[], int numElems, int value)
{
   int first = 0,                        // First array element
       last = numElems - 1,              // Last array element
       middle,                           // Midpoint of search
       position = -1;                    // Position of search value
   bool found = false;                   // Flag

   while (!found && first <= last)
   {
      middle = (first + last) / 2;       // Calculate midpoint
      if (array[middle] == value)        // If value is found at mid
      {
         found = true;
         position = middle;
      }
      else if (array[middle] > value)    // If value is in lower half
         last = middle - 1;
       else
         first = middle + 1;             // If value is in upper half
   }
   return position;
}
```

Program 8-2 is a complete program using the `binarySearch` function. It searches an array of employee ID numbers for a specific value.

Program 8-2

```
 1  // This program demonstrates the binarySearch function, which
 2  // performs a binary search on an integer array.
 3  #include <iostream>
 4  using namespace std;
 5
 6  // Function prototype
 7  int binarySearch(int [], int, int);
 8  const int SIZE = 20;
 9
10  int main()
11  {
12     // Array with employee IDs sorted in ascending order.
13     int idNums[SIZE] = {101, 142, 147, 189, 199, 207, 222,
14                         234, 289, 296, 310, 319, 388, 394,
15                         417, 429, 447, 521, 536, 600};
16     int results;   // To hold the search results
17     int empID;     // To hold an employee ID
18
19     // Get an employee ID to search for.
20     cout << "Enter the employee ID you wish to search for: ";
21     cin >> empID;
22
23     // Search for the ID.
24     results = binarySearch(idNums, SIZE, empID);
25
26     // If results contains -1 the ID was not found.
27     if (results == -1)
28        cout << "That number does not exist in the array.\n";
29     else
30     {
31        // Otherwise results contains the subscript of
32        // the specified employee ID in the array.
33        cout << "That ID is found at element " << results;
34        cout << " in the array.\n";
35     }
36     return 0;
37  }
38
39  //****************************************************************
40  // The binarySearch function performs a binary search on an     *
41  // integer array. array, which has a maximum of size elements,  *
42  // is searched for the number stored in value. If the number is *
43  // found, its array subscript is returned. Otherwise, -1 is     *
44  // returned indicating the value was not in the array.          *
45  //****************************************************************
46
```

```
47  int binarySearch(int array[], int size, int value)
48  {
49     int first = 0,              // First array element
50         last = size - 1,        // Last array element
51         middle,                 // Midpoint of search
52         position = -1;          // Position of search value
53     bool found = false;         // Flag
54
55     while (!found && first <= last)
56     {
57        middle = (first + last) / 2;    // Calculate midpoint
58        if (array[middle] == value)     // If value is found at mid
59        {
60           found = true;
61           position = middle;
62        }
63        else if (array[middle] > value)  // If value is in lower half
64           last = middle - 1;
65        else
66           first = middle + 1;           // If value is in upper half
67     }
68     return position;
69  }
```

Program Output with Example Input Shown in Bold
Enter the employee ID you wish to search for: **199 [Enter]**
That ID is found at element 4 in the array.

 WARNING! Notice that the array in Program 8-2 is initialized with its values already sorted in ascending order. The binary search algorithm will not work properly unless the values in the array are sorted.

The Efficiency of the Binary Search

Obviously, the binary search is much more efficient than the linear search. Every time it makes a comparison and fails to find the desired item, it eliminates half of the remaining portion of the array that must be searched. For example, consider an array with 1,000 elements. If the binary search fails to find an item on the first attempt, the number of elements that remains to be searched is 500. If the item is not found on the second attempt, the number of elements that remains to be searched is 250. This process continues until the binary search has either located the desired item or determined that it is not in the array. With 1,000 elements, this takes no more than 10 comparisons. (Compare this to the linear search, which would make an average of 500 comparisons!)

Powers of 2 are used to calculate the maximum number of comparisons the binary search will make on an array of any size. (A power of 2 is 2 raised to the power of some number.) Simply find the smallest power of 2 that is greater than or equal to the number of elements in the array. For example, a maximum of 16 comparisons will be made on an array of 50,000 elements ($2^{16} = 65,536$), and a maximum of 20 comparisons will be made on an array of 1,000,000 elements ($2^{20} = 1,048,576$).

8.2   Focus on Problem Solving and Program Design: A Case Study

The Demetris Leadership Center (DLC, Inc.) publishes the books, DVDs, and audio CDs listed in Table 8-1.

Table 8-1

Product Title	Product Description	Product Number	Unit Price
Six Steps to Leadership	Book	914	$12.95
Six Steps to Leadership	Audio CD	915	$14.95
The Road to Excellence	DVD	916	$18.95
Seven Lessons of Quality	Book	917	$16.95
Seven Lessons of Quality	Audio CD	918	$21.95
Seven Lessons of Quality	DVD	919	$31.95
Teams Are Made, Not Born	Book	920	$14.95
Leadership for the Future	Book	921	$14.95
Leadership for the Future	Audio CD	922	$16.95

The manager of the Telemarketing Group has asked you to write a program that will help order-entry operators look up product prices. The program should prompt the user to enter a product number, and will then display the title, description, and price of the product.

Variables

Table 8-2 lists the variables needed:

Table 8-2

Variable	Description
NUM_PRODS	A constant integer initialized with the number of products the Demetris Leadership Center sells. This value will be used in the definition of the program's array.
TITLE_SIZE	A constant integer initialized with the maximum size of a product's title.
DESC_SIZE	A constant integer initialized with the maximum size of a product's description.
MIN_PRODNUM	A constant integer initialized with the lowest product number.
MAX_PRODNUM	A constant integer initialized with the highest product number.
id	Array of integers. Holds each product's number.
title	Array of strings, initialized with the titles of products.
description	Array of strings, initialized with the descriptions of each product.
prices	Array of doubles. Holds each product's price.

Modules

The program will consist of the functions listed in Table 8-3.

Table 8-3

Function	Description
main	The program's main function. It calls the program's other functions.
getProdNum	Prompts the user to enter a product number. The function validates input and rejects any value outside the range of correct product numbers.
binarySearch	A standard binary search routine. Searches an array for a specified value. If the value is found, its subscript is returned. If the value is not found, −1 is returned.
displayProd	Uses a common subscript into the title, description, and prices arrays to display the title, description, and price of a product.

Function main

Function main contains the variable definitions and calls the other functions. Here is its pseudocode:

```
do
    Call getProdNum.
    Call binarySearch.
    If binarySearch returned -1
        Inform the user that the product number was not found.
    else
        Call displayProd.
    End If.
    Ask the user if the program should repeat.
While the user wants to repeat the program.
```

Here is its actual C++ code.

```
do
{
    // Get the desired product number.
    prodNum = getProdNum();

    // Search for the product number.
    index = binarySearch(id, NUM_PRODS, prodNum);

    // Display the results of the search.
    if (index == -1)
        cout << "That product number was not found.\n";
    else
        displayProd(title, description, prices, index);

    // Does the user want to do this again?
    cout << "Would you like to look up another product? (y/n) ";
    cin >> again;
} while (again == 'y' || again == 'Y');
```

The named constants NUM_PRODS, TITLE_SIZE, and DESC_SIZE are defined globally and initialized to the values 9, 26, and 12 respectively. The arrays id, title, description, and prices will already be initialized with data.

The getProdNum Function

The getProdNum function prompts the user to enter a product number. It tests the value to ensure it is in the range of 914–922 (which are the valid product numbers). If an invalid value is entered, it is rejected and the user is prompted again. When a valid product number is entered, the function returns it. The pseudocode is shown below.

```
Display a prompt to enter a product number.
Read prodNum.
While prodNum is invalid
   Display an error message.
   Read prodNum.
End While.
Return prodNum.
```

Here is the actual C++ code.

```cpp
int getProdNum()
{
    int prodNum;

    cout << "Enter the item's product number: ";
    cin >> prodNum;
    // Validate input.
    while (prodNum < MIN_PRODNUM || prodNum > MAX_PRODNUM)
    {
        cout << "Enter a number in the range of " << MIN_PRODNUM;
        cout <<" through " << MAX_PRODNUM << ".\n";
        cin >> prodNum;
    }
    return prodNum;
}
```

The binarySearch Function

The binarySearch function is identical to the function discussed earlier in this chapter.

The displayProd Function

The displayProd function has parameter variables named title, desc, price, and index. These accept as arguments (respectively) the title, description, and price arrays, and a subscript value. The function displays the data stored in each array at the subscript passed into index. Here is the C++ code.

```
void displayProd(char title[][TITLE_SIZE], char desc[][DESC_SIZE],
                 double price[], int index)
{
   cout << "Title: " << title[index] << endl;
   cout << "Description: " << desc[index] << endl;
   cout << "Price: $" << price[index] << endl;
}
```

The Entire Program

Program 8-3 shows the entire program's source code.

Program 8-3

```
 1  // Demetris Leadership Center (DLC) product lookup program
 2  // This program allows the user to enter a product number
 3  // and then displays the title, description, and price of
 4  // that product.
 5  #include <iostream>
 6  using namespace std;
 7
 8  const int NUM_PRODS = 9;        // The number of products produced
 9  const int TITLE_SIZE = 26;      // The max size of a title string
10  const int DESC_SIZE = 12;       // The max size of a desc. string
11  const int MIN_PRODNUM = 914;    // The lowest product number
12  const int MAX_PRODNUM = 922;    // The highest product number
13
14  // Function prototypes
15  int getProdNum();
16  int binarySearch(int [], int, int);
17  void displayProd(char [][TITLE_SIZE], char [][DESC_SIZE], double [], int);
18
19  int main()
20  {
21     // Array of product IDs
22     int id[NUM_PRODS] = {914, 915, 916, 917, 918, 919, 920,
23                          921, 922};
24
25     // Array of product titles
26     char title[NUM_PRODS][TITLE_SIZE] =
27             {  "Six Steps to Leadership",
28                "Six Steps to Leadership",
29                "The Road to Excellence",
30                "Seven Lessons of Quality",
31                "Seven Lessons of Quality",
32                "Seven Lessons of Quality",
33                "Teams Are Made, Not Born",
34                "Leadership for the Future",
35                "Leadership for the Future"
36             };
37
```

(program continues)

Program 8-3 *(continued)*

```cpp
38     // Array of product descriptions
39     char description[NUM_PRODS][DESC_SIZE] =
40              {  "Book", "Audio CD", "DVD",
41                 "Book", "Audio CD", "DVD",
42                 "Book", "Book", "Audio CD"
43              };
44
45     // Array of product prices
46     double prices[NUM_PRODS] = {12.95, 14.95, 18.95, 16.95, 21.95,
47                                 31.95, 14.95, 14.95, 16.95};
48
49     int prodNum;  // To hold a product number
50     int index;    // To hold search results
51     char again;   // To hold a Y or N answer
52
53     do
54     {
55        // Get the desired product number.
56        prodNum = getProdNum();
57
58        // Search for the product number.
59        index = binarySearch(id, NUM_PRODS, prodNum);
60
61        // Display the results of the search.
62        if (index == -1)
63           cout << "That product number was not found.\n";
64        else
65           displayProd(title, description, prices, index);
66
67        // Does the user want to do this again?
68        cout << "Would you like to look up another product? (y/n) ";
69        cin >> again;
70     } while (again == 'y' || again == 'Y');
71     return 0;
72  }
73
74  //****************************************************
75  // Definition of getProdNum function                *
76  // The getProdNum function asks the user to enter a *
77  // product number. The input is validated, and when *
78  // a valid number is entered, it is returned.       *
79  //****************************************************
80
81  int getProdNum()
82  {
83     int prodNum;  // Product number
84
85     cout << "Enter the item's product number: ";
86     cin >> prodNum;
```

```
 87     // Validate input
 88     while (prodNum < MIN_PRODNUM || prodNum > MAX_PRODNUM)
 89     {
 90        cout << "Enter a number in the range of " << MIN_PRODNUM;
 91        cout <<" through " << MAX_PRODNUM << ".\n";
 92        cin >> prodNum;
 93     }
 94     return prodNum;
 95 }
 96
 97 //*************************************************************
 98 // Definition of binarySearch function                       *
 99 // The binarySearch function performs a binary search on an   *
100 // integer array. array, which has a maximum of numElems      *
101 // elements, is searched for the number stored in value. If the *
102 // number is found, its array subscript is returned. Otherwise, *
103 // -1 is returned indicating the value was not in the array.    *
104 //*************************************************************
105
106 int binarySearch(int array[], int numElems, int value)
107 {
108    int first = 0,              // First array element
109        last = numElems - 1,    // Last array element
110        middle,                 // Midpoint of search
111        position = -1;          // Position of search value
112    bool found = false;         // Flag
113
114    while (!found && first <= last)
115    {
116       middle = (first + last) / 2;  // Calculate midpoint
117       if (array[middle] == value)   // If value is found at mid
118       {
119          found = true;
120          position = middle;
121       }
122       else if (array[middle] > value) // If value is in lower half
123          last = middle - 1;
124       else
125          first = middle + 1;         // If value is in upper half
126    }
127    return position;
128 }
129
130 //*************************************************************
131 // The displayProd function accepts three arrays and an int. *
132 // The arrays parameters are expected to hold the title,      *
133 // description, and prices arrays defined in main. The        *
134 // ndx parameter holds a subscript. This function displays    *
135 // the information in each array contained at the subscript.  *
136 //*************************************************************
137
```

(program continues)

Program 8-3 *(continued)*

```
138 void displayProd(char title[][TITLE_SIZE], char desc[][DESC_SIZE],
139                  double price[], int index)
140 {
141    cout << "Title: " << title[index] << endl;
142    cout << "Description: " << desc[index] << endl;
143    cout << "Price: $" << price[index] << endl;
144 }
```

Program Output with Example Input Shown in Bold
```
Enter the item's product number: 916 [Enter]
Title: The Road to Excellence
Description: DVD
Price: $18.95
Would you like to look up another product? (y/n) y [Enter]
Enter the item's product number: 920 [Enter]
Title: Teams Are Made, Not Born
Description: Book
Price: $14.95
Would you like to look up another product? (y/n) n [Enter]
```

Checkpoint

8.1 Describe the difference between the linear search and the binary search.

8.2 On average, with an array of 20,000 elements, how many comparisons will the linear search perform? (Assume the items being searched for are consistently found in the array.)

8.3 With an array of 20,000 elements, what is the maximum number of comparisons the binary search will perform?

8.4 If a linear search is performed on an array, and it is known that some items are searched for more frequently than others, how can the contents of the array be reordered to improve the average performance of the search?

8.3

Focus on Software Engineering: Introduction to Sorting Algorithms

CONCEPT: Sorting algorithms are used to arrange data into some order.

Often the data in an array must be sorted in some order. Customer lists, for instance, are commonly sorted in alphabetical order. Student grades might be sorted from highest to lowest. Product codes could be sorted so all the products of the same color are stored together. To sort the data in an array, the programmer must use an appropriate *sorting algorithm*. A sorting algorithm is a technique for scanning through an array and rearranging its contents in some specific order. This section will introduce two simple sorting algorithms: the *bubble sort* and the *selection sort*.

The Bubble Sort

The bubble sort is an easy way to arrange data in *ascending* or *descending order*. If an array is sorted in ascending order, it means the values in the array are stored from lowest to highest. If the values are sorted in descending order, they are stored from highest to lowest. Let's see how the bubble sort is used in arranging the following array's elements in ascending order:

7	2	3	8	9	1
Element 0	Element 1	Element 2	Element 3	Element 4	Element 5

The bubble sort starts by comparing the first two elements in the array. If element 0 is greater than element 1, they are exchanged. After the exchange, the array shown above would appear as:

2	7	3	8	9	1
Element 0	Element 1	Element 2	Element 3	Element 4	Element 5

This method is repeated with elements 1 and 2. If element 1 is greater than element 2, they are exchanged. The array above would then appear as:

2	3	7	8	9	1
Element 0	Element 1	Element 2	Element 3	Element 4	Element 5

Next, elements 2 and 3 are compared. In this array, these two elements are already in the proper order (element 2 is less than element 3), so no exchange takes place.

As the cycle continues, elements 3 and 4 are compared. Once again, no exchange is necessary because they are already in the proper order.

When elements 4 and 5 are compared, however, an exchange must take place because element 4 is greater than element 5. The array now appears as:

2	3	7	8	1	9
Element 0	Element 1	Element 2	Element 3	Element 4	Element 5

At this point, the entire array has been scanned, but its contents aren't quite in the right order yet. So, the sort starts over again with elements 0 and 1. Because those two are in the proper order, no exchange takes place. Elements 1 and 2 are compared next, but once again, no exchange takes place. This continues until elements 3 and 4 are compared. Because element 3 is greater than element 4, they are exchanged. The array now appears as

2	3	7	1	8	9
Element 0	Element 1	Element 2	Element 3	Element 4	Element 5

By now you should see how the sort will eventually cause the elements to appear in the correct order. The sort repeatedly passes through the array until no exchanges are made. Ultimately, the array will appear as

1	2	3	7	8	9
Element 0	Element 1	Element 2	Element 3	Element 4	Element 5

Here is the bubble sort in pseudocode:

```
Do
    Set swap flag to false.
    For count is set to each subscript in array from 0 through the
            next-to-last subscript
        If array[count] is greater than array[count + 1]
            Swap the contents of array[count] and array[count + 1].
            Set swap flag to true.
        End If.
    End For.
While any elements have been swapped.
```

The C++ code below implements the bubble sort as a function. The parameter array is an integer array to be sorted. size contains the number of elements in array.

```cpp
void sortArray(int array[], int size)
{
    bool swap;
    int temp;

    do
    {
        swap = false;
        for (int count = 0; count < (size - 1); count++)
        {
            if (array[count] > array[count + 1])
            {
                temp = array[count];
                array[count] = array[count + 1];
                array[count + 1] = temp;
                swap = true;
            }
        }
    } while (swap);
}
```

Inside the function is a for loop nested inside a do-while loop. The for loop sequences through the entire array, comparing each element with its neighbor, and swapping them if necessary. Anytime two elements are exchanged, the flag variable swap is set to true.

The for loop must be executed repeatedly until it can sequence through the entire array without making any exchanges. This is why it is nested inside a do-while loop. The do-while loop sets swap to false, and then executes the for loop. If swap is set to true after the for loop has finished, the do-while loop repeats.

Here is the starting line of the for loop:

```cpp
for (int count = 0; count < (size - 1); count++)
```

The variable count holds the array subscript values. It starts at zero and is incremented as long as it is less than size - 1. The value of size is the number of elements in the array, and count stops just short of reaching this value because the following line compares each element with the one after it:

```cpp
if (array[count] > array[count + 1])
```

When array[count] is the next-to-last element, it will be compared to the last element. If the for loop were allowed to increment count past size - 1, the last element in the array would be compared to a value outside the array.

Let's look at the if statement in its entirety:

```cpp
if (array[count] > array[count + 1])
{
    temp = array[count];
    array[count] = array[count + 1];
    array[count + 1] = temp;
    swap = true;
}
```

If array[count] is greater than array[count + 1], the two elements must be exchanged. First, the contents of array[count] are copied into the variable temp. Then the contents of array[count + 1] is copied into array[count]. The exchange is made complete when the contents of temp (the previous contents of array[count]) are copied to array[count + 1]. Last, the swap flag variable is set to true. This indicates that an exchange has been made.

Program 8-4 demonstrates the bubble sort function in a complete program.

Program 8-4

```cpp
 1 // This program uses the bubble sort algorithm to sort an
 2 // array in ascending order.
 3 #include <iostream>
 4 using namespace std;
 5
 6 // Function prototypes
 7 void sortArray(int [], int);
 8 void showArray(int [], int);
 9
10 int main()
11 {
12     // Array of unsorted values
13     int values[6] = {7, 2, 3, 8, 9, 1};
14
15     // Display the values.
16     cout << "The unsorted values are:\n";
17     showArray(values, 6);
18
19     // Sort the values.
20     sortArray(values, 6);
```

(program continues)

Program 8-4 *(continued)*

```
21
22      // Display them again.
23      cout << "The sorted values are:\n";
24      showArray(values, 6);
25      return 0;
26  }
27
28  //*************************************************************
29  // Definition of function sortArray                          *
30  // This function performs an ascending order bubble sort on  *
31  // array. size is the number of elements in the array.       *
32  //*************************************************************
33
34  void sortArray(int array[], int size)
35  {
36      bool swap;
37      int temp;
38
39      do
40      {
41          swap = false;
42          for (int count = 0; count < (size - 1); count++)
43          {
44              if (array[count] > array[count + 1])
45              {
46                  temp = array[count];
47                  array[count] = array[count + 1];
48                  array[count + 1] = temp;
49                  swap = true;
50              }
51          }
52      } while (swap);
53  }
54
55  //*************************************************************
56  // Definition of function showArray.                         *
57  // This function displays the contents of array. size is the *
58  // number of elements.                                       *
59  //*************************************************************
60
61  void showArray(int array[], int size)
62  {
63      for (int count = 0; count < size; count++)
64          cout << array[count] << " ";
65      cout << endl;
66  }
```

Program Output

```
The unsorted values are:
7 2 3 8 9 1
The sorted values are:
1 2 3 7 8 9
```

The Selection Sort

The bubble sort is inefficient for large arrays because items only move by one element at a time. The selection sort, however, usually performs fewer exchanges because it moves items immediately to their final position in the array. It works like this: The smallest value in the array is located and moved to element 0. Then the next smallest value is located and moved to element 1. This process continues until all of the elements have been placed in their proper order.

VideoNote

The Selection Sort

Let's see how the selection sort works when arranging the elements of the following array:

5	7	2	8	9	1
Element 0	Element 1	Element 2	Element 3	Element 4	Element 5

The selection sort scans the array, starting at element 0, and locates the element with the smallest value. The contents of this element are then swapped with the contents of element 0. In this example, the 1 stored in element 5 is swapped with the 5 stored in element 0. After the exchange, the array would appear as

1	7	2	8	9	5
Element 0	Element 1	Element 2	Element 3	Element 4	Element 5

The algorithm then repeats the process, but because element 0 already contains the smallest value in the array, it can be left out of the procedure. This time, the algorithm begins the scan at element 1. In this example, the contents of element 2 are exchanged with those of element 1. The array would then appear as

1	2	7	8	9	5
Element 0	Element 1	Element 2	Element 3	Element 4	Element 5

Once again the process is repeated, but this time the scan begins at element 2. The algorithm will find that element 5 contains the next smallest value. This element's contents are exchanged with those of element 2, causing the array to appear as

1	2	5	8	9	7
Element 0	Element 1	Element 2	Element 3	Element 4	Element 5

Next, the scanning begins at element 3. Its contents are exchanged with those of element 5, causing the array to appear as

1	2	5	7	9	8
Element 0	Element 1	Element 2	Element 3	Element 4	Element 5

At this point there are only two elements left to sort. The algorithm finds that the value in element 5 is smaller than that of element 4, so the two are swapped. This puts the array in its final arrangement:

1	2	5	7	8	9
Element 0	Element 1	Element 2	Element 3	Element 4	Element 5

Here is the selection sort algorithm in pseudocode:

```
For startScan is set to each subscript in array from 0 through the
            next-to-last subscript
    Set index variable to startScan.
    Set minIndex variable to startScan.
    Set minValue variable to array[startScan].

    For index is set to each subscript in array from (startScan + 1)
            through the last subscript
        If array[index] is less than minValue
            Set minValue to array[index].
            Set minIndex to index.
        End If.
    End For.
    Set array[minIndex] to array[startScan].
    Set array[startScan] to minValue.
End For.
```

The following C++ code implements the selection sort in a function. It accepts two arguments: `array` and `size`. `array` is an integer array and `size` is the number of elements in the array. The function uses the selection sort to arrange the values in the array in ascending order.

```cpp
void selectionSort(int array[], int size)
{
    int startScan, minIndex, minValue;

    for (startScan = 0; startScan < (size - 1); startScan++)
    {
        minIndex = startScan;
        minValue = array[startScan];
        for(int index = startScan + 1; index < size; index++)
        {
            if (array[index] < minValue)
            {
                minValue = array[index];
                minIndex = index;
            }
        }
        array[minIndex] = array[startScan];
        array[startScan] = minValue;
    }
}
```

Inside the function are two `for` loops, one nested inside the other. The inner loop sequences through the array, starting at `array[startScan + 1]`, searching for the element with the smallest value. When the element is found, its subscript is stored in the variable `minIndex` and its value is stored in `minValue`. The outer loop then exchanges the contents of this element with `array[startScan]` and increments `startScan`. This procedure repeats until the contents of every element have been moved to their proper location.

Program 8-5 demonstrates the selection sort function in a complete program.

Program 8-5

```cpp
1  // This program uses the selection sort algorithm to sort an
2  // array in ascending order.
3  #include <iostream>
4  using namespace std;
5
6  // Function prototypes
7  void selectionSort(int [], int);
8  void showArray(int [], int);
9
10 int main()
11 {
12    // Define an array with unsorted values
13    const int SIZE = 6;
14    int values[SIZE] = {5, 7, 2, 8, 9, 1};
15
16    // Display the values.
17    cout << "The unsorted values are\n";
18    showArray(values, SIZE);
19
20    // Sort the values.
21    selectionSort(values, SIZE);
22
23    // Display the values again.
24    cout << "The sorted values are\n";
25    showArray(values, SIZE);
26    return 0;
27 }
28
29 //**********************************************************
30 // Definition of function selectionSort.                   *
31 // This function performs an ascending order selection sort on *
32 // array. size is the number of elements in the array.     *
33 //**********************************************************
34
35 void selectionSort(int array[], int size)
36 {
37    int startScan, minIndex, minValue;
38
39    for (startScan = 0; startScan < (size - 1); startScan++)
40    {
41       minIndex = startScan;
42       minValue = array[startScan];
43       for(int index = startScan + 1; index < size; index++)
44       {
45          if (array[index] < minValue)
46          {
47             minValue = array[index];
48             minIndex = index;
49          }
50       }
```

(program continues)

Program 8-5   *(continued)*

```
51          array[minIndex] = array[startScan];
52          array[startScan] = minValue;
53      }
54  }
55
56  //*************************************************************
57  // Definition of function showArray.                         *
58  // This function displays the contents of array. size is the *
59  // number of elements.                                       *
60  //*************************************************************
61
62  void showArray(int array[], int size)
63  {
64      for (int count = 0; count < size; count++)
65          cout << array[count] << " ";
66      cout << endl;
67  }
```

Program Output
```
The unsorted values are
5 7 2 8 9 1
The sorted values are
1 2 5 7 8 9
```

8.4 Focus on Problem Solving and Program Design: A Case Study

Like the previous case study, this is a program developed for the Demetris Leadership Center. Recall that DLC, Inc., publishes books, DVDs, and audio CDs. (See Table 8-1 for a complete list of products, with title, description, product number, and price.) Table 8-4 shows the number of units of each product sold during the past six months.

Table 8-4

Product Number	Units Sold
914	842
915	416
916	127
917	514
918	437
919	269
920	97
921	492
922	212

The vice president of sales has asked you to write a sales reporting program that displays the following information:

- A list of the products in the order of their sales dollars (NOT units sold), from highest to lowest
- The total number of all units sold
- The total sales for the six-month period

Variables

Table 8-5 lists the variables needed:

Table 8-5

Variable	Description
NUM_PRODS	A constant integer initialized with the number of products that DLC, Inc., sells. This value will be used in the definition of the program's array.
prodNum	Array of ints. Holds each product's number.
units	Array of ints. Holds each product's number of units sold.
prices	Array of doubles. Holds each product's price.
sales	Array of doubles. Holds the computed sales amounts (in dollars) of each product.

The elements of the four arrays, prodNum, units, prices, and sales will correspond with each other. For example, the product whose number is stored in prodNum[2] will have sold the number of units stored in units[2]. The sales amount for the product will be stored in sales[2].

Modules

The program will consist of the functions listed in Table 8-6.

Table 8-6

Function	Description
main	The program's main function. It calls the program's other functions.
calcSales	Calculates each product's sales.
dualSort	Sorts the sales array so the elements are ordered from highest to lowest. The prodNum array is ordered so the product numbers correspond with the correct sales figures in the sorted sales array.
showOrder	Displays a list of the product numbers and sales amounts from the sorted sales and prodNum arrays.
showTotals	Displays the total number of units sold and the total sales amount for the period.

Function `main`

Function `main` is very simple. It contains the variable definitions and calls the other functions. Here is the pseudocode for its executable statements:

```
Call calcSales.
Call dualSort.
Set display mode to fixed point output with two decimal places of
        precision.
Call showOrder.
Call showTotals.
```

Here is its actual C++ code:

```cpp
// Calculate each product's sales.
calcSales(units, prices, sales, NUM_PRODS);

// Sort the elements in the sales array in descending
// order and shuffle the ID numbers in the id array to
// keep them in parallel.
dualSort(id, sales, NUM_PRODS);

// Set the numeric output formatting.
cout << setprecision(2) << fixed << showpoint;

// Display the products and sales amounts.
showOrder(sales, id, NUM_PRODS);

// Display total units sold and total sales.
showTotals(sales, units, NUM_PRODS);
```

The named constant `NUM_PRODS` will be defined globally and initialized to the value 9.

The arrays `id`, `units`, and `prices` will already be initialized with data. (It will be left as an exercise for you to modify this program so the user may enter these values.)

The `calcSales` Function

The `calcSales` function multiplies each product's units sold by its price. The resulting amount is stored in the `sales` array. Here is the function's pseudocode:

```
For index is set to each subscript in the arrays from 0 through the
        last subscript.
    Set sales[index] to units[index] times prices[index].
End For.
```

And here is the function's actual C++ code:

```cpp
void calcSales(int units[], double prices[], double sales[], int num)
{
    for (int index = 0; index < num; index++)
        sales[index] = units[index] * prices[index];
}
```

The `dualSort` Function

The `dualSort` function is a modified version of the selection sort algorithm shown in Program 8-5. The `dualSort` function accepts two arrays as arguments: the `sales` array and the `id` array. The function actually performs the selection sort on the `sales` array. When the function moves an element in the `sales` array, however, it also moves the corresponding element in the `id` array. This is to ensure that the product numbers in the `id` array still have subscripts that match their sales figures in the `sales` array.

The `dualSort` function is also different in another way: It sorts the array in descending order.

Here is the pseudocode for the `dualSort` function:

```
For startScan variable is set to each subscript in array from 0 through
the next-to-last subscript
    Set index variable to startScan.
    Set maxIndex variable to startScan.
    Set tempId variable to id[startScan].
    Set maxValue variable to sales[startScan].
    For index variable is set to each subscript in array from
                (startScan + 1) through the last subscript
        If sales[index] is greater than maxValue
            Set maxValue to sales[index].
            Set tempId to tempId[index].
            Set maxIndex to index.
        End If.
    End For.
    Set sales[maxIndex] to sales[startScan].
    Set id[maxIndex] = id[startScan].
    Set sales[startScan] to maxValue.
    Set id[startScan] = tempId.
End For.
```

Here is the actual C++ code for the `dualSort` function:

```cpp
void dualSort(int id[], double sales[], int size)
{
    int startScan, maxIndex, tempId;
    double maxValue;

    for (startScan = 0; startScan < (size - 1); startScan++)
    {
        maxIndex = startScan;
        maxValue = sales[startScan];
        tempId = id[startScan];
        for(int index = startScan + 1; index < size; index++)
        {
            if (sales[index] > maxValue)
            {
                maxValue = sales[index];
                tempId = id[index];
                maxIndex = index;
            }
        }
```

```
            sales[maxIndex] = sales[startScan];
            id[maxIndex] = id[startScan];
            sales[startScan] = maxValue;
            id[startScan] = tempId;
        }
    }
```

 NOTE: Once the dualSort function is called, the id and sales arrays are no longer synchronized with the units and prices arrays. Because this program doesn't use units and prices together with id and sales after this point, it will not be noticed in the final output. However, it is never a good programming practice to sort parallel arrays in such a way that they are out of synchronization. It will be left as an exercise for you to modify the program so all the arrays are synchronized and used in the final output of the program.

The showOrder Function

The showOrder function displays a heading and the sorted list of product numbers and their sales amounts. It accepts the id and sales arrays as arguments. Here is its pseudocode:

```
Display heading.
For index variable is set to each subscript of the arrays from 0
through the last subscript
    Display id[index].
    Display sales[index].
End For.
```

Here is the function's actual C++ code:

```
void showOrder(double sales[], int id[], int num)
{
    cout << "Product Number\tSales\n";

    cout << "---------------------------------\n";
    for (int index = 0; index < num; index++)
    {
        cout << id[index] << "\t\t$";
        cout << setw(8) << sales[index] << endl;
    }
    cout << endl;
}
```

The showTotals Function

The showTotals function displays the total number of units of all products sold and the total sales for the period. It accepts the units and sales arrays as arguments. Here is its pseudocode:

```
Set totalUnits variable to 0.
Set totalSales variable to 0.0.
For index variable is set to each subscript in the arrays from 0
through the last subscript
    Add units[index] to totalUnits[index].
    Add sales[index] to totalSales.
```

```
End For.
Display totalUnits with appropriate heading.
Display totalSales with appropriate heading.
```

Here is the function's actual C++ code:

```cpp
void showTotals(double sales[], int units[], int num)
{
    int totalUnits = 0;
    double totalSales = 0.0;
    for (int index = 0; index < num; index++)
    {
        totalUnits += units[index];
        totalSales += sales[index];
    }
    cout << "Total Units Sold:  " << totalUnits << endl;
    cout << "Total Sales:      $" << totalSales << endl;
}
```

The Entire Program

Program 8-6 shows the entire program's source code.

Program 8-6

```cpp
1  // This program produces a sales report for DLC, Inc.
2  #include <iostream>
3  #include <iomanip>
4  using namespace std;
5
6  // Function prototypes
7  void calcSales(int [], double [], double [], int);
8  void showOrder(double [], int [], int);
9  void dualSort(int [], double [], int);
10 void showTotals(double [], int [], int);
11
12 // NUM_PRODS is the number of products produced.
13 const int NUM_PRODS = 9;
14
15 int main()
16 {
17    // Array with product ID numbers
18    int id[NUM_PRODS] = {914, 915, 916, 917, 918, 919, 920,
19                         921, 922};
20
21    // Array with number of units sold for each product
22    int units[NUM_PRODS] = {842, 416, 127, 514, 437, 269, 97,
23                            492, 212};
24
25    // Array with product prices
26    double prices[NUM_PRODS] = {12.95, 14.95, 18.95, 16.95, 21.95,
27                               31.95, 14.95, 14.95, 16.95};
28
```

(program continues)

Program 8-6   *(continued)*

```
29       // Array to hold the computed sales amounts
30       double sales[NUM_PRODS];
31
32       // Calculate each product's sales.
33       calcSales(units, prices, sales, NUM_PRODS);
34
35       // Sort the elements in the sales array in descending
36       // order and shuffle the ID numbers in the id array to
37       // keep them in parallel.
38       dualSort(id, sales, NUM_PRODS);
39
40       // Set the numeric output formatting.
41       cout << setprecision(2) << fixed << showpoint;
42
43       // Display the products and sales amounts.
44       showOrder(sales, id, NUM_PRODS);
45
46       // Display total units sold and total sales.
47       showTotals(sales, units, NUM_PRODS);
48       return 0;
49    }
50
51    //****************************************************************
52    // Definition of calcSales. Accepts units, prices, and sales   *
53    // arrays as arguments. The size of these arrays is passed      *
54    // into the num parameter. This function calculates each        *
55    // product's sales by multiplying its units sold by each unit's *
56    // price. The result is stored in the sales array.              *
57    //****************************************************************
58
59    void calcSales(int units[], double prices[], double sales[], int num)
60    {
61       for (int index = 0; index < num; index++)
62          sales[index] = units[index] * prices[index];
63    }
64
65    //****************************************************************
66    // Definition of function dualSort. Accepts id and sales arrays *
67    // as arguments. The size of these arrays is passed into size.  *
68    // This function performs a descending order selection sort on  *
69    // the sales array. The elements of the id array are exchanged  *
70    // identically as those of the sales array. size is the number  *
71    // of elements in each array.                                   *
72    //****************************************************************
73
74    void dualSort(int id[], double sales[], int size)
75    {
76       int startScan, maxIndex, tempid;
77       double maxValue;
78
```

```
 79      for (startScan = 0; startScan < (size - 1); startScan++)
 80      {
 81         maxIndex = startScan;
 82         maxValue = sales[startScan];
 83         tempid = id[startScan];
 84         for(int index = startScan + 1; index < size; index++)
 85         {
 86            if (sales[index] > maxValue)
 87            {
 88               maxValue = sales[index];
 89               tempid = id[index];
 90               maxIndex = index;
 91            }
 92         }
 93         sales[maxIndex] = sales[startScan];
 94         id[maxIndex] = id[startScan];
 95         sales[startScan] = maxValue;
 96         id[startScan] = tempid;
 97      }
 98 }
 99
100 //************************************************************
101 // Definition of showOrder function. Accepts sales and id arrays *
102 // as arguments. The size of these arrays is passed into num.    *
103 // The function first displays a heading, then the sorted list   *
104 // of product numbers and sales.                                 *
105 //************************************************************
106
107 void showOrder(double sales[], int id[], int num)
108 {
109    cout << "Product Number\tSales\n";
110    cout << "--------------------------------\n";
111    for (int index = 0; index < num; index++)
112    {
113       cout << id[index] << "\t\t$";
114       cout << setw(8) << sales[index] << endl;
115    }
116    cout << endl;
117 }
118
119 //************************************************************
120 // Definition of showTotals function. Accepts sales and id arrays *
121 // as arguments. The size of these arrays is passed into num.     *
122 // The function first calculates the total units (of all          *
123 // products) sold and the total sales. It then displays these     *
124 // amounts.                                                       *
125 //************************************************************
126
```

(program continues)

Program 8-6   *(continued)*

```
127 void showTotals(double sales[], int units[], int num)
128 {
129    int totalUnits = 0;
130    double totalSales = 0.0;
131
132    for (int index = 0; index < num; index++)
133    {
134       totalUnits += units[index];
135       totalSales += sales[index];
136    }
137    cout << "Total Units Sold:  " << totalUnits << endl;
138    cout << "Total Sales:      $" << totalSales << endl;
139 }
```

Program Output

```
Product Number                Sales
-----------------------------------
914                        $10903.90
918                        $ 9592.15
917                        $ 8712.30
919                        $ 8594.55
921                        $ 7355.40
915                        $ 6219.20
922                        $ 3593.40
916                        $ 2406.65
920                        $ 1450.15
Total Units Sold:           3406
Total Sales:               $58827.70
```

8.5

If You Plan to Continue in Computer Science: Sorting and Searching vectors (Continued from Section 7.12)

CONCEPT: The sorting and searching algorithms you have studied in this chapter may be applied to STL **vectors** as well as arrays.

Once you have properly defined an STL vector and populated it with values, you may sort and search the vector with the algorithms presented in this chapter. Simply substitute the vector syntax for the array syntax when necessary. Program 8-7, which illustrates this, is a modification of the case study in Program 8-6.

Program 8-7

```cpp
 1  // This program produces a sales report for DLC, Inc.
 2  // This version of the program uses STL vectors instead of arrays.
 3  #include <iostream>
 4  #include <iomanip>
 5  #include <vector>
 6  using namespace std;
 7
 8  // Function prototypes
 9  void initVectors(vector<int> &, vector<int> &, vector<double> &);
10  void calcSales(vector<int>, vector<double>, vector<double> &);
11  void showOrder(vector<double>, vector<int>);
12  void dualSort(vector<int> &, vector<double> &);
13  void showTotals(vector<double>, vector<int>);
14
15  int main()
16  {
17      vector<int> id;            // Product ID numbers
18      vector<int> units;         // Units sold
19      vector<double> prices;     // Product prices
20      vector<double> sales;      // To hold product sales
21
22      // Must provide an initialization routine.
23      initVectors(id, units, prices);
24
25      // Calculate each product's sales.
26      calcSales(units, prices, sales);
27
28      // Sort the elements in the sales array in descending
29      // order and shuffle the ID numbers in the id array to
30      // keep them in parallel.
31      dualSort(id, sales);
32
33      // Set the numeric output formatting.
34      cout << fixed << showpoint << setprecision(2);
35
36      // Display the products and sales amounts.
37      showOrder(sales, id);
38
39      // Display total units sold and total sales.
40      showTotals(sales, units);
41      return 0;
42  }
43
44  //*****************************************************************
45  // Definition of initVectors. Accepts id, units, and prices      *
46  // vectors as reference arguments. This function initializes each *
47  // vector to a set of starting values.                           *
48  //*****************************************************************
49
```

(program continues)

Program 8-7 *(continued)*

```cpp
50 void initVectors(vector<int> &id, vector<int> &units,
51                   vector<double> &prices)
52 {
53    // Initialize the id vector with the ID numbers
54    // 914 through 922.
55    for (int value = 914; value <= 922; value++)
56       id.push_back(value);
57
58    // Initialize the units vector with data.
59    units.push_back(842);
60    units.push_back(416);
61    units.push_back(127);
62    units.push_back(514);
63    units.push_back(437);
64    units.push_back(269);
65    units.push_back(97);
66    units.push_back(492);
67    units.push_back(212);
68
69    // Initialize the prices vector.
70    prices.push_back(12.95);
71    prices.push_back(14.95);
72    prices.push_back(18.95);
73    prices.push_back(16.95);
74    prices.push_back(21.95);
75    prices.push_back(31.95);
76    prices.push_back(14.95);
77    prices.push_back(14.95);
78    prices.push_back(16.95);
79 }
80
81
82 //****************************************************************
83 // Definition of calcSales. Accepts units, prices, and sales    *
84 // vectors as arguments. The sales vector is passed into a      *
85 // reference parameter. This function calculates each product's *
86 // sales by multiplying its units sold by each unit's price. The *
87 // result is stored in the sales vector.                        *
88 //****************************************************************
89
90 void calcSales(vector<int> units, vector<double> prices,
91                vector<double> &sales)
92 {
93    for (int index = 0; index < units.size(); index++)
94       sales.push_back(units[index] * prices[index]);
95 }
96
```

```
 97  //*****************************************************************
 98  // Definition of function dualSort. Accepts id and sales vectors *
 99  // as reference arguments. This function performs a descending   *
100  // order selection sort on the sales vector. The elements of the *
101  // id vector are exchanged identically as those of the sales     *
102  // vector.                                                        *
103  //*****************************************************************
104
105  void dualSort(vector<int> &id, vector<double> &sales)
106  {
107     int startScan, maxIndex, tempid, size;
108     double maxValue;
109
110     size = id.size();
111     for (startScan = 0; startScan < (size - 1); startScan++)
112     {
113        maxIndex = startScan;
114        maxValue = sales[startScan];
115        tempid = id[startScan];
116        for(int index = startScan + 1; index < size; index++)
117        {
118           if (sales[index] > maxValue)
119           {
120              maxValue = sales[index];
121              tempid = id[index];
122              maxIndex = index;
123           }
124        }
125        sales[maxIndex] = sales[startScan];
126        id[maxIndex] = id[startScan];
127        sales[startScan] = maxValue;
128        id[startScan] = tempid;
129     }
130  }
131
132  //*****************************************************************
133  // Definition of showOrder function. Accepts sales and id vectors *
134  // as arguments. The function first displays a heading, then the  *
135  // sorted list of product numbers and sales.                      *
136  //*****************************************************************
137
138  void showOrder(vector<double> sales, vector<int> id)
139  {
140     cout << "Product Number\tSales\n";
141     cout << "----------------------------------\n";
142     for (int index = 0; index < id.size(); index++)
143     {
144        cout << id[index] << "\t\t$";
145        cout << setw(8) << sales[index] << endl;
146     }
147     cout << endl;
148  }
```

(program continues)

Program 8-7   *(continued)*

```
149
150 //*********************************************************************
151 // Definition of showTotals function. Accepts sales and id vectors  *
152 // as arguments. The function first calculates the total units (of   *
153 // all products) sold and the total sales. It then displays these    *
154 // amounts.                                                          *
155 //*********************************************************************
156
157 void showTotals(vector<double> sales, vector<int> units)
158 {
159     int totalUnits = 0;
160     double totalSales = 0.0;
161
162     for (int index = 0; index < units.size(); index++)
163     {
164         totalUnits += units[index];
165         totalSales += sales[index];
166     }
167     cout << "Total Units Sold:  " << totalUnits << endl;
168     cout << "Total Sales:      $" << totalSales << endl;
169 }
```

Program Output

```
Product Number              Sales
----------------------------------
914                     $10903.90
918                     $ 9592.15
917                     $ 8712.30
919                     $ 8594.55
921                     $ 7355.40
915                     $ 6219.20
922                     $ 3593.40
916                     $ 2406.65
920                     $ 1450.15
Total Units Sold:        3406
Total Sales:            $58827.70
```

There are some differences between this program and Program 8-6. First, the initVectors function was added. In Program 8-6, this was not necessary because the id, units, and prices arrays had initialization lists. vectors do not accept initialization lists, so this function stores the necessary initial values in the id, units, and prices vectors.

Now, look at the function header for initVectors:

```
void initVectors(vector<int> &id, vector<int> &units,
                 vector<double> &prices)
```

Notice that the vector parameters are references (as indicated by the & that precedes the parameter name). This brings up an important difference between vectors and arrays: By default, vectors are passed by value, whereas arrays are only passed by reference. If you want to change a value in a vector argument, it *must* be passed into a reference parameter. Reference vector parameters are also used in the calcSales and dualSort functions.

Also, notice that each time a value is added to a vector, the push_back member function is called. This is because the [ ] operator cannot be used to store a new element in a vector. It can only be used to store a value in an existing element or read a value from an existing element.

The code in this function appears cumbersome because it calls each vector's push_back member function once for each value that is to be stored in the vector. This code can be simplified by storing the vector initialization values in arrays, and then using loops to call the push_back member function, storing the values in the arrays in the vectors. The following code shows an alternative initVectors function that takes this approach.

```cpp
void initVectors(vector<int> &id, vector<int> &units,
                 vector<double> &prices)
{
    const int NUM_PRODS = 9;
    int count;
    int unitsSold[NUM_PRODS] = {842, 416, 127, 514, 437, 269, 97,
                                492, 212};
    double productPrices[NUM_PRODS] = {12.95, 14.95, 18.95, 16.95,
                                       21.95, 31.95, 14.95, 14.95,
                                       16.95};

    // Initialize the id vector
    for (int value = 914; value <= 922; value++)
        id.push_back(value);

    // Initialize the units vector
    for (count = 0; count < NUM_PRODS; count++)
        units.push_back(unitsSold[count]);

    // Initialize the prices vector
    for (count = 0; count < NUM_PRODS; count++)
        prices.push_back(productPrices[count]);
}
```

Next, notice that the calcSales, showOrder, dualSort, and showTotals functions do not accept an argument indicating the number of elements in the vectors. This is not necessary because vectors have the size member function, which returns the number of elements in the vector. The following code segment, which is taken from the calcSales function, shows the units.size() member function being used to control the number of loop iterations.

```cpp
for (int index = 0; index < units.size(); index++)
    sales.push_back(units[index] * prices[index]);
```

Review Questions and Exercises

Short Answer

1. Why is the linear search also called "sequential search"?

2. If a linear search function is searching for a value that is stored in the last element of a 10,000-element array, how many elements will the search code have to read to locate the value?

3. In an average case involving an array of N elements, how many times will a linear search function have to read the array to locate a specific value?

4. A binary search function is searching for a value that is stored in the middle element of an array. How many times will the function read an element in the array before finding the value?

5. What is the maximum number of comparisons that a binary search function will make when searching for a value in a 1,000-element array?

6. Why is the bubble sort inefficient for large arrays?

7. Why is the selection sort more efficient than the bubble sort on large arrays?

Fill-in-the-Blank

8. The _____ search algorithm steps sequentially through an array, comparing each item with the search value.

9. The _____ search algorithm repeatedly divides the portion of an array being searched in half.

10. The _____ search algorithm is adequate for small arrays but not large arrays.

11. The _____ search algorithm requires that the array's contents be sorted.

12. If an array is sorted in _____ order, the values are stored from lowest to highest.

13. If an array is sorted in _____ order, the values are stored from highest to lowest.

True or False

14. T   F   If data are sorted in ascending order, it means they are ordered from lowest value to highest value.

15. T   F   If data are sorted in descending order, it means they are ordered from lowest value to highest value.

16. T   F   The *average* number of comparisons performed by the linear search on an array of N elements is N/2 (assuming the search values are consistently found).

17. T   F   The *maximum* number of comparisons performed by the linear search on an array of N elements is N/2 (assuming the search values are consistently found).

18. Complete the following table calculating the average and maximum number of comparisons the linear search will perform, and the maximum number of comparisons the binary search will perform.

Array Size →	50 Elements	500 Elements	10,000 Elements	100,000 Elements	10,000,000 Elements
Linear Search (Average Comparisons)					
Linear Search (Maximum Comparisons)					
Binary Search (Maximum Comparisons)					

Programming Challenges

1. Charge Account Validation

Write a program that lets the user enter a charge account number. The program should determine if the number is valid by checking for it in the following list:

```
5658845    4520125    7895122    8777541    8451277    1302850
8080152    4562555    5552012    5050552    7825877    1250255
1005231    6545231    3852085    7576651    7881200    4581002
```

The list of numbers above should be initialized in a single-dimensional array. A simple linear search should be used to locate the number entered by the user. If the user enters a number that is in the array, the program should display a message saying that the number is valid. If the user enters a number that is not in the array, the program should display a message indicating that the number is invalid.

2. Lottery Winners

A lottery ticket buyer purchases 10 tickets a week, always playing the same 10 5-digit "lucky" combinations. Write a program that initializes an array or a vector with these numbers and then lets the player enter this week's winning 5-digit number. The program should perform a linear search through the list of the player's numbers and report whether or not one of the tickets is a winner this week. Here are the numbers:

```
13579   26791   26792   33445   55555
62483   77777   79422   85647   93121
```

3. Lottery Winners Modification

Modify the program you wrote for Programming Challenge 2 (Lottery Winners) so it performs a binary search instead of a linear search.

4. Charge Account Validation Modification

Modify the program you wrote for Problem 1 (Charge Account Validation) so it performs a binary search to locate valid account numbers. Use the selection sort algorithm to sort the array before the binary search is performed.

5. Rainfall Statistics Modification

Modify the Rainfall Statistics program you wrote for Programming Challenge 2 of Chapter 7. The program should display a list of months, sorted in order of rainfall, from highest to lowest.

VideoNote

Solving the Charge Account Validation Modification Problem

6. **String Selection Sort**

Modify the selectionSort function presented in this chapter so it searches an array of strings instead of an array of ints. Test the function with a driver program. Use Program 8-8 as a skeleton to complete.

Program 8-8

```cpp
#include <iostream>
using namespace std;

int main()
{
    const int NUM_NAMES = 20, SIZE = 17;
    char names[NUM_NAMES][SIZE] = {"Collins, Bill", "Smith, Bart", "Allen, Jim",
                                   "Griffin, Jim", "Stamey, Marty", "Rose, Geri",
                                   "Taylor, Terri", "Johnson, Jill",
                                   "Allison, Jeff", "Looney, Joe", "Wolfe, Bill",
                                   "James, Jean", "Weaver, Jim", "Pore, Bob",
                                   "Rutherford, Greg", "Javens, Renee",
                                   "Harrison, Rose", "Setzer, Cathy",
                                   "Pike, Gordon", "Holland, Beth" };

    // Insert your code to complete this program

    return 0;
}
```

7. **Binary String Search**

Modify the binarySearch function presented in this chapter so it searches an array of strings instead of an array of ints. Test the function with a driver program. Use Program 8-8 as a skeleton to complete. (The array must be sorted before the binary search will work.)

8. **Search Benchmarks**

Write a program that has an array of at least 20 integers. It should call a function that uses the linear search algorithm to locate one of the values. The function should keep a count of the number of comparisons it makes until it finds the value. The program then should call a function that uses the binary search algorithm to locate the same value. It should also keep count of the number of comparisons it makes. Display these values on the screen.

9. **Sorting Benchmarks**

Write a program that uses two identical arrays of at least 20 integers. It should call a function that uses the bubble sort algorithm to sort one of the arrays in ascending order. The function should keep a count of the number of exchanges it makes. The program then should call a function that uses the selection sort algorithm to sort the other array. It should also keep count of the number of exchanges it makes. Display these values on the screen.

10. **Sorting Orders**

Write a program that uses two identical arrays of just eight integers. It should display the contents of the first array, then call a function to sort the array using an ascending order bubble sort modified to print out the array contents after each pass of the sort. Next, the program should display the contents of the second array, then call a function to sort the array using an ascending order selection sort modified to print out the array contents after each pass of the sort.

11. **Using Files—String Selection Sort Modification**

Modify the program you wrote for Programming Challenge 6 so it reads in 20 strings from a file. The data can be found in the `names.dat` file.

9 Pointers

TOPICS

9.1 Getting the Address of a Variable

CONCEPT: The address operator (&) returns the memory address of a variable.

Every variable is allocated a section of memory large enough to hold a value of the variable's data type. On a PC, for instance, it's common for one byte to be allocated for chars, two bytes for shorts , four bytes for ints, longs, and floats, and eight bytes for doubles.

Each byte of memory has a unique *address*. A variable's address is the address of the first byte allocated to that variable. Suppose the following variables are defined in a program:

```
char letter;
short number;
float amount;
```

Figure 9-1 illustrates how they might be arranged in memory and shows their addresses.

Figure 9-1

In Figure 9-1, the variable `letter` is shown at address 1200, `number` is at address 1201, and `amount` is at address 1203.

NOTE: The addresses of the variables shown in Figure 9-1 are arbitrary values used only for illustration purposes.

Getting the address of a variable is accomplished with an operator in C++. When the address operator (`&`) is placed in front of a variable name, it returns the address of that variable. Here is an expression that returns the address of the variable `amount`:

```
&amount
```

And here is a statement that displays the variable's address on the screen:

```
cout << &amount;
```

NOTE: Do not confuse the address operator with the `&` symbol used when defining a reference variable.

Program 9-1 demonstrates the use of the address operator to display the address, size, and contents of a variable.

Program 9-1

```
 1   // This program uses the & operator to determine a variable's
 2   // address and the sizeof operator to determine its size.
 3   #include <iostream>
 4   using namespace std;
 5
 6   int main()
 7   {
 8      int x = 25;
 9
10      cout << "The address of x is " << &x << endl;
11      cout << "The size of x is " << sizeof(x) << " bytes\n";
12      cout << "The value in x is " << x << endl;
13      return 0;
14   }
```

Program Output
```
The address of x is 0x8f05
The size of x is 4 bytes
The value in x is 25
```

 NOTE: The address of the variable x is displayed in hexadecimal. This is the way addresses are normally shown in C++.

9.2 Pointer Variables

CONCEPT: *Pointer variables*, which are often just called *pointers*, are designed to hold memory addresses. With pointer variables you can indirectly manipulate data stored in other variables.

A *pointer variable*, which often is just called a *pointer*, is a special variable that holds a memory address. Just as int variables are designed to hold integers, and double variables are designed to hold floating-point numbers, pointer variables are designed to hold memory addresses.

Memory addresses identify specific locations in the computer's memory. Because a pointer variable holds a memory address, it can be used to hold the location of some other piece of data. This should give you a clue as to why it is called a pointer: It "points" to some piece of data that is stored in the computer's memory. Pointer variables also allow you to work with the data that they point to.

We've already used memory addresses in this book to work with data. Recall from Chapter 6 that when we pass an array as an argument to a function, we are actually passing the array's beginning address. For example, suppose we have an array named numbers and we call the showValues function as shown here.

```
const int SIZE = 5;
int numbers[SIZE] = { 1, 2, 3, 4, 5 };
showValues(numbers, SIZE);
```

In this code we are passing the name of the array, numbers, and its size as arguments to the showValues function. Here is the definition for the showValues function:

```
void showValues(int values[], int size)
{
    for (int count = 0; count < size; count++)
        cout << values[count] << endl;
}
```

In the function, the values parameter receives the address of the numbers array. It works like a pointer because it "points" to the numbers array, as shown in Figure 9-2.

Figure 9-2

```
numbers array
```

Inside the showValues function, anything that is done to the values parameter is actually done to the numbers array. We can say that the values parameter references the numbers array.

Also recall from Chapter 6 that we discussed reference variables. A reference variable acts as an alias for another variable. It is called a reference variable because it references another variable in the program. Anything that you do to the reference variable is actually done to the variable it references. For example, suppose we have the variable jellyDonuts and we pass the variable to the getOrder function, as shown here:

```
int jellyDonuts;
getOrder(jellyDonuts);
```

Here is the definition for the getOrder function:

```
void getOrder(int &donuts)
{
    cout << "How many doughnuts do you want? ";
    cin >> donuts;
}
```

In the function, the donuts parameter is a reference variable, and it receives the address of the jellyDonuts variable. It works like a pointer because it "points" to the jellyDonuts variable as shown in Figure 9-3.

Inside the getOrder function, the donuts parameter references the jellyDonuts variable. Anything that is done to the donuts parameter is actually done to the jellyDonuts variable. When the user enters a value, the cin statement uses the donuts reference variable to indirectly store the value in the jellyDonuts variable.

Notice that the connection between the donuts reference variable and the jellyDonuts argument is automatically established by C++ when the function is called. When you are writing this code, you don't have go to the trouble of finding the memory address of the

Figure 9-3

jellyDonuts variable

```
getOrder(jellyDonuts);
```

address

```
void getOrder(int &donuts)
{
    cout << "How many doughnuts do you want? ";
    cin >> donuts;
}
```

jellyDonuts variable and then properly storing that address in the donuts reference variable. When you are storing a value in the donuts variable, you don't have to specify that the value should actually be stored in the jellyDonuts variable. C++ handles all of that automatically.

In C++, pointer variables are yet another mechanism for using memory addresses to work with pieces of data. Pointer variables are similar to reference variables, but pointer variables operate at a lower level. By this, I mean that C++ does not automatically do as much work for you with pointer variables as it does with reference variables. In order to make a pointer variable reference another item in memory, you have to write code that fetches the memory address of that item and assigns the address to the pointer variable. Also, when you use a pointer variable to store a value in the memory location that the pointer references, your code has to specify that the value should be stored in the location referenced by the pointer variable, and not in the pointer variable itself.

Because reference variables are easier to work with, you might be wondering why you would ever use pointers at all. In C++, pointers are useful, and even necessary, for many operations. One such operation is dynamic memory allocation. When you are writing a program that will need to work with an unknown amount of data, dynamic memory allocation allows you to create variables, arrays, and more complex data structures in memory while the program is running. We will discuss dynamic memory allocation in greater detail in this chapter. Pointers are also very useful in algorithms that manipulate arrays and C-strings. In object-oriented programming, which you will learn about in Chapters 13, 14, and 15, pointers are very useful for creating and working with objects and for sharing access to those objects.

Creating and Using Pointer Variables

The definition of a pointer variable looks pretty much like any other definition. Here is an example:

```
int *ptr;
```

The asterisk in front of the variable name indicates that ptr is a pointer variable. The int data type indicates that ptr can be used to hold the address of an integer variable. The definition statement above would read "ptr is a pointer to an int."

 NOTE: In this definition, the word int does not mean that ptr is an integer variable. It means that ptr can hold the address of an integer variable. Remember, pointers only hold one kind of value: an address.

Some programmers prefer to define pointers with the asterisk next to the type name, rather than the variable name. For example, the previous definition shown above could be written as:

```
int* ptr;
```

This style of definition might visually reinforce the fact that ptr's data type is not int, but pointer-to-int. Both definition styles are correct.

Program 9-2 demonstrates a very simple usage of a pointer: storing and printing the address of another variable.

Program 9-2

```
 1   // This program stores the address of a variable in a pointer.
 2   #include <iostream>
 3   using namespace std;
 4
 5   int main()
 6   {
 7      int x = 25;     // int variable
 8      int *ptr;       // Pointer variable, can point to an int
 9
10      ptr = &x;       // Store the address of x in ptr
11      cout << "The value in x is " << x << endl;
12      cout << "The address of x is " << ptr << endl;
13      return 0;
14   }
```

Program Output
```
The value in x is 25
The address of x is 0x7e00
```

In Program 9-2, two variables are defined: x and ptr. The variable x is an int and the variable ptr is a pointer to an int. The variable x is initialized with the value 25. The variable ptr is assigned the address of x with the following statement in line 10:

```
ptr = &x;
```

Figure 9-4 illustrates the relationship between `ptr` and `x`.

Figure 9-4

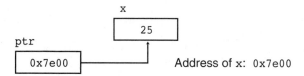

As shown in Figure 9-4, x, which is located at memory address 0x7e00, contains the number 25. `ptr` contains the address 0x7e00. In essence, it "points" to the variable x.

The real benefit of pointers is that they allow you to indirectly access and modify the variable being pointed to. In Program 9-2, for instance, `ptr` could be used to change the contents of the variable x. This is done with the *indirection operator*, which is an asterisk (*). When the indirection operator is placed in front of a pointer variable name, it *dereferences* the pointer. When you are working with a dereferenced pointer, you are actually working with the value the pointer is pointing to. This is demonstrated in Program 9-3.

Program 9-3

```
 1   // This program demonstrates the use of the indirection operator.
 2   #include <iostream>
 3   using namespace std;
 4
 5   int main()
 6   {
 7       int x = 25;     // int variable
 8       int *ptr;       // Pointer variable, can point to an int
 9
10       ptr = &x;       // Store the address of x in ptr
11
12       // Use both x and ptr to display the value in x.
13       cout << "Here is the value in x, printed twice:\n";
14       cout << x << endl;      // Displays the contents of x
15       cout << *ptr << endl;   // Displays the contents of x
16
17       // Assign 100 to the location pointed to by ptr. This
18       // will actually assign 100 to x.
19       *ptr = 100;
20
21       // Use both x and ptr to display the value in x.
22       cout << "Once again, here is the value in x:\n";
23       cout << x << endl;      // Displays the contents of x
24       cout << *ptr << endl;   // Displays the contents of x
25       return 0;
26   }
```

(program output continues)

Program 9-3   *(continued)*

Program Output
```
Here is the value in x, printed twice:
25
25
Once again, here is the value in x:
100
100
```

Take a closer look at the statement in line 10:

```
ptr = &x;
```

This statement assigns the address of the x variable to the ptr variable. Now look at line 15:

```
cout << *ptr << endl;   // Displays the contents of x
```

When you apply the indirection operator (*) to a pointer variable, you are working, not with the pointer variable itself, but with the item it points to. Because this statement sends the expression *ptr to the cout object, it does not display the value in ptr, but the value that ptr points to. Since ptr points to the x variable, this statement displays the contents of the x variable.

Suppose the statement did not use the indirection operator. Suppose that statement had been written as:

```
cout << ptr << endl;    // Displays an address
```

Because the indirection operator is not applied to ptr in this statement, it works directly with the ptr variable. This statement would display the address that is stored in ptr.

Now take a look at the following statement, which appears in line 19:

```
*ptr = 100;
```

Notice the indirection operator being used with ptr. That means the statement is not affecting ptr, but the item that ptr points to. This statement assigns 100 to the item ptr points to, which is the x variable. After this statement executes, 100 will be stored in the x variable.

Program 9-4 demonstrates that pointers can point to different variables.

Program 9-4

```
 1   // This program demonstrates a pointer variable referencing
 2   // different variables.
 3   #include <iostream>
 4   using namespace std;
 5
 6   int main()
 7   {
 8      int x = 25, y = 50, z = 75;   // Three int variables
 9      int *ptr;                     // Pointer variable
10
```

```
11        // Display the contents of x, y, and z.
12        cout << "Here are the values of x, y, and z:\n";
13        cout << x << " " << y << " " << z << endl;
14
15        // Use the pointer to manipulate x, y, and z.
16
17        ptr = &x;       // Store the address of x in ptr.
18        *ptr += 100;    // Add 100 to the value in x.
19
20        ptr = &y;       // Store the address of y in ptr.
21        *ptr += 100;    // Add 100 to the value in y.
22
23        ptr = &z;       // Store the address of z in ptr.
24        *ptr += 100;    // Add 100 to the value in z.
25
26        // Display the contents of x, y, and z.
27        cout << "Once again, here are the values of x, y, and z:\n";
28        cout << x << " " << y << " " << z << endl;
29        return 0;
30   }
```

Program Output
```
Here are the values of x, y, and z:
25 50 75
Once again, here are the values of x, y, and z:
125 150 175
```

Take a closer look at the statement in line 17:

```
ptr = &x;
```

This statement assigns the address of the x variable to the ptr variable. Now look at line 18:

```
*ptr += 100;
```

In this statement notice that the indirection operator (*) is used with the ptr variable. When we apply the indirection operator to ptr, we are working, not with ptr, but with the item that ptr points to. When this statement executes, ptr is pointing at x, so the statement in line 18 adds 100 to the contents of x. Then the following statement, in line 20, executes:

```
ptr = &y;
```

This statement assigns the address of the y variable to the ptr variable. After this statement executes, ptr is no longer pointing at x. Rather, it will be pointing at y. The statement in line 21, shown here, adds 100 to the y variable.

```
*ptr += 100;
```

These steps are repeated with the z variable in lines 23 and 24.

NOTE: So far you've seen three different uses of the asterisk in C++:

- As the multiplication operator, in statements such as
  ```
  distance = speed * time;
  ```

- In the definition of a pointer variable, such as
  ```
  int *ptr;
  ```

- As the indirection operator, in statements such as
  ```
  *ptr = 100;
  ```

9.3 The Relationship Between Arrays and Pointers

CONCEPT: Array names can be used as constant pointers, and pointers can be used as array names.

You learned in Chapter 7 that an array name, without brackets and a subscript, actually represents the starting address of the array. This means that an array name is really a pointer. Program 9-5 illustrates this by showing an array name being used with the indirection operator.

Program 9-5

```
 1   // This program shows an array name being dereferenced with the *
 2   // operator.
 3   #include <iostream>
 4   using namespace std;
 5
 6   int main()
 7   {
 8      short numbers[] = {10, 20, 30, 40, 50};
 9
10      cout << "The first element of the array is ";
11      cout << *numbers << endl;
12      return 0;
13   }
```

Program Output
```
The first element of the array is 10
```

Because numbers works like a pointer to the starting address of the array, the first element is retrieved when numbers is dereferenced. So how could the entire contents of an array be retrieved using the indirection operator? Remember, array elements are stored together in memory, as illustrated in Figure 9-5.

It makes sense that if numbers is the address of numbers[0], values could be added to numbers to get the addresses of the other elements in the array. It's important to know, however, that pointers do not work like regular variables when used in mathematical statements. In C++, when you add a value to a pointer, you are actually adding that value *times the size of the data type being referenced by the pointer.* In other words, if you add

Figure 9-5

one to numbers, you are actually adding 1 * sizeof(short) to numbers. If you add two to numbers, the result is numbers + 2 * sizeof(short), and so forth. On a PC, this means the following are true, because short integers typically use two bytes:

```
*(numbers + 1) is actually *(numbers + 1 * 2)
*(numbers + 2) is actually *(numbers + 2 * 2)
*(numbers + 3) is actually *(numbers + 3 * 2)
```

and so forth.

This automatic conversion means that an element in an array can be retrieved by using its subscript or by adding its subscript to a pointer to the array. If the expression *numbers, which is the same as *(numbers + 0), retrieves the first element in the array, then *(numbers + 1) retrieves the second element. Likewise, *(numbers + 2) retrieves the third element, and so forth. Figure 9-6 shows the equivalence of subscript notation and pointer notation.

Figure 9-6

 NOTE: The parentheses are critical when adding values to pointers. The * operator has precedence over the + operator, so the expression *number + 1 is not equivalent to *(number + 1). *number + 1 adds one to the contents of the first element of the array, while *(number + 1) adds one to the address in number, then dereferences it.

Program 9-6 shows the entire contents of the array being accessed, using pointer notation.

Program 9-6

```
1   // This program processes an array using pointer notation.
2   #include <iostream>
3   using namespace std;
4
```

(program continues)

Program 9-6   *(continued)*

```
 5   int main()
 6   {
 7      const int SIZE = 5;   // Size of the array
 8      int numbers[SIZE];    // Array of integers
 9      int count;            // Counter variable
10
11      // Get values to store in the array.
12      // Use pointer notation instead of subscripts.
13      cout << "Enter " << SIZE << " numbers: ";
14      for (count = 0; count < SIZE; count++)
15         cin >> *(numbers + count);
16
17      // Display the values in the array.
18      // Use pointer notation instead of subscripts.
19      cout << "Here are the numbers you entered:\n";
20      for (count = 0; count < SIZE; count++)
21         cout << *(numbers + count)<< " ";
22      cout << endl;
23      return 0;
24   }
```

Program Output with Example Input Shown in Bold
```
Enter 5 numbers: 5 10 15 20 25 [Enter]
Here are the numbers you entered:
5 10 15 20 25
```

When working with arrays, remember the following rule:

array[index] is equivalent to *(*array* + index)

 WARNING! Remember that C++ performs no bounds checking with arrays. When stepping through an array with a pointer, it's possible to give the pointer an address outside of the array.

To demonstrate just how close the relationship is between array names and pointers, look at Program 9-7. It defines an array of doubles and a double pointer, which is assigned the starting address of the array. Not only is pointer notation then used with the array name, but subscript notation is used with the pointer!

Program 9-7

```
1   // This program uses subscript notation with a pointer variable and
2   // pointer notation with an array name.
3   #include <iostream>
4   #include <iomanip>
5   using namespace std;
6
```

```
 7   int main()
 8   {
 9      const int NUM_COINS = 5;
10      double coins[NUM_COINS] = {0.05, 0.1, 0.25, 0.5, 1.0};
11      double *doublePtr;    // Pointer to a double
12      int count;            // Array index
13
14      // Assign the address of the coins array to doublePtr.
15      doublePtr = coins;
16
17      // Display the contents of the coins array. Use subscripts
18      // with the pointer!
19      cout << "Here are the values in the coins array:\n";
20      for (count = 0; count < NUM_COINS; count++)
21         cout << doublePtr[count] << " ";
22
23      // Display the contents of the array again, but this time
24      // use pointer notation with the array name!
25      cout << "\nAnd here they are again:\n";
26      for (count = 0; count < NUM_COINS; count++)
27         cout << *(coins + count) << " ";
28      cout << endl;
29      return 0;
30   }
```

Program Output
```
Here are the values in the coins array:
0.05 0.1 0.25 0.5 1
And here they are again:
0.05 0.1 0.25 0.5 1
```

Notice that the address operator is not needed when an array's address is assigned to a pointer. Because the name of an array is already an address, use of the & operator would be incorrect. You can, however, use the address operator to get the address of an individual element in an array. For instance, &numbers[1] gets the address of numbers[1]. This technique is used in Program 9-8.

Program 9-8

```
 1   // This program uses the address of each element in the array.
 2   #include <iostream>
 3   #include <iomanip>
 4   using namespace std;
 5
 6   int main()
 7   {
 8      const int NUM_COINS = 5;
 9      double coins[NUM_COINS] = {0.05, 0.1, 0.25, 0.5, 1.0};
10      double *doublePtr; // Pointer to a double
11      int count;         // Array index
12
```

(program continues)

Program 9-8   *(continued)*

```
13      // Use the pointer to display the values in the array.
14      cout << "Here are the values in the coins array:\n";
15      for (count = 0; count < NUM_COINS; count++)
16      {
17         // Get the address of an array element.
18         doublePtr = &coins[count];
19
20         // Display the contents of the element.
21         cout << *doublePtr << " ";
22      }
23      cout << endl;
24      return 0;
25   }
```

Program Output

```
Here are the values in the coins array:
0.05 0.1 0.25 0.5 1
```

The only difference between array names and pointer variables is that you cannot change the address an array name points to. For example, consider the following definitions:

```
double readings[20], totals[20];
double *dptr;
```

These statements are legal:

```
dptr = readings; // Make dptr point to readings.
dptr = totals;   // Make dptr point to totals.
```

But these are illegal:

```
readings = totals;  // ILLEGAL! Cannot change readings.
totals = dptr;      // ILLEGAL! Cannot change totals.
```

Array names are *pointer constants*. You can't make them point to anything but the array they represent.

9.4   Pointer Arithmetic

CONCEPT: Some mathematical operations may be performed on pointers.

The contents of pointer variables may be changed with mathematical statements that perform addition or subtraction. This is demonstrated in Program 9-9. The first loop increments the pointer variable, stepping it through each element of the array. The second loop decrements the pointer, stepping it through the array backward.

Program 9-9

```cpp
1   // This program uses a pointer to display the contents of an array.
2   #include <iostream>
3   using namespace std;
4
5   int main()
6   {
7      const int SIZE = 8;
8      int set[SIZE] = {5, 10, 15, 20, 25, 30, 35, 40};
9      int *numPtr;    // Pointer
10     int count;      // Counter variable for loops
11
12     // Make numPtr point to the set array.
13     numPtr = set;
14
15     // Use the pointer to display the array contents.
16     cout << "The numbers in set are:\n";
17     for (count = 0; count < SIZE; count++)
18     {
19        cout << *numPtr << " ";
20        numPtr++;
21     }
22
23     // Display the array contents in reverse order.
24     cout << "\nThe numbers in set backward are:\n";
25     for (count = 0; count < SIZE; count++)
26     {
27        numPtr--;
28        cout << *numPtr << " ";
29     }
30     return 0;
31  }
```

Program Output
```
The numbers in set are:
5 10 15 20 25 30 35 40
The numbers in set backward are:
40 35 30 25 20 15 10 5
```

NOTE: Because numPtr is a pointer to an integer, the increment operator adds the size of one integer to numPtr, so it points to the next element in the array. Likewise, the decrement operator subtracts the size of one integer from the pointer.

Not all arithmetic operations may be performed on pointers. For example, you cannot multiply or divide a pointer. The following operations are allowable:

- The ++ and -- operators may be used to increment or decrement a pointer variable.
- An integer may be added to or subtracted from a pointer variable. This may be performed with the + and – operators, or the += and –= operators.
- A pointer may be subtracted from another pointer.

9.5   Initializing Pointers

CONCEPT: Pointers may be initialized with the address of an existing object.

Remember that a pointer is designed to point to an object of a specific data type. When a pointer is initialized with an address, it must be the address of an object the pointer can point to. For instance, the following definition of `pint` is legal because `myValue` is an integer:

```cpp
int myValue;
int *pint = &myValue;
```

The following is also legal because `ages` is an array of integers:

```cpp
int ages[20];
int *pint = ages;
```

But the following definition of `pint` is illegal because `myFloat` is not an `int`:

```cpp
float myFloat;
int *pint = &myFloat;    // Illegal!
```

Pointers may be defined in the same statement as other variables of the same type. The following statement defines an integer variable, `myValue`, and then defines a pointer, `pint`, which is initialized with the address of `myValue`:

```cpp
int myValue, *pint = &myValue;
```

And the following statement defines an array, `readings`, and a pointer, `marker`, which is initialized with the address of the first element in the array:

```cpp
double readings[50], *marker = readings;
```

Of course, a pointer can only be initialized with the address of an object that has already been defined. The following is illegal because `pint` is being initialized with the address of an object that does not exist yet:

```cpp
int *pint = &myValue;    // Illegal!
int myValue;
```

 Checkpoint

9.1   Write a statement that displays the address of the variable `count`.

9.2   Write the definition statement for a variable `fltPtr`. The variable should be a pointer to a `float`.

9.3   List three uses of the * symbol in C++.

9.4   What is the output of the following code?

```cpp
int x = 50, y = 60, z = 70;
int *ptr;

cout << x << "  " << y << "  " << z << endl;
ptr = &x;
```

```
*ptr *= 10;
ptr = &y;
*ptr *= 5;
ptr = &z;
*ptr *= 2;
cout << x << "  " << y << "  " << z << endl;
```

9.5   Rewrite the following loop so it uses pointer notation (with the indirection opera-
       tor) instead of subscript notation.

```
for (int x = 0; x < 100; x++)
   cout << arr[x] << endl;
```

9.6   Assume `ptr` is a pointer to an `int`, and holds the address 12000. On a system
       with 4-byte integers, what address will be in `ptr` after the following statement?

```
ptr += 10;
```

9.7   Assume `pint` is a pointer variable. Is each of the following statements valid or
       invalid? If any is invalid, why?
       A) `pint++;`
       B) `--pint;`
       C) `pint /= 2;`
       D) `pint *= 4;`
       E) `pint += x;   // Assume x is an int.`

9.8   Is each of the following definitions valid or invalid? If any is invalid, why?
       A) `int ivar;`
          `int *iptr = &ivar;`
       B) `int ivar, *iptr = &ivar;`
       C) `float fvar;`
          `int *iptr = &fvar;`
       D) `int nums[50], *iptr = nums;`
       E) `int *iptr = &ivar;`
          `int ivar;`

9.6   Comparing Pointers

CONCEPT: If one address comes before another address in memory, the first address
is considered "less than" the second. C++'s relational operators may be
used to compare pointer values.

Pointers may be compared by using any of C++'s relational operators:

> < == != >= <=

In an array, all the elements are stored in consecutive memory locations, so the address of
element 1 is greater than the address of element 0. This is illustrated in Figure 9-7.

Figure 9-7

An array of five integers

arr[0]	arr[1]	arr[2]	arr[3]	arr[4]

0x5A00   0x5A04   0x5A08   0x5A0C   0x5A10
(Addresses)

Because the addresses grow larger for each subsequent element in the array, the following `if` statements are all true:

```
if (&arr[1] > &arr[0])
if (arr < &arr[4])
if (arr == &arr[0])
if (&arr[2] != &arr[3])
```

NOTE: Comparing two pointers is not the same as comparing the values the two pointers point to. For example, the following `if` statement compares the addresses stored in the pointer variables `ptr1` and `ptr2`:

```
if (ptr1 < ptr2)
```

The following statement, however, compares the values that `ptr1` and `ptr2` point to:

```
if (*ptr1 < *ptr2)
```

The capability of comparing addresses gives you another way to be sure a pointer does not go beyond the boundaries of an array. Program 9-10 initializes the pointer `nums` with the starting address of the array `set`. The `nums` pointer is then stepped through the array `set` until the address it contains is equal to the address of the last element of the array. Then the pointer is stepped backward through the array until it points to the first element.

Program 9-10

```cpp
1   // This program uses a pointer to display the contents
2   // of an integer array.
3   #include <iostream>
4   using namespace std;
5
6   int main()
7   {
8       int set[8] = {5, 10, 15, 20, 25, 30, 35, 40};
9       int *nums = set;     // Make nums point to set
10
11      // Display the numbers in the array.
12      cout << "The numbers in set are:\n";
13      cout << *nums << " ";   // Display first element
```

```
14      while (nums < &set[7])
15      {
16         // Advance nums to point to the next element.
17         nums++;
18         // Display the value pointed to by nums.
19         cout << *nums << " ";
20      }
21
22      // Display the numbers in reverse order.
23      cout << "\nThe numbers in set backward are:\n";
24      cout << *nums << " ";    // Display first element
25      while (nums > set)
26      {
27         // Move backward to the previous element.
28         nums--;
29         // Display the value pointed to by nums.
30         cout << *nums << " ";
31      }
32      return 0;
33   }
```

Program Output

```
The numbers in set are:
5 10 15 20 25 30 35 40
The numbers in set backward are:
40 35 30 25 20 15 10 5
```

9.7 Pointers as Function Parameters

CONCEPT: A pointer can be used as a function parameter. It gives the function access to the original argument, much like a reference parameter does.

In Chapter 6 you were introduced to the concept of reference variables being used as function parameters. A reference variable acts as an alias to the original variable used as an argument. This gives the function access to the original argument variable, allowing it to change the variable's contents. When a variable is passed into a reference parameter, the argument is said to be passed by reference.

Another way to pass an argument by reference is to use a pointer variable as the parameter. Admittedly, reference variables are much easier to work with than pointers. Reference variables hide all the "mechanics" of dereferencing and indirection. You should still learn to use pointers as function arguments, however, because some tasks, especially when you are dealing with strings, are best done with pointers.* Also, the C++ library has many functions that use pointers as parameters.

---

* It is also important to learn this technique in case you ever need to write a C program. In C, the only way to pass a variable by reference is to use a pointer.

Here is the definition of a function that uses a pointer parameter:

```
void doubleValue(int *val)
{
    *val *= 2;
}
```

The purpose of this function is to double the variable pointed to by `val` with the following statement:

```
*val *= 2;
```

When `val` is dereferenced, the `*=` operator works on the variable pointed to by `val`. This statement multiplies the original variable, whose address is stored in `val`, by two. Of course, when the function is called, the address of the variable that is to be doubled must be used as the argument, not the variable itself. Here is an example of a call to the `doubleValue` function:

```
doubleValue(&number);
```

This statement uses the address operator (`&`) to pass the address of `number` into the `val` parameter. After the function executes, the contents of `number` will have been multiplied by two. The use of this function is illustrated in Program 9-11.

Program 9-11

```
1   // This program uses two functions that accept addresses of
2   // variables as arguments.
3   #include <iostream>
4   using namespace std;
5
6   // Function prototypes
7   void getNumber(int *);
8   void doubleValue(int *);
9
10  int main()
11  {
12      int number;
13
14      // Call getNumber and pass the address of number.
15      getNumber(&number);
16
17      // Call doubleValue and pass the address of number.
18      doubleValue(&number);
19
20      // Display the value in number.
21      cout << "That value doubled is " << number << endl;
22      return 0;
23  }
24
```

```
25   //*************************************************************
26   // Definition of getNumber. The parameter, input, is a pointer. *
27   // This function asks the user for a number. The value entered   *
28   // is stored in the variable pointed to by input.                *
29   //*************************************************************
30
31   void getNumber(int *input)
32   {
33      cout << "Enter an integer number: ";
34      cin >> *input;
35   }
36
37   //*************************************************************
38   // Definition of doubleValue. The parameter, val, is a pointer. *
39   // This function multiplies the variable pointed to by val by    *
40   // two.                                                          *
41   //*************************************************************
42
43   void doubleValue(int *val)
44   {
45      *val *= 2;
46   }
```

Program Output with Example Input Shown in Bold
Enter an integer number: **10 [Enter]**
That value doubled is 20

Program 9-11 has two functions that use pointers as parameters. Notice the function pro totypes:

```
void getNumber(int *);
void doubleValue(int *);
```

Each one uses the notation int * to indicate the parameter is a pointer to an int. As with all other types of parameters, it isn't necessary to specify the name of the variable in the prototype. The * is required, though.

The getNumber function asks the user to enter an integer value. The following cin state-ment, in line 34, stores the value entered by the user in memory:

```
cin >> *input;
```

The indirection operator causes the value entered by the user to be stored, not in input, but in the variable pointed to by input.

 WARNING! It's critical that the indirection operator be used in the statement above. Without it, cin would store the value entered by the user in input, as if the value were an address. If this happens, input will no longer point to the number variable in function main. Subsequent use of the pointer will result in erroneous, if not disastrous, results.

When the `getNumber` function is called in line 15, the address of the `number` variable in function `main` is passed as the argument. After the function executes, the value entered by the user is stored in `number`. Next, the `doubleValue` function is called in line 18, with the address of `number` passed as the argument. This causes `number` to be multiplied by two.

Pointer variables can also be used to accept array addresses as arguments. Either subscript or pointer notation may then be used to work with the contents of the array. This is demonstrated in Program 9-12.

Program 9-12

```cpp
 1   // This program demonstrates that a pointer may be used as a
 2   // parameter to accept the address of an array.
 3   #include <iostream>
 4   #include <iomanip>
 5   using namespace std;
 6
 7   // Function prototypes
 8   void getSales(double *, int);
 9   double totalSales(double *, int);
10
11   int main()
12   {
13      const int QTRS = 4;
14      double sales[QTRS];
15
16      // Get the sales data for all quarters.
17      getSales(sales, QTRS);
18
19      // Set the numeric output formatting.
20      cout << fixed << showpoint << setprecision(2);
21
22      // Display the total sales for the year.
23      cout << "The total sales for the year are $";
24      cout << totalSales(sales, QTRS) << endl;
25      return 0;
26   }
27
28   //*****************************************************************
29   // Definition of getSales. This function uses a pointer to accept *
30   // the address of an array of doubles. The function asks the user *
31   // to enter sales figures and stores them in the array.           *
32   //*****************************************************************
33   void getSales(double *arr, int size)
34   {
35      for (int count = 0; count < size; count++)
36      {
37         cout << "Enter the sales figure for quarter ";
38         cout << (count + 1) << ": ";
39         cin >> arr[count];
40      }
41   }
42
```

```
43  //************************************************************
44  // Definition of totalSales. This function uses a pointer to    *
45  // accept the address of an array. The function returns the total *
46  // of the elements in the array.                                  *
47  //************************************************************
48  double totalSales(double *arr, int size)
49  {
50      double sum = 0.0;
51
52      for (int count = 0; count < size; count++)
53      {
54          sum += *arr;
55          arr++;
56      }
57      return sum;
58  }
```

Program Output with Example Input Shown in Bold
Enter the sales figure for quarter 1: **10263.98 [Enter]**
Enter the sales figure for quarter 2: **12369.69 [Enter]**
Enter the sales figure for quarter 3: **11542.13 [Enter]**
Enter the sales figure for quarter 4: **14792.06 [Enter]**
The total sales for the year are $48967.86

Notice that in the getSales function in Program 9-12, even though the parameter arr is defined as a pointer, subscript notation is used in the cin statement in line 39:

```
cin >> arr[count];
```

In the totalSales function, arr is used with the indirection operator in line 54:

```
sum += *arr;
```

And in line 55, the address in arr is incremented to point to the next element:

```
arr++;
```

> **NOTE:** The two previous statements could be combined into the following statement:
>
> ```
> sum += *arr++;
> ```
>
> The * operator will first dereference arr, then the ++ operator will increment the address in arr.

Pointers to Constants

You have seen how an item's address can be passed into a pointer parameter, and how the pointer can be used to modify the item that was passed as an argument. Sometimes it is necessary to pass the address of a const item into a pointer. When this is the case, the pointer must be defined as a pointer to a const item. For example, consider the following array definition:

```
const int SIZE = 6;
const double payRates[SIZE] = { 18.55, 17.45,
                                12.85, 14.97,
                                10.35, 18.89 };
```

In this code, payRates is an array of const doubles. This means that each element in the array is a const double, and the compiler will not allow us to write code that changes the array's contents. If we want to pass the payRates array into a pointer parameter, the parameter must be declared as a pointer to const double. The following function shows such an example:

```
void displayPayRates(const double *rates, int size)
{
    // Set numeric output formatting.
    cout << setprecision(2) << fixed << showpoint;

    // Display all the pay rates.
    for (int count = 0; count < size; count++)
    {
        cout << "Pay rate for employee " << (count + 1)
             << " is $" << *(rates + count) << endl;
    }
}
```

In the function header, notice that the rates parameter is defined as a pointer to const double. It should be noted that the word const is applied to the thing that rates points to, not rates itself. This is illustrated in Figure 9-8.

Figure 9-8

Because rates is a pointer to a const, the compiler will not allow us to write code that changes the thing that rates points to.

In passing the address of a constant into a pointer variable, the variable must be defined as a pointer to a constant. If the word const had been left out of the definition of the rates parameter, a compiler error would have resulted.

Passing a Nonconstant Argument into a Pointer to a Constant

Although a constant's address can be passed only to a pointer to const, a pointer to const can also receive the address of a nonconstant item. For example, look at Program 9-13.

Program 9-13

```cpp
1  // This program demonstrates a pointer to const parameter
2  #include <iostream>
3  using namespace std;
4
5  void displayValues(const int *, int);
6
7  int main()
8  {
9     // Array sizes
10    const int SIZE = 6;
11
12    // Define an array of const ints.
13    const int array1[SIZE] = { 1, 2, 3, 4, 5, 6 };
14
15    // Define an array of nonconst ints.
16    int array2[SIZE] = { 2, 4, 6, 8, 10, 12 };
17
18    // Display the contents of the const array.
19    displayValues(array1, SIZE);
20
21    // Display the contents of the nonconst array.
22    displayValues(array2, SIZE);
23    return 0;
24 }
25
26 //*************************************************
27 // The displayValues function uses a pointer to    *
28 // parameter to display the contents of an array.  *
29 //*************************************************
30
31 void displayValues(const int *numbers, int size)
32 {
33    // Display all the values.
34    for (int count = 0; count < size; count++)
35    {
36       cout << *(numbers + count) << " ";
37    }
38    cout << endl;
39 }
```

Program Output
```
1 2 3 4 5 6
2 4 6 8 10 12
```

 NOTE: When you are writing a function that uses a pointer parameter, and the function is not intended to change the data the parameter points to, it is always a good idea to make the parameter a pointer to const. Not only will this protect you from writing code in the function that accidentally changes the argument, but the function will be able to accept the addresses of both constant and nonconstant arguments.

Constant Pointers

In the previous section we discussed pointers to `const`. That is, pointers that point to `const` data. You can also use the `const` key word to define a constant pointer. Here is the difference between a pointer to `const` and a `const` pointer:

- A pointer to `const` points to a constant item. The data that the pointer points to cannot change, but the pointer itself can change.
- With a `const` pointer, it is the pointer itself that is constant. Once the pointer is initialized with an address, it cannot point to anything else.

The following code shows an example of a `const` pointer.

```
int value = 22;
int * const ptr = &value;
```

Notice in the definition of `ptr` the word `const` appears after the asterisk. This means that `ptr` is a `const` pointer. This is illustrated in Figure 9-9. In the code, `ptr` is initialized with the address of the `value` variable. Because `ptr` is a constant pointer, a compiler error will result if we write code that makes `ptr` point to anything else. An error will not result, however, if we use `ptr` to change the contents of `value`. This is because `value` is not constant, and `ptr` is not a pointer to `const`.

Figure 9-9

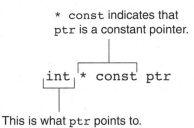

Constant pointers must be initialized with a starting value, as shown in the previous example code. If a constant pointer is used as a function parameter, the parameter will be initialized with the address that is passed as an argument into it, and cannot be changed to point to anything else while the function is executing. Here is an example that attempts to violate this rule:

```
void setToZero(int * const ptr)
{
    ptr = 0;  // ERROR!! Cannot change the contents of ptr.
}
```

This function's parameter, `ptr`, is a `const` pointer. It will not compile because we cannot have code in the function that changes the contents of `ptr`. However, `ptr` does not point to a `const`, so we can have code that changes the data that `ptr` points to. Here is an example of the function that will compile:

```
void setToZero(int * const ptr)
{
    *ptr = 0;
}
```

Although the parameter is const pointer, we can call the function multiple times with different arguments. The following code will successfully pass the addresses of x, y, and z to the setToZero function:

```
int x, y, z;
// Set x, y, and z to 0.
setToZero(&x);
setToZero(&y);
setToZero(&z);
```

Constant Pointers to Constants

So far, when using const with pointers we've seen pointers to constants and we've seen constant pointers. You can also have constant pointers to constants. For example, look at the following code:

```
int value = 22;
const int * const ptr = &value;
```

In this code ptr is a const pointer to a const int. Notice the word const appears before int, indicating that ptr points to a const int, and it appears after the asterisk, indicating that ptr is a constant pointer. This is illustrated in Figure 9-10.

Figure 9-10

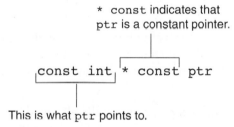

In the code, ptr is initialized with the address of value. Because ptr is a const pointer, we cannot write code that makes ptr point to anything else. Because ptr is a pointer to const, we cannot use it to change the contents of value. The following code shows one more example of a const pointer to a const. This is another version of the displayValues function in Program 9-13.

```
void displayValues(const int * const numbers, int size)
{
    // Display all the values.
    for (int count = 0; count < size; count++)
    {
        cout << *(numbers + count) << " ";
    }
    cout << endl;
}
```

In this code, the parameter numbers is a const pointer to a const int. Although we can call the function with different arguments, the function itself cannot change what numbers points to, and it cannot use numbers to change the contents of an argument.

9.8 Focus on Software Engineering: Dynamic Memory Allocation

> **CONCEPT:** Variables may be created and destroyed while a program is running.

As long as you know how many variables you will need during the execution of a program, you can define those variables up front. For example, a program to calculate the area of a rectangle will need three variables: one for the rectangle's length, one for the rectangle's width, and one to hold the area. If you are writing a program to compute the payroll for 30 employees, you'll probably create an array of 30 elements to hold the amount of pay for each person.

But what about those times when you don't know how many variables you need? For instance, suppose you want to write a test-averaging program that will average any number of tests. Obviously the program would be very versatile, but how do you store the individual test scores in memory if you don't know how many variables to define? Quite simply, you allow the program to create its own variables "on the fly." This is called *dynamic memory allocation*, and is only possible through the use of pointers.

To dynamically allocate memory means that a program, while running, asks the computer to set aside a chunk of unused memory large enough to hold a variable of a specific data type. Let's say a program needs to create an integer variable. It will make a request to the computer that it allocate enough bytes to store an `int`. When the computer fills this request, it finds and sets aside a chunk of unused memory large enough for the variable. It then gives the program the starting address of the chunk of memory. The program can only access the newly allocated memory through its address, so a pointer is required to use those bytes.

The way a C++ program requests dynamically allocated memory is through the `new` operator. Assume a program has a pointer to an `int` defined as

```
int *iptr;
```

Here is an example of how this pointer may be used with the `new` operator:

```
iptr = new int;
```

This statement is requesting that the computer allocate enough memory for a new `int` variable. The operand of the `new` operator is the data type of the variable being created. Once the statement executes, `iptr` will contain the address of the newly allocated memory. This is illustrated in Figure 9-11. A value may be stored in this new variable by dereferencing the pointer:

```
*iptr = 25;
```

Any other operation may be performed on the new variable by simply using the dereferenced pointer. Here are some example statements:

```
cout << *iptr;      // Display the contents of the new variable.
cin >> *iptr;       // Let the user input a value.
total += *iptr;     // Use the new variable in a computation.
```

Figure 9-11

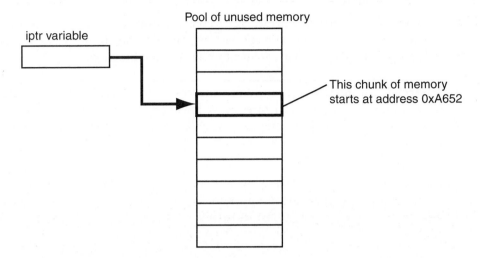

Although the statements above illustrate the use of the new operator, there's little purpose in dynamically allocating a single variable. A more practical use of the new operator is to dynamically create an array. Here is an example of how a 100-element array of integers may be allocated:

```
iptr = new int[100];
```

VideoNote

Dynamically
Allocating an
Array

Once the array is created, the pointer may be used with subscript notation to access it. For instance, the following loop could be used to store the value 1 in each element:

```
for (int count = 0; count < 100; count++)
    iptr[count] = 1;
```

But what if there isn't enough free memory to accommodate the request? What if the program asks for a chunk large enough to hold a 100,000-element array of floats, and that much memory isn't available? When memory cannot be dynamically allocated, C++ throws an exception and terminates the program. *Throwing an exception* means the program signals that an error has occurred.

Programs created with older C++ compilers behave differently when memory cannot be dynamically allocated. Under older compilers, the new operator returns the address 0, or NULL when it fails to allocate the requested amount of memory. (NULL is a named constant, defined in the iostream file, that stands for address 0.) A program created with an older compiler should always check to see if the new operator returns NULL, as shown in the following code:

```
iptr = new int[100];
if (iptr == NULL)
{
    cout << "Error allocating memory!\n";
    return;
}
```

NOTE: A pointer that contains the address 0 is called a *null pointer.*

The `if` statement determines whether `iptr` points to address 0. If it does, then the `new` operator was unable to allocate enough memory for the array. In this case, an error message is displayed and the `return` statement terminates the function.

 WARNING! The address 0 is considered an unusable address. Most computers store special operating system data structures in the lower areas of memory. Anytime you use the `new` operator with an older compiler, you should always test the pointer for the `NULL` address before you use it.

When a program is finished using a dynamically allocated chunk of memory, it should release it for future use. The `delete` operator is used to free memory that was allocated with `new`. Here is an example of how `delete` is used to free a single variable, pointed to by `iptr`:

```
delete iptr;
```

If `iptr` points to a dynamically allocated array, the `[]` symbol must be placed between `delete` and `iptr`:

```
delete [] iptr;
```

 WARNING! Only use pointers with `delete` that were previously used with `new`. If you use a pointer with `delete` that does not reference dynamically allocated memory, unexpected problems could result!

Program 9-14 demonstrates the use of `new` and `delete`. It asks for sales figures for any number of days. The figures are stored in a dynamically allocated array, and then totaled and averaged.

 Appendix F on the Student CD discusses garbage collection in .NET.

Program 9-14

```cpp
1   // This program totals and averages the sales figures for any
2   // number of days. The figures are stored in a dynamically
3   // allocated array.
4   #include <iostream>
5   #include <iomanip>
6   using namespace std;
7
8   int main()
9   {
10     double *sales,      // To dynamically allocate an array
11            total = 0.0, // Accumulator
12            average;     // To hold average sales
```

```
13       int numDays,          // To hold the number of days of sales
14           count;            // Counter variable
15
16       // Get the number of days of sales.
17       cout << "How many days of sales figures do you wish ";
18       cout << "to process? ";
19       cin >> numDays;
20
21       // Dynamically allocate an array large enough to hold
22       // that many days of sales amounts.
23       sales = new double[numDays];
24
25       // Get the sales figures for each day.
26       cout << "Enter the sales figures below.\n";
27       for (count = 0; count < numDays; count++)
28       {
29          cout << "Day " << (count + 1) << ": ";
30          cin >> sales[count];
31       }
32
33       // Calculate the total sales
34       for (count = 0; count < numDays; count++)
35       {
36          total += sales[count];
37       }
38
39       // Calculate the average sales per day
40       average = total / numDays;
41
42       // Display the results
43       cout << fixed << showpoint << setprecision(2);
44       cout << "\n\nTotal Sales: $" << total << endl;
45       cout << "Average Sales: $" << average << endl;
46
47       // Free dynamically allocated memory
48       delete [] sales;
49       sales = 0;          // Make sales point to null.
50
51       return 0;
52    }
```

Program Output with Example Input Shown in Bold

```
How many days of sales figures do you wish to process? 5 [Enter]
Enter the sales figures below.
Day 1: 898.63 [Enter]
Day 2: 652.32 [Enter]
Day 3: 741.85 [Enter]
Day 4: 852.96 [Enter]
Day 5: 921.37 [Enter]

Total Sales: $4067.13
Average Sales: $813.43
```

The statement in line 23 dynamically allocates memory for an array of doubles, using the value in numDays as the number of elements. The new operator returns the starting address of the chunk of memory, which is assigned to the sales pointer variable. The sales variable is then used throughout the program to store the sales amounts in the array and perform the necessary calculations. In line 48 the delete operator is used to free the allocated memory.

Notice that in line 49 the value 0 is assigned to the sales pointer. It is a good practice to store 0 in a pointer variable after using delete on it. First, it prevents code from inadvertently using the pointer to access the area of memory that was freed. Second, it prevents errors from occurring if delete is accidentally called on the pointer again. The delete operator is designed to have no effect when used on a null pointer.

9.9 Focus on Software Engineering: Returning Pointers from Functions

CONCEPT: Functions can return pointers, but you must be sure the item the pointer references still exists.

Like any other data type, functions may return pointers. For example, the following function locates the null terminator in a string and returns a pointer to it.

```
char *findNull(char *str)
{
    char *ptr = str;

    while (*ptr != '\0')
        ptr++;
    return ptr;
}
```

The char * return type in the function header indicates the function returns a pointer to a char:

```
char *findNull(char *str)
```

When writing functions that return pointers, however, you should take care not to create elusive bugs. For instance, see if you can determine what's wrong with the following function.

```
char *getName()
{
    char name[81];
    cout << "Enter your name: ";
    cin.getline(name, 81);
    return name;
}
```

The problem, of course, is that the function returns a pointer to an array that no longer exists. Because name is defined locally, it is destroyed when the function terminates. Attempting to use the pointer will result in erroneous and unpredictable results.

You should only return a pointer from a function if it is

- A pointer to an item that was passed into the function as an argument
- A pointer to a dynamically allocated chunk of memory

For instance, the following function is acceptable:

```cpp
char *getName(char *name)
{
    cout << "Enter your name: ";
    cin.getline(name, 81);
    return name;
}
```

This function accepts a pointer to the memory location where the user's input is to be stored. Because the pointer references a memory location that was valid prior to the function being called, it is safe to return a pointer to the same location. Here is another acceptable function:

```cpp
char *getName()
{
    char *name;

    name = new char[81];
    cout << "Enter your name: ";
    cin.getline(name, 81);
    return name;
}
```

This function uses the new operator to allocate a section of memory. This memory will remain allocated until the delete operator is used or the program ends, so it's safe to return a pointer to it.

Program 9-15 shows another example. This program uses a function, getRandomNumbers, to get a pointer to an array of random numbers. The function accepts an integer argument that is the number of random numbers in the array. The function dynamically allocates an array, uses the system clock to seed the random number generator, populates the array with random values, and then returns a pointer to the array.

Program 9-15

```cpp
 1  // This program demonstrates a function that returns
 2  // a pointer.
 3  #include <iostream>
 4  #include <cstdlib>   // For rand and srand
 5  #include <ctime>     // For the time function
 6  using namespace std;
 7
 8  // Function prototype
 9  int *getRandomNumbers(int);
10
```

(program continues)

Program 9-15   *(continued)*

```
11   int main()
12   {
13      int *numbers;  // To point to the numbers
14
15      // Get an array of five random numbers.
16      numbers = getRandomNumbers(5);
17
18      // Display the numbers.
19      for (int count = 0; count < 5; count++)
20         cout << numbers[count] << endl;
21
22      // Free the memory.
23      delete [] numbers;
24      numbers = 0;
25      return 0;
26   }
27
28   //**************************************************
29   // The getRandomNumbers function returns a pointer *
30   // to an array of random integers. The parameter   *
31   // indicates the number of numbers requested.      *
32   //**************************************************
33
34   int *getRandomNumbers(int num)
35   {
36      int *arr;    // Array to hold the numbers
37
38      // Return null if num is zero or negative.
39      if (num <= 0)
40         return NULL;
41
42      // Dynamically allocate the array.
43      arr = new int[num];
44
45      // Seed the random number generator by passing
46      // the return value of time(0) to srand.
47      srand( time(0) );
48
49      // Populate the array with random numbers.
50      for (int count = 0; count < num; count++)
51         arr[count] = rand();
52
53      // Return a pointer to the array.
54      return arr;
55   }
```

Program Output

```
2712
9656
24493
12483
7633
```

In the Spotlight

Suppose you are developing a program that works with arrays of integers, and you find that you frequently need to duplicate the arrays. Rather than rewriting the array-duplicating code each time you need it, you decide to write a function that accepts an array and its size as arguments, creates a new array that is a copy of the argument array, and returns a pointer to the new array. The function will work as follows:

Accept an array and its size as arguments.
Dynamically allocate a new array that is the same size as the argument array.
Copy the elements of the argument array to the new array.
Return a pointer to the new array.

Program 9-16 demonstrates the function, which is named `duplicateArray`.

Program 9-16

```
 1  // This program uses a function to duplicate
 2  // an int array of any size.
 3  #include <iostream>
 4  using namespace std;
 5
 6  // Function prototype
 7  int *duplicateArray(const int *, int);
 8  void displayArray(int[], int);
 9
10  int main()
11  {
12     // Define constants for the array sizes.
13     const int SIZE1 = 5, SIZE2 = 7, SIZE3 = 10;
14
15     // Define three arrays of different sizes.
16     int array1[SIZE1] = { 100, 200, 300, 400, 500 };
17     int array2[SIZE2] = { 10, 20, 30, 40, 50, 60, 70 };
18     int array3[SIZE3] = { 1, 2, 3, 4, 5, 6, 7, 8, 9, 10 };
19
20     // Define three pointers for the duplicate arrays.
21     int *dup1, *dup2, *dup3;
22
23     // Duplicate the arrays.
24     dup1 = duplicateArray(array1, SIZE1);
25     dup2 = duplicateArray(array2, SIZE2);
26     dup3 = duplicateArray(array3, SIZE3);
27
28     // Display the original arrays.
29     cout << "Here are the original array contents:\n";
30     displayArray(array1, SIZE1);
31     displayArray(array2, SIZE2);
32     displayArray(array3, SIZE3);
33
34     // Display the new arrays.
```

(program continues)

Program 9-16   *(continued)*

```cpp
35     cout << "\nHere are the duplicate arrays:\n";
36     displayArray(dup1, SIZE1);
37     displayArray(dup2, SIZE2);
38     displayArray(dup3, SIZE3);
39
40     // Free the dynamically allocated memory and
41     // set the pointers to 0.
42     delete [] dup1;
43     delete [] dup2;
44     delete [] dup3;
45     dup1 = 0;
46     dup2 = 0;
47     dup3 = 0;
48     return 0;
49  }
50  //********************************************************
51  // The duplicateArray function accepts an int array     *
52  // and an int that indicates the array's size. The      *
53  // function creates a new array that is a duplicate     *
54  // of the argument array and returns a pointer to the   *
55  // new array. If an invalid size is passed the          *
56  // function returns null.                                *
57  //********************************************************
58
59  int *duplicateArray(const int *arr, int size)
60  {
61     int *newArray;
62
63     // Validate the size. If 0 or a negative
64     // number was passed, return null.
65     if (size <= 0)
66        return NULL;
67
68     // Allocate a new array.
69     newArray = new int[size];
70
71     // Copy the array's contents to the
72     // new array.
73     for (int index = 0; index < size; index++)
74        newArray[index] = arr[index];
75
76     // Return a pointer to the new array.
77     return newArray;
78  }
79
80  //**************************************************
81  // The displayArray function accepts an int array  *
82  // and its size as arguments and displays the      *
83  // contents of the array.                           *
84  //**************************************************
85
86  void displayArray(int arr[], int size)
```

```
87  {
88     for (int index = 0; index < size; index++)
89        cout << arr[index] << " ";
90     cout << endl;
91  }
```

Program Output
```
Here are the original array contents:
100 200 300 400 500
10 20 30 40 50 60 70
1 2 3 4 5 6 7 8 9 10

Here are the duplicate arrays:
100 200 300 400 500
10 20 30 40 50 60 70
1 2 3 4 5 6 7 8 9 10
```

The duplicateArray function appears in lines 59 through 78. The if statement in lines 65 through 66 validates that size contains a valid array size. If size is 0 or less, the function immediately returns NULL to indicate that an invalid size was passed.

Line 69 allocates a new array and assigns its address to the newArray pointer. Then the loop in lines 73 through 74 copies the elements of the arr parameter to the new array. Then the return statement in line 77 returns a pointer to the new array.

Checkpoint

9.9 Assuming arr is an array of ints, will each of the following program segments display "True" or "False"?

A) ```
if (arr < &arr[1])
    cout << "True";
else
    cout << "False";
```

B) ```
if (&arr[4] < &arr[1])
    cout << "True";
else
    cout << "False";
```

C) ```
if (arr != &arr[2])
    cout << "True";
else
    cout << "False";
```

D) ```
if (arr != &arr[0])
    cout << "True";
else
    cout << "False";
```

9.10 Give an example of the proper way to call the following function:

```
void makeNegative(int *val)
{
    if (*val > 0)
```

```
        *val = -(*val);
     }
```

9.11   Complete the following program skeleton. When finished, the program will ask the user for a length (in inches), convert that value to centimeters, and display the result. You are to write the function convert. (*Note:* 1 inch = 2.54 cm. Do not modify function main.)

```
#include <iostream>
#include <iomanip>
using namespace std;

// Write your function prototype here.

int main()
{
    double measurement;

    cout << "Enter a length in inches, and I will convert\n";
    cout << "it to centimeters: ";
    cin >> measurement;
    convert(&measurement);
    cout << fixed << setprecision(4);
    cout << "Value in centimeters: " << measurement << endl;
    return 0;
}
//
// Write the function convert here.
//
```

9.12   Look at the following array definition:

```
const int numbers[SIZE] = { 18, 17, 12, 14 };
```

Suppose we want to pass the array to the function processArray in the following manner:

```
processArray(numbers, SIZE);
```

Which of the following function headers is the correct one for the processArray function?

A) void processArray(const int *arr, int size)

B) void processArray(int * const arr, int size)

9.13   Assume ip is a pointer to an int. Write a statement that will dynamically allocate an integer variable and store its address in ip. Write a statement that will free the memory allocated in the statement you wrote above.

9.14   Assume ip is a pointer to an int. Then, write a statement that will dynamically allocate an array of 500 integers and store its address in ip. Write a statement that will free the memory allocated in the statement you just wrote.

9.15   What is a null pointer?

9.16   Give an example of a function that correctly returns a pointer.

9.17   Give an example of a function that incorrectly returns a pointer.

9.10 Focus on Problem Solving and Program Design: A Case Study

CONCEPT: This case study demonstrates how an array of pointers can be used to display the contents of a second array in sorted order, without sorting the second array.

The United Cause, a charitable relief agency, solicits donations from businesses. The local United Cause office received the following donations from the employees of CK Graphics, Inc.:

$5, $100, $5, $25, $10, $5, $25, $5, $5, $100, $10, $15, $10, $5, $10

The donations were received in the order they appear. The United Cause manager has asked you to write a program that displays the donations in ascending order, as well as in their original order.

Variables

Table 9-1 shows the major variables needed.

Table 9-1

Variable	Description
NUM_DONATIONS	A constant integer initialized with the number of donations received from CK Graphics, Inc. This value will be used in the definition of the program's arrays.
donations	An array of integers containing the donation amounts.
arrPtr	An array of pointers to integers. This array has the same number of elements as the donations array. Each element of arrPtr will be initialized to point to an element of the donations array.

Programming Strategy

In this program the donations array will contain the donations in the order they were received. The elements of the arrPtr array are pointers to integers. They will point to the elements of the donations array, as illustrated in Figure 9-12.

Figure 9-12

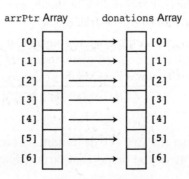

The arrPtr array will initially be set up to point to the elements of the donations array in their natural order. In other words, arrPtr[0] will point to donations[0], arrPtr[1] will point to donations[1], and so forth. In that arrangement, the following statement would cause the contents of donations[5] to be displayed:

```
cout << *(arrPtr[5]) << endl;
```

After the arrPtr array is sorted, however, arrPtr[0] will point to the smallest element of donations, arrPtr[1] will point to the next-to-smallest element of donations, and so forth. This is illustrated in Figure 9-13.

Figure 9-13

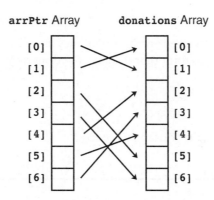

This technique gives us access to the elements of the donations array in a sorted order without actually disturbing the contents of the donations array itself.

Modules

The program will consist of the functions listed in Table 9-2.

Table 9-2

Function	Description
main	The program's main function. It calls the program's other functions.
arrSelectSort	Performs an ascending order selection sort on its parameter, arr, which is an array of pointers. Each element of arr points to an element of a second array. After the sort, arr will point to the elements of the second array in ascending order.
showArray	Displays the contents of its parameter, arr, which is an array of integers. This function is used to display the donations in their original order.
showArrPtr	Accepts an array of pointers to integers as an argument. Displays the contents of what each element of the array points to. This function is used to display the contents of the donations array in sorted order.

Function main

In addition to containing the variable definitions, function main sets up the arrPtr array to point to the elements of the donations array. Then the function arrSelectSort is called to sort the elements of `arrPtr`. Last, the functions `showArrPtr` and `showArray` are called to display the donations. Here is the pseudocode for `main`'s executable statements:

```
For count is set to the values 0 through the number of donations
    Set arrPtr[count] to the address of donations[count].
End For
Call arrSelectSort.
Call showArrPtr.
Call showArray.
```

The `arrSelectSort` Function

The `arrSelectSort` function is a modified version of the selection sort algorithm shown in Chapter 8. The only difference is that `arr` is now an array of pointers. Instead of sorting on the contents of `arr`'s elements, `arr` is sorted on the contents of what its elements point to. Here is the pseudocode:

```
For startScan is set to the values 0 up to (but not including) the
          next-to-last subscript in arr
    Set index variable to startScan.
    Set minIndex variable to startScan.
    Set minElem pointer to arr[startScan].
    For index variable is set to the values from (startScan + 1) through
               the last subscript in arr
        If *(arr[index]) is less than *minElem
            Set minElem to arr[index].
            Set minIndex to index.
        End If.
    End For.
    Set arr[minIndex] to arr[startScan].
    Set arr[startScan] to minElem.
End For.
```

The `showArrPtr` Function

The `showArrPtr` function accepts an array of pointers as its argument. It displays the values pointed to by the elements of the array. Here is its pseudocode:

```
For every element in the arr
    Dereference the element and display what it points to.
End For.
```

The `showArray` Function

The `showArray` function simply displays the contents of `arr` sequentially. Here is its pseudocode:

```
For every element in arr
    Display the element's contents
End For.
```

The Entire Program

Program 9-17 shows the entire program's source code.

Program 9-17

```
 1  // This program shows the donations made to the United Cause
 2  // by the employees of CK Graphics, Inc. It displays
 3  // the donations in order from lowest to highest
 4  // and in the original order they were received.
 5  #include <iostream>
 6  using namespace std;
 7
 8  // Function prototypes
 9  void arrSelectSort(int *[], int);
10  void showArray(int [], int);
11  void showArrPtr(int *[], int);
12
13  int main()
14  {
15     const int NUM_DONATIONS = 15;   // Number of donations
16
17     // An array containing the donation amounts.
18     int donations[NUM_DONATIONS] = {5,   100, 5,   25, 10,
19                                     5,   25,  5,   5,  100,
20                                     10,  15,  10,  5,  10 };
21
22     // An array of pointers to int.
23     int *arrPtr[NUM_DONATIONS];
24
25     // Each element of arrPtr is a pointer to int. Make each
26     // element point to an element in the donations array.
27     for (int count = 0; count < NUM_DONATIONS; count++)
28        arrPtr[count] = &donations[count];
29
30     // Sort the elements of the array of pointers.
31     arrSelectSort(arrPtr, NUM_DONATIONS);
32
33     // Display the donations using the array of pointers. This
34     // will display them in sorted order.
35     cout << "The donations, sorted in ascending order, are: \n";
36     showArrPtr(arrPtr, NUM_DONATIONS);
37
38     // Display the donations in their original order.
39     cout << "The donations, in their original order, are: \n";
40     showArray(donations, NUM_DONATIONS);
41     return 0;
42  }
43
44  //************************************************************
45  // Definition of function arrSelectSort.                    *
```

```
46 // This function performs an ascending order selection sort on    *
47 // arr, which is an array of pointers. Each element of arr        *
48 // points to an element of a second array. After the sort,        *
49 // arr will point to the elements of the second array in          *
50 // ascending order.                                               *
51 //****************************************************************
52
53 void arrSelectSort(int *arr[], int size)
54 {
55    int startScan, minIndex;
56    int *minElem;
57
58    for (startScan = 0; startScan < (size - 1); startScan++)
59    {
60       minIndex = startScan;
61       minElem = arr[startScan];
62       for(int index = startScan + 1; index < size; index++)
63       {
64          if (*(arr[index]) < *minElem)
65          {
66             minElem = arr[index];
67             minIndex = index;
68          }
69       }
70       arr[minIndex] = arr[startScan];
71       arr[startScan] = minElem;
72    }
73 }
74
75 //****************************************************************
76 // Definition of function showArray.                            *
77 // This function displays the contents of arr. size is the      *
78 // number of elements.                                          *
79 //****************************************************************
80
81 void showArray(int arr[], int size)
82 {
83    for (int count = 0; count < size; count++)
84       cout << arr[count] << " ";
85    cout << endl;
86 }
87
88 //****************************************************************
89 // Definition of function showArrPtr.                           *
90 // This function displays the contents of the array pointed to  *
91 // by arr. size is the number of elements.                      *
92 //****************************************************************
93
94 void showArrPtr(int *arr[], int size)
95 {
96    for (int count = 0; count < size; count++)
```

(program continues)

Program 9-17   *(continued)*

```
97          cout << *(arr[count]) << " ";
98     cout << endl;
99 }
```

Program Output

```
The donations, sorted in ascending order, are:
5 5 5 5 5 5 5 10 10 10 10 15 25 25 100 100
The donations, in their original order, are:
5 100 5 25 10 5 25 5 5 100 10 15 10 5 10
```

Review Questions and Exercises

Short Answer

1. What does the indirection operator do?

2. Look at the following code.

   ```
   int x = 7;
   int *iptr = &x;
   ```

   What will be displayed if you send the expression *iptr to cout? What happens if you send the expression ptr to cout?

3. So far you have learned three different uses for the * operator. What are they?

4. What math operations are allowed on pointers?

5. Assuming that ptr is a pointer to an int, what happens when you add 4 to ptr?

6. Look at the following array definition.

   ```
   int numbers[] = { 2, 4, 6, 8, 10 };
   ```

   What will the following statement display?

   ```
   cout << *(numbers + 3) << endl;
   ```

7. What is the purpose of the new operator?

8. What happens when a program uses the new operator to allocate a block of memory, but the amount of requested memory isn't available? How do programs written with older compilers handle this?

9. What is the purpose of the delete operator?

10. Under what circumstances can you successfully return a pointer from a function?

11. What is the difference between a pointer to a constant and a constant pointer?

12. What are two advantages of declaring a pointer parameter as a constant pointer?

Fill-in-the-Blank

13. Each byte in memory is assigned a unique _____.

14. The _____ operator can be used to determine a variable's address.

15. _____ variables are designed to hold addresses.

16. The _____ operator can be used to work with the variable a pointer points to.

17. Array names can be used as _____, and vice versa.

18. Creating variables while a program is running is called _____.

19. The _____ operator is used to dynamically allocate memory.

20. Under older compilers, if the new operator cannot allocate the amount of memory requested, it returns _____.

21. A pointer that contains the address 0 is called a(n) _____ pointer.

22. When a program is finished with a chunk of dynamically allocated memory, it should free it with the _____ operator.

23. You should only use pointers with delete that were previously used with _____.

Algorithm Workbench

24. Look at the following code.

```
double value = 29.7;
double *ptr = &value;
```

Write a cout statement that uses the ptr variable to display the contents of the value variable.

25. Look at the following array definition.

```
int set[10];
```

Write a statement using pointer notation that stores the value 99 in set[7];

26. Write code that dynamically allocates an array of 20 integers, then uses a loop to allow the user to enter values for each element of the array.

27. Assume that tempNumbers is a pointer that points to a dynamically allocated array. Write code that releases the memory used by the array.

28. Look at the following function definition.

```
void getNumber(int &n)
{
   cout << "Enter a number: ";
   cin >> n;
}
```

In this function, the parameter n is a reference variable. Rewrite the function so that n is a pointer.

29. Write the definition of ptr, a pointer to a constant int.

30. Write the definition of ptr, a constant pointer to an int.

True or False

31. T F Each byte of memory is assigned a unique address.

32. T F The * operator is used to get the address of a variable.

33. T F Pointer variables are designed to hold addresses.

34. T F   The & symbol is called the indirection operator.

35. T F   The & operator dereferences a pointer.

36. T F   When the indirection operator is used with a pointer variable, you are actually working with the value the pointer is pointing to.

37. T F   Array names cannot be dereferenced with the indirection operator.

38. T F   When you add a value to a pointer, you are actually adding that number times the size of the data type referenced by the pointer.

39. T F   The address operator is not needed to assign an array's address to a pointer.

40. T F   You can change the address that an array name points to.

41. T F   Any mathematical operation, including multiplication and division, may be performed on a pointer.

42. T F   Pointers may be compared using the relational operators.

43. T F   When used as function parameters, reference variables are much easier to work with than pointers.

44. T F   The new operator dynamically allocates memory.

45. T F   A pointer variable that has not been initialized is called a null pointer.

46. T F   The address 0 is generally considered unusable.

47. T F   In using a pointer with the delete operator, it is not necessary for the pointer to have been previously used with the new operator.

Find the Error

Each of the following definitions and program segments has errors. Locate as many as you can.

48.
```
int ptr*;
```

49.
```
int x, *ptr;
&x = ptr;
```

50.
```
int x, *ptr;
*ptr = &x;
```

51.
```
int x, *ptr;
ptr = &x;
ptr = 100; // Store 100 in x
cout << x << endl;
```

52.
```
int numbers[] = {10, 20, 30, 40, 50};
cout << "The third element in the array is ";
cout << *numbers + 3 << endl;
```

53.
```
int values[20], *iptr;
iptr = values;
iptr *= 2;
```

54.
```
float level;
int fptr = &level;
```

55.
```
int *iptr = &ivalue;
int ivalue;
```

56.
```
void doubleVal(int val)
{
    *val *= 2;
}
```

57. ```cpp
    int *pint;
    new pint;
    ```

58. ```cpp
    int *pint;
    pint = new int;
    if (pint == NULL)
        *pint = 100;
    else
        cout << "Memory allocation error\n";
    ```

59. ```cpp
    int *pint;
    pint = new int[100]; // Allocate memory
      .
      .
      .
    ```
    Code that processes the array.
    ```cpp
      .
      .
      .
    delete pint;    // Free memory
    ```

60. ```cpp
    int *getNum()
    {
        int wholeNum;

        cout << "Enter a number: ";
        cin >> wholeNum;
        return &wholeNum;
    }
    ```

61. ```cpp
    const int arr[] = { 1, 2, 3 };
    int *ptr = arr;
    ```

62. ```cpp
    void doSomething(int * const ptr)
    {
        int localArray[] = { 1, 2, 3 };
        ptr = localArray;
    }
    ```

Programming Challenges

1. Array Allocator

Write a function that dynamically allocates an array of integers. The function should accept an integer argument indicating the number of elements to allocate. The function should return a pointer to the array.

2. Test Scores #1

Write a program that dynamically allocates an array large enough to hold a user-defined number of test scores. Once all the scores are entered, the array should be passed to a function that sorts them in ascending order. Another function should be called that calculates the average score. The program should display the sorted list of scores and averages with appropriate headings. Use pointer notation rather than array notation whenever possible.

Input Validation: Do not accept negative numbers for test scores.

3. Drop Lowest Score

Modify Problem 2 above so the lowest test score is dropped. This score should not be included in the calculation of the average.

4. **Test Scores #2**

   Modify the program of Programming Challenge 2 to allow the user to enter name-score pairs. For each student taking a test, the user types the student's name followed by the student's integer test score. Modify the sorting function so it takes an array holding the student names and an array holding the student test scores. When the sorted list of scores is displayed, each student's name should be displayed along with his or her score. In stepping through the arrays, use pointers rather than array subscripts.

VideoNote

Solving the
getString
Function
Problem

5. **getString Function**

   Write a function named getString that has a local char array of 80 elements. The function should ask the user to enter a sentence, and store the sentence in the array. Then the function should dynamically allocate a char array just large enough to hold the sentence, plus the null terminator. It should copy the sentence to the dynamically allocated array, and then return a pointer to the array. Demonstrate the function in a complete program.

6. **Case Study Modification #1**

   Modify Program 9-17 (the United Cause case study program) so it can be used with any set of donations. The program should dynamically allocate the donations array and ask the user to input its values.

7. **Case Study Modification #2**

   Modify Program 9-17 (the United Cause case study program) so the arrptr array is sorted in descending order instead of ascending order.

8. **Mode Function**

   In statistics, the *mode* of a set of values is the value that occurs most often or with the greatest frequency. Write a function that accepts as arguments the following:

   A) An array of integers

   B) An integer that indicates the number of elements in the array

   The function should determine the mode of the array. That is, it should determine which value in the array occurs most often. The mode is the value the function should return. If the array has no mode (none of the values occur more than once), the function should return -1. (Assume the array will always contain nonnegative values.)

   Demonstrate your pointer prowess by using pointer notation instead of array notation in this function.

9. **Median Function**

   In statistics, when a set of values is sorted in ascending or descending order, its *median* is the middle value. If the set contains an even number of values, the median is the mean, or average, of the two middle values. Write a function that accepts as arguments the following:

   A) An array of integers

   B) An integer that indicates the number of elements in the array

The function should determine the median of the array. This value should be returned as a `double`. (Assume the values in the array are already sorted.)

Demonstrate your pointer prowess by using pointer notation instead of array notation in this function.

10. **Reverse Array**

Write a function that accepts an `int` array and the array's size as arguments. The function should create a copy of the array, except that the element values should be reversed in the copy. The function should return a pointer to the new array. Demonstrate the function in a complete program.

11. **Pointer Rewrite**

The following function uses reference variables as parameters. Rewrite the function so it uses pointers instead of reference variables, and then demonstrate the function in a complete program.

```
int doSomething(int &x, int &y)
{
    int temp = x;
    x = y * 10;
    y = temp * 10;
    return x + y;
}
```

12. **Array Expander**

Write a function that accepts an `int` array and the array's size as arguments. The function should create a new array that is twice the size of the argument array. The function should copy the contents of the argument array to the new array, and initialize the unused elements of the second array with 0. The function should return a pointer to the new array.

13. **Element Shifter**

Write a function that accepts an `int` array and the array's size as arguments. The function should create a new array that is one element larger than the argument array. The first element of the new array should be set to 0. Element 0 of the argument array should be copied to element 1 of the new array, element 1 of the argument array should be copied to element 2 of the new array, and so forth. The function should return a pointer to the new array.

14. **Movie Statistics**

Write a program that can be used to gather statistical data about the number of movies college students see in a month. The program should perform the following steps:

A) Ask the user how many students were surveyed. An array of integers with this many elements should then be dynamically allocated.

B) Allow the user to enter the number of movies each student saw into the array.

C) Calculate and display the average, median, and mode of the values entered. (Use the functions you wrote in Problems 8 and 9 to calculate the median and mode.)

Input Validation: Do not accept negative numbers for input.

10 Characters, Strings, and the **string** Class

TOPICS

10.1 Character Testing

CONCEPT: The C++ library provides several functions for testing characters. To use these functions you must include the **cctype** header file.

The C++ library provides several functions that allow you to test the value of a character. These functions test a single char argument and return either true or false.* For example, the following program segment uses the isupper function to determine whether the character passed as an argument is an uppercase letter. If it is, the function returns true. Otherwise, it returns false.

```cpp
char letter = 'a';
if (isupper(letter))
    cout << "Letter is uppercase.\n";
else
    cout << "Letter is lowercase.\n";
```

---

* These functions actually return an int value. The return value is nonzero to indicate true, or zero to indicate false.

Because the variable letter, in this example, contains a lowercase character, isupper returns false. The if statement will cause the message "Letter is lowercase" to be displayed.

Table 10-1 lists several character-testing functions. Each of these is prototyped in the cctype header file, so be sure to include that file when using the functions.

Table 10-1

Character Function	Description
isalpha	Returns true (a nonzero number) if the argument is a letter of the alphabet. Returns 0 if the argument is not a letter.
isalnum	Returns true (a nonzero number) if the argument is a letter of the alphabet or a digit. Otherwise it returns 0.
isdigit	Returns true (a nonzero number) if the argument is a digit from 0 through 9. Otherwise it returns 0.
islower	Returns true (a nonzero number) if the argument is a lowercase letter. Otherwise, it returns 0.
isprint	Returns true (a nonzero number) if the argument is a printable character (including a space). Returns 0 otherwise.
ispunct	Returns true (a nonzero number) if the argument is a printable character other than a digit, letter, or space. Returns 0 otherwise.
isupper	Returns true (a nonzero number) if the argument is an uppercase letter. Otherwise, it returns 0.
isspace	Returns true (a nonzero number) if the argument is a whitespace character. Whitespace characters are any of the following: space ' ' vertical tab '\v' newline '\n' tab '\t' Otherwise, it returns 0.

Program 10-1 uses several of the functions shown in Table 10-1. It asks the user to input a character and then displays various messages, depending upon the return value of each function.

Program 10-1

```
1  // This program demonstrates some character-testing functions.
2  #include <iostream>
3  #include <cctype>
4  using namespace std;
5
6  int main()
7  {
8     char input;
9
```

```
10      cout << "Enter any character: ";
11      cin.get(input);
12      cout << "The character you entered is: " << input << endl;
13      if (isalpha(input))
14         cout << "That's an alphabetic character.\n";
15      if (isdigit(input))
16         cout << "That's a numeric digit.\n";
17      if (islower(input))
18         cout << "The letter you entered is lowercase.\n";
19      if (isupper(input))
20         cout << "The letter you entered is uppercase.\n";
21      if (isspace(input))
22         cout << "That's a whitespace character.\n";
23      return 0;
24   }
```

Program Output with Example Input Shown in Bold
```
Enter any character: A [Enter]
The character you entered is: A
That's an alphabetic character.
The letter you entered is uppercase.
```

Program Output with Different Example Input Shown in Bold
```
Enter any character: 7 [Enter]
The character you entered is: 7
That's a numeric digit.
```

Program 10-2 shows a more practical application of the character testing functions. It tests a seven-character customer number to determine whether it is in the proper format.

Program 10-2

```
1   // This program tests a customer number to determine whether
2   // it is in the proper format.
3   #include <iostream>
4   #include <cctype>
5   using namespace std;
6
7   // Function prototype
8   bool testNum(char [], int);
9
10  int main()
11  {
12     const int SIZE = 8;    // Array size
13     char customer[SIZE];   // To hold a customer number
14
15     // Get the customer number.
16     cout << "Enter a customer number in the form ";
17     cout << "LLLNNNN\n";
18     cout << "(LLL = letters and NNNN = numbers): ";
19     cin.getline(customer, SIZE);
```

(program continues)

Program 10-2   *(continued)*

```
20
21      // Determine whether it is valid.
22      if (testNum(customer, SIZE))
23         cout << "That's a valid customer number.\n";
24      else
25      {
26         cout << "That is not the proper format of the ";
27         cout << "customer number.\nHere is an example:\n";
28         cout << "   ABC1234\n";
29      }
30      return 0;
31   }
32
33   //***********************************************************
34   // Definition of function testNum.                          *
35   // This function determines whether the custNum parameter   *
36   // holds a valid customer number. The size parameter is     *
37   // the size of the custNum array.                           *
38   //***********************************************************
39
40   bool testNum(char custNum[], int size)
41   {
42      int count;  // Loop counter
43
44      // Test the first three characters for alphabetic letters.
45      for (count = 0; count < 3; count++)
46      {
47         if (!isalpha(custNum[count]))
48            return false;
49      }
50
51      // Test the remaining characters for numeric digits.
52      for (count = 3; count < size - 1; count++)
53      {
54         if (!isdigit(custNum[count]))
55            return false;
56      }
57      return true;
58   }
```

Program Output with Example Input Shown in Bold
```
Enter a customer number in the form LLLNNNN
(LLL = letters and NNNN = numbers): RQS4567 [Enter]
That's a valid customer number.
```

Program Output with Different Example Input Shown in Bold
```
Enter a customer number in the form LLLNNNN
(LLL = letters and NNNN = numbers): AX467T9 [Enter]
That is not the proper format of the customer number.
Here is an example:
   ABC1234
```

In this program, the customer number is expected to consist of three alphabetic letters followed by four numeric digits. The `testNum` function accepts an array argument and tests the first three characters with the following loop in lines 45 through 49:

```
for (count = 0; count < 3; count++)
{
   if (!isalpha(custNum[count]))
      return false;
}
```

The `isalpha` function returns `true` if its argument is an alphabetic character. The `!` operator is used in the `if` statement to determine whether the tested character is NOT alphabetic. If this is so for any of the first three characters, the function `testNum` returns `false`. Likewise, the next four characters are tested to determine whether they are numeric digits with the following loop in lines 52 through 56:

```
for (count = 3; count < size - 1; count++)
{
   if (!isdigit(custNum[count]))
      return false;
}
```

The `isdigit` function returns `true` if its argument is the character representation of any of the digits 0 through 9. Once again, the `!` operator is used to determine whether the tested character is *not* a digit. If this is so for any of the last four characters, the function `testNum` returns `false`. If the customer number is in the proper format, the function will cycle through both the loops without returning `false`. In that case, the last line in the function is the `return true` statement, which indicates the customer number is valid.

10.2 Character Case Conversion

CONCEPT: The C++ library offers functions for converting a character to upper- or lowercase.

The C++ library provides two functions, `toupper` and `tolower`, for converting the case of a character. The functions are described in Table 10-2. (These functions are prototyped in the header file `cctype`, so be sure to include it.)

Table 10-2

Function	Description
`toupper`	Returns the uppercase equivalent of its argument.
`tolower`	Returns the lowercase equivalent of its argument.

Each of the functions in Table 10-2 accepts a single character argument. If the argument is a lowercase letter, the `toupper` function returns its uppercase equivalent. For example, the following statement will display the character A on the screen:

```
cout << toupper('a');
```

If the argument is already an uppercase letter, toupper returns it unchanged. The following statement causes the character Z to be displayed:

```
cout << toupper('Z');
```

Any nonletter argument passed to toupper is returned as it is. Each of the following statements display toupper's argument without any change:

```
cout << toupper('*');   // Displays *
cout << toupper ('&');  // Displays &
cout << toupper('%');   // Displays %
```

toupper and tolower don't actually cause the character argument to change, they simply return the upper- or lowercase equivalent of the argument. For example, in the following program segment, the variable letter is set to the value 'A'. The tolower function returns the character 'a', but letter still contains 'A'.

```
char letter = 'A';
cout << tolower(letter) << endl;
cout << letter << endl;
```

These statements will cause the following to be displayed:

```
a
A
```

Program 10-3 demonstrates the toupper function in an input validation loop.

Program 10-3

```
 1  // This program calculates the area of a circle. It asks the user
 2  // if he or she wishes to continue. A loop that demonstrates the
 3  // toupper function repeats until the user enters 'y', 'Y',
 4  // 'n', or 'N'.
 5  #include <iostream>
 6  #include <cctype>
 7  #include <iomanip>
 8  using namespace std;
 9
10  int main()
11  {
12     const double PI = 3.14159;  // Constant for pi
13     double radius;              // The circle's radius
14     char goAgain;               // To hold Y or N
15
16     cout << "This program calculates the area of a circle.\n";
17     cout << fixed << setprecision(2);
18
19     do
20     {
21        // Get the radius and display the area.
22        cout << "Enter the circle's radius: ";
23        cin >> radius;
24        cout << "The area is " << (PI * radius * radius);
25        cout << endl;
```

```
26
27          // Does the user want to do this again?
28          cout << "Calculate another? (Y or N) ";
29          cin >> goAgain;
30
31          // Validate the input.
32          while (toupper(goAgain) != 'Y' && toupper(goAgain) != 'N')
33          {
34              cout << "Please enter Y or N: ";
35              cin >> goAgain;
36          }
37
38      } while (toupper(goAgain) == 'Y');
39      return 0;
40  }
```

Program Output with Example Input Shown in Bold
This program calculates the area of a circle.
Enter the circle's radius: **10 [Enter]**
The area is 314.16
Calculate another? (Y or N) **b Enter]**
Please enter Y or N: **y [Enter]**
Enter the circle's radius: **1 [Enter]**
The area is 3.14
Calculate another? (Y or N) **n [Enter]**

In lines 28 and 29 the user is prompted to enter either Y or N to indicate whether he or she wants to calculate another area. We don't want the program to be so picky that it accepts only uppercase Y or uppercase N. Lowercase y or lowercase n are also acceptable. The input validation loop must be written so to reject anything except 'Y', 'y', 'N', or 'n'. One way to do this would be to test the goAgain variable in four relational expressions, as shown here:

```
while (goAgain != 'Y' && goAgain != 'y' &&
       goAgain != 'N' && goAgain != 'N')
```

Although there is nothing wrong with this code, we could use the toupper function to get the uppercase equivalent of goAgain, and make only two comparisons. This is the approach taken in line 32:

```
while (toupper(goAgain) != 'Y' && toupper(goAgain) != 'N')
```

Another approach would have been to use the tolower function to get the lowercase equivalent of goAgain. Here is an example:

```
while (tolower(goAgain) != 'y' && tolower(goAgain) != 'n')
```

Either approach will yield the same results.

Checkpoint

10.1   Write a short description of each of the following functions:

```
isalpha
isalnum
isdigit
islower
isprint
ispunct
isupper
isspace
toupper
tolower
```

10.2   Write a statement that will convert the contents of the `char` variable `big` to lowercase. The converted value should be assigned to the variable `little`.

10.3   Write an `if` statement that will display the word "digit" if the variable `ch` contains a numeric digit. Otherwise, it should display "Not a digit."

10.4   What is the output of the following statement?

```
cout << toupper(tolower('A'));
```

10.5   Write a loop that asks the user `"Do you want to repeat the program or quit? (R/Q)"`. The loop should repeat until the user has entered an R or Q (either uppercase or lowercase).

10.3   Review of the Internal Storage of C-Strings

CONCEPT: In C++, a C-string is a sequence of characters stored in consecutive memory locations, terminated by a null character.

In this section we will discuss strings, string literals, and C-strings. Although you have previously encountered these terms, make sure you understand what each means and the differences between them.

String is a generic term that describes any consecutive sequence of characters. A word, a sentence, a person's name, and the title of a song are all strings. In a program, a string may be constant or variable in nature, and may be stored in a variety of ways.

A *string literal* or *string constant* is the literal representation of a string in a program. In C++, string literals are enclosed in double quotation marks, such as:

```
"What is your name?"
```

The term *C-string* describes a string whose characters are stored in consecutive memory locations and are followed by a null character, or null terminator. Recall that a null character or null terminator is a byte holding the ASCII code 0. For example, Figure 10-1 illustrates how the string "Bailey" is stored in memory, as a C-string.

Figure 10-1

| B | a | i | l | e | y | \0 |

NOTE: Remember that \0 ("slash zero") is the escape sequence representing the null terminator. It stands for the ASCII code 0.

The purpose of the null terminator is to mark the end of the C-string. Without it, there would be no way for a function to know the length of a C-string argument.

String Literals

A string literal or string constant is enclosed in a set of double quotation marks (" "). For example, here are five string literals:

```
"Have a nice day."
"What is your name?"
"John Smith"
"Please enter your age:"
"Part Number 45Q1789"
```

All of a program's string literals are stored in memory as C-strings, with the null terminator automatically appended. For example, look at Program 10-4.

Program 10-4

```
 1   // This program contains string literals.
 2   #include <iostream>
 3   using namespace std;
 4
 5   int main()
 6   {
 7      char again;
 8
 9      do
10      {
11         cout << "C++ programming is great fun!" << endl;
12         cout << "Do you want to see the message again? ";
13         cin >> again;
14      } while (again == 'Y' || again == 'y');
15      return 0;
16   }
```

This program contains two string literals:

```
"C++ programming is great fun!"
"Do you want to see the message again? "
```

Although the strings are not stored in arrays, they are still part of the program's data. The first string occupies 30 bytes of memory (including the null terminator), and the second string occupies 39 bytes. They appear in memory in the following forms:

| C | + | + | | p | r | o | g | r | a | m | m | i | n | g | | i | s | | g | r | e | a | t | | f | u | n | ! | \0 |

| D | o | | y | o | u | | w | a | n | t | | t | o | | s | e | e | | t | h | e | | m | e | s | s | a | g |
| e | | a | g | a | i | n | ? | | \0 |

It's important to realize that a string literal has its own storage location, just like a variable or an array. When a string literal appears in a statement, it's actually its memory address that C++ uses. Look at the following example:

```
cout << "Do you want to see the message again? ";
```

In this statement, the memory address of the string literal "Do you want to see the message again? " is passed to the `cout` object. `cout` displays the consecutive characters found at this address. It stops displaying the characters when a null terminator is encountered.

Strings Stored in Arrays

Quite often programs need to accept string input, change the contents of a string, or access a string for performing comparisons. One method of storing nonliteral strings is in character arrays, as C-strings. When defining a character array for holding a C-string, be sure the array is large enough for the null terminator. For example, the following 12-element array can hold a string of no more than 11 characters:

```
char company[12];
```

String input can be performed by the `cin` object. For example, the following statement allows the user to enter a string (with no whitespace characters) into the `company` array:

```
cin >> company;
```

Recall from Chapter 7 that an array name with no brackets and no subscript is converted into the beginning address of the array. In the previous statement, `company` indicates the address in memory where the string is to be stored. Of course, `cin` has no way of knowing that `company` only has 12 elements. If the user enters a string of 30 characters, `cin` will write past the end of the array. This can be prevented by using `cin`'s `getline` member function. Assume the following array has been defined in a program:

```
char line[80];
```

The following statement uses `cin`'s `getline` member function to get a line of input (including whitespace characters) and store it in the `line` array:

```
cin.getline(line, 80);
```

As you will recall from Chapter 3, the first argument tells `getline` where to store the string input. This statement indicates the starting address of the `line` array as the storage location for the string. The second argument (80) indicates the maximum length of the string, including the null terminator. `cin` will read 79 characters, or until the user presses the **[Enter]** key, whichever comes first. `cin` will automatically append the null terminator to the end of the string.

Once a string is stored in an array, it can be processed using standard subscript notation. For example, Program 10-5 displays a string stored in an array. It uses a loop to display each character in the array until the null terminator is encountered.

Program 10-5

```
 1   // This program displays a string stored in a char array.
 2   #include <iostream>
 3   using namespace std;
 4
 5   int main()
 6   {
 7      const int SIZE = 80;    // Array size
 8      char line[SIZE];        // To hold a line of input
 9      int count = 0;          // Loop counter variable
10
11      // Get a line of input.
12      cout << "Enter a sentence of no more than "
13           << (SIZE - 1) << " characters:\n";
14      cin.getline(line, SIZE);
15
16      // Display the input one character at a time.
17      cout << "The sentence you entered is:\n";
18      while (line[count] != '\0')
19      {
20         cout << line[count];
21         count++;
22      }
23      return 0;
24   }
```

Program Output with Example Input Shown in Bold
```
Enter a sentence of no more than 79 characters:
```
C++ is challenging but fun! [Enter]
```
The sentence you entered is:
C++ is challenging but fun!
```

10.4 Library Functions for Working with C-Strings

> **CONCEPT:** The C++ library has numerous functions for handling C-strings. These functions perform various tests and manipulations, and require that the **cstring** header file be included.

The `strlen` Function

Working with C-strings can be tedious. As discussed in Chapter 7, just copying a C-string from one array to another isn't a simple matter. Fortunately, the C++ library provides many functions for manipulating and testing strings. For instance, the following program segment uses the `strlen` function to determine the length of the string stored in name:

```
char name[50] = "Thomas Edison";
int length;
length = strlen(name);
```

The `strlen` function accepts a pointer to a C-string as its argument. It returns the length of the string, which is the number of characters up to, but not including, the null terminator. As a result, the variable `length` will have the number 13 stored in it. The length of a string isn't to be confused with the size of the array holding it. Remember, the only information being passed to `strlen` is the beginning address of a C-string. It doesn't know where the array ends, so it looks for the null terminator to indicate the end of the string.

NOTE: `strlen`, as well as the other functions discussed in this section, require the `cstring` header file to be included.

When using a C-string handling function, you must pass one or more C-strings as arguments. This means passing the address of the C-string, which may be accomplished by using any of the following as arguments:

- The name of the array holding the C-string
- A pointer variable that holds the address of the C-string
- A literal string

Anytime a literal string is used as an argument to a function, the address of the literal string is passed. Here is an example of the `strlen` function being used with such an argument:

```
length = strlen("Thomas Edison");
```

The `strcat` Function

The `strcat` function accepts two pointers to C-strings as its arguments. The function *concatenates*, or appends one string to another. The following code shows an example of its use:

```
char string1[13] = "Hello ";
char string2[7] = "World!";
cout << string1 << endl;
cout << string2 << endl;
strcat(string1, string2);
cout << string1 << endl;
```

These statements will cause the following output:

```
Hello
World!
Hello World!
```

The `strcat` function copies the contents of `string2` to the end of `string1`. In this example, `string1` contains the string "Hello " before the call to `strcat`. After the call, it contains the string "Hello World!". Figure 10-2 shows the contents of both arrays before and after the function call.

Notice the last character in `string1` (before the null terminator) is a space. The `strcat` function doesn't insert a space, so it's the programmer's responsibility to make sure one is already there, if needed. It's also the programmer's responsibility to make sure the array holding `string1` is large enough to hold `string1` plus `string2` plus a null terminator.

Figure 10-2

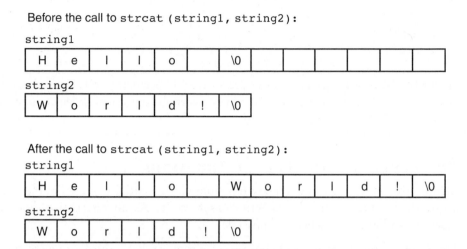

Before the call to strcat (string1, string2):

Here is a program segment that uses the sizeof operator to test an array's size before strcat is called:

```
if (sizeof(string1) >= (strlen(string1) + strlen(string2) + 1))
    strcat(string1, string2);
else
    cout << "String1 is not large enough for both strings.\n";
```

WARNING! If the array holding the first string isn't large enough to hold both strings, strcat will overflow the boundaries of the array.

The strcpy Function

Recall from Chapter 7 that one array cannot be assigned to another with the = operator. Each individual element must be assigned, usually inside a loop. The strcpy function can be used to copy one string to another. Here is an example of its use:

```
char name[20];
strcpy(name, "Albert Einstein");
```

The strcpy function's two arguments are C-string addresses. The second C-string is copied to the first C-string, including the null terminator. (The first argument usually references an array.) In this example, the strcpy function will copy the string "Albert Einstein" to the name array.

If anything is already stored in the location referenced by the first argument, it is overwritten, as shown in the following program segment:

```
char string1[10] = "Hello", string2[10] = "World!";
cout << string1 << endl;
cout << string2 << endl;
strcpy(string1, string2);
cout << string1 << endl;
cout << string2 << endl;
```

Here is the output:

```
Hello
World!
World!
World!
```

 WARNING! Being true to C++'s nature, `strcpy` performs no bounds checking. The array specified by the first argument will be overflowed if it isn't large enough to hold the string specified by the second argument.

The `strncat` and `strncpy` Functions

Because the the `strcat` and `strcpy` functions can potentially overwrite the bounds of an array, they make it possible to write unsafe code. As an alternative, you should use `strncat` and `strncpy` whenever possible.

The `strncat` functions works like `strcat`, except it takes a third argument specifying the maximum number of characters from the second string to append to the first. Here is an example call to `strncat`:

```
strncat(string1, string2, 10);
```

When this statement executes, `strncat` will append no more than 10 characters from `string2` to `string1`. The following code shows an example of calculating the maximum number of characters that can be appended to an array.

```
int maxChars;
char string1[17] = "Welcome ";
char string2[18] = "to North Carolina";

cout << string1 << endl;
cout << string2 << endl;

maxChars = sizeof(string1) - (strlen(string1) + 1);

strncat(string1, string2, maxChars);
cout << string1 << endl;
```

The sixth statement in this code calculates the number of empty elements in `string1`. It does this by subtracting the length of the string stored in the array plus 1 for the null terminator. This code will cause the following output:

```
Welcome
to North Carolina
Welcome to North
```

The `strncpy` function allows you to copy a specified number of characters from a string to a destination. Calling `strncpy` is similar to calling `strcpy`, except you pass a third argument specifying the maximum number of characters from the second string to copy to the first. Here is an example call to `strncpy`:

```
strncpy(string1, string2, 5);
```

When this statement executes, strncpy will copy no more than five characters from string2 to string1. However, if the specified number of characters is less than or equal to the length of string2, a null terminator is not appended to string1. If the specified number of characters is greater than the length of string2, then string1 is padded with null terminators, up to the specified number of characters. The following code shows an example using the strncpy function.

```
int maxChars;
char string1[11];
char string2[] = "I love C++ programming!";

maxChars = sizeof(string1) - 1;
strncpy(string1, string2, maxChars);

// Put the null terminator at the end.
string1[10] = '\0';
cout << string1 << endl;
```

Notice that a statement was written to put the null terminator at the end of string1. This is because maxChars was less than the length of string2, and strncpy did not automatically place a null terminator there.

The strstr Function

The strstr function searches for a string inside of a string. For instance, it could be used to search for the string "seven" inside the larger string "Four score and seven years ago." The function's first argument is the string to be searched, and the second argument is the string to look for. If the function finds the second string inside the first, it returns the address of the occurrence of the second string within the first string. Otherwise it returns the address 0, or the NULL address. Here is an example:

```
char arr[] = "Four score and seven years ago";
char *strPtr;
cout << arr << endl;
strPtr = strstr(arr, "seven"); // search for "seven"
cout << strPtr << endl;
```

In this code, strstr will locate the string "seven" inside the string "Four score and seven years ago." It will return the address of the first character in "seven" which will be stored in the pointer variable strPtr. If run as part of a complete program, this segment will display the following:

```
Four score and seven years ago
seven years ago
```

The strstr function can be useful in any program that must locate data inside one or more strings. Program 10-6, for example, stores a list of product numbers and descriptions in an array of C-strings. It allows the user to look up a product description by entering all or part of its product number.

Program 10-6

```
 1   // This program uses the strstr function to search an array.
 2   #include <iostream>
 3   #include <cstring>        // For strstr
 4   using namespace std;
 5
 6   int main()
 7   {
 8      // Constants for array lengths
 9      const int NUM_PRODS = 5;   // Number of products
10      const int LENGTH = 27;     // String length
11
12      // Array of products
13      char products[NUM_PRODS][LENGTH] =
14                       { "TV327 31-inch Television",
15                         "CD257 CD Player",
16                         "TA677 Answering Machine",
17                         "CS109 Car Stereo",
18                         "PC955 Personal Computer" };
19
20      char lookUp[LENGTH];  // To hold user's input
21      char *strPtr = NULL;  // To point to the found product
22      int index;            // Loop counter
23
24      // Prompt the user for a product number.
25      cout << "\tProduct Database\n\n";
26      cout << "Enter a product number to search for: ";
27      cin.getline(lookUp, LENGTH);
28
29      // Search the array for a matching substring
30      for (index = 0; index < NUM_PRODS; index++)
31      {
32         strPtr = strstr(products[index], lookUp);
33         if (strPtr != NULL)
34            break;
35      }
36
37      // If a matching substring was found, display the product info.
38      if (strPtr != NULL)
39         cout << products[index] << endl;
40      else
41         cout << "No matching product was found.\n";
42
43      return 0;
44   }
```

Program Output with Example Input Shown in Bold
```
    Product Database

Enter a product to search for: CS [Enter]
CS109  Car Stereo
```

Program Output with Different Example Input Shown in Bold
```
      Product Database

Enter a product to search for: AB [Enter]
No matching product was found.
```

Table 10-3 summarizes the string-handling functions discussed here, as well as the `strcmp` function that was discussed in Chapter 4. (All the functions listed require the `cstring` header file.)

In Program 10-6, the `for` loop in lines 30 through 35 cycles through each C-string in the array calling the following statement:

```
strPtr = strstr(prods[index], lookUp);
```

The `strstr` function searches the string referenced by `prods[index]` for the name entered by the user, which is stored in `lookUp`. If `lookUp` is found inside `prods[index]`, the function returns its address. In that case, the following `if` statement causes the `for` loop to terminate:

```
if (strPtr != NULL)
    break;
```

Outside the loop, the following `if else` statement in lines 38 through 41 determines whether the string entered by the user was found in the array. If not, it informs the user that no matching product was found. Otherwise, the product number and description are displayed:

```
if (strPtr == NULL)
    cout << "No matching product was found.\n";
else
    cout << prods[index] << endl;
```

Table 10-3

Function	Description
strlen	Accepts a C-string or a pointer to a C-string as an argument. Returns the length of the C-string (not including the null terminator.) *Example Usage:* `len = strlen(name);`
strcat	Accepts two C-strings or pointers to two C-strings as arguments. The function appends the contents of the second string to the first C-string. (The first string is altered, the second string is left unchanged.) *Example Usage:* `strcat(string1, string2);`
strcpy	Accepts two C-strings or pointers to two C-strings as arguments. The function copies the second C-string to the first C-string. The second C-string is left unchanged. *Example Usage:* `strcpy(string1, string2);`

(table continues)

Table 10-3 *(continued)*

Function	Description
strncat	Accepts two C-strings or pointers to two C-strings, and an integer argument. The third argument, an integer, indicates the maximum number of characters to copy from the second C-string to the first C-string. *Example Usage:* `strncat(string1, string2, n);`
strncpy	Accepts two C-strings or pointers to two C-strings, and an integer argument. The third argument, an integer, indicates the maximum number of characters to copy from the second C-string to the first C-string. If n is less than the length of `string2`, the null terminator is not automatically appended to `string1`. If n is greater than the length of `string2`, `string1` is padded with '\0' characters. *Example Usage:* `strncpy(string1, string2, n);`
strcmp	Accepts two C-strings or pointers to two C-strings arguments. If `string1` and `string2` are the same, this function returns 0. If `string2` is alphabetically greater than `string1`, it returns a negative number. If `string2` is alphabetically less than `string1`, it returns a positive number. *Example Usage:* `if (strcmp(string1, string2))`
strstr	Accepts two C-strings or pointers to two C-strings as arguments. Searches for the first occurrence of `string2` in `string1`. If an occurrence of `string2` is found, the function returns a pointer to it. Otherwise, it returns a NULL pointer (address 0). *Example Usage:* `cout << strstr(string1, string2);`

 Checkpoint

10.6   Write a short description of each of the following functions:

```
strlen
strcat
strcpy
strncat
strncpy
strcmp
strstr
```

10.7   What will the following program segment display?

```
char dog[] = "Fido";
cout << strlen(dog) << endl;
```

10.8   What will the following program segment display?

```
char string1[16] = "Have a ";
char string2[9] = "nice day";
strcat(string1, string2);
cout << string1 << endl;
cout << string2 << endl;
```

10.9   Write a statement that will copy the string "Beethoven" to the array `composer`.

10.10   When complete, the following program skeleton will search for the string "Windy" in the array place. If place contains "Windy" the program will display the message "Windy found." Otherwise it will display "Windy not found."

```cpp
#include <iostream>
// include any other necessary header files
using namespace std;

int main()
{
    char place[] = "The Windy City";
    // Complete the program. It should search the array place
    // for the string "Windy" and display the message "Windy
    // found" if it finds the string. Otherwise, it should
    // display the message "Windy not found."
    return 0;
}
```

10.5 String/Numeric Conversion Functions

CONCEPT: The C++ library provides functions for converting a string representation of a number to a numeric data type and vice versa. These functions require the cstdlib header file to be included.

There is a great difference between a number that is stored as a string and one stored as a numeric value. The string "26792" isn't actually a number, but a series of ASCII codes representing the individual digits of the number. It uses six bytes of memory (including the null terminator). Because it isn't an actual number, it's not possible to perform mathematical operations with it, unless it is first converted to a numeric value.

Several functions exist in the C++ library for converting string representations of numbers into numeric values, and vice versa. Table 10-4 shows some of these. Note that all of these functions require the cstdlib header file.

Table 10-4

Function	Description
atoi	Accepts a C-string as an argument. The function converts the C-string to an integer and returns that value. *Example Usage:* num = atoi("4569");
atol	Accepts a C-string as an argument. The function converts the C-string to a long integer and returns that value. *Example Usage:* lnum = atol("500000");
atof	Accepts a C-string as an argument. The function converts the C-string to a double and returns that value. *Example Usage:* fnum = atof("3.14159");
itoa	Converts an integer to a C-string.* The first argument, value, is the integer. The result will be stored at the location pointed to by the second argument, string. The third argument, base, is an integer. It specifies the numbering system that the converted integer should be expressed in (8 = octal, 10 = decimal, 16 = hexadecimal, etc.). *Example Usage:* itoa(value, string, base);

*The itoa function is not supported by all compilers.

The atoi Function

The atoi function converts a string to an integer. It accepts a C-string argument and returns the converted integer value. Here is an example of how to use it:

```
int num;
num = atoi("1000");
```

In these statements, atoi converts the string "1000" into the integer 1000. Once the variable num is assigned this value, it can be used in mathematical operations or any task requiring a numeric value.

The atol Function

The atol function works just like atoi, except the return value is a long integer. Here is an example:

```
long bigNum;
bigNum = atol("500000");
```

The atof Function

The atof function accepts a C-string argument and converts it to a double. The numeric double value is returned, as shown here:

```
double num;
num = atof("12.67");
```

Although the atof function returns a double, you can still use it to convert a C-string to a float. For example, look at the following code.

```
float x;
x = atof("3.4");
```

The atof function converts the string "3.4" to the double value 3.4. Because 3.4 is within the range of a float, it can be stored in a float variable without the loss of data.

> **NOTE:** If a string that cannot be converted to a numeric value is passed to any of these functions, the function's behavior is undefined by C++. Many compilers, however, will perform the conversion process until an invalid character is encountered. For example, atoi("123x5") might return the integer 123. It is possible that these functions will return 0 if they cannot successfully convert their argument.

The itoa Function

The itoa function is similar to atoi, but it works in reverse. It converts a numeric integer into a string representation of the integer. The itoa function accepts three arguments: the integer value to be converted, a pointer to the location in memory where the string is to be stored, and a number that represents the base of the converted value. Here is an example:

```
char numArray[10];
itoa(1200, numArray, 10);
cout << numArray << endl;
```

This program segment converts the integer value 1200 to a string. The string is stored in the array numArray. The third argument, 10, means the number should be written in decimal, or base 10 notation. The output of the cout statement is

    1200

 WARNING! As always, C++ performs no array bounds checking. Make sure the array whose address is passed to itoa is large enough to hold the converted number, including the null terminator.

Now let's look at Program 10-7, which uses a string-to-number conversion function, atoi. It allows the user to enter a series of values, or the letters Q or q to quit. The average of the numbers is then calculated and displayed.

Program 10-7

```
1   // This program demonstrates the strcmp and atoi functions.
2   #include <iostream>
3   #include <cctype>        // For tolower
4   #include <cstring>       // For strcmp
5   #include <cstdlib>       // For atoi
6   using namespace std;
7
8   int main()
9   {
10     const int SIZE = 20;   // Array size
11     char input[SIZE];      // To hold user input
12     int total = 0;         // Accumulator
13     int count = 0;         // Loop counter
14     double average;        // To hold the average of numbers
15
16     // Get the first number.
17     cout << "This program will average a series of numbers.\n";
18     cout << "Enter the first number or Q to quit: ";
19     cin.getline(input, SIZE);
20
21     // Process the number and subsequent numbers.
22     while (tolower(input[0]) != 'q')
23     {
24        total += atoi(input);   // Keep a running total
25        count++;                // Count the numbers entered
26        // Get the next number.
27        cout << "Enter the next number or Q to quit: ";
28        cin.getline(input, SIZE);
29     }
30
31     // If any numbers were entered, display their average.
32     if (count != 0)
33     {
34        average = static_cast<double>(total) / count;
35        cout << "Average: " << average << endl;
36     }
37     return 0;
38  }
```

(program output continues)

Program 10-7 *(continued)*

Program Output with Example Input Shown in Bold
```
This program will average a series of numbers.
Enter the first number or Q to quit: 74 [Enter]
Enter the next number or Q to quit: 98 [Enter]
Enter the next number or Q to quit: 23 [Enter]
Enter the next number or Q to quit: 54 [Enter]
Enter the next number or Q to quit: Q [Enter]
Average: 62.25
```

In line 22, the following `while` statement uses the `tolower` function to determine whether the first character entered by the user is "q" or "Q".

```
while (tolower(input[0]) != 'q')
```

If the user hasn't entered 'Q' or 'q' the loop performs an iteration. The following statement, in line 24, uses `atoi` to convert the string in input to an integer and adds its value to `total`:

```
total += atoi(input);  // Keep a running total
```

The counter is updated in line 25 and then the user is asked for the next number. When all the numbers are entered, the user terminates the loop by entering 'Q' or 'q'. If one or more numbers are entered, their average is displayed.

The string-to numeric conversion functions can also help with a common input problem. Recall from Chapter 3 that using `cin >>` and then calling `cin.get` causes problems because the `>>` operator leaves the newline character in the keyboard buffer. When the `cin.get` function executes, the first character it sees in the keyboard buffer is the newline character, so it reads no further.

The same problem exists when a program uses `cin >>` and then calls `cin.getline` to read a line of input. For example, look at the following code. (Assume `idNumber` is an `int` and name is a `char` array.)

```
1     // Get the user's ID number.
2     cout << "What is your ID number? ";
3     cin >> idNumber;
4
5     // Get the user's name.
6     cout << "What is your name? ";
7     cin.getline(name, NAME_SIZE);
```

Let's say the user enters 25 and presses Enter when the `cin >>` statement in line 3 executes. The value 25 will be stored in `idNumber`, and the newline character will be left in the keyboard buffer. When the `cin.getline` function is called in line 7, the first character it sees in the keyboard buffer is the newline character, so it reads no further. It will appear that the statement in line 7 was skipped.

One work-around that we have used in this book is to call `cin.ignore` to skip over the newline character just before calling `cin.getline`. Another approach is to use cin.getline to read all of a program's input, including numbers. When numeric input is needed, it is read into a char array as a string, and then converted to the appropriate numeric data type. Because you aren't mixing cin >> with cin.getline, the problem of the remaining newline character doesn't exist. Program 10-8 shows an example.

Program 10-8

```cpp
 1  // This program demonstrates how the getline function can
 2  // be used for all of a program's input.
 3  #include <iostream>
 4  #include <cstdlib>
 5  #include <iomanip>
 6  using namespace std;
 7
 8  int main()
 9  {
10      const int INPUT_SIZE = 81;    // Size of input array
11      const int NAME_SIZE = 30;     // Size of name array
12      char input[INPUT_SIZE];       // To hold a line of input
13      char name[NAME_SIZE];         // To hold a name
14      int idNumber;                 // To hold an ID number
15      int age;                      // To hold an age
16      double income;                // To hold income
17
18      // Get the user's ID number.
19      cout << "What is your ID number? ";
20      cin.getline(input, INPUT_SIZE); // Read as a string
21      idNumber = atoi(input);         // Convert to int
22
23      // Get the user's name. No conversion necessary.
24      cout << "What is your name? ";
25      cin.getline(name, NAME_SIZE);
26
27      // Get the user's age.
28      cout << "How old are you? ";
29      cin.getline(input, INPUT_SIZE); // Read as a string
30      age = atoi(input);              // Convert to int
31
32      // Get the user's income.
33      cout << "What is your annual income? ";
34      cin.getline(input, INPUT_SIZE); // Read as a string
35      income = atof(input);           // Convert to double
36
37      // Show the resulting data.
38      cout << setprecision(2) << fixed << showpoint;
39      cout << "Your name is " << name
40          <<", you are " << age
41          << " years old,\nand you make $"
42          << income << " per year.\n";
43
44      return 0;
45  }
```

(program output continues)

Program 10-8 *(continued)*

Program Output with Example Input Shown in Bold
```
What is your ID number? 1234 [Enter]
What is your name? Janice Smith [Enter]
How old are you? 25 [Enter]
What is your annual income? 60000 [Enter]
Your name is Janice Smith, you are 25 years old,
and you make $60000.00 per year.
```

 Checkpoint

10.11   Write a short description of each of the following functions:

```
atoi
atol
atof
itoa
```

10.12   Write a statement that will convert the string "`10`" to an integer and store the result in the variable num.

10.13   Write a statement that will convert the string "`100000`" to a `long` and store the result in the variable num.

10.14   Write a statement that will convert the string "`7.2389`" to a `double` and store the result in the variable num.

10.15   Write a statement that will convert the integer 127 to a string, stored in base-10 notation in the array `value`.

10.6

Focus on Software Engineering: Writing Your Own C-String-Handling Functions

CONCEPT: You can design your own specialized functions for manipulating strings.

VideoNote

Writing a C-String-Handling Function

By being able to pass arrays as arguments, you can write your own functions for processing C-strings. For example, Program 10-9 uses a function to copy a C-string from one array to another.

Program 10-9

```
1   // This program uses a function to copy a C-string into an array.
2   #include <iostream>
3   using namespace std;
4
5   void stringCopy(char [], char []);  // Function prototype
6
```

```
 7   int main()
 8   {
 9      const int LENGTH = 30;   // Size of the arrays
10      char first[LENGTH];      // To hold the user's input
11      char second[LENGTH];     // To hold the copy
12
13      // Get a string from the user and store in first.
14      cout << "Enter a string with no more than "
15           << (LENGTH - 1) << " characters:\n";
16      cin.getline(first, LENGTH);
17
18      // Copy the contents of first to second.
19      stringCopy(first, second);
20
21      // Display the copy.
22      cout << "The string you entered is:\n" << second << endl;
23      return 0;
24   }
25
26   //*********************************************************
27   // Definition of the stringCopy function.                 *
28   // This function copies the C-string in string1 to string2. *
29   //*********************************************************
30
31   void stringCopy(char string1[], char string2[])
32   {
33      int index = 0;   // Loop counter
34
35      // Step through string1, copying each element to
36      // string2. Stop when the null character is encountered.
37      while (string1[index] != '\0')
38      {
39         string2[index] = string1[index];
40         index++;
41      }
42
43      // Place a null character in string2.
44      string2[index] = '\0';
45   }
```

Program Output with Example Input Shown in Bold
Enter a string with no more than 29 characters:
Thank goodness it's Friday! [Enter]
The string you entered is:
Thank goodness it's Friday!

Notice the function stringCopy does not accept an argument indicating the size of the arrays. It simply copies the characters from string1 into string2 until it encounters a null terminator in string1. When the null terminator is found, the loop has reached the end of the C-string. The last statement in the function assigns a null terminator (the '\0' character) to the end of string2, so it is properly terminated.

WARNING! Because the `stringCopy` function doesn't know the size of the second array, it's the programmer's responsibility to make sure the second array is large enough to hold the string in the first array.

Program 10-10 uses another C-string-handling function: `nameSlice`. The program asks the user to enter his or her first and last names, separated by a space. The function searches the string for the space, and replaces it with a null terminator. In effect, this "cuts" the last name off of the string.

Program 10-10

```
1   // This program uses the function nameSlice to cut the last
2   // name off of a string that contains the user's first and
3   // last names.
4   #include <iostream>
5   using namespace std;
6
7   void nameSlice(char []); // Function prototype
8
9   int main()
10  {
11     const int SIZE = 41;  // Array size
12     char name[SIZE];       // To hold the user's name
13
14     cout << "Enter your first and last names, separated ";
15     cout << "by a space:\n";
16     cin.getline(name, SIZE);
17     nameSlice(name);
18     cout << "Your first name is: " << name << endl;
19     return 0;
20  }
21
22  //************************************************************
23  // Definition of function nameSlice. This function accepts a   *
24  // character array as its argument. It scans the array looking *
25  // for a space. When it finds one, it replaces it with a null  *
26  // terminator.                                                 *
27  //************************************************************
28
29  void nameSlice(char userName[])
30  {
31     int count = 0;  // Loop counter
32
33     // Locate the first space, or the null terminator if there
34     // are no spaces.
35     while (userName[count] != ' ' && userName[count] != '\0')
36        count++;
37
38     // If a space was found, replace it with a null terminator.
39     if (userName[count] == ' ')
40        userName[count] = '\0';
41  }
```

Program Output with Example Input Shown in Bold
```
Enter your first and last names, separated by a space:
Jimmy Jones [Enter]
Your first name is: Jimmy
```

The following loop in lines 35 and 36 starts at the first character in the array and scans the string searching for either a space or a null terminator:

```
while (userName[count] != ' ' && userName[count] != '\0')
    count++;
```

If the character in userName[count] isn't a space or the null terminator, count is incremented, and the next character is examined. With the example input "Jimmy Jones," the loop finds the space separating "Jimmy" and "Jones" at userName[5]. When the loop stops, count is set to 5. This is illustrated in Figure 10-3.

Figure 10-3

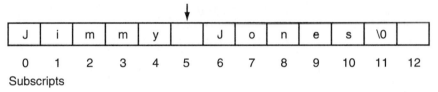

The loop stops when count reaches 5 because userName[5] contains a space

J	i	m	m	y		J	o	n	e	s	\0	
0	1	2	3	4	5	6	7	8	9	10	11	12

Subscripts

NOTE: The loop will also stop if it encounters a null terminator. This is so it will not go beyond the boundary of the array if the user didn't enter a space.

Once the loop has finished, userName[count] will either contain a space or a null terminator. If it contains a space, the following if statement, in lines 39 and 40, replaces it with a null terminator:

```
if (userName[count] == ' ')
    userName[count] = '\0';
```

This is illustrated in Figure 10-4.

Figure 10-4

The space is replaced with a null terminator. This now becomes the end of the string.

J	i	m	m	y	\0	J	o	n	e	s	\0	
0	1	2	3	4	5	6	7	8	9	10	11	12

Subscripts

The new null terminator now becomes the end of the string.

Using Pointers to Pass C-String Arguments

Pointers are extremely useful for writing functions that process C-strings. If the starting address of a string is passed into a pointer parameter variable, it can be assumed that all the characters, from that address up to the byte that holds the null terminator, are part of the string. (It isn't necessary to know the length of the array that holds the string.)

Program 10-11 demonstrates a function, `countChars`, that uses a pointer to count the number of times a specific character appears in a C-string.

Program 10-11

```cpp
 1  // This program demonstrates a function, countChars, that counts
 2  // the number of times a specific character appears in a string.
 3  #include <iostream>
 4  using namespace std;
 5
 6  int countChars(char *, char);  // Function prototype
 7
 8  int main()
 9  {
10     const int SIZE = 51;    // Array size
11     char userString[SIZE];  // To hold a string
12     char letter;            // The character to count
13
14     // Get a string from the user.
15     cout << "Enter a string (up to 50 characters): ";
16     cin.getline(userString, SIZE);
17
18     // Choose a character whose occurrences within the string will be counted.
19     cout << "Enter a character and I will tell you how many\n";
20     cout << "times it appears in the string: ";
21     cin >> letter;
22
23     // Display the number of times the character appears.
24     cout << letter << " appears ";
25     cout << countChars(userString, letter) << " times.\n";
26     return 0;
27  }
28
29  //******************************************************************
30  // Definition of countChars. The parameter strPtr is a pointer   *
31  // that points to a string. The parameter Ch is a character that *
32  // the function searches for in the string. The function returns *
33  // the number of times the character appears in the string.      *
34  //******************************************************************
35
36  int countChars(char *strPtr, char ch)
37  {
38     int times = 0;  // Number of times ch appears in the string
39
```

```
40      // Step through the string counting occurrences of ch.
41      while (*strPtr != '\0')
42      {
43          if (*strPtr == ch)   // If the current character equals ch...
44              times++;          // ... increment the counter
45          strPtr++;             // Go to the next char in the string.
46      }
47
48      return times;
49  }
```

Program Output with Example Input Shown in Bold
Enter a string (up to 50 characters): **Starting Out with C++ [Enter]**
Enter a character and I will tell you how many
times it appears in the string: **t [Enter]**
t appears 4 times.

In the function countChars, strPtr points to the C-string that is to be searched and ch contains the character to look for. The while loop in lines 41 through 46 repeats as long as the character that strPtr points to is not the null terminator:

```
while (*strPtr != '\0')
```

Inside the loop, the if statement in line 43 compares the character that strPtr points to with the character in ch:

```
if (*strPtr == ch)
```

If the two are equal, the variable times is incremented in line 44. (times keeps a running total of the number of times the character appears.) The last statement in the loop is

```
strPtr++;
```

This statement increments the address in strPtr. This causes strPtr to point to the next character in the string. Then, the loop starts over. When strPtr finally reaches the null terminator, the loop terminates and the function returns the value in times.

 See the Student CD for the String Manipulation Case Study.

 Checkpoint

10.16 What is the output of the following program?

```
#include <iostream>
using namespace std;

// Function Prototype
void mess(char []);

int main()
{
    char stuff[] = "Tom Talbert Tried Trains";
```

```
        cout << stuff << endl;
        mess(stuff);
        cout << stuff << endl;
        return 0;
    }

    // Definition of function mess
    void mess(char str[])
    {
        int step = 0;

        while (str[step] != '\0')
        {
            if (str[step] == 'T')
                str[step] = 'D';
            step++;
        }
    }
```

10.7   The C++ string Class

CONCEPT: Standard C++ provides a special data type for storing and working with strings.

VideoNote
Using the
string Class

C++ provides two ways of storing and working with strings. One method is to store them as C-strings in character array variables. Another way is to store them in string class objects. Although string class objects are much easier to work with than C-strings, some prestandard compilers do not support them. Because you are likely to encounter programs in the workplace that use one or the other approach to handling strings, this book teaches both.

What Is the string Class?

The string class is an abstract data type. This means it is not a built-in, primitive data type like int or char. Instead, it is a programmer-defined data type that accompanies the C++ language. It provides many capabilities that make storing and working with strings easy and intuitive.

Using the string Class

The first step in using the string class is to #include the string header file. This is accomplished with the following preprocessor directive:

```
#include <string>
```

Now you are ready to define a string object. Defining a string object is similar to defining a variable of a primitive type. For example, the following statement defines a string object named movieTitle.

```
string movieTitle;
```

You assign a string value to the movieTitle object with the assignment operator, as shown in the following statement.

```
movieTitle = "Wheels of Fury";
```

The contents of movieTitle is displayed on the screen with the cout object, as shown in the next statement:

```
cout << "My favorite movie is " << movieTitle << endl;
```

Program 10-12 is a complete program that demonstrates the statements shown above.

Program 10-12

```
 1   // This program demonstrates the string class.
 2   #include <iostream>
 3   #include <string>     // Required for the string class.
 4   using namespace std;
 5
 6   int main()
 7   {
 8       string movieTitle;
 9
10       movieTitle = "Wheels of Fury";
11       cout << "My favorite movie is " << movieTitle << endl;
12       return 0;
13   }
```

Program Output
```
My favorite movie is Wheels of Fury
```

As you can see, working with string objects is similar to working with variables of other types. For example, Program 10-13 demonstrates how you can use cin to read a value from the keyboard into a string object.

Program 10-13

```
 1   // This program demonstrates how cin can read a string into
 2   // a string class object.
 3   #include <iostream>
 4   #include <string>
 5   using namespace std;
 6
 7   int main()
 8   {
 9       string name;
10
11       cout << "What is your name? ";
12       cin >> name;
13       cout << "Good morning " << name << endl;
14       return 0;
15   }
```

(program output continues)

Program 10-13   *(continued)*

Program Output with Example Input Shown in Bold
```
What is your name? Peggy [Enter]
Good morning Peggy
```

Reading a Line of Input into a string Object

If you want to read a line of input (with spaces) into a string object, use the getline() function. Here is an example:

```
string name;
cout << "What is your name? ";
getline(cin, name);
```

The getline() function's first argument is the name of a stream object you wish to read the input from. The function call above passes the cin object to getline(), so the function reads a line of input from the keyboard. The second argument is the name of a string object. This is where getline() stores the input that it reads.

Comparing and Sorting string Objects

There is no need to use a function such as strcmp to compare string objects. You may use the <, >, <=, >=, ==, and != relational operators. For example, assume the following definitions exist in a program:

```
string set1 = "ABC";
string set2 = "XYZ";
```

The object set1 is considered less than the object set2 because the characters "ABC" alphabetically precede the characters "XYZ." So, the following if statement will cause the message "set1 is less than set2" to be displayed on the screen.

```
if (set1 < set2)
   cout << "set1 is less than set2.\n";
```

Relational operators perform comparisons on string objects in a fashion similar to the way the strcmp function compares C-strings. One by one, each character in the first operand is compared with the character in the corresponding position in the second operand. If all the characters in both strings match, the two strings are equal. Other relationships can be determined if two characters in corresponding positions do not match. The first operand is less than the second operand if the mismatched character in the first operand is less than its counterpart in the second operand. Likewise, the first operand is greater than the second operand if the mismatched character in the first operand is greater than its counterpart in the second operand.

For example, assume a program has the following definitions:

```
string name1 = "Mary";
string name2 = "Mark";
```

The value in name1, "Mary," is greater than the value in name2, "Mark." This is because the "y" in "Mary" has a greater ASCII value than the "k" in "Mark."

string objects can also be compared to C-strings with relational operators. Assuming str is a string object, all of the following are valid relational expressions:

```
str > "Joseph"
"Kimberly" < str
str == "William"
```

Program 10-14 demonstrates string objects and relational operators.

Program 10-14

```
 1   // This program uses the == operator to compare the string entered
 2   // by the user with the valid stereo part numbers.
 3   #include <iostream>
 4   #include <iomanip>
 5   #include <string>
 6   using namespace std;
 7
 8   int main()
 9   {
10      const double APRICE = 249.0;    // Price for part A
11      const double BPRICE = 299.0;    // Price for part B
12      string partNum;                 // Part number
13
14      cout << "The stereo part numbers are:\n";
15      cout << "\tBoom Box, part number S147-29A\n";
16      cout << "\tShelf Model, part number S147-29B\n";
17      cout << "Enter the part number of the stereo you\n";
18      cout << "wish to purchase: ";
19      cin >> partNum;
20      cout << fixed << showpoint << setprecision(2);
21
22      if (partNum == "S147-29A")
23         cout << "The price is $" << APRICE << endl;
24      else if (partNum == "S147-29B")
25         cout << "The price is $" << BPRICE << endl;
26      else
27         cout << partNum << " is not a valid part number.\n";
28      return 0;
29   }
```

Program Output with Example Input Shown in Bold
```
The stereo part numbers are:
        Boom Box, part number S147-29A
        Shelf Model, part number S147-29B
Enter the part number of the stereo you
wish to purchase: S147-29A [Enter]
The price is $249.00
```

You may also use relational operators to sort string objects. Program 10-15 demonstrates this.

Program 10-15

```
 1   // This program uses relational operators to alphabetically
 2   // sort two strings entered by the user.
 3   #include <iostream>
 4   #include <string>
 5   using namespace std;
 6
 7   int main ()
 8   {
 9      string name1, name2;
10
11      // Get a name.
12      cout << "Enter a name (last name first): ";
13      getline(cin, name1);
14
15      // Get another name.
16      cout << "Enter another name: ";
17      getline(cin, name2);
18
19      // Display them in alphabetical order.
20      cout << "Here are the names sorted alphabetically:\n";
21      if (name1 < name2)
22         cout << name1 << endl << name2 << endl;
23      else if (name1 > name2)
24         cout << name2 << endl << name1 << endl;
25      else
26         cout << "You entered the same name twice!\n";
27      return 0;
28   }
```

Program Output with Example Input Shown in Bold
```
Enter a name (last name first): Smith, Richard [Enter]
Enter another name: Jones, John [Enter]
Here are the names sorted alphabetically:
Jones, John
Smith, Richard
```

Other Ways to Define `string` Objects

There are a variety of ways to initialize a `string` object when you define it. Table 10-5 shows several example definitions, and describes each. Program 10-16 demonstrates a `string` object initialized with the string "William Smith."

Program 10-16

```
 1   // This program initializes a string object.
 2   #include <iostream>
 3   #include <string>
 4   using namespace std;
 5
```

```
6   int main()
7   {
8       string greeting;
9       string name("William Smith");
10
11      greeting = "Hello ";
12      cout << greeting << name << endl;
13      return 0;
14  }
```

Program Output

```
Hello William Smith
```

Table 10-5

Definition	Description
`string address;`	Defines an empty `string` object named `address`.
`string name("William Smith");`	Defines a `string` object named `name`, initialized with "William Smith."
`string person1(person2);`	Defines a `string` object named `person1`, which is a copy of `person2`. `person2` may be either a `string` object or character array.
`string set1(set2, 5);`	Defines a `string` object named `set1`, which is initialized to the first five characters in the character array `set2`.
`string lineFull('z', 10);`	Defines a `string` object named `lineFull` initialized with 10 `'z'` characters.
`string firstName(fullName, 0, 7);`	Defines a `string` object named `firstName`, initialized with a substring of the `string` `fullName`. The substring is seven characters long, beginning at position 0.

Notice in Program 10-16 the use of the = operator to assign a value to the `string` object. The `string` class supports several operators, which are described in Table 10-6.

Table 10-6

Supported Operator	Description
`>>`	Extracts characters from a stream and inserts them into the `string`. Characters are copied until a whitespace or the end of the string is encountered.
`<<`	Inserts the `string` into a stream.
`=`	Assigns the `string` on the right to the `string` object on the left.
`+=`	Appends a copy of the `string` on the right to the `string` object on the left.
`+`	Returns a `string` that is the concatenation of the two `string` operands.
`[ ]`	Implements array-subscript notation, as in `name[x]`. A reference to the character in the `x` position is returned.
Relational Operators	Each of the relational operators is implemented:
	`< > <= >= == !=`

Program 10-17 demonstrates some of the string operators.

Program 10-17

```cpp
1   // This program demonstrates the C++ string class.
2   #include <iostream>
3   #include <string>
4   using namespace std;
5
6   int main ()
7   {
8      // Define three string objects.
9      string str1, str2, str3;
10
11     // Assign values to all three.
12     str1 = "ABC";
13     str2 = "DEF";
14     str3 = str1 + str2;
15
16     // Display all three.
17     cout << str1 << endl;
18     cout << str2 << endl;
19     cout << str3 << endl;
20
21     // Concatenate a string onto str3 and display it.
22     str3 += "GHI";
23     cout << str3 << endl;
24     return 0;
25  }
```

Program Output
```
ABC
DEF
ABCDEF
ABCDEFGHI
```

Using string Class Member Functions

The string class also has member functions. For example, the length member function returns the length of the string stored in the object. The value is returned as an unsigned integer.

Assume the following string object definition exists in a program:

```cpp
string town = "Charleston";
```

The following statement in the same program would assign the value 10 to the variable x.

```cpp
x = town.length();
```

Program 10-18 further demonstrates the length member function.

Program 10-18

```
 1   // This program demonstrates a string
 2   // object's length member function.
 3   #include <iostream>
 4   #include <string>
 5   using namespace std;
 6
 7   int main ()
 8   {
 9      string town;
10
11      cout << "Where do you live? ";
12      cin >> town;
13      cout << "Your town's name has " << town.length() ;
14      cout << " characters\n";
15      return 0;
16   }
```

Program Output with Example Input Shown in Bold
Where do you live? **Jacksonville [Enter]**
Your town's name has 12 characters

The size function returns the length of the string. It is demonstrated in the for loop in Program 10-19.

Program 10-19

```
 1   // This program demonstrates the C++ string class.
 2   #include <iostream>
 3   #include <string>
 4   using namespace std;
 5
 6   int main()
 7   {
 8      // Define three string objects.
 9      string str1, str2, str3;
10
11      // Assign values to all three.
12      str1 = "ABC";
13      str2 = "DEF";
14      str3 = str1 + str2;
15
16      // Use subscripts to display str3 one character
17      // at a time.
18      for (int x = 0; x < str3.size(); x++)
19         cout << str3[x];
20      cout << endl;
21
```

(program continues)

Program 10-19   *(continued)*

```
22      // Compare str1 with str2.
23      if (str1 < str2)
24         cout << "str1 is less than str2\n";
25      else
26         cout << "str1 is not less than str2\n";
27      return 0;
28   }
```

Program Output
```
ABCDEF
str1 is less than str2
```

Table 10-7 lists many of the string class member functions and their overloaded variations. In the examples, assume theString is the name of a string object.

Table 10-7

Member Function Example	Description
theString.append(n, 'z');	Appends n copies of 'z' to theString.
theString.append(str);	Appends str to theString. str can be a string object or character array.
theString.append(str, n);	The first n characters of the character array str are appended to theString.
theString.append(str, x, n);	n number of characters from str, starting at position x, are appended to theString. If theString is too small, the function will copy as many characters as possible.
theString.assign(n, 'z');	Assigns n copies of 'z' to theString.
theString.assign(str);	Assigns str to theString. str can be a string object or character array.
theString.assign(str, n);	The first n characters of the character array str are assigned to theString.
theString.assign(str, x, n);	n number of characters from str, starting at position x, are assigned to theString. If theString is too small, the function will copy as many characters as possible.
theString.at(x);	Returns the character at position x in the string.
theString.begin();	Returns an iterator pointing to the first character in the string.
theString.c_str();	Returns a character array containing a null terminated string, as stored in theString.
theString.capacity();	Returns the size of the storage allocated for the string.
theString.clear();	Clears the string by deleting all the characters stored in it.

Table 10-7   *(continued)*

Member Function Example	Description
`theString.compare(str);`	Performs a comparison like the `strcmp` function (see Chapter 4), with the same return values. `str` can be a `string` object or a character array.
`theString.compare(x, n, str);`	Compares `theString` and `str`, starting at position x, and continuing for n characters. The return value is like `strcmp`. `str` can be a `string` object or character array.
`theString.copy(str, x, n);`	Copies the character array `str` to `theString`, beginning at position x, for n characters. If `theString` is too small, the function will copy as many characters as possible.
`theString.empty();`	Returns true if `theString` is empty.
`theString.end();`	Returns an iterator pointing to the last character of the string in `theString`.
`theString.erase(x, n);`	Erases n characters from `theString`, beginning at position x.
`theString.find(str, x);`	Returns the first position at or beyond position x where the string `str` is found in `theString`. `str` may be either a `string` object or a character array.
`theString.find('z', x);`	Returns the first position at or beyond position x where 'z' is found in `theString`.
`theString.insert(x, n, 'z');`	Inserts 'z' n times into `theString` at position x.
`theString.insert(x, str);`	Inserts a copy of `str` into `theString`, beginning at position x. `str` may be either a `string` object or a character array.
`theString.length();`	Returns the length of the string in `theString`.
`theString.replace(x, n, str);`	Replaces the n characters in `theString` beginning at position x with the characters in string object `str`.
`theString.resize(n, 'z');`	Changes the size of the allocation in `theString` to n. If n is less than the current size of the string, the string is truncated to n characters. If n is greater, the string is expanded and 'z' is appended at the end enough times to fill the new spaces.
`theString.size();`	Returns the length of the string in `theString`.
`theString.substr(x, n);`	Returns a copy of a substring. The substring is n characters long and begins at position x of `theString`.
`theString.swap(str);`	Swaps the contents of `theString` with `str`.

Focus on Problem Solving and Program Design: A Case Study

10.8

As a programmer for the Home Software Company, you are asked to develop a function named `dollarFormat` that inserts commas and a $ sign at the appropriate locations in a `string` object containing an unformatted dollar amount. As an argument, the function should accept a reference to a `string` object. You may assume the `string` object contains a value such as 1084567.89. The function should modify the `string` object so it contains a formatted dollar amount, such as $1,084,567.89.

The code for the `dollarFormat` function follows.

```cpp
void dollarFormat(string &currency)
{
    int dp;

    dp = currency.find('.');   // Find decimal point
    if (dp > 3)                // Insert commas
    {
        for (int x = dp - 3; x > 0; x -= 3)
            currency.insert(x, ",");
    }
    currency.insert(0, "$");   // Insert dollar sign
}
```

The function defines an `int` variable named `dp`. This variable is used to hold the position of the unformatted number's decimal point. This is accomplished with the statement:

```cpp
dp = currency.find('.');
```

The `string` class' `find` member function returns the position number in the string where the '.' character is found. An `if` statement determines if the number has more than three numbers preceding the decimal point:

```cpp
if (dp > 3)
```

If the decimal point is at a position greater than 3, then the function inserts commas in the string with the following loop:

```cpp
for (int x = dp - 3; x > 0; x -= 3)
    currency.insert(x, ",");
```

Finally, a $ symbol is inserted at position 0 (the first character in the `string`).

Program 10-20 demonstrates the function.

Program 10-20

```
 1   // This program lets the user enter a number. The
 2   // dollarFormat function formats the number as
 3   // a dollar amount.
 4   #include <iostream>
 5   #include <string>
 6   using namespace std;
 7
 8   // Function prototype
 9   void dollarFormat(string &);
10
11   int main ()
12   {
13      string input;
14
15      // Get the dollar amount from the user.
16      cout << "Enter a dollar amount in the form nnnnn.nn : ";
17      cin >> input;
18      dollarFormat(input);
19      cout << "Here is the amount formatted:\n";
20      cout << input << endl;
21      return 0;
22   }
23
24   //***********************************************************
25   // Definition of the dollarFormat function. This function   *
26   // accepts a string reference object, which is assumed      *
27   // to hold a number with a decimal point. The function      *
28   // formats the number as a dollar amount with commas and    *
29   // a $ symbol.                                              *
30   //***********************************************************
31
32   void dollarFormat(string &currency)
33   {
34      int dp;
35
36      dp = currency.find('.');    // Find decimal point
37      if (dp > 3)                  // Insert commas
38      {
39         for (int x = dp - 3; x > 0; x -= 3)
40            currency.insert(x, ",");
41      }
42      currency.insert(0, "$");    // Insert dollar sign
43   }
```

Program Output with Example Input Shown in Bold
```
Enter a dollar amount in the form nnnnn.nn: 1084567.89 [Enter]
Here is the amount formatted:
$1,084,567.89
```

Review Questions and Exercises

Short Answer

1. What header file must you include in a program using character testing functions such as `isalpha` and `isdigit`?

2. What header file must you include in a program using the character conversion functions `toupper` and `tolower`?

3. Assume `c` is a char variable. What value does `c` hold after each of the following statements executes?

   Statement   *Contents of* `c`

   ```
   c = toupper('a');_____
   c = toupper('B');_____
   c = tolower('D');_____
   c = toupper('e');_____
   ```

4. Look at the following code. What value will be stored in `s` after the code executes?

   ```
   char name[10];
   int s;
   strcpy(name, "Jimmy");
   s = strlen(name);
   ```

5. What header file must you include in a program using string functions such as `strlen` and `strcpy`?

6. What header file must you include in a program using string/numeric conversion functions such as `atoi` and `atof`?

7. What header file must you include in a program using `string` class objects?

8. How do you compare `string` class objects?

Fill-in-the-Blank

9. The _____ function returns true if the character argument is uppercase.

10. The _____ function returns true if the character argument is a letter of the alphabet.

11. The _____ function returns true if the character argument is a digit.

12. The _____ function returns true if the character argument is a whitespace character.

13. The _____ function returns the uppercase equivalent of its character argument.

14. The _____ function returns the lowercase equivalent of its character argument.

15. The _____ file must be included in a program that uses character testing functions.

16. The _____ function returns the length of a string.

17. To _____ two strings means to append one string to the other.

18. The _____ function concatenates two strings.

19. The _____ function copies one string to another.

20. The _____ function searches for a string inside of another one.

21. The _____ function compares two strings.

22. The _____ function copies, at most, *n* number of characters from one string to another.

23. The _____ function returns the value of a string converted to an integer.

24. The _____ function returns the value of a string converted to a long integer.

25. The _____ function returns the value of a string converted to a float.

26. The _____ function converts an integer to a string.

Algorithm Workbench

27. The following `if` statement determines whether choice is equal to 'Y' or 'y'.

```
if (choice == 'Y' || choice == 'y')
```

Simplify this statement by using either the `toupper` or `tolower` function.

28. Assume `input` is a `char` array holding a C-string. Write code that counts the number of elements in the array that contain an alphabetic character.

29. Look at the following array definition.

```
char str[10];
```

Assume that `name` is also a `char` array, and it holds a C-string. Write code that copies the contents of `name` to `str` if the C-string in `name` is not too big to fit in `str`.

30. Look at the following statements.

```
char str[] = "237.89";
double value;
```

Write a statement that converts the string in `str` to a double and stores the result in `value`.

31. Write a function that accepts a pointer to a C-string as its argument. The function should count the number of times the character 'w' occurs in the argument and return that number.

32. Assume that `str1` and `str2` are string class objects. Write code that displays "They are the same!" if the two objects contain the same string.

True or False

33. T F Character testing functions, such as `isupper`, accept strings as arguments and test each character in the string.

34. T F If `toupper`'s argument is already uppercase, it is returned as is, with no changes.

35. T F If `tolower`'s argument is already lowercase, it will be inadvertently converted to uppercase.

36. T F The `strlen` function returns the size of the array containing a string.

37. T F If the starting address of a string is passed into a pointer parameter, it can be assumed that all the characters, from that address up to the byte that holds the null terminator, are part of the string.

38. T F String-handling functions accept as arguments pointers to strings (array names or pointer variables), or literal strings.

39. T   F   The strcat function checks to make sure the first string is large enough to hold both strings before performing the concatenation.

40. T   F   The strcpy function will overwrite the contents of its first string argument.

41. T   F   The strcpy function performs no bounds checking on the first argument.

42. T   F   There is no difference between "847" and 847.

Find the Errors

Each of the following programs or program segments has errors. Find as many as you can.

43.
```
char str[] = "Stop";
if (isupper(str) == "STOP")
    exit(0);
```

44.
```
char numeric[5];
int x = 123;
numeric = atoi(x);
```

45.
```
char string1[] = "Billy";
char string2[] = " Bob Jones";
strcat(string1, string2);
```

46.
```
char x = 'a', y = 'a';
if (strcmp(x, y) == 0)
    exit(0);
```

Programming Challenges

1. **String Length**

    Write a function that returns an integer and accepts a pointer to a C-string as an argument. The function should count the number of characters in the string and return that number. Demonstrate the function in a simple program that asks the user to input a string, passes it to the function, and then displays the function's return value.

VideoNote

Solving the
Backward
String
Problem

2. **Backward String**

    Write a function that accepts a pointer to a C-string as an argument and displays its contents backward. For instance, if the string argument is "Gravity" the function should display "ytivarG". Demonstrate the function in a program that asks the user to input a string and then passes it to the function.

3. **Word Counter**

    Write a function that accepts a pointer to a C-string as an argument and returns the number of words contained in the string. For instance, if the string argument is "Four score and seven years ago" the function should return the number 6. Demonstrate the function in a program that asks the user to input a string and then passes it to the function. The number of words in the string should be displayed on the screen. *Optional Exercise:* Write an overloaded version of this function that accepts a string class object as its argument.

4. **Average Number of Letters**

    Modify the program you wrote for Problem 3 (Word Counter), so it also displays the average number of letters in each word.

5. **Sentence Capitalizer**

Write a function that accepts a pointer to a C-string as an argument and capitalizes the first character of each sentence in the string. For instance, if the string argument is "hello. my name is Joe. what is your name?" the function should manipulate the string so it contains "Hello. My name is Joe. What is your name?" Demonstrate the function in a program that asks the user to input a string and then passes it to the function. The modified string should be displayed on the screen. *Optional Exercise:* Write an overloaded version of this function that accepts a string class object as its argument.

6. **Vowels and Consonants**

Write a function that accepts a pointer to a C-string as its argument. The function should count the number of vowels appearing in the string and return that number.

Write another function that accepts a pointer to a C-string as its argument. This function should count the number of consonants appearing in the string and return that number.

Demonstrate these two functions in a program that performs the following steps:

1. The user is asked to enter a string.

2. The program displays the following menu:
   A) Count the number of vowels in the string
   B) Count the number of consonants in the string
   C) Count both the vowels and consonants in the string
   D) Enter another string
   E) Exit the program

3. The program performs the operation selected by the user and repeats until the user selects E to exit the program.

7. **Name Arranger**

Write a program that asks for the user's first, middle, and last names. The names should be stored in three different character arrays. The program should then store, in a fourth array, the name arranged in the following manner: the last name followed by a comma and a space, followed by the first name and a space, followed by the middle name. For example, if the user entered "Carol Lynn Smith", it should store "Smith, Carol Lynn" in the fourth array. Display the contents of the fourth array on the screen.

8. **Sum of Digits in a String**

Write a program that asks the user to enter a series of single digit numbers with nothing separating them. Read the input as a C-string or a `string` object. The program should display the sum of all the single-digit numbers in the string. For example, if the user enters 2514, the program should display 12, which is the sum of 2, 5, 1, and 4. The program should also display the highest and lowest digits in the string.

9. **Most Frequent Character**

Write a function that accepts either a pointer to a C-string, or a string object, as its argument. The function should return the character that appears most frequently in the string. Demonstrate the function in a complete program.

10. **replaceSubstring Function**

Write a function named replaceSubstring. The function should accept three C-string or string object arguments. Let's call them *string1*, *string2*, and *string3*. It should search *string1* for all occurrences of *string2*. When it finds an occurrence of *string2*, it should replace it with *string3*. For example, suppose the three arguments have the following values:

string1:	"the dog jumped over the fence"
string2:	"the"
string3:	"that"

With these three arguments, the function would return a string object with the value "that dog jumped over that fence." Demonstrate the function in a complete program.

11. **Case Manipulator**

Write a program with three functions: upper, lower, and reverse. The upper function should accept a pointer to a C-string as an argument. It should step through each character in the string, converting it to uppercase. The lower function, too, should accept a pointer to a C-string as an argument. It should step through each character in the string, converting it to lowercase. Like upper and lower, reverse should also accept a pointer to a string. As it steps through the string, it should test each character to determine whether it is upper- or lowercase. If a character is uppercase, it should be converted to lowercase. Likewise, if a character is lowercase, it should be converted to uppercase.

Test the functions by asking for a string in function main, then passing it to them in the following order: reverse, lower, and upper.

12. **Password Verifier**

Imagine you are developing a software package that requires users to enter their own passwords. Your software requires that users' passwords meet the following criteria:

- The password should be at least six characters long.
- The password should contain at least one uppercase and at least one lowercase letter.
- The password should have at least one digit.

Write a program that asks for a password and then verifies that it meets the stated criteria. If it doesn't, the program should display a message telling the user why.

13. **Date Printer**

Write a program that reads a string from the user containing a date in the form mm/dd/yyyy. It should print the date in the form March 12, 2010.

14. **Word Separator**

Write a program that accepts as input a sentence in which all of the words are run together, but the first character of each word is uppercase. Convert the sentence to a string in which the words are separated by spaces and only the first word starts with an uppercase letter. For example the string "StopAndSmellTheRoses." would be converted to "Stop and smell the roses."

15. **Character Analysis**

On the student CD you will find a file named `text.txt`. Write a program that reads the file's contents and determines the following:

- The number of uppercase letters in the file
- The number of lowercase letters in the file
- The number of digits in the file
- The number of whitespace characters in the file

16. **Pig Latin**

Write a program that reads a sentence as input and converts each word to "Pig Latin." In one version, to convert a word to Pig Latin you remove the first letter and place that letter at the end of the word. Then you append the string "ay" to the word. Here is an example:

English: I SLEPT MOST OF THE NIGHT

Pig Latin: IAY LEPTSAY OSTMAY FOAY HETAY IGHTNAY

17. **Morse Code Converter**

Morse code is a code where each letter of the English alphabet, each digit, and various punctuation characters are represented by a series of dots and dashes. Table 10-8 shows part of the code.

Write a program that asks the user to enter a string, and then converts that string to Morse code. (Use hyphens for dashes and periods for dots.)

Table 10-8   Morse Code

Character	Code	Character	Code	Character	Code	Character	Code
space	*space*	6	-....	G	--.	Q	--.-
comma	--..--	7	--...	H	....	R	.-.
period	.-.-.-	8	---..	I	..	S	...
question mark	..--..	9	----.	J	.---	T	-
0	-----	A	.-	K	-.-	U	..-
1	.----	B	-...	L	.-..	V	...-
2	..---	C	-.-.	M	--	W	.--
3	...--	D	-..	N	-.	X	-..-
4	....-	E	.	O	---	Y	-.--
5	.....	F	..-.	P	.--.	Z	--..

18. **Phone Number List**

Write a program that has an array of at least 10 string objects that hold people's names and phone numbers. You may make up your own strings, or use the following:

```
"Becky Warren, 555-1223"
"Joe Looney, 555-0097"
"Geri Palmer, 555-8787"
"Lynn Presnell, 555-1212"
"Holly Gaddis, 555-8878"
"Sam Wiggins, 555-0998"
"Bob Kain, 555-8712"
"Tim Haynes, 555-7676"
"Warren Gaddis, 555-9037"
"Jean James, 555-4939"
"Ron Palmer, 555-2783"
```

The program should ask the user to enter a name or partial name to search for in the array. Any entries in the array that match the string entered should be displayed. For example, if the user enters "Palmer" the program should display the following names from the list:

```
Geri Palmer, 555-8787
Ron Palmer, 555-2783
```

19. **Check Writer**

Write a program that displays a simulated paycheck. The program should ask the user to enter the date, the payee's name, and the amount of the check. It should then display a simulated check with the dollar amount spelled out, as shown here:

```
                                              Date: 11/24/09


Pay to the Order of: John Phillips            $1920.85

One thousand nine hundred twenty and 85 cents
```

Be sure to format the numeric value of the check in fixed-point notation with two decimal places of precision. Be sure the decimal place always displays, even when the number is zero or has no fractional part. Use either C-strings or string class objects in this program.

Input Validation: Do not accept negative dollar amounts, or amounts over $10,000.

11 Structured Data

TOPICS

11.1 Abstract Data Types

CONCEPT: Abstract data types (ADTs) are data types created by the programmer. ADTs have their own range (or domain) of data and their own sets of operations that may be performed on them.

The term *abstract data type,* or ADT, is very important in computer science and is especially significant in object-oriented programming. This chapter introduces you to the structure, which is one of C++'s mechanisms for creating abstract data types.

Abstraction

An *abstraction* is a general model of something. It is a definition that includes only the general characteristics of an object. For example, the term "dog" is an abstraction. It defines a general type of animal. The term captures the essence of what all dogs are without specifying the detailed characteristics of any particular type of dog. According to *Webster's New Collegiate Dictionary,* a dog is a highly variable carnivorous domesticated mammal (*Canis familiaris*) probably descended from the common wolf.

In real life, however, there is no such thing as a mere "dog." There are specific types of dogs, each with its own set of characteristics. There are poodles, cocker spaniels, Great Danes, rottweilers, and many other breeds. There are small dogs and large dogs. There are gentle dogs and ferocious dogs. They come in all shapes, sizes, and dispositions. A real-life dog is not abstract. It is concrete.

Data Types

C++ has several *primitive data types*, or data types that are defined as a basic part of the language, as shown in Table 11-1.

Table 11-1

bool	int	unsigned long int
char	long int	float
unsigned char	unsigned short int	double
short int	unsigned int	long double

A data type defines what values a variable may hold. Each data type listed in Table 11-1 has its own range of values, such as −32,768 to +32,767 for shorts, and so forth. Data types also define what values a variable may not hold. For example, integer variables may not be used to hold fractional numbers.

In addition to defining a range or domain of values that a variable may hold, data types also define the operations that may be performed on a value. All of the data types listed in Table 11-1 allow the following mathematical and relational operators to be used with them:

```
+   -   *   /   >   <   >=   <=   ==   !=
```

Only the integer data types, however, allow operations with the modulus operator (%). So, a data type defines what values an object may hold and the operations that may be performed on the object.

The primitive data types are abstract in the sense that a data type and an object of that data type are not the same thing. For example, consider the following variable definition:

```
int x = 1, y = 2, z = 3;
```

In the statement above the integer variables x, y, and z are defined. They are three separate instances of the data type int. Each variable has its own characteristics (x is set to 1, y is set to 2, and z is set to 3). In this example, the data type int is the abstraction and the variables x, y, and z are concrete occurrences.

Abstract Data Types

An abstract data type (ADT) is a data type created by the programmer and is composed of one or more primitive data types. The programmer decides what values are acceptable for the data type, as well as what operations may be performed on the data type. In many cases, the programmer designs his or her own specialized operations.

For example, suppose a program is created to simulate a 12-hour clock. The program could contain three ADTs: Hours, Minutes, and Seconds. The range of values for the Hours data type would be the integers 1 through 12. The range of values for the Minutes and Seconds data types would be 0 through 59. If an Hours object is set to 12 and then incremented, it will then take on the value 1. Likewise if a Minutes object or a Seconds object is set to 59 and then incremented, it will take on the value 0.

Abstract data types often combine several values. In the clock program, the Hours, Minutes, and Seconds objects could be combined to form a single Clock object. In this chapter you will learn how to combine variables of primitive data types to form your own data structures, or ADTs.

11.2 Focus on Software Engineering: Combining Data into Structures

CONCEPT: C++ allows you to group several variables together into a single item known as a structure.

So far you've written programs that keep data in individual variables. If you need to group items together, C++ allows you to create arrays. The limitation of arrays, however, is that all the elements must be of the same data type. Sometimes a relationship exists between items of different types. For example, a payroll system might keep the variables shown in Table 11-2. These variables hold data for a single employee.

Table 11-2

Variable Definition	Data Held
`int empNumber;`	Employee number
`char name[SIZE];`	Employee's name
`double hours;`	Hours worked
`double payRate;`	Hourly pay rate
`double grossPay;`	Gross pay

VideoNote

Creating a Structure

All of the variables listed in Table 11-2 are related because they can hold data about the same employee. Their definition statements, though, do not make it clear that they belong together. To create a relationship between variables, C++ gives you the ability to package them together into a *structure*.

Before a structure can be used, it must be declared. Here is the general format of a structure declaration:

```
struct tag
{
    variable declaration;
    // ... more declarations
    //     may follow...
};
```

The *tag* is the name of the structure. As you will see later, it's used like a data type name. The variable declarations that appear inside the braces declare *members* of the structure. Here is an example of a structure declaration that holds the payroll data listed in Table 11-2:

```
const int SIZE = 25; // Array size

struct PayRoll
{
    int empNumber;     // Employee number
    char name[SIZE];   // Employee's name
    double hours;      // Hours worked
    double payRate;    // Hourly pay rate
    double grossPay;   // Gross pay
};
```

This declaration declares a structure named `PayRoll`. The structure has five members: `empNumber`, `name`, `hours`, `payRate`, and `grossPay`.

WARNING! Notice that a semicolon is required after the closing brace of the structure declaration.

NOTE: In this text we begin the names of structure tags with an uppercase letter. Later you will see the same convention used with unions. This visually differentiates these names from the names of variables.

NOTE: The structure declaration shown contains three `double` members, each declared on a separate line. The three could also have been declared on the same line, as

```
const int SIZE = 25;

struct PayRoll
{
    int empNumber;
    char name[SIZE];
    double hours, payRate, grossPay;
};
```

Many programmers prefer to place each member declaration on a separate line, however, for increased readability.

It's important to note that the structure declaration in our example does not define a variable. It simply tells the compiler what a `PayRoll` structure is made of. In essence, it creates a new data type named `PayRoll`. You can define variables of this type with simple definition statements, just as you would with any other data type. For example, the following statement defines a variable named `deptHead`:

```
PayRoll deptHead;
```

The data type of deptHead is the PayRoll structure. The structure tag, PayRoll, is listed before the variable name just as the word int or double would be listed to define variables of those types.

Remember that structure variables are actually made up of other variables known as members. Because deptHead is a PayRoll structure it contains the following members:

    empNumber, an int
    name, a 25-element character array
    hours, a double
    payRate, a double
    grossPay, a double

Figure 11-1 illustrates this.

Figure 11-1

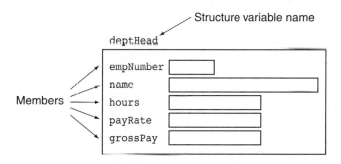

Just as it's possible to define multiple int or double variables, it's possible to define multiple structure variables in a program. The following statement defines three PayRoll variables: deptHead, foreman, and associate:

    PayRoll deptHead, foreman, associate;

Figure 11-2 illustrates the existence of these three variables.

Figure 11-2

deptHead

empNumber	
name	
hours	
payRate	
grossPay	

foreman

empNumber	
name	
hours	
payRate	
grossPay	

associate

empNumber	
name	
hours	
payRate	
grossPay	

Each of the variables defined in this example is a separate *instance* of the `PayRoll` structure and contains its own members. An instance of a structure is a variable that exists in memory. It contains within it all the members described in the structure declaration.

Although the structure variables in the example are separate, each contains members with the same name. (In the next section you'll see how to access these members.) Here are some other examples of structure declarations and variable definitions:

```
struct Time                              struct Date
{                                        {
   int hour;                                int day;
   int minutes;                             int month;
   int seconds;                             int year;
};                                       };

// Definition of the                     // Definition of the structure
// structure variable now.               // variable today.
Time now;                                Date today;
```

In review, there are typically two steps to implementing structures in a program:

- Create the structure declaration. This establishes the tag (or name) of the structure and a list of items that are members.
- Define variables (or instances) of the structure and use them in the program to hold data.

11.3   Accessing Structure Members

CONCEPT: The *dot operator* (.) allows you to access structure members in a program.

C++ provides the dot operator (a period) to access the individual members of a structure. Using our example of `deptHead` as a `PayRoll` structure variable, the following statement demonstrates how to access the `empNumber` member:

```
deptHead.empNumber = 475;
```

In this statement, the number 475 is assigned to the `empNumber` member of `deptHead`. The dot operator connects the name of the member variable with the name of the structure variable it belongs to. The following statements assign values to the `empNumber` members of the `deptHead`, `foreman`, and `associate` structure variables:

```
deptHead.empNumber = 475;
foreman.empNumber = 897;
associate.empNumber = 729;
```

With the dot operator you can use member variables just like regular variables. For example these statements display the contents of deptHead's members:

```
cout << deptHead.empNumber << endl;
cout << deptHead.name << endl;
cout << deptHead.hours << endl;
cout << deptHead.payRate << endl;
cout << deptHead.grossPay << endl;
```

Program 11-1 is a complete program that uses the PayRoll structure.

Program 11-1

```
 1   // This program demonstrates the use of structures.
 2   #include <iostream>
 3   #include <iomanip>
 4   using namespace std;
 5
 6   const int SIZE = 25; // Array size
 7
 8   struct PayRoll
 9   {
10      int empNumber;     // Employee number
11      char name[SIZE];   // Employee's name
12      double hours;      // Hours worked
13      double payRate;    // Hourly pay rate
14      double grossPay;   // Gross pay
15   };
16
17   int main()
18   {
19      PayRoll employee; // employee is a PayRoll structure.
20
21      // Get the employee's number.
22      cout << "Enter the employee's number: ";
23      cin >> employee.empNumber;
24
25      // Get the employee's name.
26      cout << "Enter the employee's name: ";
27      cin.ignore();  // To skip the remaining '\n' character
28      cin.getline(employee.name, SIZE);
29
30      // Get the hours worked by the employee.
31      cout << "How many hours did the employee work? ";
32      cin >> employee.hours;
33
34      // Get the employee's hourly pay rate.
35      cout << "What is the employee's hourly pay rate? ";
36      cin >> employee.payRate;
37
38      // Calculate the employee's gross pay.
39      employee.grossPay = employee.hours * employee.payRate;
40
```

(program continues)

Program 11-1 *(continued)*

```
41      // Display the employee data.
42      cout << "Here is the employee's payroll data:\n";
43      cout << "Name: " << employee.name << endl;
44      cout << "Number: " << employee.empNumber << endl;
45      cout << "Hours worked: " << employee.hours << endl;
46      cout << "Hourly pay rate: " << employee.payRate << endl;
47      cout << fixed << showpoint << setprecision(2);
48      cout << "Gross pay: $" << employee.grossPay << endl;
49      return 0;
50  }
```

Program Output with Example Input Shown in Bold
```
Enter the employee's number: 489 [Enter]
Enter the employee's name: Jill Smith [Enter]
How many hours did the employee work? 40 [Enter]
What is the employee's hourly pay rate? 20 [Enter]
Here is the employee's payroll data:
Name: Jill Smith
Number: 489
Hours worked: 40
Hourly pay rate: 20
Gross pay: $800.00
```

NOTE: Program 11-1 has the following call, in line 27, to cin's ignore member function:

```
cin.ignore();
```

Recall that the ignore function causes cin to ignore the next character in the input buffer. This is necessary for the cin.getline statement to work properly in the program.

NOTE: The contents of a structure variable cannot be displayed by passing the entire variable to cout. For example, assuming employee is a PayRoll structure variable, the following statement will not work:

```
cout << employee << endl;  // Will not work!
```

Instead, each member must be separately passed to cout.

As you can see from Program 11-1, structure members that are of a primitive data type can be used with cin, cout, mathematical statements, and any operation that can be performed with regular variables. The only difference is that the structure variable name and the dot operator must precede the name of a member. Program 11-2 shows the member of a structure variable being passed to the pow function.

Program 11-2

```
 1   // This program stores data about a circle in a structure.
 2   #include <iostream>
 3   #include <cmath>  // For the pow function
 4   #include <iomanip>
 5   using namespace std;
 6
 7   // Constant for pi.
 8   const double PI = 3.14159;
 9
10   // Structure declaration
11   struct Circle
12   {
13      double radius;      // A circle's radius
14      double diameter;    // A circle's diameter
15      double area;        // A circle's area
16   };
17
18   int main()
19   {
20      Circle c;     // Define a structure variable
21
22      // Get the circle's diameter.
23      cout << "Enter the diameter of a circle: ";
24      cin >> c.diameter;
25
26      // Calculate the circle's radius.
27      c.radius = c.diameter / 2;
28
29      // Calculate the circle's area.
30      c.area = PI * pow(c.radius, 2.0);
31
32      // Display the circle data.
33      cout << fixed << showpoint << setprecision(2);
34      cout << "The radius and area of the circle are:\n";
35      cout << "Radius: " << c.radius << endl;
36      cout << "Area: " << c.area << endl;
37      return 0;
38   }
```

Program Output with Example Input Shown in Bold
```
Enter the diameter of a circle: 10 [Enter]
The radius and area of the circle are:
Radius: 5
Area: 78.54
```

Comparing Structure Variables

You cannot perform comparison operations directly on structure variables. For example, assume that `circle1` and `circle2` are `Circle` structure variables. The following statement will cause an error.

```
if (circle1 == circle2)   // Error!
```

In order to compare two structures, you must compare the individual members, as shown in the following code.

```
if (circle1.radius == circle2.radius &&
    circle1.diameter == circle2.diameter &&
    circle1.area == circle2.area)
```

Strings as Structure Members

When a character array is a structure member, you can use the same string manipulation techniques with it as you would with any other character array. For example, assume `product.description` is a character array. The following statement copies into it the string "19-inch television":

```
strcpy(product.description, "19-inch television");
```

Also, assume that `product.partNum` is a 15-element character array. The following statement reads into it a line of input:

```
cin.getline(product.partNum, 15);
```

Program 11-3 demonstrates the use of a structure containing string data.

Program 11-3

```
 1   // This program uses a structure to hold someone's first,
 2   // middle, and last name.
 3   #include <iostream>
 4   #include <cstring>
 5   using namespace std;
 6
 7   // Constants for array lengths
 8   const int LENGTH = 15;
 9   const int FULL_LENGTH = 45;
10
11   struct Name
12   {
13      char first[LENGTH];      // To hold the first name
14      char middle[LENGTH];     // To hold the middle name
15      char last[LENGTH];       // To hold the last name
16      char full[FULL_LENGTH];  // To hold the full name
17   };
18
```

```
19   int main()
20   {
21       // personName is a Name structure variable
22       Name personName;
23
24       // Get the first name.
25       cout << "Enter your first name: ";
26       cin >> personName.first;
27
28       // Get the middle name.
29       cout << "Enter your middle name: ";
30       cin >> personName.middle;
31
32       // Get the last name.
33       cout << "Enter your last name: ";
34       cin >> personName.last;
35
36       // Assemble the full name.
37       strcpy(personName.full, personName.first);
38       strcat(personName.full, " ");
39       strcat(personName.full, personName.middle);
40       strcat(personName.full, " ");
41       strcat(personName.full, personName.last);
42
43       // Display the full name.
44       cout << "\nYour full name is " << personName.full << endl;
45       return 0;
46   }
```

Program Output with Example Input Shown in Bold
Enter your first name: **Josephine [Enter]**
Enter your middle name: **Yvonne [Enter]**
Enter your last name: **Smith [Enter]**

Your full name is Josephine Yvonne Smith

11.4 Initializing a Structure

CONCEPT: The members of a structure variable may be initialized with starting values when the structure variable is defined.

A structure variable may be initialized when it is defined, in a fashion similar to the initialization of an array. Assume the following structure declaration exists in a program:

```
struct CityInfo
{
    char cityName[30];
    char state[3];
    long population;
    int distance;
};
```

A variable may then be defined with an initialization list, as shown in the following:

```
CityInfo location = {"Asheville", "NC", 50000, 28};
```

This statement defines the variable `location`. The first value in the initialization list is assigned to the first declared member, the second value in the initialization list is assigned to the second member, and so on. The `location` variable is initialized in the following manner:

The string "Asheville" is assigned to `location.cityName`
The string "NC" is assigned to `location.state`
50000 is assigned to `location.population`
28 is assigned to `location.distance`

You do not have to provide initializers for all the members of a structure variable. For example, the following statement only initializes the `cityName` member of `location`:

```
CityInfo location = {"Tampa"};
```

The `state`, `population`, and `distance` members are left uninitialized. The following statement only initializes the `cityName` and `state` members, while leaving `population` and `distance` uninitialized:

```
CityInfo location = {"Atlanta", "GA"};
```

If you leave a structure member uninitialized, you must leave all the members that follow it uninitialized as well. C++ does not provide a way to skip members in a structure. For example, the following statement, which attempts to skip the initialization of the `population` member, is *not* legal:

```
CityInfo location = {"Knoxville", "TN", , 90};  // Illegal!
```

Program 11-4 demonstrates the use of partially initialized structure variables.

Program 11-4

```
1  // This program demonstrates partially initialized
2  // structure variables.
3  #include <iostream>
4  #include <iomanip>
5  using namespace std;
6
7  const int LENGTH = 25;  // Array size
8
```

```
 9   struct EmployeePay
10   {
11      char name[LENGTH];    // Employee name
12      int empNum;           // Employee number
13      double payRate;       // Hourly pay rate
14      double hours;         // Hours worked
15      double grossPay;      // Gross pay
16   };
17
18   int main()
19   {
20      EmployeePay employee1 = {"Betty Ross", 141, 18.75};
21      EmployeePay employee2 = {"Jill Sandburg", 142, 17.50};
22
23      cout << fixed << showpoint << setprecision(2);
24
25      // Calculate pay for employee1
26      cout << "Name: " << employee1.name << endl;
27      cout << "Employee Number: " << employee1.empNum << endl;
28      cout << "Enter the hours worked by this employee: ";
29      cin >> employee1.hours;
30      employee1.grossPay = employee1.hours * employee1.payRate;
31      cout << "Gross Pay: " << employee1.grossPay << endl << endl;
32
33      // Calculate pay for employee2
34      cout << "Name: " << employee2.name << endl;
35      cout << "Employee Number: " << employee2.empNum << endl;
36      cout << "Enter the hours worked by this employee: ";
37      cin >> employee2.hours;
38      employee2.grossPay = employee2.hours * employee2.payRate;
39      cout << "Gross Pay: " << employee2.grossPay << endl;
40      return 0;
41   }
```

Program Output with Example Input Shown in Bold
```
Name: Betty Ross
Employee Number: 141
Enter the hours worked by this employee: 40 [Enter]
Gross Pay: 750.00

Name: Jill Sandburg
Employee Number: 142
Enter the hours worked by this employee: 20 [Enter]
Gross Pay: 350.00
```

It's important to note that you cannot initialize a structure member in the declaration of the structure. For instance, the following declaration is illegal:

```
// Illegal structure declaration
struct CityInfo
{
    char cityName[30] = "Asheville";    // Error!
    char state[3] = "NC";               // Error!
    long population = 50000;            // Error!
    int distance = 28;                  // Error!
};
```

Remember that a structure declaration doesn't actually create the member variables. It only declares what the structure "looks like." The member variables are created in memory when a structure variable is defined. Because no variables are created by the structure declaration, there's nothing that can be initialized there.

Checkpoint

11.1   Write a structure declaration to hold the following data about a savings account:

Account Number (15-element character string)
Account Balance (`double`)
Interest Rate (`double`)
Average Monthly Balance (`double`)

11.2   Write a definition statement for a variable of the structure you declared in question 11.1. Initialize the members with the following data:

Account Number: ACZ42137-B12-7
Account Balance: $4512.59
Interest Rate: 4%
Average Monthly Balance: $4217.07

11.3   The following program skeleton, when complete, asks the user to enter these data about his or her favorite movie:

Name of movie
Name of the movie's director
Name of the movie's producer
The year the movie was released

Complete the program by declaring the structure that holds this data, defining a structure variable, and writing the individual statements necessary.

```
#include <iostream>
using namespace std;

// Write the structure declaration here to hold the movie data.

int main()
{
    // define the structure variable here.
```

```
        cout << "Enter the following data about your\n";
        cout << "favorite movie.\n";
        cout << "name: ";
        // Write a statement here that lets the user enter the
        // name of a favorite movie. Store the name in the
        // structure variable.
        cout << "Director: ";
        // Write a statement here that lets the user enter the
        // name of the movie's director. Store the name in the
        // structure variable.
        cout << "Producer: ";
        // Write a statement here that lets the user enter the
        // name of the movie's producer. Store the name in the
        // structure variable.
        cout << "Year of release: ";
        // Write a statement here that lets the user enter the
        // year the movie was released. Store the year in the
        // structure variable.
        cout << "Here is data on your favorite movie:\n";
        // Write statements here that display the data.
        // just entered into the structure variable.
        return 0;
}
```

11.5 Arrays of Structures

CONCEPT: Arrays of structures can simplify some programming tasks.

In Chapter 7 you saw that data can be stored in two or more arrays, with a relationship established between the arrays through their subscripts. Because structures can hold several items of varying data types, a single array of structures can be used in place of several arrays of regular variables.

An array of structures is defined like any other array. Assume the following structure declaration exists in a program:

```
struct BookInfo
{
    char title[50];
    char author[30];
    char publisher[25];
    double price;
};
```

The following statement defines an array, bookList, that has 20 elements. Each element is a BookInfo structure.

```
BookInfo bookList[20];
```

Each element of the array may be accessed through a subscript. For example, bookList[0] is the first structure in the array, bookList[1] is the second, and so forth. To access a member of any element, simply place the dot operator and member name after the subscript. For example, the following expression refers to the `title` member of `bookList[5]`:

```
bookList[5].title
```

The following loop steps through the array, displaying the data stored in each element:

```
for (int index = 0; index < 20; index++)
{
    cout << bookList[index].title << endl;
    cout << bookList[index].author << endl;
    cout << bookList[index].publisher << endl;
    cout << bookList[index].price << endl << endl;
}
```

Because the members `title`, `author`, and `publisher` are also arrays, their individual elements may be accessed as well. The following statement displays the character that is the first element of the `title` member of `bookList[10]`:

```
cout << bookList[10].title[0];
```

And the following statement stores the character 't' in the fourth element of the `publisher` member of `bookList[2]`:

```
bookList[2].publisher[3] = 't';
```

Program 11-5 calculates and displays payroll data for three employees. It uses a single array of structures.

Program 11-5

```
 1   // This program uses an array of structures.
 2   #include <iostream>
 3   #include <iomanip>
 4   using namespace std;
 5
 6   struct PayInfo
 7   {
 8      int hours;         // Hours worked
 9      double payRate;    // Hourly pay rate
10   };
11
12   int main()
13   {
14      const int NUM_WORKERS = 3;   // Number of workers
15      PayInfo workers[NUM_WORKERS]; // Array of structures
16      int index;                    // Loop counter
17
```

```
18        // Get employee pay data.
19        cout << "Enter the hours worked by " << NUM_WORKERS
20            << " employees and their hourly rates.\n";
21
22        for (index = 0; index < NUM_WORKERS; index++)
23        {
24            // Get the hours worked by an employee.
25            cout << "Hours worked by employee #" << (index + 1);
26            cout << ": ";
27            cin >> workers[index].hours;
28
29            // Get the employee's hourly pay rate.
30            cout << "Hourly pay rate for employee #";
31            cout << (index + 1) << ": ";
32            cin >> workers[index].payRate;
33            cout << endl;
34        }
35
36        // Display each employee's gross pay.
37        cout << "Here is the gross pay for each employee:\n";
38        cout << fixed << showpoint << setprecision(2);
39        for (index - 0; index < NUM_WORKERS; index++)
40        {
41            double gross;
42            gross = workers[index].hours * workers[index].payRate;
43            cout << "Employee #" << (index + 1);
44            cout << ": $" << gross << endl;
45        }
46        return 0;
47    }
```

Program Output with Example Input Shown in Bold

```
Enter the hours worked by 3 employees and their hourly rates.
Hours worked by employee #1: 10 [Enter]
Hourly pay rate for employee #1: 9.75 [Enter]

Hours worked by employee #2: 20 [Enter]
Hourly pay rate for employee #2: 10.00 [Enter]

Hours worked by employee #3: 40 [Enter]
Hourly pay rate for employee #3: 20.00 [Enter]

Here is the gross pay for each employee:
Employee #1: $97.50
Employee #2: $200.00
Employee #3: $800.00
```

Initializing a Structure Array

To initialize a structure array, simply provide an initialization list for one or more of the elements. For example, the array in Program 11-5 could have been initialized as follows:

```
PayInfo workers[NUM_WORKERS] = {
                                {10, 9.75 },
                                {15, 8.62 },
                                {20, 10.50},
                                {40, 18.75},
                                {40, 15.65}
                               };
```

As in all single-dimensional arrays, you can initialize all or part of the elements in an array of structures, as long as you do not skip elements.

11.6 Focus on Software Engineering: Nested Structures

CONCEPT: It's possible for a structure variable to be a member of another structure variable.

Sometimes it's helpful to nest structures inside other structures. For example, consider the following structure declarations:

```
struct Costs
{
   double wholesale;
   double retail;
};

struct Item
{
   char partNum[10];
   char description[25];
   Costs pricing;
};
```

The `Costs` structure has two members: `wholesale` and `retail`, both `doubles`. Notice that the third member of the `Item` structure, `pricing`, is a `Costs` structure. Assume the variable `widget` is defined as follows:

```
Item widget;
```

The following statements show examples of accessing members of the `pricing` variable, which is inside `widget`:

```
widget.pricing.wholesale = 100.0;
widget.pricing.retail = 150.0;
```

Program 11-6 gives a more elaborate illustration of nested structures.

Program 11-6

```
 1   // This program uses nested structures.
 2   #include <iostream>
 3   using namespace std;
 4
 5   // Constants for char array sizes
 6   const int ADDR_LENGTH = 50;    // Address length
 7   const int CITY_LENGTH = 20;    // City length
 8   const int STATE_LENGTH = 15;   // State length
 9   const int ZIP_LENGTH = 11;     // ZIP code length
10   const int NAME_LENGTH = 50;    // Name length
11
12   // The Date structure holds data about a date.
13   struct Date
14   {
15      int month;
16      int day;
17      int year;
18   };
19
20   // The Place structure holds a physical address.
21   struct Place
22   {
23      char address[ADDR_LENGTH];
24      char city[CITY_LENGTH];
25      char state[STATE_LENGTH];
26      char zip[ZIP_LENGTH];
27   };
28
29   // The EmployeeInfo structure holds an employee's data.
30   struct EmployeeInfo
31   {
32      char name[NAME_LENGTH];
33      int employeeNumber;
34      Date birthDate;            // Nested structure
35      Place residence;           // Nested structure
36   };
37
38   int main()
39   {
40      // Define a structure variable to hold info about the manager.
41      EmployeeInfo manager;
42
43      // Get the manager's name and employee number
44      cout << "Enter the manager's name: ";
45      cin.getline(manager.name, NAME_LENGTH);
46      cout << "Enter the manager's employee number: ";
47      cin >> manager.employeeNumber;
48
```

(program continues)

Program 11-6 *(continued)*

```
49        // Get the manager's birth date
50        cout << "Now enter the manager's date of birth.\n";
51        cout << "Month (up to 2 digits): ";
52        cin >> manager.birthDate.month;
53        cout << "Day (up to 2 digits): ";
54        cin >> manager.birthDate.day;
55        cout << "Year (2 digits): ";
56        cin >> manager.birthDate.year;
57        cin.ignore();   // Skip the remaining newline character
58
59        // Get the manager's residence information
60        cout << "Enter the manager's street address: ";
61        cin.getline(manager.residence.address, ADDR_LENGTH);
62        cout << "City: ";
63        cin.getline(manager.residence.city, CITY_LENGTH);
64        cout << "State: ";
65        cin.getline(manager.residence.state, STATE_LENGTH);
66        cout << "ZIP Code: ";
67        cin.getline(manager.residence.zip, ZIP_LENGTH);
68
69        // Display the information just entered
70        cout << "\nHere is the manager's information:\n";
71        cout << manager.name << endl;
72        cout << "Employee number " << manager.employeeNumber << endl;
73        cout << "Date of birth: ";
74        cout << manager.birthDate.month << "-";
75        cout << manager.birthDate.day << "-";
76        cout << manager.birthDate.year << endl;
77        cout << "Place of residence:\n";
78        cout << manager.residence.address << endl;
79        cout << manager.residence.city << ", ";
80        cout << manager.residence.state << " ";
81        cout << manager.residence.zip << endl;
82        return 0;
83  }
```

Program Output with Example Input Shown in Bold

```
Enter the manager's name: John Smith [Enter]
Enter the manager's employee number: 789 [Enter]
Now enter the manager's date of birth.
Month (up to 2 digits): 10 [Enter]
Day (up to 2 digits): 14 [Enter]
Year (2 digits): 65 [Enter]
Enter the manager's street address: 190 Disk Drive [Enter]
City: Redmond [Enter]
State: WA [Enter]
ZIP Code: 98052 [Enter]
```

```
Here is the manager's information:
John Smith
Employee number 789
Date of birth: 10-14-65
Place of residence:
190 Disk Drive
Redmond, WA  98052
```

 ## Checkpoint

For questions 11.4–11.7 below, assume the `Product` structure is declared as follows:

```
struct Product
{
    char description[50];    // Product description
    int partNum;             // Part number
    double cost;             // Product cost
},
```

11.4 Write a definition for an array of 100 `Product` structures. Do not initialize the array.

11.5 Write a loop that will step through the entire array you defined in Question 11.4, setting all the product descriptions to a null string, all part numbers to zero, and all costs to zero.

11.6 Write the statements that will store the following data in the first element of the array you defined in Question 11.4:

Description: Claw hammer
Part Number: 547
Part Cost: $8.29

11.7 Write a loop that will display the contents of the entire array you created in Question 11.4.

11.8 Write a structure declaration named `Measurement`, with the following members:

miles, an integer
meters, a long integer

11.9 Write a structure declaration named `Destination`, with the following members:

city, a 35-element character array
distance, a `Measurement` structure (declared in Question 11.8)

Also define a variable of this structure type.

11.10 Write statements that store the following data in the variable you defined in Question 11.9:

City: Tupelo
Miles: 375
Meters: 603,375

VideoNote

Passing a
Structure to a
Function

11.7   Structures as Function Arguments

CONCEPT: Structure variables may be passed as arguments to functions.

Like other variables, the individual members of a structure variable may be used as function arguments. For example, assume the following structure declaration exists in a program:

```
struct Rectangle
{
    double length;
    double width;
    double area;
};
```

Let's say the following function definition exists in the same program:

```
double multiply(double x, double y)
{
    return x * y;
}
```

Assuming that box is a variable of the Rectangle structure type, the following function call will pass box.length into x and box.width into y. The return value will be stored in box.area.

```
box.area = multiply(box.length, box.width);
```

Sometimes it's more convenient to pass an entire structure variable into a function instead of individual members. For example, the following function definition uses a Rectangle structure variable as its parameter:

```
void showRect(Rectangle r)
{
    cout << r.length << endl;
    cout << r.width << endl;
    cout << r.area << endl;
}
```

The following function call passes the box variable into r:

```
showRect(box);
```

Inside the function showRect, r's members contain a copy of box's members. This is illustrated in Figure 11-3.

Once the function is called, r.length contains a copy of box.length, r.width contains a copy of box.width, and r.area contains a copy of box.area.

Structures, like all variables, are normally passed by value into a function. If a function is to access the members of the original argument, a reference variable may be used as the parameter. Program 11-7 uses two functions that accept structures as arguments. Arguments are passed to the getItem function by reference, and to the showItem function by value.

Figure 11-3

```
                          showRect(box);
                                 └─────────────┐
                                               ↓
                          void showRect(Rectangle r)
                          {
                                cout << r.length << endl;
                                cout << r.width << endl;
                                cout << r.area << endl;
                          }
```

Program 11-7

```
 1   // This program has functions that accept structure variables
 2   // as arguments.
 3   #include <iostream>
 4   #include <iomanip>
 5   using namespace std;
 6
 7   const int DESC_SIZE = 50;        // Array size
 8
 9   struct InventoryItem
10   {
11      int partNum;                  // Part number
12      char description[DESC_SIZE];  // Item description
13      int onHand;                   // Units on hand
14      double price;                 // Unit price
15   };
16
17   // Function Prototypes
18   void getItem(InventoryItem&);    // Argument passed by reference
19   void showItem(InventoryItem);    // Argument passed by value
20
21   int main()
22   {
23      InventoryItem part;
24
25      getItem(part);
26      showItem(part);
27      return 0;
28   }
29
30   //*********************************************************
31   // Definition of function getItem. This function uses      *
32   // a structure reference variable as its parameter. It asks *
33   // the user for information to store in the structure.      *
34   //*********************************************************
35
```

(program continues)

Program 11-7 *(continued)*

```
36   void getItem(InventoryItem &p)     // Uses a reference parameter
37   {
38      // Get the part number.
39      cout << "Enter the part number: ";
40      cin >> p.partNum;
41
42      // Get the part description.
43      cout << "Enter the part description: ";
44      cin.ignore():                    // Ignore the remaining newline character.
45      cin.getline(p.description, DESC_SIZE);
46
47      // Get the quantity on hand.
48      cout << "Enter the quantity on hand: ";
49      cin >> p.onHand;
50
51      // Get the unit price.
52      cout << "Enter the unit price: ";
53      cin >> p.price;
54   }
55
56   //***********************************************************
57   // Definition of function showItem. This function accepts   *
58   // an argument of the InventoryItem structure type. The     *
59   // contents of the structure is displayed.                  *
60   //***********************************************************
61
62   void showItem(InventoryItem p)
63   {
64      cout << fixed << showpoint << setprecision(2);
65      cout << "Part Number: " << p.partNum << endl;
66      cout << "Description: " << p.description << endl;
67      cout << "Units on Hand: " << p.onHand << endl;
68      cout << "Price: $" << p.price << endl;
69   }
```

Program Output with Example Input Shown in Bold
```
Enter the part number: 800 [Enter]
Enter the part description: Screwdriver [Enter]
Enter the quantity on hand: 135 [Enter]
Enter the unit price: 1.25 [Enter]
Part Number: 800
Description: Screwdriver
Units on Hand: 135
Price: $1.25
```

Notice that the InventoryItem structure declaration in Program 11-7 appears before both the prototypes and the definitions of the getItem and showItem functions. This is because both functions use an InventoryItem structure variable as their parameter. The compiler must know what InventoryItem is before it encounters any definitions for variables of that type. Otherwise, an error will occur.

Constant Reference Parameters

Sometimes structures can be quite large. Passing large structures by value can decrease a program's performance because a copy of the structure has to be created. When a structure is passed by reference, however, it isn't copied. A reference that points to the original argument is passed instead. So, it's often preferable to pass large objects such as structures by reference.

Of course, the disadvantage of passing an object by reference is that the function has access to the original argument. It can potentially alter the argument's value. This can be prevented, however, by passing the argument as a constant reference. The showItem function from Program 11-7 is shown here, modified to use a constant reference parameter.

```cpp
void showItem(const InventoryItem &p)
{
    cout << fixed << showpoint << setprecision(2);
    cout << "Part Number: " << p.partNum << endl;
    cout << "Description: " << p.description << endl;
    cout << "Units on Hand: " << p.onHand << endl;
    cout << "Price: $" << p.price << endl;
}
```

This version of the function is more efficient than the original version because the amount of time and memory consumed in the function call is reduced. Because the parameter is defined as a constant, the function cannot accidentally corrupt the value of the argument.

The prototype for this version of the function follows.

```cpp
void showItem(const InventoryItem&);
```

11.8 Returning a Structure from a Function

CONCEPT: A function may return a structure.

Just as functions can be written to return an int, long, double, or other data type, they can also be designed to return a structure. Recall the following structure declaration from Program 11-2:

```cpp
struct Circle
{
    double radius;
    double diameter;
    double area;
};
```

A function, such as the following, could be written to return a variable of the Circle data type:

```
Circle getCircleData()
{
    Circle temp;                // Temporary Circle structure

    temp.radius = 10.0;     // Store the radius
    temp.diameter = 20.0;   // Store the diameter
    temp.area = 314.159;    // Store the area
    return temp;            // Return the temporary structure
}
```

Notice that the `getCircleData` function has a return data type of `Circle`. That means the function returns an entire `Circle` structure when it terminates. The return value can be assigned to any variable that is a `Circle` structure. The following statement, for example, assigns the function's return value to the `Circle` structure variable named `myCircle`:

```
myCircle = getCircleData();
```

After this statement executes, `myCircle.radius` will be set to 10.0, `myCircle.diameter` will be set to 20.0, and `myCircle.area` will be set to 314.159.

When a function returns a structure, it is always necessary for the function to have a local structure variable to hold the member values that are to be returned. In the `getCircleData` function, the values for `diameter`, `radius`, and `area` are stored in the local variable `temp`. The `temp` variable is then returned from the function.

Program 11-8 is a modification of Program 11-2. The function `getInfo` gets the circle's diameter from the user and calculates the circle's radius. The diameter and radius are stored in a local structure variable, `round`, which is returned from the function.

Program 11-8

```
 1  // This program uses a function to return a structure. This
 2  // is a modification of Program 11-2.
 3  #include <iostream>
 4  #include <iomanip>
 5  #include <cmath>  // For the pow function
 6  using namespace std;
 7
 8  // Constant for pi.
 9  const double PI = 3.14159;
10
11  // Structure declaration
12  struct Circle
13  {
14      double radius;       // A circle's radius
15      double diameter;     // A circle's diameter
16      double area;         // A circle's area
17  };
18
19  // Function prototype
20  Circle getInfo();
21
22  int main()
23  {
24      Circle c;        // Define a structure variable
```

```
25
26      // Get data about the circle.
27      c = getInfo();
28
29      // Calculate the circle's area.
30      c.area = PI * pow(c.radius, 2.0);
31
32      // Display the circle data.
33      cout << "The radius and area of the circle are:\n";
34      cout << fixed << setprecision(2);
35      cout << "Radius: " << c.radius << endl;
36      cout << "Area: " << c.area << endl;
37      return 0;
38  }
39
40  //****************************************************************
41  // Definition of function getInfo. This function uses a local   *
42  // variable, tempCircle, which is a circle structure. The user  *
43  // enters the diameter of the circle, which is stored in        *
44  // tempCircle.diameter. The function then calculates the radius *
45  // which is stored in tempCircle.radius. tempCircle is then     *
46  // returned from the function.                                  *
47  //****************************************************************
48
49  Circle getInfo()
50  {
51      Circle tempCircle;  // Temporary structure variable
52
53      // Store circle data in the temporary variable.
54      cout << "Enter the diameter of a circle: ";
55      cin >> tempCircle.diameter;
56      tempCircle.radius = tempCircle.diameter / 2.0;
57
58      // Return the temporary variable.
59      return tempCircle;
60  }
```

Program Output with Example Input Shown in Bold
```
Enter the diameter of a circle: 10 [Enter]
The radius and area of the circle are:
Radius: 5.00
Area: 78.54
```

NOTE: In Chapter 6 you learned that C++ only allows you to return a single value from a function. Structures, however, provide a way around this limitation. Even though a structure may have several members, it is technically a single value. By packaging multiple values inside a structure, you can return as many variables as you need from a function.

11.9   Pointers to Structures

CONCEPT: You may take the address of a structure variable and create variables that are pointers to structures.

Defining a variable that is a pointer to a structure is as simple as defining any other pointer variable: The data type is followed by an asterisk and the name of the pointer variable. Here is an example:

```
Circle *cirPtr;
```

This statement defines `cirPtr` as a pointer to a `Circle` structure. Look at the following code:

```
Circle myCircle = { 10.0, 20.0, 314.159 };
Circle *cirPtr;
cirPtr = &myCircle;
```

The first two lines define `myCircle`, a structure variable, and `cirPtr`, a pointer. The third line assigns the address of `myCircle` to `cirPtr`. After this line executes, `cirPtr` will point to the `myCircle` structure. This is illustrated in Figure 11-4.

Figure 11-4

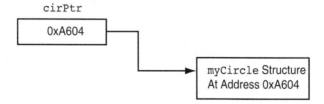

Indirectly accessing the members of a structure through a pointer can be clumsy, however, if the indirection operator is used. One might think the following statement would access the `radius` member of the structure pointed to by `cirPtr`, but it doesn't:

```
*cirPtr.radius = 10;
```

The dot operator has higher precedence than the indirection operator, so the indirection operator tries to dereference `cirPtr.radius`, not `cirPtr`. To dereference the `cirPtr` pointer, a set of parentheses must be used.

```
(*cirPtr).radius = 10;
```

Because of the awkwardness of this notation, C++ has a special operator for dereferencing structure pointers. It's called the *structure pointer operator*, and it consists of a hyphen (-) followed by the greater-than symbol (>). The previous statement, rewritten with the structure pointer operator, looks like this:

```
cirPtr->radius = 10;
```

The structure pointer operator takes the place of the dot operator in statements using pointers to structures. The operator automatically dereferences the structure pointer on its left. There is no need to enclose the pointer name in parentheses.

NOTE: The structure pointer operator is supposed to look like an arrow, thus visually indicating that a "pointer" is being used.

Program 11-9 shows that a pointer to a structure may be used as a function parameter, allowing the function to access the members of the original structure argument.

Program 11-9

```
1   // This program demonstrates a function that uses a
2   // pointer to a structure variable as a parameter.
3   #include <iostream>
4   #include <iomanip>
5   using namespace std;
6
7   const int NAME_LENGTH = 35; // Array size
8
9   struct Student
10  {
11      char name[NAME_LENGTH]; // Student's name
12      int idNum;              // Student ID number
13      int creditHours;        // Credit hours enrolled
14      double gpa;             // Current GPA
15  };
16
17  void getData(Student *);  // Function prototype
18
19  int main()
20  {
21      Student freshman;
22
23      // Get the student data.
24      cout << "Enter the following student data:\n";
25      getData(&freshman);     // Pass the address of freshman.
26      cout << "\nHere is the student data you entered:\n";
27
28      // Now display the data stored in freshman
29      cout << setprecision(2);
30      cout << "Name: " << freshman.name << endl;
31      cout << "ID Number: " << freshman.idNum << endl;
32      cout << "Credit Hours: " << freshman.creditHours << endl;
33      cout << "GPA: " << freshman.gpa << endl;
34      return 0;
35  }
36
```

(program continues)

Program 11-9   *(continued)*

```
37   //**********************************************************
38   // Definition of function getData. Uses a pointer to a  *
39   // Student structure variable. The user enters student  *
40   // information, which is stored in the variable.         *
41   //**********************************************************
42
43   void getData(Student *s)
44   {
45      // Get the student name.
46      cout << "Student Name: ";
47      cin.getline(s->name, NAME_LENGTH);
48
49      // Get the student ID number.
50      cout << "Student ID Number: ";
51      cin >> s->idNum;
52
53      // Get the credit hours enrolled.
54      cout << "Credit Hours Enrolled: ";
55      cin >> s->creditHours;
56
57      // Get the GPA.
58      cout << "Current GPA: ";
59      cin >> s->gpa;
60   }
```

Program Output with Example Input Shown in Bold

```
Enter the following student data:
Student Name: Frank Smith [Enter]
Student ID Number: 4876 [Enter]
Credit Hours Enrolled: 12 [Enter]
Current GPA: 3.45 [Enter]

Here is the student data you entered:
Name: Frank Smith
ID Number: 4876
Credit Hours: 12
GPA: 3.45
```

Dynamically Allocating a Structure

You can also use a structure pointer and the new operator to dynamically allocate a structure. For example, the following code defines a Circle pointer named cirPtr and dynamically allocates a Circle structure. Values are then stored in the dynamically allocated structure's members.

```
Circle *cirPtr;           // Define a Circle pointer
cirPtr = new Circle;      // Dynamically allocate a Circle structure
cirPtr->radius = 10;      // Store a value in the radius member
cirPtr->diameter = 20;    // Store a value in the diameter member
cirPtr->area = 314.159;   // Store a value in the area member
```

You can also dynamically allocate an array of structures. The following code shows an array of five Circle structures being allocated.

```
Circle *circles;
circles = new Circle[5];
for (int count = 0; count < 5; count++)
{
    cout << "Enter the radius for circle "
         << (count + 1) << ": ";
    cin >> circles[count].radius;
}
```

11.10 Focus on Software Engineering: When to Use ., When to Use ->, and When to Use *

Sometimes structures contain pointers as members. For example, the following structure declaration has an int pointer member:

```
struct GradeInfo
{
    char name[25];          // Student names
    int *testScores;        // Dynamically allocated array
    float average;          // Test average
};
```

It is important to remember that the structure pointer operator (->) is used to dereference a pointer to a structure, not a pointer that is a member of a structure. If a program dereferences the testScores pointer in this structure, the indirection operator must be used. For example, assume that the following variable has been defined:

```
GradeInfo student1;
```

The following statement will display the value pointed to by the testScores member:

```
cout << *student1.testScores;
```

It is still possible to define a pointer to a structure that contains a pointer member. For instance, the following statement defines stPtr as a pointer to a GradeInfo structure:

```
GradeInfo *stPtr;
```

Assuming that stPtr points to a valid GradeInfo variable, the following statement will display the value pointed to by its testScores member:

```
cout << *stPtr->testScores;
```

In this statement, the * operator dereferences stPtr->testScores, while the -> operator dereferences stPtr. It might help to remember that the following expression:

```
stPtr->testScores
```

is equivalent to

```
(*stPtr).testScores
```

So, the expression

```
*stPtr->testScores
```

is the same as

```
*(*stPtr).testScores
```

The awkwardness of this last expression shows the necessity of the -> operator. Table 11-3 lists some expressions using the *, ->, and . operators, and describes what each references.

Table 11-3

Expression	Description
s->m	s is a structure pointer and m is a member. This expression accesses the m member of the structure pointed to by s.
*a.p	a is a structure variable and p, a pointer, is a member. This expression dereferences the value pointed to by p.
(*s).m	s is a structure pointer and m is a member. The * operator dereferences s, causing the expression to access the m member of the structure pointed to by s. This expression is the same as s->m.
*s->p	s is a structure pointer and p, a pointer, is a member of the structure pointed to by s. This expression accesses the value pointed to by p. (The -> operator dereferences s and the * operator dereferences p.)
*(*s).p	s is a structure pointer and p, a pointer, is a member of the structure pointed to by s. This expression accesses the value pointed to by p. (*s) dereferences s and the outermost * operator dereferences p. The expression *s->p is equivalent.

Checkpoint

Assume the following structure declaration exists for questions 11.11–11.15:

```
struct Rectangle
{
   int length;
   int width;
};
```

11.11 Write a function that accepts a Rectangle structure as its argument and displays the structure's contents on the screen.

11.12 Write a function that uses a Rectangle structure reference variable as its parameter and stores the user's input in the structure's members.

11.13 Write a function that returns a Rectangle structure. The function should store the user's input in the members of the structure before returning it.

11.14 Write the definition of a pointer to a Rectangle structure.

11.15 Assume rptr is a pointer to a Rectangle structure. Which of the expressions, A, B, or C, is equivalent to the following expression:

```
   rptr->width
```

A)   *rptr.width

B)   (*rptr).width

C)   rptr.(*width)

11.11 Unions

CONCEPT: A *union* is like a structure, except all the members occupy the same memory area.

A union, in almost all regards, is just like a structure. The difference is that all the members of a union use the same memory area, so only one member can be used at a time. A union might be used in an application where the program needs to work with two or more values (of different data types), but only needs to use one of the values at a time. Unions conserve memory by storing all their members in the same memory location.

Unions are declared just like structures, except the key word union is used instead of struct. Here is an example:

```
union PaySource
{
    short hours;
    float sales;
};
```

A union variable of the data type shown above can then be defined as

```
PaySource employee1;
```

The PaySource union variable defined here has two members: hours (a short), and sales (a float). The entire variable will only take up as much memory as the largest member (in this case, a float). The way this variable is stored on a typical PC is illustrated in Figure 11-5.

Figure 11-5

employee1: a PaySource union variable

First two bytes are used by hours, a short

All four bytes are used by sales, a float

As shown in Figure 11-5, the union uses four bytes on a typical PC. It can store a short or a float, depending on which member is used. When a value is stored in the sales member, all four bytes are needed to hold the data. When a value is stored in the hours member, however, only the first two bytes are used. Obviously, both members can't hold values at the same time. This union is demonstrated in Program 11-10.

Program 11-10

```cpp
 1   // This program demonstrates a union.
 2   #include <iostream>
 3   #include <iomanip>
 4   using namespace std;
 5
 6   union PaySource
 7   {
 8      int hours;           // Hours worked
 9      float sales;         // Amount of sales
10   };
11
12   int main()
13   {
14      PaySource employee1;       // Define a union variable
15      char payType;              // To hold the pay type
16      float payRate;             // Hourly pay rate
17      float grossPay;            // Gross pay
18
19      cout << fixed << showpoint << setprecision(2);
20      cout << "This program calculates either hourly wages or\n";
21      cout << "sales commission.\n";
22
23      // Get the pay type, hourly or commission.
24      cout << "Enter H for hourly wages or C for commission: ";
25      cin >> payType;
26
27      // Determine the gross pay, depending on the pay type.
28      if (payType == 'H' || payType == 'h')
29      {
30         // This is an hourly paid employee. Get the
31         // pay rate and hours worked.
32         cout << "What is the hourly pay rate? ";
33         cin >> payRate;
34         cout << "How many hours were worked? ";
35         cin >> employee1.hours;
36
37         // Calculate and display the gross pay.
38         grossPay = employee1.hours * payRate;
39         cout << "Gross pay: $" << grossPay << endl;
40      }
41      else if (payType == 'C' || payType == 'c')
42      {
43         // This is a commission-paid employee. Get the
44         // amount of sales.
45         cout << "What are the total sales for this employee? ";
46         cin >> employee1.sales;
47
48         // Calculate and display the gross pay.
49         grossPay = employee1.sales * 0.10;
50         cout << "Gross pay: $" << grossPay << endl;
51      }
```

```
52      else
53      {
54          // The user made an invalid selection.
55          cout << payType << " is not a valid selection.\n";
56      }
57      return 0;
58  }
```

Program Output with Example Input Shown in Bold
```
This program calculates either hourly wages or
sales commission.
Enter H for hourly wages or C for commission: C [Enter]
What are the total sales for this employee? 5000 [Enter]
Gross pay: $500.00
```

Program Output with Different Example Input Shown in Bold
```
This program calculates either hourly wages or
sales commission.
Enter H for hourly wages or C for commission: H [Enter]
What is the hourly pay rate? 20 [Enter]
How many hours were worked? 40 [Enter]
Gross pay: $800.00
```

Everything else you already know about structures applies to unions. For example, arrays of unions may be defined. A union may be passed as an argument to a function or returned from a function. Pointers to unions may be defined and the members of the union referenced by the pointer can be accessed with the -> operator.

Anonymous Unions

The members of an anonymous union have names, but the union itself has no name. Here is the general format of an anonymous union declaration:

```
union
{
    member declaration;
    ...
};
```

An anonymous union declaration actually creates the member variables in memory, so there is no need to separately define a union variable. Anonymous unions are simple to use because the members may be accessed without the dot operator. Program 11-11, which is a modification of Program 11-10, demonstrates the use of an anonymous union.

Program 11-11

```
1   // This program demonstrates an anonymous union.
2   #include <iostream>
3   #include <iomanip>
4   using namespace std;
```

(program continues)

Program 11-11 *(continued)*

```cpp
 5
 6   int main()
 7   {
 8      union                      // Anonymous union
 9      {
10         int hours;
11         float sales;
12      };
13
14      char payType;             // To hold the pay type
15      float payRate;            // Hourly pay rate
16      float grossPay;           // Gross pay
17
18      cout << fixed << showpoint << setprecision(2);
19      cout << "This program calculates either hourly wages or\n";
20      cout << "sales commission.\n";
21
22      // Get the pay type, hourly or commission.
23      cout << "Enter H for hourly wages or C for commission: ";
24      cin >> payType;
25
26      // Determine the gross pay, depending on the pay type.
27      if (payType == 'H' || payType == 'h')
28      {
29         // This is an hourly paid employee. Get the
30         // pay rate and hours worked.
31         cout << "What is the hourly pay rate? ";
32         cin >> payRate;
33         cout << "How many hours were worked? ";
34         cin >> hours; // Anonymous union member
35
36         // Calculate and display the gross pay.
37         grossPay = hours * payRate;
38         cout << "Gross pay: $" << grossPay << endl;
39      }
40      else if (payType == 'C' || payType == 'c')
41      {
42         // This is a commission-paid employee. Get the
43         // amount of sales.
44         cout << "What are the total sales for this employee? ";
45         cin >> sales; // Anonymous union member
46
47         // Calculate and display the gross pay.
48         grossPay = sales * 0.10;
49         cout << "Gross pay: $" << grossPay << endl;
50      }
51      else
52      {
53         // The user made an invalid selection.
54         cout << payType << " is not a valid selection.\n";
55      }
56      return 0;
57   }
```

Program Output with Example Input Shown in Bold
```
This program calculates either hourly wages or
sales commission.
Enter H for hourly wages or C for commission: C [Enter]
What are the total sales for this employee? 12000 [Enter]
Gross pay: $1200.00
```

 NOTE: Notice the anonymous union in Program 11-11 is declared inside function `main`. If an anonymous union is declared globally (outside all functions), it must be declared static. This means the word `static` must appear before the word `union`.

 Checkpoint

11.16   Declare a union named `ThreeTypes` with the following members:

   `letter:`   A character
   `whole:`   An integer
   `real:`   A double

11.17   Write the definition for an array of 50 of the `ThreeTypes` structures you declared in Question 11.16.

11.18   Write a loop that stores the floating point value 2.37 in all the elements of the array you defined in Question 11.17.

11.19   Write a loop that stores the character 'A' in all the elements of the array you defined in Question 11.17.

11.20   Write a loop that stores the integer 10 in all the elements of the array you defined in Question 11.17.

11.12   Enumerated Data Types

CONCEPT: An enumerated data type is a programmer-defined data type. It consists of values known as enumerators, which represent integer constants.

Using the enum key word you can create your own data type and specify the values that belong to that type. Such a type is known as an *enumerated data type*. Here is an example of an enumerated data type declaration:

```
enum Day { MONDAY, TUESDAY, WEDNESDAY, THURSDAY, FRIDAY };
```

An enumerated type declaration begins with the key word enum, followed by the name of the type, followed by a list of identifiers inside braces, and is terminated with a semicolon. The example declaration creates an enumerated data type named `Day`. The identifiers `MONDAY`, `TUESDAY`, `WEDNESDAY`, `THURSDAY`, and `FRIDAY`, which are listed inside the braces, are known as *enumerators*. They represent the values that belong to the Day data type. Here is the general format of an enumerated type declaration:

> enum *TypeName* { *One or more enumerators* };

Note that the enumerators are not enclosed in quotation marks, therefore they are not strings. Enumerators must be legal C++ identifiers.

Once you have created an enumerated data type in your program, you can define variables of that type. For example, the following statement defines workDay as a variable of the Day type:

```
Day workDay;
```

Because workDay is a variable of the Day data type, we may assign any of the enumerators MONDAY, TUESDAY, WEDNESDAY, THURSDAY, or FRIDAY to it. For example, the following statement assigns the value WEDNESDAY to the workDay variable.

```
Day workDay = WEDNESDAY;
```

So just what are these enumerators MONDAY, TUESDAY, WEDNESDAY, THURSDAY, and FRIDAY? You can think of them as integer named constants. Internally, the compiler assigns integer values to the enumerators, beginning with 0. The enumerator MONDAY is stored in memory as the number 0, TUESDAY is stored in memory as the number 1, WEDNESDAY is stored in memory as the number 2, and so forth. To prove this, look at the following code.

```
cout << MONDAY << endl << TUESDAY << endl
     << WEDNESDAY << endl << THURSDAY << endl
     << FRIDAY << endl;
```

This statement will produce the following output:

```
0
1
2
3
4
```

> **NOTE:** When making up names for enumerators, it is not required that they be written in all uppercase letters. For example, we could have written the enumerators of the Days type as monday, tuesday, etc. Because they represent constant values, however, many programmers prefer to write them in all uppercase letters. This is strictly a preference of style.

Assigning an Integer to an enum Variable

Even though the enumerators of an enumerated data type are stored in memory as integers, you cannot directly assign an integer value to an enum variable. For example, assuming that workDay is a variable of the Day data type previously described, the following assignment statement is illegal.

```
workDay = 3;    // Error!
```

Compiling this statement will produce an error message such as "Cannot convert `int` to `Day`." When assigning a value to an `enum` variable, you should use a valid enumerator. However, if circumstances require that you store an integer value in an `enum` variable, you can do so by casting the integer. Here is an example:

```
workDay = static_cast<Day>(3);
```

This statement will produce the same results as:

```
workDay = THURSDAY;
```

Assigning an Enumerator to an `int` Variable

Although you cannot directly assign an integer value to an `enum` variable, you can directly assign an enumerator to an integer variable. For example, the following code will work just fine.

```
enum Day { MONDAY, TUESDAY, WEDNESDAY, THURSDAY, FRIDAY };
int x;
x = THURSDAY;
cout << x << endl;
```

When this code runs it will display 3. You can also assign a variable of an enumerated type to an integer variable, as shown here:

```
Day workDay = FRIDAY;
int x = workDay;
cout << x << endl;
```

When this code runs it will display 4.

Comparing Enumerator Values

Enumerator values can be compared using the relational operators. For example, using the `Day` data type we have been discussing, the following expression is `true`.

```
FRIDAY > MONDAY
```

The expression is `true` because the enumerator `FRIDAY` is stored in memory as 4 and the enumerator `MONDAY` is stored as 0. The following code will display the message "Friday is greater than Monday."

```
if (FRIDAY > MONDAY)
    cout << "Friday is greater than Monday.\n";
```

You can also compare enumerator values with integer values. For example, the following code will display the message "Monday is equal to zero."

```
if (MONDAY == 0)
    cout << "Monday is equal to zero.\n";
```

Let's look at a complete program that uses much of what we have learned so far. Program 11-12 uses the `Day` data type that we have been discussing.

Program 11-12

```cpp
 1    // This program demonstrates an enumerated data type.
 2    #include <iostream>
 3    #include <iomanip>
 4    using namespace std;
 5
 6    enum Day { MONDAY, TUESDAY, WEDNESDAY, THURSDAY, FRIDAY };
 7
 8    int main()
 9    {
10       const int NUM_DAYS = 5;     // The number of days
11       double sales[NUM_DAYS];     // To hold sales for each day
12       double total = 0.0;         // Accumulator
13       int index;                  // Loop counter
14
15       // Get the sales for each day.
16       for (index = MONDAY; index <= FRIDAY; index++)
17       {
18          cout << "Enter the sales for day "
19               << index << ": ";
20          cin >> sales[index];
21       }
22
23       // Calculate the total sales.
24       for (index = MONDAY; index <= FRIDAY; index++)
25          total += sales[index];
26
27       // Display the total.
28       cout << "The total sales are $" << setprecision(2)
29            << fixed << total << endl;
30
31       return 0;
32    }
```

Program Output with Example Input Shown in Bold

```
Enter the sales for day 0: 1525.00 [Enter]
Enter the sales for day 1: 1896.50 [Enter]
Enter the sales for day 2: 1975.63 [Enter]
Enter the sales for day 3: 1678.33 [Enter]
Enter the sales for day 4: 1498.52 [Enter]
The total sales are $8573.98
```

Anonymous Enumerated Types

Notice that Program 11-12 does not define a variable of the Day data type. Instead it uses the Day data type's enumerators in the for loops. The counter variable index is initialized to MONDAY (which is 0), and the loop iterates as long as index is less than or equal to FRIDAY (which is 4). When you do not need to define variables of an enumerated type, you can actually make the type anonymous. An *anonymous enumerated type* is simply one that does not have a name. For example, in Program 11-12 we could have declared the enumerated type as:

```cpp
enum { MONDAY, TUESDAY, WEDNESDAY, THURSDAY, FRIDAY };
```

This declaration still creates the enumerators. We just can't use the data type to define variables because the type does not have a name.

Using Math Operators to Change the Value of an `enum` Variable

Even though enumerators are really integers, and `enum` variables really hold integer values, you can run into problems when trying to perform math operations with them. For example, look at the following code.

```
Day day1, day2;    // Defines two Day variables.
day1 = TUESDAY;    // Assign TUESDAY to day1.
day2 = day1 + 1;   // ERROR! This will not work!
```

The third statement causes a problem because the expression `day1 + 1` results in the integer value 2. The assignment operator then attempts to assign the integer value 2 to the `enum` variable `day2`. Because C++ cannot implicitly convert an `int` to a `Day`, an error occurs. You can fix this by using a cast to explicitly convert the result to `Day`, as shown here:

```
day2 = static_cast<Day>(day1 + 1);   // This works.
```

Using an `enum` Variable to Step Through an Array's Elements

Because enumerators are stored in memory as integers, you can use them as array subscripts. For example, look at the following code.

```
enum Day { MONDAY, TUESDAY, WEDNESDAY, THURSDAY, FRIDAY };
const int NUM_DAYS = 5;
double sales[NUM_DAYS];
sales[MONDAY] = 1525.0;      // Stores 1525.0 in sales[0].
sales[TUESDAY] = 1896.5;     // Stores 1896.5 in sales[1].
sales[WEDNESDAY] = 1975.63;  // Stores 1975.63 in sales[2].
sales[THURSDAY] = 1678.33;   // Stores 1678.33 in sales[3].
sales[FRIDAY] = 1498.52;     // Stores 1498.52 in sales[4].
```

This code stores values in all five elements of the `sales` array. Because enumerator values can be used as array subscripts, you can use an `enum` variable in a loop to step through the elements of an array. However, using an `enum` variable for this purpose is not as straightforward as using an `int` variable. This is because you cannot use the `++` or `--` operators directly on an `enum` variable. To understand what I mean, first look at the following code taken from Program 11-12:

```
for (index = MONDAY; index <= FRIDAY; index++)
{
    cout << "Enter the sales for day "
         << index << ": ";
    cin >> sales[index];
}
```

In this code, `index` is an `int` variable used to step through each element of the array. It is reasonable to expect that we could use a `Day` variable instead, as shown in the following code.

```
Day workDay;  // Define a Day variable

// ERROR!!! This code will NOT work.
for (workDay = MONDAY; workDay <= FRIDAY; workDay++)
{
   cout << "Enter the sales for day "
        << workDay << ": ";
   cin >> sales[workDay];
}
```

Notice that the for loop's update expression uses the ++ operator to increment workDay. Although this works fine with an int variable, the ++ operator cannot be used with an enum variable. Instead, you must convert workDay++ to an equivalent expression that will work. The expression workDay++ attempts to do the same thing as:

```
workDay = workDay + 1;  // Good idea, but still won't work.
```

However, this still will not work. We have to use a cast to explicitly convert the expression workDay + 1 to the Day data type, like this:

```
workDay = static_cast<Day>(workDay + 1);
```

This is the expression that we must use in the for loop instead of workDay++. The corrected for loop looks like this:

```
for (workDay = MONDAY; workDay <= FRIDAY;
            workDay = static_cast<Day>(workDay + 1))
{
   cout << "Enter the sales for day "
        << workDay << ": ";
   cin >> sales[workDay];
}
```

Program 11-13 is a version of Program 11-12 that is modified to use a Day variable to step through the elements of the sales array.

Program 11-13

```
 1  // This program demonstrates an enumerated data type.
 2  #include <iostream>
 3  #include <iomanip>
 4  using namespace std;
 5
 6  enum Day { MONDAY, TUESDAY, WEDNESDAY, THURSDAY, FRIDAY };
 7
 8  int main()
 9  {
10     const int NUM_DAYS = 5;    // The number of days
11     double sales[NUM_DAYS];     // To hold sales for each day
12     double total = 0.0;         // Accumulator
13     Day workDay;                // Loop counter
14
```

```
15      // Get the sales for each day.
16      for (workDay = MONDAY; workDay <= FRIDAY;
17                       workDay = static_cast<Day>(workDay + 1))
18      {
19         cout << "Enter the sales for day "
20              << workDay << ": ";
21         cin >> sales[workDay];
22      }
23
24      // Calculate the total sales.
25      for (workDay = MONDAY; workDay <= FRIDAY;
26                       workDay = static_cast<Day>(workDay + 1))
27         total += sales[workDay];
28
29      // Display the total.
30      cout << "The total sales are $" << setprecision(2)
31           << fixed << total << endl;
32
33      return 0;
34  }
```

Program Output with Example Input Shown in Bold
```
Enter the sales for day 0: 1525.00 [Enter]
Enter the sales for day 1: 1896.50 [Enter]
Enter the sales for day 2: 1975.63 [Enter]
Enter the sales for day 3: 1678.33 [Enter]
Enter the sales for day 4: 1498.52 [Enter]
The total sales are $8573.98
```

Using Enumerators to Output Values

As you have already seen, sending an enumerator to cout causes the enumerator's integer value to be displayed. For example, assuming we are using the Day type previously described, the following statement displays 0.

```
cout << MONDAY << endl;
```

If you wish to use the enumerator to display a string such as "Monday," you'll have to write code that produces the desired string. For example, in the following code assume that workDay is a Day variable that has been initialized to some value. The switch statement displays the name of a day, based upon the value of the variable.

```
switch(workDay)
{
    case MONDAY    : cout << "Monday";
                     break;
    case TUESDAY   : cout << "Tuesday";
                     break;
    case WEDNESDAY : cout << "Wednesday";
                     break;
    case THURSDAY  : cout << "Thursday";
                     break;
    case FRIDAY    : cout << "Friday";
}
```

Program 11-14 shows this type of code used in a function. Instead of asking the user to enter the sales for day 0, day 1, and so forth, it displays the names of the days.

Program 11-14

```cpp
 1  // This program demonstrates an enumerated data type.
 2  #include <iostream>
 3  #include <iomanip>
 4  using namespace std;
 5
 6  enum Day { MONDAY, TUESDAY, WEDNESDAY, THURSDAY, FRIDAY };
 7
 8  // Function prototype
 9  void displayDayName(Day);
10
11  int main()
12  {
13     const int NUM_DAYS = 5;    // The number of days
14     double sales[NUM_DAYS];    // To hold sales for each day
15     double total = 0.0;        // Accumulator
16     Day workDay;               // Loop counter
17
18     // Get the sales for each day.
19     for (workDay = MONDAY; workDay <= FRIDAY;
20                        workDay = static_cast<Day>(workDay + 1))
21     {
22        cout << "Enter the sales for day ";
23        displayDayName(workDay);
24        cout << ": ";
25        cin >> sales[workDay];
26     }
27
28     // Calculate the total sales.
29     for (workDay = MONDAY; workDay <= FRIDAY;
30                        workDay = static_cast<Day>(workDay + 1))
31        total += sales[workDay];
32
33     // Display the total.
34     cout << "The total sales are $" << setprecision(2)
35         << fixed << total << endl;
36
37     return 0;
38  }
39
40  //***********************************************************
41  // Definition of the displayDayName function                *
42  // This function accepts an argument of the Day type and     *
43  // displays the corresponding name of the day.              *
44  //***********************************************************
45
```

```
46  void displayDayName(Day d)
47  {
48     switch(d)
49     {
50        case MONDAY     : cout << "Monday";
51                           break;
52        case TUESDAY    : cout << "Tuesday";
53                           break;
54        case WEDNESDAY  : cout << "Wednesday";
55                           break;
56        case THURSDAY   : cout << "Thursday";
57                           break;
58        case FRIDAY     : cout << "Friday";
59     }
60  }
```

Program Output with Example Input Shown in Bold
```
Enter the sales for Monday: 1525.00 [Enter]
Enter the sales for Tuesday: 1896.50 [Enter]
Enter the sales for Wednesday: 1975.63 [Enter]
Enter the sales for Thursday: 1678.33 [Enter]
Enter the sales for Friday: 1498.52 [Enter]
The total sales are $8573.98
```

Specifying Integer Values for Enumerators

By default, the enumerators in an enumerated data type are assigned the integer values 0, 1, 2, and so forth. If this is not appropriate, you can specify the values to be assigned, as in the following example.

```
enum Water { FREEZING = 32, BOILING = 212 };
```

In this example, the FREEZING enumerator is assigned the integer value 32 and the BOILING enumerator is assigned the integer value 212. Program 11-15 demonstrates how this enumerated type might be used.

Program 11-15

```
1   // This program demonstrates an enumerated data type.
2   #include <iostream>
3   #include <iomanip>
4   using namespace std;
5
6   int main()
7   {
8      enum Water { FREEZING = 32, BOILING = 212 };
9      int waterTemp; // To hold the water temperature
10
```

(program continues)

Program 11-15 *(continued)*

```
11      cout << "Enter the current water temperature: ";
12      cin >> waterTemp;
13      if (waterTemp <= FREEZING)
14        cout << "The water is frozen.\n";
15      else if (waterTemp >= BOILING)
16        cout << "The water is boiling.\n";
17      else
18        cout << "The water is not frozen or boiling.\n";
19
20      return 0;
21  }
```

Program Output with Example Input Shown in Bold
```
Enter the current water temperature: 10 [Enter]
The water is frozen.
```

Program Output with Example Input Shown in Bold
```
Enter the current water temperature: 300 [Enter]
The water is boiling.
```

Program Output with Example Input Shown in Bold
```
Enter the current water temperature: 92 [Enter]
The water is not frozen or boiling.
```

If you leave out the value assignment for one or more of the enumerators, it will be assigned a default value. Here is an example:

```
enum Colors { RED, ORANGE, YELLOW = 9, GREEN, BLUE };
```

In this example the enumerator RED will be assigned the value 0, ORANGE will be assigned the value 1, YELLOW will be assigned the value 9, GREEN will be assigned the value 10, and BLUE will be assigned the value 11.

Enumerators Must Be Unique Within the Same Scope

Enumerators are identifiers just like variable names, named constants, and function names. As with all identifiers, they must be unique within the same scope. For example, an error will result if both of the following enumerated types are declared within the same scope. The reason is that ROOSEVELT is declared twice.

```
enum Presidents { MCKINLEY, ROOSEVELT, TAFT };
enum VicePresidents { ROOSEVELT, FAIRBANKS, SHERMAN };  // Error!
```

The following declarations will also cause an error if they appear within the same scope.

```
enum Status { OFF, ON };
const int OFF = 0;        // Error!
```

Declaring the Type and Defining the Variables in One Statement

The following code uses two lines to declare an enumerated data type and define a variable of the type.

```
enum Car { PORSCHE, FERRARI, JAGUAR };
Car sportsCar;
```

C++ allows you to declare an enumerated data type and define one or more variables of the type in the same statement. The previous code could be combined into the following statement:

```
enum Car { PORSCHE, FERRARI, JAGUAR } sportsCar;
```

The following statement declares the `Car` data type and defines two variables: `myCar` and `yourCar`.

```
enum Car { PORSCHE, FERRARI, JAGUAR } myCar, yourCar;
```

 See the High Adventure Travel Part 2 Case Study on the Student CD.

Checkpoint

11.21   Look at the following declaration.
```
enum Flower { ROSE, DAISY, PETUNIA };
```
In memory, what value will be stored for the enumerator ROSE? For DAISY? For PETUNIA?

11.22   What will the following code display?
```
enum { HOBBIT, ELF = 7, DRAGON };
cout << HOBBIT << " " << ELF << " " << DRAGON << endl;
```

11.23   Does the enumerated data type declared in Checkpoint Question 11.22 have a name, or is it anonymous?

11.24   What will the following code display?
```
enum Letters { Z, Y, X };
if (Z > X)
    cout << "Z is greater than X.\n";
else
    cout << "Z is not greater than X.\n";
```

11.25   Will the following code cause an error, or will it compile without any errors? If it causes an error, rewrite it so it compiles.
```
enum Color { RED, GREEN, BLUE };
Color c;
c = 0;
```

11.26   Will the following code cause an error, or will it compile without any errors? If it causes an error, rewrite it so it compiles.
```
enum Color { RED, GREEN, BLUE };
Color c = RED;
c++;
```

Review Questions and Exercises

Short Answer

1. What is a primitive data type?

2. Does a structure declaration cause a structure variable to be created?

3. Both arrays and structures are capable of storing multiple values. What is the difference between an array and a structure?

4. Look at the following structure declaration.

```
struct Point
{
    int x;
    int y;
};
```

Write statements that

A) define a Point structure variable named center

B) assign 12 to the x member of center

C) assign 7 to the y member of center

D) display the contents of the x and y members of center

5. Look at the following structure declaration.

```
struct FullName
{
    char lastName[26];
    char middleName[26];
    char firstName[26];
};
```

Write statements that

A) Define a FullName structure variable named info

B) Assign your last, middle, and first name to the members of the info variable

C) Display the contents of the members of the info variable

6. Look at the following code.

```
struct PartData
{
    char partName[51];
    int idNumber;
};


PartData inventory[100];
```

Write a statement that displays the contents of the partName member of element 49 of the inventory array.

7. Look at the following code.

```
struct Town
{
    char townName[51];
    char countyName[51];
    double population;
    double elevation;
};
```

```
Town t = { "Canton", "Haywood", 9478 };
```

A) What value is stored in t.townName?

B) What value is stored in t.countyName?

C) What value is stored in t.population?

D) What value is stored in t.elevation?

8. Look at the following code.

```
structure Rectangle
{
    int length;
    int width;
};
```

```
Rectangle *r;
```

Write statements that

A) Dynamically allocate a Rectangle structure variable and use r to point to it.

B) Assign 10 to the structure's length member and 14 to the structure's width member.

9. What is the difference between a union and a structure?

10. Look at the following code.

```
union Values
{
    int ivalue;
    double dvalue;
};
```

```
Values v;
```

Assuming that an int uses four bytes and a double uses eight bytes, how much memory does the variable v use?

11. What will the following code display?

```
enum { POODLE, BOXER, TERRIER };
cout << POODLE << " " << BOXER << " " << TERRIER << endl;
```

12. Look at the following declaration.

```
enum Person { BILL, JOHN, CLAIRE, BOB };
Person p;
```

Indicate whether each of the following statements or expressions is valid or invalid.

A) `p = BOB;`

B) `p++;`

C) `BILL > BOB`

D) `p = 0;`

E) `int x = BILL;`

F) `p = static_cast<Person>(3);`

G) `cout << CLAIRE << endl;`

Fill-in-the-Blank

13. Before a structure variable can be created, the structure must be _____.

14. The _____ is the name of the structure type.

15. The variables declared inside a structure declaration are called _____.

16. A(n) _____ is required after the closing brace of a structure declaration.

17. In the definition of a structure variable, the _____ is placed before the variable name, just like the data type of a regular variable is placed before its name.

18. The _____ operator allows you to access structure members.

Algorithm Workbench

19. The structure `Car` is declared as follows:

```
struct Car
{
    char carMake[20];
    char carModel[20];
    int yearModel;
    double cost;
};
```

Write a definition statement that defines a `Car` structure variable initialized with the following data:

Make: Ford
Model: Mustang
Year Model: 1997
Cost: $20,000

20. Define an array of 25 of the `Car` structure variables (the structure is declared in Question 19).

21. Define an array of 35 of the `Car` structure variables. Initialize the first three elements with the following data:

Make	Model	Year	Cost
Ford	Taurus	1997	$21,000
Honda	Accord	1992	$11,000
Lamborghini	Countach	1997	$200,000

22. Write a loop that will step through the array you defined in Question 21, displaying the contents of each element.

23. Declare a structure named `TempScale`, with the following members:

    ```
    fahrenheit: a double
    centigrade: a double
    ```

    Next, declare a structure named `Reading`, with the following members:

    ```
    windSpeed: an int
    humidity: a double
    temperature: a TempScale structure variable
    ```

    Next define a `Reading` structure variable.

24. Write statements that will store the following data in the variable you defined in Question 23.

    Wind Speed: 37 mph
    Humidity: 32%
    Fahrenheit temperature: 32 degrees
    Centigrade temperature: 0 degrees

25. Write a function called `showReading`. It should accept a `Reading` structure variable (see Question 23) as its argument. The function should display the contents of the variable on the screen.

26. Write a function called `findReading`. It should use a `Reading` structure reference variable (see Question 23) as its parameter. The function should ask the user to enter values for each member of the structure.

27. Write a function called `getReading`, which returns a `Reading` structure (see Question 23). The function should ask the user to enter values for each member of a `Reading` structure, then return the structure.

28. Write a function called `recordReading`. It should use a `Reading` structure pointer variable (see Question 23) as its parameter. The function should ask the user to enter values for each member of the structure pointed to by the parameter.

29. Rewrite the following statement using the structure pointer operator:

    ```
    (*rptr).windSpeed = 50;
    ```

30. Rewrite the following statement using the structure pointer operator:

    ```
    *(*strPtr).num = 10;
    ```

31. Write the declaration of a union called `Items` with the following members:

    ```
    alpha        a character
    num          an integer
    bigNum       a long integer
    real         a float
    ```

    Next, write the definition of an `Items` union variable.

32. Write the declaration of an anonymous union with the same members as the union you declared in Question 31.

33. Write a statement that stores the number 452 in the `num` member of the anonymous union you declared in Question 32.

34. Look at the following statement.

```
enum Color { RED, ORANGE, GREEN, BLUE };
```

   A) What is the name of the data type declared by this statement?
   B) What are the enumerators for this type?
   C) Write a statement that defines a variable of this type and initializes it with a valid value.

35. A pet store sells dogs, cats, birds, and hamsters. Write a declaration for an anonymous enumerated data type that can represent the types of pets the store sells.

True or False

36. T F A semicolon is required after the closing brace of a structure or union declaration.

37. T F A structure declaration does not define a variable.

38. T F The contents of a structure variable can be displayed by passing the structure variable to the cout object.

39. T F Structure variables may not be initialized.

40. T F In a structure variable's initialization list, you do not have to provide initializers for all the members.

41. T F You may skip members in a structure's initialization list.

42. T F The following expression refers to the element 5 in the array carInfo:
    carInfo.model[5]

43. T F An array of structures may be initialized.

44. T F A structure variable may not be a member of another structure.

45. T F A structure member variable may be passed to a function as an argument.

46. T F An entire structure may not be passed to a function as an argument.

47. T F A function may return a structure.

48. T F When a function returns a structure, it is always necessary for the function to have a local structure variable to hold the member values that are to be returned.

49. T F The indirection operator has higher precedence than the dot operator.

50. T F The structure pointer operator does not automatically dereference the structure pointer on its left.

51. T F In a union, all the members are stored in different memory locations.

52. T F All the members of a union may be used simultaneously.

53. T F You may define arrays of unions.

54. T F You may not define pointers to unions.

55. T F An anonymous union has no name.

56. T F If an anonymous union is defined globally (outside all functions), it must be declared static.

Find the Errors

Each of the following declarations, programs, and program segments has errors. Locate as many as you can.

57. ```cpp
    struct
    {
        int x;
        float y;
    };
    ```

58. ```cpp
    struct Values
    {
        char name[30];
        int age;
    }
    ```

59. ```cpp
    struct TwoVals
    {
        int a, b;
    };
    int main ()
    {
        TwoVals.a = 10;
        TwoVals.b = 20;
        return 0;
    }
    ```

60. ```cpp
    #include <iostream>
    using namespace std;

    struct ThreeVals
    {
        int a, b, c;
    };
    int main()
    {
        ThreeVals vals = {1, 2, 3};
        cout << vals << endl;
        return 0;
    }
    ```

61. ```cpp
    #include <iostream>
    using namespace std;

    struct names
    {
        char first[20];
        char last[20];
    };
    int main ()
    {
        names customer = "Smith", "Orley";
        cout << names.first << endl;
        cout << names.last << endl;
        return 0;
    }
    ```
    ```

62.
```cpp
struct FourVals
{
    int a, b, c, d;
};
int main ()
{
    FourVals nums = {1, 2, , 4};
    return 0;
}
```

63.
```cpp
#include <iostream>
using namespace std;

struct TwoVals
{
    int a = 5;
    int b = 10;
};
int main()
{
    TwoVals v;

    cout << v.a << " " << v.b;
    return 0;
}
```

64.
```cpp
struct TwoVals
{
    int a = 5;
    int b = 10;
};

int main()
{
    TwoVals varray[10];

    varray.a[0] = 1;
    return 0;
}
```

65.
```cpp
struct TwoVals
{
    int a;
    int b;
};
TwoVals getVals()
{
    TwoVals.a = TwoVals.b = 0;
}
```

66.
```cpp
struct ThreeVals
{
    int a, b, c;
};

int main ()
{
    TwoVals s, *sptr;
```

```
        sptr = &s;
        *sptr.a = 1;
        return 0;
    }
```

67.
```
    #include <iostream>
    using namespace std;

    union Compound
    {
        int x;
        float y;
    };

    int main()
    {
        Compound u;
        u.x = 1000;
        cout << u.y << endl;
        return 0;
    }
```

Programming Challenges

1. Movie Data

Write a program that uses a structure named MovieData to store the following information about a movie:

>   Title
>   Director
>   Year Released
>   Running Time (in minutes)

The program should create two MovieData variables, store values in their members, and pass each one, in turn, to a function that displays the information about the movie in a clearly formatted manner.

2. Movie Profit

Modify the Movie Data program written for Programming Challenge 1 to include two additional members that hold the movie's production costs and first-year revenues. Modify the function that displays the movie data to display the title, director, release year, running time, and first year's profit or loss.

3. Corporate Sales Data

Write a program that uses a structure to store the following data on a company division:

>   Division Name (such as East, West, North, or South)
>   First-Quarter Sales
>   Second-Quarter Sales
>   Third-Quarter Sales
>   Fourth-Quarter Sales
>   Total Annual Sales
>   Average Quarterly Sales

The program should use four variables of this structure. Each variable should represent one of the following corporate divisions: East, West, North, and South. The user should be asked for the four quarters' sales figures for each division. Each division's total and average sales should be calculated and stored in the appropriate member of each structure variable. These figures should then be displayed on the screen.

Input Validation: Do not accept negative numbers for any sales figures.

VideoNote

Solving the
Weather
Statistics
Problem

4. **Weather Statistics**

Write a program that uses a structure to store the following weather data for a particular month:

Total Rainfall
High Temperature
Low Temperature
Average Temperature

The program should have an array of 12 structures to hold weather data for an entire year. When the program runs, it should ask the user to enter data for each month. (The average temperature should be calculated.) Once the data are entered for all the months, the program should calculate and display the average monthly rainfall, the total rainfall for the year, the highest and lowest temperatures for the year (and the months they occurred in), and the average of all the monthly average temperatures.

Input Validation: Only accept temperatures within the range between –100 and +140 degrees Fahrenheit.

5. **Weather Statistics Modification**

Modify the program that you wrote for Programming Challenge 4 so it defines an enumerated data type with enumerators for the months (JANUARY, FEBRUARY, etc.). The program should use the enumerated type to step through the elements of the array.

6. **Soccer Scores**

Write a program that stores the following data about a soccer player in a structure:

Player's Name
Player's Number
Points Scored by Player

The program should keep an array of 12 of these structures. Each element is for a different player on a team. When the program runs it should ask the user to enter the data for each player. It should then show a table that lists each player's number, name, and points scored. The program should also calculate and display the total points earned by the team. The number and name of the player who has earned the most points should also be displayed.

Input Validation: Do not accept negative values for players' numbers or points scored.

7. **Customer Accounts**

   Write a program that uses a structure to store the following data about a customer account:

   > Name
   > Address
   > City, State, and ZIP
   > Telephone Number
   > Account Balance
   > Date of Last Payment

   The program should use an array of at least 20 structures. It should let the user enter data into the array, change the contents of any element, and display all the data stored in the array. The program should have a menu-driven user interface.

   Input Validation: When the data for a new account is entered, be sure the user enters data for all the fields. No negative account balances should be entered.

8. **Search Function for Customer Accounts Program**

   Add a function to Programming Challenge 7 that allows the user to search the structure array for a particular customer's account. It should accept part of the customer's name as an argument and then search for an account with a name that matches it. All accounts that match should be displayed. If no account matches, a message saying so should be displayed.

9. **Speakers' Bureau**

   Write a program that keeps track of a speakers' bureau. The program should use a structure to store the following data about a speaker:

   > Name
   > Telephone Number
   > Speaking Topic
   > Fee Required

   The program should use an array of at least 10 structures. It should let the user enter data into the array, change the contents of any element, and display all the data stored in the array. The program should have a menu-driven user interface.

   Input Validation: When the data for a new speaker is entered, be sure the user enters data for all the fields. No negative amounts should be entered for a speaker's fee.

10. **Search Function for the Speakers' Bureau Program**

    Add a function to Programming Challenge 9 that allows the user to search for a speaker on a particular topic. It should accept a key word as an argument and then search the array for a structure with that key word in the Speaking Topic field. All structures that match should be displayed. If no structure matches, a message saying so should be displayed.

11. Monthly Budget

A student has established the following monthly budget:

Housing	500.00
Utilities	150.00
Household Expenses	65.00
Transportation	50.00
Food	250.00
Medical	30.00
Insurance	100.00
Entertainment	150.00
Clothing	75.00
Miscellaneous	50.00

Write a program that has a `MonthlyBudget` structure designed to hold each of these expense categories. The program should pass the structure to a function that asks the user to enter the amounts spent in each budget category during a month. The program should then pass the structure to a function that displays a report indicating the amount over or under in each category, as well as the amount over or under for the entire monthly budget.

12. Course Grade

Write a program that uses a structure to store the following data:

Member Name	Description
Name	Student name
Idnum	Student ID number
Tests	Pointer to an array of test scores
Average	Average test score
Grade	Course grade

The program should keep a list of test scores for a group of students. It should ask the user how many test scores there are to be and how many students there are. It should then dynamically allocate an array of structures. Each structure's `Tests` member should point to a dynamically allocated array that will hold the test scores.

After the arrays have been dynamically allocated, the program should ask for the ID number and all the test scores for each student. The average test score should be calculated and stored in the `average` member of each structure. The course grade should be computed on the basis of the following grading scale:

Average Test Grade	Course Grade
91–100	A
81–90	B
71–80	C
61–70	D
60 or below	F

The course grade should then be stored in the Grade member of each structure. Once all this data is calculated, a table should be displayed on the screen listing each student's name, ID number, average test score, and course grade.

Input Validation: Be sure all the data for each student is entered. Do not accept negative numbers for any test score.

13. **Drink Machine Simulator**

Write a program that simulates a soft drink machine. The program should use a structure that stores the following data:

> Drink Name
> Drink Cost
> Number of Drinks in Machine

The program should create an array of five structures. The elements should be initialized with the following data:

Drink Name	Cost	Number in Machine
Cola	.75	20
Root Beer	.75	20
Lemon-Lime	.75	20
Grape Soda	.80	20
Cream Soda	.80	20

Each time the program runs, it should enter a loop that performs the following steps: A list of drinks is displayed on the screen. The user should be allowed to either quit the program or pick a drink. If the user selects a drink, he or she will next enter the amount of money that is to be inserted into the drink machine. The program should display the amount of change that would be returned and subtract one from the number of that drink left in the machine. If the user selects a drink that has sold out, a message should be displayed. The loop then repeats. When the user chooses to quit the program it should display the total amount of money the machine earned.

Input Validation: When the user enters an amount of money, do not accept negative values, or values greater than $1.00.

14. **Inventory Bins**

Write a program that simulates inventory bins in a warehouse. Each bin holds a number of the same type of parts. The program should use a structure that keeps the following data:

> Description of the part kept in the bin
> Number of parts in the bin

The program should have an array of 10 bins, initialized with the following data:

Part Description	Number of Parts in the Bin
Valve	10
Bearing	5
Bushing	15
Coupling	21
Flange	7
Gear	5
Gear Housing	5
Vacuum Gripper	25
Cable	18
Rod	12

The program should have the following functions:

AddParts: a function that increases a specific bin's part count by a specified number.

RemoveParts: a function that decreases a specific bin's part count by a specified number.

When the program runs, it should repeat a loop that performs the following steps: The user should see a list of what each bin holds and how many parts are in each bin. The user can choose to either quit the program or select a bin. When a bin is selected, the user can either add parts to it or remove parts from it. The loop then repeats, showing the updated bin data on the screen.

Input Validation: No bin can hold more than 30 parts, so don't let the user add more than a bin can hold. Also, don't accept negative values for the number of parts being added or removed.

15. **Multipurpose Payroll**

Write a program that calculates pay for either an hourly paid worker or a salaried worker. Hourly paid workers are paid their hourly pay rate times the number of hours worked. Salaried workers are paid their regular salary plus any bonus they may have earned. The program should declare two structures for the following data:

> **Hourly Paid:**
> HoursWorked
> HourlyRate
>
> **Salaried:**
> Salary
> Bonus

The program should also declare a union with two members. Each member should be a structure variable: one for the hourly paid worker and another for the salaried worker.

The program should ask the user whether he or she is calculating the pay for an hourly paid worker or a salaried worker. Regardless of which the user selects, the appropriate members of the union will be used to store the data that will be used to calculate the pay.

Input Validation: Do not accept negative numbers. Do not accept values greater than 80 for HoursWorked.

12 Advanced File Operations

TOPICS

12.1 File Operations

CONCEPT: A file is a collection of data that is usually stored on a computer's disk. Data can be saved to files and then later reused.

Almost all real-world programs use files to store and retrieve data. Here are a few examples of familiar software packages that use files extensively.

- **Word Processors:** Word processing programs are used to write letters, memos, reports, and other documents. The documents are then saved in files so they can be edited and reprinted.

- **Database Management Systems:** DBMSs are used to create and maintain databases. Databases are files that contain large collections of data, such as payroll records, inventories, sales statistics, and customer records.

- **Spreadsheets:** Spreadsheet programs are used to work with numerical data. Numbers and mathematical formulas can be inserted into the rows and columns of the spreadsheet. The spreadsheet can then be saved to a file for use later.

- **Compilers:** Compilers translate the source code of a program, which is saved in a file, into an executable file. Throughout the previous chapters of this book you have created many C++ source files and compiled them to executable files.

Chapter 3 introduced you to file operations using the `ifstream` and `ofstream` data types. You saw how to open a file for input with an `ifstream` object, and how to open a file for output with an `ofstream` object. That chapter also explained that the stream extraction operator (>>) may be used with an `ifstream` object to read data from a file, and that the stream insertion operator (<<) may be used with an `ofstream` object to write data to a file. Chapter 4 discussed how to test for errors when a file is opened, and Chapter 5 explained how to detect whether the end of a file has been encountered. That chapter also demonstrated techniques for using loops with files.

Chapters 3, 4, and 5 provided enough information for you to write programs that perform simple file operations. This chapter covers more advanced file operations, and focuses primarily on the `fstream` data type. As a review, Table 12-1 compares the `ifstream`, `ofstream`, and `fstream` data types. All of these data types require the `fstream` header file.

Table 12-1 File Stream

Data Type	Description
ifstream	Input File Stream. This data type can be used only to read data from files into memory.
ofstream	Output File Stream. This data type can be used to create files and write data to them.
fstream	File Stream. This data type can be used to create files, write data to them, and read data from them.

Using the `fstream` Data Type

You define an `fstream` object just as you define objects of other data types. The following statement defines an `fstream` object named `dataFile`.

```
fstream dataFile;
```

As with `ifstream` and `ofstream` objects, you use an `fstream` object's `open` function to open a file. An `fstream` object's `open` function requires two arguments, however. The first argument is a string containing the name of the file. The second argument is a file access flag that indicates the mode in which you wish to open the file. Here is an example.

```
dataFile.open("info.txt", ios::out);
```

The first argument in this function call is the name of the file, `info.txt`. The second argument is the file access flag `ios::out`. This tells C++ to open the file in output mode. Output mode allows data to be written to a file. The following statement uses the `ios::in` access flag to open a file in input mode, which allows data to be read from the file.

```
dataFile.open("info.txt", ios::in);
```

There are many file access flags, as listed in Table 12-2.

Table 12-2

File Access Flag	Meaning
`ios::app`	Append mode. If the file already exists, its contents are preserved and all output is written to the end of the file. By default, this flag causes the file to be created if it does not exist.
`ios::ate`	If the file already exists, the program goes directly to the end of it. Output may be written anywhere in the file.
`ios::binary`	Binary mode. When a file is opened in binary mode, data are written to or read from it in pure binary format. (The default mode is text.)
`ios::in`	Input mode. Data will be read from the file. If the file does not exist, it will not be created and the open function will fail.
`ios::out`	Output mode. Data will be written to the file. By default, the file's contents will be deleted if it already exists.
`ios::trunc`	If the file already exists, its contents will be deleted (truncated). This is the default mode used by `ios::out`.

Several flags may be used together if they are connected with the | operator. For example, assume `dataFile` is an fstream object in the following statement:

```
dataFile.open("info.txt", ios::in | ios::out);
```

This statement opens the file `info.txt` in both input and output modes. This means data may be written to and read from the file.

NOTE: When used by itself, the `ios::out` flag causes the file's contents to be deleted if the file already exists. When used with the `ios::in` flag, however, the file's existing contents are preserved. If the file does not already exist, it will be created.

The following statement opens the file in such a way that data will only be written to its end:

```
dataFile.open("info.txt", ios::out | ios::app);
```

By using different combinations of access flags, you can open files in many possible modes.

Program 12-1 uses an fstream object to open a file for output, and then writes data to the file.

Program 12-1

```
1    // This program uses an fstream object to write data to a file.
2    #include <iostream>
3    #include <fstream>
4    using namespace std;
5
6    int main()
7    {
8        fstream dataFile;
9
```

(program continues)

Program 12-1   *(continued)*

```
10      cout << "Opening file...\n";
11      dataFile.open("demofile.txt", ios::out);    // Open for output
12      cout << "Now writing data to the file.\n";
13      dataFile << "Jones\n";                       // Write line 1
14      dataFile << "Smith\n";                       // Write line 2
15      dataFile << "Willis\n";                      // Write line 3
16      dataFile << "Davis\n";                       // Write line 4
17      dataFile.close();                            // Close the file
18      cout << "Done.\n";
19      return 0;
20  }
```

Program Output

```
Opening file...
Now writing data to the file.
Done.
```

Output to File `demofile.txt`

```
Jones
Smith
Willis
Davis
```

The file output is shown for Program 12-1 the way it would appear if the file contents were displayed on the screen. The \n characters cause each name to appear on a separate line. The actual file contents, however, appear as a stream of characters as shown in Figure 12-1.

Figure 12-1

As you can see from the figure, \n characters are written to the file along with all the other characters. The characters are added to the file sequentially, in the order they are written by the program. The very last character is an *end-of-file marker*. It is a character that marks the end of the file and is automatically written when the file is closed. (The actual character used to mark the end of a file depends upon the operating system being used. It is always a nonprinting character. For example, some systems use control-Z.)

Program 12-2 is a modification of Program 12-1 that further illustrates the sequential nature of files. The file is opened, two names are written to it, and it is closed. The file is then reopened by the program in append mode (with the `ios::app` access flag). When a file is opened in append mode, its contents are preserved and all subsequent output is appended to the file's end. Two more names are added to the file before it is closed and the program terminates.

Program 12-2

```
1   // This program writes data to a file, closes the file,
2   // then reopens the file and appends more data.
3   #include <iostream>
4   #include <fstream>
5   using namespace std;
6
7   int main()
8   {
9      ofstream dataFile;
10
11     cout << "Opening file...\n";
12     // Open the file in output mode.
13     dataFile.open("demofile.txt", ios::out);
14     cout << "Now writing data to the file.\n";
15     dataFile << "Jones\n";                       // Write line 1
16     dataFile << "Smith\n";                       // Write line 2
17     cout << "Now closing the file.\n";
18     dataFile.close();                            // Close the file
19
20     cout << "Opening the file again...\n";
21     // Open the file in append mode.
22     dataFile.open("demofile.txt", ios::out | ios::app);
23     cout << "Writing more data to the file.\n";
24     dataFile << "Willis\n";                      // Write line 3
25     dataFile << "Davis\n";                       // Write line 4
26     cout << "Now closing the file.\n";
27     dataFile.close();                            // Close the file
28
29     cout << "Done.\n";
30     return 0;
31  }
```

Output to File demofile.txt
```
Jones
Smith
Willis
Davis
```

The first time the file is opened, the names are written as shown in Figure 12-2.

Figure 12-2

The file is closed and an end-of-file character is automatically written. When the file is reopened, the new output is appended to the end of the file, as shown in Figure 12-3.

Figure 12-3

NOTE: If the `ios::out` flag had been alone, without `ios::app` the second time the file was opened, the file's contents would have been deleted. If this had been the case, the names Jones and Smith would have been erased and the file would only have contained the names Willis and Davis.

File Open Modes with `ifstream` and `ofstream` Objects

The `ifstream` and `ofstream` data types each have a default mode in which they open files. This mode determines the operations that may be performed on the file, and what happens if the file that is being opened already exists. Table 12-3 describes each data type's default open mode.

Table 12-3

File Type	Default Open Mode
ofstream	The file is opened for output only. Data may be written to the file, but not read from the file. If the file does not exist, it is created. If the file already exists, its contents are deleted (the file is truncated).
ifstream	The file is opened for input only. Data may be read from the file, but not written to it. The file's contents will be read from its beginning. If the file does not exist, the open function fails.

You cannot change the fact that `ifstream` files may only be read from, and `ofstream` files may only be written to. You can, however, vary the way operations are carried out on these files by providing a file access flag as an optional second argument to the `open` function. The following code shows an example using an `ofstream` object.

```
ofstream outputFile;
outputFile.open("values.txt", ios::out|ios::app);
```

The `ios::app` flag specifies that data written to the `values.txt` file should be appended to its existing contents.

Checking for a File's Existence Before Opening It

Sometimes you want to determine whether a file already exists before opening it for output. You can do this by first attempting to open the file for input. If the file does not exist, the open operation will fail. In that case, you can create the file by opening it for output. The following code gives an example.

```
fstream dataFile;
dataFile.open("values.txt", ios::in);
if (dataFile.fail())
{
        // The file does not exist, so create it.
        dataFile.open("values.txt", ios::out);
        //
        // Continue to process the file...
        //
}
```

```
else    // The file already exists.
{
        dataFile.close();
        cout << "The file values.txt already exists.\n";
}
```

Opening a File with the File Stream Object Definition Statement

An alternative to using the open member function is to use the file stream object definition statement to open the file. Here is an example:

```
fstream dataFile("names.txt", ios::in | ios::out);
```

This statement defines an fstream object named dataFile and uses it to open the file names.txt. The file is opened in both input and output modes. This technique eliminates the need to call the open function when your program knows the name and access mode of the file at the time the object is defined. You may also use this technique with ifstream and ofstream objects, as shown in the following examples.

```
ifstream inputFile("info.txt");
ofstream outputFile("addresses.txt");
ofstream dataFile("customers.txt", ios::out|ios::app);
```

You may also test for errors after you have opened a file with this technique. The following code shows an example.

```
ifstream inputFile("SalesData.txt");
if (!inputFile)
    cout << "Error opening SalesData.txt.\n";
```

More About File Names

Each operating system has its own rules for naming files. Most systems allow long file names such as

SalesInfoFrom1997
CorpSalesReport
VehicleRegistrations

Some systems only allow shorter file names. The older MS-DOS operating system, for example, allowed file names of no more than eight characters with an optional three character extension.

Extensions are commonly used with file names. The name and extension are separated by a period, known as a "dot." While the file name identifies the file's purpose, the extension usually identifies the type of data contained in the file. For example, the .txt extension identifies a text file that may be opened with a text editor such as Notepad. The .cpp extension identifies a C++ program. The file name payroll.cpp would identify a payroll program written in C++. Table 12-4 lists other example file names and the types of data they contain.

Table 12-4

File Name and Extension	File Contents
myprog.bas	BASIC program
menu.bat	Windows batch file
install.doc	Microsoft Word document
crunch.exe	Executable file
bob.html	HTML (Hypertext Markup Language) file
3dmodel.java	Java program or applet
vacation.jpg	JPEG image file
invent.obj	Object file
instructions.pdf	Adobe Portable Document Format file
prog1.prj	Borland C++ project file
ansi.sys	System device driver
readme.txt	Text file

 Checkpoint

12.1 Which file access flag would you use if you want all output to be written to the end of an existing file?

12.2 How do you use more than one file access flag?

12.3 Assuming that `diskInfo` is an `fstream` object, write a statement that opens the file `names.dat` for output.

12.4 Assuming that `diskInfo` is an `fstream` object, write a statement that opens the file `customers.txt` for output, where all output will be written to the end of the file.

12.5 Assuming that `diskInfo` is an `fstream` object, write a statement that opens the file `payable.txt` for both input and output.

12.6 Write a statement that defines an `fstream` object named `dataFile` and opens a file named `salesfigures.txt` for input. (*Note:* The file should be opened with the definition statement, not an `open` function call.)

12.2 File Output Formatting

CONCEPT: File output may be formatted in the same way that screen output is formatted.

The same output formatting techniques that are used with `cout`, which are covered in Chapter 3, may also be used with file stream objects. For example, the `setprecision` and `fixed` manipulators may be called to establish the number of digits of precision that floating point values are rounded to. Program 12-3 demonstrates this.

Program 12-3

```
 1  // This program uses the setprecision and fixed
 2  // manipulators to format file output.
 3  #include <iostream>
 4  #include <iomanip>
 5  #include <fstream>
 6  using namespace std;
 7
 8  int main()
 9  {
10     fstream dataFile;
11     double num = 17.816392;
12
13     dataFile.open("numfile.txt", ios::out);   // Open in output mode
14
15     dataFile << fixed;            // Format for fixed-point notation
16     dataFile << num << endl;      // Write the number
17
18     dataFile << setprecision(4);  // Format for 4 decimal places
19     dataFile << num << endl;      // Write the number
20
21     dataFile << setprecision(3);  // Format for 3 decimal places
22     dataFile << num << endl;      // Write the number
23
24     dataFile << setprecision(2);  // Format for 2 decimal places
25     dataFile << num << endl;      // Write the number
26
27     dataFile << setprecision(1);  // Format for 1 decimal place
28     dataFile << num << endl;      // Write the number
29
30     cout << "Done.\n";
31     dataFile.close();             // Close the file
32     return 0;
33  }
```

Contents of File `numfile.txt`
```
17.816392
17.8164
17.816
17.82
17.8
```

Notice the file output is formatted just as `cout` would format screen output. Program 12-4 shows the `setw` stream manipulator being used to format file output into columns.

Program 12-4

```
 1  // This program writes three rows of numbers to a file.
 2  #include <iostream>
 3  #include <fstream>
 4  #include <iomanip>
 5  using namespace std;
```

(program continues)

Program 12-4 *(continued)*

```
 6
 7  int main()
 8  {
 9     const int ROWS = 3;    // Rows to write
10     const int COLS = 3;    // Columns to write
11     int nums[ROWS][COLS] = { 2897, 5, 837,
12                              34, 7, 1623,
13                              390, 3456, 12 };
14     fstream outFile("table.txt", ios::out);
15
16     // Write the three rows of numbers with each
17     // number in a field of 8 character spaces.
18     for (int row = 0; row < ROWS; row++)
19     {
20        for (int col = 0; col < COLS; col++)
21        {
22           outFile << setw(8) << nums[row][col];
23        }
24        outFile << endl;
25     }
26     outFile.close();
27     cout << "Done.\n";
28     return 0;
29  }
```

Contents of File `table.txt`

```
    2897       5     837
      34       7    1623
     390    3456      12
```

Figure 12-4 shows the way the characters appear in the file.

Figure 12-4

12.3 Passing File Stream Objects to Functions

CONCEPT: File stream objects may be passed by reference to functions.

When writing actual programs, you'll want to create modularized code for handling file operations. File stream objects may be passed to functions, but they should always be passed by reference. The `openFile` function shown below uses an `fstream` reference object parameter:

VideoNote

Passing
File Stream
Objects to
Functions

```cpp
bool openFileIn(fstream &file, char *name)
{
   bool status;

   file.open(name, ios::in);
   if (file.fail())
      status = false;
   else
      status = true;
   return status;
}
```

The internal state of file stream objects changes with most every operation. They should always be passed to functions by reference to ensure internal consistency. Program 12-5 shows an example of how file stream objects may be passed as arguments to functions.

Program 12-5

```cpp
 1  // This program demonstrates how file stream objects may
 2  // be passed by reference to functions.
 3  #include <iostream>
 4  #include <fstream>
 5  using namespace std;
 6
 7  // Maximum amount to read from a line in the file
 8  const int MAX_LINE_SIZE = 81;
 9
10  // Function prototypes
11  bool openFileIn(fstream &, char *);
12  void showContents(fstream &);
13
14  int main()
15  {
16     fstream dataFile;
17
18     if (!openFileIn(dataFile,"demofile.txt"))
19     {
20        cout << "File open error!" << endl;
21        return 0;   // Exit the program on error.
22     }
```

(program continues)

Program 12-5   *(continued)*

```cpp
23        cout << "File opened successfully.\n";
24        cout << "Now reading data from the file.\n\n";
25        showContents(dataFile);
26        dataFile.close();
27        cout << "\nDone.\n";
28        return 0;
29    }
30
31    //************************************************************
32    // Definition of function openFileIn. Accepts a reference   *
33    // to an fstream object as its argument. The file is opened *
34    // for input. The function returns true upon success, false *
35    // upon failure.                                            *
36    //************************************************************
37
38    bool openFileIn(fstream &file, char *name)
39    {
40        file.open(name, ios::in);
41        if (file.fail())
42           return false;
43        else
44           return true;
45    }
46
47    //************************************************************
48    // Definition of function showContents. Accepts an fstream  *
49    // reference as its argument. Uses a loop to read each name *
50    // from the file and displays it on the screen.             *
51    //************************************************************
52
53    void showContents(fstream &file)
54    {
55        char line[MAX_LINE_SIZE];
56
57        while (file >> line)
58        {
59           cout << line << endl;
60        }
61    }
```

Program Output

```
File opened successfully.
Now reading data from the file.

Jones
Smith
Willis
Davis

Done.
```

12.4 More Detailed Error Testing

> **CONCEPT:** All stream objects have error state bits that indicate the condition of the stream.

All stream objects contain a set of bits that act as flags. These flags indicate the current state of the stream. Table 12-5 lists these bits.

Table 12-5

Bit	Description
`ios::eofbit`	Set when the end of an input stream is encountered.
`ios::failbit`	Set when an attempted operation has failed.
`ios::hardfail`	Set when an unrecoverable error has occurred.
`ios::badbit`	Set when an invalid operation has been attempted.
`ios::goodbit`	Set when all the flags above are not set. Indicates the stream is in good condition.

These bits can be tested by the member functions listed in Table 12-6. (You've already learned about the `fail()` function.) One of the functions listed in the table, `clear()`, can be used to set a status bit.

Table 12-6

Function	Description
`eof()`	Returns true (nonzero) if the `eofbit` flag is set, otherwise returns false.
`fail()`	Returns true (nonzero) if the `failbit` or `hardfail` flags are set, otherwise returns false.
`bad()`	Returns true (nonzero) if the `badbit` flag is set, otherwise returns false.
`good()`	Returns true (nonzero) if the `goodbit` flag is set, otherwise returns false.
`clear()`	When called with no arguments, clears all the flags listed above. Can also be called with a specific flag as an argument.

The function `showState`, shown here, accepts a file stream reference as its argument. It shows the state of the file by displaying the return values of the `eof()`, `fail()`, `bad()`, and `good()` member functions:

```
void showState(fstream &file)
{
    cout << "File Status:\n";
    cout << "  eof bit: " << file.eof() << endl;
    cout << "  fail bit: " << file.fail() << endl;
    cout << "  bad bit: " << file.bad() << endl;
    cout << "  good bit: " << file.good() << endl;
    file.clear();        // Clear any bad bits
}
```

Program 12-6 uses the `showState` function to display `testFile`'s status after various operations. First, the file is created and the integer value 10 is stored in it. The file is then closed and reopened for input. The integer is read from the file, and then a second read operation is performed. Because there is only one item in the file, the second read operation will result in an error.

Program 12-6

```
1   // This program demonstrates the return value of the stream
2   // object error testing member functions.
3   #include <iostream>
4   #include <fstream>
5   using namespace std;
6
7   // Function prototype
8   void showState(fstream &);
9
10  int main()
11  {
12      int num = 10;
13
14      // Open the file for output.
15      fstream testFile("stuff.dat", ios::out);
16      if (testFile.fail())
17      {
18          cout << "ERROR: Cannot open the file.\n";
19          return 0;
20      }
21
22      // Write a value to the file.
23      cout << "Writing the value " << num << " to the file.\n";
24      testFile << num;
25
26      // Show the bit states.
27      showState(testFile);
28
29      // Close the file.
30      testFile.close();
31
32      // Reopen the file for input.
33      testFile.open("stuff.dat", ios::in);
34      if (testFile.fail())
35      {
36          cout << "ERROR: Cannot open the file.\n";
37          return 0;
38      }
39
40      // Read the only value from the file.
41      cout << "Reading from the file.\n";
42      testFile >> num;
43      cout << "The value " << num << " was read.\n";
44
45      // Show the bit states.
46      showState(testFile);
47
```

```
48        // No more data in the file, but force an invalid read operation.
49        cout << "Forcing a bad read operation.\n";
50        testFile >> num;
51
52        // Show the bit states.
53        showState(testFile);
54
55        // Close the file.
56        testFile.close();
57        return 0;
58   }
59
60   //*****************************************************************
61   // Definition of function showState. This function uses          *
62   // an fstream reference as its parameter. The return values of   *
63   // the eof(), fail(), bad(), and good() member functions are     *
64   // displayed. The clear() function is called before the function *
65   // returns.                                                      *
66   //*****************************************************************
67
68   void showState(fstream &file)
69   {
70      cout << "File Status:\n";
71      cout << "   eof bit: " << file.eof() << endl;
72      cout << "  fail bit: " << file.fail() << endl;
73      cout << "   bad bit: " << file.bad() << endl;
74      cout << "  good bit: " << file.good() << endl;
75      file.clear();   // Clear any bad bits
76   }
```

Program Output
```
Writing the value 10 to the file.
File Status:
  eof bit: 0
  fail bit: 0
  bad bit: 0
  good bit: 1
Reading from the file.
The value 10 was read.
File Status:
  eof bit: 1
  fail bit: 0
  bad bit: 0
  good bit: 1
Forcing a bad read operation.
File Status:
  eof bit: 1
  fail bit: 1
  bad bit: 0
  good bit: 0
```

12.5 Member Functions for Reading and Writing Files

> **CONCEPT:** File stream objects have member functions for more specialized file reading and writing.

If whitespace characters are part of the data in a file, a problem arises when the file is read by the >> operator. Because the operator considers whitespace characters as delimiters, it does not read them. For example, consider the file murphy.txt, which contains the following data:

> Jayne Murphy
> 47 Jones Circle
> Almond, NC 28702

Figure 12-5 shows the way the data is recorded in the file.

Figure 12-5

| J | a | y | n | e | | M | u | r | p | h | y | \n | 4 | 7 |

| | J | o | n | e | s | | C | i | r | c | l | e | \n | A |

| l | m | o | n | d | , | | N | C | | | 2 | 8 | 7 | 0 |

| 2 | \n | <EOF> |

The problem that arises from the use of the >> operator is evident in the output of Program 12-7.

Program 12-7

```
 1   // This program demonstrates how the >> operator should not
 2   // be used to read data that contain whitespace characters
 3   // from a file.
 4   #include <iostream>
 5   #include <fstream>
 6   using namespace std;
 7
 8   int main()
 9   {
10      const int SIZE = 81;   // Size of input array
11      char input[SIZE];      // To hold file input
12      fstream nameFile;      // File stream object
13
```

```
14      // Open the file in input mode.
15      nameFile.open("murphy.txt", ios::in);
16      if (!nameFile)
17      {
18         cout << "ERROR: Cannot open file.\n";
19         return 0;
20      }
21
22      // Read the file contents.
23      while (nameFile >> input)
24      {
25         cout << input;
26      }
27
28      // Close the file.
29      nameFile.close();
30      return 0;
31   }
```

Program Output

JayneMurphy47JonesCircleAlmond,NC28702

The `getline` Member Function

The problem with Program 12-7 can be solved by using the file stream object's `getline` member function. The function reads a "line" of data, including whitespace characters. Here is an example of the function call:

```
dataFile.getline(str, 81, '\n');
```

The three arguments in this statement are explained as follows:

str	This is the name of a character array, or a pointer to a section of memory. The data read from the file will be stored here.
81	This number is one greater than the maximum number of characters to be read. In this example, a maximum of 80 characters will be read.
'\n'	This is a delimiter character of your choice. If this delimiter is encountered, it will cause the function to stop reading before it has read the maximum number of characters. (This argument is optional. If it's left out, '\n' is the default.)

The statement is an instruction to read a line of characters from the file. The function will read until it has read 80 characters or encounters a \n, whichever happens first. The line of characters will be stored in the `str` array.

Program 12-8 is a modification of Program 12-7. It uses the `getline` member function to read whole lines of data from the file.

Program 12-8

```
 1   // This program uses the file stream object's getline member
 2   // function to read a line of data from the file.
 3   #include <iostream>
 4   #include <fstream>
 5   using namespace std;
 6
 7   int main()
 8   {
 9      const int SIZE = 81;   // Size of input array
10      char input[SIZE];      // To hold file input
11      fstream nameFile;      // File stream object
12
13      // Open the file in input mode.
14      nameFile.open("murphy.txt", ios::in);
15      if (!nameFile)
16      {
17         cout << "ERROR: Cannot open file.\n";
18         return 0;
19      }
20
21      // Read the file contents.
22      nameFile.getline(input, SIZE);   // Use \n as a delimiter.
23      while (!nameFile.eof())
24      {
25         cout << input << endl;
26         nameFile.getline(input, SIZE);   // Use \n as a delimiter.
27      }
28
29      // Close the file.
30      nameFile.close();
31      return 0;
32   }
```

Program Output
```
Jayne Murphy
47 Jones Circle
Almond, NC 28702
```

Because the third argument of the getline function was left out in Program 12-8, its default value is \n. Sometimes you might want to specify another delimiter. For example, consider a file that contains multiple names and addresses, and that is internally formatted in the following manner:

Contents of names2.txt
```
Jayne Murphy$47 Jones Circle$Almond, NC 28702\n$Bobbie Smith$
217 Halifax Drive$Canton, NC 28716\n$Bill Hammet$PO Box 121$
Springfield, NC 28357\n$
```

Think of this file as consisting of three records. A record is a complete set of data about a single item. Also, the records in the file above are made of three fields. The first field is the person's name. The second field is the person's street address or PO box number. The third field contains the person's city, state, and ZIP code. Notice that each field ends with a $

character, and each record ends with a \n character. Program 12-9 demonstrates how a getline function can be used to detect the $ characters.

Program 12-9

```
 1   // This file demonstrates the getline function with a user-
 2   // specified delimiter.
 3   #include <iostream>
 4   #include <fstream>
 5   using namespace std;
 6
 7   int main()
 8   {
 9      const int SIZE = 81;   // Size of input array
10      char input[SIZE];      // To hold file input
11
12      // Open the file for input.
13      fstream dataFile("names2.txt", ios::in);
14
15      // Read items from the file using $ as a delimiter.
16      dataFile.getline(input, SIZE, '$');
17      while (!dataFile.eof())
18      {
19         cout << input << endl;
20         dataFile.getline(input, SIZE, '$');
21      }
22
23      // Close the file.
24      dataFile.close();
25      return 0;
26   }
```

Program Output
```
Jayne Murphy
47 Jones Circle
Almond, NC 28702

Bobbie Smith
217 Halifax Drive
Canton, NC 28716

Bill Hammet
PO Box 121
Springfield, NC 28357
```

Notice that the \n characters, which mark the end of each record, are also part of the output. They cause an extra blank line to be printed on the screen, separating the records.

NOTE: When using a printable character, such as $, to delimit data in a file, be sure to select a character that will not actually appear in the data itself. Since it's doubtful that anyone's name or address contains a $ character, it's an acceptable delimiter. If the file contained dollar amounts, however, another delimiter would have been chosen.

The get Member Function

Another useful member function is get. It reads a single character from the file. Here is an example of its usage:

```
inFile.get(ch);
```

In this example, ch is a char variable. A character will be read from the file and stored in ch. Program 12-10 shows the function used in a complete program. The user is asked for the name of a file. The file is opened and the get function is used in a loop to read the file's contents, one character at a time.

Program 12-10

```
 1    // This program asks the user for a file name. The file is
 2    // opened and its contents are displayed on the screen.
 3    #include <iostream>
 4    #include <fstream>
 5    using namespace std;
 6
 7    int main()
 8    {
 9       const int SIZE = 51;    // Array size for file name
10       char fileName[SIZE];    // To hold the file name
11       char ch;                // To hold a character
12       fstream file;           // File stream object
13
14       // Get the file name.
15       cout << "Enter a file name: ";
16       cin >> fileName;
17
18       // Open the file.
19       file.open(fileName, ios::in);
20       if (!file)
21       {
22          cout << fileName << " could not be opened.\n";
23          return 0;
24       }
25
26       // Get each character from the file and display them.
27       file.get(ch);
28       while (!file.eof())
29       {
30          cout << ch;
31          file.get(ch);
32       }
33
34       // Close the file.
35       file.close();
36       return 0;
37    }
```

Program 12-10 will display the contents of any file. The get function even reads whitespaces, so all the characters will be shown exactly as they appear in the file.

The put Member Function

The put member function writes a single character to the file. Here is an example of its usage:

```
outFile.put(ch);
```

In this statement, the variable ch is assumed to be a char variable. Its contents will be written to the file associated with the file stream object outFile. Program 12-11 demonstrates the put function.

Program 12-11

```
 1   // This program demonstrates the put member function.
 2   #include <iostream>
 3   #include <fstream>
 4   using namespace std;
 5
 6   int main()
 7   {
 8      char ch;  // To hold a character
 9
10      // Open the file for output.
11      fstream dataFile("sentence.txt", ios::out);
12
13      cout << "Type a sentence and be sure to end it with a ";
14      cout << "period.\n";
15
16      // Get a sentence from the user one character at a time
17      // and write each character to the file.
18      cin.get(ch);
19      while (ch != '.')
20      {
21         dataFile.put(ch);
22         cin.get(ch);
23      }
24      dataFile.put(ch); // Write the period.
25
26      // Close the file.
27      dataFile.close();
28      return 0;
29   }
```

Program Output with Example Input Shown in Bold

Type a sentence and be sure to end it with a period.
I am on my way to becoming a great programmer. [Enter]

Resulting Contents of the File sentence.txt:

I am on my way to becoming a great programmer.

Checkpoint

12.7   Assume the file `input.txt` contains the following characters:

R	u	n		S	p	o	t		r	u	n	\n	S	e

e		S	p	o	t		r	u	n	\n	\<EOF\>

What will the following program display on the screen?

```cpp
#include <iostream>
#include <fstream>
using namespace std;

int main()
{
   const int SIZE = 81;
   fstream inFile("input.txt", ios::in);
   char item[SIZE];

   inFile >> item;
   while (!inFile.eof())
   {
      cout << item << endl;
      inFile >> item;
   }
   inFile.close();
   return 0;
}
```

12.8   Describe the difference between reading a file with the `>>` operator and the `getline` member function.

12.9   What will be stored in the file `out.txt` after the following program runs?

```cpp
include <iostream>
#include <fstream>
#include <iomanip>
using namespace std;

int main()
{
   const int SIZE = 5;
   ofstream outFile("out.txt");
   double nums[SIZE] = {100.279, 1.719, 8.602, 7.777, 5.099};

   outFile << fixed << setprecision(2);
   for (int count = 0; count < 5; count++)
   {
      outFile << setw(8) << nums[count];
   }
   outFile.close();
   return 0;
}
```

12.6 Focus on Software Engineering: Working with Multiple Files

CONCEPT: It's possible to have more than one file open at once in a program.

VideoNote

Working with
Multiple Files

Quite often you will need to have multiple files open at once. In many real-world applications, data about a single item are categorized and written to several different files. For example, a payroll system might keep the following files:

emp.dat   A file that contains the following data about each employee: name, job title, address, telephone number, employee number, and the date hired.

pay.dat   A file that contains the following data about each employee: employee number, hourly pay rate, overtime rate, and number of hours worked in the current pay cycle.

withold.dat   A file that contains the following data about each employee: employee number, dependents, and extra withholdings.

When the system is writing paychecks, you can see that it will need to open each of the files listed above and read data from them. (Notice that each file contains the employee number. This is how the program can locate a specific employee's data.)

In C++, you open multiple files by defining multiple file stream objects. For example, if you need to read from three files, you can define three file stream objects, such as:

```
ifstream file1, file2, file3;
```

Sometimes you will need to open one file for input and another file for output. For example, Program 12-12 asks the user for a file name. The file is opened and read. Each character is converted to uppercase and written to a second file called out.txt. This type of program can be considered a *filter*. Filters read the input of one file, changing the data in some fashion, and write it out to a second file. The second file is a modified version of the first file.

Program 12-12

```
1   // This program demonstrates reading from one file and writing
2   // to a second file.
3   #include <iostream>
4   #include <fstream>
5   #include <cctype> // Needed for the toupper function.
6   using namespace std;
7
8   int main()
9   {
10      const int SIZE = 51;   // Array size for file name
11      char fileName[SIZE];   // To hold the file name
12      char ch;               // To hold a character
13      ifstream inFile;       // Input file
14
```

(program continues)

Program 12-12 *(continued)*

```
15      // Open a file for output.
16      ofstream outFile("out.txt");
17
18      // Get the input file name.
19      cout << "Enter a file name: ";
20      cin >> fileName;
21
22      // Open the file for input.
23      inFile.open(fileName);
24      if (!inFile)
25      {
26         cout << "Cannot open " << fileName << endl;
27         return 0;
28      }
29
30      // Process the files.
31      inFile.get(ch);                  // Get a char from file 1
32      while (!inFile.eof())            // Test for end of file
33      {
34         outFile.put(toupper(ch)); // Write uppercase char to file 2
35         inFile.get(ch);               // Get another char from file 1
36      }
37
38      // Close the files.
39      inFile.close();
40      outFile.close();
41      cout << "File conversion done.\n";
42      return 0;
43   }
```

Program Output with Example Input Shown in Bold
```
Enter a file name: hownow.txt [Enter]
File conversion done.
```

Contents of `hownow.txt`
```
how now brown cow.
How Now?
```

Resulting Contents of `out.txt`
```
HOW NOW BROWN COW.
HOW NOW?
```

12.7 Binary Files

CONCEPT: Binary files contain data that is not necessarily stored as ASCII text.

All the files you've been working with so far have been text files. That means the data stored in the files has been formatted as ASCII text. Even a number, when stored in a file with the << operator, is converted to text. For example, consider the following program segment:

```
ofstream file("num.dat");
short x = 1297;
file << x;
```

The last statement writes the contents of x to the file. When the number is written, however, it is stored as the characters '1', '2', '9', and '7'. This is illustrated in Figure 12-6.

Figure 12-6

1297 expressed in ASCII

| 49 | 50 | 57 | 55 | <EOF> |

The number 1297 isn't stored in memory (in the variable x) in the fashion depicted in the figure above, however. It is formatted as a binary number, occupying two bytes on a typical PC. Figure 12-7 shows how the number is represented in memory, using binary or hexadecimal.

Figure 12-7

1297 as a short integer, in binary

| 00000101 | 00010001 |

1297 as a short integer, in hexadecimal

| 05 | 11 |

The representation of the number shown in Figure 12-7 is the way the "raw" data is stored in memory. Data can be stored in a file in its pure, binary format. The first step is to open the file in binary mode. This is accomplished by using the ios::binary flag. Here is an example:

```
file.open("stuff.dat", ios::out | ios::binary);
```

Notice the ios::out and ios::binary flags are joined in the statement with the | operator. This causes the file to be opened in both output and binary modes.

NOTE: By default, files are opened in text mode.

The write **and** read **Member Functions**

The file stream object's write member function is used to write binary data to a file. The general format of the write member function is

```
fileObject.write(address, size);
```

Let's look at the parts of this function call format.

- *fileObject* is the name of a file stream object.
- *address* is the starting address of the section of memory that is to be written to the file. This argument is expected to be the address of a char (or a pointer to a char).
- *size* is the number of bytes of memory to write. This argument must be an integer value.

For example, the following code uses a file stream object named file to write a character to a binary file.

```
char letter = 'A';
file.write(&letter, sizeof(letter));
```

The first argument passed to the write function is the address of the letter variable. This tells the write function where the data that is to be written to the file is located. The second argument is the size of the letter variable, which is returned from the sizeof operator. This tells the write function the number of bytes of data to write to the file. Because the sizes of data types can vary among systems, it is best to use the sizeof operator to determine the number of bytes to write. After this function call executes, the contents of the letter variable will be written to the binary file associated with the file object.

The following code shows another example. This code writes an entire char array to a binary file.

```
char data[] = {'A', 'B', 'C', 'D'};
file.write(data, sizeof(data));
```

In this code, the first argument is the name of the data array. By passing the name of the array we are passing a pointer to the beginning of the array. Because data is an array of char values, the name of the array is a pointer to a char. The second argument passes the name of the array to the sizeof operator. When the name of an array is passed to the sizeof operator, the operator returns the number of bytes allocated to the array. After this function call executes, the contents of the data array will be written to the binary file associated with the file object.

The read member function is used to read binary data from a file into memory. The general format of the read member function is

```
fileObject.read(address, size);
```

Here are the parts of this function call format:

- *fileObject* is the name of a file stream object.
- *address* is the starting address of the section of memory where the data being read from the file is to be stored. This is expected to be the address of a char (or a pointer to a char).
- *size* is the number of bytes of memory to read from the file. This argument must be an integer value.

For example, suppose we want to read a single character from a binary file and store that character in the letter variable. The following code uses a file stream object named file to do just that.

```
char letter;
file.read(&letter, sizeof(letter));
```

The first argument passed to the `read` function is the address of the `letter` variable. This tells the `read` function where to store the value that is read from the file. The second argument is the size of the `letter` variable. This tells the `read` function the number of bytes to read from the file. After this function executes, the `letter` variable will contain a character that was read from the file.

The following code shows another example. This code reads enough data from a binary file to fill an entire `char` array.

```
char data[4];
file.read(data, sizeof(data));
```

In this code, the first argument is the address of the `data` array. The second argument is the number of bytes allocated to the array. On a system that uses 1-byte characters, this function will read four bytes from the file and store them in the `data` array.

Program 12-13 demonstrates writing a `char` array to a file and then reading the data from the file back into memory.

Program 12-13

```
 1  // This program uses the write and read functions.
 2  #include <iostream>
 3  #include <fstream>
 4  using namespace std;
 5
 6  int main()
 7  {
 8     const int SIZE = 4;
 9     char data[SIZE] = {'A', 'B', 'C', 'D'};
10     fstream file;
11
12     // Open the file for output in binary mode.
13     file.open("test.dat", ios::out | ios::binary);
14
15     // Write the contents of the array to the file.
16     cout << "Writing the characters to the file.\n";
17     file.write(data, sizeof(data));
18
19     // Close the file.
20     file.close();
21
22     // Open the file for input in binary mode.
23     file.open("test.dat", ios::in | ios::binary);
24
25     // Read the contents of the file into the array.
26     cout << "Now reading the data back into memory.\n";
27     file.read(data, sizeof(data));
28
```

(program continues)

Program 12-13 *(continued)*

```
29      // Display the contents of the array.
30      for (int count = 0; count < SIZE; count++)
31        cout << data[count] << " ";
32      cout << endl;
33
34      // Close the file.
35      file.close();
36      return 0;
37   }
```

Program Output
```
Writing the characters to the file.
Now reading the data back into memory.
A B C D
```

Writing Data Other Than char to Binary Files

Because the write and read member functions expect their first argument to be a pointer to a char, you must use a type cast when writing and reading items that are of other data types. To convert a pointer from one type to another you should use the reinterpret_cast type cast. The general format of the type cast is

```
reinterpret_cast<dataType>(value)
```

where *dataType* is the data type that you are converting to, and *value* is the value that you are converting. For example, the following code uses the type cast to store the address of an int in a char pointer variable.

```
int x = 65;
char *ptr;
ptr = reinterpret_cast<char *>(&x);
```

The following code shows how to use the type cast to pass the address of an integer as the first argument to the write member function.

```
int x = 27;
file.write(reinterpret_cast<char *>(&x), sizeof(x));
```

After the function executes, the contents of the variable x will be written to the binary file associated with the file object. The following code shows an int array being written to a binary file.

```
const int SIZE = 10;
int numbers[SIZE] = {1, 2, 3, 4, 5, 6, 7, 8, 9, 10};
file.write(reinterpret_cast<char *>(numbers), sizeof(numbers));
```

After this function call executes, the contents of the numbers array will be written to the binary file. The following code shows values being read from the file and stored into the numbers array.

```
const int SIZE = 10;
int numbers[SIZE];
file.read(reinterpret_cast<char *>(numbers), sizeof(numbers));
```

Program 12-14 demonstrates writing an `int` array to a file and then reading the data from the file back into memory.

Program 12-14

```
 1  // This program uses the write and read functions.
 2  #include <iostream>
 3  #include <fstream>
 4  using namespace std;
 5
 6  int main()
 7  {
 8     const int SIZE = 10;
 9     fstream file;
10     int numbers[SIZE] = {1,  2,  3,  4,  5,  6,  7,  8,  9,  10};
11
12     // Open the file for output in binary mode.
13     file.open("numbers.dat", ios::out | ios::binary);
14
15     // Write the contents of the array to the file.
16     cout << "Writing the data to the file.\n";
17     file.write(reinterpret_cast<char *>(numbers), sizeof(numbers));
18
19     // Close the file.
20     file.close();
21
22     // Open the file for input in binary mode.
23     file.open("numbers.dat", ios::in | ios::binary);
24
25     // Read the contents of the file into the array.
26     cout << "Now reading the data back into memory.\n";
27     file.read(reinterpret_cast<char *>(numbers), sizeof(numbers));
28
29     // Display the contents of the array.
30     for (int count = 0; count < SIZE; count++)
31        cout << numbers[count] << " ";
32     cout << endl;
33
34     // Close the file.
35     file.close();
36     return 0;
37  }
```

Program Output
```
Writing the data to the file.
Now reading the data back into memory.
1 2 3 4 5 6 7 8 9 10
```

12.8   Creating Records with Structures

CONCEPT: Structures may be used to store fixed-length records to a file.

Earlier in this chapter the concept of fields and records was introduced. A field is an individual piece of data pertaining to a single item. A record is made up of fields and is a complete set of data about a single item. For example, a set of fields might be a person's name, age, address, and phone number. Together, all those fields that pertain to one person make up a record.

In C++, structures provide a convenient way to organize data into fields and records. For example, the following code could be used to create a record containing data about a person.

```
const int NAME_SIZE = 51, ADDR_SIZE = 51, PHONE_SIZE = 14;

struct Info
{
   char name[NAME_SIZE];
   int  age;
   char address1[ADDR_SIZE];
   char address2[ADDR_SIZE];
   char phone[PHONE_SIZE];
};
```

Besides providing an organizational structure for data, structures also package data into a single unit. For example, assume the structure variable `person` is defined as

```
Info person;
```

Once the members (or fields) of `person` are filled with data, the entire variable may be written to a file using the `write` function:

```
file.write(reinterpret_cast<char *>(&person), sizeof(person));
```

The first argument is the address of the `person` variable. The `reinterpret_cast` operator is used to convert the address to a `char` pointer. The second argument is the `sizeof` operator with `person` as its `argument`. This returns the number of bytes used by the `person` structure. Program 12-15 demonstrates this technique.

NOTE: Because structures can contain a mixture of data types, you should always use the `ios::binary` mode when opening a file to store them.

Program 12-15

```
1  // This program uses a structure variable to store a record to a file.
2  #include <iostream>
3  #include <fstream>
4  using namespace std;
5
```

```
 6   // Array sizes
 7   const int NAME_SIZE = 51, ADDR_SIZE = 51, PHONE_SIZE = 14;
 8
 9   // Declare a structure for the record.
10   struct Info
11   {
12      char name[NAME_SIZE];
13      int  age;
14      char address1[ADDR_SIZE];
15      char address2[ADDR_SIZE];
16      char phone[PHONE_SIZE];
17   };
18
19   int main()
20   {
21      Info person;    // To hold info about a person
22      char again;     // To hold Y or N
23
24      // Open a file for binary output.
25      fstream people("people.dat", ios::out | ios::binary);
26
27      do
28      {
29         // Get data about a person.
30         cout << "Enter the following data about a "
31              << "person:\n";
32         cout << "Name: ";
33         cin.getline(person.name, NAME_SIZE);
34         cout << "Age: ";
35         cin >> person.age;
36         cin.ignore(); // Skip over the remaining newline.
37         cout << "Address line 1: ";
38         cin.getline(person.address1, ADDR_SIZE);
39         cout << "Address line 2: ";
40         cin.getline(person.address2, ADDR_SIZE);
41         cout << "Phone: ";
42         cin.getline(person.phone, PHONE_SIZE);
43
44         // Write the contents of the person structure to the file.
45         people.write(reinterpret_cast<char *>(&person),
46                      sizeof(person));
47
48         // Determine whether the user wants to write another record.
49         cout << "Do you want to enter another record? ";
50         cin >> again;
51         cin.ignore();  // Skip over the remaining newline.
52      } while (again == 'Y' || again == 'y');
53
54      // Close the file.
55      people.close();
56      return 0;
57   }
```

(program output continues)

Program 12-15   (continued)

Program Output with Example Input Shown in Bold

```
Enter the following data about a person:
Name: Charlie Baxter [Enter]
Age: 42 [Enter]
Address line 1: 67 Kennedy Bvd. [Enter]
Address line 2: Perth, SC 38754 [Enter]
Phone: (803)555-1234 [Enter]
Do you want to enter another record? Y [Enter]
Enter the following data about a person:
Name: Merideth Murney [Enter]
Age: 22 [Enter]
Address line 1: 487 Lindsay Lane [Enter]
Address line 2: Hazelwood, NC 28737 [Enter]
Phone: (828)555-9999 [Enter]
Do you want to enter another record? N [Enter]
```

Program 12-15 allows you to build a file by filling the members of the person variable, and then writing the variable to the file. Program 12-16 opens the file and reads each record into the person variable, then displays the data on the screen.

Program 12-16

```
 1   // This program uses a structure variable to read a record from a file.
 2   #include <iostream>
 3   #include <fstream>
 4   using namespace std;
 5
 6   const int NAME_SIZE = 51, ADDR_SIZE = 51, PHONE_SIZE = 14;
 7
 8   // Declare a structure for the record.
 9   struct Info
10   {
11      char name[NAME_SIZE];
12      int age;
13      char address1[ADDR_SIZE];
14      char address2[ADDR_SIZE];
15      char phone[PHONE_SIZE];
16   };
17
18   int main()
19   {
20      Info person;     // To hold info about a person
21      char again;      // To hold Y or N
22      fstream people;  // File stream object
23
24      // Open the file for input in binary mode.
25      people.open("people.dat", ios::in | ios::binary);
26
```

```
27        // Test for errors.
28        if (!people)
29        {
30           cout << "Error opening file. Program aborting.\n";
31           return 0;
32        }
33
34
35        cout << "Here are the people in the file:\n\n";
36        // Read the first record from the file.
37        people.read(reinterpret_cast<char *>(&person),
38                    sizeof(person));
39
40        // While not at the end of the file, display
41        // the records.
42        while (!people.eof())
43        {
44           // Display the record.
45           cout << "Name: ";
46           cout << person.name << endl;
47           cout << "Age: ";
48           cout << person.age << endl;
49           cout << "Address line 1: ";
50           cout << person.address1 << endl;
51           cout << "Address line 2: ";
52           cout << person.address2 << endl;
53           cout << "Phone: ";
54           cout << person.phone << endl;
55
56           // Wait for the user to press the Enter key.
57           cout << "\nPress the Enter key to see the next record.\n";
58           cin.get(again);
59
60           // Read the next record from the file.
61           people.read(reinterpret_cast<char *>(&person),
62                       sizeof(person));
63        }
64
65        cout << "That's all the data in the file!\n";
66        people.close();
67        return 0;
68     }
```

Program Output (Using the same file created by Program 12-15 as input)

```
Here are the people in the file:

Name: Charlie Baxter
Age: 42
Address line 1: 67 Kennedy Bvd.
Address line 2: Perth, SC  38754
Phone: (803)555-1234
```

(program output continues)

Program 12-16   *(continued)*

```
Press the Enter key to see the next record.

Name: Merideth Murney
Age: 22
Address line 1: 487 Lindsay Lane
Address line 2: Hazelwood, NC  28737
Phone: (828)555-9999

Press the Enter key to see the next record.

That's all the data in the file!
```

12.9   Random-Access Files

CONCEPT: Random Access means nonsequentially accessing data in a file.

All of the programs created so far in this chapter have performed *sequential file access*. When a file is opened, the position where reading and/or writing will occur is at the file's beginning (unless the `ios::app` mode is used, which causes data to be written to the end of the file). If the file is opened for output, bytes are written to it one after the other. If the file is opened for input, data is read beginning at the first byte. As the reading or writing continues, the file stream object's read/write position advances sequentially through the file's contents.

The problem with sequential file access is that in order to read a specific byte from the file, all the bytes that precede it must be read first. For instance, if a program needs data stored at the hundredth byte of a file, it will have to read the first 99 bytes to reach it. If you've ever listened to a cassette tape player, you understand sequential access. To listen to a song at the end of the tape, you have to listen to all the songs that come before it, or fast-forward over them. There is no way to immediately jump to that particular song.

Although sequential file access is useful in many circumstances, it can slow a program down tremendously. If the file is very large, locating data buried deep inside it can take a long time. Alternatively, C++ allows a program to perform *random file access*. In random file access, a program may immediately jump to any byte in the file without first reading the preceding bytes. The difference between sequential and random file access is like the difference between a cassette tape and a compact disc. When listening to a CD, there is no need to listen to or fast forward over unwanted songs. You simply jump to the track that you want to listen to. This is illustrated in Figure 12-8.

The seekp and seekg Member Functions

File stream objects have two member functions that are used to move the read/write position to any byte in the file. They are `seekp` and `seekg`. The `seekp` function is used with files opened for output and `seekg` is used with files opened for input. (It makes sense if

Figure 12-8

you remember that "p" stands for "put" and "g" stands for "get." seekp is used with files that you put data into, and seekg is used with files you get data out of.)

Here is an example of seekp's usage:

```
file.seekp(20L, ios::beg);
```

The first argument is a long integer representing an offset into the file. This is the number of the byte you wish to move to. In this example, 20L is used. (Remember, the L suffix forces the compiler to treat the number as a long integer.) This statement moves the file's write position to byte number 20. (All numbering starts at 0, so byte number 20 is actually the twenty-first byte.)

The second argument is called the mode, and it designates where to calculate the offset *from*. The flag ios::beg means the offset is calculated from the beginning of the file. Alternatively, the offset can be calculated from the end of the file or the current position in the file. Table 12-7 lists the flags for all three of the random-access modes.

Table 12-7

Mode Flag	Description
ios::beg	The offset is calculated from the beginning of the file.
ios::end	The offset is calculated from the end of the file.
ios::cur	The offset is calculated from the current position.

Table 12-8 shows examples of seekp and seekg using the various mode flags.

Notice that some of the examples in Table 12-8 use a negative offset. Negative offsets result in the read or write position being moved backward in the file, while positive offsets result in a forward movement.

Assume the file letters.txt contains the following data:

```
abcdefghijklmnopqrstuvwxyz
```

Program 12-17 uses the seekg function to jump around to different locations in the file, retrieving a character after each stop.

Table 12-8

Statement	How It Affects the Read/Write Position
`file.seekp(32L, ios::beg);`	Sets the write position to the 33rd byte (byte 32) from the beginning of the file.
`file.seekp(-10L, ios::end);`	Sets the write position to the 10th byte from the end of the file.
`file.seekp(120L, ios::cur);`	Sets the write position to the 121st byte (byte 120) from the current position.
`file.seekg(2L, ios::beg);`	Sets the read position to the 3rd byte (byte 2) from the beginning of the file.
`file.seekg(-100L, ios::end);`	Sets the read position to the 100th byte from the end of the file.
`file.seekg(40L, ios::cur);`	Sets the read position to the 41st byte (byte 40) from the current position.
`file.seekg(0L, ios::end);`	Sets the read position to the end of the file.

Program 12-17

```
 1  // This program demonstrates the seekg function.
 2  #include <iostream>
 3  #include <fstream>
 4  using namespace std;
 5
 6  int main()
 7  {
 8     char ch;  // To hold a character
 9
10     // Open the file for input.
11     fstream file("letters.txt", ios::in);
12
13     // Move to byte 5 from the beginning of the file
14     // (the 6th byte) and read the character there.
15     file.seekg(5L, ios::beg);
16     file.get(ch);
17     cout << "Byte 5 from beginning: " << ch << endl;
18
19     // Move to the 10th byte from the end of the file
20     // and read the character there.
21     file.seekg(-10L, ios::end);
22     file.get(ch);
23     cout << "10th byte from end: " << ch << endl;
24
25     // Move to byte 3 from the current position
26     // (the 4th byte) and read the character there.
27     file.seekg(3L, ios::cur);
28     file.get(ch);
29     cout << "Byte 3 from current: " << ch << endl;
30
31     file.close();
32     return 0;
33  }
```

Program Screen Output

```
Byte 5 from beginning: f
10th byte from end: q
Byte 3 from current: u
```

Program 12-18 shows a more robust example of the seekg function. It opens the people.dat file created by Program 12-15. The file contains two records. Program 12-18 displays record 1 (the second record) first, then displays record 0.

The program has two important functions other than main. The first, byteNum, takes a record number as its argument and returns that record's starting byte. It calculates the record's starting byte by multiplying the record number by the size of the Info structure. This returns the offset of that record from the beginning of the file. The second function, showRec, accepts an Info structure as its argument and displays its contents on the screen.

Program 12-18

```cpp
 1   // This program randomly reads a record of data from a file.
 2   #include <iostream>
 3   #include <fstream>
 4   using namespace std;
 5
 6   const int NAME_SIZE = 51, ADDR_SIZE = 51, PHONE_SIZE = 14;
 7
 8   // Declare a structure for the record.
 9   struct Info
10   {
11       char name[NAME_SIZE];
12       int age;
13       char address1[ADDR_SIZE];
14       char address2[ADDR_SIZE];
15       char phone[PHONE_SIZE];
16   };
17
18   // Function Prototypes
19   long byteNum(int);
20   void showRec(Info);
21
22   int main()
23   {
24       Info person;     // To hold info about a person
25       fstream people;  // File stream object
26
27       // Open the file for input in binary mode.
28       people.open("people.dat", ios::in | ios::binary);
29
```

(program continues)

Program 12-18   *(continued)*

```
30      // Test for errors.
31      if (!people)
32      {
33         cout << "Error opening file. Program aborting.\n";
34         return 0;
35      }
36
37      // Read and display record 1 (the second record).
38      cout << "Here is record 1:\n";
39      people.seekg(byteNum(1), ios::beg);
40      people.read(reinterpret_cast<char *>(&person), sizeof(person));
41      showRec(person);
42
43      // Read and display record 0 (the first record).
44      cout << "\nHere is record 0:\n";
45      people.seekg(byteNum(0), ios::beg);
46      people.read(reinterpret_cast<char *>(&person), sizeof(person));
47      showRec(person);
48
49      // Close the file.
50      people.close();
51      return 0;
52   }
53
54   //*********************************************************
55   // Definition of function byteNum. Accepts an integer as   *
56   // its argument. Returns the byte number in the file of the *
57   // record whose number is passed as the argument.          *
58   //*********************************************************
59
60   long byteNum(int recNum)
61   {
62      return sizeof(Info) * recNum;
63   }
64
65   //*********************************************************
66   // Definition of function showRec. Accepts an Info structure *
67   // as its argument, and displays the structure's contents.   *
68   //*********************************************************
69
70   void showRec(Info record)
71   {
72      cout << "Name: ";
73      cout << record.name << endl;
74      cout << "Age: ";
75      cout << record.age << endl;
76      cout << "Address line 1: ";
77      cout << record.address1 << endl;
78      cout << "Address line 2: ";
79      cout << record.address2 << endl;
```

```
80        cout << "Phone: ";
81        cout << record.phone << endl;
82  }
```

Program Output (Using the same file created by Program 12–19 as input)
```
Here is record 1:
Name: Merideth Murney
Age: 22
Address line 1: 487 Lindsay Lane
Address line 2: Hazelwood, NC   28737
Phone: (828)555-9999

Here is record 0:
Name: Charlie Baxter
Age: 42
Address line 1: 67 Kennedy Bvd.
Address line 2: Perth, SC   38754
Phone: (803)555-1234
```

 WARNING! If a program has read to the end of a file, you must call the file stream object's clear member function before calling seekg or seekp. This clears the file stream object's eof flag. Otherwise, the seekg or seekp function will not work.

The tellp and tellg Member Functions

File stream objects have two more member functions that may be used for random file access: tellp and tellg. Their purpose is to return, as a long integer, the current byte number of a file's read and write position. As you can guess, tellp returns the write position and tellg returns the read position. Assuming pos is a long integer, here is an example of the functions' usage:

```
pos = outFile.tellp();
pos = inFile.tellg();
```

One application of these functions is to determine the number of bytes that a file contains. The following example demonstrates how to do this using the tellg function.

```
file.seekg(0L, ios::end);
numBytes = file.tellg();
cout << "The file has " << numBytes << " bytes.\n";
```

First the seekg member function is used to move the read position to the last byte in the file. Then the tellg function is used to get the current byte number of the read position.

Program 12-19 demonstrates the tellg function. It opens the letters.txt file, which was also used in Program 12-17. The file contains the following characters:

```
abcdefghijklmnopqrstuvwxyz
```

Program 12-19

```cpp
1   // This program demonstrates the tellg function.
2   #include <iostream>
3   #include <fstream>
4   using namespace std;
5
6   int main()
7   {
8      long offset;     // To hold an offset amount
9      long numBytes;   // To hold the file size
10     char ch;         // To hold a character
11     char again;      // To hold Y or N
12
13     // Open the file for input.
14     fstream file("letters.txt", ios::in);
15
16     // Determine the number of bytes in the file.
17     file.seekg(0L, ios::end);
18     numBytes = file.tellg();
19     cout << "The file has " << numBytes << " bytes.\n";
20
21     // Go back to the beginning of the file.
22     file.seekg(0L, ios::beg);
23
24     // Let the user move around within the file.
25     do
26     {
27        // Display the current read position.
28        cout << "Currently at position " << file.tellg() << endl;
29
30        // Get a byte number from the user.
31        cout << "Enter an offset from the beginning of the file: ";
32        cin >> offset;
33
34        // Move the read position to that byte, read the
35        // character there, and display it.
36        if (offset >= numBytes)     // Past the end of the file?
37           cout << "Cannot read past the end of the file.\n";
38        else
39        {
40           file.seekg(offset, ios::beg);
41           file.get(ch);
42           cout << "Character read: " << ch << endl;
43        }
44
45        // Does the user want to try this again?
46        cout << "Do it again? ";
47        cin >> again;
48     } while (again == 'Y' || again == 'y');
49
50     // Close the file.
51     file.close();
52     return 0;
53  }
```

Program 12-19

Program Output with Example Input Shown in Bold
```
The file has 26 bytes.
Currently at position 0
Enter an offset from the beginning of the file: 5 [Enter]
Character read: f
Do it again? y [Enter]
Currently at position 6
Enter an offset from the beginning of the file: 0 [Enter]
Character read: a
Do it again? y [Enter]
Currently at position 1
Enter an offset from the beginning of the file: 26 [Enter]
Cannot read past the end of the file.
Do it again? n [Enter]
```

Rewinding a Sequential-Access File with seekg

Sometimes when processing a sequential file, it is necessary for a program to read the contents of the file more than one time. For example, suppose a program searches a file for an item specified by the user. The program must open the file, read its contents, and determine if the specified item is in the file. If the user needs to search the file again for another item, the program must read the file's contents again.

One simple approach for reading a file's contents more than once is to close and reopen the file, as shown in the following code example.

```cpp
dataFile.open("file.txt", ios::in);      // Open the file.

//
// Read and process the file's contents.
//

dataFile.close();                        // Close the file.
dataFile.open("file.txt", ios::in);      // Open the file again.

//
// Read and process the file's contents again.
//

dataFile.close();                        // Close the file.
```

Each time the file is reopened, its read position is located at the beginning of the file. The read position is the byte in the file that will be read with the next read operation.

Another approach is to "rewind" the file. This means moving the read position to the beginning of the file without closing and reopening it. This is accomplished with the file stream object's seekg member function to move the read position back to the beginning of the file. The following example code demonstrates.

```cpp
dataFile.open("file.txt", ios::in);      // Open the file.

//
// Read and process the file's contents.
//
```

```
dataFile.clear();                          // Clear the eof flag.
dataFile.seekg(0L, ios::beg);              // Rewind the read position.

//
// Read and process the file's contents again.
//

dataFile.close();                    // Close the file.
```

Notice that prior to calling the `seekg` member function, the `clear` member function is called. As previously mentioned this clears the file object's `eof` flag and is necessary only if the program has read to the end of the file. This approach eliminates the need to close and reopen the file each time the file's contents are processed.

12.10 Opening a File for Both Input and Output

CONCEPT: You may perform input and output on an `fstream` file without closing it and reopening it.

Sometimes you'll need to perform both input and output on a file without closing and reopening it. For example, consider a program that allows you to search for a record in a file and then make changes to it. A read operation is necessary to copy the data from the file to memory. After the desired changes have been made to the data in memory, a write operation is necessary to replace the old data in the file with the new data in memory.

Such operations are possible with `fstream` objects. The `ios::in` and `ios::out` file access flags may be joined with the | operator, as shown in the following statement.

```
fstream file("data.dat", ios::in | ios::out)
```

The same operation may be accomplished with the `open` member function:

```
file.open("data.dat", ios::in | ios::out);
```

You may also specify the `ios::binary` flag if binary data is to be written to the file. Here is an example:

```
file.open("data.dat", ios::in | ios::out | ios::binary);
```

When an `fstream` file is opened with both the `ios::in` and `ios::out` flags, the file's current contents are preserved and the read/write position is initially placed at the beginning of the file. If the file does not exist, it is created.

Programs 12-20, 12-21, and 12-22 demonstrate many of the techniques we have discussed. Program 12-20 sets up a file with five blank inventory records. Each record is a structure with members for holding a part description, quantity on hand, and price. Program 12-21 displays the contents of the file on the screen. Program 12-22 opens the file in both input and output modes, and allows the user to change the contents of a specific record.

Program 12-20

```
1   // This program sets up a file of blank inventory records.
2   #include <iostream>
3   #include <fstream>
4   using namespace std;
5
6   // Constants
7   const int DESC_SIZE = 31;   // Description size
8   const int NUM_RECORDS = 5;  // Number of records
9
10  // Declaration of InventoryItem structure
11  struct InventoryItem
12  {
13     char desc[DESC_SIZE];
14     int qty;
15     double price;
16  };
17
18  int main()
19  {
20     // Create an empty InventoryItem structure.
21     InventoryItem record = { "", 0, 0.0 };
22
23     // Open the file for binary output.
24     fstream inventory("Inventory.dat", ios::out | ios::binary);
25
26     // Write the blank records
27     for (int count = 0; count < NUM_RECORDS; count++)
28     {
29        cout << "Now writing record " << count << endl;
30        inventory.write(reinterpret_cast<char *>(&record),
31                     sizeof(record));
32     }
33
34     // Close the file.
35     inventory.close();
36     return 0;
37  }
```

Program Output
```
Now writing record 0
Now writing record 1
Now writing record 2
Now writing record 3
Now writing record 4
```

Program 12-21 simply displays the contents of the inventory file on the screen. It can be used to verify that Program 12-20 successfully created the blank records, and that Program 12-22 correctly modified the designated record.

Program 12-21

```
 1   // This program displays the contents of the inventory file.
 2   #include <iostream>
 3   #include <fstream>
 4   using namespace std;
 5
 6   const int DESC_SIZE = 31;   // Description size
 7
 8   // Declaration of InventoryItem structure
 9   struct InventoryItem
10   {
11      char desc[DESC_SIZE];
12      int qty;
13      double price;
14   };
15
16   int main()
17   {
18      InventoryItem record; // To hold an inventory record
19
20      // Open the file for binary input.
21      fstream inventory("Inventory.dat", ios::in | ios::binary);
22
23      // Now read and display the records
24      inventory.read(reinterpret_cast<char *>(&record),
25                  sizeof(record));
26      while (!inventory.eof())
27      {
28         cout << "Description: ";
29         cout << record.desc << endl;
30         cout << "Quantity: ";
31         cout << record.qty << endl;
32         cout << "Price: ";
33         cout << record.price << endl << endl;
34         inventory.read(reinterpret_cast<char *>(&record),
35                     sizeof(record));
36      }
37
38      // Close the file.
39      inventory.close();
40      return 0;
41   }
```

Here is the screen output of Program 12-21 if it is run immediately after Program 12-20 sets up the file of blank records.

Program 12-21

Program Output

```
Description:
Quantity: 0
Price: 0.0
```

```
Description:
Quantity: 0
Price: 0.0

Description:
Quantity: 0
Price: 0.0

Description:
Quantity: 0
Price: 0.0

Description:
Quantity: 0
Price: 0.0
```

Program 12-22 allows the user to change the contents of an individual record in the inventory file.

Program 12-22

```cpp
 1   // This program allows the user to edit a specific record.
 2   #include <iostream>
 3   #include <fstream>
 4   using namespace std;
 5
 6   const int DESC_SIZE = 31;   // Description size
 7
 8   // Declaration of InventoryItem structure
 9   struct InventoryItem
10   {
11      char desc[DESC_SIZE];
12      int qty;
13      double price;
14   };
15
16   int main()
17   {
18      InventoryItem record;   // To hold an inventory record
19      long recNum;            // To hold a record number
20
21      // Open the file in binary mode for input and output
22      fstream inventory("Inventory.dat",
23                        ios::in | ios::out | ios::binary);
24
25      // Get the record number of the desired record.
26      cout << "Which record do you want to edit? ";
27      cin >> recNum;
28
29      // Move to the record and read it.
30      inventory.seekg(recNum * sizeof(record), ios::beg);
31      inventory.read(reinterpret_cast<char *>(&record),
32                  sizeof(record));
```

(program continues)

Program 12-22   *(continued)*

```
33
34      // Display the record contents.
35      cout << "Description: ";
36      cout << record.desc << endl;
37      cout << "Quantity: ";
38      cout << record.qty << endl;
39      cout << "Price: ";
40      cout << record.price << endl;
41
42      // Get the new record data.
43      cout << "Enter the new data:\n";
44      cout << "Description: ";
45      cin.ignore();
46      cin.getline(record.desc, DESC_SIZE);
47      cout << "Quantity: ";
48      cin >> record.qty;
49      cout << "Price: ";
50      cin >> record.price;
51
52      // Move back to the beginning of this record's position.
53      inventory.seekp(recNum * sizeof(record), ios::beg);
54
55      // Write the new record over the current record.
56      inventory.write(reinterpret_cast<char *>(&record),
57                  sizeof(record));
58
59      // Close the file.
60      inventory.close();
61      return 0;
62  }
```

Program Output with Example Input Shown in Bold
```
Which record do you want to edit? 2 [Enter]
Description:
Quantity: 0
Price: 0.0
Enter the new data:
Description: Wrench [Enter]
Quantity: 10 [Enter]
Price: 4.67 [Enter]
```

 Checkpoint

12.10   Describe the difference between the seekg and the seekp functions.

12.11   Describe the difference between the tellg and the tellp functions.

12.12   Describe the meaning of the following file access flags:
        ios::beg
        ios::end
        ios::cur

12.13   What is the number of the first byte in a file?

12.14   Briefly describe what each of the following statements does:
```
file.seekp(100L, ios::beg);
file.seekp(-10L, ios::end);
file.seekg(-25L, ios::cur);
file.seekg(30L, ios::cur);
```

12.15   Describe the mode that each of the following statements causes a file to be opened in:
```
file.open("info.dat", ios::in | ios::out);
file.open("info.dat", ios::in | ios::app);
file.open("info.dat", ios::in | ios::out | ios::ate);
file.open("info.dat", ios::in | ios::out | ios::binary);
```

 See the Student CD for the High Adventure Travel Part 3 Case Study.

Review Questions and Exercises

Short Answer

1. What capability does the `fstream` data type provide that the `ifstream` and `ofstream` data types do not?

2. Which file access flag do you use to open a file when you want all output written to the end of the file's existing contents?

3. Assume that the file `data.txt` already exists, and the following statement executes. What happens to the file?

    ```
    fstream file("data.txt", ios::out);
    ```

4. How do you combine multiple file access flags when opening a file?

5. Should file stream objects be passed to functions by value or by reference? Why?

6. Under what circumstances is a file stream object's `ios::hardfail` bit set? What member function reports the state of this bit?

7. Under what circumstances is a file stream object's `ios::eofbit` bit set? What member function reports the state of this bit?

8. Under what circumstances is a file stream object's `ios::badbit` bit set? What member function reports the state of this bit?

9. How do you read the contents of a text file that contains whitespace characters as part of its data?

10. What arguments do you pass to a file stream object's `write` member function?

11. What arguments do you pass to a file stream object's `read` member function?

12. What type cast do you use to convert a pointer from one type to another?

13. What is the difference between the `seekg` and `seekp` member functions?

14. How do you get the byte number of a file's current read position? How do you get the byte number of a file's current write position?

15. If a program has read to the end of a file, what must you do before using either the `seekg` or `seekp` member functions?

16. How do you determine the number of bytes that a file contains?

17. How do you rewind a sequential-access file?

Fill-in-the-Blank

18. The _____ file stream data type is for output files, input files, or files that perform both input and output.

19. If a file fails to open, the file stream object will be set to _____.

20. The same formatting techniques used with _____ may also be used when writing data to a file.

21. The _____ member function reads a line of text from a file.

22. The _____ member function reads a single character from a file.

23. The _____ member function writes a single character to a file.

24. _____ files contain data that is unformatted and not necessarily stored as ASCII text.

25. _____ files contain data formatted as _____.

26. A(n) _____ is a complete set of data about a single item and is made up of _____.

27. In C++, _____ provide a convenient way to organize data into fields and records.

28. The _____ member function writes "raw" binary data to a file.

29. The _____ member function reads "raw" binary data from a file.

30. The _____ operator is necessary if you pass anything other than a pointer-to-char as the first argument of the two functions mentioned in questions 26 and 27.

31. In _____ file access, the contents of the file are read in the order they appear in the file, from the file's start to its end.

32. In _____ file access, the contents of a file may be read in any order.

33. The _____ member function moves a file's read position to a specified byte in the file.

34. The _____ member function moves a file's write position to a specified byte in the file.

35. The _____ member function returns a file's current read position.

36. The _____ member function returns a file's current write position.

37. The _____ mode flag causes an offset to be calculated from the beginning of a file.

38. The _____ mode flag causes an offset to be calculated from the end of a file.

39. The _____ mode flag causes an offset to be calculated from the current position in the file.

40. A negative offset causes the file's read or write position to be moved _____ in the file from the position specified by the mode.

Algorithm Workbench

41. Write a statement that defines a file stream object named `places`. The object will be used for both output and input.

42. Write two statements that use a file stream object named `people` to open a file named `people.dat`. (Show how to open the file with a member function and at the definition of the file stream object.) The file should be opened for output.

43. Write two statements that use a file stream object named `pets` to open a file named `pets.dat`. (Show how to open the file with a member function and at the definition of the file stream object.) The file should be opened for input.

44. Write two statements that use a file stream object named `places` to open a file named `places.dat`. (Show how to open the file with a member function and at the definition of the file stream object.) The file should be opened for both input and output.

45. Write a program segment that defines a file stream object named `employees`. The file should be opened for both input and output (in binary mode). If the file fails to open, the program segment should display an error message.

46. Write code that opens the file `data.txt` for both input and output, but first determines if the file exists. If the file does not exist, the code should create it, then open it for both input and output.

47. Write code that determines the number of bytes contained in the file associated with the file stream object `dataFile`.

48. The `infoFile` file stream object is used to sequentially access data. The program has already read to the end of the file. Write code that rewinds the file.

True or False

49. T   F   Different operating systems have different rules for naming files.
50. T   F   `fstream` objects are only capable of performing file output operations.
51. T   F   `ofstream` objects, by default, delete the contents of a file if it already exists when opened.
52. T   F   `ifstream` objects, by default, create a file if it doesn't exist when opened.
53. T   F   Several file access flags may be joined by using the | operator.
54. T   F   A file may be opened in the definition of the file stream object.
55. T   F   If a file is opened in the definition of the file stream object, no mode flags may be specified.
56. T   F   A file stream object's `fail` member function may be used to determine if the file was successfully opened.
57. T   F   The same output formatting techniques used with `cout` may also be used with file stream objects.
58. T   F   The >> operator expects data to be delimited by whitespace characters.
59. T   F   The `getline` member function can be used to read text that contains whitespaces.
60. T   F   It is not possible to have more than one file open at once in a program.
61. T   F   Binary files contain unformatted data, not necessarily stored as text.
62. T   F   Binary is the default mode in which files are opened.
63. T   F   The `tellp` member function tells a file stream object which byte to move its write position to.
64. T   F   It is possible to open a file for both input and output.

Find the Error

Each of the following programs or program segments has errors. Find as many as you can.

65. ```cpp
fstream file(ios::in | ios::out);
file.open("info.dat");
if (!file)
{
    cout << "Could not open file.\n";
}
```

66. ```cpp
ofstream file;
file.open("info.dat", ios::in);
if (file)
{
    cout << "Could not open file.\n";
}
```

67. ```cpp
fstream file("info.dat");
if (!file)
{
    cout << "Could not open file.\n";
}
```

68. ```cpp
fstream dataFile("info.dat", ios:in | ios:binary);
int x = 5;
dataFile << x;
```

69. ```cpp
fstream dataFile("info.dat", ios:in);
int x;
while (dataFile.eof())
{
    dataFile >> x;
    cout << x << endl;
}
```

70. ```cpp
fstream dataFile("info.dat", ios:in);
char line[81];
dataFile.getline(line);
```

71. ```cpp
fstream dataFile("info.dat", ios:in);
char stuff[81];
dataFile.get(stuff);
```

72. ```cpp
fstream dataFile("info.dat", ios:in);
char stuff[81] = "abcdefghijklmnopqrstuvwxyz";
dataFile.put(stuff);
```

73. ```cpp
fstream dataFile("info.dat", ios:out);
struct Date
{
    int month;
    int day;
    int year;
};
Date dt = { 4, 2, 98 };
dataFile.write(&dt, sizeof(int));
```
```

```
74. fstream inFile("info.dat", ios:in);
    int x;
    inFile.seekp(5);
    inFile >> x;
```

Programming Challenges

1. File Head Program

Write a program that asks the user for the name of a file. The program should display the first 10 lines of the file on the screen (the "head" of the file). If the file has fewer than 10 lines, the entire file should be displayed, with a message indicating the entire file has been displayed.

NOTE: Using an editor, you should create a simple text file that can be used to test this program.

2. File Display Program

Write a program that asks the user for the name of a file. The program should display the contents of the file on the screen. If the file's contents won't fit on a single screen, the program should display 24 lines of output at a time, and then pause. Each time the program pauses, it should wait for the user to strike a key before the next 24 lines are displayed.

NOTE: Using an editor, you should create a simple text file that can be used to test this program.

3. Punch Line

Write a program that reads and prints a joke and its punch line from two different files. The first file contains a joke, but not its punch line. The second file has the punch line as its last line, preceded by "garbage." The main function of your program should open the two files and then call two functions, passing each one the file it needs. The first function should read and display each line in the file it is passed (the joke file). The second function should display only the last line of the file it is passed (the punch line file). It should find this line by seeking to the end of the file and then backing up to the beginning of the last line. Data to test your program can be found in the joke.txt and punchline.txt files.

4. Tail Program

Write a program that asks the user for the name of a file. The program should display the last 10 lines of the file on the screen (the "tail" of the file). If the file has fewer than 10 lines, the entire file should be displayed, with a message indicating the entire file has been displayed.

NOTE: Using an editor, you should create a simple text file that can be used to test this program.

5. Line Numbers

(This assignment could be done as a modification of the program in Programming Challenge 2.) Write a program that asks the user for the name of a file. The program should display the contents of the file on the screen. Each line of screen output should be preceded with a line number, followed by a colon. The line numbering should start at 1. Here is an example:

```
1:George Rolland
2:127 Academy Street
3:Brasstown, NC  28706
```

If the file's contents won't fit on a single screen, the program should display 24 lines of output at a time, and then pause. Each time the program pauses, it should wait for the user to strike a key before the next 24 lines are displayed.

 NOTE: Using an editor, you should create a simple text file that can be used to test this program.

6. String Search

Write a program that asks the user for a file name and a string to search for. The program should search the file for every occurrence of a specified string. When the string is found, the line that contains it should be displayed. After all the occurrences have been located, the program should report the number of times the string appeared in the file.

 NOTE: Using an editor, you should create a simple text file that can be used to test this program.

 ## 7. Sentence Filter

Write a program that asks the user for two file names. The first file will be opened for input and the second file will be opened for output. (It will be assumed that the first file contains sentences that end with a period.) The program will read the contents of the first file and change all the letters to lowercase except the first letter of each sentence, which should be made uppercase. The revised contents should be stored in the second file.

 NOTE: Using an editor, you should create a simple text file that can be used to test this program.

8. Array/File Functions

Write a function named `arrayToFile`. The function should accept three arguments: the name of a file, a pointer to an int array, and the size of the array. The function should open the specified file in binary mode, write the contents of the array to the file, and then close the file.

Write another function named `fileToArray`. This function should accept three arguments: the name of a file, a pointer to an int array, and the size of the array. The function should open the specified file in binary mode, read its contents into the array, and then close the file.

Write a complete program that demonstrates these functions by using the `arrayToFile` function to write an array to a file, and then using the `fileToArray` function to read the data from the same file. After the data are read from the file into the array, display the array's contents on the screen.

9. **File Encryption Filter**

VideoNote

Solving
the File
Encryption
Filter Problem

File encryption is the science of writing the contents of a file in a secret code. Your encryption program should work like a filter, reading the contents of one file, modifying the data into a code, and then writing the coded contents out to a second file. The second file will be a version of the first file, but written in a secret code.

Although there are complex encryption techniques, you should come up with a simple one of your own. For example, you could read the first file one character at a time, and add 10 to the ASCII code of each character before it is written to the second file.

10. **File Decryption Filter**

Write a program that decrypts the file produced by the program in Programming Challenge 9. The decryption program should read the contents of the coded file, restore the data to its original state, and write it to another file.

11. **Corporate Sales Data Output**

Write a program that uses a structure to store the following data on a company division:

   Division Name (such as East, West, North, or South)
   Quarter (1, 2, 3, or 4)
   Quarterly Sales

The user should be asked for the four quarters' sales figures for the East, West, North, and South divisions. The data for each quarter for each division should be written to a file.

Input Validation: Do not accept negative numbers for any sales figures.

12. **Corporate Sales Data Input**

Write a program that reads the data in the file created by the program in Programming Challenge 11. The program should calculate and display the following figures:

- Total corporate sales for each quarter
- Total yearly sales for each division
- Total yearly corporate sales
- Average quarterly sales for the divisions
- The highest and lowest quarters for the corporation

13. **Inventory Program**

Write a program that uses a structure to store the following inventory data in a file:

   Item Description
   Quantity on Hand
   Wholesale Cost
   Retail Cost
   Date Added to Inventory

The program should have a menu that allows the user to perform the following tasks:

- Add new records to the file.
- Display any record in the file.
- Change any record in the file.

Input Validation: The program should not accept quantities, or wholesale or retail costs, less than 0. The program should not accept dates that the programmer determines are unreasonable.

14. **Inventory Screen Report**

Write a program that reads the data in the file created by the program in Programming Challenge 13. The program should calculate and display the following data:

- The total wholesale value of the inventory
- The total retail value of the inventory
- The total quantity of all items in the inventory

15. **Average Number of Words**

On the student CD you will find a file named `text.txt`. The text that is in the file is stored as one sentence per line. Write a program that reads the file's contents and calculates the average number of words per sentence.

Group Project

16. **Customer Accounts**

This program should be designed and written by a team of students. Here are some suggestions:

- One student should design function `main`, which will call other program functions. The remainder of the functions will be designed by other members of the team.
- The requirements of the program should be analyzed so each student is given about the same workload.

Write a program that uses a structure to store the following data about a customer account:

> Name
> Address
> City, State, and ZIP
> Telephone Number
> Account Balance
> Date of Last Payment

The structure should be used to store customer account records in a file. The program should have a menu that lets the user perform the following operations:

- Enter new records into the file.
- Search for a particular customer's record and display it.
- Search for a particular customer's record and delete it.
- Search for a particular customer's record and change it.
- Display the contents of the entire file.

Input Validation: When the data for a new account is entered, be sure the user enters data for all the fields. No negative account balances should be entered.

TOPICS

13.1 Procedural and Object-Oriented Programming

CONCEPT: Procedural programming is a method of writing software. It is a programming practice centered on the procedures or actions that take place in a program. Object-oriented programming is centered around the object. Objects are created from abstract data types that encapsulate data and functions together.

There are two common programming methods in practice today: procedural programming and object-oriented programming (or OOP). Up to this chapter, you have learned to write procedural programs.

In a procedural program, you typically have data stored in a collection of variables and/or structures, coupled with a set of functions that perform operations on the data. The data and the functions are separate entities. For example, in a program that works with the geometry of a rectangle you might have the variables in Table 13-1:

Table 13-1

Variable Definition	Description
`double width;`	Holds the rectangle's width
`double length;`	Holds the rectangle's length

In addition to the variables listed in Table 13-1, you might also have the functions listed in Table 13-2:

Table 13-2

Function Name	Description
`setData()`	Stores values in `width` and `length`
`displayWidth()`	Displays the rectangle's width
`displayLength()`	Displays the rectangle's length
`displayArea()`	Displays the rectangle's area

Usually the variables and data structures in a procedural program are passed to the functions that perform the desired operations. As you might imagine, the focus of procedural programming is on creating the functions that operate on the program's data.

Procedural programming has worked well for software developers for many years. However, as programs become larger and more complex, the separation of a program's data and the code that operates on the data can lead to problems. For example, the data in a procedural program are stored in variables, as well as more complex structures that are created from variables. The procedures that operate on the data must be designed with those variables and data structures in mind. But, what happens if the format of the data is altered? Quite often, a program's specifications change, resulting in redesigned data structures. When the structure of the data changes, the code that operates on the data must also change to accept the new format. This results in additional work for programmers and a greater opportunity for bugs to appear in the code.

This problem has helped influence the shift from procedural programming to object-oriented programming (OOP). Whereas procedural programming is centered on creating procedures or functions, object-oriented programming is centered on creating objects. An *object* is a software entity that contains both data and procedures. The data that are contained in an object are known as the object's *attributes*. The procedures that an object performs are called *member functions*. The object is, conceptually, a self-contained unit consisting of attributes (data) and procedures (functions). This is illustrated in Figure 13-1.

OOP addresses the problems that can result from the separation of code and data through encapsulation and data hiding. *Encapsulation* refers to the combining of data and code into a single object. *Data hiding* refers to an object's ability to hide its data from code that

Figure 13-1

Object

Data (Attributes)

Functions That
Operate on the Data

 NOTE: In other programming languages, the procedures that an object performs are often called *methods*.

is outside the object. Only the object's member functions may directly access and make changes to the object's data. An object typically hides its data, but allows outside code to access its member functions. As shown in Figure 13-2, the object's member functions provide programming statements outside the object with indirect access to the object's data.

Figure 13-2

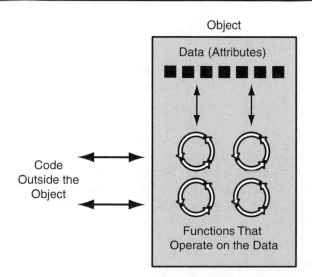

Object

Data (Attributes)

Code
Outside the
Object

Functions That
Operate on the Data

When an object's internal data are hidden from outside code, and access to that data is restricted to the object's member functions, the data are protected from accidental corruption. In addition, the programming code outside the object does not need to know about the format or internal structure of the object's data. The code only needs to interact with the object's functions. When a programmer changes the structure of an object's internal data, he or she also modifies the object's member functions so they may properly operate on the data. The way in which outside code interacts with the member functions, however, does not change.

An everyday example of object-oriented technology is the automobile. It has a rather simple interface that consists of an ignition switch, steering wheel, gas pedal, brake pedal, and a gear shift. Vehicles with manual transmissions also provide a clutch pedal. If you want to drive an automobile (to become its user), you only have to learn to operate these elements of its interface. To start the motor, you simply turn the key in the ignition switch. What happens internally is irrelevant to the user. If you want to steer the auto to the left, you rotate the steering wheel left. The movements of all the linkages connecting the steering wheel to the front tires occur transparently.

Because automobiles have simple user interfaces, they can be driven by people who have no mechanical knowledge. This is good for the makers of automobiles because it means more people are likely to become customers. It's good for the users of automobiles because they can learn just a few simple procedures and operate almost any vehicle.

These are also valid concerns in software development. A real-world program is rarely written by only one person. Even the programs you have created so far weren't written entirely by you. If you incorporated C++ library functions, or objects like `cin` and `cout`, you used code written by someone else. In the world of professional software development, programmers commonly work in teams, buy and sell their code, and collaborate on projects. With OOP, programmers can create objects with powerful engines tucked away "under the hood," protected by simple interfaces that safeguard the object's algorithms.

Object Reusability

In addition to solving the problems of code/data separation, the use of OOP has also been encouraged by the trend of *object reusability*. An object is not a stand-alone program, but is used by programs that need its service. For example, Sharon is a programmer who has developed an object for rendering 3D images. She is a math whiz and knows a lot about computer graphics, so her object is coded to perform all the necessary 3D mathematical operations and handle the computer's video hardware. Tom, who is writing a program for an architectural firm, needs his application to display 3D images of buildings. Because he is working under a tight deadline and does not possess a great deal of knowledge about computer graphics, he can use Sharon's object to perform the 3D rendering (for a small fee, of course!).

Classes and Objects

Now let's discuss how objects are created in software. Before an object can be created, it must be designed by a programmer. The programmer determines the attributes and functions that are necessary, and then creates a class. A *class* is code that specifies the attributes and member functions that a particular type of object may have. Think of a class as a "blueprint" that objects may be created from. It serves a similar purpose as the blueprint for a house. The blueprint itself is not a house, but is a detailed description of a house. When we use the blueprint to build an actual house, we could say we are building an instance of the house described by the blueprint. If we so desire, we can build several identical houses from the same blueprint. Each house is a separate instance of the house described by the blueprint. This idea is illustrated in Figure 13-3.

Figure 13-3

Blueprint that describes a house.

Instances of the house described by the blueprint.

So, a class is not an object, but it is a description of an object. When the program is running, it uses the class to create, in memory, as many objects of a specific type as needed. Each object that is created from a class is called an *instance* of the class.

For example, Jessica is an entomologist (someone who studies insects) and she also enjoys writing computer programs. She designs a program to catalog different types of insects. As part of the program, she creates a class named `Insect`, which specifies attributes and member functions for holding and manipulating data common to all types of insects. The `Insect` class is not an object, but a specification that objects may be created from. Next, she writes programming statements that create a `housefly` object, which is an instance of the `Insect` class. The `housefly` object is an entity that occupies computer memory and stores data about a housefly. It has the attributes and member functions specified by the `Insect` class. Then she writes programming statements that create a `mosquito` object. The `mosquito` object is also an instance of the `Insect` class. It has its own area in memory, and stores data about a mosquito. Although the `housefly` and `mosquito` objects are two separate entities in the computer's memory, they were both created from the `Insect` class. This means that each of the objects has the attributes and member functions described by the `Insect` class. This is illustrated in Figure 13-4.

Figure 13-4

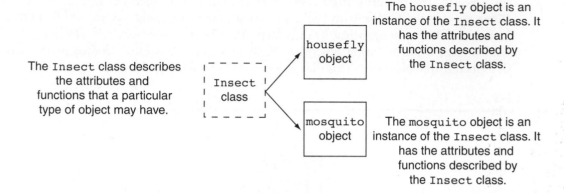

The Insect class describes the attributes and functions that a particular type of object may have.

Insect class

housefly object

The housefly object is an instance of the Insect class. It has the attributes and functions described by the Insect class.

mosquito object

The mosquito object is an instance of the Insect class. It has the attributes and functions described by the Insect class.

At the beginning of this section we discussed how a procedural program that works with rectangles might have variables to hold the rectangle's width and length, and separate functions to do things like store values in the variables and make calculations. The program would pass the variables to the functions as needed. In an object-oriented program, we would create a Rectangle class which would encapsulate the data (width and length) and the functions that work with the data. Figure 13-5 shows a representation of such a class.

Figure 13-5

```
Member Variables
    double width;
    double length;

Member Functions
    void setWidth(double w)
    { ... function code ...}

    void setLength(double len)
    { ... function code ...}

    double getWidth()
    { ... function code ...}

    double getLength()
    { ... function code ...}

    double getArea()
    { ... function code ...}
```

In the object-oriented approach, the variables and functions are all members of the Rectangle class. When we need to work with a rectangle in our program, we create a Rectangle object, which is an instance of the Rectangle class. When we need to perform an operation on the Rectangle object's data, we use that object to call the appropriate member function. For example, if we need to get the area of the rectangle, we use the object to call the getArea member function. The getArea member function would be designed to calculate the area of that object's rectangle, and return the value.

Using a Class You Already Know

Before we go any further, let's review the basics of a class that you have already learned something about. Chapter 10 introduced you to the `string` class, which allows you to create `string` objects. First, recall that you must have the following `#include` directive in any program that uses the `string` class:

```
#include <string>
```

This is necessary because the `string` class is declared in the `string` header file. Next, you can define a `string` object with a statement such as

```
string cityName;
```

This creates a `string` object named `cityName`. The `cityName` object is an instance of the `string` class.

Once a `string` object has been created, you can store data in it. Because the `string` class is designed to work with the assignment operator, you can assign a C-string to a `string` object. Here is an example:

```
cityName = "Charleston";
```

After this statement executes, the string `"Charleston"` will be stored in the `cityName` object. `"Charleston"` will become the object's data.

The `string` class specifies numerous member functions that perform operations on the data that a `string` object holds. In Chapter 10 we discussed a member function named `length`, which returns the length of the string stored in a `string` object. The following code demonstrates:

```
string cityName;           // Create a string object named cityName
int strSize;               // To hold the length of a string
cityName = "Charleston";   // Assign "Charleston" to cityName
strSize = cityName.length(); // Store the string length in strSize
```

The last statement calls the `length` member function, which returns the length of a string. The expression `cityName.length()` returns the length of the string stored in the `cityName` object. After this statement executes, the `strSize` variable will contain the value 10, which is the length of the string `"Charleston"`.

The `string` class also specifies a member function named `append`, which appends an additional string onto the string already stored in an object. The following code demonstrates.

```
string cityName;
cityName = "Charleston";
cityName.append(" South Carolina");
```

In the second line, the string `"Charleston"` is assigned to the `cityName` object. In the third line, the `append` member function is called and `" South Carolina"` is passed as an argument. The argument is appended to the string that is already stored in `cityName`. After this statement executes, the `cityName` object will contain the string `"Charleston South Carolina"`.

13.2 Introduction to Classes

> **CONCEPT:** In C++, the class is the construct primarily used to create objects.

A *class* is similar to a structure. It is a data type defined by the programmer, consisting of variables and functions. Here is the general format of a class declaration:

VideoNote

Writing
a Class

```
class ClassName
{
   declaration;
   // ... more declarations
   // may follow...
};
```

The declaration statements inside a class declaration are for the variables and functions that are members of that class. For example, the following code declares a class named `Rectangle` with two member variables: `width` and `length`.

```
class Rectangle
{
   double width;
   double length;
};                      // Don't forget the semicolon.
```

There is a problem with this class, however. Unlike structures, the members of a class are *private* by default. Private class members cannot be accessed by programming statements outside the class. So, no statements outside this `Rectangle` class can access the `width` and `length` members.

Recall from our earlier discussion on object-oriented programming that an object can perform data hiding, which means that critical data stored inside the object are protected from code outside the object. In C++, a class's private members are hidden, and can be accessed only by functions that are members of the same class. A class's *public* members may be accessed by code outside the class.

Access Specifiers

C++ provides the key words `private` and `public` which you may use in class declarations. These key words are known as *access specifiers* because they specify how class members may be accessed. The following is the general format of a class declaration that uses the `private` and `public` access specifiers.

```
class ClassName
{
   private:
      // Declarations of private
      // members appear here.
   public:
      // Declarations of public
      // members appear here.
};
```

Notice that the access specifiers are followed by a colon (:), and then followed by one or more member declarations. In this general format, the `private` access specifier is used first. All of the declarations that follow it, up to the `public` access specifier, are for private members. Then, all of the declarations that follow the `public` access specifier are for public members.

Public Member Functions

To allow access to a class's private member variables, you create public member functions that work with the private member variables. For example, consider the `Rectangle` class. To allow access to a `Rectangle` object's `width` and `length` member variables, we will add the member functions listed in Table 13-3.

Table 13-3

Member Function	Description
setWidth	This function accepts an argument which is assigned to the `width` member variable.
setLength	This function accepts an argument which is assigned to the `length` member variable.
getWidth	This function returns the value stored in the `width` member variable.
getLength	This function returns the value stored in the `length` member variable.
getArea	This function returns the product of the `width` member variable multiplied by the `length` member variable. This value is the area of the rectangle.

For the moment we will not actually define the functions described in Table 13-3. We leave that for later. For now we will only include declarations, or prototypes, for the functions in the class declaration:

```
class Rectangle
{
    private:
        double width;
        double length;
    public:
        void setWidth(double);
        void setLength(double);
        double getWidth() const;
        double getLength() const;
        double getArea() const;
};
```

In this declaration, the member variables `width` and `length` are declared as `private`, which means they can be accessed only by the class's member functions. The member functions, however, are declared as `public`, which means they can be called from statements outside the class. If code outside the class needs to store a width or a length in a `Rectangle` object, it must do so by calling the object's `setWidth` or `setLength` member functions. Likewise, if code outside the class needs to retrieve a width or length stored in a `Rectangle` object, it must do so with the object's `getWidth` or `getLength` member functions. These public functions provide an interface for code outside the class to use `Rectangle` objects.

> **NOTE:** Even though the default access of a class is private, it's still a good idea to use the `private` key word to explicitly declare private members. This clearly documents the access specification of all the members of the class.

Using `const` with Member Functions

Notice that the key word `const` appears in the declarations of the `getWidth`, `getLength`, and `getArea` member functions, as shown here:

```
double getWidth() const;
double getLength() const;
double getArea() const;
```

When the key word `const` appears after the parentheses in a member function declaration, it specifies that the function will not change any data stored in the calling object. If you inadvertently write code in the function that changes the calling object's data, the compiler will generate an error. As you will see momentarily, the `const` key word must also appear in the function header.

Placement of `public` and `private` Members

There is no rule requiring you to declare private members before public members. The `Rectangle` class could be declared as follows:

```
class Rectangle
{
   public:
      void setWidth(double);
      void setLength(double);
      double getWidth() const;
      double getLength() const;
      double getArea() const;
   private:
      double width;
      double length;
};
```

In addition, it is not required that all members of the same access specification be declared in the same place. Here is yet another declaration of the `Rectangle` class.

```
class Rectangle
{
   private:
      double width;
   public:
      void setWidth(double);
      void setLength(double);
      double getWidth() const;
      double getLength() const;
      double getArea() const;
   private:
      double length;
};
```

Although C++ gives you freedom in arranging class member declarations, you should adopt a consistent standard. Most programmers choose to group member declarations of the same access specification together.

 NOTE: Notice in our example that the first character of the class name is written in uppercase. This is not required, but serves as a visual reminder that the class name is not a variable name.

Defining Member Functions

The `Rectangle` class declaration contains declarations or prototypes for five member functions: `setWidth`, `setLength`, `getWidth`, `getLength`, and `getArea`. The definitions of these functions are written outside the class declaration:

```cpp
//*************************************************************
// setWidth assigns its argument to the private member width. *
//*************************************************************

void Rectangle::setWidth(double w)
{
   width = w;
}



//**************************************************************
// setLength assigns its argument to the private member length. *
//**************************************************************

void Rectangle::setLength(double len)
{
   length = len;
}

//*************************************************************
// getWidth returns the value in the private member width.   *
//*************************************************************

double Rectangle::getWidth() const
{
   return width;
}

//************************************************************
// getLength returns the value in the private member length. *
//************************************************************

double Rectangle::getLength() const
{
   return length;
}
```

```
//******************************************************
// getArea returns the product of width times length.   *
//******************************************************

double Rectangle::getArea() const
{
   return width * length;
}
```

In each function definition, the following precedes the name of each function:

```
Rectangle::
```

The two colons are called the *scope resolution operator*. When `Rectangle::` appears before the name of a function in a function header, it identifies the function as a member of the `Rectangle` class.

Here is the general format of the function header of any member function defined outside the declaration of a class:

> *ReturnType ClassName::functionName(ParameterList)*

In the general format, *ReturnType* is the function's return type. *ClassName* is the name of the class that the function is a member of. *functionName* is the name of the member function. *ParameterList* is an optional list of parameter variable declarations.

WARNING! Remember, the class name and scope resolution operator extends the name of the function. They must appear after the return type and immediately before the function name in the function header. The following would be incorrect:

```
Rectangle::double getArea() //Incorrect!
```

In addition, if you leave the class name and scope resolution operator out of a member function's header, the function will not become a member of the class.

```
double getArea() // Not a member of the Rectangle class!
```

Accessors and Mutators

As mentioned earlier, it is a common practice to make all of a class's member variables private and to provide public member functions for accessing and changing them. This ensures that the object owning the member variables is in control of all changes being made to them. A member function that gets a value from a class's member variable but does not change it is known as an *accessor*. A member function that stores a value in member variable or changes the value of member variable in some other way is known as a *mutator*. In the `Rectangle` class, the member functions `getLength` and `getWidth` are accessors, and the member functions `setLength` and `setWidth` are mutators.

Some programmers refer to mutators as *setter functions* because they set the value of an attribute, and accessors as *getter functions* because they get the value of an attribute.

Using `const` with Accessors

Notice that the key word `const` appears in the headers of the `getWidth`, `getLength`, and `getArea` member functions, as shown here:

```
double Rectangle::getWidth() const
double Rectangle::getLength() const
double Rectangle::getArea() const
```

Recall that these functions were also declared in the class with the `const` key word. When you mark a member function as `const`, the `const` key word must appear in both the declaration and the function header.

In essence, when you mark a member function as `const`, you are telling the compiler that the calling object is a constant. The compiler will generate an error if you inadvertently write code in the function that changes the calling object's data. Because this decreases the chances of having bugs in your code, it is a good practice to mark all accessor functions as `const`.

13.3 Defining an Instance of a Class

CONCEPT: Class objects must be defined after the class is declared.

VideoNote

Defining
an Instance
of a Class

Like structure variables, class objects are not created in memory until they are defined. This is because a class declaration by itself does not create an object, but is merely the description of an object. We can use it to create one or more objects, which are instances of the class.

Class objects are created with simple definition statements, just like variables. Here is the general format of a simple object definition statement:

> *ClassName objectName;*

In the general format, *ClassName* is the name of a class and *objectName* is the name we are giving the object.

For example, the following statement defines `box` as an object of the `Rectangle` class:

```
Rectangle box;
```

Defining a class object is called the *instantiation* of a class. In this statement, `box` is an *instance* of the `Rectangle` class.

Accessing an Object's Members

The `box` object that we previously defined is an instance of the `Rectangle` class. Suppose we want to change the value in the `box` object's `width` variable. To do so, we must use the `box` object to call the `setWidth` member function, as shown here:

```
box.setWidth(12.7);
```

Just as you use the dot operator to access a structure's members, you use the dot operator to call a class's member functions. This statement uses the `box` object to call the `setWidth` member function, passing 12.7 as an argument. As a result, the box object's width variable will be set to 12.7. Here are other examples of statements that use the box object to call member functions:

```
box.setLength(4.8);      // Set box's length to 4.8.
x = box.getWidth();      // Assign box's width to x.
cout << box.getLength(); // Display box's length.
cout << box.getArea();   // Display box's area.
```

NOTE: Notice that inside the Rectangle class's member functions, the dot operator is not used to access any of the class's member variables. When an object is used to call a member function, the member function has direct access to that object's member variables.

A Class Demonstration Program

Program 13-1 is a complete program that demonstrates the Rectangle class.

Program 13-1

```
1   // This program demonstrates a simple class.
2   #include <iostream>
3   using namespace std;
4
5   // Rectangle class declaration.
6   class Rectangle
7   {
8      private:
9         double width;
10        double length;
11     public:
12        void setWidth(double);
13        void setLength(double);
14        double getWidth() const;
15        double getLength() const;
16        double getArea() const;
17  };
18
19  //***************************************************
20  // setWidth assigns a value to the width member.   *
21  //***************************************************
22
23  void Rectangle::setWidth(double w)
24  {
25     width = w;
26  }
27
28  //***************************************************
29  // setLength assigns a value to the length member. *
30  //***************************************************
31
```

```
32    void Rectangle::setLength(double len)
33    {
34        length = len;
35    }
36
37    //***************************************************
38    // getWidth returns the value in the width member. *
39    //***************************************************
40
41    double Rectangle::getWidth() const
42    {
43        return width;
44    }
45
46    //****************************************************
47    // getLength returns the value in the length member. *
48    //****************************************************
49
50    double Rectangle::getLength() const
51    {
52        return length;
53    }
54
55    //*****************************************************
56    // getArea returns the product of width times length. *
57    //*****************************************************
58
59    double Rectangle::getArea() const
60    {
61        return width * length;
62    }
63
64    //*****************************************************
65    // Function main                                      *
66    //*****************************************************
67
68    int main()
69    {
70        Rectangle box;      // Define an instance of the Rectangle class
71        double rectWidth;   // Local variable for width
72        double rectLength;  // Local variable for length
73
74        // Get the rectangle's width and length from the user.
75        cout << "This program will calculate the area of a\n";
76        cout << "rectangle. What is the width? ";
77        cin >> rectWidth;
78        cout << "What is the length? ";
79        cin >> rectLength;
80
81        // Store the width and length of the rectangle
82        // in the box object.
83        box.setWidth(rectWidth);
84        box.setLength(rectLength);
```

(program continues)

Program 13-1 *(continued)*

```
85
86      // Display the rectangle's data.
87      cout << "Here is the rectangle's data:\n";
88      cout << "Width: " << box.getWidth() << endl;
89      cout << "Length: " << box.getLength() << endl;
90      cout << "Area: " << box.getArea() << endl;
91      return 0;
92   }
```

Program Output with Example Input Shown in Bold

This program will calculate the area of a
rectangle. What is the width? **10 [Enter]**
What is the length? **5 [Enter]**
Here is the rectangle's data:
Width: 10
Length: 5
Area: 50

The `Rectangle` class declaration, along with the class's member functions, appears in lines 6 through 62. Inside the `main` function, in line 70, the following statement creates a `Rectangle` object named `box`.

```
Rectangle box;
```

The `box` object is illustrated in Figure 13-6. Notice that the `width` and `length` member variables do not yet hold meaningful values. An object's member variables are not automatically initialized to 0. When an object's member variable is first created, it holds whatever random value happens to exist at the variable's memory location. We commonly refer to such a random value as "garbage."

Figure 13-6

The box object when first created

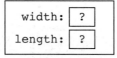

In lines 75 through 79 the program prompts the user to enter the width and length of a rectangle. The width that is entered is stored in the `rectWidth` variable, and the length that is entered is stored in the `rectLength` variable. In line 83 the following statement uses the `box` object to call the `setWidth` member function, passing the value of the `rectWidth` variable as an argument:

```
box.setWidth(rectWidth);
```

This sets `box`'s `width` member variable to the value in `rectWidth`. Assuming `rectWidth` holds the value 10, Figure 13-7 shows the state of the `box` object after this statement executes.

Figure 13-7

The box object with `width` set to 10

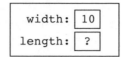

In line 84 the following statement uses the `box` object to call the `setLength` member function, passing the value of the `rectLength` variable as an argument.

        box.setLength(rectLength);

This sets `box`'s `length` member variable to the value in `rectLength`. Assuming `rectLength` holds the value 5, Figure 13-8 shows the state of the `box` object after this statement executes.

Figure 13-8

The box object with `width` set to 10
and `length` set to 5

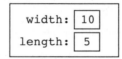

Lines 88, 89, and 90 use the `box` object to call the `getWidth`, `getLength`, and `getArea` member functions, displaying their return values on the screen.

NOTE: Figures 13-6 through 13-8 show the state of the box object at various times during the execution of the program. An object's *state* is simply the data that is stored in the object's attributes at any given moment.

Program 13-1 creates only one `Rectangle` object. It is possible to create many instances of the same class, each with its own data. For example, Program 13-2 creates three `Rectangle` objects, named `kitchen`, `bedroom`, and `den`. Note that lines 6 through 62 have been left out of the listing because they contain the `Rectangle` class declaration and the definitions for the class's member functions. These lines are identical to those same lines in Program 13-1.

Program 13-2

```
1 // This program creates three instances of the Rectangle class.
2 #include <iostream>
3 using namespace std;
4
5 // Rectangle class declaration.
```

        Lines 6 through 62 have been left out.

(program continues)

Program 13-2   *(continued)*

```cpp
63
64 //*****************************************************
65 // Function main                                     *
66 //*****************************************************
67
68 int main()
69 {
70    double number;        // To hold a number
71    double totalArea;     // The total area
72    Rectangle kitchen;    // To hold kitchen dimensions
73    Rectangle bedroom;    // To hold bedroom dimensions
74    Rectangle den;        // To hold den dimensions
75
76    // Get the kitchen dimensions.
77    cout << "What is the kitchen's length? ";
78    cin >> number;                          // Get the length
79    kitchen.setLength(number);              // Store in kitchen object
80    cout << "What is the kitchen's width? ";
81    cin >> number;                          // Get the width
82    kitchen.setWidth(number);               // Store in kitchen object
83
84    // Get the bedroom dimensions.
85    cout << "What is the bedroom's length? ";
86    cin >> number;                          // Get the length
87    bedroom.setLength(number);              // Store in bedroom object
88    cout << "What is the bedroom's width? ";
89    cin >> number;                          // Get the width
90    bedroom.setWidth(number);               // Store in bedroom object
91
92    // Get the den dimensions.
93    cout << "What is the den's length? ";
94    cin >> number;                          // Get the length
95    den.setLength(number);                  // Store in den object
96    cout << "What is the den's width? ";
97    cin >> number;                          // Get the width
98    den.setWidth(number);                   // Store in den object
99
100   // Calculate the total area of the three rooms.
101   totalArea = kitchen.getArea() + bedroom.getArea()
102            + den.getArea();
103
104   // Display the total area of the three rooms.
105   cout << "The total area of the three rooms is "
106        << totalArea << endl;
107
108   return 0;
109 }
```

Program Output with Example Input Shown in Bold
```
What is the kitchen's length? 10 [Enter]
What is the kitchen's width? 14 [Enter]
What is the bedroom's length? 15 [Enter]
What is the bedroom's width? 12 [Enter]
What is the den's length? 20 [Enter]
What is the den's width? 30 [Enter]
The total area of the three rooms is 920
```

In lines 72, 73, and 74, the following code defines three `Rectangle` variables. This creates three objects, each an instance of the `Rectangle` class:

```
Rectangle kitchen;     // To hold kitchen dimensions
Rectangle bedroom;     // To hold bedroom dimensions
Rectangle den;         // To hold den dimensions
```

In the example output, the user enters 10 and 14 as the length and width of the kitchen, 15 and 12 as the length and width of the bedroom, and 20 and 30 as the length and width of the den. Figure 13-9 shows the states of the objects after these values are stored in them.

Figure 13-9

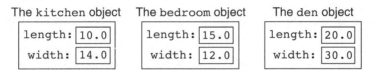

Notice from Figure 13-9 that each instance of the `Rectangle` class has its own `length` and `width` variables. Every instance of a class has its own set of member variables that can hold their own values. The class's member functions can perform operations on specific instances of the class. For example, look at the following statement in line 79 of Program 13-2:

```
kitchen.setLength(number);
```

This statement calls the `setLength` member function, which stores a value in the `kitchen` object's `length` variable. Now look at the following statement in line 87:

```
bedroom.setLength(number);
```

This statement also calls the `setLength` member function, but this time it stores a value in the `bedroom` object's `length` variable. Likewise, the following statement in line 95 calls the `setLength` member function to store a value in the `den` object's `length` variable:

```
den.setLength(number);
```

The `setLength` member function stores a value in a specific instance of the `Rectangle` class. All of the other `Rectangle` class member functions work in a similar way. They access one or more member variables of a specific `Rectangle` object.

Avoiding Stale Data

In the Rectangle class, the getLength and getWidth member functions return the values stored in member variables, but the getArea member function returns the result of a calculation. You might be wondering why the area of the rectangle is not stored in a member variable, like the length and the width. The area is not stored in a member variable because it could potentially become stale. When the value of an item is dependent on other data and that item is not updated when the other data are changed, it is said that the item has become *stale*. If the area of the rectangle were stored in a member variable, the value of the member variable would become incorrect as soon as either the length or width member variables changed.

When designing a class, you should take care not to store in a member variable calculated data that could potentially become stale. Instead, provide a member function that returns the result of the calculation.

Pointers to Objects

You can also define pointers to class objects. For example, the following statement defines a pointer variable named rectPtr:

```
Rectangle *rectPtr;
```

The rectPtr variable is not an object, but it can hold the address of a Rectangle object. The following code shows an example.

```
Rectangle myRectangle;   // A Rectangle object
Rectangle *rectPtr;      // A Rectangle pointer
rectPtr = &myRectangle;  // rectPtr now points to myRectangle
```

The first statement creates a Rectangle object named myRectangle. The second statement creates a Rectangle pointer named rectPtr. The third statement stores the address of the myRectangle object in the rectPtr pointer. This is illustrated in Figure 13-10.

Figure 13-10

The rectPtr pointer can then be used to call member functions by using the -> operator. The following statements show examples.

```
rectPtr->setWidth(12.5);
rectPtr->setLength(4.8);
```

The first statement calls the setWidth member function, passing 12.5 as an argument. Because rectPtr points to the myRectangle object, this will cause 12.5 to be stored in the myRectangle object's width variable. The second statement calls the setLength member function, passing 4.8 as an argument. This will cause 4.8 to be stored in the myRectangle object's `length` variable. Figure 13-11 shows the state of the `myRectangle` object after these statements have executed.

Figure 13-11

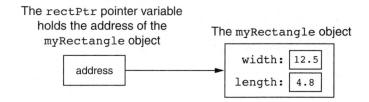

The `rectPtr` pointer variable holds the address of the `myRectangle` object

The `myRectangle` object

address

width: 12.5

length: 4.8

Class object pointers can be used to dynamically allocate objects. The following code shows an example.

```
1   // Define a Rectangle pointer.
2   Rectangle *rectPtr;
3
4   // Dynamically allocate a Rectangle object.
5   rectPtr = new Rectangle;
6
7   // Store values in the object's width and length.
8   rectPtr->setWidth(10.0);
9   rectPtr->setLength(15.0);
10
11  // Delete the object from memory.
12  delete rectPtr;
13  rectPtr = 0;
```

Line 2 defines `rectPtr` as a Rectangle pointer. Line 5 uses the new operator to dynamically allocate a Rectangle object and assign its address to `rectPtr`. Lines 8 and 9 store values in the dynamically allocated object's `width` and `length` variables. Figure 13-12 shows the state of the dynamically allocated object after these statements have executed.

Figure 13-12

The `rectPtr` pointer variable holds the address of a dynamically allocated `Rectangle` object

A `Rectangle` object

address

width: 10.0

length: 15.0

Line 12 deletes the object from memory and line 13 stores the address 0 in `rectPtr`. Recall from Chapter 9 that this prevents code from inadvertently using the pointer to access the area of memory that has been freed. It also prevents errors from occurring if `delete` is accidentally called on the pointer again.

Program 13-3 is a modification of Program 13-2. In this program, `kitchen`, `bedroom`, and `den` are Rectangle pointers. They are used to dynamically allocate Rectangle objects. The output is the same as Program 13-2.

Program 13-3

```
1  // This program creates three instances of the Rectangle class.
2  #include <iostream>
3  using namespace std;
4
5  // Rectangle class declaration.
```

            Lines 6 through 62 have been left out.

```
63
64  //****************************************************
65  // Function main                                     *
66  //****************************************************
67
68  int main()
69  {
70     double number;        // To hold a number
71     double totalArea;     // The total area
72     Rectangle *kitchen;   // To point to kitchen dimensions
73     Rectangle *bedroom;   // To point to bedroom dimensions
74     Rectangle *den;       // To point to den dimensions
75
76     // Dynamically allocate the objects.
77     kitchen = new Rectangle;
78     bedroom = new Rectangle;
79     den = new Rectangle;
80
81     // Get the kitchen dimensions.
82     cout << "What is the kitchen's length? ";
83     cin >> number;                           // Get the length
84     kitchen->setLength(number);              // Store in kitchen object
85     cout << "What is the kitchen's width? ";
86     cin >> number;                           // Get the width
87     kitchen->setWidth(number);               // Store in kitchen object
88
89     // Get the bedroom dimensions.
90     cout << "What is the bedroom's length? ";
91     cin >> number;                           // Get the length
92     bedroom->setLength(number);              // Store in bedroom object
93     cout << "What is the bedroom's width? ";
94     cin >> number;                           // Get the width
95     bedroom->setWidth(number);               // Store in bedroom object
96
97     // Get the den dimensions.
98     cout << "What is the den's length? ";
99     cin >> number;                           // Get the length
100    den->setLength(number);                  // Store in den object
101    cout << "What is the den's width? ";
102    cin >> number;                           // Get the width
103    den->setWidth(number);                   // Store in den object
104
105    // Calculate the total area of the three rooms.
106    totalArea = kitchen->getArea() + bedroom->getArea()
107             + den->getArea();
108
```

```
109    // Display the total area of the three rooms.
110    cout << "The total area of the three rooms is "
111         << totalArea << endl;
112
113    // Delete the objects from memory.
114    delete kitchen;
115    delete bedroom;
116    delete den;
117    kitchen = 0;    // Make kitchen point to null.
118    bedroom = 0;    // Make bedroom point to null.
119    den = 0;        // Make den point to null.
120
121    return 0;
122 }
```

 ## Checkpoint

13.1   True or False: You must declare all private members of a class before the public members.

13.2   Assume that `RetailItem` is the name of a class, and the class has a `void` member function named `setPrice` which accepts a `double` argument. Which of the following shows the correct use of the scope resolution operator in the member function definition?

     A) `RetailItem::void setPrice(double p)`

     B) `void RetailItem::setPrice(double p)`

13.3   An object's private member variables are accessed from outside the object by

     A) public member functions

     B) any function

     C) the dot operator

     D) the scope resolution operator

13.4   Assume that `RetailItem` is the name of a class, and the class has a `void` member function named `setPrice` which accepts a `double` argument. If `soap` is an instance of the `RetailItem` class, which of the following statements properly uses the `soap` object to call the `setPrice` member function?

     A) `RetailItem::setPrice(1.49);`

     B) `soap::setPrice(1.49);`

     C) `soap.setPrice(1.49);`

     D) `soap:setPrice(1.49);`

13.5   Complete the following code skeleton to declare a class named `Date`. The class should contain variables and functions to store and retrieve a date in the form 4/2/2010.

```
class Date
{
   private:


   public:


}
```

13.4 Why Have Private Members?

CONCEPT: In object-oriented programming, an object should protect its important data by making it private and providing a public interface to access that data.

You might be questioning the rationale behind making the member variables in the Rectangle class private. You might also be questioning why member functions were defined for such simple tasks as setting variables and getting their contents. After all, if the member variables were declared as public, the member functions wouldn't be needed.

As mentioned earlier in this chapter, classes usually have variables and functions that are meant only to be used internally. They are not intended to be accessed by statements outside the class. This protects critical data from being accidentally modified or used in a way that might adversely affect the state of the object. When a member variable is declared as private, the only way for an application to store values in the variable is through a public member function. Likewise, the only way for an application to retrieve the contents of a private member variable is through a public member function. In essence, the public members become an interface to the object. They are the only members that may be accessed by any application that uses the object.

In the Rectangle class, the width and length member variables hold critical data. Therefore they are declared as private and an interface is constructed with public member functions. If a program creates a Rectangle object, the program must use the setWidth and getWidth member functions to access the object's width member. To access the object's length member, the program must use the setLength and getLength member functions. This idea is illustrated in Figure 13-13.

Figure 13-13

The public member functions can be written to filter out invalid data. For example, look at the following version of the setWidth member function.

```
void Rectangle::setWidth(double w)
{
    if (w >= 0)
        width = w;
```

```
      else
      {
         cout << "Invalid width\n";
         exit(EXIT_FAILURE);
      }

   }
```

Notice that this version of the function doesn't just assign the parameter value to the width variable. It first tests the parameter to make sure it is 0 or greater. If a negative number was passed to the function, an error message is displayed and then the standard library function exit is called to abort the program. The setLength function could be written in a similar way:

```
   void Rectangle::setLength(double len)
   {
      if (len >= 0)
         length = len;
      else
      {
         cout << "Invalid length\n";
         exit(EXIT_FAILURE);
      }
   }
```

The point being made here is that mutator functions can do much more than simply store values in attributes. They can also validate those values to ensure that only acceptable data is stored in the object's attributes. Keep in mind, however, that calling the exit function, as we have done in these examples, is not the best way to deal with invalid data. There are more advanced techniques that professional programmers use for handling these types of errors, but those techniques are beyond the scope of this book. Because you are just starting to learn about classes and OOP, we will keep our code simple by using only rudimentary data validation techniques.

Focus on Software Engineering: Separating Class Specification from Implementation

13.5

CONCEPT: Usually class declarations are stored in their own header files. Member function definitions are stored in their own .cpp files.

In the programs we've looked at so far, the class declaration, member function definitions, and application program are all stored in one file. A more conventional way of designing C++ programs is to store class declarations and member function definitions in their own separate files. Typically, program components are stored in the following fashion:

- Class declarations are stored in their own header files. A header file that contains a class declaration is called a *class specification* file. The name of the class specification file is usually the same as the name of the class, with a .h extension. For example, the Rectangle class would be declared in the file Rectangle.h.

- The member function definitions for a class are stored in a separate .cpp file called the *class implementation* file. The file usually has the same name as the class, with the .cpp extension. For example, the Rectangle class's member functions would be defined in the file Rectangle.cpp.
- Any program that uses the class should #include the class's header file. The class's .cpp file (that which contains the member function definitions) should be compiled and linked with the main program. This process can be automated with a project or make utility. Integrated development environments such as Visual Studio also provide the means to create the multi-file projects.

Let's see how we could rewrite Program 13-1 using this design approach. First, the Rectangle class declaration would be stored in the following Rectangle.h file. (This file is stored in the Student Source Code Folder Chapter 13\Rectangle Version 1.)

Contents of Rectangle.h (Version 1)

```
1 // Specification file for the Rectangle class.
2 #ifndef RECTANGLE_H
3 #define RECTANGLE_H
4
5 // Rectangle class declaration.
6
7 class Rectangle
8 {
9    private:
10       double width;
11       double length;
12    public:
13       void setWidth(double);
14       void setLength(double);
15       double getWidth() const;
16       double getLength() const;
17       double getArea() const;
18 };
19
20 #endif
```

This is the specification file for the Rectangle class. It contains only the declaration of the Rectangle class. It does not contain any member function definitions. When we write other programs that use the Rectangle class, we can have an #include directive that includes this file. That way, we won't have to write the class declaration in every program that uses the Rectangle class.

This file also introduces two new preprocessor directives: #ifndef and #endif. The #ifndef directive that appears in line 2 is called an *include guard*. It prevents the header file from accidentally being included more than once. When your main program file has an #include directive for a header file, there is always the possibility that the header file will have an #include directive for a second header file. If your main program file also has an #include directive for the second header file, then the preprocessor will include the second header file twice. Unless an include guard has been written into the second header file, an error will occur because the compiler will process the declarations in the second header file twice. Let's see how an include guard works.

The word `ifndef` stands for "if not defined." It is used to determine whether a specific constant has not been defined with a `#define` directive. When the `Rectangle.h` file is being compiled, the `#ifndef` directive checks for the existence of a constant named `RECTANGLE_H`. If the constant has not been defined, it is immediately defined in line 3 and the rest of the file is included. If the constant has been defined, it means that the file has already been included. In that case, everything between the `#ifndef` and `#endif` directives is skipped. This is illustrated in Figure 13-14.

Figure 13-14

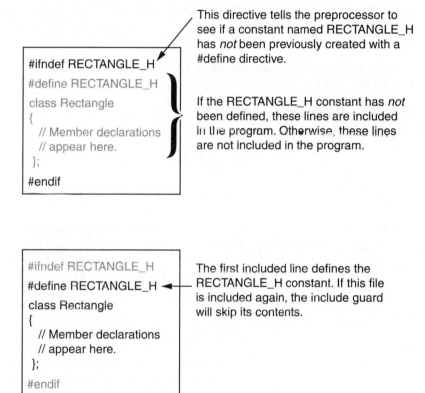

#ifndef RECTANGLE_H

This directive tells the preprocessor to see if a constant named RECTANGLE_H has *not* been previously created with a #define directive.

#define RECTANGLE_H
class Rectangle
{
   // Member declarations
   // appear here.
};
#endif

If the RECTANGLE_H constant has *not* been defined, these lines are included in the program. Otherwise, these lines are not included in the program.

#ifndef RECTANGLE_H
#define RECTANGLE_H
class Rectangle
{
   // Member declarations
   // appear here.
};
#endif

The first included line defines the RECTANGLE_H constant. If this file is included again, the include guard will skip its contents.

Next we need an implementation file that contains the class's member function definitions. The implementation file for the `Rectangle` class is `Rectangle.cpp`. (This file is stored in the Student Source Code Folder `Chapter 13\Rectangle Version 1`.)

Contents of `Rectangle.cpp` (Version 1)

```
1   // Implementation file for the Rectangle class.
2   #include "Rectangle.h"    // Needed for the Rectangle class
3   #include <iostream>       // Needed for cout
4   #include <cstdlib>        // Needed for the exit function
5   using namespace std;
6
7   //*********************************************************
8   // setWidth sets the value of the member variable width.   *
9   //*********************************************************
10
```

```
11  void Rectangle::setWidth(double w)
12  {
13     if (w >= 0)
14        width = w;
15     else
16     {
17        cout << "Invalid width\n";
18        exit(EXIT_FAILURE);
19     }
20  }
21
22  //************************************************************
23  // setLength sets the value of the member variable length.  *
24  //************************************************************
25
26  void Rectangle::setLength(double len)
27  {
28     if (len >= 0)
29        length = len;
30     else
31     {
32        cout << "Invalid length\n";
33        exit(EXIT_FAILURE);
34     }
35  }
36
37  //************************************************************
38  // getWidth returns the value in the member variable width. *
39  //************************************************************
40
41  double Rectangle::getWidth() const
42  {
43     return width;
44  }
45
46  //*************************************************************
47  // getLength returns the value in the member variable length. *
48  //*************************************************************
49
50  double Rectangle::getLength() const
51  {
52     return length;
53  }
54
55  //***********************************************************
56  // getArea returns the product of width times length.      *
57  //***********************************************************
58
59  double Rectangle::getArea() const
60  {
61     return width * length;
62  }
```

Look at line 2, which has the following #include directive:

```
#include "Rectangle.h"
```

This directive includes the Rectangle.h file, which contains the Rectangle class declaration. Notice that the name of the header file is enclosed in double-quote characters (" ") instead of angled brackets (< >). When you are including a C++ system header file, such as iostream, you enclose the name of the file in angled brackets. This indicates that the file is located in the compiler's *include file directory*. The include file directory is the directory or folder where all of the standard C++ header files are located. When you are including a header file that you have written, such as a class specification file, you enclose the name of the file in double-quote marks. This indicates that the file is located in the current project directory.

Any file that uses the Rectangle class must have an #include directive for the Rectangle.h file. We need to include Rectangle.h in the class specification file because the functions in this file belong to the Rectangle class. Before the compiler can process a function with Rectangle:: in its name, it must have already processed the Rectangle class declaration.

Now that we have the Rectangle class stored in its own specification and implementation files, we can see how to use them in a program. Program 13-4 shows a modified version of Program 13-1. This version of the program does not contain the Rectangle class declaration, or the definitions of any of the class's member functions. Instead, it is designed to be compiled and linked with the class specification and implementation files. (This file is stored in the Student Source Code Folder Chapter 13\Rectangle Version 1.)

Program 13-4

```
 1  // This program uses the Rectangle class, which is declared in
 2  // the Rectangle.h file. The member Rectangle class's member
 3  // functions are defined in the Rectangle.cpp file. This program
 4  // should be compiled with those files in a project.
 5  #include <iostream>
 6  #include "Rectangle.h"  // Needed for Rectangle class
 7  using namespace std;
 8
 9  int main()
10  {
11     Rectangle box;      // Define an instance of the Rectangle class
12     double rectWidth;   // Local variable for width
13     double rectLength;  // Local variable for length
14
15     // Get the rectangle's width and length from the user.
16     cout << "This program will calculate the area of a\n";
17     cout << "rectangle. What is the width? ";
18     cin >> rectWidth;
19     cout << "What is the length? ";
20     cin >> rectLength;
21
```

(program continues)

Program 13-4   *(continued)*

```
22      // Store the width and length of the rectangle
23      // in the box object.
24      box.setWidth(rectWidth);
25      box.setLength(rectLength);
26
27      // Display the rectangle's data.
28      cout << "Here is the rectangle's data:\n";
29      cout << "Width: " << box.getWidth() << endl;
30      cout << "Length: " << box.getLength() << endl;
31      cout << "Area: " << box.getArea() << endl;
32      return 0;
33  }
```

Notice that Program 13-4 has an #include directive for the Rectangle.h file in line 6. This causes the declaration for the Rectangle class to be included in the file. To create an executable program from this file, the following steps must be taken:

- The implementation file, Rectangle.cpp, must be compiled. Rectangle.cpp is not a complete program, so you cannot create an executable file from it alone. Instead, you compile Rectangle.cpp to an object file which contains the compiled code for the Rectangle class. This file would typically be named Rectangle.obj.
- The main program file, Pr13-4.cpp, must be compiled. This file is not a complete program either, because it does not contain any of the implementation code for the Rectangle class. So, you compile this file to an object file such as Pr13-4.obj.
- The object files, Pr13-4.obj and Rectangle.obj, are linked together to create an executable file, which would be named something like Pr13-4.exe.

This process is illustrated in Figure 13-15.

The exact details on how these steps take place are different for each C++ development system. Fortunately, most systems perform all of these steps automatically for you. For example, in Microsoft Visual C++ you create a project, and then you simply add all of the files to the project. When you compile the project, the steps are taken care of for you and an executable file is generated.

NOTE: Appendix L on the Student CD gives step-by-step instructions for creating multi-file projects in Microsoft Visual C++ 2008 Express Edition.

Separating a class into a specification file and an implementation file provides a great deal of flexibility. First, if you wish to give your class to another programmer, you don't have to share all of your source code with that programmer. You can give him or her the specification file and the compiled object file for the class's implementation. The other programmer simply inserts the necessary #include directive into his or her program, compiles it, and links it with your class's object file. This prevents the other programmer, who might not know all the details of your code, from making changes that will introduce bugs.

Figure 13-15

Separating a class into specification and implementation files also makes things easier when the class's member functions must be modified. It is only necessary to modify the implementation file and recompile it to a new object file. Programs that use the class don't have to be completely recompiled, just linked with the new object file.

13.6 Inline Member Functions

CONCEPT: When the body of a member function is written inside a class declaration, it is declared inline.

When the body of a member function is small, it is usually more convenient to place the function's definition, instead of its prototype, in the class declaration. For example, in the `Rectangle` class the member functions `getWidth`, `getLength`, and `getArea` each have only one statement. The `Rectangle` class could be revised as shown in the following listing. (This file is stored in the Student Source Code Folder `Chapter 13\Rectangle Version 2`.)

Contents of `Rectangle.h` (Version 2)

```
1   // Specification file for the Rectangle class
2   // This version uses some inline member functions.
3   #ifndef RECTANGLE_H
4   #define RECTANGLE_H
5
6   class Rectangle
7   {
8      private:
9         double width;
10        double length;
```

```
11      public:
12         void setWidth(double);
13         void setLength(double);
14
15         double getWidth() const
16            { return width; }
17
18         double getLength() const
19            { return length; }
20
21         double getArea() const
22            { return width * length; }
23   };
24   #endif
```

When a member function is defined in the declaration of a class, it is called an *inline function*. Notice that because the function definitions are part of the class, there is no need to use the scope resolution operator and class name in the function header.

Notice that the getWidth, getLength, and getArea functions are declared inline, but the setWidth and setLength functions are not. They are still defined outside the class declaration. The following listing shows the implementation file for the revised Rectangle class. (This file is also stored in the Student Source Code Folder Chapter 13\ Rectangle Version 2.)

Contents of `Rectangle.cpp` (Version 2)

```
1    // Implementation file for the Rectangle class.
2    // In this version of the class, the getWidth, getLength,
3    // and getArea functions are written inline in Rectangle.h.
4    #include "Rectangle.h"    // Needed for the Rectangle class
5    #include <iostream>       // Needed for cout
6    #include <cstdlib>        // Needed for the exit function
7    using namespace std;
8
9    //**********************************************************
10   // setWidth sets the value of the member variable width.   *
11   //**********************************************************
12
13   void Rectangle::setWidth(double w)
14   {
15      if (w >= 0)
16         width = w;
17      else
18      {
19         cout << "Invalid width\n";
20         exit(EXIT_FAILURE);
21      }
22   }
23
24   //**********************************************************
25   // setLength sets the value of the member variable length.  *
26   //**********************************************************
27
```

```
28   void Rectangle::setLength(double len)
29   {
30      if (len >= 0)
31         length = len;
32      else
33      {
34         cout << "Invalid length\n";
35         exit(EXIT_FAILURE);
36      }
37   }
```

Inline Functions and Performance

A lot goes on "behind the scenes" each time a function is called. A number of special items, such as the function's return address in the program and the values of arguments, are stored in a section of memory called the *stack*. In addition, local variables are created and a location is reserved for the function's return value. All this overhead, which sets the stage for a function call, takes precious CPU time. Although the time needed is minuscule, it can add up if a function is called many times, as in a loop.

Inline functions are compiled differently than other functions. In the executable code, inline functions aren't "called" in the conventional sense. In a process known as *inline expansion*, the compiler replaces the call to an inline function with the code of the function itself. This means that the overhead needed for a conventional function call isn't necessary for an inline function, and can result in improved performance.[*] Because the inline function's code can appear multiple times in the executable program, however, the size of the program can increase.[†]

 Checkpoint

13.6   Why would you declare a class's member variables `private`?

13.7   When a class's member variables are declared `private`, how does code outside the class store values in, or retrieve values from, the member variables?

13.8   What is a class specification file? What is a class implementation file?

13.9   What is the purpose of an include guard?

13.10   Assume the following class components exist in a program:

BasePay class declaration
BasePay member function definitions
Overtime class declaration
Overtime member function definitions

In what files would you store each of these components?

13.11   What is an inline member function?

---

[*] Because inline functions cause code to increase in size, they can decrease performance on systems that use paging.
[†] Writing a function inline is a request to the compiler. The compiler will ignore the request if inline expansion is not possible or practical.

13.7   Constructors

CONCEPT: A constructor is a member function that is automatically called when a class object is created.

A constructor is a member function that has the same name as the class. It is automatically called when the object is created in memory, or instantiated. It is helpful to think of constructors as initialization routines. They are very useful for initializing member variables or performing other setup operations.

To illustrate how constructors work, look at this Demo class declaration:

```
class Demo
{
public:
    Demo(); // Constructor
};

Demo::Demo()
{
    cout << "Welcome to the constructor!\n";
}
```

The class Demo only has one member: a function also named Demo. This function is the constructor. When an instance of this class is defined, the function Demo is automatically called. This is illustrated in Program 13-5.

Program 13-5

```
 1  // This program demonstrates a constructor.
 2  #include <iostream>
 3  using namespace std;
 4
 5  // Demo class declaration.
 6
 7  class Demo
 8  {
 9  public:
10      Demo();        // Constructor
11  };
12
13  Demo::Demo()
14  {
15      cout << "Welcome to the constructor!\n";
16  }
17
```

```
18   //*****************************************
19   // Function main.                         *
20   //*****************************************
21
22   int main()
23   {
24       Demo demoObject;   // Define a Demo object;
25
26       cout << "This program demonstrates an object\n";
27       cout << "with a constructor.\n";
28       return 0;
29   }
```

Program Output

```
Welcome to the constructor!
This program demonstrates an object
with a constructor.
```

Notice that the constructor's function header looks different than that of a regular member function. There is no return type—not even void. This is because constructors are not executed by explicit function calls and cannot return a value. The function header of a constructor's external definition takes the following form:

> *ClassName*::*ClassName*(*ParameterList*)

In the general format, *ClassName* is the name of the class and *ParameterList* is an optional list of parameter variable declarations.

In Program 13-5, demoObject's constructor executes automatically when the object is defined. Because the object is defined before the cout statements in function main, the constructor displays its message first. Suppose we had defined the Demo object between two cout statements, as shown here.

```
cout << "This is displayed before the object is created.\n";
Demo demoObject;// Define a Demo object.
cout << "\nThis is displayed after the object is created.\n";
```

This code would produce the following output:

```
This is displayed before the object is created.
Welcome to the constructor!
This is displayed after the object is created.
```

This simple Demo example illustrates when a constructor executes. More importantly, you should understand why a class should have a constructor. A constructor's purpose is to initialize an object's attributes. Because the constructor executes as soon as the object is created, it can initialize the object's data members to valid values before those members are used by other code. It is a good practice to always write a constructor for every class.

For example, the `Rectangle` class that we looked at earlier could benefit from having a constructor. A program could define a `Rectangle` object and then use that object to call the `getArea` function before any values were stored in `width` and `length`. Because the `width` and `length` member variables are not initialized, the function would return garbage. The following code shows a better version of the `Rectangle` class, equipped with a constructor. The constructor initializes both `width` and `length` to 0.0. (These files are stored in the Student Source Code Folder `Chapter 13\Rectangle Version 3`.)

Contents of `Rectangle.h` (Version 3)

```
 1  // Specification file for the Rectangle class
 2  // This version has a constructor.
 3  #ifndef RECTANGLE_H
 4  #define RECTANGLE_H
 5
 6  class Rectangle
 7  {
 8     private:
 9        double width;
10        double length;
11     public:
12        Rectangle();              // Constructor
13        void setWidth(double);
14        void setLength(double);
15
16        double getWidth() const
17           { return width; }
18
19        double getLength() const
20           { return length; }
21
22        double getArea() const
23           { return width * length; }
24  };
25  #endif
```

Contents of `Rectangle.cpp` (Version 3)

```
 1  // Implementation file for the Rectangle class.
 2  // This version has a constructor.
 3  #include "Rectangle.h"   // Needed for the Rectangle class
 4  #include <iostream>      // Needed for cout
 5  #include <cstdlib>       // Needed for the exit function
 6  using namespace std;
 7
 8  //***********************************************************
 9  // The constructor initializes width and length to 0.0.     *
10  //***********************************************************
11
12  Rectangle::Rectangle()
13  {
14     width = 0.0;
15     length = 0.0;
16  }
```

```
17
18   //**********************************************************
19   // setWidth sets the value of the member variable width.    *
20   //**********************************************************
21
22   void Rectangle::setWidth(double w)
23   {
24      if (w >= 0)
25         width = w;
26      else
27      {
28         cout << "Invalid width\n";
29         exit(EXIT_FAILURE);
30      }
31   }
32
33   //**********************************************************
34   // setLength sets the value of the member variable length.  *
35   //**********************************************************
36
37   void Rectangle::setLength(double len)
38   {
39      if (len >= 0)
40         length = len;
41      else
42      {
43         cout << "Invalid length\n";
44         exit(EXIT_FAILURE);
45      }
46   }
```

Program 13-6 demonstrates this new version of the class. It creates a `Rectangle` object and then displays the values returned by the `getWidth`, `getLength`, and `getArea` member functions. (This file is also stored in the Student Source Code Folder `Chapter 13\Rectangle Version 3`.)

Program 13-6

```
1    // This program uses the Rectangle class's constructor.
2    #include <iostream>
3    #include "Rectangle.h"  // Needed for Rectangle class
4    using namespace std;
5
6    int main()
7    {
8       Rectangle box;      // Define an instance of the Rectangle class
9
10      // Display the rectangle's data.
11      cout << "Here is the rectangle's data:\n";
12      cout << "Width: " << box.getWidth() << endl;
13      cout << "Length: " << box.getLength() << endl;
14      cout << "Area: " << box.getArea() << endl;
15      return 0;
16   }
```

(program output continues)

Program 13-6   *(continued)*

Program Output
```
Here is the rectangle's data:
Width: 0
Length: 0
Area: 0
```

The Default Constructor

All of the examples we have looked at in this section demonstrate default constructors. A *default constructor* is a constructor that takes no arguments. Like regular functions, constructors may accept arguments, have default arguments, be declared inline, and be overloaded. We will see examples of these as we progress through the chapter.

If you write a class with no constructor whatsoever, when the class is compiled C++ will automatically write a default constructor that does nothing. For example, the first version of the `Rectangle` class had no constructor; so, when the class was compiled C++ generated the following constructor:

```
Rectangle::Rectangle()
{ }
```

Default Constructors and Dynamically Allocated Objects

Earlier we discussed how class objects may be dynamically allocated in memory. For example, assume the following pointer is defined in a program:

```
Rectangle *rectPtr;
```

This statement defines `rectPtr` as a `Rectangle` pointer. It can hold the address of any `Rectangle` object. But because this statement does not actually create a `Rectangle` object, the constructor does not execute. Suppose we use the pointer in a statement that dynamically allocates a `Rectangle` object, as shown in the following code.

```
rectPtr = new Rectangle;
```

This statement creates a `Rectangle` object. When the `Rectangle` object is created by the new operator, its default constructor is automatically executed.

13.8 Passing Arguments to Constructors

CONCEPT: A constructor can have parameters, and can accept arguments when an object is created.

Constructors may accept arguments in the same way as other functions. When a class has a constructor that accepts arguments, you can pass initialization values to the constructor when you create an object. For example, the following code shows yet another version of the `Rectangle` class. This version has a constructor that accepts arguments for the rectangle's width and length. (These files are stored in the Student Source Code Folder `Chapter 13\Rectangle Version 4`.)

Contents of `Rectangle.h` (Version 4)

```
 1   // Specification file for the Rectangle class
 2   // This version has a constructor.
 3   #ifndef RECTANGLE_H
 4   #define RECTANGLE_H
 5
 6   class Rectangle
 7   {
 8      private:
 9         double width;
10         double length;
11      public:
12         Rectangle(double, double);   // Constructor
13         void setWidth(double);
14         void setLength(double);
15
16         double getWidth() const
17            { return width; }
18
19         double getLength() const
20            { return length; }
21
22         double getArea() const
23            { return width * length; }
24   };
25   #endif
```

Contents of `Rectangle.cpp` (Version 4)

```
 1   // Implementation file for the Rectangle class.
 2   // This version has a constructor that accepts arguments.
 3   #include "Rectangle.h"   // Needed for the Rectangle class
 4   #include <iostream>      // Needed for cout
 5   #include <cstdlib>       // Needed for the exit function
 6   using namespace std;
 7
 8   //************************************************************
 9   // The constructor accepts arguments for width and length.  *
10   //************************************************************
11
12   Rectangle::Rectangle(double w, double len)
13   {
14      width = w;
15      length = len;
16   }
17
18   //************************************************************
19   // setWidth sets the value of the member variable width.    *
20   //************************************************************
21
22   void Rectangle::setWidth(double w)
23   {
24      if (w >= 0)
25         width = w;
```

```
26         else
27         {
28            cout << "Invalid width\n";
29            exit(EXIT_FAILURE);
30         }
31    }
32
33    //**********************************************************
34    // setLength sets the value of the member variable length.  *
35    //**********************************************************
36
37    void Rectangle::setLength(double len)
38    {
39       if (len >= 0)
40          length = len;
41       else
42       {
43          cout << "Invalid length\n";
44          exit(EXIT_FAILURE);
45       }
46    }
```

The constructor, which appears in lines 12 through 16 of `Rectangle.cpp`, accepts two arguments, which are passed into the w and len parameters. The parameters are assigned to the `width` and `length` member variables. Because the constructor is automatically called when a `Rectangle` object is created, the arguments are passed to the constructor as part of the object definition. Here is an example:

```
Rectangle box(10.0, 12.0);
```

This statement defines `box` as an instance of the `Rectangle` class. The constructor is called with the value 10.0 passed into the w parameter and 12.0 passed into the len parameter. As a result, the object's `width` member variable will be assigned 10.0 and the `length` member variable will be assigned 12.0. This is illustrated in Figure 13-16.

Figure 13-16

```
Rectangle box(10.0, 12.0);
```

The box object is initialized with `width` set to 10.0 and `length` set to 12.0

width: 10.0
length: 12.0

Program 13-7 demonstrates the class. (This file is also stored in the Student Source Code Folder `Chapter 13\Rectangle Version 4`.)

Program 13-7

```
 1   // This program calls the Rectangle class constructor.
 2   #include <iostream>
 3   #include <iomanip>
 4   #include "Rectangle.h"
 5   using namespace std;
 6
 7   int main()
 8   {
 9      double houseWidth,    // To hold the room width
10             houseLength;   // To hold the room length
11
12      // Get the width of the house.
13      cout << "In feet, how wide is your house? ";
14      cin >> houseWidth;
15
16      // Get the length of the house.
17      cout << "In feet, how long is your house? ";
18      cin >> houseLength;
19
20      // Create a Rectangle object.
21      Rectangle house(houseWidth, houseLength);
22
23      // Display the house's width, length, and area.
24      cout << setprecision(2) << fixed;
25      cout << "The house is " << house.getWidth()
26           << " feet wide.\n";
27      cout << "The house is " << house.getLength()
28           << " feet long.\n";
29      cout << "The house is " << house.getArea()
30           << " square feet in area.\n";
31      return 0;
32   }
```

Program Output with Example Input Shown in Bold
```
In feet, how wide is your house? 30 [Enter]
In feet, how long is your house? 60 [Enter]
The house is 30.00 feet wide.
The house is 60.00 feet long.
The house is 1800.00 square feet in area.
```

The statement in line 21 creates a Rectangle object, passing the values in houseWidth and houseLength as arguments.

The following code shows another example: the Sale class. This class might be used in a retail environment where sales transactions take place. An object of the Sale class represents the sale of an item. (This file is stored in the Student Source Code Folder Chapter 13\ Sale Version 1.)

Contents of `Sale.h` (Version 1)

```
1   // Specification file for the Sale class.
2   #ifndef SALE_H
3   #define SALE_H
4
5   class Sale
6   {
7   private:
8      double itemCost;      // Cost of the item
9      double taxRate;       // Sales tax rate
10  public:
11     Sale(double cost, double rate)
12        { itemCost = cost;
13          taxRate = rate; }
14
15     double getItemCost() const
16        { return itemCost; }
17
18     double getTaxRate() const
19        { return taxRate; }
20
21     double getTax() const
22        { return (itemCost * taxRate); }
23
24     double getTotal() const
25        { return (itemCost + getTax()); }
26  };
27  #endif
```

The `itemCost` member variable, declared in line 8, holds the selling price of the item. The `taxRate` member variable, declared in line 9, holds the sales tax rate. The constructor appears in lines 11 through 13. Notice that the constructor is written inline. It accepts two arguments, the item cost and the sales tax rate. These arguments are used to initialize the `itemCost` and `taxRate` member variables. The `getItemCost` member function, in lines 15 through 16, returns the value in `itemCost`, and the `getTaxRate` member function, in lines 18 through 19, returns the value in `taxRate`. The `getTax` member function, in lines 21 through 22, calculates and returns the amount of sales tax for the purchase. The `getTotal` member function, in lines 24 through 25, calculates and returns the total of the sale. The total is the item cost plus the sales tax. Program 13-8 demonstrates the class. (This file is stored in the Student Source Code Folder `Chapter 13\Sale Version 1`.)

Program 13-8

```
1   // This program demonstrates passing an argument to a constructor.
2   #include <iostream>
3   #include <iomanip>
4   #include "Sale.h"
5   using namespace std;
6
```

```
 7   int main()
 8   {
 9      const double TAX_RATE = 0.06;   // 6 percent sales tax rate
10      double cost;                    // To hold the item cost
11
12      // Get the cost of the item.
13      cout << "Enter the cost of the item: ";
14      cin >> cost;
15
16      // Create a Sale object for this transaction.
17      Sale itemSale(cost, TAX_RATE);
18
19      // Set numeric output formatting.
20      cout << fixed << showpoint << setprecision(2);
21
22      // Display the sales tax and total.
23      cout << "The amount of sales tax is $"
24           << itemSale.getTax() << endl;
25      cout << "The total of the sale is $";
26      cout << itemSale.getTotal() << endl;
27      return 0;
28   }
```

Program Output with Example Input Shown in Bold

```
Enter the cost of the item: 10.00 [Enter]
The amount of sales tax is $0.60
The total of the sale is $10.60
```

In the example run of the program the user enters 10.00 as the cost of the item. This value is stored in the local variable cost. In line 17 the itemSale object is created. The values of the cost variable and the TAX_RATE constant are passed as arguments to the constructor. As a result, the object's cost member variable is initialized with the value 10.0 and the rate member variable is initialized with the value 0.06. This is illustrated in Figure 13-17.

Figure 13-17

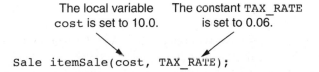

The local variable cost is set to 10.0.   The constant TAX_RATE is set to 0.06.

Sale itemSale(cost, TAX_RATE);

The itemSale object is initialized with the cost member set to 10.0 and the rate member set to 0.06

cost: 10.0
rate: 0.06

Using Default Arguments with Constructors

Like other functions, constructors may have default arguments. Recall from Chapter 6 that default arguments are passed to parameters automatically if no argument is provided in the function call. The default value is listed in the parameter list of the function's declaration or the function header. The following code shows a modified version of the Sale class. This version's constructor uses a default argument for the tax rate. (This file is stored in the Student Source Code Folder Chapter 13\Sale Version 2.)

Contents of `Sale.h` (Version 2)

```
 1   // This version of the Sale class uses a default argument
 2   // in the constructor.
 3   #ifndef SALE_H
 4   #define SALE_H
 5
 6   class Sale
 7   {
 8   private:
 9      double itemCost;      // Cost of the item
10      double taxRate;       // Sales tax rate
11   public:
12      Sale(double cost, double rate = 0.05)
13         { itemCost = cost;
14            taxRate = rate; }
15
16      double getItemCost() const
17         { return itemCost; }
18
19      double getTaxRate() const
20         { return taxRate; }
21
22      double getTax() const
23         { return (itemCost * taxRate); }
24
25      double getTotal() const
26         { return (itemCost + getTax()); }
27   };
28   #endif
```

If an object of this Sale class is defined with only one argument (for the cost parameter) passed to the constructor, the default argument 0.05 will be provided for the rate parameter. This is demonstrated in Program 13-9. (This file is stored in the Student Source Code Folder Chapter 13\Sale Version 2.)

Program 13-9

```
1   // This program uses a constructor's default argument.
2   #include <iostream>
3   #include <iomanip>
4   #include "Sale.h"
5   using namespace std;
6
```

```
 7   int main()
 8   {
 9      double cost;    // To hold the item cost
10
11      // Get the cost of the item.
12      cout << "Enter the cost of the item: ";
13      cin >> cost;
14
15      // Create a Sale object for this transaction.
16      // Specify the item cost, but use the default
17      // tax rate of 5 percent.
18      Sale itemSale(cost);
19
20      // Set numeric output formatting.
21      cout << fixed << showpoint << setprecision(2);
22
23      // Display the sales tax and total.
24      cout << "The amount of sales tax is $"
25           << itemSale.getTax() << endl;
26      cout << "The total of the sale is $";
27      cout << itemSale.getTotal() << endl;
28      return 0;
29   }
```

Program Output with Example Input Shown in Bold
```
Enter the cost of the item: 10.00 [Enter]
The amount of sales tax is $0.50
The total of the sale is $10.50
```

More About the Default Constructor

It was mentioned earlier that when a constructor doesn't accept arguments, it is known as the default constructor. If a constructor has default arguments for all its parameters, it can be called with no explicit arguments. It then becomes the default constructor. For example, suppose the constructor for the Sale class had been written as the following:

```
Sale(double cost = 0.0, double rate = 0.05)
  { itemCost = cost;
     taxRate = rate; }
```

This constructor has default arguments for each of its parameters. As a result, the constructor can be called with no arguments, as shown here:

```
Sale itemSale;
```

This statement defines a Sale object. No arguments were passed to the constructor, so the default arguments for both parameters are used. Because this constructor can be called with no arguments, it is the default constructor.

Classes with No Default Constructor

When all of a class's constructors require arguments, then the class does not have a default constructor. In such a case you must pass the required arguments to the constructor when creating an object. Otherwise, a compiler error will result.

13.9   Destructors

CONCEPT: A destructor is a member function that is automatically called when an object is destroyed.

Destructors are member functions with the same name as the class, preceded by a tilde character (~). For example, the destructor for the Rectangle class would be named ~Rectangle.

Destructors are automatically called when an object is destroyed. In the same way that constructors set things up when an object is created, destructors perform shutdown procedures when the object goes out of existence. For example, a common use of destructors is to free memory that was dynamically allocated by the class object.

Program 13-10 shows a simple class with a constructor and a destructor. It illustrates when, during the program's execution, each is called.

Program 13-10

```
 1   // This program demonstrates a destructor.
 2   #include <iostream>
 3   using namespace std;
 4
 5   class Demo
 6   {
 7   public:
 8      Demo();      // Constructor
 9      ~Demo();     // Destructor
10   };
11
12   Demo::Demo()
13   {
14      cout << "Welcome to the constructor!\n";
15   }
16
17   Demo::~Demo()
18   {
19      cout << "The destructor is now running.\n";
20   }
21
```

```
22   //*********************************************
23   // Function main.                             *
24   //*********************************************
25
26   int main()
27   {
28      Demo demoObject;  // Define a demo object;
29
30      cout << "This program demonstrates an object\n";
31      cout << "with a constructor and destructor.\n";
32      return 0;
33   }
```

Program Output

```
Welcome to the constructor!
This program demonstrates an object
with a constructor and destructor.
The destructor is now running.
```

The following code shows a more practical example of a class with a destructor. The InventoryItem class holds the following data about an item that is stored in inventory:

- The item's description
- The item's cost
- The number of units in inventory

The constructor accepts arguments for all three items. The description is passed as a pointer to a C-string. Rather than storing the description in a char array with a fixed size, the constructor gets the length of the C-string and dynamically allocates just enough memory to hold it. The destructor frees the allocated memory when the object is destroyed. (This file is stored in the Student Source Code Folder Chapter 13\ InventoryItem Version 1.)

Contents of InventoryItem.h (Version 1)

```
1    // Specification file for the InventoryItem class.
2    #ifndef INVENTORYITEM_H
3    #define INVENTORYITEM_H
4    #include <cstring>   // Needed for strlen and strcpy
5
6    // InventoryItem class declaration.
7    class InventoryItem
8    {
9    private:
10      char *description;  // The item description
11      double cost;        // The item cost
12      int units;          // Number of units on hand
```

```
13   public:
14       // Constructor
15       InventoryItem(char *desc, double c, int u)
16          { // Allocate just enough memory for the description.
17             description = new char [strlen(desc) + 1];
18
19             // Copy the description to the allocated memory.
20             strcpy(description, desc);
21
22             // Assign values to cost and units.
23             cost = c;
24             units = u;}
25
26       // Destructor
27       ~InventoryItem()
28          { delete [] description; }
29
30       const char *getDescription() const
31          { return description; }
32
33       double getCost() const
34          { return cost; }
35
36       int getUnits() const
37          { return units; }
38   };
39   #endif
```

Notice that the return type of the getDescription function in lines 30 through 31 is const char *. This means that the function returns a pointer to a constant char. This is a security measure. It prevents any code that calls the function from changing the string that the pointer points to.

Program 13-11 demonstrates the class. (This file is also stored in the Student Source Code Folder Chapter 13\InventoryItem Version 1.)

Program 13-11

```
1   // This program demonstrates a class with a destructor.
2   #include <iostream>
3   #include <iomanip>
4   #include "InventoryItem.h"
5   using namespace std;
6
7   int main()
8   {
9       // Define an InventoryItem object with the following data:
10      // Description: Wrench   Cost: 8.75    Units on hand: 20
11      InventoryItem stock("Wrench", 8.75, 20);
12
13      // Set numeric output formatting.
14      cout << setprecision(2) << fixed << showpoint;
15
```

```
16      // Display the object's data.
17      cout << "Item Description: " << stock.getDescription() << endl;
18      cout << "Cost: $" << stock.getCost() << endl;
19      cout << "Units on hand: " << stock.getUnits() << endl;
20      return 0;
21  }
```

Program Output
```
Item Description: Wrench
Cost: $8.75
Units on hand: 20
```

In addition to the fact that destructors are automatically called when an object is destroyed, the following points should be mentioned:

- Like constructors, destructors have no return type.
- Destructors cannot accept arguments, so they never have a parameter list.

Destructors and Dynamically Allocated Class Objects

If a class object has been dynamically allocated by the new operator, its memory should be released when the object is no longer needed. For example, in the following code objectPtr is a pointer to a dynamically allocated InventoryItem class object.

```
// Define an InventoryItem pointer.
InventoryItem *objectPtr;

// Dynamically create an InventoryItem object.
objectPtr = new InventoryItem("Wrench", 8.75, 20);
```

The following statement shows the delete operator being used to destroy the dynamically created object.

```
delete objectPtr;
```

When the object pointed to by objectPtr is destroyed, its destructor is automatically called.

 Checkpoint

13.12   Briefly describe the purpose of a constructor.

13.13   Briefly describe the purpose of a destructor.

13.14   A member function that is never declared with a return data type, but that may have arguments is
   A) The constructor
   B) The destructor
   C) Both the constructor and the destructor
   D) Neither the constructor nor the destructor

13.15 A member function that is never declared with a return data type and can never have arguments is

A) The constructor

B) The destructor

C) Both the constructor and the destructor

D) Neither the constructor nor the destructor

13.16 Destructor function names always start with

A) A number

B) Tilde character (~)

C) A data type name

D) None of the above

13.17 A constructor that requires no arguments is called

A) A default constructor

B) An overloaded constructor

C) A null constructor

D) None of the above

13.18 TRUE or FALSE: Constructors are never declared with a return data type.

13.19 TRUE or FALSE: Destructors are never declared with a return type.

13.20 TRUE or FALSE: Destructors may take any number of arguments.

13.10 Overloading Constructors

CONCEPT: A class can have more than one constructor.

Recall from Chapter 6 that when two or more functions share the same name, the function is said to be overloaded. Multiple functions with the same name may exist in a C++ program, as long as their parameter lists are different.

A class's member functions may be overloaded, including the constructor. One constructor might take an integer argument, for example, while another constructor takes a `double`. There could even be a third constructor taking two integers. As long as each constructor takes a different list of parameters, the compiler can tell them apart. For example, the `string` class, which was introduced in Chapter 10, has several overloaded constructors. The following statement creates a `string` object with no arguments passed to the constructor:

```
string str;
```

This executes the `string` class's default constructor, which stores an empty string in the object. Another way to create a `string` object is to pass a string literal as an argument to the constructor, as shown here:

```
string str("Hello");
```

This executes an overloaded constructor, which stores the string "Hello" in the object.

A new version of the `InventoryItem` class appears in the following code listing with three constructors. To simplify the code listing, all the member functions are written inline. (This file is stored in the Student Source Code Folder `Chapter 13\InventoryItem Version 2`.)

Contents of `InventoryItem.h` (Version 2)

```
1   // This class has overloaded constructors.
2   #ifndef INVENTORYITEM_H
3   #define INVENTORYITEM_H
4   #include <cstring>   // Needed for strlen and strcpy
5
6   // Constant for the description's default size
7   const int DEFAULT_SIZE = 51;
8
9   class InventoryItem
10  {
11  private:
12     char *description;   // The item description
13     double cost;         // The item cost
14     int units;           // Number of units on hand
15  public:
16     // Constructor #1
17     InventoryItem()
18        { // Allocate the default amount of memory for description.
19          description = new char [DEFAULT_SIZE];
20
21          // Store a null terminator in the first character.
22          *description = '\0';
23
24          // Initialize cost and units.
25          cost = 0.0;
26          units = 0; }
27
28     // Constructor #2
29     InventoryItem(char *desc)
30        { // Allocate just enough memory for the description.
31          description = new char [strlen(desc) + 1];
32
33          // Copy the description to the allocated memory.
34          strcpy(description, desc);
35
36          // Initialize cost and units.
37          cost = 0.0;
38          units = 0; }
39
40     // Constructor #3
41     InventoryItem(char *desc, double c, int u)
42        { // Allocate just enough memory for the description.
43          description = new char [strlen(desc) + 1];
44
45          // Copy the description to the allocated memory.
46          strcpy(description, desc);
47
```

```
48              // Assign values to cost and units.
49              cost = c;
50              units = u; }
51
52          // Destructor
53          ~InventoryItem()
54              { delete [] description; }
55
56          // Mutator functions
57          void setDescription(char *d)
58              { strcpy(description, d); }
59
60          void setCost(double c)
61              { cost = c; }
62
63          void setUnits(int u)
64              { units = u; }
65
66          // Accessor functions
67          const char *getDescription() const
68              { return description; }
69
70          double getCost() const
71              { return cost; }
72
73          int getUnits() const
74              { return units; }
75      };
76      #endif
```

The first constructor appears in lines 17 through 26. It takes no arguments, so it is the default constructor. It dynamically allocates a block of memory large enough to hold 51 characters and stores the address of the block in the description pointer. The cost and units variables are initialized to 0.

The second constructor appears in lines 29 through 38. This constructor accepts only one argument, a pointer to the item description. The cost and units variables are initialized to 0.

The third constructor appears in lines 41 through 50. This constructor, which is the same one that appeared in the first version of the class, accepts arguments for the description, cost, and units.

We have also added mutator functions that set values for description, cost, and units. Program 13-12 demonstrates the class. (This file is also stored in the Student Source Code Folder Chapter 13\InventoryItem Version 2.)

Program 13-12

```
1   // This program demonstrates a class with overloaded constructors.
2   #include <iostream>
3   #include <iomanip>
4   #include "InventoryItem.h"
5   using namespace std;
6
```

```
 7   int main()
 8   {
 9       // Create an InventoryItem object and call
10       // the default constructor.
11       InventoryItem item1;
12       item1.setDescription("Hammer"); // Set the description
13       item1.setCost(6.95);            // Set the cost
14       item1.setUnits(12);             // Set the units
15
16       // Create an InventoryItem object and call
17       // constructor #2.
18       InventoryItem item2("Pliers");
19
20       // Create an InventoryItem object and call
21       // constructor #3.
22       InventoryItem item3("Wrench", 8.75, 20);
23
24       cout << "The following items are in inventory:\n";
25       cout << setprecision(2) << fixed << showpoint;
26
27       // Display the data for item 1.
28       cout << "Description: " << item1.getDescription() << endl;
29       cout << "Cost: $" << item1.getCost() << endl;
30       cout << "Units on Hand: " << item1.getUnits() << endl << endl;
31
32       // Display the data for item 2.
33       cout << "Description: " << item2.getDescription() << endl;
34       cout << "Cost: $" << item2.getCost() << endl;
35       cout << "Units on Hand: " << item2.getUnits() << endl << endl;
36
37       // Display the data for item 3.
38       cout << "Description: " << item3.getDescription() << endl;
39       cout << "Cost: $" << item3.getCost() << endl;
40       cout << "Units on Hand: " << item3.getUnits() << endl;
41       return 0;
42   }
```

Program Output
```
The following items are in inventory:
Description: Hammer
Cost: $6.95
Units on Hand: 12

Description: Pliers
Cost: $0.00
Units on Hand: 0

Description: Wrench
Cost: $8.75
Units on Hand: 20
```

Only One Default Constructor and One Destructor

When an object is defined without an argument list for its constructor, the compiler automatically calls the default constructor. For this reason, a class may have only one default constructor. If there were more than one constructor that could be called without an argument, the compiler would not know which one to call by default.

Remember, a constructor whose parameters all have a default argument is considered a default constructor. It would be an error to create a constructor that accepts no parameters along with another constructor that has default arguments for all its parameters. In such a case the compiler would not be able to resolve which constructor to execute.

Classes may also only have one destructor. Because destructors take no arguments, the compiler has no way to distinguish different destructors.

Other Overloaded Member Functions

Member functions other than constructors can also be overloaded. This can be useful because sometimes you need several different ways to perform the same operation. For example, in the `InventoryItem` class we could have overloaded the `setCost` function as shown here:

```
void setCost(double c)
   { cost = c; }

void setCost(char *c)
   { cost = atof(c); }
```

The first version of the function accepts a `double` argument and assigns it to `cost`. The second version of the function accepts a `char` pointer. This could be used where you have the cost of the item stored in a string. The function calls the `atof` function to convert the string to a `double`, and assigns its value to `cost`.

13.11 Private Member Functions

CONCEPT: A private member function may only be called from a function that is a member of the same class.

Sometimes a class will contain one or more member functions that are necessary for internal processing, but should not be called by code outside the class. For example, a class might have a member function that performs a calculation only when a value is stored in a particular member variable, and should not be performed at any other time. That function should not be directly accessible by code outside the class because it might get called at the wrong time. In this case, the member function should be declared `private`. When a member function is declared `private`, it may only be called internally.

For example, consider the following version of the `InventoryItem` class. (This file is stored in the Student Source Code Folder `Chapter 13\InventoryItem Version 3`.)

Contents of `InventoryItem.h` (Version 3)

```cpp
1    // This class has a private member function.
2    #ifndef INVENTORYITEM_H
3    #define INVENTORYITEM_H
4    #include <cstring>    // Needed for strlen and strcpy
5
6    // Constant for the description's default size
7    const int DEFAULT_SIZE = 51;
8
9    class InventoryItem
10   {
11   private:
12      char *description;   // The item description
13      double cost;         // The item cost
14      int units;           // Number of units on hand
15
16      // Private member function.
17      void createDescription(int size, char *value)
18         { // Allocate the default amount of memory for description.
19            description = new char [size];
20
21            // Store a value in the memory.
22            strcpy(description, value); }
23
24   public:
25      // Constructor #1
26      InventoryItem()
27         { // Store an empty string in the description
28            // attribute.
29            createDescription(DEFAULT_SIZE, "");
30
31            // Initialize cost and units.
32            cost = 0.0;
33            units = 0; }
34
35      // Constructor #2
36      InventoryItem(char *desc)
37         { // Allocate memory and store the description.
38            createDescription(strlen(desc), desc);
39
40            // Initialize cost and units.
41            cost = 0.0;
42            units = 0; }
43
44      // Constructor #3
45      InventoryItem(char *desc, double c, int u)
46         { // Allocate memory and store the description.
47            createDescription(strlen(desc), desc);
48
49            // Assign values to cost and units.
50            cost = c;
51            units = u; }
52
```

```
53      // Destructor
54      ~InventoryItem()
55         { delete [] description; }
56
57      // Mutator functions
58      void setDescription(char *d)
59         { strcpy(description, d); }
60
61      void setCost(double c)
62         { cost = c; }
63
64      void setUnits(int u)
65         { units = u; }
66
67      // Accessor functions
68      const char *getDescription() const
69         { return description; }
70
71      double getCost() const
72         { return cost; }
73
74      int getUnits() const
75         { return units; }
76   };
77   #endif
```

This version of the class has a private member function named `createDescription`. The purpose of the function is to allocate a specified amount of memory for the `description` pointer and copy a string to the allocated memory. The function is called from all three of the constructors. You can see why this function should be private. If it were ever called by code outside the class, the value already stored for the item description would be lost.

13.12 Arrays of Objects

CONCEPT: You may define and work with arrays of class objects.

As with any other data type in C++, you can define arrays of class objects. An array of `InventoryItem` objects could be created to represent a business's inventory records. Here is an example of such a definition:

```
InventoryItem inventory[40];
```

This statement defines an array of 40 `InventoryItem` objects. The name of the array is `inventory`, and the default constructor is called for each object in the array.

If you wish to define an array of objects and call a constructor that requires arguments, you must specify the arguments for each object individually in an initializer list. Here is an example:

```
InventoryItem inventory[3] = {"Hammer", "Wrench", "Pliers"};
```

The compiler treats each item in the initializer list as an argument for an array element's constructor. Recall that the second constructor in the InventoryItem class declaration takes the item description as an argument. So, this statement defines an array of three objects and calls that constructor for each object. The constructor for inventory[0] is called with "Hammer" as its argument, the constructor for inventory[1] is called with "Wrench" as its argument, and the constructor for inventory[2] is called with "Pliers" as its argument.

WARNING! If the class does not have a default constructor you must provide an initializer for each object in the array.

If a constructor requires more than one argument, the initializer must take the form of a function call. For example, look at the following definition statement.

```
InventoryItem inventory[3] = { InventoryItem("Hammer", 6.95, 12),
                               InventoryItem("Wrench", 8.75, 20),
                               InventoryItem("Pliers", 3.75, 10) };
```

This statement calls the third constructor in the InventoryItem class declaration for each object in the inventory array.

It isn't necessary to call the same constructor for each object in an array. For example, look at the following statement.

```
InventoryItem inventory[3] = { "Hammer",
                               InventoryItem("Wrench", 8.75, 20),
                               "Pliers" };
```

This statement calls the second constructor for inventory[0] and inventory[2], and calls the third constructor for inventory[1].

If you do not provide an initializer for all of the objects in an array, the default constructor will be called for each object that does not have an initializer. For example, the following statement defines an array of three objects, but only provides initializers for the first two. The default constructor is called for the third object.

```
InventoryItem inventory[3] = { "Hammer",
                               InventoryItem("Wrench", 8.75, 20) };
```

In summary, if you use an initializer list for class object arrays, there are three things to remember:

- If there is no default constructor you must furnish an initializer for each object in the array.
- If there are fewer initializers in the list than objects in the array, the default constructor will be called for all the remaining objects.
- If a constructor requires more than one argument, the initializer takes the form of a constructor function call.

Accessing Members of Objects in an Array

Objects in an array are accessed with subscripts, just like any other data type in an array. For example, to call the setUnits member function of inventory[2], the following statement could be used:

```
inventory[2].setUnits(30);
```

This statement sets the units variable of inventory[2] to the value 30. Program 13-13 shows an array of InventoryItem objects being used in a complete program. (This file is stored in the Student Source Code Folder Chapter 13\InventoryItem Version 3.)

Program 13-13

```cpp
 1  // This program demonstrates an array of class objects.
 2  #include <iostream>
 3  #include <iomanip>
 4  #include "InventoryItem.h"
 5  using namespace std;
 6
 7  int main()
 8  {
 9     const int NUM_ITEMS = 5;
10     InventoryItem inventory[NUM_ITEMS] = {
11                  InventoryItem("Hammer", 6.95, 12),
12                  InventoryItem("Wrench", 8.75, 20),
13                  InventoryItem("Pliers", 3.75, 10),
14                  InventoryItem("Ratchet", 7.95, 14),
15                  InventoryItem("Screwdriver", 2.50, 22) };
16
17     cout << setw(14) <<"Inventory Item"
18          << setw(8) << "Cost" << setw(8)
19          << setw(16) << "Units on Hand\n";
20     cout << "-----------------------------------\n";
21
22     for (int i = 0; i < NUM_ITEMS; i++)
23     {
24        cout << setw(14) << inventory[i].getDescription();
25        cout << setw(8) << inventory[i].getCost();
26        cout << setw(7) << inventory[i].getUnits() << endl;
27     }
28
29     return 0;
30  }
```

Program Output

```
Inventory Item    Cost  Units on Hand
-----------------------------------
        Hammer    6.95      12
        Wrench    8.75      20
        Pliers    3.75      10
       Ratchet    7.95      14
    Screwdriver    2.5      22
```

Checkpoint

13.21   What will the following program display on the screen?

```cpp
#include <iostream>
using namespace std;

class Tank
{
private:
   int gallons;
public:
   Tank()
       { gallons = 50; }
   Tank(int gal)
       { gallons = gal; }
   int getGallons()
       { return gallons; }
};

int main()
{
   Tank storage[3] = { 10, 20 };

   for (int index = 0; index < 3; index++)
      cout << storage[index].getGallons() << endl;
   return 0;
}
```

13.22   What will the following program display on the screen?

```cpp
#include <iostream>
using namespace std;

class Package
{
private:
   int value;
public:
   Package()
       { value = 7; cout << value << endl; }
   Package(int v)
       { value = v; cout << value << endl; }
   ~Package()
       { cout << value << endl; }
};

int main()
{
   Package obj1(4);
   Package obj2();
   Package obj3(2);
   return 0;
}
```

13.23   In your answer for Checkpoint 13.22 indicate for each line of output whether the line is displayed by constructor #1, constructor #2, or the destructor.

13.24   Why would a member function be declared private?

13.25   Define an array of three InventoryItem objects.

13.26   Complete the following program so it defines an array of Yard objects. The program should use a loop to ask the user for the length and width of each Yard.

```
#include <iostream>
using namespace std;

class Yard
{
private:
   int length, width;
public:
   Yard()
      { length = 0; width = 0; }
   setLength(int len)
      { length = len; }
   setWidth(int w)
      { width = w; }
};

int main()
{
   // Finish this program
}
```

13.13 Focus on Problem Solving and Program Design: An OOP Case Study

You are a programmer for the Home Software Company. You have been assigned to develop a class that models the basic workings of a bank account. The class should perform the following tasks:

- Save the account balance.
- Save the number of transactions performed on the account.
- Allow deposits to be made to the account.
- Allow withdrawals to be taken from the account.
- Calculate interest for the period.
- Report the current account balance at any time.
- Report the current number of transactions at any time.

Private Member Variables

Table 13-4 lists the private member variables needed by the class.

Table 13-4

Variable	Description
balance	A double that holds the current account balance.
interestRate	A double that holds the interest rate for the period.
interest	A double that holds the interest earned for the current period.
transactions	An integer that holds the current number of transactions.

Public Member Functions

Table 13-5 lists the public member functions needed by the class.

Table 13-5

Function	Description
Constructor	Takes arguments to be initially stored in the balance and interestRate members. The default value for the balance is zero and the default value for the interest rate is 0.045.
setInterestRate	Takes a double argument which is stored in the interestRate member.
makeDeposit	Takes a double argument, which is the amount of the deposit. This argument is added to balance.
withdraw	Takes a double argument which is the amount of the withdrawal. This value is subtracted from the balance, unless the withdrawal amount is greater than the balance. If this happens, the function reports an error.
calcInterest	Takes no arguments. This function calculates the amount of interest for the current period, stores this value in the interest member, and then adds it to the balance member.
getInterestRate	Returns the current interest rate (stored in the interestRate member).
getBalance	Returns the current balance (stored in the balance member).
getInterest	Returns the interest earned for the current period (stored in the interest member).
getTransactions	Returns the number of transactions for the current period (stored in the transactions member).

The Class Declaration

The following listing shows the class declaration.

Contents of `Account.h`

```
 1   // Specification file for the Account class.
 2   #ifndef ACCOUNT_H
 3   #define ACCOUNT_H
 4
 5   class Account
 6   {
 7   private:
 8      double balance;        // Account balance
 9      double interestRate;   // Interest rate for the period
10      double interest;       // Interest earned for the period
11      int transactions;      // Number of transactions
12   public:
13      Account(double iRate = 0.045, double bal = 0)
14         { balance = bal;
15            interestRate = iRate;
16            interest = 0;
17            transactions = 0; }
18
```

```
19      void setInterestRate(double iRate)
20         { interestRate = iRate; }
21
22      void makeDeposit(double amount)
23         { balance += amount; transactions++; }
24
25      void withdraw(double amount); // Defined in Account.cpp
26
27      void calcInterest()
28         { interest = balance * interestRate; balance += interest; }
29
30      double getInterestRate() const
31         { return interestRate; }
32
33      double getBalance() const
34         { return balance; }
35
36      double getInterest() const
37         { return interest; }
38
39      int getTransactions() const
40         { return transactions; }
41   };
42   #endif
```

The withdraw Member Function

The only member function not written inline in the class declaration is withdraw. The purpose of that function is to subtract the amount of a withdrawal from the balance member. If the amount to be withdrawn is greater than the current balance, however, no withdrawal is made. The function returns true if the withdrawal is made, or false if there is not enough in the account.

Contents of Account.cpp

```
1   // Implementation file for the Account class.
2   #include "Account.h"
3
4   bool Account::withdraw(double amount)
5   {
6      if (balance < amount)
7         return false; // Not enough in the account
8      else
9      {
10        balance -= amount;
11        transactions++;
12        return true;
13     }
14  }
```

The Class's Interface

The `balance`, `interestRate`, `interest`, and `transactions` member variables are private, so they are hidden from the world outside the class. The reason is that a programmer with direct access to these variables might unknowingly commit any of the following errors:

- A deposit or withdrawal might be made without the `transactions` member being incremented.
- A withdrawal might be made for more than is in the account. This will cause the `balance` member to have a negative value.
- The interest rate might be calculated and the `balance` member adjusted, but the amount of interest might not get recorded in the `interest` member.
- The wrong interest rate might be used.

Because of the potential for these errors, the class contains public member functions that ensure the proper steps are taken when the account is manipulated.

Implementing the Class

Program 13-14 shows an implementation of the `Account` class. It presents a menu for displaying a savings account's balance, number of transactions, and interest earned. It also allows the user to deposit an amount into the account, make a withdrawal from the account, and calculate the interest earned for the current period.

Program 13-14

```cpp
 1 // This program demonstrates the Account class.
 2 #include <iostream>
 3 #include <cctype>
 4 #include <iomanip>
 5 #include "Account.h"
 6 using namespace std;
 7
 8 // Function prototypes
 9 void displayMenu();
10 void makeDeposit(Account &);
11 void withdraw(Account &);
12
13 int main()
14 {
15    Account savings;    // Savings account object
16    char choice;        // Menu selection
17
18    // Set numeric output formatting.
19     cout << fixed << showpoint << setprecision(2);
20
21    do
22    {
23       // Display the menu and get a valid selection.
24       displayMenu();
25       cin >> choice;
```

(program continues)

Program 13-14   *(continued)*

```
26          while (toupper(choice) < 'A' || toupper(choice) > 'G')
27          {
28             cout << "Please make a choice in the range "
29                  << "of A through G:";
30             cin >> choice;
31          }
32
33          // Process the user's menu selection.
34          switch(choice)
35          {
36          case 'a':
37          case 'A': cout << "The current balance is $";
38                    cout << savings.getBalance() << endl;
39                    break;
40          case 'b':
41          case 'B': cout << "There have been ";
42                    cout << savings.getTransactions()
43                         << " transactions.\n";
44                    break;
45          case 'c':
46          case 'C': cout << "Interest earned for this period: $";
47                    cout << savings.getInterest() << endl;
48                    break;
49          case 'd':
50          case 'D': makeDeposit(savings);
51                    break;
52          case 'e':
53          case 'E': withdraw(savings);
54                    break;
55          case 'f':
56          case 'F': savings.calcInterest();
57                    cout << "Interest added.\n";
58          }
59       } while (toupper(choice) != 'G');
60
61       return 0;
62    }
63
64    //*****************************************************
65    // Definition of function displayMenu. This function *
66    // displays the user's menu on the screen.           *
67    //*****************************************************
68
```

```cpp
 69 void displayMenu()
 70 {
 71    cout << "\n                    MENU\n";
 72    cout << "----------------------------------------\n";
 73    cout << "A) Display the account balance\n";
 74    cout << "B) Display the number of transactions\n";
 75    cout << "C) Display interest earned for this period\n";
 76    cout << "D) Make a deposit\n";
 77    cout << "E) Make a withdrawal\n";
 78    cout << "F) Add interest for this period\n";
 79    cout << "G) Exit the program\n\n";
 80    cout << "Enter your choice: ";
 81 }
 82
 83 //************************************************************
 84 // Definition of function makeDeposit. This function accepts  *
 85 // a reference to an Account object. The user is prompted for *
 86 // the dollar amount of the deposit, and the makeDeposit      *
 87 // member of the Account object is then called.               *
 88 //************************************************************
 89
 90 void makeDeposit(Account &acnt)
 91 {
 92    double dollars;
 93
 94    cout << "Enter the amount of the deposit: ";
 95    cin >> dollars;
 96    cin.ignore();
 97    acnt.makeDeposit(dollars);
 98 }
 99
100 //************************************************************
101 // Definition of function withdraw. This function accepts     *
102 // a reference to an Account object. The user is prompted for *
103 // the dollar amount of the withdrawal, and the withdraw      *
104 // member of the Account object is then called.               *
105 //************************************************************
106
107 void withdraw(Account &acnt)
108 {
109    double dollars;
110
111    cout << "Enter the amount of the withdrawal: ";
112    cin >> dollars;
113    cin.ignore();
114    if (!acnt.withdraw(dollars))
115       cout << "ERROR: Withdrawal amount too large.\n\n";
116 }
```

(program output continues)

Program 13-14 *(continued)*

Program Output with Example Input Shown in Bold

```
                    MENU
-------------------------------------------
A) Display the account balance
B) Display the number of transactions
C) Display interest earned for this period
D) Make a deposit
E) Make a withdrawal
F) Add interest for this period
G) Exit the program

Enter your choice: d [Enter]
Enter the amount of the deposit: 500 [Enter]

                    MENU
-------------------------------------------
A) Display the account balance
B) Display the number of transactions
C) Display interest earned for this period
D) Make a deposit
E) Make a withdrawal
F) Add interest for this period
G) Exit the program

Enter your choice: a [Enter]
The current balance is $500.00

                    MENU
-------------------------------------------
A) Display the account balance
B) Display the number of transactions
C) Display interest earned for this period
D) Make a deposit
E) Make a withdrawal
F) Add interest for this period
G) Exit the program

Enter your choice: e [Enter]
Enter the amount of the withdrawal: 700 [Enter]
ERROR: Withdrawal amount too large.

                    MENU
-------------------------------------------
A) Display the account balance
B) Display the number of transactions
C) Display interest earned for this period
D) Make a deposit
E) Make a withdrawal
F) Add interest for this period
G) Exit the program

Enter your choice: e [Enter]
Enter the amount of the withdrawal: 200 [Enter]
```

```
                MENU
-------------------------------------------
A) Display the account balance
B) Display the number of transactions
C) Display interest earned for this period
D) Make a deposit
E) Make a withdrawal
F) Add interest for this period
G) Exit the program

Enter your choice: f [Enter]
Interest added.

                MENU
-------------------------------------------
A) Display the account balance
B) Display the number of transactions
C) Display interest earned for this period
D) Make a deposit
E) Make a withdrawal
F) Add interest for this period
G) Exit the program

Enter your choice: a [Enter]
The current balance is $313.50

                MENU
-------------------------------------------
A) Display the account balance
B) Display the number of transactions
C) Display interest earned for this period
D) Make a deposit
E) Make a withdrawal
F) Add interest for this period
G) Exit the program

Enter your choice: g [Enter]
```

13.14 Focus on Object-Oriented Programming: Creating an Abstract Array Data Type

CONCEPT: The absence of array bounds checking in C++ is a source of potential hazard. In this section we examine a simple integer list class that provides bounds checking.

One of the benefits of object-oriented programming is the ability to create abstract data types that are improvements on built-in data types. As you know, arrays provide no bounds checking in C++. You can, however, create a class that has array-like characteristics and performs bounds checking. For example, look at the following IntegerList class.

Contents of `IntegerList.h`

```
1   // Specification file for the IntegerList class.
2   #ifndef INTEGERLIST_H
3   #define INTEGERLIST_H
4
5   class IntegerList
6   {
7   private:
8      int *list;              // Pointer to the array.
9      int numElements;        // Number of elements.
10     bool isValid(int);      // Validates subscripts.
11  public:
12     IntegerList(int);         // Constructor
13     ~IntegerList();           // Destructor
14     void setElement(int, int);  // Sets an element to a value.
15     void getElement(int, int&); // Returns an element.
16  };
17  #endif
```

Contents of `IntegerList.cpp`

```
1  // Implementation file for the IntegerList class.
2  #include <iostream>
3  #include <cstdlib>
4  #include "IntegerList.h"
5  using namespace std;
6
7  //**********************************************************
8  // The constructor sets each element to zero.              *
9  //**********************************************************
10
11 IntegerList::IntegerList(int size)
12 {
13    list = new int[size];
14    numElements = size;
15    for (int ndx = 0; ndx < size; ndx++)
16       list[ndx] = 0;
17 }
18
19 //**********************************************************
20 // The destructor releases allocated memory.               *
21 //**********************************************************
22
23 IntegerList::~IntegerList()
24 {
25    delete [] list;
26 }
27
```

```
28  //**********************************************************
29  // isValid member function.                                *
30  // This private member functon returns true if the argument *
31  // is a valid subscript, or false otherwise.               *
32  //**********************************************************
33
34  bool IntegerList::isValid(int element) const
35  {
36     bool status;
37
38     if (element < 0 || element >= numElements)
39        status = false;
40     else
41        status = true;
42     return status;
43  }
44
45  //**********************************************************
46  // setElement member function.                             *
47  // Stores a value in a specific element of the list. If an  *
48  // invalid subscript is passed, the program aborts.        *
49  //**********************************************************
50
51  void IntegerList::setElement(int element, int value)
52  {
53     if (isValid(element))
54        list[element] = value;
55     else
56     {
57        cout << "Error: Invalid subscript\n";
58        exit(EXIT_FAILURE);
59     }
60  }
61
62  //**********************************************************
63  // getElement member function.                             *
64  // Returns the value stored at the specified element.      *
65  // If an invalid subscript is passed, the program aborts.  *
66  //**********************************************************
67
68  int IntegerList::getElement(int element) const
69  {
70     if (isValid(element))
71        return list[element];
72     else
73     {
74        cout << "Error: Invalid subscript\n";
75        exit(EXIT_FAILURE);
76     }
77  }
```

The `IntegerList` class allows you to store and retrieve numbers in a dynamically allocated array of integers. Here is a synopsis of the members.

`list`	A pointer to an `int`. This member points to the dynamically allocated array of integers.
`numElements`	An integer that holds the number of elements in the dynamically allocated array.
`isValid`	This function validates a subscript into the array. It accepts a subscript value as an argument, and returns boolean `true` if the subscript is in the range 0 through `numElements - 1`. If the value is outside that range, boolean `false` is returned.
Constructor	The class constructor accepts an `int` argument that is the number of elements to allocate for the array. The array is allocated and each element is set to zero.
`setElement`	The `setElement` member function sets a specific element of the `list` array to a value. The first argument is the element subscript, and the second argument is the value to be stored in that element. The function uses `isValid` to validate the subscript. If an invalid subscript is passed to the function, the program aborts.
`getElement`	The `getElement` member function retrieves a value from a specific element in the `list` array. The argument is the subscript of the element whose value is to be retrieved. The function uses `isValid` to validate the subscript. If the subscript is valid, the value is returned. If the subscript is invalid, the program aborts.

Program 13-15 demonstrates the class. A loop uses the `setElement` member to fill the array with 9s and prints an asterisk on the screen each time a 9 is successfully stored. Then another loop uses the `getElement` member to retrieve the values from the array and prints them on the screen. Finally, a statement uses the `setElement` member to demonstrate the subscript validation by attempting to store a value in element 50.

Program 13-15

```
 1   // This program demonstrates the IntegerList class.
 2   #include <iostream>
 3   #include "IntegerList.h"
 4   using namespace std;
 5
 6   int main()
 7   {
 8      const int SIZE = 20;
 9      IntegerList numbers(SIZE);
10      int val, x;
11
```

```
12      // Store 9s in the list and display an asterisk
13      // each time a 9 is successfully stored.
14      for (x = 0; x < SIZE; x++)
15      {
16         numbers.setElement(x, 9);
17         cout << "* ";
18      }
19      cout << endl;
20
21      // Display the 9s.
22      for (x = 0; x < SIZE; x++)
23      {
24         val = numbers.getElement(x);
25         cout << val << " ";
26      }
27      cout << endl;
28
29      // Attempt to store a value outside the list's bounds.
30      numbers.setElement(50, 9);
31
32      // Will this message display?
33      cout << "Element 50 successfully set.\n";
34      return 0;
35   }
```

Program Output

```
* * * * * * * * * * * * * * * * * * * * *
9 9 9 9 9 9 9 9 9 9 9 9 9 9 9 9 9 9 9 9 9
Error: Invalid subscript
```

13.15 Focus on Object-Oriented Design: The Unified Modeling Language (UML)

CONCEPT: The Unified Modeling Language provides a standard method for graphically depicting an object-oriented system.

When designing a class it is often helpful to draw a UML diagram. *UML* stands for *Unified Modeling Language*. The UML provides a set of standard diagrams for graphically depicting object-oriented systems. Figure 13-18 shows the general layout of a UML diagram for a class. Notice that the diagram is a box that is divided into three sections. The top section is where you write the name of the class. The middle section holds a list of the class's member variables. The bottom section holds a list of the class's member functions.

Figure 13-18

Class name goes here ⟶

Member variables are listed here ⟶

Member functions are listed here ⟶

Earlier in this chapter you studied a `Rectangle` class that could be used in a program that works with rectangles. The first version of the `Rectangle` class that you studied had the following member variables:

- `width`
- `length`

The class also had the following member functions:

- `setWidth`
- `setLength`
- `getWidth`
- `getLength`
- `getArea`

From this information alone we can construct a simple UML diagram for the class, as shown in Figure 13-19.

Figure 13-19

```
            Rectangle

   width
   length

   setWidth()
   setLength()
   getWidth()
   getLength()
   getArea()
```

The UML diagram in Figure 13-19 tells us the name of the class, the names of the member variables, and the names of the member functions. The UML diagram in Figure 13-19 does not convey many of the class details, however, such as access specification, member variable data types, parameter data types, and function return types. The UML provides optional notation for these types of details.

Showing Access Specification in UML Diagrams

The UML diagram in Figure 13-19 lists all of the members of the `Rectangle` class but does not indicate which members are private and which are public. In a UML diagram you may optionally place a – character before a member name to indicate that it is private, or a + character to indicate that it is public. Figure 13-20 shows the UML diagram modified to include this notation.

Figure 13-20

```
          ┌─────────────────────────┐
          │        Rectangle        │
          ├─────────────────────────┤
          │ - width                 │
          │ - length                │
          ├─────────────────────────┤
          │ + setWidth()            │
          │ + setLength()           │
          │ + getWidth()            │
          │ + getLength()           │
          │ + getArea()             │
          └─────────────────────────┘
```

Data Type and Parameter Notation in UML Diagrams

The Unified Modeling Language also provides notation that you may use to indicate the data types of member variables, member functions, and parameters. To indicate the data type of a member variable, place a colon followed by the name of the data type after the name of the variable. For example, the width variable in the Rectangle class is a double. It could be listed as follows in the UML diagram:

```
- width : double
```

 NOTE: In UML notation the variable name is listed first, then the data type. This is the opposite of C++ syntax, which requires the data type to appear first.

The return type of a member function can be listed in the same manner: After the function's name, place a colon followed by the return type. The Rectangle class's getLength function returns a double, so it could be listed as follows in the UML diagram:

```
+ getLength() : double
```

Parameter variables and their data types may be listed inside a member function's parentheses. For example, the Rectangle class's setLength function has a double parameter named len, so it could be listed as follows in the UML diagram:

```
+ setLength(len : double) : void
```

Figure 13-21 shows a UML diagram for the Rectangle class with parameter and data type notation.

Figure 13-21

```
          ┌───────────────────────────────┐
          │           Rectangle           │
          ├───────────────────────────────┤
          │ - width : double              │
          │ - length : double             │
          ├───────────────────────────────┤
          │ + setWidth(w : double) : void │
          │ + setLength(len : double) : void │
          │ + getWidth() : double         │
          │ + getLength() : double        │
          │ + getArea() : double          │
          └───────────────────────────────┘
```

Showing Constructors and Destructors in a UML Diagram

There is more than one accepted way of showing a class constructor in a UML diagram. In this book we will show a constructor just as any other function, except we will list no return type. For example, Figure 13-22 shows a UML diagram for the third version of the InventoryItem class that we looked at.

Figure 13-22

InventoryItem
- description : char*   - cost : double   - units : int   - createDescription(size : int,   value : char*) : void
+ InventoryItem() :   + InventoryItem(desc : char*) :   + InventoryItem(desc : char*,   c : double, u : int) :   + ~InventoryItem() :   + setDescription(d : char*) : void   + setCost(c : double) : void   + setUnits(u : int) : void   + getDescription() : char*   + getCost() : double   + getUnits() : int

13.16 Focus on Object-Oriented Design: Finding the Classes and Their Responsibilities

CONCEPT: One of the first steps in creating an object-oriented application is determining the classes that are necessary, and their responsibilities within the application.

So far you have learned the basics of writing a class, creating an object from the class, and using the object to perform operations. This knowledge is necessary to create an object-oriented application, but it is not the first step in designing the application. The first step is to analyze the problem that you are trying to solve and determine the classes that you will need. In this section we will discuss a simple technique for finding the classes in a problem and determining their responsibilities.

Finding the Classes

When developing an object-oriented application, one of your first tasks is to identify the classes that you will need to create. Typically, your goal is to identify the different types of real-world objects that are present in the problem, and then create classes for those types of objects within your application.

Over the years, software professionals have developed numerous techniques for finding the classes in a given problem. One simple and popular technique involves the following steps.

1. Get a written description of the problem domain.

2. Identify all the nouns (including pronouns and noun phrases) in the description. Each of these is a potential class.

3. Refine the list to include only the classes that are relevant to the problem.

Let's take a closer look at each of these steps.

Write a Description of the Problem Domain

The *problem domain* is the set of real-world objects, parties, and major events related to the problem. If you adequately understand the nature of the problem you are trying to solve, you can write a description of the problem domain yourself. If you do not thoroughly understand the nature of the problem, you should have an expert write the description for you.

For example, suppose we are programming an application that the manager of Joe's Automotive Shop will use to print service quotes for customers. Here is a description that an expert, perhaps Joe himself, might have written:

Joe's Automotive Shop services foreign cars and specializes in servicing cars made by Mercedes, Porsche, and BMW. When a customer brings a car to the shop, the manager gets the customer's name, address, and telephone number. The manager then determines the make, model, and year of the car, and gives the customer a service quote. The service quote shows the estimated parts charges, estimated labor charges, sales tax, and total estimated charges.

The problem domain description should include any of the following:

- Physical objects such as vehicles, machines, or products
- Any role played by a person, such as manager, employee, customer, teacher, student, etc.
- The results of a business event, such as a customer order, or in this case a service quote
- Recordkeeping items, such as customer histories and payroll records

Identify All of the Nouns

The next step is to identify all of the nouns and noun phrases. (If the description contains pronouns, include them too.) Here's another look at the previous problem domain description. This time the nouns and noun phrases appear in bold.

Joe's Automotive Shop services **foreign cars,** and specializes in servicing **cars** made by **Mercedes, Porsche,** and **BMW.** When a **customer** brings a **car** to the **shop,** the **manager** gets the **customer's name, address,** and **telephone number.** The **manager** then determines the **make, model,** and **year** of the **car,** and gives the **customer** a **service quote.** The **service quote** shows the **estimated parts charges, estimated labor charges, sales tax,** and **total estimated charges.**

Notice that some of the nouns are repeated. The following list shows all of the nouns without duplicating any of them.

address
BMW
car
cars
customer
estimated labor charges
estimated parts charges
foreign cars
Joe's Automotive Shop
make
manager
Mercedes
model
name
Porsche
sales tax
service quote
shop
telephone number
total estimated charges
year

Refine the List of Nouns

The nouns that appear in the problem description are merely candidates to become classes. It might not be necessary to make classes for them all. The next step is to refine the list to include only the classes that are necessary to solve the particular problem at hand. We will look at the common reasons that a noun can be eliminated from the list of potential classes.

1. Some of the nouns really mean the same thing.

In this example, the following sets of nouns refer to the same thing:

- **cars** and **foreign cars**
  These both refer to the general concept of a car.
- **Joe's Automotive Shop** and **shop**
  Both of these refer to the company "Joe's Automotive Shop."

We can settle on a single class for each of these. In this example we will arbitrarily eliminate **foreign cars** from the list, and use the word **cars**. Likewise we will eliminate **Joe's Automotive Shop** from the list and use the word **shop**. The updated list of potential classes is:

address
BMW
car
cars
customer
estimated labor charges
estimated parts charges
~~foreign cars~~
~~Joe's Automotive Shop~~
make
manager
Mercedes
model
name
Porsche
sales tax
service quote
shop
telephone number
total estimated charges
year

Because **cars** and **foreign cars** mean the same thing in this problem, we have eliminated **foreign cars**. Also, because **Joe's Automotive Shop** and **shop** mean the same thing, we have eliminated **Joe's Automotive Shop**.

2. **Some nouns might represent items that we do not need to be concerned with in order to solve the problem.**

A quick review of the problem description reminds us of what our application should do: print a service quote. In this example we can eliminate two unnecessary classes from the list:

- We can cross **shop** off the list because our application only needs to be concerned with individual service quotes. It doesn't need to work with or determine any company-wide information. If the problem description asked us to keep a total of all the service quotes, then it would make sense to have a class for the shop.
- We will not need a class for the **manager** because the problem statement does not direct us to process any information about the manager. If there were multiple shop managers, and the problem description had asked us to record which manager generated each service quote, then it would make sense to have a class for the manager.

The updated list of potential classes at this point is:

address
BMW
car
cars
customer
estimated labor charges
estimated parts charges
~~foreign cars~~
~~Joe's Automotive Shop~~
make
~~manager~~
Mercedes
model
name
Porsche
sales tax
service quote
~~shop~~
telephone number
total estimated charges
year

Our problem description does not direct us to process any information about the **shop**, or any information about the **manager**, so we have eliminated those from the list.

3. Some of the nouns might represent objects, not classes.

We can eliminate **Mercedes, Porsche,** and **BMW** as classes because, in this example, they all represent specific cars, and can be considered instances of a **cars** class. Also, we can eliminate the word **car** from the list. In the description it refers to a specific car brought to the shop by a customer. Therefore, it would also represent an instance of a **cars** class. At this point the updated list of potential classes is:

address
~~BMW~~
~~car~~
cars
customer
estimated labor charges
estimated parts charges
~~foreign cars~~
~~Joe's Automotive Shop~~
~~manager~~
make
~~Mercedes~~
model
name
~~Porsche~~
sales tax
service quote
~~shop~~
telephone number
total estimated charges
year

We have eliminated **Mercedes, Porsche, BMW,** and **car** because they are all instances of a **cars** class. That means that these nouns identify objects, not classes.

NOTE: Some object-oriented designers take note of whether a noun is plural or singular. Sometimes a plural noun will indicate a class and a singular noun will indicate an object.

4. **Some of the nouns might represent simple values that can be stored in a variable and do not require a class.**

Remember, a class contains attributes and member functions. Attributes are related items that are stored within an object of the class, and define the object's state. Member functions are actions or behaviors that may be performed by an object of the class. If a noun represents a type of item that would not have any identifiable attributes or member functions, then it can probably be eliminated from the list. To help determine whether a noun represents an item that would have attributes and member functions, ask the following questions about it:

- Would you use a group of related values to represent the item's state?
- Are there any obvious actions to be performed by the item?

If the answers to both of these questions are no, then the noun probably represents a value that can be stored in a simple variable. If we apply this test to each of the nouns that remain in our list, we can conclude that the following are probably not classes: **address, estimated labor charges, estimated parts charges, make, model, name, sales tax, telephone number, total estimated charges** and **year**. These are all simple string or numeric values that can be stored in variables. Here is the updated list of potential classes:

~~address~~
~~BMW~~
~~car~~
cars
customer
~~estimated labor charges~~
~~estimated parts charges~~
~~foreign cars~~
~~Joe's Automotive Shop~~   We have eliminated **address, estimated labor charges,**
~~make~~   **estimated parts charges, make, model, name, sales**
~~manager~~   **tax, telephone number, total estimated charges,** and
~~Mercedes~~   **year** as classes because they represent simple values that can
~~model~~   be stored in variables.
~~name~~
~~Porsche~~
~~sales tax~~
service quote
~~shop~~
~~telephone number~~
~~total estimated charges~~
~~year~~

As you can see from the list, we have eliminated everything except **cars, customer,** and **service quote**. This means that in our application, we will need classes to represent cars, customers, and service quotes. Ultimately, we will write a `Car` class, a `Customer` class, and a `ServiceQuote` class.

Identifying a Class's Responsibilities

Once the classes have been identified, the next task is to identify each class's responsibilities. A class's *responsibilities* are

- the things that the class is responsible for knowing
- the actions that the class is responsible for doing

When you have identified the things that a class is responsible for knowing, then you have identified the class's attributes. Likewise, when you have identified the actions that a class is responsible for doing, you have identified its member functions.

It is often helpful to ask the questions "In the context of this problem, what must the class know? What must the class do?" The first place to look for the answers is in the description of the problem domain. Many of the things that a class must know and do will be mentioned. Some class responsibilities, however, might not be directly mentioned in the problem domain, so brainstorming is often required. Let's apply this methodology to the classes we previously identified from our problem domain.

The `Customer` class

In the context of our problem domain, what must the `Customer` class know? The description directly mentions the following items, which are all attributes of a customer:

- the customer's name
- the customer's address
- the customer's telephone number

These are all values that can be represented as strings and stored in the class's member variables. The `Customer` class can potentially know many other things. One mistake that can be made at this point is to identify too many things that an object is responsible for knowing. In some applications, a `Customer` class might know the customer's email address. This particular problem domain does not mention that the customer's email address is used for any purpose, so we should not include it as a responsibility.

Now let's identify the class's member functions. In the context of our problem domain, what must the `Customer` class do? The only obvious actions are to

- create an object of the `Customer` class
- set and get the customer's name
- set and get the customer's address
- set and get the customer's telephone number

From this list we can see that the `Customer` class will have a constructor, as well as accessor and mutator functions for each of its attributes. Figure 13-23 shows a UML diagram for the `Customer` class.

Figure 13-23

```
                    Customer
    - name : String
    - address : String
    - phone : String
    + Customer() :
    + setName(n : String) : void
    + setAddress(a : String) : void
    + setPhone(p : String) : void
    + getName() : String
    + getAddress() : String
    + getPhone() : String
```

The Car **Class**

In the context of our problem domain, what must an object of the Car class know? The following items are all attributes of a car, and are mentioned in the problem domain:

- the car's make
- the car's model
- the car's year

Now let's identify the class's member functions. In the context of our problem domain, what must the Car class do? Once again, the only obvious actions are the standard set of member functions that we will find in most classes (constructors, accessors, and mutators). Specifically, the actions are:

- create an object of the Car class
- set and get the car's make
- set and get the car's model
- set and get the car's year

Figure 13-24 shows a UML diagram for the Car class at this point.

Figure 13-24

```
                    Car
    - make : String
    - model : String
    - year : int
    + Car() :
    + setMake(m : String) : void
    + setModel(m : String) : void
    + setYear(y : int) : void
    + getMake() : String
    + getModel() : String
    + getYear() : int
```

The ServiceQuote Class

In the context of our problem domain, what must an object of the ServiceQuote class know? The problem domain mentions the following items:

- the estimated parts charges
- the estimated labor charges
- the sales tax
- the total estimated charges

Careful thought and a little brainstorming will reveal that two of these items are the results of calculations: sales tax and total estimated charges. These items are dependent on the values of the estimated parts and labor charges. In order to avoid the risk of holding stale data, we will not store these values in member variables. Rather, we will provide member functions that calculate these values and return them. The other member functions that we will need for this class are a constructor and the accessors and mutators for the estimated parts charges and estimated labor charges attributes. Figure 13-25 shows a UML diagram for the ServiceQuote class.

Figure 13-25

```
┌─────────────────────────────────┐
│          ServiceQuote           │
├─────────────────────────────────┤
│ - partsCharges : double         │
│ - laborCharges : double         │
├─────────────────────────────────┤
│ + ServiceQuote() :              │
│ + setPartsCharges(c : double) : │
│     void                        │
│ + setLaborCharges(c : double) : │
│     void                        │
│ + getPartsCharges() : double    │
│ + getLaborCharges() : double    │
│ + getSalesTax() : double        │
│ + getTotalCharges() : double    │
└─────────────────────────────────┘
```

This Is Only the Beginning

You should look at the process that we have discussed in this section as merely a starting point. It's important to realize that designing an object-oriented application is an iterative process. It may take you several attempts to identify all of the classes that you will need, and determine all of their responsibilities. As the design process unfolds, you will gain a deeper understanding of the problem, and consequently you will see ways to improve the design.

 Checkpoint

13.27   What is a problem domain?

13.28   When designing an object-oriented application, who should write a description of the problem domain?

13.29   How do you identify the potential classes in a problem domain description?

13.30   What are a class's responsibilities?

13.31   What two questions should you ask to determine a class's responsibilities?

13.32   Will all of a class's actions always be directly mentioned in the problem domain description?

13.33   Look at the following description of a problem domain:

A doctor sees patients in her practice. When a patient comes to the practice, the doctor performs one or more procedures on the patient. Each procedure that the doctor performs has a description and a standard fee. As the patient leaves the practice, he or she receives a statement from the office manager. The statement shows the patient's name and address, as well as the procedures that were performed, and the total charge for the procedures.

Assume that you are writing an application to generate a statement that can be printed and given to the patient.

A) Identify all of the potential classes in this problem domain.

B) Refine the list to include only the necessary class or classes for this problem.

C) Identify the responsibilities of the class or classes that you identified in step B.

Review Questions and Exercises

Short Answer

1. What is the difference between a class and an instance of the class?

2. What is the difference between the following `Person` structure and `Person` class?

```
struct Person
{
    char name[51];
    int age;
};

class Person
{
    char name[51];
    int age;
};
```

3. What is the default access specification of class members?

4. Look at the following function header for a member function.

```
void Circle::getRadius()
```

What is the name of the function?

What class is the function a member of?

5. A contractor uses a blueprint to build a set of identical houses. Are classes analogous to the blueprint or the houses?

6. What is a mutator function? What is an accessor function?

7. Is it a good idea to make member variables private? Why or why not?

8. Can you think of a good reason to avoid writing statements in a class member function that use `cout` or `cin`?

9. Under what circumstances should a member function be private?

10. What is a constructor? What is a destructor?

11. What is a default constructor? Is it possible to have more than one default constructor?

12. Is it possible to have more than one constructor? Is it possible to have more than one destructor?

13. If a class object is dynamically allocated in memory, does its constructor execute? If so, when?

14. When defining an array of class objects, how do you pass arguments to the constructor for each object in the array?

15. What are a class's responsibilities?

16. How do you identify the classes in a problem domain description?

Fill-in-the-Blank

17. The two common programming methods in practice today are _____ and _____.

18. _____ programming is centered around functions or procedures.

19. _____ programming is centered around objects.

20. _____ is an object's ability to contain and manipulate its own data.

21. In C++ the _____ is the construct primarily used to create objects.

22. A class is very similar to a(n) _____.

23. A(n) _____ is a key word inside a class declaration that establishes a member's accessibility.

24. The default access specification of class members is _____.

25. The default access specification of a struct in C++ is _____.

26. Defining a class object is often called the _____ of a class.

27. Members of a class object may be accessed through a pointer to the object by using the _____ operator.

28. If you were writing the declaration of a class named Canine, what would you name the file it was stored in? _____

29. If you were writing the external definitions of the Canine class's member functions, you would save them in a file named _____.

30. When a member function's body is written inside a class declaration, the function is _____.

31. A(n) _____ is automatically called when an object is created.

32. A(n) _____ is a member function with the same name as the class.

33. _____ are useful for performing initialization or setup routines in a class object.

34. Constructors cannot have a(n) _____ type.

35. A(n) _____ constructor is one that requires no arguments.

36. A(n) _____ is a member function that is automatically called when an object is destroyed.

37. A destructor has the same name as the class, but is preceded by a(n) _____ character.

38. Like constructors, destructors cannot have a(n) _____ type.

39. A constructor whose arguments all have default values is a(n) _____ constructor.

40. A class may have more than one constructor, as long as each has a different _____.

41. A class may only have one default _____ and one _____.

42. A(n) _____ may be used to pass arguments to the constructors of elements in an object array.

Algorithm Workbench

43. Write a class declaration named `Circle` with a private member variable named `radius`. Write set and get functions to access the `radius` variable, and a function named `getArea` that returns the area of the circle. The area is calculated as

    ```
    3.14159 * radius * radius
    ```

44. Add a default constructor to the `Circle` class in question 43. The constructor should initialize the `radius` member to 0.

45. Add an overloaded constructor to the `Circle` class in question 44. The constructor should accept an argument and assign its value to the `radius` member variable.

46. Write a statement that defines an array of five objects of the `Circle` class in question 45. Let the default constructor execute for each element of the array.

47. Write a statement that defines an array of five objects of the `Circle` class in question 45. Pass the following arguments to the elements' constructor: 12, 7, 9, 14, and 8.

48. Write a `for` loop that displays the radius and area of the circles represented by the array you defined in question 47.

49. If the items on the following list appeared in a problem domain description, which would be potential classes?

Animal	Medication	Nurse
Inoculate	Operate	Advertise
Doctor	Invoice	Measure
Patient	Client	Customer

50. Look at the following description of a problem domain:

    The bank offers the following types of accounts to its customers: savings accounts, checking accounts, and money market accounts. Customers are allowed to deposit money into an account (thereby increasing its balance), withdraw money from an account (thereby decreasing its balance), and earn interest on the account. Each account has an interest rate.

    Assume that you are writing an application that will calculate the amount of interest earned for a bank account.

    A) Identify the potential classes in this problem domain.

    B) Refine the list to include only the necessary class or classes for this problem.

    C) Identify the responsibilities of the class or classes.

True or False

51. T F Private members must be declared before public members.

52. T F Class members are private by default.

53. T F Members of a `struct` are private by default.

54. T F Classes and structures in C++ are very similar.

55. T F All private members of a class must be declared together.

56. T F All public members of a class must be declared together.

57. T F It is legal to define a pointer to a class object.

58. T F You can use the `new` operator to dynamically allocate an instance of a class.

59. T F A private member function may be called from a statement outside the class, as long as the statement is in the same program as the class declaration.

60. T F Constructors do not have to have the same name as the class.

61. T F Constructors may not have a return type.

62. T F Constructors cannot take arguments.

63. T F Destructors cannot take arguments.

64. T F Destructors may return a value.

65. T F Constructors may have default arguments.

66. T F Member functions may be overloaded.

67. T F Constructors may not be overloaded.

68. T F A class may not have a constructor with no parameter list, and a constructor whose arguments all have default values.

69. T F A class may only have one destructor.

70. T F When an array of objects is defined, the constructor is only called for the first element.

71. T F To find the classes needed for an object-oriented application, you identify all of the verbs in a description of the problem domain.

72. T F A class's responsibilities are the things the class is responsible for knowing, and actions the class must perform.

Find the Errors

Each of the following class declarations or programs contain errors. Find as many as possible.

73.
```cpp
class Circle:
{
private
   double centerX;
   double centerY;
   double radius;
public
   setCenter(double, double);
   setRadius(double);
}
```

74.
```cpp
#include <iostream>
using namespace std;

Class Moon;
{
Private;
    double earthWeight;
    double moonWeight;
Public;
    moonWeight(double ew);
        { earthWeight = ew; moonWeight = earthWeight / 6; }
    double getMoonWeight();
        { return moonWeight; }
}

int main()
{
    double earth;
    cout >> "What is your weight? ";
    cin << earth;
    Moon lunar(earth);
    cout << "On the moon you would weigh "
        <<lunar.getMoonWeight() << endl;
    return 0;
}
```

75.
```cpp
#include <iostream>
using namespace std;

class DumbBell;
{
    int weight;
public:
    void setWeight(int);
};
void setWeight(int w)
{
    weight = w;
}

int main()
{
    DumBell bar;

    DumbBell(200);
    cout << "The weight is " << bar.weight << endl;
    return 0;
}
```

76.
```cpp
class Change
{
public:
    int pennies;
    int nickels;
    int dimes;
    int quarters;
    Change()
```

```
            { pennies = nickels = dimes = quarters = 0; }
        Change(int p = 100, int n = 50, d = 50, q = 25);
};

void Change::Change(int p, int n, d, q)
{
    pennies = p;
    nickels = n;
    dimes = d;
    quarters = q;
}
```

Programming Challenges

1. Date

Design a class called Date. The class should store a date in three integers: month, day, and year. There should be member functions to print the date in the following forms:

12/25/10
December 25, 2010
25 December 2010

Demonstrate the class by writing a complete program implementing it.

Input Validation: Do not accept values for the day greater than 31 or less than 1. Do not accept values for the month greater than 12 or less than 1.

2. Employee Class

VideoNote
Solving the
Employee
Class Problem

Write a class named Employee that has the following member variables:

- **name.** A string that holds the employee's name.
- **idNumber.** An int variable that holds the employee's ID number.
- **department.** A string that holds the name of the department where the employee works.
- **position.** A string that holds the employee's job title.

The class should have the following constructors:

- A constructor that accepts the following values as arguments and assigns them to the appropriate member variables: employee's name, employee's ID number, department, and position.
- A constructor that accepts the following values as arguments and assigns them to the appropriate member variables: employee's name and ID number. The department and position fields should be assigned an empty string (" ").
- A default constructor that assigns empty strings (" ") to the name, department, and position member variables, and 0 to the idNumber member variable.

Write appropriate mutator functions that store values in these member variables and accessor functions that return the values in these member variables. Once you have written the class, write a separate program that creates three Employee objects to hold the following data.

Name	ID Number	Department	Position
Susan Meyers	47899	Accounting	Vice President
Mark Jones	39119	IT	Programmer
Joy Rogers	81774	Manufacturing	Engineer

The program should store this data in the three objects and then display the data for each employee on the screen.

3. **Car** Class

Write a class named `Car` that has the following member variables:

- **yearModel.** An int that holds the car's year model.
- **make.** A string that holds the make of the car.
- **speed.** An int that holds the car's current speed.

In addition, the class should have the following constructor and other member functions.

- **Constructor.** The constructor should accept the car's year model and make as arguments. These values should be assigned to the object's yearModel and make member variables. The constructor should also assign 0 to the speed member variables.
- **Accessor.** Appropriate accessor functions to get the values stored in an object's yearModel, make, and speed member variables.
- **accelerate.** The accelerate function should add 5 to the speed member variable each time it is called.
- **brake.** The brake function should subtract 5 from the speed member variable each time it is called.

Demonstrate the class in a program that creates a `Car` object, and then calls the accelerate function five times. After each call to the accelerate function, get the current speed of the car and display it. Then, call the brake function five times. After each call to the brake function, get the current speed of the car and display it.

4. **Personal Information Class**

Design a class that holds the following personal data: name, address, age, and phone number. Write appropriate accessor and mutator functions. Demonstrate the class by writing a program that creates three instances of it. One instance should hold your information, and the other two should hold your friends' or family members' information.

5. **RetailItem** Class

Write a class named `RetailItem` that holds data about an item in a retail store. The class should have the following member variables:

- **description.** A string that holds a brief description of the item.
- **unitsOnHand.** An int that holds the number of units currently in inventory.
- **price.** A double that holds the item's retail price.

Write a constructor that accepts arguments for each member variable, appropriate mutator functions that store values in these member variables, and accessor functions that return the values in these member variables. Once you have written the class, write a separate program that creates three `RetailItem` objects and stores the following data in them.

	Description	Units On Hand	Price
Item #1	Jacket	12	59.95
Item #2	Designer Jeans	40	34.95
Item #3	Shirt	20	24.95

6. **Inventory Class**

Design an `Inventory` class that can hold information and calculate data for items in a retail store's inventory. The class should have the following *private* member variables:

Variable Name	Description
`itemNumber`	An `int` that holds the item's item number.
`quantity`	An `int` for holding the quantity of the items on hand.
`cost`	A `double` for holding the wholesale per-unit cost of the item
`totalCost`	A `double` for holding the total inventory cost of the item (calculated as `quantity` times `cost`).

The class should have the following *public* member functions:

Member Function	Description
Default Constructor	Sets all the member variables to 0.
Constructor #2	Accepts an item's number, cost, and quantity as arguments. The function should copy these values to the appropriate member variables and then call the `setTotalCost` function.
`setItemNumber`	Accepts an integer argument that is copied to the `itemNumber` member variable.
`setQuantity`	Accepts an integer argument that is copied to the `quantity` member variable.
`setCost`	Accepts a `double` argument that is copied to the `cost` member variable.
`setTotalCost`	Calculates the total inventory cost for the item (`quantity` times `cost`) and stores the result in `totalCost`.
`getItemNumber`	Returns the value in `itemNumber`.
`getQuantity`	Returns the value in `quantity`.
`getCost`	Returns the value in `cost`.
`getTotalCost`	Returns the value in `totalCost`.

Demonstrate the class in a driver program.

Input Validation: Do not accept negative values for item number, quantity, or cost.

7. **Widget Factory**

Design a class for a widget manufacturing plant. Assuming that 10 widgets may be produced each hour, the class object will calculate how many days it will take to produce any number of widgets. (The plant operates two shifts of eight hours each per day.) Write a program that asks the user for the number of widgets that have been ordered and then displays the number of days it will take to produce them.

Input Validation: Do not accept negative values for the number of widgets ordered.

8. **`TestScores` Class**

Design a `TestScores` class that has member variables to hold three test scores. The class should have a constructor, accessor, and mutator functions for the test score fields, and a member function that returns the average of the test scores. Demonstrate the class by writing a separate program that creates an instance of the class. The program should ask the user to enter three test scores, which are stored in the `TestScores` object. Then the program should display the average of the scores, as reported by the `TestScores` object.

9. **Circle Class**

Write a `Circle` class that has the following member variables:

- `radius`: a double
- `pi`: a double initialized with the value 3.14159

The class should have the following member functions:

- **Default Constructor.** A default constructor that sets `radius` to 0.0.
- **Constructor.** Accepts the radius of the circle as an argument.
- **`setRadius`.** A mutator function for the radius variable.
- **`getRadius`.** An accessor function for the radius variable.
- **`getArea`.** Returns the area of the circle, which is calculated as
  `area = pi * radius * radius`
- **`getDiameter`.** Returns the diameter of the circle, which is calculated as
  `diameter = radius * 2`
- **`getCircumference`.** Returns the circumference of the circle, which is calculated as
  `circumference = 2 * pi * radius`

Write a program that demonstrates the `Circle` class by asking the user for the circle's radius, creating a `Circle` object, and then reporting the circle's area, diameter, and circumference.

10. **Population**

In a population, the birth rate and death rate are calculated as follows:

Birth Rate = Number of Births ÷ Population
Death Rate = Number of Deaths ÷ Population

For example, in a population of 100,000 that has 8,000 births and 6,000 deaths per year, the birth rate and death rate are:

Birth Rate = 8,000 ÷ 100,000 = 0.08
Death Rate = 6,000 ÷ 100,000 = 0.06

Design a `Population` class that stores a population, number of births, and number of deaths for a period of time. Member functions should return the birth rate and death rate. Implement the class in a program.

Input Validation: Do not accept population figures less than 1, or birth or death numbers less than 0.

11. **Number Array Class**

Design a class that has an array of floating-point numbers. The constructor should accept an integer argument and dynamically allocate the array to hold that many numbers. The destructor should free the memory held by the array. In addition, there should be member functions to perform the following operations:

- Store a number in any element of the array
- Retrieve a number from any element of the array
- Return the highest value stored in the array
- Return the lowest value stored in the array
- Return the average of all the numbers stored in the array

Demonstrate the class in a program.

12. **Payroll**

Design a `PayRoll` class that has data members for an employee's hourly pay rate, number of hours worked, and total pay for the week. Write a program with an array of seven `PayRoll` objects. The program should ask the user for the number of hours each employee has worked and will then display the amount of gross pay each has earned.

Input Validation: Do not accept values greater than 60 for the number of hours worked.

13. **Mortgage Payment**

Design a class that will determine the monthly payment on a home mortgage. The monthly payment with interest compounded monthly can be calculated as follows:

$$\text{Payment} = \frac{\text{Loan} \times \dfrac{\text{Rate}}{12} \times \text{Term}}{\text{Term} - 1}$$

where

$$\text{Term} = \left(1 + \frac{\text{Rate}}{12}\right)^{12 \times \text{Years}}$$

Payment = the monthly payment
Loan = the dollar amount of the loan
Rate = the annual interest rate
Years = the number of years of the loan

The class should have member functions for setting the loan amount, interest rate, and number of years of the loan. It should also have member functions for returning the monthly payment amount and the total amount paid to the bank at the end of the loan period. Implement the class in a complete program.

Input Validation: Do not accept negative numbers for any of the loan values.

14. **Freezing and Boiling Points**

The following table lists the freezing and boiling points of several substances.

Substance	Freezing Point	Boiling Point
Ethyl Alcohol	−173	172
Oxygen	−362	−306
Water	32	212

Design a class that stores a temperature in a `temperature` member variable and has the appropriate accessor and mutator functions. In addition to appropriate constructors, the class should have the following member functions:

- **isEthylFreezing.** This function should return the `bool` value `true` if the temperature stored in the `temperature` field is at or below the freezing point of ethyl alcohol. Otherwise, the function should return `false`.
- **isEthylBoiling.** This function should return the `bool` value `true` if the temperature stored in the `temperature` field is at or above the boiling point of ethyl alcohol. Otherwise, the function should return `false`.
- **isOxygenFreezing.** This function should return the `bool` value `true` if the temperature stored in the `temperature` field is at or below the freezing point of oxygen. Otherwise, the function should return `false`.
- **isOxygenBoiling.** This function should return the `bool` value `true` if the temperature stored in the `temperature` field is at or above the boiling point of oxygen. Otherwise, the function should return `false`.
- **isWaterFreezing.** This function should return the `bool` value `true` if the temperature stored in the `temperature` field is at or below the freezing point of water. Otherwise, the function should return `false`.
- **isWaterBoiling.** This function should return the `bool` value `true` if the temperature stored in the `temperature` field is at or above the boiling point of water. Otherwise, the function should return `false`.

Write a program that demonstrates the class. The program should ask the user to enter a temperature, and then display a list of the substances that will freeze at that temperature and those that will boil at that temperature. For example, if the temperature is -20 the class should report that water will freeze and oxygen will boil at that temperature.

15. **Cash Register**

Design a `CashRegister` class that can be used with the `InventoryItem` class discussed in this chapter. The `CashRegister` class should perform the following:

1. Ask the user for the item and quantity being purchased.

2. Get the item's cost from the `InventoryItem` object.

3. Add a 30% profit to the cost to get the item's unit price.

4. Multiply the unit price times the quantity being purchased to get the purchase subtotal.

5. Compute a 6% sales tax on the subtotal to get the purchase total.

6. Display the purchase subtotal, tax, and total on the screen.

7. Subtract the quantity being purchased from the `onHand` variable of the `InventoryItem` class object.

Implement both classes in a complete program. Feel free to modify the `InventoryItem` class in any way necessary.

Input Validation: Do not accept a negative value for the quantity of items being purchased.

16. **Trivia Game**

In this programming challenge you will create a simple trivia game for two players. The program will work like this:

- Starting with player 1, each player gets a turn at answering five trivia questions. (There are a total of 10 questions.) When a question is displayed, four possible answers are also displayed. Only one of the answers is correct, and if the player selects the correct answer he or she earns a point.
- After answers have been selected for all of the questions, the program displays the number of points earned by each player and declares the player with the highest number of points the winner.

In this program you will design a `Question` class to hold the data for a trivia question. The `Question` class should have member variables for the following data:

- A trivia question
- Possible answer #1
- Possible answer #2
- Possible answer #3
- Possible answer #4
- The number of the correct answer (1, 2, 3, or 4)

The `Question` class should have appropriate constructor(s), accessor, and mutator functions.

The program should create an array of 10 `Question` objects, one for each trivia question. Make up your own trivia questions on the subject or subjects of your choice for the objects.

Group Project

17. **Patient Fees**

1. This program should be designed and written by a team of students. Here are some suggestions:

   – One or more students may work on a single class.
   – The requirements of the program should be analyzed so each student is given about the same workload.

- The parameters and return types of each function and class member function should be decided in advance.
- The program will be best implemented as a multi-file program.

2. You are to write a program that computes a patient's bill for a hospital stay. The different components of the program are

The `PatientAccount` class
The `Surgery` class
The `Pharmacy` class
The `main` program

- The `PatientAccount` class will keep a total of the patient's charges. It will also keep track of the number of days spent in the hospital. The group must decide on the hospital's daily rate.
- The `Surgery` class will have stored within it the charges for at least five types of surgery. It can update the charges variable of the `PatientAccount` class.
- The `Pharmacy` class will have stored within it the price of at least five types of medication. It can update the charges variable of the `PatientAccount` class.
- The student who designs the main program will design a menu that allows the user to enter a type of surgery and a type of medication, and check the patient out of the hospital. When the patient checks out, the total charges should be displayed.

14.1   Instance and Static Members

CONCEPT: Each instance of a class has its own copies of the class's instance variables. If a member variable is declared **static**, however, all instances of that class have access to that variable. If a member function is declared **static**, it may be called without any instances of the class being defined.

Instance Variables

Each class object (an instance of a class) has its own copy of the class's member variables. An object's member variables are separate and distinct from the member variables of other objects of the same class. For example, recall that the Rectangle class discussed in Chapter 13 has two member variables: width and length. Suppose that we define two objects of the Rectangle class and set their width and length member variables as shown in the following code.

```
Rectangle box1, box2;

// Set the width and length for box1.
box1.setWidth(5);
box1.setLength(10);
```

```
// Set the width and length for box2.
box2.setWidth(500);
box2.setLength(1000);
```

This code creates `box1` and `box2`, which are two distinct objects. Each has its own `width` and `length` member variables, as illustrated in Figure 14-1.

Figure 14-1

When the `getWidth` member function is called, it returns the value stored in the calling object's `width` member variable. For example, the following statement displays 5 500.

```
cout << box1.getWidth() << " " << box2.getWidth() << endl;
```

In object-oriented programming, member variables such as the `Rectangle` class's `width` and `length` members are known as *instance variables*. They are called instance variables because each instance of the class has its own copies of the variables.

Static Members

It is possible to create a member variable or member function that does not belong to any instance of a class. Such members are known as a *static member variables* and *static member functions*. When a value is stored in a static member variable, it is not stored in an instance of the class. In fact, an instance of the class doesn't even have to exist in order for values to be stored in the class's static member variables. Likewise, static member functions do not operate on instance variables. Instead, they can operate only on static member variables. You can think of static member variables and static member functions as belonging to the class instead of to an instance of the class. In this section, we will take a closer look at static members. First we will examine static member variables.

Static Member Variables

When a member variable is declared with the key word `static`, there will be only one copy of the member variable in memory, regardless of the number of instances of the class that might exist. A single copy of a class's static member variable is shared by all instances of the class. For example, the following `Tree` class uses a static member variable to keep count of the number of instances of the class that are created.

Contents of `Tree.h`

```
1   // Tree class
2   class Tree
3   {
4   private:
5       static int objectCount;   // Static member variable.
```

```
 6    public:
 7        // Constructor
 8        Tree()
 9            { objectCount++; }
10
11        // Accessor function for objectCount
12        int getObjectCount() const
13            { return objectCount; }
14    };
15
16    // Definition of the static member variable, written
17    // outside the class.
18    int Tree::objectCount = 0;
```

First, notice in line 5 the declaration of the static member variable named objectCount: A static member variable is created by placing the key word static before the variable's data type. Also notice that in line 18 we have written a definition statement for the objectCount variable, and that the statement is outside the class declaration. This external definition statement causes the variable to be created in memory, and is required. In line 18 we have explicitly initialized the objectCount variable with the value 0. We could have left out the initialization because C++ automatically stores 0 in all uninitialized static member variables. It is a good practice to initialize the variable anyway, so it is clear to anyone reading the code that the variable starts out with the value 0.

Next, look at the constructor in lines 8 and 9. In line 9 the ++ operator is used to increment objectCount. Each time an instance of the Tree class is created, the constructor will be called and the objectCount member variable will be incremented. As a result, the objectCount member variable will contain the number of instances of the Tree class that have been created. The getObjectCount function, in lines 12 and 13, returns the value in objectCount. Program 14-1 demonstrates this class.

Program 14-1

```
 1    // This program demonstrates a static member variable.
 2    #include <iostream>
 3    #include "Tree.h"
 4    using namespace std;
 5
 6    int main()
 7    {
 8        // Define three Tree objects.
 9        Tree oak;
10        Tree elm;
11        Tree pine;
12
13        // Display the number of Tree objects we have.
14        cout << "We have " << pine.getObjectCount()
15            << " trees in our program!\n";
16        return 0;
17    }
```

Program Output
```
We have 3 trees in our program!
```

The program creates three instances of the `Tree` class, stored in the variables `oak`, `elm`, and `pine`. Although there are three instances of the class, there is only one copy of the static `objectCount` variable. This is illustrated in Figure 14-2.

Figure 14-2

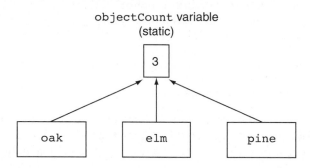

Instances of the `Tree` class

In line 14 the program calls the `getObjectCount` member function to retrieve the number of instances that have been created. Although the program uses the `pine` object to call the member function, the same value would be returned if any of the objects had been used. For example, all three of the following `cout` statements would display the same thing.

```
cout << "We have " << oak.getObjectCount() << " trees\n";
cout << "We have " << elm.getObjectCount() << " trees\n";
cout << "We have " << pine.getObjectCount() << " trees\n";
```

A more practical use of a static member variable is demonstrated in Program 14-2. The `Budget` class is used to gather the budget requests for all the divisions of a company. The class uses a static member, `corpBudget`, to hold the amount of the overall corporate budget. When the member function `addBudget` is called, its argument is added to the current contents of `corpBudget`. By the time the program is finished, `corpBudget` will contain the total of all the values placed there by all the `Budget` class objects. (These files are stored in the Student Source Code Folder `Chapter 14\Budget Version 1`.)

Contents of `Budget.h` (Version 1)

```
 1   #ifndef BUDGET_H
 2   #define BUDGET_H
 3
 4   // Budget class declaration
 5   class Budget
 6   {
 7   private:
 8      static double corpBudget;    // Static member
 9      double divisionBudget;       // Instance member
10   public:
11      Budget()
12         { divisionBudget = 0; }
13
```

```
14        void addBudget(double b)
15           { divisionBudget += b;
16             corpBudget += b; }
17
18        double getDivisionBudget() const
19           { return divisionBudget; }
20
21        double getCorpBudget() const
22           { return corpBudget; }
23   };
24
25   // Definition of static member variable corpBudget
26   double Budget::corpBudget = 0;
27
28   #endif
```

Program 14-2

```
1    // This program demonstrates a static class member variable.
2    #include <iostream>
3    #include <iomanip>
4    #include "Budget.h"
5    using namespace std;
6
7    int main()
8    {
9       int count;                       // Loop counter
10      const int NUM_DIVISIONS = 4;     // Number of divisions
11      Budget divisions[NUM_DIVISIONS]; // Array of Budget objects
12
13      // Get the budget requests for each division.
14      for (count = 0; count < NUM_DIVISIONS; count++)
15      {
16         double budgetAmount;
17         cout << "Enter the budget request for division ";
18         cout << (count + 1) << ": ";
19         cin >> budgetAmount;
20         divisions[count].addBudget(budgetAmount);
21      }
22
23      // Display the budget requests and the corporate budget.
24      cout << fixed << showpoint << setprecision(2);
25      cout << "\nHere are the division budget requests:\n";
26      for (count = 0; count < NUM_DIVISIONS; count++)
27      {
28         cout << "\tDivision " << (count + 1) << "\t$ ";
29         cout << divisions[count].getDivisionBudget() << endl;
30      }
31      cout << "\tTotal Budget Requests:\t$ ";
32      cout << divisions[0].getCorpBudget() << endl;
33
34      return 0;
35   }
```

(program output continues)

Program 14-2   *(continued)*

Program Output with Example Input Shown in Bold
```
Enter the budget request for division 1: 100000 [Enter]
Enter the budget request for division 2: 200000 [Enter]
Enter the budget request for division 3: 300000 [Enter]
Enter the budget request for division 4: 400000 [Enter]

Here are the division budget requests:
    Division 1    $ 100000.00
    Division 2    $ 200000.00
    Division 3    $ 300000.00
    Division 4    $ 400000.00
    Total Budget Requests: $ 1000000.00
```

Static Member Functions

You declare a static member function by placing the `static` keyword in the function's prototype. Here is the general form:

```
static ReturnType FunctionName (ParameterTypeList);
```

A function that is a static member of a class cannot access any nonstatic member data in its class. With this limitation in mind, you might wonder what purpose static member functions serve. The following two points are important for understanding their usefulness:

- Even though static member variables are declared in a class, they are actually defined outside the class declaration. The lifetime of a class's static member variable is the lifetime of the program. This means that a class's static member variables come into existence before any instances of the class are created.
- A class's static member functions can be called before any instances of the class are created. This means that a class's static member functions can access the class's static member variables *before* any instances of the class are defined in memory. This gives you the ability to create very specialized setup routines for class objects.

Program 14-3, a modification of Program 14-2, demonstrates this feature. It asks the user to enter the main office's budget request before any division requests are entered. The `Budget` class has been modified to include a static member function named `mainOffice`. This function adds its argument to the static `corpBudget` variable, and is called before any instances of the `Budget` class are defined. (These files are stored in the Student Source Code Folder `Chapter 14\Budget Version 2`.)

Contents of `Budget.h` (Version 2)

```
1   #ifndef BUDGET_H
2   #define BUDGET_H
3
4   // Budget class declaration
5   class Budget
6   {
7   private:
8       static double corpBudget;     // Static member variable
9       double divisionBudget;        // Instance member variable
```

```
10   public:
11      Budget()
12         { divisionBudget = 0; }
13
14      void addBudget(double b)
15         { divisionBudget += b;
16           corpBudget += b; }
17
18      double getDivisionBudget() const
19         { return divisionBudget; }
20
21      double getCorpBudget() const
22         { return corpBudget; }
23
24      static void mainOffice(double);  // Static member function
25   };
26
27   #endif
```

Contents of `Budget.cpp`

```
1   #include "Budget.h"
2
3   // Definition of corpBudget static member variable
4   double Budget::corpBudget = 0;
5
6   //*********************************************************
7   // Definition of static member function mainOffice.      *
8   // This function adds the main office's budget request to *
9   // the corpBudget variable.                              *
10  //*********************************************************
11
12  void Budget::mainOffice(double moffice)
13  {
14      corpBudget += moffice;
15  }
```

Program 14-3

```
1   // This program demonstrates a static member function.
2   #include <iostream>
3   #include <iomanip>
4   #include "Budget.h"
5   using namespace std;
6
7   int main()
8   {
9      int count;                      // Loop counter
10     double mainOfficeRequest;       // Main office budget request
11     const int NUM_DIVISIONS = 4;    // Number of divisions
12
```

(program continues)

Program 14-3   *(continued)*

```
13        // Get the main office's budget request.
14        // Note that no instances of the Budget class have been defined.
15        cout << "Enter the main office's budget request: ";
16        cin >> mainOfficeRequest;
17        Budget::mainOffice(mainOfficeRequest);
18
19        Budget divisions[NUM_DIVISIONS]; // An array of Budget objects.
20
21        // Get the budget requests for each division.
22        for (count = 0; count < NUM_DIVISIONS; count++)
23        {
24           double budgetAmount;
25           cout << "Enter the budget request for division ";
26           cout << (count + 1) << ": ";
27           cin >> budgetAmount;
28           divisions[count].addBudget(budgetAmount);
29        }
30
31        // Display the budget requests and the corporate budget.
32        cout << fixed << showpoint << setprecision(2);
33        cout << "\nHere are the division budget requests:\n";
34        for (count = 0; count < NUM_DIVISIONS; count++)
35        {
36           cout << "\tDivision " << (count + 1) << "\t$ ";
37           cout << divisions[count].getDivisionBudget() << endl;
38        }
39        cout << "\tTotal Budget Requests:\t$ ";
40        cout << divisions[0].getCorpBudget() << endl;
41
42        return 0;
43     }
```

Program Output with Example Input Shown in Bold
```
Enter the main office's budget request: 100000 [Enter]
Enter the budget request for division 1: 100000 [Enter]
Enter the budget request for division 2: 200000 [Enter]
Enter the budget request for division 3: 300000 [Enter]
Enter the budget request for division 4: 400000 [Enter]

Here are the division budget requests:
     Division 1    $ 100000.00
     Division 2    $ 200000.00
     Division 3    $ 300000.00
     Division 4    $ 400000.00
     Total Requests (including main office): $ 1100000.00
```

Notice in line 17 the statement that calls the static function mainOffice:

```
Budget::mainOffice(amount);
```

Calls to static member functions do not use the regular notation of connecting the function name to an object name with the dot operator. Instead, static member functions are called by connecting the function name to the class name with the scope resolution operator.

NOTE: If an instance of a class with a static member function exists, the static member function can be called with the class object name and the dot operator, just like any other member function.

14.2 Friends of Classes

CONCEPT: A friend is a function or class that is not a member of a class, but has access to the private members of the class.

Private members are hidden from all parts of the program outside the class, and accessing them requires a call to a public member function. Sometimes you will want to create an exception to that rule. A *friend* function is a function that is not part of a class, but that has access to the class's private members. In other words, a friend function is treated as if it were a member of the class. A friend function can be a regular stand-alone function, or it can be a member of another class. (In fact, an entire class can be declared a friend of another class.)

In order for a function or class to become a friend of another class, it must be declared as such by the class granting it access. Classes keep a "list" of their friends, and only the external functions or classes whose names appear in the list are granted access. A function is declared a friend by placing the key word `friend` in front of a prototype of the function. Here is the general format:

```
friend ReturnType FunctionName (ParameterTypeList)
```

In the following declaration of the `Budget` class, the `addBudget` function of another class, `AuxiliaryOffice` has been declared a friend. (This file is stored in the Student Source Code Folder `Chapter 14\Budget Version 3`.)

Contents of `Budget.h` (Version 3)

```
 1  #ifndef BUDGET_H
 2  #define BUDGET_H
 3  #include "Auxil.h"
 4
 5  // Budget class declaration
 6  class Budget
 7  {
 8  private:
 9     static double corpBudget;  // Static member variable
10     double divisionBudget;     // Instance member variable
11  public:
12     Budget()
13        { divisionBudget = 0; }
14
15     void addBudget(double b)
16        { divisionBudget += b;
17          corpBudget += b; }
```

```
18
19        double getDivisionBudget() const
20           { return divisionBudget; }
21
22        double getCorpBudget() const
23           { return corpBudget; }
24
25        // Static member function
26        static void mainOffice(double);
27
28        // Friend function
29        friend void AuxiliaryOffice::addBudget(double, Budget &);
30   };
31
32   #endif
```

Let's assume another class, `AuxiliaryOffice`, represents a division's auxiliary office, perhaps in another country. The auxiliary office makes a separate budget request, which must be added to the overall corporate budget. The friend declaration of the `AuxiliaryOffice::addBudget` function tells the compiler that the function is to be granted access to `Budget`'s private members. Notice the function takes two arguments: a `double` and a reference object of the `Budget` class. The `Budget` class object that is to be modified by the function is passed to it, by reference, as an argument. The following code shows the declaration of the `AuxillaryOffice` class. (This file is stored in the Student Source Code Folder `Chapter 14\Budget Version 3`.)

Contents of `Auxil.h`

```
1    #ifndef AUXIL_H
2    #define AUXIL_H
3
4    class Budget;   // Forward declaration of Budget class
5
6    // Aux class declaration
7
8    class AuxiliaryOffice
9    {
10   private:
11      double auxBudget;
12   public:
13      AuxiliaryOffice()
14         { auxBudget = 0; }
15
16      double getDivisionBudget() const
17         { return auxBudget; }
18
19      void addBudget(double, Budget &);
20   };
21
22   #endif
```

Contents of `Auxil.cpp`

```
1   #include "Auxil.h"
2   #include "Budget.h"
3
4   //*********************************************************
5   // Definition of member function mainOffice.             *
6   // This function is declared a friend by the Budget class. *
7   // It adds the value of argument b to the static corpBudget *
8   // member variable of the Budget class.                  *
9   //*********************************************************
10
11  void AuxiliaryOffice::addBudget(double b, Budget &div)
12  {
13      auxBudget += b;
14      div.corpBudget += b;
15  }
```

Notice the `Auxil.h` file contains the following statement in line 4:

```
class Budget; // Forward declaration of Budget class
```

This is a *forward declaration* of the `Budget` class. It simply tells the compiler that a class named `Budget` will be declared later in the program. This is necessary because the compiler will process the `Auxil.h` file before it processes the `Budget` class declaration. When it is processing the `Auxil.h` file it will see the following function declaration in line 19:

```
void addBudget(double, Budget &);
```

The `addBudget` function's second parameter is a `Budget` reference variable. At this point, the compiler has not processed the `Budget` class declaration, so, without the forward declaration, it wouldn't know what a `Budget` reference variable is.

The following code shows the definition of the `addBudget` function. (This file is also stored in the Student Source Code Folder `Chapter 14\Budget Version 3`.)

Contents of `Auxil.cpp`

```
1   #include "Auxil.h"
2   #include "Budget.h"
3
4   //*********************************************************
5   // Definition of member function mainOffice.             *
6   // This function is declared a friend by the Budget class. *
7   // It adds the value of argument b to the static corpBudget *
8   // member variable of the Budget class.                  *
9   //*********************************************************
10
11  void AuxiliaryOffice::addBudget(double b, Budget &div)
12  {
13      auxBudget += b;
14      div.corpBudget += b;
15  }
```

The parameter `div`, a reference to a `Budget` class object, is used in line 14. This statement adds the parameter `b` to `div.corpBudget`. Program 14-4 demonstrates the classes.

Program 14-4

```cpp
1   // This program demonstrates a static member function.
2   #include <iostream>
3   #include <iomanip>
4   #include "Budget.h"
5   using namespace std;
6
7   int main()
8   {
9      int count;                      // Loop counter
10     double mainOfficeRequest;       // Main office budget request
11     const int NUM_DIVISIONS = 4;    // Number of divisions
12
13     // Get the main office's budget request.
14     cout << "Enter the main office's budget request: ";
15     cin >> mainOfficeRequest;
16     Budget::mainOffice(mainOfficeRequest);
17
18     Budget divisions[NUM_DIVISIONS]; // Array of Budget objects
19     AuxiliaryOffice auxOffices[4];   // Array of AuxiliaryOffice
20
21     // Get the budget requests for each division
22     // and their auxiliary offices.
23     for (count = 0; count < NUM_DIVISIONS; count++)
24     {
25        double budgetAmount;  // To hold input
26
27        // Get the request for the division office.
28        cout << "Enter the budget request for division ";
29        cout << (count + 1) << ": ";
30        cin >> budgetAmount;
31        divisions[count].addBudget(budgetAmount);
32
33        // Get the request for the auxiliary office.
34        cout << "Enter the budget request for that division's\n";
35        cout << "auxiliary office: ";
36        cin >> budgetAmount;
37        auxOffices[count].addBudget(budgetAmount, divisions[count]);
38     }
39
40     // Display the budget requests and the corporate budget.
41     cout << fixed << showpoint << setprecision(2);
42     cout << "\nHere are the division budget requests:\n";
43     for (count = 0; count < NUM_DIVISIONS; count++)
44     {
45        cout << "\tDivision " << (count + 1) << "\t\t$";
46        cout << divisions[count].getDivisionBudget() << endl;
47        cout << "\tAuxiliary office:\t$";
48        cout << auxOffices[count].getDivisionBudget() << endl << endl;
49     }
50     cout << "Total Budget Requests:\t$ ";
51     cout << divisions[0].getCorpBudget() << endl;
52     return 0;
53  }
```

Program Output with Example Input Shown in Bold
```
Enter the main office's budget request: 100000 [Enter]
Enter the budget request for division 1: 100000 [Enter]
Enter the budget request for that division's
auxiliary office: 50000 [Enter]
Enter the budget request for division 2: 200000 [Enter]
Enter the budget request for that division's
auxiliary office: 40000 [Enter]
Enter the budget request for division 3: 300000 [Enter]
Enter the budget request for that division's
auxiliary office: 70000 [Enter]
Enter the budget request for division 4: 400000 [Enter]
Enter the budget request for that division's
auxiliary office: 65000 [Enter]

Here are the division budget requests:
        Division 1              $100000.00
        Auxiliary office:       $50000.00

        Division 2              $200000.00
        Auxiliary office:       $40000.00

        Division 3              $300000.00
        Auxiliary office:       $70000.00

        Division 4              $400000.00
        Auxiliary office:       $65000.00

Total Budget Requests:  $ 1325000.00
```

As mentioned before, it is possible to make an entire class a friend of another class. The Budget class could make the AuxiliaryOffice class its friend with the following declaration:

```
friend class AuxiliaryOffice;
```

This may not be a good idea, however. Every member function of AuxiliaryOffice (including ones that may be added later) would have access to the private members of Budget. The best practice is to declare as friends only those functions that must have access to the private members of the class.

 Checkpoint

14.1   What is the difference between an instance member variable and a static member variable?

14.2   Static member variables are declared inside the class declaration. Where are static member variables defined?

14.3   Does a static member variable come into existence in memory before, at the same time as, or after any instances of its class?

14.4   What limitation does a static member function have?

14.5 What action is possible with a static member function that isn't possible with an instance member function?

14.6 If class X declares function f as a friend, does function f become a member of class X?

14.7 Class Y is a friend of class X, which means the member functions of class Y have access to the private members of class X. Does the friend key word appear in class Y's declaration or in class X's declaration?

14.3 Memberwise Assignment

CONCEPT: The = operator may be used to assign one object's data to another object, or to initialize one object with another object's data. By default, each member of one object is copied to its counterpart in the other object.

Like other variables (except arrays), objects may be assigned to one another using the = operator. As an example, consider Program 14-5 which uses the Rectangle class (version 4) that we discussed in Chapter 13. Recall that the Rectangle class has two member variables: width and length. The constructor accepts two arguments, one for width and one for length.

Program 14-5

```
 1   // This program demonstrates memberwise assignment.
 2   #include <iostream>
 3   #include "Rectangle.h"
 4   using namespace std;
 5
 6   int main()
 7   {
 8      // Define two Rectangle objects.
 9      Rectangle box1(10.0, 10.0);   // width = 10.0, length = 10.0
10      Rectangle box2 (20.0, 20.0);  // width = 20.0, length = 20.0
11
12      // Display each object's width and length.
13      cout << "box1's width and length: " << box1.getWidth()
14          << " " << box1.getLength() << endl;
15      cout << "box2's width and length: " << box2.getWidth()
16          << " " << box2.getLength() << endl << endl;
17
18      // Assign the members of box1 to box2.
19      box2 = box1;
20
21      // Display each object's width and length again.
22      cout << "box1's width and length: " << box1.getWidth()
23          << " " << box1.getLength() << endl;
24      cout << "box2's width and length: " << box2.getWidth()
25          << " " << box2.getLength() << endl;
26
27      return 0;
28   }
```

Program Output
```
box1's width and length: 10 10
box2's width and length: 20 20

box1's width and length: 10 10
box2's width and length: 10 10
```

The following statement, which appears in line 19, copies the width and length member variables of box1 directly into the width and length member variables of box2:

```
box2 = box1;
```

Memberwise assignment also occurs when one object is initialized with another object's values. Remember the difference between assignment and initialization: assignment occurs between two objects that already exist, and initialization happens to an object being created. Consider the following code:

```
// Define box1.
Rectangle box1(100.0, 50.0);

// Define box2, initialize with box1's values
Rectangle box2 = box1;
```

The last statement defines a Rectangle object, box2, and initializes it to the values stored in box1. Because memberwise assignment takes place, the box2 object will contain the exact same values as the box1 object.

14.4 Copy Constructors

CONCEPT: A copy constructor is a special constructor that is called whenever a new object is created and initialized with another object's data.

Most of the time, the default memberwise assignment behavior in C++ is perfectly acceptable. There are instances, however, where memberwise assignment cannot be used. For example, consider the following class. (This file is stored in the Student Source Code Folder Chapter 14\PersonInfo Version 1.)

Contents of `PersonInfo.h` (Version 1)

```
1   #include <cstring>
2
3   class PersonInfo
4   {
5   private:
6      char *name;
7      int age;
8
```

```
 9   public:
10      PersonInfo(char *n, int a)
11         { name = new char[strlen(n) + 1];
12           strcpy(name, n);
13           age = a; }
14
15      ~PersonInfo()
16         { delete [] name; }
17
18      const char *getName()
19         { return name; }
20
21      int getAge()
22         { return age; }
23   };
```

A potential problem with this class lies in the fact that one of its members, name, is a pointer. The constructor performs a critical operation with the pointer: it dynamically allocates a section of memory and copies a string to it. For instance, the following statement creates a personInfo object named person1, whose name member references dynamically allocated memory holding the string "Maria Jones-Tucker":

```
PersonInfo person1("Maria Jones-Tucker", 25);
```

This is depicted in Figure 14-3.

Figure 14-3

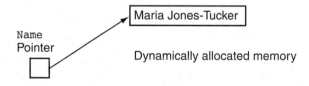

Consider what happens when another PersonInfo object is created and initialized with the person1 object, as in the following statement:

```
PersonInfo person2 = person1;
```

In the statement above, person2's constructor isn't called. Instead, memberwise assignment takes place, copying each of person1's member variables into person2. This means that a separate section of memory is not allocated for person2's name member. It simply gets a copy of the address stored in person1's name member. Both pointers will point to the same address, as depicted in Figure 14-4.

In this situation, either object can manipulate the string, causing the changes to show up in the other object. Likewise, one object can be destroyed, causing its destructor to be called, which frees the allocated memory. The remaining object's name pointer would still reference this section of memory, although it should no longer be used.

Figure 14-4

The solution to this problem is to create a *copy constructor* for the object. A copy constructor is a special constructor that's called when an object is initialized with another object's data. It has the same form as other constructors, except it has a reference parameter of the same class type as the object itself. For example, here is a copy constructor for the `PersonInfo` class:

```
PersonInfo(PersonInfo &obj)
   { name = new char[strlen(obj.name) + 1];
     strcpy(name, obj.name);
     age = obj.age; }
```

When the = operator is used to initialize a `PersonInfo` object with the contents of another `PersonInfo` object, the copy constructor is called. The `PersonInfo` object that appears on the right side of the = operator is passed as an argument to the copy constructor. For example, look at the following statement:

```
PersonInfo person1("Molly McBride", 27);
PersonInfo person2 = person1;
```

In this code, the `person1` object is passed as an argument to the `person2` object's copy constructor.

 NOTE: C++ requires that a copy constructor's parameter be a reference object.

As you can see from studying the copy constructor's code, `person2`'s `name` member will properly reference its own dynamically allocated memory. There will be no danger of `person1` inadvertently destroying or corrupting `person2`'s data.

Using `const` Parameters in Copy Constructors

Because copy constructors are required to use reference parameters, they have access to their argument's data. Since the purpose of a copy constructor is to make a copy of the argument, there is no reason the constructor should modify the argument's data. With this in mind, it's a good idea to make copy constructors' parameters constant by specifying the `const` key word in the parameter list. Here is an example:

```
PersonInfo(const PersonInfo &obj)
   { name = new char[strlen(obj.name) + 1];
     strcpy(name, obj.name);
     age = obj.age; }
```

The const key word ensures that the function cannot change the contents of the parameter. This will prevent you from inadvertently writing code that corrupts data.

The complete listing for the revised PersonInfo class is shown here. (This file is stored in the Student Source Code Folder Chapter 14\PersonInfo Version 2.)

Contents of PersonInfo.h (Version 2)

```
 1    #include <cstring>
 2
 3    class PersonInfo
 4    {
 5    private:
 6       char *name;
 7       int age;
 8
 9    public:
10       // Constructor
11       PersonInfo(char *n, int a)
12          { name = new char[strlen(n) + 1];
13            strcpy(name, n);
14            age = a; }
15
16       // Copy Constructor
17       PersonInfo(const PersonInfo &obj)
18          { name = new char[strlen(obj.name) + 1];
19            strcpy(name, obj.name);
20            age = obj.age; }
21
22       ~PersonInfo()
23          { delete [] name; }
24
25       const char *getName()
26          { return name; }
27
28       int getAge()
29          { return age; }
30    };
```

Copy Constructors and Function Parameters

When a class object is passed by value as an argument to a function, it is passed to a parameter that is also a class object, and the copy constructor of the function's parameter is called. Remember that when a nonreference class object is used as a function parameter it is created when the function is called, and it is initialized with the argument's value.

This is why C++ requires the parameter of a copy constructor to be a reference object. If an object were passed to the copy constructor by value, the copy constructor would create a copy of the argument and store it in the parameter object. When the parameter object is created, its copy constructor will be called, thus causing another parameter object to be created. This process will continue indefinitely (or at least until the available memory fills up, causing the program to halt).

To prevent the copy constructor from calling itself an infinite number of times, C++ requires its parameter to be a reference object.

The Default Copy Constructor

Although you may not realize it, you have seen the action of a copy constructor before. If a class doesn't have a copy constructor, C++ creates a *default copy constructor* for it. The default copy constructor performs the memberwise assignment discussed in the previous section.

 ## Checkpoint

14.8 Briefly describe what is meant by memberwise assignment.

14.9 Describe two instances when memberwise assignment occurs.

14.10 Describe a situation in which memberwise assignment should not be used.

14.11 When is a copy constructor called?

14.12 How does the compiler know that a member function is a copy constructor?

14.13 What action is performed by a class's default copy constructor?

 # 14.5 Operator Overloading

CONCEPT: C++ allows you to redefine how standard operators work when used with class objects.

VideoNote
Operator
Overloading

C++ provides many operators to manipulate data of the primitive data types. However, what if you wish to use an operator to manipulate class objects? For example, assume that a class named Date exists, and objects of the Date class hold the month, day, and year in member variables. Suppose the Date class has a member function named add. The add member function adds a number of days to the date, and adjusts the member variables if the date goes to another month or year. For example, the following statement adds five days to the date stored in the today object:

```
today.add(5);
```

Although it might be obvious that the statement is adding five days to the date stored in today, the use of an operator might be more intuitive. For example, look at the following statement:

```
today += 5;
```

This statement uses the standard += operator to add 5 to today. This behavior does not happen automatically, however. The += operator must be *overloaded* for this action to occur. In this section, you will learn to overload many of C++'s operators to perform specialized operations on class objects.

NOTE: You have already experienced the behavior of an overloaded operator. The / operator performs two types of division: floating point and integer. If one of the / operator's operands is a floating point type, the result will be a floating point value. If both of the / operator's operands are integers, however, a different behavior occurs: the result is an integer and any fractional part is thrown away.

Overloading the = Operator

Although copy constructors solve the initialization problems inherent with objects containing pointer members, they do not work with simple assignment statements. Copy constructors are just that—constructors. They are only invoked when an object is created. Statements like the following still perform memberwise assignment:

```
person2 = person1;
```

In order to change the way the assignment operator works, it must be overloaded. Operator overloading permits you to redefine an existing operator's behavior when used with a class object.

C++ allows a class to have special member functions called *operator functions*. If you wish to redefine the way a particular operator works with an object, you define a function for that operator. The Operator function is then executed any time the operator is used with an object of that class. For example, the following version of the PersonInfo class overloads the = operator. (This file is stored in the Student Source Code Folder Chapter 14\ PersonInfo Version 3.)

Contents of PersonInfo.h (Version 3)

```
 1    #include <cstring>
 2
 3    class PersonInfo
 4    {
 5    private:
 6        char *name;
 7        int age;
 8
 9    public:
10        // Constructor
11        PersonInfo(char *n, int a)
12            { name = new char[strlen(n) + 1];
13              strcpy(name, n);
14              age = a; }
15
16        // Copy Constructor
17        PersonInfo(const PersonInfo &obj)
18            { name = new char[strlen(obj.name) + 1];
19              strcpy(name, obj.name);
20              age = obj.age; }
21
22        // Destructor
23        ~PersonInfo()
24            { delete [] name; }
25
```

```
26        // Accessor functions
27        const char *getName()
28           { return name; }
29
30        int getAge()
31           { return age; }
32
33        // Overloaded = operator
34        void operator=(const PersonInfo &right)
35           { delete [] name;
36             name = new char[strlen(right.name) + 1];
37             strcpy(name, right.name);
38             age = right.age; }
39   };
```

Let's examine the operator function to understand how it works. First look at the function header:

Return   Function   Parameter for object
type   name   on the right side of operator

void operator=(const PersonInfo &right)

The name of the function is `operator=`. This specifies that the function overloads the = operator. Because it is a member of the `PersonInfo` class, this function will be called only when an assignment statement executes where the object on the left side of the = operator is a `PersonInfo` object.

> **NOTE:** You can, if you choose, put spaces around the operator symbol. For instance, the function header above could also read:

```
void operator = (const PersonInfo &right)
```

The function has one parameter: a constant reference object named `right`. This parameter references the object on the right side of the operator. For example, when the statement below is executed, `right` will reference the `person1` object:

```
person2 = person1;
```

It is not required that the parameter of an operator function be a reference object. The `PersonInfo` example declares `right` as a `const` reference for the following reasons:

- It was declared as a reference for efficiency purposes. This prevents the compiler from making a copy of the object being passed into the function.
- It was declared constant so the function will not accidentally change the contents of the argument.

> **NOTE:** In the example, the parameter was named `right` simply to illustrate that it references the object on the right side of the operator. You can name the parameter anything you wish. It will always take the object on the operator's right as its argument.

In learning the mechanics of operator overloading, it is helpful to know that the following two statements do the same thing:

```
person2 = person1;              // Call operator= function
person2.operator=(person1);     // Call operator= function
```

In the last statement you can see exactly what is going on in the function call. The `person1` object is being passed to the function's parameter, `right`. Inside the function, the values in `right`'s members are used to initialize `person2`. Notice that the `operator=` function has access to the `right` parameter's private members. Because the `operator=` function is a member of the `PersonInfo` class, it has access to the private members of any `PersonInfo` object that is passed into it.

NOTE: C++ allows operator functions to be called with regular function call notation, or by using the operator symbol.

Program 14-6 demonstrates the `PersonInfo` class with its overloaded assignment operator. (This file is stored in the Student Source Code Folder `Chapter 14\PersonInfo Version 3`.)

Program 14-6

```
 1   // This program demonstrates the overloaded = operator.
 2   #include <iostream>
 3   #include <cstring>
 4   #include "PersonInfo.h"
 5   using namespace std;
 6
 7   int main()
 8   {
 9      // Create and initialize the jim object.
10      PersonInfo jim("Jim Young", 27);
11
12      // Create and initialize the bob object.
13      PersonInfo bob("Bob Faraday", 32);
14
15      // Create the clone object and initialize with jim.
16      PersonInfo clone = jim;
17
18      // Display the contents of the jim object.
19      cout << "The jim Object contains: " << jim.getName();
20      cout << ", " << jim.getAge() << endl;
21
22      // Display the contents of the bob object.
23      cout << "The bob Object contains: " << bob.getName();
24      cout << ", " << bob.getAge() << endl;
25
26      // Display the contents of the clone object.
27      cout << "The clone Object contains: " << clone.getName();
28      cout << ", " << clone.getAge() << endl << endl;
29
```

```
30      // Assign bob to clone.
31      cout << "Now the clone will change to bob and ";
32      cout << "bob will change to jim.\n\n";
33      clone = bob;    // Call overloaded = operator
34      bob = jim;      // Call overloaded = operator
35
36      // Display the contents of the jim object.
37      cout << "The jim Object contains: " << jim.getName();
38      cout << ", " << jim.getAge() << endl;
39
40      // Display the contents of the bob object.
41      cout << "The bob Object contains: " << bob.getName();
42      cout << ", " << bob.getAge() << endl;
43
44      // Display the contents of the clone object.
45      cout << "The clone Object contains: " << clone.getName();
46      cout << ", " << clone.getAge() << endl;
47
48      return 0;
49  }
```

Program Output
```
The jim Object contains: Jim Young, 27
The bob Object contains: Bob Faraday, 32
The clone Object contains: Jim Young, 27

Now the clone will change to bob and bob will change to jim.

The jim Object contains: Jim Young, 27
The bob Object contains: Jim Young, 27
The clone Object contains: Bob Faraday, 32
```

The = Operator's Return Value

There is only one problem with the overloaded = operator shown in Program 14-6: it has a void return type. C++'s built-in = operator allows multiple assignment statements such as:

```
a = b = c;
```

In this statement, the expression b = c causes c to be assigned to b and then returns the value of c. The return value is then stored in a. If a class object's overloaded = operator is to function this way, it too must have a valid return type.

For example, the PersonInfo class's operator= function could be written as:

```
const PersonInfo operator=(const PersonInfo &right)
        { delete [] name;
          name = new char[strlen(right.name) + 1];
          strcpy(name, right.name);
          age = right.age;
          return *this;
        }
```

The data type of the operator function specifies that a `const PersonInfo` object is returned. Look at the last statement in the function:

```
return *this;
```

This statement returns the value of a dereferenced pointer: `this`. But what is `this`? Read on.

The `this` Pointer

The `this` pointer is a special built-in pointer that is available to a class's member functions. It always points to the instance of the class making the function call. For example, if `person1` and `person2` are both `PersonInfo` objects, the following statement causes the `getName` function to operate on `person1`:

```
cout << person1.getName() << endl;
```

Likewise, the following statement causes `getName` to operate on `person2`:

```
cout << person2.getName() << endl;
```

When `getName` is operating on `person1`, the `this` pointer is pointing to `person1`. When `getName` is operating on `person2`, `this` is pointing to `person2`. The `this` pointer always points to the object that is being used to call the member function.

 NOTE: The `this` pointer is passed as a hidden argument to all nonstatic member functions.

The overloaded = operator function is demonstrated in Program 14-7. The multiple assignment statement in line 20 causes the `operator=` function to execute. (This file and the revised version of the `PersonInfo` class is stored in the Student Source Code Folder `Chapter 14\PersonInfo Version 4`.)

Program 14-7

```
 1   // This program demonstrates the overloaded = operator
 2   // with a return value.
 3   #include <iostream>
 4   #include <cstring>
 5   #include "PersonInfo.h"
 6   using namespace std;
 7
 8   int main()
 9   {
10      // Create and initialize the jim object.
11      PersonInfo jim("Jim Young", 27);
12
13      // Create and initialize the bob object.
14      PersonInfo bob("Bob Faraday", 32);
15
16      // Create the clone object and initialize with jim.
17      PersonInfo clone = jim;
18
```

```
19       // Assign jim to bob and clone.
20       clone = bob = jim;    // Call overloaded = operator
21
22       // Display the contents of the jim object.
23       cout << "The jim Object contains: " << jim.getName();
24       cout << ", " << jim.getAge() << endl;
25
26       // Display the contents of the bob object.
27       cout << "The bob Object contains: " << bob.getName();
28       cout << ", " << bob.getAge() << endl;
29
30       // Display the contents of the clone object.
31       cout << "The clone Object contains: " << clone.getName();
32       cout << ", " << clone.getAge() << endl;
33
34       return 0;
35  }
```

Program Output

```
The jim Object contains: Jim Young, 27
The bob Object contains: Jim Young, 27
The clone Object contains: Jim Young, 27
```

Some General Issues of Operator Overloading

Now that you have had a taste of operator overloading, let's look at some of the general issues involved in this programming technique.

Although it is not a good programming practice, you can change an operator's entire meaning if that's what you wish to do. There is nothing to prevent you from changing the = symbol from an assignment operator to a "display" operator. For instance, the following class does just that:

```
class Weird
{
private:
    int value;
public:
    Weird(int v)
        {value = v; }
    void operator=(const weird &right)
        { cout << right.value << endl; }
};
```

Although the operator= function in the Weird class overloads the assignment operator, the function doesn't perform an assignment. Instead, it displays the contents of right.value. Consider the following program segment:

```
Weird a(5), b(10);
a = b;
```

Although the statement a = b looks like an assignment statement, it actually causes the contents of b's `value` member to be displayed on the screen:

```
10
```

Another operator overloading issue is that you cannot change the number of operands taken by an operator. The = symbol must always be a binary operator. Likewise, ++ and -- must always be unary operators.

The last issue is that although you may overload most of the C++ operators, you cannot overload all of them. Table 14-1 shows all of the C++ operators that may be overloaded.

Table 14-1

+	-	*	/	%	^	&	|	~	!	=	<
>	+=	-=	*=	/=	%=	^=	&=	|=	<<	>>	>>=
<<=	==	!=	<=	>=	&&	||	++	--	->*	,	->
[]	()	new	delete								

> **NOTE:** Some of the operators in Table 14-1 are beyond the scope of this book and are not covered.

The only operators that cannot be overloaded are

```
?:    .    .*    ::    sizeof
```

Overloading Math Operators

Many classes would benefit not only from an overloaded assignment operator, but also from overloaded math operators. To illustrate this, consider the `FeetInches` class shown in the following two files. (These files are stored in the Student Source Code Folder `Chapter 14\FeetInches Version 1.`)

Contents of `FeetInches.h` (Version 1)

```
1   #ifndef FEETINCHES_H
2   #define FEETINCHES_H
3
4   // The FeetInches class holds distances or measurements
5   // expressed in feet and inches.
6
7   class FeetInches
8   {
9   private:
10      int feet;      // To hold a number of feet
11      int inches;    // To hold a number of inches
12      void simplify(); // Defined in FeetInches.cpp
13  public:
14      // Constructor
15      FeetInches(int f = 0, int i = 0)
16         { feet = f;
17           inches = i;
18           simplify(); }
19
```

```
20      // Mutator functions
21      void setFeet(int f)
22         { feet = f; }
23
24      void setInches(int i)
25         { inches = i;
26           simplify(); }
27
28      // Accessor functions
29      int getFeet() const
30         { return feet; }
31
32      int getInches() const
33         { return inches; }
34
35      // Overloaded operator functions
36      FeetInches operator + (const FeetInches &); // Overloaded +
37      FeetInches operator - (const FeetInches &); // Overloaded -
38    };
39
40    #endif
```

Contents of `FeetInches.cpp` (Version 1)

```
1    // Implementation file for the FeetInches class
2    #include <cstdlib>        // Needed for abs()
3    #include "FeetInches.h"
4
5    //**********************************************************
6    // Definition of member function simplify. This function    *
7    // checks for values in the inches member greater than      *
8    // twelve or less than zero. If such a value is found,       *
9    // the numbers in feet and inches are adjusted to conform    *
10   // to a standard feet & inches expression. For example,      *
11   // 3 feet 14 inches would be adjusted to 4 feet 2 inches and *
12   // 5 feet -2 inches would be adjusted to 4 feet 10 inches.   *
13   //**********************************************************
14
15   void FeetInches::simplify()
16   {
17      if (inches >= 12)
18      {
19         feet += (inches / 12);
20         inches = inches % 12;
21      }
22      else if (inches < 0)
23      {
24         feet -= ((abs(inches) / 12) + 1);
25         inches = 12 - (abs(inches) % 12);
26      }
27   }
28
```

```
29   //**********************************************
30   // Overloaded binary + operator.              *
31   //**********************************************
32
33   FeetInches FeetInches::operator + (const FeetInches &right)
34   {
35      FeetInches temp;
36
37      temp.inches = inches + right.inches;
38      temp.feet = feet + right.feet;
39      temp.simplify();
40      return temp;
41   }
42
43   //**********************************************
44   // Overloaded binary - operator.              *
45   //**********************************************
46
47   FeetInches FeetInches::operator - (const FeetInches &right)
48   {
49      FeetInches temp;
50
51      temp.inches = inches - right.inches;
52      temp.feet = feet - right.feet;
53      temp.simplify();
54      return temp;
55   }
```

The FeetInches class is designed to hold distances or measurements expressed in feet and inches. It consists of eight member functions:

- A constructor that allows the feet and inches members to be set. The default values for these members is zero.
- A setFeet function for storing a value in the feet member.
- A setInches function for storing a value in the inches member.
- A getFeet function for returning the value in the feet member.
- A getInches function for returning the value in the inches member.
- A simplify function for normalizing the values held in feet and inches. This function adjusts any set of values where the inches member is greater than 12 or less than 0.
- An operator + function that overloads the standard + math operator.
- An operator - function that overloads the standard - math operator.

NOTE: The simplify function uses the standard library function abs() to get the absolute value of the inches member. The abs() function requires that cstdlib be included.

The overloaded + and − operators allow one `FeetInches` object to be added to or subtracted from another. For example, assume the `length1` and `length2` objects are defined and initialized as follows:

```
FeetInches length1(3, 5), length2(6, 3);
```

The `length1` object is holding the value 3 feet 5 inches, and the `length2` object is holding the value 6 feet 3 inches. Because the + operator is overloaded, we can add these two objects in a statement such as:

```
length3 = length1 + length2;
```

This statement will add the values of the `length1` and `length2` objects and store the result in the `length3` object. After the statement executes, the `length3` object will be set to 9 feet 8 inches.

The member function that overloads the + operator appears in lines 33 through 41 of the `FeetInches.cpp` file.

This function is called anytime the + operator is used with two `FeetInches` objects. Just like the overloaded = operator we defined in the previous section, this function has one parameter: a constant reference object named `right`. This parameter references the object on the right side of the operator. For example, when the following statement is executed, `right` will reference the `length2` object:

```
length3 = length1 + length2;
```

As before, it might be helpful to think of the statement above as the following function call:

```
length3 = length1.operator+(length2);
```

The `length2` object is being passed to the function's parameter, `right`. When the function finishes, it will return a `FeetInches` object to `length3`. Now let's see what is happening inside the function. First, notice that a `FeetInches` object named `temp` is defined locally in line 35:

```
FeetInches temp;
```

This object is a temporary location for holding the results of the addition. Next, line 37 adds `inches` to `right.inches` and stores the result in `temp.inches`:

```
temp.inches = inches + right.inches;
```

The `inches` variable is a member of `length1`, the object making the function call. It is the object on the left side of the operator. `right.inches` references the `inches` member of `length2`. The next statement, in line 38, is very similar. It adds `feet` to `right.feet` and stores the result in `temp.feet`:

```
temp.feet = feet + right.feet;
```

At this point in the function, `temp` contains the sum of the `feet` and `inches` members of both objects in the expression. The next step is to adjust the values so they conform to a normal value expressed in feet and inches. This is accomplished in line 39 by calling `temp.simplify()`:

```
temp.simplify();
```

The last step, in line 40, is to return the value stored in `temp`:

```
return temp;
```

In the statement `length3 = length1 + length2`, the return statement in the operator function causes the values stored in `temp` to be returned to the `length3` object.

Program 14-8 demonstrates the overloaded operators. (This file is stored in the student source code folder `Chapter 14\FeetInches Version 1`.)

Program 14-8

```
 1   // This program demonstrates the FeetInches class's overloaded
 2   // + and - operators.
 3   #include <iostream>
 4   #include "FeetInches.h"
 5   using namespace std;
 6
 7   int main()
 8   {
 9       int feet, inches;  // To hold input for feet and inches
10
11       // Create three FeetInches objects. The default arguments
12       // for the constructor will be used.
13       FeetInches first, second, third;
14
15       // Get a distance from the user.
16       cout << "Enter a distance in feet and inches: ";
17       cin >> feet >> inches;
18
19       // Store the distance in the first object.
20       first.setFeet(feet);
21       first.setInches(inches);
22
23       // Get another distance from the user.
24       cout << "Enter another distance in feet and inches: ";
25       cin >> feet >> inches;
26
27       // Store the distance in second.
28       second.setFeet(feet);
29       second.setInches(inches);
30
31       // Assign first + second to third.
32       third = first + second;
33
34       // Display the result.
35       cout << "first + second = ";
36       cout << third.getFeet() << " feet, ";
37       cout << third.getInches() << " inches.\n";
38
```

```
39      // Assign first - second to third.
40      third = first - second;
41
42      // Display the result.
43      cout << "first - second = ";
44      cout << third.getFeet() << " feet, ";
45      cout << third.getInches() << " inches.\n";
46
47      return 0;
48  }
```

Program Output with Example Input Shown in Bold
Enter a distance in feet and inches: **6 5 [Enter]**
Enter another distance in feet and inches: **3 10 [Enter]**
first + second = 10 feet, 3 inches.
first - second = 2 feet, 7 inches.

Overloading the Prefix ++ Operator

Unary operators, such as ++ and ––, are overloaded in a fashion similar to the way binary operators are implemented. Because unary operators only affect the object making the operator function call, however, there is no need for a parameter. For example, let's say you wish to have a prefix increment operator for the FeetInches class. Assume the FeetInches object distance is set to the values 7 feet and 5 inches. A ++ operator function could be designed to increment the object's inches member. The following statement would cause distance to have the value 7 feet 6 inches:

```
++distance;
```

The following function overloads the prefix ++ operator to work in this fashion:

```
FeetInches FeetInches::operator++()
{
    ++inches;
    simplify();
    return *this;
}
```

This function first increments the object's inches member. The simplify() function is called and then the dereferenced this pointer is returned. This allows the operator to perform properly in statements like this:

```
distance2 = ++distance1;
```

Remember, the statement above is equivalent to

```
distance2 = distance1.operator++();
```

Overloading the Postfix ++ Operator

Overloading the postfix ++ operator is only slightly different than overloading the prefix version. Here is the function that overloads the postfix operator with the `FeetInches` class:

```
FeetInches FeetInches::operator++(int)
{
    FeetInches temp(feet, inches);
    inches++;
    simplify();
    return temp;
}
```

The first difference you will notice is the use of a *dummy parameter*. The word `int` in the function's parentheses establishes a nameless integer parameter. When C++ sees this parameter in an operator function, it knows the function is designed to be used in postfix mode. The second difference is the use of a temporary local variable, the `temp` object. `temp` is initialized with the `feet` and `inches` values of the object making the function call. `temp`, therefore, is a copy of the object being incremented, but before the increment takes place. After `inches` is incremented and the `simplify` function is called, the contents of `temp` is returned. This causes the postfix operator to behave correctly in a statement like this:

```
distance2 = distance1++;
```

You will find a version of the `FeetInches` class with the overloaded prefix and postfix ++ operators stored in the Student Source Code Folder `Chapter 14\FeetInches Version 2`. In that folder you will also find Program 14-9, which demonstrates these overloaded operators.

Program 14-9

```
 1   // This program demonstrates the FeetInches class's overloaded
 2   // prefix and postfix ++ operators.
 3   #include <iostream>
 4   #include "FeetInches.h"
 5   using namespace std;
 6
 7   int main()
 8   {
 9       int count;   // Loop counter
10
11       // Define a FeetInches object with the default
12       // value of 0 feet, 0 inches.
13       FeetInches first;
14
15       // Define a FeetInches object with 1 foot 5 inches.
16       FeetInches second(1, 5);
17
```

```
18        // Use the prefix ++ operator.
19        cout << "Demonstrating prefix ++ operator.\n";
20        for (count = 0; count < 12; count++)
21        {
22           first = ++second;
23           cout << "first: " << first.getFeet() << " feet, ";
24           cout << first.getInches() << " inches. ";
25           cout << "second: " << second.getFeet() << " feet, ";
26           cout << second.getInches() << " inches.\n";
27        }
28
29        // Use the postfix ++ operator.
30        cout << "\nDemonstrating postfix ++ operator.\n";
31        for (count = 0; count < 12; count++)
32        {
33           first = second++;
34           cout << "first: " << first.getFeet() << " feet, ";
35           cout << first.getInches() << " inches. ";
36           cout << "second: " << second.getFeet() << " feet, ";
37           cout << second.getInches() << " inches.\n";
38        }
39
40        return 0;
41  }
```

Program Output

```
Demonstrating prefix ++ operator.
first: 1 feet 6 inches. second: 1 feet 6 inches.
first: 1 feet 7 inches. second: 1 feet 7 inches.
first: 1 feet 8 inches. second: 1 feet 8 inches.
first: 1 feet 9 inches. second: 1 feet 9 inches.
first: 1 feet 10 inches. second: 1 feet 10 inches.
first: 1 feet 11 inches. second: 1 feet 11 inches.
first: 2 feet 0 inches. second: 2 feet 0 inches.
first: 2 feet 1 inches. second: 2 feet 1 inches.
first: 2 feet 2 inches. second: 2 feet 2 inches.
first: 2 feet 3 inches. second: 2 feet 3 inches.
first: 2 feet 4 inches. second: 2 feet 4 inches.
first: 2 feet 5 inches. second: 2 feet 5 inches.

Demonstrating postfix ++ operator.
first: 2 feet 5 inches. second: 2 feet 6 inches.
first: 2 feet 6 inches. second: 2 feet 7 inches.
first: 2 feet 7 inches. second: 2 feet 8 inches.
first: 2 feet 8 inches. second: 2 feet 9 inches.
first: 2 feet 9 inches. second: 2 feet 10 inches.
first: 2 feet 10 inches. second: 2 feet 11 inches.
first: 2 feet 11 inches. second: 3 feet 0 inches.
first: 3 feet 0 inches. second: 3 feet 1 inches.
first: 3 feet 1 inches. second: 3 feet 2 inches.
first: 3 feet 2 inches. second: 3 feet 3 inches.
first: 3 feet 3 inches. second: 3 feet 4 inches.
first: 3 feet 4 inches. second: 3 feet 5 inches.
```

Checkpoint

14.14 Assume there is a class named `Pet`. Write the prototype for a member function of `Pet` that overloads the = operator.

14.15 Assume that `dog` and `cat` are instances of the `Pet` class, which has overloaded the = operator. Rewrite the following statement so it appears in function call notation instead of operator notation:

```
dog = cat;
```

14.16 What is the disadvantage of an overloaded = operator returning `void`?

14.17 Describe the purpose of the `this` pointer.

14.18 The `this` pointer is automatically passed to what type of functions?

14.19 Assume there is a class named `Animal` that overloads the = and + operators. In the following statement, assume `cat`, `tiger`, and `wildcat` are all instances of the `Animal` class:

```
wildcat = cat + tiger;
```

Of the three objects, `wildcat`, `cat`, or `tiger`, which is calling the `operator+` function? Which object is passed as an argument into the function?

14.20 What does the use of a dummy parameter in a unary operator function indicate to the compiler?

Overloading Relational Operators

In addition to the assignment and math operators, relational operators may be overloaded. This capability allows classes to be compared in statements that use relational expressions such as:

```
if (distance1 < distance2)
{
    ... code ...
}
```

Overloaded relational operators are implemented like other binary operators. The only difference is that a relational operator function should always return a `true` or `false` value. The `FeetInches` class in the Student Source Code Folder `Chapter 14\ FeetInches Version 3` contains functions to overload the >, <, and == relational operators. Here is the function for overloading the > operator:

```
bool FeetInches::operator > (const FeetInches &right)
{
    bool status;

    if (feet > right.feet)
        status = true;
    else if (feet == right.feet && inches > right.inches)
        status = true;
    else
        status = false;

    return status;
}
```

As you can see, the function compares the `feet` member (and if necessary, the `inches` member) with that of the parameter. If the calling object contains a value greater than that of the parameter, `true` is returned. Otherwise, `false` is returned.

Here is the code that overloads the < operator:

```cpp
bool FeetInches::operator < (const FeetInches &right)
{
    bool status;

    if (feet < right.feet)
        status = true;
    else if (feet == right.feet && inches < right.inches)
        status = true;
    else
        status = false;

    return status;
}
```

Here is the code that overloads the == operator:

```cpp
bool FeetInches::operator == (const FeetInches &right)
{
    bool status;

    if (feet == right.feet && inches == right.inches)
        status = true;
    else
        status = false;

    return status;
}
```

Program 14-10 demonstrates these overloaded operators. (This file is also stored in the Student Source Code Folder `Chapter 14\FeetInches Version 3`.)

Program 14-10

```cpp
 1  // This program demonstrates the FeetInches class's overloaded
 2  // relational operators.
 3  #include <iostream>
 4  #include "FeetInches.h"
 5  using namespace std;
 6
 7  int main()
 8  {
 9      int feet, inches;  // To hold input for feet and inches
10
11      // Create two FeetInches objects. The default arguments
12      // for the constructor will be used.
13      FeetInches first, second;
14
15      // Get a distance from the user.
16      cout << "Enter a distance in feet and inches: ";
17      cin >> feet >> inches;
18
```

(program continues)

Program 14-10   *(continued)*

```
19      // Store the distance in first.
20      first.setFeet(feet);
21      first.setInches(inches);
22
23      // Get another distance.
24      cout << "Enter another distance in feet and inches: ";
25      cin >> feet >> inches;
26
27      // Store the distance in second.
28      second.setFeet(feet);
29      second.setInches(inches);
30
31      // Compare the two objects.
32      if (first == second)
33        cout << "first is equal to second.\n";
34      if (first > second)
35        cout << "first is greater than second.\n";
36      if (first < second)
37        cout << "first is less than second.\n";
38
39      return 0;
40   }
```

Program Output with Example Input Shown in Bold
Enter a distance in feet and inches: **6 5 [Enter]**
Enter another distance in feet and inches: **3 10 [Enter]**
first is greater than second.

Program Output with Different Example Input Shown in Bold
Enter a distance in feet and inches: **5 5 [Enter]**
Enter another distance in feet and inches: **5 5 [Enter]**
first is equal to second.

Program Output with Different Example Input Shown in Bold
Enter a distance in feet and inches: **3 4 [Enter]**
Enter another distance in feet and inches: **3 7 [Enter]**
first is less than second.

Overloading the << and >> Operators

Overloading the math and relational operators gives you the ability to write those types of expressions with class objects just as naturally as with integers, floats, and other built-in data types. If an object's primary data members are private, however, you still have to make explicit member function calls to send their values to cout. For example, assume distance is a FeetInches object. The following statements display its internal values:

```
cout << distance.getFeet() << " feet, ";
cout << distance.getInches() << "inches";
```

It is also necessary to explicitly call member functions to set a FeetInches object's data. For instance, the following statements set the distance object to user-specified values:

```
cout << "Enter a value in feet: ";
cin >> f;
distance.setFeet(f);
cout << "Enter a value in inches: ";
cin >> i;
distance.setInches(i);
```

By overloading the stream insertion operator (<<), you could send the `distance` object to `cout`, as shown in the following code, and have the screen output automatically formatted in the correct way.

```
cout << distance;
```

Likewise, by overloading the stream extraction operator (>>), the `distance` object could take values directly from `cin`, as shown here.

```
cin >> distance;
```

Overloading these operators is done in a slightly different way, however, than overloading other operators. These operators are actually part of the `ostream` and `istream` classes defined in the C++ runtime library. (The `cout` and `cin` objects are instances of `ostream` and `istream`.) You must write operator functions to overload the `ostream` version of `<<` and the `istream` version of `>>`, so they work directly with a class such as `FeetInches`. The `FeetInches` class in the Student Source Code Folder `Chapter 14\FeetInches Version 4` contains functions to overload the `<<` and `>>` operators. Here is the function that overloads the `<<` operator:

```
ostream &operator << (ostream &strm, const FeetInches &obj)
{
    strm << obj.feet << " feet, " << obj.inches << " inches";
    return strm;
}
```

Notice the function has two parameters: an `ostream` reference object and a `const FeetInches` reference object. The `ostream` parameter will be a reference to the actual `ostream` object on the left side of the `<<` operator. The second parameter is a reference to a `FeetInches` object. This parameter will reference the object on the right side of the `<<` operator. This function tells C++ how to handle any expression that has the following form:

```
ostreamObject << FeetInchesObject
```

So, when C++ encounters the following statement, it will call the overloaded `operator<<` function:

```
cout << distance;
```

Notice that the function's return type is `ostream &`. This means that the function returns a reference to an `ostream` object. When the `return strm;` statement executes, it doesn't return a copy of `strm`, but a reference to it. This allows you to chain together several expressions using the overloaded `<<` operator, such as:

```
cout << distance1 << " " << distance2 << endl;
```

Here is the function that overloads the stream extraction operator to work with the `FeetInches` class:

```
istream &operator >> (istream &strm, FeetInches &obj)
{
    // Prompt the user for the feet.
    cout << "Feet: ";
    strm >> obj.feet;

    // Prompt the user for the inches.
    cout << "Inches: ";
    strm >> obj.inches;

    // Normalize the values.
    obj.simplify();

    return strm;
}
```

The same principles hold true for this operator. It tells C++ how to handle any expression in the following form:

> *istreamObject* >> *FeetInchesObject*

Once again, the function returns a reference to an `istream` object so several of these expressions may be chained together.

You have probably realized that neither of these functions is quite ready to work, though. Both functions attempt to directly access the `FeetInches` object's private members. Because the functions aren't themselves members of the `FeetInches` class, they don't have this type of access. The next step is to make the operator functions friends of `FeetInches`. This is shown in the following listing of the `FeetInches` class declaration. (This file is stored in the Student Source Code Folder `Chapter 14\FeetInches Version 4`.)

NOTE: Some compilers require you to prototype the >> and << operator functions outside the class. For this reason, we have added the following statements to the `FeetInches.h` class specification file.

```
class FeetInches;                        // Forward Declaration

// Function Prototypes for Overloaded Stream Operators
ostream &operator << (ostream &, const FeetInches &);
istream &operator >> (istream &, FeetInches &);
```

Contents of `FeetInches.h` (Version 4)

```
 1   #ifndef FEETINCHES_H
 2   #define FEETINCHES_H
 3
 4   #include <iostream>
 5   using namespace std;
 6
 7   class FeetInches; // Forward Declaration
 8
 9   // Function Prototypes for Overloaded Stream Operators
10   ostream &operator << (ostream &, const FeetInches &);
11   istream &operator >> (istream &, FeetInches &);
```

```
12
13    // The FeetInches class holds distances or measurements
14    // expressed in feet and inches.
15
16    class FeetInches
17    {
18    private:
19       int feet;        // To hold a number of feet
20       int inches;      // To hold a number of inches
21       void simplify(); // Defined in FeetInches.cpp
22    public:
23       // Constructor
24       FeetInches(int f = 0, int i = 0)
25          { feet = f;
26            inches = i;
27            simplify(); }
28
29       // Mutator functions
30       void setFeet(int f)
31          { feet = f; }
32
33       void setInches(int i)
34          { inches = i;
35            simplify(); }
36
37       // Accessor functions
38       int getFeet() const
39          { return feet; }
40
41       int getInches() const
42          { return inches; }
43
44       // Overloaded operator functions
45       FeetInches operator + (const FeetInches &); // Overloaded +
46       FeetInches operator - (const FeetInches &); // Overloaded -
47       FeetInches operator ++ ();              // Prefix ++
48       FeetInches operator ++ (int);           // Postfix ++
49       bool operator > (const FeetInches &);      // Overloaded >
50       bool operator < (const FeetInches &);      // Overloaded <
51       bool operator == (const FeetInches &);     // Overloaded ==
52
53       // Friends
54       friend ostream &operator << (ostream &, const FeetInches &);
55       friend istream &operator >> (istream &, FeetInches &);
56    };
57
58    #endif
```

Lines 54 and 55 in the class declaration tell C++ to make the overloaded << and >> operator functions friends of the FeetInches class:

```
friend ostream &operator<<(ostream &, const FeetInches &);
friend istream &operator>>(istream &, FeetInches &);
```

These statements give the operator functions direct access to the FeetInches class's private members. Program 14-11 demonstrates how the overloaded operators work. (This file is also stored in the Student Source Code Folder Chapter 14\FeetInches Version 4.)

Program 14-11

```
 1   // This program demonstrates the << and >> operators,
 2   // overloaded to work with the FeetInches class.
 3   #include <iostream>
 4   #include "FeetInches.h"
 5   using namespace std;
 6
 7   int main()
 8   {
 9      FeetInches first, second;   // Define two objects.
10
11      // Get a distance for the first object.
12      cout << "Enter a distance in feet and inches.\n";
13      cin >> first;
14
15      // Get a distance for the second object.
16      cout << "Enter another distance in feet and inches.\n";
17      cin >> second;
18
19      // Display the values in the objects.
20      cout << "The values you entered are:\n";
21      cout << first << " and " << second << endl;
22      return 0;
23   }
```

Program Output with Example Input Shown in Bold
```
Enter a distance in feet and inches.
Feet: 6 [Enter]
Inches: 5 [Enter]
Enter another distance in feet and inches.
Feet: 3 [Enter]
Inches: 10 [Enter]
The values you entered are:
6 feet, 5 inches and 3 feet, 10 inches
```

Overloading the [] Operator

In addition to the traditional operators, C++ allows you to change the way the [] symbols work. This gives you the ability to write classes that have array-like behaviors. For example, the string class overloads the [] operator so you can access the individual characters stored in string class objects. Assume the following definition exists in a program:

```
string name = "William";
```

The first character in the string, 'W,' is stored at name[0], so the following statement will display W on the screen.

```
cout << name[0];
```

You can use the overloaded `[]` operator to create an array class, like the following one. The class behaves like a regular array, but performs the bounds-checking that C++ lacks.

Contents of `IntArray.h`

```
1   // Specification file for the IntArray class
2   #ifndef INTARRAY_H
3   #define INTARRAY_H
4
5   class IntArray
6   {
7   private:
8      int *aptr;                    // Pointer to the array
9      int arraySize;                // Holds the array size
10     void subscriptError();        // Handles invalid subscripts
11  public:
12     IntArray(int);                // Constructor
13     IntArray(const IntArray &);   // Copy constructor
14     ~IntArray();                  // Destructor
15
16     int size() const              // Returns the array size
17        { return arraySize; }
18
19     int &operator[](const int &); // Overloaded [] operator
20  };
21  #endif
```

Contents of `IntArray.cpp`

```
1   // Implementation file for the IntArray class
2   #include <iostream>
3   #include <cstdlib>   // For the exit function
4   #include "IntArray.h"
5   using namespace std;
6
7   //*****************************************************
8   // Constructor for IntArray class. Sets the size of the *
9   // array and allocates memory for it.                   *
10  //*****************************************************
11
12  IntArray::IntArray(int s)
13  {
14     arraySize = s;
15     aptr = new int [s];
16     for (int count = 0; count < arraySize; count++)
17        *(aptr + count) = 0;
18  }
19
20  //*****************************************************
21  // Copy Constructor for IntArray class.               *
22  //*****************************************************
23
```

```
24    IntArray::IntArray(const IntArray &obj)
25    {
26       arraySize = obj.arraySize;
27       aptr = new int [arraySize];
28       for(int count = 0; count < arraySize; count++)
29          *(aptr + count) = *(obj.aptr + count);
30    }
31
32    //*****************************************************
33    // Destructor for IntArray class.                     *
34    //*****************************************************
35
36    IntArray::~IntArray()
37    {
38       if (arraySize > 0)
39          delete [] aptr;
40    }
41
42    //***********************************************************
43    // subscriptError function. Displays an error message and   *
44    // terminates the program when a subscript is out of range. *
45    //***********************************************************
46
47    void IntArray::subscriptError()
48    {
49       cout << "ERROR: Subscript out of range.\n";
50       exit(0);
51    }
52
53    //*********************************************************
54    // Overloaded [] operator. The argument is a subscript. *
55    // This function returns a reference to the element     *
56    // in the array indexed by the subscript.               *
57    //*********************************************************
58
59    int &IntArray::operator[](const int &sub)
60    {
61       if (sub < 0 || sub >= arraySize)
62          subscriptError();
63       return aptr[sub];
64    }
```

Before focusing on the overloaded operator, let's look at the constructors and the destructor. The code for the first constructor in lines 12 through 18 of the IntArray.cpp file follows:

```
IntArray::IntArray(int s)
{
   arraySize = s;
   aptr = new int [s];
   for (int count = 0; count < arraySize; count++)
      *(aptr + count) = 0;
}
```

When an instance of the class is defined, the number of elements the array is to have is passed into the constructor's parameter, s. This value is copied to the arraySize member, and then used to dynamically allocate enough memory for the array. The constructor's final step is to store zeros in all of the array's elements:

```
for (int count = 0; count < arraySize; count++)
    *(aptr + count) = 0;
```

The class also has a copy constructor in lines 24 through 30, which is used when a class object is initialized with another object's data:

```
IntArray::IntArray(const IntArray &obj)
{
    arraySize = obj.arraySize;
    aptr = new int [arraySize];
    for(int count = 0; count < arraySize; count++)
        *(aptr + count) = *(obj.aptr + count);
}
```

A reference to the initializing object is passed into the parameter obj. Once the memory is successfully allocated for the array, the constructor copies all the values in obj's array into the calling object's array.

The destructor, in lines 36 through 40, simply frees the memory allocated by the class's constructors. First, however, it checks the value in arraySize to be sure the array has at least one element:

```
IntArray::~IntArray()
{
    if (arraySize > 0)
        delete [] aptr;
}
```

The [] operator is overloaded similarly to other operators. The definition of the operator[] function appears in lines 59 through 64:

```
int &IntArray::operator[](const int &sub)
{
    if (sub < 0 || sub >= arraySize)
        subscriptError();
    return aptr[sub];
}
```

The operator[] function can have only a single parameter. The one shown uses a constant reference to an integer. This parameter holds the value placed inside the brackets in an expression. For example, if table is an IntArray object, the number 12 will be passed into the sub parameter in the following statement:

```
cout << table[12];
```

Inside the function, the value in the sub parameter is tested by the following if statement:

```
if (sub < 0 || sub >= arraySize)
    subscriptError();
```

This statement determines whether sub is within the range of the array's subscripts. If sub is less than 0 or greater than or equal to arraySize, it's not a valid subscript, so the subscriptError function is called. If sub is within range, the function uses it as an offset into the array, and returns a reference to the value stored at that location.

One critically important aspect of the function above is its return type. It's crucial that the function return not simply an integer, but a *reference* to an integer. The reason for this is that expressions such as the following must be possible:

```
table[5] = 27;
```

Remember, the built-in = operator requires the object on its left to be an lvalue. An lvalue must represent a modifiable memory location, such as a variable. The integer return value of a function is not an lvalue. If the operator[] function merely returns an integer, it cannot be used to create expressions placed on the left side of an assignment operator.

A reference to an integer, however, is an lvalue. If the operator[] function returns a reference, it can be used to create expressions like the following:

```
table[7] = 52;
```

In this statement, the operator[] function is called with 7 passed as its argument. Assuming 7 is within range, the function returns a reference to the integer stored at (aptr + 7). In essence, the statement above is equivalent to:

```
*(aptr + 7) = 52;
```

Because the operator[] function returns actual integers stored in the array, it is not necessary for math or relational operators to be overloaded. Even the stream operators << and >> will work just as they are with the IntArray class.

Program 14-12 demonstrates how the class works.

Program 14-12

```cpp
 1  // This program demonstrates an overloaded [] operator.
 2  #include <iostream>
 3  #include "IntArray.h"
 4  using namespace std;
 5
 6  int main()
 7  {
 8     const int SIZE = 10;  // Array size
 9
10     // Define an IntArray with 10 elements.
11     IntArray table(SIZE);
12
13     // Store values in the array.
14     for (int x = 0; x < SIZE; x++)
15        table[x] = (x * 2);
16
17     // Display the values in the array.
18     for (int x = 0; x < SIZE; x++)
19        cout << table[x] << " ";
20     cout << endl;
21
22     // Use the standard + operator on array elements.
23     for (int x = 0; x < SIZE; x++)
24        table[x] = table[x] + 5;
25
```

```
26      // Display the values in the array.
27      for (int x = 0; x < SIZE; x++)
28         cout << table[x] << " ";
29      cout << endl;
30
31      // Use the standard ++ operator on array elements.
32      for (int x = 0; x < SIZE; x++)
33         table[x]++;
34
35      // Display the values in the array.
36      for (int x = 0; x < SIZE; x++)
37         cout << table[x] << " ";
38      cout << endl;
39
40      return 0;
41   }
```

Program Output
```
0 2 4 6 8 10 12 14 16 18
5 7 9 11 13 15 17 19 21 23
6 8 10 12 14 16 18 20 22 24
```

Program 14-13 demonstrates the IntArray class's bounds-checking capability.

Program 14-13

```
1  // This program demonstrates the IntArray class's bounds-checking ability.
2  #include <iostream>
3  #include "IntArray.h"
4  using namespace std;
5
6  int main()
7  {
8     const int SIZE = 10;   // Array size
9
10    // Define an IntArray with 10 elements.
11    IntArray table(SIZE);
12
13    // Store values in the array.
14    for (int x = 0; x < SIZE; x++)
15       table[x] = x;
16
17    // Display the values in the array.
18    for (int x = 0; x < SIZE; x++)
19       cout << table[x] << " ";
20    cout << endl;
21
22    // Attempt to use an invalid subscript.
23    cout << "Now attempting to use an invalid subscript.\n";
24    table[SIZE + 1] = 0;
25    return 0;
26 }
```

(program output continues)

Program 14-13   *(continued)*

Program Output
```
0  1  2  3  4  5  6  7  8  9
Now attempting to use an invalid subscript.
ERROR: Subscript out of range.
```

Checkpoint

14.21   Describe the values that should be returned from functions that overload relational operators.

14.22   What is the advantage of overloading the << and >> operators?

14.23   What type of object should an overloaded << operator function return?

14.24   What type of object should an overloaded >> operator function return?

14.25   If an overloaded << or >> operator accesses a private member of a class, what must be done in that class's declaration?

14.26   Assume the class `NumList` has overloaded the `[ ]` operator. In the expression below, `list1` is an instance of the `NumList` class:

```
list1[25]
```

Rewrite the expression above to explicitly call the function that overloads the `[ ]` operator.

14.6   Object Conversion

CONCEPT: Special operator functions may be written to convert a class object to any other type.

As you've already seen, operator functions allow classes to work more like built-in data types. Another capability that operator functions can give classes is automatic type conversion.

Data type conversion happens "behind the scenes" with the built-in data types. For instance, suppose a program uses the following variables:

```
int i;
double d;
```

The statement below automatically converts the value in `i` to a floating-point number and stores it in `d`:

```
d = i;
```

Likewise, the following statement converts the value in `d` to an integer (truncating the fractional part) and stores it in `i`:

```
i = d;
```

The same functionality can also be given to class objects. For example, assuming `distance` is a `FeetInches` object and `d` is a `double`, the following statement would conveniently convert `distance`'s value into a floating-point number and store it in `d`, if `FeetInches` is properly written:

```
d = distance;
```

To be able to use a statement such as this, an operator function must be written to perform the conversion. The Student Source Code Folder `Chapter 14\FeetInches Version 5` contains a version of the `FeetInches` class with such an operator function. Here is the code for the operator function that converts a `FeetInches` object to a `double`:

```
FeetInches::operator double()
{
    double temp = feet;

    temp += (inches / 12.0);
    return temp;
}
```

This function contains an algorithm that will calculate the decimal equivalent of a feet and inches measurement. For example, the value 4 feet 6 inches will be converted to 4.5. This value is stored in the local variable `temp`. The `temp` variable is then returned.

NOTE: No return type is specified in the function header. Because the function is a `FeetInches`-to-double conversion function, it will always return a `double`. Also, because the function takes no arguments, there are no parameters.

The revised `FeetInches` class also has an operator function that converts a `FeetInches` object to an `int`. The function, shown here, simply returns the `feet` member, thus truncating the `inches` value:

```
FeetInches:: operator int()
{
    return feet;
}
```

Program 14-14 demonstrates both of these conversion functions. (This file is also stored in the Student Source Code Folder `Chapter 14\FeetInches Version 5`.)

Program 14-14

```
1   // This program demonstrates the the FeetInches class's
2   // conversion functions.
3   #include <iostream>
4   #include "FeetInches.h"
5   using namespace std;
6
7   int main()
8   {
9       double d;  // To hold double input
10      int i;     // To hold int input
11
```

(program continues)

Program 14-14   *(continued)*

```
12       // Define a FeetInches object.
13       FeetInches distance;
14
15       // Get a distance from the user.
16       cout << "Enter a distance in feet and inches:\n";
17       cin >> distance;
18
19       // Convert the distance object to a double.
20       d = distance;
21
22       // Convert the distance object to an int.
23       i = distance;
24
25       // Display the values.
26       cout << "The value " << distance;
27       cout << " is equivalent to " << d << " feet\n";
28       cout << "or " << i << " feet, rounded down.\n";
29       return 0;
30    }
```

Program Output with Example Input Shown in Bold
```
Enter a distance in feet and inches:
Feet: 8 [Enter]
Inches: 6 [Enter]
The value 8 feet, 6 inches is equivalent to 8.5 feet
or 8 feet, rounded down.
```

 See the Case Study on Creating a String Class on the Student CD.

Checkpoint

14.27   When overloading a binary operator such as + or –, what object is passed into the operator function's parameter?

14.28   Explain why overloaded prefix and postfix ++ and -- operator functions should return a value.

14.29   How does C++ tell the difference between an overloaded prefix and postfix ++ or -- operator function?

14.30   Write member functions of the FeetInches class that overload the prefix and postfix -- operators. Demonstrate the functions in a simple program similar to Program 14-14.

14.7   Aggregation

CONCEPT: Aggregation occurs when a class contains an instance of another class.

VideoNote
Class
Aggregation

In real life, objects are frequently made of other objects. A house, for example, is made of door objects, window objects, wall objects, and much more. It is the combination of all these objects that makes a house object.

When designing software, it sometimes makes sense to create an object from other objects. For example, suppose you need an object to represent a course that you are taking in college. You decide to create a `Course` class, which will hold the following information:

- The course name
- The instructor's last name, first name, and office number
- The textbook's title, author, and publisher

In addition to the course name, the class will hold items related to the instructor and the textbook. You could put attributes for each of these items in the `Course` class. However, a good design principle is to separate related items into their own classes. In this example, an `Instructor` class could be created to hold the instructor-related data and a `TextBook` class could be created to hold the textbook-related data. Instances of these classes could then be used as attributes in the `Course` class.

Let's take a closer look at how this might be done. To keep things simple, the `Instructor` class will have only the following functions:

- A default constructor that assigns empty strings to the instructor's last name, first name, and office number.
- A constructor that accepts arguments for the instructor's last name, first name, and office number
- A set function that can be used to set all of the class's attributes
- A print function that displays the object's attribute values

The code for the `Instructor` class is shown here:

Contents of `Instructor.h`

```
1   #ifndef INSTRUCTOR
2   #define INSTRUCTOR
3   #include <iostream>
4   #include <cstring>
5   using namespace std;
6
7   // Constants for array sizes
8   const int NAME_SIZE = 51;
9   const int OFFICE_NUM_SIZE = 21;
10
11  // Instructor class
12  class Instructor
13  {
14  private:
15     char lastName[NAME_SIZE];           // Last name
16     char firstName[NAME_SIZE];          // First name
17     char officeNumber[OFFICE_NUM_SIZE]; // Office number
18  public:
19     // The default constructor stores empty strings
20     // in the char arrays.
21     Instructor()
22        { set("", "", ""); }
23
24     // Constructor
25     Instructor(char *lname, char *fname, char *office)
```

```
26                    { set(lname, fname, office); }
27
28          // set function
29          void set(const char *lname, const char *fname,
30                    const char *office)
31            { strncpy(lastName, lname, NAME_SIZE);
32              lastName[NAME_SIZE - 1] = '\0';
33
34              strncpy(firstName, fname, NAME_SIZE);
35              firstName[NAME_SIZE - 1] = '\0';
36
37              strncpy(officeNumber, office, OFFICE_NUM_SIZE);
38              officeNumber[OFFICE_NUM_SIZE - 1] = '\0'; }
39
40          // print function
41          void print() const
42            { cout << "Last name: " << lastName << endl;
43              cout << "First name: " << firstName << endl;
44              cout << "Office number: " << officeNumber << endl; }
45       };
46       #endif
```

The code for the TextBook class is shown next. As before, we want to keep the class simple. The only functions it has are a default constructor, a constructor that accepts arguments, a set function, and a print function.

Contents of `TextBook.h`

```
1    #ifndef TEXTBOOK
2    #define TEXTBOOK
3    #include <iostream>
4    #include <cstring>
5    using namespace std;
6
7    // Constant for array sizes
8    const int PUB_SIZE = 51;
9
10   // TextBook class
11   class TextBook
12   {
13   private:
14      char title[PUB_SIZE];      // Book title
15      char author[PUB_SIZE];     // Author name
16      char publisher[PUB_SIZE];  // Publisher name
17   public:
18      // The default constructor stores empty strings
19      // in the char arrays.
20      TextBook()
21        { set("", "", ""); }
22
23      // Constructor
24      TextBook(char *textTitle, char *auth, char *pub)
25        { set(textTitle, auth, pub); }
26
27      // set function
```

```
28      void set(const char *textTitle, const char *auth,
29              const char *pub)
30        { strncpy(title, textTitle, PUB_SIZE);
31          title[NAME_SIZE - 1] = '\0';
32
33          strncpy(author, auth, PUB_SIZE);
34          author[NAME_SIZE - 1] = '\0';
35
36          strncpy(publisher, pub, PUB_SIZE);
37          publisher[OFFICE_NUM_SIZE - 1] = '\0'; }
38
39      // print function
40      void print() const
41        {  cout << "Title: " << title << endl;
42           cout << "Author: " << author << endl;
43           cout << "Publisher: " << publisher << endl; }
44   };
45   #endif
```

The `Course` class is shown next. Notice that the `Course` class has an `Instructor` object and a `TextBook` object as member variables. Those objects are used as attributes of the `Course` object. Making an instance of one class an attribute of another class is called *object aggregation*. The word *aggregate* means "a whole that is made of constituent parts." In this example, the `Course` class is an aggregate class because an instance of it is made of constituent objects.

When an instance of one class is a member of another class, it is said that there is a "has a" relationship between the classes. For example, the relationships that exist among the `Course`, `Instructor`, and `TextBook` classes can be described as follows:

- The course *has an* instructor.
- The course *has a* textbook.

The "has a" relationship is sometimes called a *whole–part relationship* because one object is part of a greater whole.

Contents of `Course.h`

```
1    #ifndef COURSE
2    #define COURSE
3    #include <iostream>
4    #include <cstring>
5    #include "Instructor.h"
6    #include "TextBook.h"
7    using namespace std;
8
9    // Constant for course name
10   const int COURSE_SIZE = 51;
11
12   class Course
13   {
14   private:
15      char courseName[COURSE_SIZE];   // Course name
16      Instructor instructor;          // Instructor
17      TextBook textbook;              // Textbook
```

```
18   public:
19      // Constructor
20      Course(const char *course, const char *instrLastName,
21           const char *instrFirstName, const char *instrOffice,
22           const char *textTitle, const char *author,
23           const char *publisher)
24      { // Assign the course name.
25        strncpy(courseName, course, COURSE_SIZE);
26        courseName[COURSE_SIZE - 1] = '\0';
27
28        // Assign the instructor.
29        instructor.set(instrLastName, instrFirstName, instrOffice);
30
31        // Assign the textbook.
32        textbook.set(textTitle, author, publisher); }
33
34      // print function
35      void print() const
36      { cout << "Course name: " << courseName << endl << endl;
37        cout << "Instructor Information:\n";
38        instructor.print();
39        cout << "\nTextbook Information:\n";
40        textbook.print();
41        cout << endl; }
42   };
43   #endif
```

Program 14-15 demonstrates the Course class.

Program 14-15

```
1    // This program demonstrates the Course class.
2    #include "Course.h"
3
4    int main()
5    {
6       // Create a Course object.
7       Course myCourse("Intro to Computer Science", // Course name
8         "Kramer", "Shawn", "RH3010",         // Instructor info
9         "Starting Out with C++", "Gaddis", // Textbook title and author
10        "Addison-Wesley");                    // Textbook publisher
11
12      // Display the course info.
13      myCourse.print();
14      return 0;
15   }
```

Program Output
```
Course name: Intro to Computer Science

Instructor Information:
Last name: Kramer
First name: Shawn
Office number: RH3010
```

```
Textbook Information:
Title: Starting Out with C++
Author: Gaddis
Publisher: Addison-Wesley
```

Aggregation in UML Diagrams

In Chapter 13 you were introduced to the Unified Modeling Language (UML) as a tool for designing classes. You show aggregation in a UML diagram by connecting two classes with a line that has an open diamond at one end. The diamond is closest to the class that is the aggregate. Figure 14-5 shows a UML diagram depicting the relationship between the Course, Instructor, and TextBook classes. The open diamond is closest to the Course class because it is the aggregate (the whole).

Figure 14-5

14.8 Focus on Object-Oriented Design: Class Collaborations

CONCEPT: It is common for classes to interact, or collaborate, with one another to perform their operations. Part of the object-oriented design process is identifying the collaborations between classes.

In an object-oriented application it is common for objects of different classes to collaborate. This simply means that objects interact with each other. Sometimes one object will need the services of another object in order to fulfill its responsibilities. For example, let's say an object needs to read a number from the keyboard and then format the number to appear as a dollar amount. The object might use the services of the `cin` object to read the number from the keyboard, and then use the services of another object that is designed to format the number.

If one object is to collaborate with another object, then it must know something about the other object's member functions and how to call them. Let's look at an example.

The following code shows a class named `Stock`. An object of this class holds data about a company's stock. This class has two attributes: `symbol` and `sharePrice`. The `symbol` attribute holds the trading symbol for the company's stock. This is a short series of characters that are used to identify the stock on the stock exchange. For example, the XYZ Company's stock might have the trading symbol XYZ. The `sharePrice` attribute holds the current price per share of the stock. The class also has the following member functions:

- A default constructor that initializes `symbol` to an empty string and `sharePrice` to 0.0.
- A constructor that accepts arguments for the symbol and share price.
- A copy constructor
- A `set` function that accepts arguments for the symbol and share price.
- A `getSymbol` function that returns the stock's trading symbol.
- A `getSharePrice` function that returns the current price of the stock.

Contents of `Stock.h`

```
 1   #ifndef STOCK
 2   #define STOCK
 3   #include <cstring>
 4
 5   // Constant for symbol array.
 6   const int SYMBOL_SIZE = 6;
 7
 8   class Stock
 9   {
10   private:
11      char symbol[SYMBOL_SIZE]; // Trading symbol of the stock
12      double sharePrice;        // Current price per share
```

```
13  public:
14      // Default Constructor
15      Stock()
16          { set("", 0.0); }
17
18      // Constructor
19      Stock(const char *sym, double price)
20          { set(sym, price); }
21
22      // Copy constructor
23      Stock(const Stock &obj)
24          { set(obj.symbol, obj.sharePrice); }
25
26      // Mutator function
27      void set(const char *sym, double price)
28          { strncpy(symbol, sym, SYMBOL_SIZE);
29            symbol[SYMBOL_SIZE - 1] = '\0';
30            sharePrice = price; }
31
32      // Accessor functions
33      const char *getSymbol() const
34          { return symbol; }
35
36      double getSharePrice() const
37          { return sharePrice; }
38  };
39  #endif
```

The following code shows another class named StockPurchase that uses an object of the Stock class to simulate the purchase of a stock. The StockPurchase class is responsible for calculating the cost of the stock purchase. To do that, the StockPurchase class must know how to call the Stock class's getSharePrice function to get the price per share of the stock.

Contents of StockPurchase.h

```
1   #ifndef STOCK_PURCHASE
2   #define STOCK_PURCHASE
3   #include "Stock.h"
4
5   class StockPurchase
6   {
7   private:
8       Stock stock;    // The stock that was purchased
9       int shares;     // The number of shares
10  public:
11      // The default constructor sets shares to 0. The stock
12      // object is initialized by its default constructor.
13      StockPurchase()
14          { shares = 0; }
15
```

```
16        // Constructor
17        StockPurchase(const Stock &stockObject, int numShares)
18          { stock = stockObject;
19            shares = numShares; }
20
21        // Accessor function
22        double getCost() const
23          {  return shares * stock.getSharePrice(); }
24     };
25     #endif
```

The second constructor for the StockPurchase class accepts a Stock object representing the stock that is being purchased, and an int representing the number of shares to purchase. In line 18 we see the first collaboration: the StockPurchase constructor makes a copy of the Stock object by using the Stock class's copy constructor. The next collaboration takes place in the getCost function. This function calculates and returns the cost of the stock purchase. In line 23 it calls the Stock class's getSharePrice function to determine the stock's price per share. Program 14-16 demonstrates this class.

Program 14-16

```
1   // Stock trader program
2   #include <iostream>
3   #include <iomanip>
4   #include "Stock.h"
5   #include "StockPurchase.h"
6   using namespace std;
7
8   int main()
9   {
10      int sharesToBuy;   // Number of shares to buy
11
12      // Create a Stock object for the company stock. The
13      // trading symbol is XYZ and the stock is currently
14      // priced at $9.62 per share.
15      Stock xyzCompany("XYZ", 9.62);
16
17      // Display the symbol and current share price.
18      cout << setprecision(2) << fixed << showpoint;
19      cout << "XYZ Company's trading symbol is "
20          << xyzCompany.getSymbol() << endl;
21      cout << "The stock is currently $"
22          << xyzCompany.getSharePrice()
23          << " per share.\n";
24
25      // Get the number of shares to purchase.
26      cout << "How many shares do you want to buy? ";
27      cin >> sharesToBuy;
28
```

```
29       // Create a StockPurchase object for the transaction.
30       StockPurchase buy(xyzCompany, sharesToBuy);
31
32       // Display the cost of the transaction.
33       cout << "The cost of the transaction is $"
34            << buy.getCost() << endl;
35       return 0;
36   }
```

Program Output with Example Input Shown in Bold
```
XYZ Company's trading symbol is XYZ
The stock is currently $9.62 per share.
How many shares do you want to buy? 100 [Enter]
The cost of the transaction is $962.00
```

Determining Class Collaborations with CRC Cards

During the object-oriented design process, you can determine many of the collaborations that will be necessary between classes by examining the responsibilities of the classes. In Chapter 13 we discussed the process of finding the classes and their responsibilities. Recall from that section that a class's responsibilities are

- the things that the class is responsible for knowing
- the actions that the class is responsible for doing

Often you will determine that the class must collaborate with another class in order to fulfill one or more of its responsibilities. One popular method of discovering a class's responsibilities and collaborations is by creating CRC cards. *CRC* stands for class, responsibilities, and collaborations.

You can use simple index cards for this procedure. Once you have gone through the process of finding the classes (which is discussed in Chapter 13), set aside one index card for each class. At the top of the index card, write the name of the class. Divide the rest of the card into two columns. In the left column, write each of the class's responsibilities. As you write each responsibility, think about whether the class needs to collaborate with another class to fulfill that responsibility. Ask yourself questions such as

- Will an object of this class need to get data from another object in order to fulfill this responsibility?
- Will an object of this class need to request another object to perform an operation in order to fulfill this responsibility?

If collaboration is required, write the name of the collaborating class in the right column, next to the responsibility that requires it. If no collaboration is required for a responsibility, simply write "None" in the right column, or leave it blank. Figure 14-6 shows an example CRC card for the StockPurchase class.

Figure 14-6

From the CRC card shown in the figure, we can see that the StockPurhcase class has the following responsibilities and collaborations:

- Responsibility: To know the stock to purchase
  Collaboration: The Stock class
- Responsibility: To know the number of shares to purchase
  Collaboration: None
- Responsibility: To calculate the cost of the purchase
  Collaboration: The Stock class

When you have completed a CRC card for each class in the application, you will have a good idea of each class's responsibilities and how the classes must interact.

 Checkpoint

14.31   What are the benefits of having operator functions that perform object conversion?

14.32   Why are no return types listed in the prototypes or headers of operator functions that perform data type conversion?

14.33   Assume there is a class named BlackBox. Write the header for a member function that converts a BlackBox object to an int.

14.34   Assume there are two classes, Big and Small. The Big class has, as a member, an instance of the Small class. Write a sentence that describes the relationship between the two classes.

Review Questions and Exercises

Short Answer

1. Describe the difference between an instance member variable and a static member variable.

2. Assume that a class named `Numbers` has the following static member function declaration:
   ```
   static void showTotal();
   ```
   Write a statement that calls the `showTotal` function.

3. A static member variable is declared in a class. Where is the static member variable defined?

4. What is a friend function?

5. Why is it not always a good idea to make an entire class a friend of another class?

6. What is memberwise assignment?

7. When is a copy constructor called?

8. How can the compiler determine if a constructor is a copy constructor?

9. Describe a situation where memberwise assignment is not desirable.

10. Why must the parameter of a copy constructor be a reference?

11. What is a default copy constructor?

12. Why would a programmer want to overload operators rather than use regular member functions to perform similar operations?

13. What is passed to the parameter of a class's `operator=` function?

14. Why shouldn't a class's overloaded = operator be implemented with a `void` operator function?

15. How does the compiler know whether an overloaded ++ operator should be used in prefix or postfix mode?

16. What is the `this` pointer?

17. What type of value should be returned from an overloaded relational operator function?

18. The class `Stuff` has both a copy constructor and an overloaded = operator. Assume that `blob` and `clump` are both instances of the `Stuff` class. For each statement below, indicate whether the copy constructor or the overloaded = operator will be called.
    ```
    Stuff blob = clump;
    clump = blob;
    blob.operator=(clump);
    showValues(blob);        // blob is passed by value.
    ```

19. Explain the programming steps necessary to make a class's member variable static.

20. Explain the programming steps necessary to make a class's member function static.

21. Consider the following class declaration:
    ```
    class Thing
    {
    private:
       int x;
    ```

```
        int y;
        static int z;
    public:
        Thing()
            { x = y = z; }
        static void putThing(int a)
            { z = a; }
    };
```

Assume a program containing the class declaration defines three Thing objects with the following statement:

```
Thing one, two, three;
```

How many separate instances of the x member exist?

How many separate instances of the y member exist?

How many separate instances of the z member exist?

What value will be stored in the x and y members of each object?

Write a statement that will call the PutThing member function *before* the objects above are defined.

22. Describe the difference between making a class a member of another class (object aggregation), and making a class a friend of another class.

23. What is the purpose of a forward declaration of a class?

24. Explain why memberwise assignment can cause problems with a class that contains a pointer member.

25. Why is a class's copy constructor called when an object of that class is passed by value into a function?

Fill-in-the-Blank

26. If a member variable is declared _____, all objects of that class have access to the same variable.

27. Static member variables are defined _____ the class.

28. A(n) _____ member function cannot access any nonstatic member variables in its own class.

29. A static member function may be called _____ any instances of its class are defined.

30. A(n) _____ function is not a member of a class, but has access to the private members of the class.

31. A(n) _____ tells the compiler that a specific class will be declared later in the program.

32. _____ is the default behavior when an object is assigned the value of another object of the same class.

33. A(n) _____ is a special constructor, called whenever a new object is initialized with another object's data.

34. _____ is a special built-in pointer that is automatically passed as a hidden argument to all nonstatic member functions.

35. An operator may be _____ to work with a specific class.

36. When overloading the _____ operator, its function must have a dummy parameter.

37. Making an instance of one class a member of another class is called _____.

38. Object aggregation is useful for creating a(n) _____ relationship between two classes.

Algorithm Workbench

39. Assume a class named `Bird` exists. Write the header for a member function that overloads the = operator for that class.

40. Assume a class named `Dollars` exists. Write the headers for member functions that overload the prefix and postfix ++ operators for that class.

41. Assume a class named `Yen` exists. Write the header for a member function that overloads the < operator for that class.

42. Assume a class named `Length` exists. Write the header for a member function that overloads cout's << operator for that class.

43. Assume a class named `Collection` exists. Write the header for a member function that overloads the [ ] operator for that class.

True or False

44. T F Static member variables cannot be accessed by nonstatic member functions.

45. T F Static member variables are defined outside their class declaration.

46. T F A static member function may refer to nonstatic member variables of the same class, but only after an instance of the class has been defined.

47. T F When a function is declared a `friend` by a class, it becomes a member of that class.

48. T F A `friend` function has access to the private members of the class declaring it a `friend`.

49. T F An entire class may be declared a `friend` of another class.

50. T F In order for a function or class to become a friend of another class, it must be declared as such by the class granting it access.

51. T F If a class has a pointer as a member, it's a good idea to also have a copy constructor.

52. T F You cannot use the = operator to assign one object's values to another object, unless you overload the operator.

53. T F If a class doesn't have a copy constructor, the compiler generates a default copy constructor for it.

54. T F If a class has a copy constructor, and an object of that class is passed by value into a function, the function's parameter will *not* call its copy constructor.

55. T F The `this` pointer is passed to static member functions.

56. T F All functions that overload unary operators must have a dummy parameter.

57. T F For an object to perform automatic type conversion, an operator function must be written.

58. T F It is possible to have an instance of one class as a member of another class.

Find the Error

Each of the following class declarations has errors. Locate as many as you can.

```
59. class Box
    {
        private:
            double width;
            double length;
            double height;
        public:
            Box(double w, l, h)
                { width = w; length = l; height = h; }
            Box(Box b) // Copy constructor
                { width = b.width;
                  length = b.length;
                  height = b.height; }

            ... Other member functions follow ...
    };

60. class Circle
    {
        private:
            double diameter;
            int centerX;
            int centerY;
        public:
            Circle(double d, int x, int y)
                { diameter = d; centerX = x; centerY = y; }
            // Overloaded = operator
            void Circle=(Circle &right)
                { diameter = right.diameter;
                  centerX = right.centerX;
                  centerY = right.centerY; }

                ... Other member functions follow ...
            };

61. class Point
    {
        private:
            int xCoord;
            int yCoord;
        public:
            Point (int x, int y)
                { xCoord = x; yCoord = y; }
            // Overloaded + operator
            void operator+(const &Point right)
                { xCoord += right.xCoord;
                  yCoord += right.yCoord;
                }

            ... Other member functions follow ...
    };
```

62. ```cpp
    class Box
    {
        private:
            double width;
            double length;
            double height;
        public:
            Box(double w, l, h)
                { width = w; length = l; height = h; }
            // Overloaded prefix ++ operator
            void operator++()
                {   ++width; ++length; }
            // Overloaded postfix ++ operator
            void operator++()
                {   width++; length++; }

        ... Other member functions follow ...
    };
    ```

63. ```cpp
    class Yard
    {
        private:
            float length;
        public:
            yard(float l)
                { length = l; }
            // float conversion function
            void operator float()
                { return length; }

        ... Other member functions follow ...
    };
    ```

Programming Challenges

1. **Numbers Class**

   Design a class Numbers that can be used to translate whole dollar amounts in the range 0 through 9999 into an English description of the number. For example, the number 713 would be translated into the string *seven hundred thirteen*, and 8203 would be translated into *eight thousand two hundred three*. The class should have a single integer member variable:

   ```cpp
   int number;
   ```

   and a static array of strings that specify how to translate key dollar amounts into the desired format. For example, you might use static strings such as

   ```cpp
   char lessThan20[20][25] = {"zero", "one", …, "eighteen", "nineteen"};
   char hundred[] = "hundred";
   char thousand[] = "thousand";
   ```

   The class should have a constructor that accepts a nonnegative integer and uses it to initialize the Numbers object. It should have a member function print() that prints the English description of the Numbers object. Demonstrate the class by writing a main program that asks the user to enter a number in the proper range and then prints out its English description.

2. **Day of the Year**

   Assuming that a year has 365 days, write a class named `DayOfYear` that takes an integer representing a day of the year and translates it to a string consisting of the month followed by day of the month. For example,

   Day 2 would be *January 2.*
   Day 32 would be *February 1.*
   Day 365 would be *December 31.*

   The constructor for the class should take as parameter an integer representing the day of the year, and the class should have a member function `print()` that prints the day in the month–day format. The class should have an integer member variable to represent the day, and should have static member variables holding strings that can be used to assist in the translation from the integer format to the month-day format.

   Test your class by inputting various integers representing days and printing out their representation in the month–day format.

3. **Day of the Year Modification**

   Modify the `DayOfYear` class, written in Programming Challenge 2, to add a constructor that takes two parameters: a string representing a month and an integer in the range 0 through 31 representing the day of the month. The constructor should then initialize the integer member of the class to represent the day specified by the month and day of month parameters. The constructor should terminate the program with an appropriate error message if the number entered for a day is outside the range of days for the month given.

   Add the following overloaded operators:

   ++   **prefix and postfix increment operators.** These operators should modify the `DayOfYear` object so that it represents the next day. If the day is already the end of the year, the new value of the object will represent the first day of the year.

   --   **prefix and postfix decrement operators.** These operators should modify the `DayOfYear` object so that it represents the previous day. If the day is already the first day of the year, the new value of the object will represent the last day of the year.

4. **`NumDays` Class**

VideoNote

Solving the
`NumDays`
Problem

   Design a class called `NumDays`. The class's purpose is to store a value that represents a number of work hours and convert it to a number of days. For example, 8 hours would be converted to 1 day, 12 hours would be converted to 1.5 days, and 18 hours would be converted to 2.25 days. The class should have a constructor that accepts a number of hours, as well as member functions for storing and retrieving the hours and days. The class should also have the following overloaded operators:

   +   *Addition operator.* When two `NumDays` objects are added together, the overloaded + operator should return the sum of the two objects' hours members.

   −   *Subtraction operator.* When one `NumDays` object is subtracted from another, the overloaded − operator should return the difference of the two objects' hours members.

++   *Prefix and postfix increment operators.* These operators should increment the number of hours stored in the object. When incremented, the number of days should be automatically recalculated.

--   *Prefix and postfix decrement operators.* These operators should decrement the number of hours stored in the object. When decremented, the number of days should be automatically recalculated.

5. **Time Off**

> **NOTE:** This assignment assumes you have already completed Programming Challenge 4.

Design a class named `TimeOff`. The purpose of the class is to track an employee's sick leave, vacation, and unpaid time off. It should have, as members, the following instances of the `NumDays` class described in Programming Challenge 4:

`maxSickDays`	A `NumDays` object that records the maximum number of days of sick leave the employee may take.
`sickTaken`	A `NumDays` object that records the number of days of sick leave the employee has already taken.
`maxVacation`	A `NumDays` object that records the maximum number of days of paid vacation the employee may take.
`vacTaken`	A `NumDays` object that records the number of days of paid vacation the employee has already taken.
`maxUnpaid`	A `NumDays` object that records the maximum number of days of unpaid vacation the employee may take.
`unpaidTaken`	A `NumDays` object that records the number of days of unpaid leave the employee has taken.

Additionally, the class should have members for holding the employee's name and identification number. It should have an appropriate constructor and member functions for storing and retrieving data in any of the member objects.

Input Validation: Company policy states that an employee may not accumulate more than 240 hours of paid vacation. The class should not allow the `maxVacation` object to store a value greater than this amount.

6. **Personnel Report**

> **NOTE:** This assignment assumes you have already completed Programming Challenges 4 and 5.

Write a program that uses an instance of the `TimeOff` class you designed in Programming Challenge 5. The program should ask the user to enter the number of months an employee has worked for the company. It should then use the `TimeOff` object to calculate and display the employee's maximum number of sick leave and vacation days. Employees earn 12 hours of vacation leave and 8 hours of sick leave per month.

7. **Month** Class

Design a class named Month. The class should have the following private members:

- name A string object that holds the name of a month, such as "January," "February," etc.
- monthNumber An integer variable that holds the number of the month. For example, January would be 1, February would be 2, etc. Valid values for this variable are 1 through 12.

In addition, provide the following member functions:

- A default constructor that sets monthNumber to 1 and name to "January."
- A constructor that accepts the name of the month as an argument. It should set name to the value passed as the argument and set monthNumber to the correct value.
- A constructor that accepts the number of the month as an argument. It should set monthNumber to the value passed as the argument and set name to the correct month name.
- Appropriate set and get functions for the name and monthNumber member variables.
- Prefix and postfix overloaded ++ operator functions that increment monthNumber and set name to the name of next month. If monthNumber is set to 12 when these functions execute, they should set monthNumber to 1 and name to "January."
- Prefix and postfix overloaded -- operator functions that decrement monthNumber and set name to the name of previous month. If monthNumber is set to 1 when these functions execute, they should set monthNumber to 12 and name to "December."

Also, you should overload cout's << operator and cin's >> operator to work with the Month class. Demonstrate the class in a program.

8. **Date** Class Modification

Modify the Date class in Programming Challenge 1 of Chapter 13. The new version should have the following overloaded operators:

++ *Prefix and postfix increment operators.* These operators should increment the object's day member.

-- *Prefix and postfix decrement operators.* These operators should decrement the object's day member.

- *Subtraction operator.* If one Date object is subtracted from another, the operator should give the number of days between the two dates. For example, if April 10, 2010 is subtracted from April 18, 2010, the result will be 8.

<< cout's *stream insertion operator.* This operator should cause the date to be displayed in the form

```
April 18, 2010
```

>> cin's *stream extraction operator.* This operator should prompt the user for a date to be stored in a Date object.

The class should detect the following conditions and handle them accordingly:

- When a date is set to the last day of the month and incremented, it should become the first day of the following month.
- When a date is set to December 31 and incremented, it should become January 1 of the following year.
- When a day is set to the first day of the month and decremented, it should become the last day of the previous month.
- When a date is set to January 1 and decremented, it should become December 31 of the previous year.

Demonstrate the class's capabilities in a simple program.

Input Validation: The overloaded >> operator should not accept invalid dates. For example, the date 13/45/09 should not be accepted.

9. **FeetInches** Modification

Modify the `FeetInches` class discussed in this chapter so it overloads the following operators:

```
<=
>=
!=
```

Demonstrate the class's capabilities in a simple program.

10. **Corporate Sales**

A corporation has six divisions, each responsible for sales to different geographic locations. Design a `DivSales` class that keeps sales data for a division, with the following members:

- An array with four elements for holding four quarters of sales figures for the division
- A private static variable for holding the total corporate sales for all divisions for the entire year.
- A member function that takes four arguments, each assumed to be the sales for a quarter. The value of the arguments should be copied into the array that holds the sales data. The total of the four arguments should be added to the static variable that holds the total yearly corporate sales.
- A function that takes an integer argument within the range of 0–3. The argument is to be used as a subscript into the division quarterly sales array. The function should return the value of the array element with that subscript.

Write a program that creates an array of six `DivSales` objects. The program should ask the user to enter the sales for four quarters for each division. After the data are entered, the program should display a table showing the division sales for each quarter. The program should then display the total corporate sales for the year.

Input Validation: Only accept positive values for quarterly sales figures.

11. **FeetInches** Class Copy Constructor and **multiply** Function

Add a copy constructor to the `FeetInches` class. This constructor should accept a `FeetInches` object as an argument. The constructor should assign to the `feet` attribute the value in the argument's `feet` attribute, and assign to the `inches` attribute the value in the argument's `inches` attribute. As a result, the new object will be a copy of the argument object.

Next, add a `multiply` member function to the `FeetInches` class. The `multiply` function should accept a `FeetInches` object as an argument. The argument object's `feet` and `inches` attributes will be multiplied by the calling object's `feet` and `inches` attributes, and a `FeetInches` object containing the result will be returned.

12. **LandTract** Class

Make a `LandTract` class that is composed of two `FeetInches` objects, one for the tract's length and one for the width. The class should have a member function that returns the tract's area. Demonstrate the class in a program that asks the user to enter the dimensions for two tracts of land. The program should display the area of each tract of land and indicate whether the tracts are of equal size.

13. **Carpet Calculator**

The Westfield Carpet Company has asked you to write an application that calculates the price of carpeting for rectangular rooms. To calculate the price, you multiply the area of the floor (width times length) by the price per square foot of carpet. For example, the area of floor that is 12 feet long and 10 feet wide is 120 square feet. To cover that floor with carpet that costs $8 per square foot would cost $960. ($12 \times 10 \times 8 = 960$.)

First, you should create a class named `RoomDimension` that has two `FeetInches` objects as attributes: one for the length of the room and one for the width. (You should use the version of the `FeetInches` class that you created in Programming Challenge 11 with the addition of a `multiply` member function. You can use this function to calculate the area of the room.) The `RoomDimension` class should have a member function that returns the area of the room as a `FeetInches` object.

Next, you should create a `RoomCarpet` class that has a `RoomDimension` object as an attribute. It should also have an attribute for the cost of the carpet per square foot. The `RoomCarpet` class should have a member function that returns the total cost of the carpet.

Once you have written these classes, use them in an application that asks the user to enter the dimensions of a room and the price per square foot of the desired carpeting. The application should display the total cost of the carpet.

14. **Parking Ticket Simulator**

For this assignment you will design a set of classes that work together to simulate a police officer issuing a parking ticket. The classes you should design are:

- **The `ParkedCar` Class:** This class should simulate a parked car. The class's responsibilities are:
    - To know the car's make, model, color, license number, and the number of minutes that the car has been parked
- **The `ParkingMeter` Class:** This class should simulate a parking meter. The class's only responsibility is:
    - To know the number of minutes of parking time that has been purchased

- The **ParkingTicket** Class: This class should simulate a parking ticket. The class's responsibilities are:
  - To report the make, model, color, and license number of the illegally parked car
  - To report the amount of the fine, which is $25 for the first hour or part of an hour that the car is illegally parked, plus $10 for every additional hour or part of an hour that the car is illegally parked
  - To report the name and badge number of the police officer issuing the ticket
- The **PoliceOfficer** Class: This class should simulate a police officer inspecting parked cars. The class's responsibilities are:
  - To know the police officer's name and badge number
  - To examine a `ParkedCar` object and a `ParkingMeter` object, and determine whether the car's time has expired
  - To issue a parking ticket (generate a `ParkingTicket` object) if the car's time has expired

Write a program that demonstrates how these classes collaborate.

15. **Car Instrument Simulator**

   For this assignment you will design a set of classes that work together to simulate a car's fuel gauge and odometer. The classes you will design are:

   - The `FuelGauge` Class: This class will simulate a fuel gauge. Its responsibilities are
     - To know the car's current amount of fuel, in gallons.
     - To report the car's current amount of fuel, in gallons.
     - To be able to increment the amount of fuel by 1 gallon. This simulates putting fuel in the car. (The car can hold a maximum of 15 gallons.)
     - To be able to decrement the amount of fuel by 1 gallon, if the amount of fuel is greater than 0 gallons. This simulates burning fuel as the car runs.

   - The `Odometer` Class: This class will simulate the car's odometer. Its responsibilities are:
     - To know the car's current mileage.
     - To report the car's current mileage.
     - To be able to increment the current mileage by 1 mile. The maximum mileage the odometer can store is 999,999 miles. When this amount is exceeded, the odometer resets the current mileage to 0.
     - To be able to work with a `FuelGuage` object. It should decrease the `FuelGauge` object's current amount of fuel by 1 gallon for every 24 miles traveled. (The car's fuel economy is 24 miles per gallon.)

   Demonstrate the classes by creating instances of each. Simulate filling the car up with fuel, and then run a loop that increments the odometer until the car runs out of fuel. During each loop iteration, print the car's current mileage and amount of fuel.

CHAPTER

15

Inheritance, Polymorphism, and Virtual Functions

TOPICS

15.1 What Is Inheritance?

CONCEPT: Inheritance allows a new class to be based on an existing class. The new class inherits all the member variables and functions (except the constructors and destructor) of the class it is based on.

Generalization and Specialization

In the real world you can find many objects that are specialized versions of other more general objects. For example, the term "insect" describes a very general type of creature with numerous characteristics. Because grasshoppers and bumblebees are insects, they have all the general characteristics of an insect. In addition, they have special characteristics of their own. For example, the grasshopper has its jumping ability, and the bumblebee has its stinger. Grasshoppers and bumblebees are specialized versions of an insect. This is illustrated in Figure 15-1.

Figure 15-1

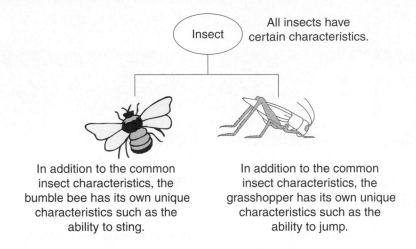

In addition to the common insect characteristics, the bumble bee has its own unique characteristics such as the ability to sting.

In addition to the common insect characteristics, the grasshopper has its own unique characteristics such as the ability to jump.

Inheritance and the "Is a" Relationship

When one object is a specialized version of another object, there is an *"is a" relationship* between them. For example, a grasshopper *is an* insect. Here are a few other examples of the "is a" relationship.

- A poodle *is a* dog.
- A car *is a* vehicle.
- A tree *is a* plant.
- A rectangle *is a* shape.
- A football player *is an* athlete.

When an "is a" relationship exists between classes, it means that the specialized class has all of the characteristics of the general class, plus additional characteristics that make it special. In object-oriented programming, *inheritance* is used to create an "is a" relationship between classes.

Inheritance involves a base class and a derived class. The *base class* is the general class and the *derived class* is the specialized class. The derived class is based on, or derived from, the base class. You can think of the base class as the parent and the derived class as the child. This is illustrated in Figure 15-2.

Figure 15-2

The derived class inherits the member variables and member functions of the base class without any of them being rewritten. Furthermore, new member variables and functions may be added to the derived class to make it more specialized than the base class.

Let's look at an example of how inheritance can be used. Most teachers assign various graded activities for their students to complete. A graded activity can receive a numeric score such as 70, 85, 90, and so on, and a letter grade such as A, B, C, D, or F. The following `GradedActivity` class is designed to hold the numeric score and letter grade of a graded activity. When a numeric score is stored by the class, it automatically determines the letter grade. (These files are stored in the Student Source Code Folder `Chapter 15\GradedActivity Version 1`.)

Contents of `GradedActivity.h` (Version 1)

```
 1   #ifndef GRADEDACTIVITY_H
 2   #define GRADEDACTIVITY_H
 3
 4   // GradedActivity class declaration
 5
 6   class GradedActivity
 7   {
 8   private:
 9      double score;    // To hold the numeric score
10   public:
11      // Default constructor
12      GradedActivity()
13         { score = 0.0; }
14
15      // Constructor
16      GradedActivity(double s)
17         { score = s; }
18
19      // Mutator function
20      void setScore(double s)
21         { score = s; }
22
23      // Accessor functions
24      double getScore() const
25         { return score; }
26
27      char getLetterGrade() const;
28   };
29   #endif
```

Contents of `GradedActivity.cpp` (Version 1)

```
 1   #include "GradedActivity.h"
 2
 3   //********************************************************
 4   // Member function GradedActivity::getLetterGrade        *
 5   //********************************************************
 6
```

```
 7  char GradedActivity::getLetterGrade() const
 8  {
 9      char letterGrade;  // To hold the letter grade
10
11      if (score > 89)
12          letterGrade = 'A';
13      else if (score > 79)
14          letterGrade = 'B';
15      else if (score > 69)
16          letterGrade = 'C';
17      else if (score > 59)
18          letterGrade = 'D';
19      else
20          letterGrade = 'F';
21
22      return letterGrade;
23  }
```

The GradedActivity class has a default constructor that initializes the score member
variable to 0.0. A second constructor accepts an argument for score. The setScore member function also accepts an argument for the score variable, and the getLetterGrade
member function returns the letter grade that corresponds to the value in score.
Program 15-1 demonstrates the GradedActivity class. (This file is also stored in the Student Source Code Folder Chapter 15\GradedActivity Version 1.)

Program 15-1

```
 1  // This program demonstrates the GradedActivity class.
 2  #include <iostream>
 3  #include "GradedActivity.h"
 4  using namespace std;
 5
 6  int main()
 7  {
 8      double testScore;   // To hold a test score
 9
10      // Create a GradedActivity object for the test.
11      GradedActivity test;
12
13      // Get a numeric test score from the user.
14      cout << "Enter your numeric test score: ";
15      cin >> testScore;
16
17      // Store the numeric score in the test object.
18      test.setScore(testScore);
19
20      // Display the letter grade for the test.
21      cout << "The grade for that test is "
22          << test.getLetterGrade() << endl;
23
24      return 0;
25  }
```

The GradedActivity class represents the general characteristics of a student's graded activity. Many different types of graded activities exist, however, such as quizzes, midterm exams, final exams, lab reports, essays, and so on. Because the numeric scores might be determined differently for each of these graded activities, we can create derived classes to handle each one. For example, the following code shows the FinalExam class, which is derived from the GradedActivity class. It has member variables for the number of questions on the exam (numQuestions), the number of points each question is worth (pointsEach), and the number of questions missed by the student (numMissed). These files are also stored in the Student Source Code Folder Chapter 15\GradedActivity Version 1.

Contents of FinalExam.h

```cpp
 1  #ifndef FINALEXAM_H
 2  #define FINALEXAM_H
 3  #include "GradedActivity.h"
 4
 5  class FinalExam : public GradedActivity
 6  {
 7  private:
 8     int numQuestions;     // Number of questions
 9     double pointsEach;    // Points for each question
10     int numMissed;        // Number of questions missed
11  public:
12     // Default constructor
13     FinalExam()
14        { numQuestions = 0;
15          pointsEach = 0.0;
16          numMissed = 0; }
17
18     // Constructor
19     FinalExam(int questions, int missed)
20        { set(questions, missed); }
21
22     // Mutator function
23     void set(int, int);  // Defined in FinalExam.cpp
24
25     // Accessor functions
26     double getNumQuestions() const
27        { return numQuestions; }
28
29     double getPointsEach() const
30        { return pointsEach; }
31
```

```
32     int getNumMissed() const
33        { return numMissed; }
34 };
35 #endif
```

Contents of `FinalExam.cpp`

```
1  #include "FinalExam.h"
2
3  //***********************************************************
4  // set function                                            *
5  // The parameters are the number of questions and the      *
6  // number of questions missed.                             *
7  //***********************************************************
8
9  void FinalExam::set(int questions, int missed)
10 {
11    double numericScore;  // To hold the numeric score
12
13    // Set the number of questions and number missed.
14    numQuestions = questions;
15    numMissed = missed;
16
17    // Calculate the points for each question.
18    pointsEach = 100.0 / numQuestions;
19
20    // Calculate the numeric score for this exam.
21    numericScore = 100.0 - (missed * pointsEach);
22
23    // Call the inherited setScore function to set
24    // the numeric score.
25    setScore(numericScore);
26 }
```

The only new notation in this code is in line 5 of the `FinalExam.h` file, which reads

```
class FinalExam : public GradedActivity
```

This line indicates the name of the class being declared and the name of the base class it is derived from. `FinalExam` is the name of the class being declared and `GradedActivity` is the name of the base class it inherits from.

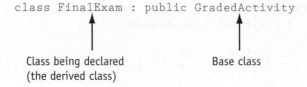

If we want to express the relationship between the two classes, we can say that a `FinalExam` *is a* `GradedActivity`.

The word `public`, which precedes the name of the base class in line 5 of the `FinalExam.h` file, is the *base class access specification*. It affects how the members of the base class are inherited by the derived class. When you create an object of a derived class, you can think of it as being built on top of an object of the base class. The members of the base class object become members of the derived class object. How the base class members appear in the derived class is determined by the base class access specification.

Although we will discuss this topic in more detail in the next section, let's see how it works in this example. The GradedActivity class has both private members and public members. The FinalExam class is derived from the GradedActivity class, using public access specification. This means that the public members of the GradedActivity class will become public members of the FinalExam class. The private members of the GradedActivity class cannot be accessed directly by code in the FinalExam class. Although the private members of the GradedActivity class are inherited, it's as though they are invisible to the code in the FinalExam class. They can only be accessed by the member functions of the GradedActivity class. Here is a list of the members of the FinalExam class:

Private Members:

int numQuestions	Declared in the FinalExam class
double pointsEach	Declared in the FinalExam class
int numMissed	Declared in the FinalExam class

Public Members:

FinalExam()	Defined in the FinalExam class
FinalExam(int, int)	Defined in the FinalExam class
set(int, int)	Defined in the FinalExam class
getNumQuestions()	Defined in the FinalExam class
getPointsEach()	Defined in the FinalExam class
getNumMissed()	Defined in the FinalExam class
setScore(double)	Inherited from GradedActivity
getScore()	Inherited from GradedActivity
getLetterGrade()	Inherited from GradedActivity

The GradedActivity class has one private member, the variable score. Notice that it is not listed as a member of the FinalExam class. It is still inherited by the derived class, but because it is a private member of the base class, only member functions of the base class may access it. It is truly private to the base class. Because the functions setScore, getScore, and getLetterGrade are public members of the base class, they also become public members of the derived class.

You will also notice that the GradedActivity class constructors are not listed among the members of the FinalExam class. Although the base class constructors still exist, it makes sense that they are not members of the derived class because their purpose is to construct objects of the base class. In the next section we discuss in more detail how base class constructors operate.

Let's take a closer look at the FinalExam class constructors. The default constructor appears in lines 13 through 16 of the FinalExam.h file. It simply assigns 0 to each of the class's member variables. Another constructor appears in lines 19 through 20. This constructor accepts two arguments, one for the number of questions on the exam, and one for the number of questions missed. This constructor merely passes those values as arguments to the set function.

The set function is defined in `FinalExam.cpp`. It accepts two arguments: the number of questions on the exam, and the number of questions missed by the student. In lines 14 and 15 these values are assigned to the `numQuestions` and `numMissed` member variables. In line 18 the number of points for each question is calculated. In line 21 the numeric test score is calculated. In line 25, the last statement in the function reads:

```cpp
setScore(numericScore);
```

This is a call to the `setScore` function. Although no `setScore` function appears in the `FinalExam` class, it is inherited from the `GradedActivity` class. Program 15-2 demonstrates the `FinalExam` class.

Program 15-2

```cpp
 1    // This program demonstrates a base class and a derived class.
 2    #include <iostream>
 3    #include <iomanip>
 4    #include "FinalExam.h"
 5    using namespace std;
 6
 7    int main()
 8    {
 9       int questions; // Number of questions on the exam
10       int missed;    // Number of questions missed by the student
11
12       // Get the number of questions on the final exam.
13       cout << "How many questions are on the final exam? ";
14       cin >> questions;
15
16       // Get the number of questions the student missed.
17       cout << "How many questions did the student miss? ";
18       cin >> missed;
19
20       // Define a FinalExam object and initialize it with
21       // the values entered.
22       FinalExam test(questions, missed);
23
24       // Display the test results.
25       cout << setprecision(2);
26       cout << "\nEach question counts " << test.getPointsEach()
27            << " points.\n";
28       cout << "The exam score is " << test.getScore() << endl;
29       cout << "The exam grade is " << test.getLetterGrade() << endl;
30
31       return 0;
32    }
```

Program Output with Example Input Shown in Bold
```
How many questions are on the final exam? 20 [Enter]
How many questions did the student miss? 3 [Enter]

Each question counts 5 points.
The exam score is 85
The exam grade is B
```

Notice in lines 28 and 29 that the public member functions of the `GradedActivity` class may be directly called by the `test` object:

```
cout << "The exam score is " << test.getScore() << endl;
cout << "The exam grade is " << test.getLetterGrade() << endl;
```

The `getScore` and `getLetterGrade` member functions are inherited as public members of the `FinalExam` class, so they may be accessed like any other public member.

Inheritance does not work in reverse. It is not possible for a base class to call a member function of a derived class. For example, the following classes will not compile in a program because the `BadBase` constructor attempts to call a function in its derived class:

```
class BadBase
{
   private:
       int x;
   public:
       BadBase() { x = getVal(); }    // Error!
};

class Derived : public BadBase
{
   private:
       int y;
   public:
       Derived(int z) { y = z; }
       int getVal() { return y; }
};
```

Checkpoint

15.1   Here is the first line of a class declaration. Circle the name of the base class:
        `class Truck : public Vehicle`

15.2   Circle the name of the derived class in the following declaration line:
        `class Truck : public Vehicle`

15.3   Suppose a program has the following class declarations:

```
class Shape
{
private:
   double area;
public:
   void setArea(double a)
       { area = a; }

   double getArea()
       { return area; }
};

class Circle : public Shape
{
private:
   double radius;
```

```
public:
    void setRadius(double r)
        { radius = r;
          setArea(3.14 * r * r); }

    double getRadius()
        { return radius; }
};
```

Answer the following questions concerning these classes:

A) When an object of the Circle class is created, what are its private members?

B) When an object of the Circle class is created, what are its public members?

C) What members of the Shape class are not accessible to member functions of the Circle class?

15.2   Protected Members and Class Access

CONCEPT: Protected members of a base class are like private members, but they may be accessed by derived classes. The base class access specification determines how private, public, and protected base class members are accessed when they are inherited by the derived classes.

Until now you have used two access specifications within a class: private and public. C++ provides a third access specification, protected. Protected members of a base class are like private members, except they may be accessed by functions in a derived class. To the rest of the program, however, protected members are inaccessible.

The following code shows a modified version of the GradedActivity class declaration. The private member of the class has been made protected. This file is stored in the Student Source Code Folder Chapter 15\GradedActivity Version 2. The implementation file, GradedActivity.cpp has not changed, so it is not shown again in this example.

Contents of GradedActivity.h (Version 2)

```
 1   #ifndef GRADEDACTIVITY_H
 2   #define GRADEDACTIVITY_H
 3
 4   // GradedActivity class declaration
 5
 6   class GradedActivity
 7   {
 8   protected:
 9       double score;    // To hold the numeric score
10   public:
11       // Default constructor
12       GradedActivity()
13           { score = 0.0; }
14
15       // Constructor
16       GradedActivity(double s)
17           { score = s; }
18
```

```
19      // Mutator function
20      void setScore(double s)
21         { score = s; }
22
23      // Accessor functions
24      double getScore() const
25         { return score; }
26
27      char getLetterGrade() const;
28   };
29   #endif
```

Now we will look at a modified version of the `FinalExam` class, which is derived from this version of the `GradedActivity` class. This version of the `FinalExam` class has a new member function named `adjustScore`. This function directly accesses the `GradedActivity` class's `score` member variable. If the content of the `score` variable has a fractional part of 0.5 or greater, the function rounds `score` up to the next whole number. The `set` function calls the `adjustScore` function after it calculates the numeric score. (These files are stored in the Student Source Code Folder `Chapter 15\GradedActivity Version 2`.)

Contents of `FinalExam.h` (Version 2)

```
1    #ifndef FINALEXAM_H
2    #define FINALEXAM_H
3    #include "GradedActivity.h"
4
5    class FinalExam : public GradedActivity
6    {
7    private:
8       int numQuestions;      // Number of questions
9       double pointsEach;     // Points for each question
10      int numMissed;         // Number of questions missed
11   public:
12      // Default constructor
13      FinalExam()
14         { numQuestions = 0;
15           pointsEach = 0.0;
16           numMissed = 0; }
17
18      // Constructor
19      FinalExam(int questions, int missed)
20         { set(questions, missed); }
21
22      // Mutator functions
23      void set(int, int);   // Defined in FinalExam.cpp
24      void adjustScore();   // Defined in FinalExam.cpp
25
26      // Accessor functions
27      double getNumQuestions() const
28         { return numQuestions; }
29
30      double getPointsEach() const
31         { return pointsEach; }
32
```

```
33        int getNumMissed() const
34           { return numMissed; }
35    };
36    #endif
```

Contents of `FinalExam.cpp` (Version 2)

```
1    #include "FinalExam.h"
2
3    //********************************************************
4    // set function                                         *
5    // The parameters are the number of questions and the    *
6    // number of questions missed.                           *
7    //********************************************************
8
9    void FinalExam::set(int questions, int missed)
10   {
11      double numericScore;  // To hold the numeric score
12
13      // Set the number of questions and number missed.
14      numQuestions = questions;
15      numMissed = missed;
16
17      // Calculate the points for each question.
18      pointsEach = 100.0 / numQuestions;
19
20      // Calculate the numeric score for this exam.
21      numericScore = 100.0 - (missed * pointsEach);
22
23      // Call the inherited setScore function to set
24      // the numeric score.
25      setScore(numericScore);
26
27      // Call the adjustScore function to adjust
28      // the score.
29      adjustScore();
30   }
31
32   //************************************************************
33   // Definition of Test::adjustScore. If score is within       *
34   // 0.5 points of the next whole point, it rounds the score up *
35   // and recalculates the letter grade.                         *
36   //************************************************************
37
38   void FinalExam::adjustScore()
39   {
40      double fraction = score - static_cast<int>(score);
41
42      if (fraction >= 0.5)
43      {
44         // Adjust the score variable in the GradedActivity class.
45         score += (1.0 - fraction);
46      }
47   }
```

Program 15-3 demonstrates these versions of the `GradedActivity` and `FinalExam` classes. (This file is also stored in the Student Source Code Folder `Chapter 15\ GradedActivity Version 2`.)

Program 15-3

```cpp
 1  // This program demonstrates a base class with a
 2  // protected member.
 3  #include <iostream>
 4  #include <iomanip>
 5  #include "FinalExam.h"
 6  using namespace std;
 7
 8  int main()
 9  {
10     int questions; // Number of questions on the exam
11     int missed;    // Number of questions missed by the student
12
13     // Get the number of questions on the final exam.
14     cout << "How many questions are on the final exam? ";
15     cin >> questions;
16
17     // Get the number of questions the student missed.
18     cout << "How many questions did the student miss? ";
19     cin >> missed;
20
21     // Define a FinalExam object and initialize it with
22     // the values entered.
23     FinalExam test(questions, missed);
24
25     // Display the adjusted test results.
26     cout << setprecision(2) << fixed;
27     cout << "\nEach question counts "
28          << test.getPointsEach() << " points.\n";
29     cout << "The adjusted exam score is "
30          << test.getScore() << endl;
31     cout << "The exam grade is "
32          << test.getLetterGrade() << endl;
33
34     return 0;
35  }
```

Program Output with Example Input Shown in Bold

How many questions are on the final exam? **16 [Enter]**
How many questions did the student miss? **5 [Enter]**

Each question counts 6.25 points.
The adjusted exam score is 69.00
The exam grade is D

The program works as planned. In the example run, the student missed five questions, which are worth 6.25 points each. The unadjusted score would be 68.75. The score was adjusted to 69.

More About Base Class Access Specification

The first line of the FinalExam class declaration reads:

```
class FinalExam : public GradedActivity
```

This declaration gives public access specification to the base class. Recall from our earlier discussion that base class access specification affects how inherited base class members are accessed. Be careful not to confuse base class access specification with member access specification. Member access specification determines how members that are *defined* within the class are accessed. Base class access specification determines how *inherited* members are accessed.

When you create an object of a derived class, it inherits the members of the base class. The derived class can have its own private, protected, and public members, but what is the access specification of the inherited members? This is determined by the base class access specification. Table 15-1 summarizes how base class access specification affects the way that base class members are inherited.

Table 15-1

Base Class Access Specification	How Members of the Base Class Appear in the Derived Class
private	Private members of the base class are inaccessible to the derived class.
	Protected members of the base class become private members of the derived class.
	Public members of the base class become private members of the derived class.
protected	Private members of the base class are inaccessible to the derived class.
	Protected members of the base class become protected members of the derived class.
	Public members of the base class become protected members of the derived class.
public	Private members of the base class are inaccessible to the derived class.
	Protected members of the base class become protected members of the derived class.
	Public members of the base class become public members of the derived class.

As you can see from Table 15-1, class access specification gives you a great deal of flexibility in determining how base class members will appear in the derived class. Think of a base class's access specification as a filter that base class members must pass through when becoming inherited members of a derived class. This is illustrated in Figure 15-3.

> **NOTE:** If the base class access specification is left out of a declaration, the default access specification is private. For example, in the following declaration, Grade is declared as a private base class:
>
> ```
> class Test : Grade
> ```

Figure 15-3

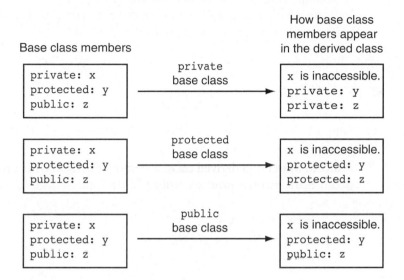

Checkpoint

15.4   What is the difference between private members and protected members?

15.5   What is the difference between member access specification and class access specification?

15.6   Suppose a program has the following class declaration:

```
// Declaration of CheckPoint class.
class CheckPoint
{
    private:
        int a;
    protected:
        int b;
        int c;
        void setA(int x) { a = x;}
    public:
        void setB(int y) { b = y;}
        void setC(int z) { c = z;}
};
```

Answer the following questions regarding the class:

A)   Suppose another class, Quiz, is derived from the CheckPoint class. Here is the first line of its declaration:

```
class Quiz : private CheckPoint
```

Indicate whether each member of the CheckPoint class is private, protected, public, or inaccessible:

    a
    b
    c
    setA
    setB
    setC

B) Suppose the Quiz class, derived from the CheckPoint class, is declared as
    class Quiz : protected Checkpoint
Indicate whether each member of the CheckPoint class is private, protected, public, or inaccessible:

    a
    b
    c
    setA
    setB
    setC

C) Suppose the Quiz class, derived from the CheckPoint class, is declared as
    class Quiz : public Checkpoint
Indicate whether each member of the CheckPoint class is private, protected, public, or inaccessible:

    a
    b
    c
    setA
    setB
    setC

D) Suppose the Quiz class, derived from the CheckPoint class, is declared as
    class Quiz : Checkpoint
Is the CheckPoint class a private, public, or protected base class?

15.3   Constructors and Destructors in Base and Derived Classes

CONCEPT: The base class's constructor is called before the derived class's constructor. The destructors are called in reverse order, with the derived class's destructor being called first.

In inheritance, the base class constructor is called before the derived class constructor. Destructors are called in reverse order. Program 15-4 shows a simple set of demonstration classes, each with a default constructor and a destructor. The DerivedClass class is derived from the BaseClass class. Messages are displayed by the constructors and destructors to demonstrate when each is called.

Program 15-4

```
 1   // This program demonstrates the order in which base and
 2   // derived class constructors and destructors are called.
 3   #include <iostream>
 4   using namespace std;
 5
 6   //*******************************
 7   // BaseClass declaration        *
 8   //*******************************
 9
```

```
10   class BaseClass
11   {
12   public:
13      BaseClass()  // Constructor
14         { cout << "This is the BaseClass constructor.\n"; }
15
16      ~BaseClass() // Destructor
17         { cout << "This is the BaseClass destructor.\n"; }
18   };
19
20   //*******************************
21   // DerivedClass declaration      *
22   //*******************************
23
24   class DerivedClass : public BaseClass
25   {
26   public:
27      DerivedClass()  // Constructor
28         { cout << "This is the DerivedClass constructor.\n"; }
29
30      ~DerivedClass()  // Destructor
31         { cout << "This is the DerivedClass destructor.\n"; }
32   };
33
34   //*******************************
35   // main function                *
36   //*******************************
37
38   int main()
39   {
40      cout << "We will now define a DerivedClass object.\n";
41
42      DerivedClass object;
43
44      cout << "The program is now going to end.\n";
45      return 0;
46   }
```

Program Output

```
We will now define a DerivedClass object.
This is the BaseClass constructor.
This is the DerivedClass constructor.
The program is now going to end.
This is the DerivedClass destructor.
This is the BaseClass destructor.
```

Passing Arguments to Base Class Constructors

In Program 15-4, both the base class and derived class have default constructors, that are called automatically. But what if the base class's constructor takes arguments? What if there is more than one constructor in the base class? The answer to these questions is to let the derived class constructor pass arguments to the base class constructor. For example, consider the following class:

Contents of `Rectangle.h`

```
1  #ifndef RECTANGLE_H
2  #define RECTANGLE_H
3
4  class Rectangle
5  {
6  private:
7     double width;
8     double length;
9  public:
10    // Default constructor
11    Rectangle()
12      { width = 0.0;
13        length = 0.0; }
14
15    // Constructor #2
16    Rectangle(double w, double len)
17      { width = w;
18        length = len; }
19
20    double getWidth() const
21      { return width; }
22
23    double getLength() const
24      { return length; }
25
26    double getArea() const
27      { return width * length; }
28  };
29  #endif
```

This class is designed to hold data about a rectangle. It specifies two constructors. The default constructor, in lines 11 through 13, simply initializes the width and length member variables to 0.0. The second constructor, in lines 16 through 18, takes two arguments, which are assigned to the width and length member variables. Now let's look at a class that is derived from the Rectangle class:

Contents of `Cube.h`

```
1  #ifndef CUBE_H
2  #define CUBE_H
3  #include "Rectangle.h"
4
5  class Cube : public Rectangle
6  {
7  protected:
8     double height;
9     double volume;
10 public:
11    // Default constructor
12    Cube() : Rectangle()
13      { height = 0.0; volume = 0.0; }
14
```

```
15      // Constructor #2
16      Cube(double w, double len, double h) : Rectangle(w, len)
17         { height = h;
18           volume = getArea() * h; }
19
20      double getHeight() const
21         { return height; }
22
23      double getVolume() const
24         { return volume; }
25  };
26  #endif
```

The Cube class is designed to hold data about cubes, which not only have a length and width, but a height and volume as well. Look at line 12, which is the first line of the Cube class's default constructor:

```
Cube() : Rectangle()
```

Notice the added notation in the header of the constructor. A colon is placed after the derived class constructor's parentheses, followed by a function call to a base class constructor. In this case, the base class's default constructor is being called. When this Cube class constructor executes, it will first call the Rectangle class's default constructor. This is illustrated here:

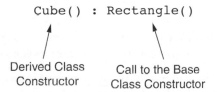

The general format of this type of constructor declaration is

> *ClassName::ClassName(ParameterList) : BaseClassName(ArgumentList)*

You can also pass arguments to the base class constructor, as shown in the Cube class's second constructor. Look at line 16:

```
Cube(double w, double len, double h) : Rectangle(w, len)
```

This Cube class constructor has three parameters: w, len, and h. Notice that the Rectangle class's constructor is called, and the w and len parameters are passed as arguments. This causes the Rectangle class's second constructor to be called.

You only write this notation in the definition of a constructor, not in a prototype. In this example, the derived class constructor is written inline (inside the class declaration), so the notation that contains the call to the base class constructor appears there. If the constructor were defined outside the class, the notation would appear in the function header. For example, the Cube class could appear as follows.

```
class Cube : public Rectangle
{
protected:
    double height;
    double volume;
public:
    // Default constructor
    Cube() : Rectangle()
       { height = 0.0; volume = 0.0; }

    // Constructor #2
    Cube(double, double, double);

    double getHeight() const
       { return height; }

    double getVolume() const
       { return volume; }
};

// Cube class constructor #2
Cube::Cube(double w, double len, double h) : Rectangle(w, len)
{
    height = h;
    volume = getArea() * h;
}
```

The base class constructor is always executed before the derived class constructor. When the `Rectangle` constructor finishes, the `Cube` constructor is then executed.

Any literal value or variable that is in scope may be used as an argument to the derived class constructor. Usually, one or more of the arguments passed to the derived class constructor are, in turn, passed to the base class constructor. The values that may be used as base class constructor arguments are

- Derived class constructor parameters
- Literal values
- Global variables that are accessible to the file containing the derived class constructor definition
- Expressions involving any of these items

Program 15-5 shows the `Rectangle` and `Cube` classes in use.

Program 15-5

```
1   // This program demonstrates passing arguments to a base
2   // class constructor.
3   #include <iostream>
4   #include "Cube.h"
5   using namespace std;
6
```

```
 7  int main()
 8  {
 9      double cubeWidth;    // To hold the cube's width
10      double cubeLength;   // To hold the cube's length
11      double cubeHeight;   // To hold the cube's height
12
13      // Get the width, length, and height of
14      // the cube from the user.
15      cout << "Enter the dimensions of a cube:\n";
16      cout << "Width: ";
17      cin >> cubeWidth;
18      cout << "Length: ";
19      cin >> cubeLength;
20      cout << "Height: ";
21      cin >> cubeHeight;
22
23      // Define a Cube object and use the dimensions
24      // entered by the user.
25      Cube myCube(cubeWidth, cubeLength, cubeHeight);
26
27      // Display the Cube object's properties.
28      cout << "Here are the cube's properties:\n";
29      cout << "Width: " << myCube.getWidth() << endl;
30      cout << "Length: " << myCube.getLength() << endl;
31      cout << "Height: " << myCube.getHeight() << endl;
32      cout << "Base area: " << myCube.getArea() << endl;
33      cout << "Volume: " << myCube.getVolume() << endl;
34
35      return 0;
36  }
```

Program Output with Example Input Shown in Bold
```
Enter the dimensions of a cube:
Width: 10 [Enter]
Length: 15 [Enter]
Height: 12 [Enter]
Here are the cube's properties:
Width: 10
Length: 15
Height: 12
Base area: 150
Volume: 1800
```

 NOTE: If the base class has no default constructor, then the derived class must have a constructor that calls one of the base class constructors.

Checkpoint

15.7   What will the following program display?

```cpp
#include <iostream>
using namespace std;

class Sky
{
public:
   Sky()
      { cout << "Entering the sky.\n"; }
   ~Sky()
      { cout << "Leaving the sky.\n"; }
};

class Ground : public Sky
{
public:
   Ground()
      { cout << "Entering the Ground.\n"; }
   ~Ground()
      { cout << "Leaving the Ground.\n"; }
};

int main()
{
   Ground object;
   return 0;
}
```

15.8   What will the following program display?

```cpp
#include <iostream>
using namespace std;

class Sky
{
public:
   Sky()
      { cout << "Entering the sky.\n"; }
   Sky(char *color)
      { cout << "The sky is " << color << endl; }
   ~Sky()
      { cout << "Leaving the sky.\n"; }
};

class Ground : public Sky
{
public:
   Ground()
      { cout << "Entering the Ground.\n"; }
   Ground(char *c1, char *c2) : Sky(c1)
      { cout << "The ground is " << c2 << endl; }
   ~Ground()
      { cout << "Leaving the Ground.\n"; }
};
```

```
int main()
{
    Ground object;
    return 0;
}
```

15.4 Redefining Base Class Functions

CONCEPT: A base class member function may be redefined in a derived class.

VideoNote

Redefining a Base Class Function in a Derived Class

Inheritance is commonly used to extend a class or give it additional capabilities. Sometimes it may be helpful to overload a base class function with a function of the same name in the derived class. For example, recall the GradedActivity class that was presented earlier in this chapter:

```
class GradedActivity
{
protected:
    char letter;            // To hold the letter grade
    double score;           // To hold the numeric score
    void determineGrade();  // Determines the letter grade
public:
    // Default constructor
    GradedActivity()
        { letter = ' '; score = 0.0; }

    // Mutator function
    void setScore(double s)
        { score = s;
          determineGrade();}

    // Accessor functions
    double getScore() const
        { return score; }

    char getLetterGrade() const
        { return letter; }
};
```

This class holds a numeric score and determines a letter grade based on that score. The setScore member function stores a value in score, then calls the determineGrade member function to determine the letter grade.

Suppose a teacher wants to "curve" a numeric score before the letter grade is determined. For example, Dr. Harrison determines that in order to curve the grades in her class she must multiply each student's score by a certain percentage. This gives an adjusted score, which is used to determine the letter grade.

The following CurvedActivity class is derived from the GradedActivity class. It multiplies the numeric score by a percentage, and passes that value as an argument to the base class's setScore function. (This file is stored in the Student Source Code Folder Chapter 15\CurvedActivity.)

Contents of `CurvedActivity.h`

```
 1   #ifndef CURVEDACTIVITY_H
 2   #define CURVEDACTIVITY_H
 3   #include "GradedActivity.h"
 4
 5   class CurvedActivity : public GradedActivity
 6   {
 7   protected:
 8      double rawScore;      // Unadjusted score
 9      double percentage;    // Curve percentage
10   public:
11      // Default constructor
12      CurvedActivity() : GradedActivity()
13         { rawScore = 0.0; percentage = 0.0; }
14
15      // Mutator functions
16      void setScore(double s)
17         { rawScore = s;
18           GradedActivity::setScore(rawScore * percentage); }
19
20      void setPercentage(double c)
21         { percentage = c; }
22
23      // Accessor functions
24      double getPercentage() const
25         { return percentage; }
26
27      double getRawScore() const
28         { return rawScore; }
29   };
30   #endif
```

This `CurvedActivity` class has the following member variables:

- `rawScore`   This variable holds the student's unadjusted score.
- `percentage`   This variable holds the value that the unadjusted score must be multiplied by to get the curved score.

It also has the following member functions:

- A default constructor that calls the `GradedActivity` default constructor, then sets `rawScore` and `percentage` to 0.0.
- `setScore`   This function accepts an argument that is the student's unadjusted score. The function stores the argument in the `rawScore` variable, then passes `rawScore * percentage` as an argument to the base class's `setScore` function.
- `setPercentage` This function stores a value in the `percentage` variable.
- `getPercentage` This function returns the value in the `percentage` variable.
- `getRawScore`   This function returns the value in the `rawScore` variable.

NOTE: Although we are not using the `CurvedActivity` class as a base class, it still has a protected member section. This is because we might want to use the `CurvedActivity` class itself as a base class, as you will see in the next section.

Notice that the `CurvedActivity` class has a `setScore` member function. This function has the same name as one of the base class member functions. When a derived class's member function has the same name as a base class member function, it is said that the derived class function *redefines* the base class function. When an object of the derived class calls the function, it calls the derived class's version of the function.

There is a distinction between redefining a function and overloading a function. An overloaded function is one with the same name as one or more other functions, but with a different parameter list. The compiler uses the arguments passed to the function to tell which version to call. Overloading can take place with regular functions that are not members of a class. Overloading can also take place inside a class when two or more member functions *of the same class* have the same name. These member functions must have different parameter lists for the compiler to tell them apart in function calls.

Redefining happens when a derived class has a function with the same name as a base class function. The parameter lists of the two functions can be the same because the derived class function is always called by objects of the derived class type.

Let's continue our look at the `CurvedActivity` class. Here is the `setScore` member function:

```
void setScore(double s)
    { rawScore = s;
      GradedActivity::setScore(rawScore * percentage); }
```

This function accepts an argument that should be the student's unadjusted numeric score, into the parameter s. This value is stored in the `rawScore` variable. Then the following statement is executed:

```
GradedActivity::setScore(rawScore * percentage);
```

This statement calls the base class's version of the `setScore` function with the expression `rawScore * percentage` passed as an argument. Notice that the name of the base class and the scope resolution operator precede the name of the function. This specifies that the base class's version of the `setScore` function is being called. A derived class function may call a base class function of the same name using this notation, which takes this form:

```
BaseClassName::functionName(ArgumentList);
```

Program 15-6 shows the `GradedActivity` and `CurvedActivity` classes used in a complete program. (This file is stored in the Student Source Code Folder Chapter 15\ CurvedActivity.)

Program 15-6

```
1  // This program demonstrates a class that redefines
2  // a base class function.
3  #include <iostream>
4  #include <iomanip>
5  #include "CurvedActivity.h"
6  using namespace std;
7
```

(program continues)

Program 15-6   *(continued)*

```
 8   int main()
 9   {
10      double numericScore;   // To hold the numeric score
11      double percentage;     // To hold curve percentage
12
13      // Define a CurvedActivity object.
14      CurvedActivity exam;
15
16      // Get the unadjusted score.
17      cout << "Enter the student's raw numeric score: ";
18      cin >> numericScore;
19
20      // Get the curve percentage.
21      cout << "Enter the curve percentage for this student: ";
22      cin >> percentage;
23
24      // Send the values to the exam object.
25      exam.setPercentage(percentage);
26      exam.setScore(numericScore);
27
28      // Display the grade data.
29      cout << fixed << setprecision(2);
30      cout << "The raw score is "
31           << exam.getRawScore() << endl;
32      cout << "The curved score is "
33           << exam.getScore() << endl;
34      cout << "The curved grade is "
35           << exam.getLetterGrade() << endl;
36
37      return 0;
38   }
```

Program Output with Example Input Shown in Bold
```
Enter the student's raw numeric score: 87 [Enter]
Enter the curve percentage for this student: 1.06 [Enter]
The raw score is 87.00
The curved score is 92.22
The curved grade is A
```

It is important to note that even though a derived class may redefine a function in the base class, objects that are defined of the base class type still call the base class version of the function. This is demonstrated in Program 15-7.

Program 15-7

```
 1   // This program demonstrates that when a derived class function
 2   // overrides a base class function, objects of the base class
 3   // still call the base class version of the function.
 4   #include <iostream>
 5   using namespace std;
 6
```

```
 7   class BaseClass
 8   {
 9   public:
10      void showMessage()
11         { cout << "This is the Base class.\n"; }
12   };
13
14   class DerivedClass : public BaseClass
15   {
16   public:
17      void showMessage()
18         { cout << "This is the Derived class.\n"; }
19   };
20
21   int main()
22   {
23      BaseClass b;
24      DerivedClass d;
25
26      b.showMessage();
27      d.showMessage();
28
29      return 0;
30   }
```

Program Output
```
This is the Base class.
This is the Derived class.
```

In Program 15-7, a class named BaseClass is declared with a member function named showMessage. A class named DerivedClass is then declared, also with a showMessage member function. As their names imply, DerivedClass is derived from BaseClass. Two objects, b and d, are defined in function main. The object b is a BaseClass object and d is a DerivedClass object. When b is used to call the showMessage function, it is the BaseClass version that is executed. Likewise, when d is used to call showMessage, the DerivedClass version is used.

15.5 Class Hierarchies

CONCEPT: A base class can also be derived from another class.

Sometimes it is desirable to establish a hierarchy of classes in which one class inherits from a second class, which in turn inherits from a third class, as illustrated by Figure 15-4. In some cases, the inheritance of classes goes on for many layers.

In Figure 15-4, ClassC inherits ClassB's members, including the ones that ClassB inherited from ClassA. Let's look at an example of such a chain of inheritance. Consider the following PassFailActivity class, which inherits from the GradedActivity class. The

Figure 15-4

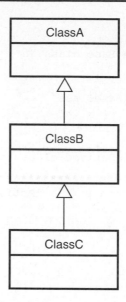

class is intended to determine a letter grade of 'P' for passing, or 'F' for failing. (This file is stored in the Student Source Code Folder Chapter 15\PassFailActivity.)

Contents of PassFailActivity.h

```
 1  #ifndef PASSFAILACTIVITY_H
 2  #define PASSFAILACTIVITY_H
 3  #include "GradedActivity.h"
 4
 5  class PassFailActivity : public GradedActivity
 6  {
 7  protected:
 8     double minPassingScore;      // Minimum passing score.
 9  public:
10     // Default constructor
11     PassFailActivity() : GradedActivity()
12        { minPassingScore = 0.0; }
13
14     // Constructor
15     PassFailActivity(double mps) : GradedActivity()
16        { minPassingScore = mps; }
17
18     // Mutator
19     void setMinPassingScore(double mps)
20        { minPassingScore = mps; }
21
22     // Accessors
23     double getMinPassingScore() const
24        { return minPassingScore; }
25
26     char getLetterGrade() const;
27  };
28  #endif
```

The `PassFailActivity` class has a private member variable named `minPassingScore`. This variable holds the minimum passing score for an activity. The default constructor, in lines 11 through 12, sets `minPassingScore` to 0.0. An overloaded constructor in lines 15 through 16 accepts a `double` argument that is the minimum passing grade for the activity. This value is stored in the `minPassingScore` variable. The `getLetterGrade` member function is defined in the following `PassFailActivity.cpp` file. (This file is also stored in the Student Source Code Folder `Chapter 15\PassFailActivity`.)

Contents of `PassFailActivity.cpp`

```
 1   #include "PassFailActivity.h"
 2
 3   //*****************************************************
 4   // Member function PassFailActivity::getLetterGrade    *
 5   // This function returns 'P' if the score is passing,  *
 6   // otherwise it returns 'F'.                           *
 7   //*****************************************************
 8
 9   char PassFailActivity::getLetterGrade() const
10   {
11      char letterGrade;
12
13      if (score >= minPassingScore)
14         letterGrade = 'P';
15      else
16         letterGrade = 'F';
17
18      return letterGrade;
19   }
```

This `getLetterGrade` member function redefines the `getLetterGrade` member function of `GradedActivity` class. This version of the function returns a grade of `'P'` if the numeric score is greater than or equal to `minPassingScore`. Otherwise, the function returns a grade of `'F'`.

The `PassFailActivity` class represents the general characteristics of a student's pass-or-fail activity. There might be numerous types of pass-or-fail activities, however. Suppose we need a more specialized class, such as one that determines a student's grade for a pass-or-fail exam. The following `PassFailExam` class is an example. This class is derived from the `PassFailActivity` class. It inherits all of the members of `PassFailActivity`, including the ones that `PassFailActivity` inherits from `GradedActivity`. The `PassFailExam` class calculates the number of points that each question on the exam is worth, as well as the student's numeric score. (These files are stored in the Student Source Code Folder `Chapter 15\PassFailActivity`.)

Contents of `PassFailExam.h`

```
 1   #ifndef PASSFAILEXAM_H
 2   #define PASSFAILEXAM_H
 3   #include "PassFailActivity.h"
 4
 5   class PassFailExam : public PassFailActivity
 6   {
```

```
 7   private:
 8      int numQuestions;    // Number of questions
 9      double pointsEach;   // Points for each question
10      int numMissed;       // Number of questions missed
11   public:
12      // Default constructor
13      PassFailExam() : PassFailActivity()
14         { numQuestions = 0;
15           pointsEach = 0.0;
16           numMissed = 0; }
17
18      // Constructor
19      PassFailExam(int questions, int missed, double mps) :
20         PassFailActivity(mps)
21         { set(questions, missed); }
22
23      // Mutator function
24      void set(int, int);  // Defined in PassFailExam.cpp
25
26      // Accessor functions
27      double getNumQuestions() const
28         { return numQuestions; }
29
30      double getPointsEach() const
31         { return pointsEach; }
32
33      int getNumMissed() const
34         { return numMissed; }
35   };
36   #endif
```

Contents of `PassFailExam.cpp`

```
 1   #include "PassFailExam.h"
 2
 3   //*********************************************************
 4   // set function                                          *
 5   // The parameters are the number of questions and the    *
 6   // number of questions missed.                           *
 7   //*********************************************************
 8
 9   void PassFailExam::set(int questions, int missed)
10   {
11      double numericScore;  // To hold the numeric score
12
13      // Set the number of questions and number missed.
14      numQuestions = questions;
15      numMissed = missed;
16
17      // Calculate the points for each question.
18      pointsEach = 100.0 / numQuestions;
19
```

```
20        // Calculate the numeric score for this exam.
21        numericScore = 100.0 - (missed * pointsEach);
22
23        // Call the inherited setScore function to set
24        // the numeric score.
25        setScore(numericScore);
26   }
```

The `PassFailExam` class inherits all of the `PassFailActivity` class's members, including the ones that `PassFailActivity` inherited from `GradedActivity`. Because the `public` base class access specification is used, all of the protected members of `PassFailActivity` become protected members of `PassFailExam`, and all of the `public` members of `PassFailActivity` become `public` members of `PassFailExam`. Table 15-2 lists all of the member variables of the `PassFailExam` class, and Table 15-3 lists all the member functions. These include the members that were inherited from the base classes.

Table 15-2

Member Variable of the `PassFailExam` Class	Access	Inherited?
numQuestions	protected	No
pointsEach	protected	No
numMissed	protected	No
minPassingScore	protected	Yes, from `PassFailActivity`
score	protected	Yes, from `PassFailActivity`, which inherited it from `GradedActivity`

Table 15-3

Member Function of the `PassFailExam` Class	Access	Inherited?
set	public	No
getNumQuestions	public	No
getPointsEach	public	No
getNumMissed	public	No
setMinPassingScore	public	Yes, from `PassFailActivity`
getMinPassingScore	public	Yes, from `PassFailActivity`
getLetterGrade	public	Yes, from `PassFailActivity`
setScore	public	Yes, from `PassFailActivity`, which inherited it from `GradedActivity`
getScore	public	Yes, from `PassFailActivity`, which inherited it from `GradedActivity`

Program 15-8 demonstrates the `PassFailExam` class. This file is also stored in the student source code folder `Chapter 15\PassFailActivity`.

Program 15-8

```
 1   // This program demonstrates the PassFailExam class.
 2   #include <iostream>
 3   #include <iomanip>
 4   #include "PassFailExam.h"
 5   using namespace std;
 6
 7   int main()
 8   {
 9      int questions;        // Number of questions
10      int missed;           // Number of questions missed
11      double minPassing;    // The minimum passing score
12
13      // Get the number of questions on the exam.
14      cout << "How many questions are on the exam? ";
15      cin >> questions;
16
17      // Get the number of questions the student missed.
18      cout << "How many questions did the student miss? ";
19      cin >> missed;
20
21      // Get the minimum passing score.
22      cout << "Enter the minimum passing score for this test: ";
23      cin >> minPassing;
24
25      // Define a PassFailExam object.
26      PassFailExam exam(questions, missed, minPassing);
27
28      // Display the test results.
29      cout << fixed << setprecision(1);
30      cout << "\nEach question counts "
31           << exam.getPointsEach() << " points.\n";
32      cout << "The minimum passing score is "
33           << exam.getMinPassingScore() << endl;
34      cout << "The student's exam score is "
35           << exam.getScore() << endl;
36      cout << "The student's grade is "
37           << exam.getLetterGrade() << endl;
38      return 0;
39   }
```

Program Output with Example Input Shown in Bold
```
How many questions are on the exam? 100 [Enter]
How many questions did the student miss? 25 [Enter]
Enter the minimum passing score for this test: 60 [Enter]

Each question counts 1.0 points.
The minimum passing score is 60.0
The student's exam score is 75.0
The student's grade is P
```

This program uses the `PassFailExam` object to call the `getLetterGrade` member function in line 37. Recall that the `PassFailActivity` class redefines the `getLetterGrade` function to report only grades of 'P' or 'F'. Because the `PassFailExam` class is derived from the `PassFailActivity` class, it inherits the redefined `getLetterGrade` function.

Software designers often use class hierarchy diagrams. Like a family tree, a class hierarchy diagram shows the inheritance relationships between classes. Figure 15-5 shows a class hierarchy for the `GradedActivity`, `FinalExam`, `PassFailActivity`, and `PassFailExam` classes. The more general classes are toward the top of the tree and the more specialized classes are toward the bottom.

Figure 15-5

15.6 Polymorphism and Virtual Member Functions

CONCEPT: Polymorphism allows an object reference variable or an object pointer to reference objects of different types, and to call the correct member functions, depending upon the type of object being referenced.

VideoNote

Polymorphism

Look at the following code for a function named `displayGrade`:

```
void displayGrade(const GradedActivity &activity)
{
    cout << setprecision(1) << fixed;
    cout << "The activity's numeric score is "
        << activity.getScore() << endl;
    cout << "The activity's letter grade is "
        << activity.getLetterGrade() << endl;
}
```

This function uses a const `GradedActivity` reference variable as its parameter. When a `GradedActivity` object is passed as an argument to this function, the function calls the object's `getScore` and `getLetterGrade` member functions to display the numeric score and letter grade. The following code shows how we might call the function.

```
GradedActivity test(88.0);   // The score is 88
displayGrade(test);          // Pass test to displayGrade
```

This code will produce the following output:

```
The activity's numeric score is 88.0
The activity's letter grade is B
```

Recall that the GradedActivity class is also the base class for the FinalExam class. Because of the "is-a" relationship between a base class and a derived class, an object of the FinalExam class is not just a FinalExam object. It is also a GradedActivity object. (A final exam *is a* graded activity.) Because of this relationship, we can also pass a FinalExam object to the displayGrade function. For example, look at the following code:

```
// There are 100 questions. The student missed 25.
FinalExam test2(100, 25);
displayGrade(test2);
```

This code will produce the following output:

```
The activity's numeric score is 75.0
The activity's letter grade is C
```

Because the parameter in the displayGrade function is a GradedActivity reference variable, it can reference any object that is derived from GradedActivity. A problem can occur with this type of code, however, when redefined member functions are involved. For example, recall that the PassFailActivity class is derived from the GradedActivity class. The PassFailActivity class redefines the getLetterGrade function. Although we can pass a PassFailActivity object as an argument to the displayGrade function, we will not get the results we wish. This is demonstrated in Program 15-9. (This file is stored in the Student Source Code Folder Chapter 15\PassFailActivity.)

Program 15-9

```
 1   #include <iostream>
 2   #include <iomanip>
 3   #include "PassFailActivity.h"
 4   using namespace std;
 5
 6   // Function prototype
 7   void displayGrade(const GradedActivity &);
 8
 9   int main()
10   {
11      // Create a PassFailActivity object. Minimum passing
12      // score is 70.
13      PassFailActivity test(70);
14
15      // Set the score to 72.
16      test.setScore(72);
17
18      // Display the object's grade data. The letter grade
19      // should be 'P'. What will be displayed?
20      displayGrade(test);
21      return 0;
22   }
```

```
23
24   //************************************************************
25   // The displayGrade function displays a GradedActivity object's *
26   // numeric score and letter grade.                               *
27   //************************************************************
28
29   void displayGrade(const GradedActivity &activity)
30   {
31      cout << setprecision(1) << fixed;
32      cout << "The activity's numeric score is "
33           << activity.getScore() << endl;
34      cout << "The activity's letter grade is "
35           << activity.getLetterGrade() << endl;
36   }
```

Program Output

```
The activity's numeric score is 72.0
The activity's letter grade is C
```

As you can see from the example output, the getLetterGrade member function returned 'C' instead of 'P'. This is because the GradedActivity class's getLetterGrade function was executed instead of the PassFailActivity class's version of the function.

This behavior happens because of the way C++ matches function calls with the correct function. This process is known as *binding*. In Program 15-9, C++ decides at compile time which version of the getLetterGrade function to execute when it encounters the call to the function in line 35. Even though we passed a PassFailActivity object to the displayGrade function, the activity parameter in the displayGrade function is a GradedActivity reference variable. Because it is of the GradedActivity type, the compiler binds the function call in line 35 with the GradedActivity class's getLetterGrade function. When the program executes, it has already been determined by the compiler that the GradedActivity class's getLetterGrade function will be called. The process of matching a function call with a function at compile time is called *static binding*.

To remedy this, the getLetterGrade function can be made *virtual*. A *virtual function* is a member function that is dynamically bound to function calls. In *dynamic binding*, C++ determines which function to call at runtime, depending on the type of the object responsible for the call. If a GradedActivity object is responsible for the call, C++ will execute the GradedActivity::getLetterGrade function. If a PassFailActivity object is responsible for the call, C++ will execute the PassFailActivity:: getLetterGrade function.

Virtual functions are declared by placing the key word virtual before the return type in the base class's function declaration, such as

```
virtual char getLetterGrade() const;
```

This declaration tells the compiler to expect getLetterGrade to be redefined in a derived class. The compiler does not bind calls to the function with the actual function. Instead, it allows the program to bind calls, at runtime, to the version of the function that belongs to the same class as the object responsible for the call.

NOTE: You place the `virtual` key word only in the function's declaration or prototype. If the function is defined outside the class, you do not place the `virtual` key word in the function header.

The following code shows an updated version of the `GradedActivity` class, with the `getLetterGrade` function declared `virtual`. This file is stored in the Student Source Code Folder `Chapter 15\GradedActivity Version 3`. The `GradedActivity.cpp` file has not changed, so it is not shown again.

Contents of `GradedActivity.h` (Version 3)

```
 1   #ifndef GRADEDACTIVITY_H
 2   #define GRADEDACTIVITY_H
 3
 4   // GradedActivity class declaration
 5
 6   class GradedActivity
 7   {
 8   protected:
 9      double score;    // To hold the numeric score
10   public:
11      // Default constructor
12      GradedActivity()
13         { score = 0.0; }
14
15      // Constructor
16      GradedActivity(double s)
17         { score = s; }
18
19      // Mutator function
20      void setScore(double s)
21         { score = s; }
22
23      // Accessor functions
24      double getScore() const
25         { return score; }
26
27      virtual char getLetterGrade() const;
28   };
29   #endif
```

The only change we have made to this class is to declare `getLetterGrade` as `virtual` in line 27. This tells the compiler not to bind calls to `getLetterGrade` with the function at compile time. Instead, calls to the function will be bound dynamically to the function at runtime.

When a member function is declared `virtual` in a base class, any redefined versions of the function that appear in derived classes automatically become `virtual`. So, it is not necessary to declare the `getLetterGrade` function in the `PassFailActivity` class as `virtual`. It is still a good idea to declare the function `virtual` in the `PassFailActivity` class for documentation purposes. A new version of the `PassFailActivity` class is shown here. This file is stored in the Student Source Code Folder `Chapter 15\GradedActivity Version 3`. The `PassFailActivity.cpp` file has not changed, so it is not shown again.

Contents of `PassFailActivity.h`

```
 1  #ifndef PASSFAILACTIVITY_H
 2  #define PASSFAILACTIVITY_H
 3  #include "GradedActivity.h"
 4
 5  class PassFailActivity : public GradedActivity
 6  {
 7  protected:
 8     double minPassingScore;     // Minimum passing score
 9  public:
10     // Default constructor
11     PassFailActivity() : GradedActivity()
12        { minPassingScore = 0.0; }
13
14     // Constructor
15     PassFailActivity(double mps) : GradedActivity()
16        { minPassingScore = mps; }
17
18     // Mutator
19     void setMinPassingScore(double mps)
20        { minPassingScore = mps; }
21
22     // Accessors
23     double getMinPassingScore() const
24        { return minPassingScore; }
25
26     virtual char getLetterGrade() const;
27  };
28  #endif
```

The only change we have made to this class is to declare `getLetterGrade` as virtual in line 26. Program 15-10 is identical to Program 15-9, except it uses the corrected version of the `GradedActivity` and `PassFailActivity` classes. This file is also stored in the student source code folder `Chapter 15\GradedActivity Version 3`.

Program 15-10

```
 1  #include <iostream>
 2  #include <iomanip>
 3  #include "PassFailActivity.h"
 4  using namespace std;
 5
 6  // Function prototype
 7  void displayGrade(const GradedActivity &);
 8
 9  int main()
10  {
11     // Create a PassFailActivity object. Minimum passing
12     // score is 70.
13     PassFailActivity test(70);
14
```

(program continues)

Program 15-10   *(continued)*

```
15      // Set the score to 72.
16      test.setScore(72);
17
18      // Display the object's grade data. The letter grade
19      // should be 'P'. What will be displayed?
20      displayGrade(test);
21      return 0;
22  }
23
24  //************************************************************
25  // The displayGrade function displays a GradedActivity object's *
26  // numeric score and letter grade.                              *
27  //************************************************************
28
29  void displayGrade(const GradedActivity &activity)
30  {
31      cout << setprecision(1) << fixed;
32      cout << "The activity's numeric score is "
33           << activity.getScore() << endl;
34      cout << "The activity's letter grade is "
35           << activity.getLetterGrade() << endl;
36  }
```

Program Output

```
The activity's numeric score is 72.0
The activity's letter grade is P
```

Now that the `getLetterGrade` function is declared `virtual`, the program works properly. This type of behavior is known as polymorphism. The term *polymorphism* means the ability to take many forms. Program 15-11 demonstrates polymorphism by passing objects of the `GradedActivity` and `PassFailExam` classes to the `displayGrade` function. This file is stored in the Student Source Code Folder `Chapter 15\GradedActivity Version 3`.

Program 15-11

```
1   #include <iostream>
2   #include <iomanip>
3   #include "PassFailExam.h"
4   using namespace std;
5
6   // Function prototype
7   void displayGrade(const GradedActivity &);
8
9   int main()
10  {
11      // Create a GradedActivity object. The score is 88.
12      GradedActivity test1(88.0);
13
```

```
14        // Create a PassFailExam object. There are 100 questions,
15        // the student missed 25 of them, and the minimum passing
16        // score is 70.
17        PassFailExam test2(100, 25, 70.0);
18
19        // Display the grade data for both objects.
20        cout << "Test 1:\n";
21        displayGrade(test1);     // GradedActivity object
22        cout << "\nTest 2:\n";
23        displayGrade(test2);     // PassFailExam object
24        return 0;
25    }
26
27    //***********************************************************
28    // The displayGrade function displays a GradedActivity object's *
29    // numeric score and letter grade.                              *
30    //***********************************************************
31
32    void displayGrade(const GradedActivity &activity)
33    {
34        cout << setprecision(1) << fixed;
35        cout << "The activity's numeric score is "
36             << activity.getScore() << endl;
37        cout << "The activity's letter grade is "
38             << activity.getLetterGrade() << endl;
39    }
```

Program Output
```
Test 1:
The activity's numeric score is 88.0
The activity's letter grade is B

Test 2:
The activity's numeric score is 75.0
The activity's letter grade is P
```

Polymorphism Requires References or Pointers

The displayGrade function in Programs 15-10 and 15-11 uses a GradedActivity reference variable as its parameter. When we call the function, we pass an object by reference. Polymorphic behavior is not possible when an object is passed by value, however. For example, suppose the displayGrade function had been written as shown here:

```
// Polymorphic behavior is not possible with this function.
void displayGrade(const GradedActivity activity)
{
    cout << setprecision(1) << fixed;
    cout << "The activity's numeric score is "
         << activity.getScore() << endl;
    cout << "The activity's letter grade is "
         << activity.getLetterGrade() << endl;
}
```

In this version of the function the `activity` parameter is an object variable, not a reference variable. Suppose we call this version of the function with the following code:

```
// Create a GradedActivity object. The score is 88.
GradedActivity test1(88.0);

// Create a PassFailExam object. There are 100 questions,
// the student missed 25 of them, and the minimum passing
// score is 70.
PassFailExam test2(100, 25, 70.0);

// Display the grade data for both objects.
cout << "Test 1:\n";
displayGrade(test1);    // Pass the GradedActivity object
cout << "\nTest 2:\n";
displayGrade(&test2);   // Pass the PassFailExam object
```

This code will produce the following output:

```
Test 1:
The activity's numeric score is 88.0
The activity's letter grade is B

Test 2:
The activity's numeric score is 75.0
The activity's letter grade is C
```

Even though the `getLetterGrade` function is declared `virtual`, static binding still takes place because `activity` is not a reference variable or a pointer.

Alternatively we could have used a `GradedActivity` pointer in the `displayGrade` function, as shown in Program 15-12. This file is also stored in the Student Source Code Folder `Chapter 15\GradedActivity Version 3`.

Program 15-12

```
 1  #include <iostream>
 2  #include <iomanip>
 3  #include "PassFailExam.h"
 4  using namespace std;
 5
 6  // Function prototype
 7  void displayGrade(const GradedActivity *);
 8
 9  int main()
10  {
11     // Create a GradedActivity object. The score is 88.
12     GradedActivity test1(88.0);
13
14     // Create a PassFailExam object. There are 100 questions,
15     // the student missed 25 of them, and the minimum passing
16     // score is 70.
17     PassFailExam test2(100, 25, 70.0);
18
```

```
19        // Display the grade data for both objects.
20        cout << "Test 1:\n";
21        displayGrade(&test1);   // Address of the GradedActivity object
22        cout << "\nTest 2:\n";
23        displayGrade(&test2);   // Address of the PassFailExam object
24        return 0;
25    }
26
27    //***************************************************************
28    // The displayGrade function displays a GradedActivity object's *
29    // numeric score and letter grade. This version of the function *
30    // uses a GradedActivity pointer as its parameter.              *
31    //***************************************************************
32
33    void displayGrade(const GradedActivity *activity)
34    {
35        cout << setprecision(1) << fixed;
36        cout << "The activity's numeric score is "
37             << activity->getScore() << endl;
38        cout << "The activity's letter grade is "
39             << activity->getLetterGrade() << endl;
40    }
```

Program Output
```
Test 1:
The activity's numeric score is 88.0
The activity's letter grade is B

Test 2:
The activity's numeric score is 75.0
The activity's letter grade is P
```

Base Class Pointers

Pointers to a base class may be assigned the address of a derived class object. For example, look at the following code:

```
GradedActivity *exam = new PassFailExam(100, 25, 70.0);
```

This statement dynamically allocates a PassFailExam object and assigns its address to exam, which is a GradedActivity pointer. We can then use the exam pointer to call member functions, as shown here:

```
cout << exam->getScore() << endl;
cout << exam->getLetterGrade() << endl;
```

Program 15-13 is an example that uses base class pointers to reference derived class objects. This file is also stored in the Student Source Code Folder Chapter 15\ GradedActivity Version 3.

Program 15-13

```cpp
 1   #include <iostream>
 2   #include <iomanip>
 3   #include "PassFailExam.h"
 4   using namespace std;
 5
 6   // Function prototype
 7   void displayGrade(const GradedActivity *);
 8
 9   int main()
10   {
11      // Constant for the size of an array.
12      const int NUM_TESTS = 4;
13
14      // tests is an array of GradedActivity pointers.
15      // Each element of tests is initialized with the
16      // address of a dynamically allocated object.
17      GradedActivity *tests[NUM_TESTS] =
18         { new GradedActivity(88.0),
19           new PassFailExam(100, 25, 70.0),
20           new GradedActivity(67.0),
21           new PassFailExam(50, 12, 60.0)
22         };
23
24      // Display the grade data for each element in the array.
25      for (int count = 0; count < NUM_TESTS; count++)
26      {
27         cout << "Test #" << (count + 1) << ":\n";
28         displayGrade(tests[count]);
29         cout << endl;
30      }
31      return 0;
32   }
33
34   //**************************************************************
35   // The displayGrade function displays a GradedActivity object's *
36   // numeric score and letter grade. This version of the function *
37   // uses a GradedActivity pointer as its parameter.             *
38   //**************************************************************
39
40   void displayGrade(const GradedActivity *activity)
41   {
42      cout << setprecision(1) << fixed;
43      cout << "The activity's numeric score is "
44           << activity->getScore() << endl;
45      cout << "The activity's letter grade is "
46           << activity->getLetterGrade() << endl;
47   }
```

Program Output
```
Test #1:
The activity's numeric score is 88.0
The activity's letter grade is B

Test #2:
The activity's numeric score is 75.0
The activity's letter grade is P

Test #3:
The activity's numeric score is 67.0
The activity's letter grade is D

Test #4:
The activity's numeric score is 76.0
The activity's letter grade is P
```

Let's take a closer look at this program. An array named tests is defined in lines 17 through 22. This is an array of GradedActivity pointers. The array elements are initialized with the addresses of dynamically allocated objects. The tests[0] element is initialized with the address of the GradedActivity object returned from this expression:

```
new GradedActivity(88.0)
```

The tests[1] element is initialized with the address of the GradedActivity object returned from this expression:

```
new PassFailExam(100, 25, 70.0)
```

The tests[2] element is initialized with the address of the GradedActivity object returned from this expression:

```
new GradedActivity(67.0)
```

Finally, the tests[3] element is initialized with the address of the GradedActivity object returned from this expression:

```
new PassFailExam(50, 12, 60.0)
```

Although each element in the array is a GradedActivity pointer, some of the elements point to GradedActivity objects and some point to PassFailExam objects. The loop in lines 25 through 30 steps through the array, passing each pointer element to the displayGrade function.

Base Class Pointers and References Know Only About Base Class Members

Although a base class pointer can reference objects of any class that derives from the base class, there are limits to what the pointer can do with those objects. Recall that the GradedActivity class has, other than its constructors, only three member functions: setScore, getScore, and getLetterGrade. So, a GradedActivity pointer can be used to call only those functions, regardless of the type of object it points to. For example, look at the following code.

```
GradedActivity *exam = new PassFailExam(100, 25, 70.0);
cout << exam->getScore() << endl;        // This works.
cout << exam->getLetterGrade() << endl;  // This works.
cout << exam->getPointsEach() << endl;   // ERROR! Won't work!
```

In this code, exam is a GradedActivity pointer, and is assigned the address of a PassFailExam object. The GradedActivity class has only the setScore, getScore, and getLetterGrade member functions, so those are the only member functions that the exam variable knows how to execute. The last statement in this code is a call to the getPointsEach member function, which is defined in the PassFailExam class. Because the exam variable only knows about member functions in the GradedActivity class, it cannot execute this function.

The "Is-a" Relationship Does Not Work in Reverse

It is important to note that the "is-a" relationship does not work in reverse. Although the statement "a final exam is a graded activity" is true, the statement "a graded activity is a final exam" is not true. This is because not all graded activities are final exams. Likewise, not all GradedActivity objects are FinalExam objects. So, the following code will not work.

```
// Create a GradedActivity object.
GradedActivity *gaPointer = new GradedActivity(88.0);

// Error! This will not work.
FinalExam *fePointer = gaPointer;
```

You cannot assign the address of a GradedActivity object to a FinalExam pointer. This makes sense because FinalExam objects have capabilities that go beyond those of a GradedActivity object. Interestingly, the C++ compiler will let you make such an assignment if you use a type cast, as shown here:

```
// Create a GradedActivity object.
GradedActivity *gaPointer = new GradedActivity(88.0);

// This will work, but with limitations.
FinalExam *fePointer = static_cast<FinalExam *>(gaPointer);
```

After this code executes, the derived class pointer fePointer will be pointing to a base class object. We can use the pointer to access members of the object, but only the members that exist. The following code demonstrates:

```
// This will work. The object has a getScore function.
cout << fePointer->getScore() << endl;

// This will work. The object has a getLetterGrade function.
cout << fePointer->getLetterGrade() << endl;

// This will compile, but an error will occur at runtime.
// The object does not have a getPointsEach function.
cout << fePointer->getPointsEach() << endl;
```

In this code `fePointer` is a `FinalExam` pointer, and it points to a `GradedActivity` object. The first two `cout` statements work because the `GradedActivity` object has `getScore` and a `getLetterGrade` member functions. The last `cout` statement will cause an error, however, because it calls the `getPointsEach` member function. The `GradedActivity` object does not have a `getPointsEach` member function.

Redefining vs. Overriding

Earlier in this chapter you learned how a derived class can redefine a base class member function. When a class redefines a virtual function, it is said that the class *overrides* the function. In C++, the difference between overriding and redefining base class functions is that overridden functions are dynamically bound, and redefined functions are statically bound. Only virtual functions can be overridden.

Virtual Destructors

When you write a class with a destructor, and that class could potentially become a base class, you should always declare the destructor `virtual`. This is because the compiler will perform static binding on the destructor if it is not declared `virtual`. This can lead to problems when a base class pointer or reference variable references a derived class object. If the derived class has its own destructor, it will not execute when the object is destroyed or goes out of scope. Only the base class destructor will execute. Program 15-14 demonstrates.

Program 15-14

```
 1   #include <iostream>
 2   using namespace std;
 3
 4   // Animal is a base class.
 5   class Animal
 6   {
 7   public:
 8      // Constructor
 9      Animal()
10         { cout << "Animal constructor executing.\n"; }
11
12      // Destructor
13      ~Animal()
14         { cout << "Animal destructor executing.\n"; }
15   };
16
17   // The Dog class is derived from Animal
18   class Dog : public Animal
19   {
20   public:
21      // Constructor
22      Dog() : Animal()
23         { cout << "Dog constructor executing.\n"; }
24
```

(program continues)

Program 15-14   *(continued)*

```
25      // Destructor
26      ~Dog()
27         { cout << "Dog destructor executing.\n"; }
28   };
29
30   //*************************************************
31   // main function                                  *
32   //*************************************************
33
34   int main()
35   {
36      // Create a Dog object, referenced by an
37      // Animal pointer.
38      Animal *myAnimal = new Dog;
39
40      // Delete the dog object.
41      delete myAnimal;
42      return 0;
43   }
```

Program Output

```
Animal constructor executing.
Dog constructor executing.
Animal destructor executing.
```

This program declares two classes: Animal and Dog. Animal is the base class and Dog is the derived class. Each class has its own constructor and destructor. In line 38, a Dog object is created and its address is stored in an Animal pointer. Both the Animal and the Dog constructors execute. In line 41 the object is deleted. When this statement executes, however, only the Animal destructor executes. The Dog destructor does not execute because the object is referenced by an Animal pointer. We can fix this problem by declaring the Animal class destructor virtual, as shown in Program 15-15.

Program 15-15

```
1    #include <iostream>
2    using namespace std;
3
4    // Animal is a base class.
5    class Animal
6    {
7    public:
8       // Constructor
9       Animal()
10          { cout << "Animal constructor executing.\n"; }
11
```

```
12       // Destructor
13       virtual ~Animal()
14          { cout << "Animal destructor executing.\n"; }
15    };
16
17    // The Dog class is derived from Animal
18    class Dog : public Animal
19    {
20    public:
21       // Constructor
22       Dog() : Animal()
23          { cout << "Dog constructor executing.\n"; }
24
25       // Destructor
26       ~Dog()
27          { cout << "Dog destructor executing.\n"; }
28    };
29
30    //*********************************************
31    // main function                             *
32    //*********************************************
33
34    int main()
35    {
36       // Create a Dog object, referenced by an
37       // Animal pointer.
38       Animal *myAnimal = new Dog;
39
40       // Delete the dog object.
41       delete myAnimal;
42       return 0;
43    }
```

Program Output
```
Animal constructor executing.
Dog constructor executing.
Dog destructor executing.
Animal destructor executing.
```

The only thing that has changed in this program is that the Animal class destructor is declared virtual in line 13. As a result, the destructor is dynamically bound at runtime. When the Dog object is destroyed, both the Animal and Dog destructors execute.

A good programming practice to follow is that any class that has a virtual member function should also have a virtual destructor. If the class doesn't require a destructor, it should have a virtual destructor that performs no statements. Remember, when a base class function is declared virtual, all overridden versions of the function in derived classes automatically become virtual. Including a virtual destructor in a base class, even one that does nothing, will ensure that any derived class destructors will also be virtual.

15.7 Abstract Base Classes and Pure Virtual Functions

CONCEPT: An abstract base class cannot be instantiated, but other classes are derived from it. A pure virtual function is a virtual member function of a base class that must be overridden. When a class contains a pure virtual function as a member, that class becomes an abstract base class.

Sometimes it is helpful to begin a class hierarchy with an *abstract base class*. An abstract base class is not instantiated itself, but serves as a base class for other classes. The abstract base class represents the generic, or abstract, form of all the classes that are derived from it.

For example, consider a factory that manufactures airplanes. The factory does not make a generic airplane, but makes three specific types of planes: two different models of prop-driven planes, and one commuter jet model. The computer software that catalogs the planes might use an abstract base class called `Airplane`. That class has members representing the common characteristics of all airplanes. In addition, it has classes for each of the three specific airplane models the factory manufactures. These classes have members representing the unique characteristics of each type of plane. The base class, `Airplane`, is never instantiated, but is used to derive the other classes.

A class becomes an abstract base class when one or more of its member functions is a *pure virtual function*. A pure virtual function is a virtual member function declared in a manner similar to the following:

```
virtual void showInfo() = 0;
```

The = 0 notation indicates that `showInfo` is a pure virtual function. Pure virtual functions have no body, or definition, in the base class. They must be overridden in derived classes. Additionally, the presence of a pure virtual function in a class prevents a program from instantiating the class. The compiler will generate an error if you attempt to define an object of an abstract base class.

For example, look at the following abstract base class `Student`. It holds data common to all students, but does not hold all the data needed for students of specific majors.

Contents of `Student.h`

```
 1   // Specification file for the Student class
 2   #ifndef STUDENT_H
 3   #define STUDENT_H
 4   #include <cstring>    // For strcpy
 5
 6   // Constants for array sizes
 7   const int NAME_SIZE = 51;
 8   const int ID_SIZE = 21;
 9
10   class Student
11   {
```

```
12  protected:
13      char name[NAME_SIZE];    // Student name
14      char idNumber[ID_SIZE];  // Student ID
15      int yearAdmitted;        // Year student was admitted
16  public:
17      // Default constructor
18      Student()
19         { name[0] = '\0';
20           idNumber[0] = '\0';
21           yearAdmitted = 0; }
22
23      // Constructor
24      Student(const char *n, const char *id, int year)
25         { set(n, id, year); }
26
27      // The set function sets the attribute data.
28      void set(const char *n, const char *id, int year)
29         { strncpy(name, n, NAME_SIZE);    // Copy the name
30           name[NAME_SIZE - 1] = '\0';     // Place a null character
31           strncpy(idNumber, n, ID_SIZE);  // Copy the ID number
32           idNumber[ID_SIZE - 1] = '\0';   // Place a null character
33           yearAdmitted = year; }          // Assign year admitted
34
35      // Accessor functions
36      const char *getName() const
37         { return name; }
38
39      const char *getIdNum() const
40         { return idNumber; }
41
42      int getYearAdmitted() const
43         { return yearAdmitted; }
44
45      // Pure virtual function
46      virtual int getRemainingHours() const = 0;
47  };
48  #endif
```

The `Student` class contains members for storing a student's name, ID number, and year admitted. It also has constructors and a mutator function for setting values in the `name`, `idNumber`, and `yearAdmitted` members. Accessor functions are provided that return the values in the `name`, `idNumber`, and `yearAdmitted` members. A pure virtual function named `getRemainingHours` is also declared.

The pure virtual function must be overridden in classes derived from the `Student` class. It was made a pure virtual function because this class is intended to be the base for classes that represent students of specific majors. For example, a `CsStudent` class might hold the data for a computer science student, and a `BiologyStudent` class might hold the data for a biology student. Computer science students must take courses in different disciplines than those taken by biology students. It stands to reason that the `CsStudent` class will calculate the number of hours taken in a different manner than the `BiologyStudent` class.

Let's look at an example of the `CsStudent` class.

Contents of `CsStudent.h`

```
1   // Specification file for the CsStudent class
2   #ifndef CSSTUDENT_H
3   #define CSSTUDENT_H
4   #include "Student.h"
5
6   // Constants for required hours
7   const int MATH_HOURS = 20;    // Math hours
8   const int CS_HOURS = 40;      // Computer science hours
9   const int GEN_ED_HOURS = 60;  // General Ed hours
10
11  class CsStudent : public Student
12  {
13  private:
14     int mathHours;    // Hours of math taken
15     int csHours;      // Hours of Computer Science taken
16     int genEdHours;   // Hours of general education taken
17
18  public:
19     // Default Constructor
20     CsStudent() : Student()
21        { mathHours = 0;
22          csHours = 0;
23          genEdHours = 0; }
24
25     // Constructor
26     CsStudent(const char *n, const char *id, int year) :
27        Student(n, id, year)
28        { mathHours = 0;
29          csHours = 0;
30          genEdHours = 0; }
31
32     // Mutator functions
33     void setMathHours(int mh)
34        { mathHours = mh; }
35
36     void setCsHours(int csh)
37        { csHours = csh; }
38
39     void setGenEdHours(int geh)
40        { genEdHours = geh; }
41
42     // Overridden getRemainingHours function,
43     // defined in CsStudent.cpp
44     virtual int getRemainingHours() const;
45  };
46  #endif
```

This file declares the following `const int` member variables in lines 7 through 9:
`MATH_HOURS`, `CS_HOURS`, and `GEN_ED_HOURS`. These variables hold the required number of
math, computer science, and general education hours for a computer science student. The
`CsStudent` class, which derives from the `Student` class, declares the following member
variables in lines 14 through 16: `mathHours`, `csHours`, and `genEdHours`. These variables

hold the number of math, computer science, and general education hours taken by the student. Mutator functions are provided to store values in these variables. In addition, the class overrides the pure virtual getRemainingHours function in the CsStudent.cpp file.

Contents of CsStudent.cpp

```
 1   #include <iostream>
 2   #include "CsStudent.h"
 3   using namespace std;
 4
 5   //********************************************************
 6   // The CsStudent::getRemainingHours function returns *
 7   // the number of hours remaining to be taken.         *
 8   //********************************************************
 9
10   int CsStudent::getRemainingHours() const
11   {
12      int reqHours,      // Total required hours
13      remainingHours;    // Remaining hours
14
15      // Calculate the required hours.
16      reqHours = MATH_HOURS + CS_HOURS + GEN_ED_HOURS;
17
18      // Calculate the remaining hours.
19      remainingHours = reqHours - (mathHours + csHours +
20                       genEdHours);
21
22      // Return the remaining hours.
23      return remainingHours;
24   }
```

Program 15-16 provides a simple demonstration of the class.

Program 15-16

```
 1   // This program demonstrates the CsStudent class, which is
 2   // derived from the abstract base class, Student.
 3   #include <iostream>
 4   #include "CsStudent.h"
 5   using namespace std;
 6
 7   int main()
 8   {
 9      // Create a CsStudent object for a student.
10      CsStudent student("Jennifer Haynes", "167W98337", 2010);
11
12      // Store values for Math, Computer Science, and General
13      // Ed hours.
14      student.setMathHours(12);  // Student has taken 12 Math hours
15      student.setCsHours(20);    // Student has taken 20 CS hours
16      student.setGenEdHours(40); // Student has taken 40 Gen Ed hours
17
```

(program continues)

Program 15-16   *(continued)*

```
18      // Display the number of remaining hours.
19      cout << "The student " << student.getName()
20          << " needs to take " << student.getRemainingHours()
21          << " more hours to graduate.\n";
22
23      return 0;
24  }
```

Program Output

The student Jennifer Haynes needs to take 48 more hours to graduate.

Remember the following points about abstract base classes and pure virtual functions:

- When a class contains a pure virtual function, it is an abstract base class.
- Pure virtual functions are declared with the = 0 notation.
- Abstract base classes cannot be instantiated.
- Pure virtual functions have no body, or definition, in the base class.
- A pure virtual function *must* be overridden at some point in a derived class in order for it to become nonabstract.

 Checkpoint

15.9   Explain the difference between overloading a function and redefining a function.

15.10   Explain the difference between static binding and dynamic binding.

15.11   Are virtual functions statically bound or dynamically bound?

15.12   What will the following program display?

```
#include <iostream.>
using namespace std;

class First
{
protected:
    int a;
public:
    First(int x = 1)
        { a = x; }

    int getVal()
        { return a; }
};

class Second : public First
{
private:
    int b;
public:
    Second(int y = 5)
        { b = y; }
    int getVal()
        { return b; }
};
```

```cpp
int main()
{
   First object1;
   Second object2;

   cout << object1.getVal() << endl;
   cout << object2.getVal() << endl;
   return 0;
}
```

15.13   What will the following program display?

```cpp
#include <iostream>
using namespace std;

class First
{
protected:
   int a;
public:
   First(int x = 1)
      { a = x; }

   void twist()
      { a *= 2; }
   int getVal()
      { twist(); return a; }
};

class Second : public First
{
private:
   int b;
public:
   Second(int y = 5)
      { b = y; }

   void twist()
      { b *= 10; }
};

int main()
{
   First object1;
   Second object2;

   cout << object1.getVal() << endl;
   cout << object2.getVal() << endl;
   return 0;
}
```

15.14   What will the following program display?

```cpp
#include <iostream>
using namespace std;

class First
{
protected:
   int a;
```

```cpp
public:
   First(int x = 1)
      { a = x; }

   virtual void twist()
      { a *= 2; }

   int getVal()
      { twist(); return a; }
};

class Second : public First
{
private:
   int b;
public:
   Second(int y = 5)
      { b = y; }
   virtual void twist()
      { b *= 10; }
};

int main()
{
   First object1;
   Second object2;

   cout << object1.getVal() << endl;
   cout << object2.getVal() << endl;
   return 0;
}
```

15.15 What will the following program display?

```cpp
#include <iostream>
using namespace std;

class Base
{
protected:
   int baseVar;
public:
   Base(int val = 2)
      { baseVar = val; }

   int getVar()
      { return baseVar; }
};

class Derived : public Base
{
private:
   int derivedVar;
public:
   Derived(int val = 100)
      { derivedVar = val; }
   int getVar()
      { return derivedVar; }
};
```

```
int main()
{
    Base *optr;
    Derived object;

    optr = &object;
    cout << optr->getVar() << endl;
    return 0;
}
```

15.8 Multiple Inheritance

CONCEPT: Multiple inheritance is when a derived class has two or more base classes.

Previously we discussed how a class may be derived from a second class that is itself derived from a third class. The series of classes establishes a chain of inheritance. In such a scheme, you might be tempted to think of the lowest class in the chain as having multiple base classes. A base class, however, should be thought of as the class that another class is directly derived from. Even though there may be several classes in a chain, each class (below the topmost class) only has one base class.

Another way of combining classes is through multiple inheritance. *Multiple inheritance* is when a class has two or more base classes. This is illustrated in Figure 15-6.

Figure 15-6

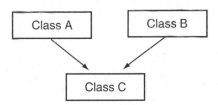

In Figure 15-6, class C is directly derived from classes A and B, and inherits the members of both. Neither class A nor B, however, inherits members from the other. Their members are only passed down to class C. Let's look at an example of multiple inheritance. Consider the two classes declared here:

Contents of `Date.h`

```
1   // Specification file for the Date class
2   #ifndef DATE_H
3   #define DATE_H
4
5   class Date
6   {
```

```
 7  protected:
 8     int day;
 9     int month;
10     int year;
11  public:
12     // Default constructor
13     Date(int d, int m, int y)
14        { day = 1; month = 1; year = 1900; }
15
16     // Constructor
17     Date(int d, int m, int y)
18        { day = d; month = m; year = y; }
19
20     // Accessors
21     int getDay() const
22        { return day; }
23
24     int getMonth() const
25        { return month; }
26
27     int getYear() const
28        { return year; }
29  };
30  #endif
```

Contents of `Time.h`

```
 1  // Specification file for the Time class
 2  #ifndef TIME_H
 3  #define TIME_H
 4
 5  class Time
 6  {
 7  protected:
 8     int hour;
 9     int min;
10     int sec;
11  public:
12     // Default constructor
13     Time()
14        { hour = 0; min = 0; sec = 0; }
15
16     // Constructor
17     Time(int h, int m, int s)
18        { hour = h; min = m; sec = s; }
19
20     // Accessor functions
21     int getHour() const
22        { return hour; }
23
```

```
24       int getMin() const
25          { return min; }
26
27       int getSec() const
28          { return sec; }
29    };
30    #endif
```

These classes are designed to hold integers that represent the date and time. They both can be used as base classes for a third class we will call `DateTime`:

Contents of `DateTime.h`

```
1    // Specification file for the DateTime class
2    #ifndef DATETIME_H
3    #define DATETIME_H
4    #include "Date.h"
5    #include "Time.h"
6
7    // Constant for string size
8    const int DT_SIZE = 20;
9
10   class DateTime : public Date, public Time
11   {
12   protected:
13      char dateTimeString[DT_SIZE];
14   public:
15      // Default constructor
16      DateTime();
17
18      // Constructor
19      DateTime(int, int, int, int, int, int);
20
21      // Accessor function
22      const char *getDateTime() const
23         { return dateTimeString; }
24   };
25   #endif
```

In line 10, the first line in the `DateTime` declaration reads

```
class DateTime : public Date, public Time
```

Notice there are two base classes listed, separated by a *comma*. Each base class has its own access specification. The general format of the first line of a class declaration with multiple base classes is

```
class DerivedClassName : AccessSpecification BaseClassName,
                         AccessSpecification BaseClassName [, ...]
```

The notation in the square brackets indicates that the list of base classes with their access specifications may be repeated. (It is possible to have several base classes.)

Contents of `DateTime.cpp`

```
 1   // Implementation file for the DateTime class
 2   #include <cstring>        // For strcpy and strcat
 3   #include <cstdlib>        // For itoa
 4   #include "DateTime.h"
 5
 6   // Constant for temp array size
 7   const int TEMP_SIZE = 10;
 8
 9   //*************************************************
10   // Default constructor                           *
11   //*************************************************
12
13   DateTime::DateTime() : Date(), Time()
14   {
15      strcpy(dateTimeString, "1/1/1900 0:0:0");
16   }
17
18   //*************************************************
19   // Constructor                                   *
20   //*************************************************
21
22   DateTime::DateTime(int dy, int mon, int yr, int hr, int mt, int sc) :
23       Date(dy, mon, yr), Time(hr, mt, sc)
24   {
25      char temp[TEMP_SIZE]; // Temporary work area for itoa()
26
27      // Store the date in dateTimeString, in the form MM/DD/YY
28      strcpy(dateTimeString, itoa(getMonth(), temp, TEMP_SIZE));
29      strcat(dateTimeString, "/");
30      strcat(dateTimeString, itoa(getDay(), temp, TEMP_SIZE));
31      strcat(dateTimeString, "/");
32      strcat(dateTimeString, itoa(getYear(), temp, TEMP_SIZE));
33      strcat(dateTimeString, " ");
34
35      // Store the time in dateTimeString, in the form HH:MM:SS
36      strcat(dateTimeString, itoa(getHour(), temp, TEMP_SIZE));
37      strcat(dateTimeString, ":");
38      strcat(dateTimeString, itoa(getMin(), temp, TEMP_SIZE));
39      strcat(dateTimeString, ":");
40      strcat(dateTimeString, itoa(getSec(), temp, TEMP_SIZE));
41   }
```

The class has two constructors: a default constructor and a constructor that accepts arguments for each component of a date and time. Let's look at the function header for the default constructor, in line 13:

```
DateTime::DateTime() : Date(), Time()
```

After the `DateTime` constructor's parentheses is a colon, followed by calls to the `Date` constructor and the `Time` constructor. The calls are separated by a comma. When using multiple inheritance, the general format of a derived class's constructor header is

```
DerivedClassName(ParameterList) : BaseClassName(ArgumentList),
                                  BaseClassName( ArgumentList)[, ...]
```

Look at the function header for the second constructor, which appears in lines 22 and 23:

```
DateTime::DateTime(int dy, int mon, int yr, int hr, int mt, int sc) :
    Date(dy, mon, yr), Time(hr, mt, sc)
```

This `DateTime` constructor accepts arguments for the day (`dy`), month (`mon`), year (`yr`), hour (`hr`), minute (`mt`), and second (`sc`). The `dy`, `mon`, and `yr` parameters are passed as arguments to the `Date` constructor. The `hr`, `mt`, and `sc` parameters are passed as arguments to the `Time` constructor.

The order that the base class constructor calls appear in the list does not matter. They are always called in the order of inheritance. That is, they are always called in the order they are listed in the first line of the class declaration. Here is line 10 from the `DateTime.h` file:

```
class DateTime : public Date, public Time
```

Because `Date` is listed before `Time` in the `DateTime` class declaration, the `Date` constructor will always be called first. If the classes use destructors, they are always called in reverse order of inheritance. Program 15-17 shows these classes in use.

Program 15-17

```
 1   // This program demonstrates a class with multiple inheritance.
 2   #include <iostream>
 3   #include "DateTime.h"
 4   using namespace std;
 5
 6   int main()
 7   {
 8      // Define a DateTime object and use the default
 9      // constructor to initialize it.
10      DateTime emptyDay;
11
12      // Display the object's date and time.
13      cout << emptyDay.getDateTime() << endl;
14
15      // Define a DateTime object and initialize it
16      // with the date 2/4/60 and the time 5:32:27.
17      DateTime pastDay(2, 4, 60, 5, 32, 27);
18
19      // Display the object's date and time.
20      cout << pastDay.getDateTime() << endl;
21      return 0;
22   }
```

(program output continues)

Program 15-17   *(continued)*

Program Output
```
1/1/1900 0:0:0
4/2/60 5:32:27
```

> **NOTE:** It should be noted that multiple inheritance opens the opportunity for a derived class to have ambiguous members. That is, two base classes may have member variables or functions of the same name. In situations like these, the derived class should always redefine or override the member functions. Calls to the member functions of the appropriate base class can be performed within the derived class using the scope resolution operator(::). The derived class can also access the ambiguously named member variables of the correct base class using the scope resolution operator. If these steps aren't taken, the compiler will generate an error when it can't tell which member is being accessed.

 Checkpoint

15.16   Does the following diagram depict multiple inheritance or a chain of inheritance?

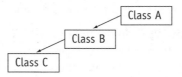

15.17   Does the following diagram depict multiple inheritance or a chain of inheritance?

15.18   Examine the following classes. The table lists the variables that are members of the `Third` class (some are inherited). Complete the table by filling in the access specification each member will have in the `Third` class. Write "inaccessible" if a member is inaccessible to the `Third` class.

```
class First
{
   private:
      int a;
   protected:
      double b;
   public:
      long c;
};

class Second : protected First
{
   private:
      int d;
   protected:
      double e;
   public:
      long f;
};
```

```
class Third : public Second
{
    private:
        int g;
    protected:
        double h;
    public:
        long i;
};
```

Member Variable	Access Specification in Third Class
a	
b	
c	
d	
e	
f	
g	
h	
i	

15.19 Examine the following class declarations:

```
class Van
{
protected:
    int passengers;
public:
    Van(int p)
    { passengers = p; }
};

class FourByFour
{
protected:
    double cargoWeight;
public:
    FourByFour(float w)
        { cargoWeight = w; }
};
```

Write the declaration of a class named SportUtility. The class should be derived from both the Van and FourByFour classes above. (This should be a case of multiple inheritance, where both Van and FourByFour are base classes.)

Review Questions and Exercises

Short Answer

1. What is an "is a" relationship?

2. A program uses two classes: `Dog` and `Poodle`. Which class is the base class and which is the derived class?

3. How does base class access specification differ from class member access specification?

4. What is the difference between a protected class member and a private class member?

5. Can a derived class ever directly access the private members of its base class?

6. Which constructor is called first, that of the derived class or the base class?

7. What is the difference between redefining a base class function and overriding a base class function?

8. When does static binding take place? When does dynamic binding take place?

9. What is an abstract base class?

10. A program has a class `Potato`, which is derived from the class `Vegetable`, which is derived from the class `Food`. Is this an example of multiple inheritance? Why or why not?

11. What base class is named in the line below?

    ```
    class Pet : public Dog
    ```

12. What derived class is named in the line below?

    ```
    class Pet : public Dog
    ```

13. What is the class access specification of the base class named below?

    ```
    class Pet : public Dog
    ```

14. What is the class access specification of the base class named below?

    ```
    class Pet : Fish
    ```

15. Protected members of a base class are like _____ members, except they may be accessed by derived classes.

16. Complete the table below by filling in private, protected, public, or inaccessible in the right-hand column:

In a private base class, this base class MEMBER access specification...	...becomes this access specification in the derived class.
private	
protected	
public	

17. Complete the table below by filling in private, protected, public, or inaccessible in the right-hand column:

In a protected base class, this base class MEMBER access specification...	...becomes this access specification in the derived class.
`private`	
`protected`	
`public`	

18. Complete the table below by filling in private, protected, public, or inaccessible in the right-hand column:

In a public base class, this base class MEMBER access specification...	...becomes this access specification in the derived class.
`private`	
`protected`	
`public`	

Fill-in-the-Blank

19. A derived class inherits the _____ of its base class.

20. When both a base class and a derived class have constructors, the base class's constructor is called _____ (first/last).

21. When both a base class and a derived class have destructors, the base class's constructor is called _____ (first/last).

22. An overridden base class function may be called by a function in a derived class by using the _____ operator.

23. When a derived class redefines a function in a base class, which version of the function do objects that are defined of the base class call? _____

24. A(n) _____ member function in a base class expects to be overridden in a derived class.

25. _____ binding is when the compiler binds member function calls at compile time.

26. _____ binding is when a function call is bound at runtime.

27. _____ is when member functions in a class hierarchy behave differently, depending upon which object performs the call.

28. When a pointer to a base class is made to point to a derived class, the pointer ignores any _____ the derived class performs, unless the function is _____.

29. A(n) _____ class cannot be instantiated.

30. A(n) _____ function has no body, or definition, in the class in which it is declared.

31. A(n) _____ of inheritance is where one class is derived from a second class, which in turn is derived from a third class.

32. _____ is where a derived class has two or more base classes.

33. In multiple inheritance, the derived class should always _____ a function that has the same name in more than one base class.

Algorithm Workbench

34. Write the first line of the declaration for a `Poodle` class. The class should be derived from the `Dog` class with public base class access.

35. Write the first line of the declaration for a `SoundSystem` class. Use multiple inheritance to base the class on the `CDplayer` class, the `Tuner` class, and the `CassettePlayer` class. Use public base class access in all cases.

36. Suppose a class named `Tiger` is derived from both the `Felis` class and the `Carnivore` class. Here is the first line of the `Tiger` class declaration:

    ```
    class Tiger : public Felis, public Carnivore
    ```

    Here is the function header for the Tiger constructor:

    ```
    Tiger(int x, int y) : Carnivore(x), Felis(y)
    ```

    Which base class constructor is called first, `Carnivore` or `Felis`?

37. Write the declaration for class `B`. The class's members should be

    - m, an integer. This variable should not be accessible to code outside the class or to member functions in any class derived from class `B`.
    - n, an integer. This variable should not be accessible to code outside the class, but should be accessible to member functions in any class derived from class `B`.
    - setM, getM, setN, and getN. These are the set and get functions for the member variables m and n. These functions should be accessible to code outside the class.
    - calc, a public virtual member function that returns the value of m times n.

    Next write the declaration for class `D`, which is derived from class `B`. The class's members should be
    - q, a `float`. This variable should not be accessible to code outside the class but should be accessible to member functions in any class derived from class `D`.
    - r, a `float`. This variable should not be accessible to code outside the class, but should be accessible to member functions in any class derived from class `D`.
    - setQ, getQ, setR, and getR. These are the set and get functions for the member variables q and r. These functions should be accessible to code outside the class.
    - calc, a public member function that overrides the base class `calc` function. This function should return the value of q times r.

True or False

38. T F The base class's access specification affects the way base class member functions may access base class member variables.

39. T F The base class's access specification affects the way the derived class inherits members of the base class.

40. T F Private members of a private base class become inaccessible to the derived class.

41. T F Public members of a private base class become private members of the derived class.

42. T F Protected members of a private base class become public members of the derived class.

43. T F Public members of a protected base class become private members of the derived class.

44. T   F   Private members of a protected base class become inaccessible to the derived class.

45. T   F   Protected members of a public base class become public members of the derived class.

46. T   F   The base class constructor is called after the derived class constructor.

47. T   F   The base class destructor is called after the derived class destructor.

48. T   F   It isn't possible for a base class to have more than one constructor.

49. T   F   Arguments are passed to the base class constructor by the derived class constructor.

50. T   F   A member function of a derived class may not have the same name as a member function of the base class.

51. T   F   Pointers to a base class may be assigned the address of a derived class object.

52. T   F   A base class may not be derived from another class.

Find the Errors

Each of the class declarations and/or member function definitions below has errors. Find as many as you can.

```
53. class Car, public Vehicle
    {
        public:
          Car();
          ~Car();
        protected:
          int passengers;
    }
```

```
54. class Truck, public : Vehicle, protected
    {
        private:
          double cargoWeight;
        public:
          Truck();
          ~Truck();
    };
```

```
55. class SnowMobile : Vehicle
    {
        protected:
          int horsePower;
          double weight;
        public:
          SnowMobile(int h, double w), Vehicle(h)
            { horsePower = h; }
          ~SnowMobile();
    };
```

```
56. class Table : public Furniture
    {
        protected:
          int numSeats;
```

```
    public:
        Table(int n) : Furniture(numSeats)
            { numSeats = n; }
        ~Table();
};
```

57. ```
class Tank : public Cylinder
{
    private:
        int fuelType;
        double gallons;
    public:
        Tank();
        ~Tank();
        void setContents(double);
        void setContents(double);
};
```

58. ```
class Three : public Two : public One
{
    protected:
        int x;
    public:
        Three(int a, int b, int c), Two(b), Three(c)
            { x = a; }
        ~Three();
};
```

Programming Challenges

VideoNote

Solving the
Employee and
**Production-
Worker** Classes
Problem

1. Employee and ProductionWorker Classes

Design a class named Employee. The class should keep the following information in member variables:

- Employee name
- Employee number
- Hire date

Write one or more constructors and the appropriate accessor and mutator functions for the class.

Next, write a class named ProductionWorker that is derived from the Employee class. The ProductionWorker class should have member variables to hold the following information:

- Shift (an integer)
- Hourly pay rate (a double)

The workday is divided into two shifts: day and night. The shift variable will hold an integer value representing the shift that the employee works. The day shift is shift 1 and the night shift is shift 2. Write one or more constructors and the appropriate accessor and mutator functions for the class. Demonstrate the classes by writing a program that uses a ProductionWorker object.

2. **ShiftSupervisor** Class

In a particular factory a shift supervisor is a salaried employee who supervises a shift. In addition to a salary, the shift supervisor earns a yearly bonus when his or her shift meets production goals. Design a ShiftSupervisor class that is derived from the Employee class you created in Programming Challenge 1. The ShiftSupervisor class should have a member variable that holds the annual salary and a member variable that holds the annual production bonus that a shift supervisor has earned. Write one or more constructors and the appropriate accessor and mutator functions for the class. Demonstrate the class by writing a program that uses a ShiftSupervisor object.

3. **TeamLeader** Class

In a particular factory, a team leader is an hourly paid production worker who leads a small team. In addition to hourly pay, team leaders earn a fixed monthly bonus. Team leaders are required to attend a minimum number of hours of training per year. Design a TeamLeader class that extends the ProductionWorker class you designed in Programming Challenge 1. The TeamLeader class should have member variables for the monthly bonus amount, the required number of training hours, and the number of training hours that the team leader has attended. Write one or more constructors and the appropriate accessor and mutator functions for the class. Demonstrate the class by writing a program that uses a TeamLeader object.

4. **Time Format**

In Program 15-17, the file Time.h contains a Time class. Design a class called MilTime that is derived from the Time class. The MilTime class should convert time in military (24-hour) format to the standard time format used by the Time class. The class should have the following member variables:

milHours: Contains the hour in 24-hour format. For example, 1:00 pm would be stored as 1300 hours, and 4:30 pm would be stored as 1630 hours.

milSeconds: Contains the seconds in standard format.

The class should have the following member functions:

Constructor: The constructor should accept arguments for the hour and seconds, in military format. The time should then be converted to standard time and stored in the hours, min, and sec variables of the Time class.

setTime: Accepts arguments to be stored in the milHour and milSeconds variables. The time should then be converted to standard time and stored in the hours, min, and sec variables of the Time class.

getHour: Returns the hour in military format.

getStandHr: Returns the hour in standard format.

Demonstrate the class in a program that asks the user to enter the time in military format. The program should then display the time in both military and standard format.

Input Validation: The MilTime class should not accept hours greater than 2359, or less than 0. It should not accept seconds greater than 59 or less than 0.

5. **Time Clock**

Design a class named `TimeClock`. The class should be derived from the `MilTime` class you designed in Programming Challenge 4. The class should allow the programmer to pass two times to it: starting time and ending time. The class should have a member function that returns the amount of time elapsed between the two times. For example, if the starting time is 900 hours (9:00 am), and the ending time is 1300 hours (1:00 pm), the elapsed time is 4 hours.

Input Validation: The class should not accept hours greater than 2359 or less than 0.

6. **Essay class**

Design an `Essay` class that is derived from the `GradedActivity` class presented in this chapter. The `Essay` class should determine the grade a student receives on an essay. The student's essay score can be up to 100, and is determined in the following manner:

- Grammar: 30 points
- Spelling: 20 points
- Correct length: 20 points
- Content: 30 points

Demonstrate the class in a simple program.

7. **PersonData and CustomerData classes**

Design a class named `PersonData` with the following member variables:

- `lastName`
- `firstName`
- `address`
- `city`
- `state`
- `zip`
- `phone`

Write the appropriate accessor and mutator functions for these member variables.

Next, design a class named `CustomerData`, which is derived from the `PersonData` class. The `CustomerData` class should have the following member variables:

- `customerNumber`
- `mailingList`

The `customerNumber` variable will be used to hold a unique integer for each customer. The `mailingList` variable should be a `bool`. It will be set to `true` if the customer wishes to be on a mailing list, or `false` if the customer does not wish to be on a mailing list. Write appropriate accessor and mutator functions for these member variables. Demonstrate an object of the `CustomerData` class in a simple program.

8. **PreferredCustomer Class**

A retail store has a preferred customer plan where customers may earn discounts on all their purchases. The amount of a customer's discount is determined by the amount of the customer's cumulative purchases in the store.

- When a preferred customer spends $500, he or she gets a 5% discount on all future purchases.

- When a preferred customer spends $1,000, he or she gets a 6% discount on all future purchases.
- When a preferred customer spends $1,500, he or she gets a 7% discount on all future purchases.
- When a preferred customer spends $2,000 or more, he or she gets a 10% discount on all future purchases.

Design a class named `PreferredCustomer`, which is derived from the `CustomerData` class you created in Programming Challenge 7. The `PreferredCustomer` class should have the following member variables:

- `purchasesAmount` (a double)
- `discountLevel` (a double)

The `purchasesAmount` variable holds the total of a customer's purchases to date. The `discountLevel` variable should be set to the correct discount percentage, according to the store's preferred customer plan. Write appropriate member functions for this class and demonstrate it in a simple program.

Input Validation: Do not accept negative values for any sales figures.

9. **File Filter**

A file filter reads an input file, transforms it in some way, and writes the results to an output file. Write an abstract file filter class that defines a pure virtual function for transforming a character. Create one derived class of your file filter class that performs encryption, another that transforms a file to all uppercase, and another that creates an unchanged copy of the original file. The class should have the following member function:

```
void doFilter(ifstream &in, ofstream &out)
```

This function should be called to perform the actual filtering. The member function for transforming a single character should have the prototype:

```
char transform(char ch)
```

The encryption class should have a constructor that takes an integer as an argument and uses it as the encryption key.

10. **File Double-Spacer**

Create a derived class of the abstract filter class of Programming Challenge 9 that double-spaces a file: that is, it inserts a blank line between any two lines of the file.

11. **Course Grades**

In a course, a teacher gives the following tests and assignments:

- A **lab activity** that is observed by the teacher and assigned a numeric score.
- A **pass/fail exam** that has 10 questions. The minimum passing score is 70.
- An **essay** that is assigned a numeric score.
- A **final exam** that has 50 questions.

Write a class named `CourseGrades`. The class should have a member named `grades` that is an array of `GradedActivity` pointers. The `grades` array should have four elements, one for each of the assignments previously described. The class should have the following member functions:

`setLab:`	This function should accept the address of a `GradedActivity` object as its argument. This object should already hold the student's score for the lab activity. Element 0 of the `grades` array should reference this object.
`setPassFailExam:`	This function should accept the address of a `PassFailExam` object as its argument. This object should already hold the student's score for the pass/fail exam. Element 1 of the `grades` array should reference this object.
`setEssay:`	This function should accept the address of an `Essay` object as its argument. (See Programming Challenge 6 for the `Essay` class. If you have not completed Programming Challenge 6, use a `GradedActivity` object instead.) This object should already hold the student's score for the essay. Element 2 of the `grades` array should reference this object.
`setPassFailExam:`	This function should accept the address of a `FinalExam` object as its argument. This object should already hold the student's score for the final exam. Element 3 of the `grades` array should reference this object.
`print:`	This function should display the numeric scores and grades for each element in the `grades` array.

Demonstrate the class in a program.

12. **`Ship`, `CruiseShip`, and `CargoShip` Classes**

Design a `Ship` class that has the following members:

- A member variable for the name of the ship (a string)
- A member variable for the year that the ship was built (a string)
- A constructor and appropriate accessors and mutators
- A virtual `print` function that displays the ship's name and the year it was built.

Design a `CruiseShip` class that is derived from the `Ship` class. The `CruiseShip` class should have the following members:

- A member variable for the maximum number of passengers (an `int`)
- A constructor and appropriate accessors and mutators
- A `print` function that overrides the `print` function in the base class. The `CruiseShip` class's print function should display only the ship's name and the maximum number of passengers.

Design a `CargoShip` class that is derived from the `Ship` class. The `CargoShip` class should have the following members:

- A member variable for the cargo capacity in tonnage (an `int`).
- A constructor and appropriate accessors and mutators.
- A `print` function that overrides the `print` function in the base class. The `CargoShip` class's print function should display only the ship's name and the ship's cargo capacity.

Demonstrate the classes in a program that has an array of `Ship` pointers. The array elements should be initialized with the addresses of dynamically allocated `Ship`,

CruiseShip, and CargoShip objects. (See Program 15-13, lines 17 through 22, for an example of how to do this.) The program should then step through the array, calling each object's print function.

13. **Pure Abstract Base Class Project**

Define a pure abstract base class called BasicShape. The BasicShape class should have the following members:

Private Member Variable:

area, a double used to hold the shape's area.

Public Member Functions:

getArea. This function should return the value in the member variable area.

calcArea. This function should be a pure virtual function.

Next, define a class named Circle. It should be derived from the BasicShape class. It should have the following members:

Private Member Variables:

centerX, a long integer used to hold the x coordinate of the circle's center.

centerY, a long integer used to hold the y coordinate of the circle's center.

radius, a double used to hold the circle's radius.

Public Member Functions:

constructor—accepts values for centerX, centerY, and radius. Should call the overridden calcArea function described below.

getCenterX—returns the value in centerX.

getCenterY—returns the value in centerY.

calcArea—calculates the area of the circle (area = 3.14159 * radius * radius) and stores the result in the inherited member area.

Next, define a class named Rectangle. It should be derived from the BasicShape class. It should have the following members:

Private Member Variables:

width, a long integer used to hold the width of the rectangle.

length, a long integer used to hold the length of the rectangle.

Public Member Functions:

constructor—accepts values for width and length. Should call the overridden calcArea function described below.

getWidth—returns the value in width.

getLength—returns the value in length.

calcArea—calculates the area of the rectangle (area = length * width) and stores the result in the inherited member area.

After you have created these classes, create a driver program that defines a Circle object and a Rectangle object. Demonstrate that each object properly calculates and reports its area.

Group Project

14. **Bank Accounts**

This program should be designed and written by a team of students. Here are some suggestions:

- One or more students may work on a single class.
- The requirements of the program should be analyzed so each student is given about the same work load.
- The parameters and return types of each function and class member function should be decided in advance.
- The program will be best implemented as a multi-file program.

Design a generic class to hold the following information about a bank account:

Balance

Number of deposits this month

Number of withdrawals

Annual interest rate

Monthly service charges

The class should have the following member functions:

Constructor:	Accepts arguments for the balance and annual interest rate.
deposit:	A virtual function that accepts an argument for the amount of the deposit. The function should add the argument to the account balance. It should also increment the variable holding the number of deposits.
withdraw:	A virtual function that accepts an argument for the amount of the withdrawal. The function should subtract the argument from the balance. It should also increment the variable holding the number of withdrawals.
calcInt:	A virtual function that updates the balance by calculating the monthly interest earned by the account, and adding this interest to the balance. This is performed by the following formulas:

Monthly Interest Rate = (Annual Interest Rate / 12)
Monthly Interest = Balance * Monthly Interest Rate
Balance = Balance + Monthly Interest

monthlyProc: A virtual function that subtracts the monthly service charges from the balance, calls the `calcInt` function, and then sets the variables that hold the number of withdrawals, number of deposits, and monthly service charges to zero.

Next, design a savings account class, derived from the generic account class. The savings account class should have the following additional member:

status (to represent an active or inactive account)

If the balance of a savings account falls below $25, it becomes inactive. (The status member could be a flag variable.) No more withdrawals may be made until the balance is raised above $25, at which time the account becomes active again. The savings account class should have the following member functions:

withdraw: A function that checks to see if the account is inactive before a withdrawal is made. (No withdrawal will be allowed if the account is not active.) A withdrawal is then made by calling the base class version of the function.

deposit: A function that checks to see if the account is inactive before a deposit is made. If the account is inactive and the deposit brings the balance above $25, the account becomes active again. The deposit is then made by calling the base class version of the function.

monthlyProc: Before the base class function is called, this function checks the number of withdrawals. If the number of withdrawals for the month is more than 4, a service charge of $1 for each withdrawal above 4 is added to the base class variable that holds the monthly service charges. (Don't forget to check the account balance after the service charge is taken. If the balance falls below $25, the account becomes inactive.)

Next, design a checking account class, also derived from the generic account class. It should have the following member functions:

withdraw: Before the base class function is called, this function will determine if a withdrawal (a check written) will cause the balance to go below $0. If the balance goes below $0, a service charge of $15 will be taken from the account. (The withdrawal will not be made.) If there isn't enough in the account to pay the service charge, the balance will become negative and the customer will owe the negative amount to the bank.

monthlyProc: Before the base class function is called, this function adds the monthly fee of $5 plus $0.10 per withdrawal (check written) to the base class variable that holds the monthly service charges.

Write a complete program that demonstrates these classes by asking the user to enter the amounts of deposits and withdrawals for a savings account and checking account. The program should display statistics for the month, including beginning balance, total amount of deposits, total amount of withdrawals, service charges, and ending balance.

 NOTE: You may need to add more member variables and functions to the classes than those listed above.

A The ASCII Character Set

| Nonprintable ASCII Characters | | | | | Printable ASCII Characters | | | |
Dec	Hex	Oct	Name of Character		Dec	Hex	Oct	Character
0	0	0	NULL		32	20	40	(Space)
1	1	1	SOH		33	21	41	!
2	2	2	STX		34	22	42	"
3	3	3	ETY		35	23	43	#
4	4	4	EOT		36	24	44	$
5	5	5	ENQ		37	25	45	%
6	6	6	ACK		38	26	46	&
7	7	7	BELL		39	27	47	'
8	8	10	BKSPC		40	28	50	(
9	9	11	HZTAB		41	29	51	)
10	a	12	NEWLN		42	2a	52	*
11	b	13	VTAB		43	2b	53	+
12	c	14	FF		44	2c	54	,
13	d	15	CR		45	2d	55	-
14	e	16	SO		46	2e	56	.
15	f	17	SI		47	2f	57	/
16	10	20	DLE		48	30	60	0
17	11	21	DC1		49	31	61	1
18	12	22	DC2		50	32	62	2
19	13	23	DC3		51	33	63	3
20	14	24	DC4		52	34	64	4
21	15	25	NAK		53	35	65	5
22	16	26	SYN		54	36	66	6
23	17	27	ETB		55	37	67	7
24	18	30	CAN		56	38	70	8
25	19	31	EM		57	39	71	9
26	1a	32	SUB		58	3a	72	:
27	1b	33	ESC		59	3b	73	;
28	1c	34	FS		60	3c	74	<
29	1d	35	GS		61	3d	75	=
30	1e	36	RS		62	3e	76	>
31	1f	37	US		63	3f	77	?
127	7f	177	DEL		64	40	100	@
					65	41	101	A
					66	42	102	B
					67	43	103	C

Printable ASCII Characters			
Dec	Hex	Oct	Character
68	44	104	D
69	45	105	E
70	46	106	F
71	47	107	G
72	48	110	H
73	49	111	I
74	4a	112	J
75	4b	113	K
76	4c	114	L
77	4d	115	M
78	4e	116	N
79	4f	117	O
80	50	120	P
81	51	121	Q
82	52	122	R
83	53	123	S
84	54	124	T
85	55	125	U
86	56	126	V
87	57	127	W
88	58	130	X
89	59	131	Y
90	5a	132	Z
91	5b	133	[
92	5c	134	\
93	5d	135	]
94	5e	136	^
95	5f	137	_
96	60	140	`
97	61	141	a
98	62	142	b
99	63	143	c
100	64	144	d
101	65	145	e
102	66	146	f
103	67	147	g
104	68	150	h
105	69	151	i
106	6a	152	j
107	6b	153	k
108	6c	154	l
109	6d	155	m
110	6e	156	n
111	6f	157	o
112	70	160	p
113	71	161	q

Printable ASCII Characters			
Dec	Hex	Oct	Character
114	72	162	r
115	73	163	s
116	74	164	t
117	75	165	u
118	76	166	v
119	77	167	w
120	78	170	x
121	79	171	y
122	7a	172	z
123	7b	173	{
124	7c	174		
125	7d	175	}
126	7e	176	~

Extended ASCII Characters			
Dec	Hex	Oct	Character
128	80	200	Ç
129	81	201	ü
130	82	202	é
131	83	203	â
132	84	204	ä
133	85	205	à
134	86	206	å
135	87	207	ç
136	88	210	ê
137	89	211	ë
138	8a	212	è
139	8b	213	ï
140	8c	214	î
141	8d	215	ì
142	8e	216	Ä
143	8f	217	Å
144	90	220	É
145	91	221	æ
146	92	222	Æ
147	93	223	ô
148	94	224	ö
149	95	225	ò
150	96	226	û
151	97	227	ù
152	98	230	ÿ
153	99	231	Ö
154	9a	232	Ü
155	9b	233	¢

Extended ASCII Characters				Extended ASCII Characters			
Dec	Hex	Oct	Character	Dec	Hex	Oct	Character
156	9c	234	£	206	ce	316	Œ
157	9d	235	ù	207	cf	317	œ
158	9e	236	û	208	d0	320	–
159	9f	237	ƒ	209	d1	321	—
160	a0	240	á	210	d2	322	"
161	a1	241	í	211	d3	323	"
162	a2	242	ó	212	d4	324	'
163	a3	243	ú	213	d5	325	'
164	a4	244	ñ	214	d6	326	÷
165	a5	245	Ñ	215	d7	327	◊
166	a6	246	ª	216	d8	330	ÿ
167	a7	247	º	217	d9	331	Ÿ
168	a8	250	¿	218	da	332	/
169	a9	251	©	219	db	333	
170	aa	252	Ñ	220	dc	334	‹
171	ab	253	´	221	dd	335	›
172	ac	254	¨	222	de	336	fi
173	ad	255	¡	223	df	337	fl
174	ae	256		224	e0	340	‡
175	af	257	»	225	e1	341	·
176	b0	260	∞	226	e2	342	‚
177	b1	261	±	227	e3	343	„
178	b2	262	≤	228	e4	344	‰
179	b3	263	≥	229	e5	345	Â
180	b4	264	¥	230	e6	346	Ê
181	b5	265	µ	231	e7	347	Á
182	b6	266	∂	232	e8	350	Ë
183	b7	267	∑	233	e9	351	È
184	b8	270	∏	234	ea	352	Í
185	b9	271	π	235	eb	353	Î
186	ba	272	∫	236	ec	354	Ï
187	bb	273	ª	237	ed	355	Ì
188	bc	274	º	238	ee	356	Ó
189	bd	275	Ω	239	ef	357	Ô
190	be	276	æ	240	f0	360	●
191	bf	277	ø	241	f1	361	Ò
192	c0	300	¿	242	f2	362	Ú
193	c1	301	¡	243	f3	363	Û
194	c2	302	¬	244	f4	364	Ù
195	c3	303	√	245	f5	365	ı
196	c4	304	ƒ	246	f6	366	^
197	c5	305	≈	247	f7	367	~
198	c6	306	∆	248	f8	370	¯
199	c7	307	»	249	f9	371	ˇ
200	c8	310	»	250	fa	372	˙
201	c9	311	…	251	fb	373	●
202	ca	312		252	fc	374	
203	cb	313	Ā	253	fd	375	˝
204	cc	314	Ã	254	fe	376	
205	cd	315	Õ	255	ff	377	˛

The operators are shown in order of precedence, from highest to lowest.

Operator	Associativity
`::`	unary: left to right
	binary: right to left
`( )  [ ]  ->  .`	left to right
`++  —  +  -  !  ~  (type)  *  &  sizeof`	right to left
`*  /  %`	left to right
`+  -`	left to right
`<<  >>`	left to right
`<  <=  >  >=`	left to right
`==  !=`	left to right
`&`	left to right
`^`	left to right
`|`	left to right
`&&`	left to right
`||`	left to right
`?:`	right to left
`=  +=  —=  *=  /=  %=  &=  ^=  |=  <<=  >>=`	right to left
`,`	left to right

Index